ANCIENT GREEK

Gavin Betts

Associate Professor of Classical Studies

&

Alan Henry

Professor of Classical Studies
Monash University, Victoria, Australia

D1059710

TEACH YOURSELF BOOKS
Hodder and Stoughton

The authors wish to acknowledge the help of
George Gellie, Deane Blackman and Adele Pretty.

First published 1989

Copyright © 1989 Gavin Betts and Alan Henry

British Library Cataloguing in Publication Data

Betts, Gavin
    Ancient Greek—(Teach yourself books)
    1. Greek language. Grammar
    I. Title   II. Henry, Alan
    485

ISBN 0 340 42298 X

Typeset by the Alden Press, Osney Mead, Oxford

Printed and bound in Great Britain
for the educational publishing division
of Hodder and Stoughton Ltd.,
Mill Road, Dunton Green, Sevenoaks, Kent
by Richard Clay Ltd, Bungay, Suffolk

Contents

Introduction
How to use this book   vii
Abbreviations   ix

Unit 1   1

1.1/1 The Greek alphabet and its pronunciation /2 Accents
.2 Exercise   .3 Excursus—The different forms of Greek

Unit 2   8

2.1/1 Nouns in Greek   /2 First declension (feminine nouns) and
the feminine definite article   /3 Basic uses of cases /4 Verbs in
Greek /5 Present and future indicative active of -ω verbs
(and corresponding infinitives) /6 Word order and elision
.2 Greek reading /1 Vocabulary

Unit 3   17

3.1/1 Second declension and the masculine and neuter definite
article /2 First declension (masculine nouns) /3 First and
second declension adjectives   /4 Adverbs   /5 Prepositions
/6 Present indicative and infinitive of εἰμί, *I am*   .2 Greek
reading /1 Vocabulary

Unit 4   25

4.1/1 Imperfect indicative active and weak aorist indicative and
infinitive active of -ω verbs   /2 First and second person pronouns,
and αὐτόν, -ήν, -ό /3 Connecting particles   .2 Greek reading

Unit 5   33

5.1/1 Third declension—consonant stem nouns (1) /2 Contracted verbs /3 Further uses of the definite article   .2 Greek
reading

Unit 6   41

6.1/1 Third declension—consonant stem nouns (2) /2 Second
declension contracted nouns and first and second declension contracted adjectives /3 Compound verbs formed with prepositional
prefixes /4 -ω verbs with stems in palatals, labials, dentals
.2 Greek reading

Unit 7   50

7.1/1 Strong aorist indicative and infinitive active of -ω verbs
/2 φημί *say* /3 Indirect speech /4 Indirect command
/5 Numerals /6 Negatives /7 Phrases expressing time and
space **.2** Greek reading

Unit 8   58

8.1/1 Middle and passive voices /2 Deponent verbs /3 Indirect statement /4 Third declension nouns—stems in ι and υ
.2 Greek reading

Unit 9   67

9.1/1 Demonstrative pronouns /2 The relative pronoun ὅς and
adjectival clauses /3 αὐτός and its uses /4 Reflexive and reciprocal pronouns /5 Possessive adjectives and pronouns
.2 Greek reading

Unit 10   77

10.1/1 Interrogative τίς and indefinite τις /2 Questions, direct
and indirect /3 First and third declension adjectives /4 Third
declension adjectives **.2** Greek reading **.3** Extra reading—
The wisdom of Socrates

Unit 11   86

11.1/1 Root aorist, aorist passive and future passive /2 Agent
and instrument /3 -ω verbs with stems in λ, μ, ν, ρ /4 Third
declension nouns—stems in ευ, αυ, ου /5 Crasis **.2** Greek
reading

Unit 12   94

12.1/1 Participles /2 Uses of participles **.2** Greek reading
.3 Extra reading—*Epigrams*

Unit 13   103

13.1/1 Oddities of declension /2 Verbs used with the genitive or
dative /3 Further particles **.2** Greek reading **.3** Extra
reading—*Plato*

Unit 14   114

14.1/1 Moods of the Greek verb /2 Subjunctive mood
/3 Optative mood /4 Uses of the subjunctive and optative
.2 Greek reading

Unit 15 123

15.1/1 Perfect indicative active /2 Verbs used with participles
.2 Greek reading **.3** Extra reading—*Prometheus Bound (1)*

Unit 16 132

16.1/1 Phrases and clauses of result /2 Pluperfect indicative active /3 Perfect and pluperfect indicative middle/passive /4 Other parts of the perfect tense **.2** Greek reading **.3** Extra reading—*Heracles*

Unit 17 142

17.1/1 Imperative mood: commands and prohibitions /2 Comparison of adjectives and adverbs /3 Meaning of the comparative and superlative /4 Constructions involving the comparative and superlative /5 Active verbs used in a passive sense **.2** Greek reading **.3** Extra reading—*Prometheus Bound (2)*

Unit 18 154

18.1/1 -μι verbs /2 δίδωμι *give*, τίθημι *put, place* /3 εἶμι *I shall come/go* /4 Other verbs with principal parts from different roots /5 Conditional sentences /6 ἄκρος, μέσος, ἔσχατος **.2** Greek reading **.3** Extra reading—*The sea, the sea!*

Unit 19 164

19.1/1 ἵστημι and its compounds /2 Potential clauses /3 Oddities in verbs **.2** Greek reading

Unit 20 173

20.1/1 Verbs in -νῡμι /2 ἵημι and its compounds /3 Genitive of price or value /4 Genitive of separation /5 Accusative of respect or specification **.2** Greek reading

Unit 21 180

21.1/1 Wishes /2 Further temporal conjunctions (ἕως, μέχρι, πρίν) /3 Further demonstrative and relative adjectives/pronouns /4 Further impersonal verbs /5 Accusative absolute **.2** Greek reading **.3** Extra reading—*Love poetry*

Unit 22 190

22.1/1 Summary of the uses of ὡς /2 Uses of cases (1)—accusative **.2** Greek reading **.3** Extra reading—*Anacreontea*

Unit 23   200

23.1/1 Uses of cases (2)—genitive /2 Uses of cases (3)—dative
.2 Greek reading   **.3** Extra reading—*Further elegaic poetry*

Unit 24   211

24.1/1 *Yes* and *no* /2 Summary of uses of οὐ and μή /3 Diminutives /4 Dual number /5 Verbal adjectives in -τος/-τός and -τέος /6 Verbs of precaution and striving /7 Verbs of hindering, preventing, forbidding, denying   **.2** Greek reading **.3** Extra reading—*The Think Tank*

Unit 25   222

25.1/1 Homeric Greek /2 Differences in phonology and morphology /3 Differences in syntax   **.2** Readings from Homer

Revision exercises   228

Suggestions for further study   230

Appendices

  1 Conjugation of λύω *loosen*   232
  2 Conjugation of contracted verbs (present and imperfect)   235
  3 Conjugation of εἰμί *be*, ἔρχομαι (and εἶμι) *come/go*, φημί *say*,
     οἶδα *know*   238
  4 Root aorists   239
  5 Conjugation of δίδωμι *give*, τίθημι *put, place*, ἵημι *let go, send
     forth*, ἵστημι *make stand*   240
  6 Conjugation of δείκνῡμι (present and imperfect)   245
  7 Table of nouns   246
  8 Numerals   248
  9 Accentuation   249
 10 Greek verse   254

Key to exercises in Greek reading and extra reading sections   257

Key to revision exercises   285

Principal parts of verbs   289

Vocabulary   295

Index   339

Introduction

How to use this book

ἀρχὴ ἥμισυ παντός   a [good] beginning is half of the whole

On one occasion when giving a speech, Hiero, a Greek ruler in ancient Sicily, was interrupted by complaints about his bad breath. This revelation of what must have been a chronic problem distressed him considerably, and on returning home he reproached his wife for not having told him of it. She indignantly justified herself by saying that she had thought that all adult males smelt as he did. To depend on a virtuous spouse to correct such faults has obvious dangers. If you are relying solely on this book to begin the study of ancient Greek there are similar pitfalls. Apart from the Key, you will have few checks on your progress, and it will be essential to follow up any doubt, however small, about meanings of words and points of grammar. To be able to do this you must make yourself completely familiar with the arrangement of the book's contents.

We assume that you are acquainted with the basics of traditional English grammar, as this is the framework we use to explain the structure of Greek. You should be familiar with the **parts of speech** (*adjective*, *adverb*, *conjunction*, *interjection*, *noun*, *preposition*, *pronoun*, *verb*) and with the meaning of such terms as *finite*, *transitive/intransitive*, *clause*, *phrase*, *subject*, *object*, etc. If these are new to you, you should consult one of the many elementary books on the subject, such as B.A. Phythian *Teach Yourself English Grammar*.

The main part of the book consists of twenty-five units. Each consists of either two or three sections. The first is taken up with grammar, the second contains sentences and passages of Greek for reading, while the third section (except in the first unit) is generally a longer Greek passage for additional reading. Revision exercises will be found on p. 228 and each of these should be done after the units to which it refers.

The grammatical sections, which are headed **.1**, are carefully graded over the course of the book in order to set out the basic features of Greek grammar in a systematic and easily digestible way. Each should be mastered before tackling the next. Very often a particular section cannot be understood without a knowledge of what has gone before.

Grammar as a whole can be divided into two parts, one involving the forms which a word can take (e.g. those of a first declension feminine noun, 2.1/2), the other dealing with the ways in which these forms are used to make up phrases and sentences (e.g. the uses of the dative case, 2.1/3e). The former we must learn by heart. The latter we can only fully understand when, after learning a general rule, we see, and are able to understand, examples of it in use. Because of the importance of such examples the sentences given to illustrate grammatical rules are nearly always original Greek, and every effort should be made to understand them fully. By reading them carefully every time you revise a unit you will not only come to understand the grammatical point involved but also extend your vocabulary.

To work through the reading exercises with one finger in the corresponding page of the Key is **not** recommended, although you should make full use of any help provided by the notes. It is only by analysing the forms of words and patiently working out the construction of clauses and sentences that you will make progress. A full translation of an exercise should be written out and then compared with the Key. When you discover you have made a mistake, you must meticulously hunt out the point of grammar concerned and see how you came to be wrong. To help you do this many cross-references have been supplied in all parts of the book (a reference of the form 22.1/2 is for the **grammatical** section (.1) of a unit, but one such as 22.2.2 is to the **reading** section (.2)). Your final step should be to read through the Greek aloud until you are able to translate it without reference to your own version or the Key. This will familiarize you with the construction employed and any new vocabulary. Some rote learning of new words is, of course, inevitable. If, however, you go to the trouble of actually memorizing some of the many famous phrases and verse passages contained in the reading you will find your grasp of the language extending itself in an enjoyable and rewarding fashion.

Appendices 1–8 give grammatical tables and other information to supplement particular units. **Appendix 9** is on accentuation and should be consulted regularly and mastered over the course of the whole book. **Appendix 10** is added to show how Greek verse was constructed; a knowledge of metre is not necessary for understanding Greek verse but obviously adds to our enjoyment of it.

The section **Principal parts of verbs** must be used in conjunction with the vocabulary after Unit 6 as the information it contains is not repeated.

For ease of reference to grammatical points an index is provided.

An additional set of exercises without a Key (Greek-English and English-Greek) for the use of teachers may be obtained from the authors (G. G. Betts and A. S. Henry, Department of Classical Studies, Monash University, Clayton, Victoria, Australia 3168).

Abbreviations

a. or acc.	accusative	m. or m	masculine
absol.	absolute	mid.	middle
act.	active	n. or n	neuter
adj.	adjective	n. or nom.	nominative
adv.	adverb	n.o.p.	no other parts
aor.	aorist	obj.	object
cap.	capital	opt.	optative
cf.	compare	pass.	passive
compar.	comparative	pers.	person
conj.	conjunction	perf.	perfect
dat.	dative	pl.	plural
esp.	especially	plpf.	pluperfect
ex.	example	poet.	poetical
f. or f	feminine	poss.	possessive
f.	following	pple.	participle
fut.	future	prep.	preposition
gen.	genitive	pres.	present
imp.	imperative	pron.	pronoun
impers.	impersonal	refl.	reflexive
impf.	imperfect	s.	singular
ind.	indicative	*sc.*	namely
indecl.	indeclinable	sub.	subject
inf.	infinitive	subj.	subjunctive
intr.	intransitive	supl.	superlative
l.	line	tr.	transitive
lit.	literally	trans.	translate
ll.	lines	v. or voc.	vocative
		viz	that is to say

Round brackets ( ) contain explanatory material or a literal translation; in the vocabulary round brackets are also used to indicate alternative forms. In the earlier units square brackets [ ] are used in translations for words which are required by English idiom but have no equivalent in the Greek original.

+ means *in conjunction with, compounded with,* or *followed by.*

< means *is derived from.*

> means *produce(s).*

* marks a word which cannot stand first in a clause or phrase.

\# indicates that the following sentence or passage is verse; in the vocabulary this sign indicates that the word to which it is attached is poetical.

† is explained in the introductory note to the vocabulary.

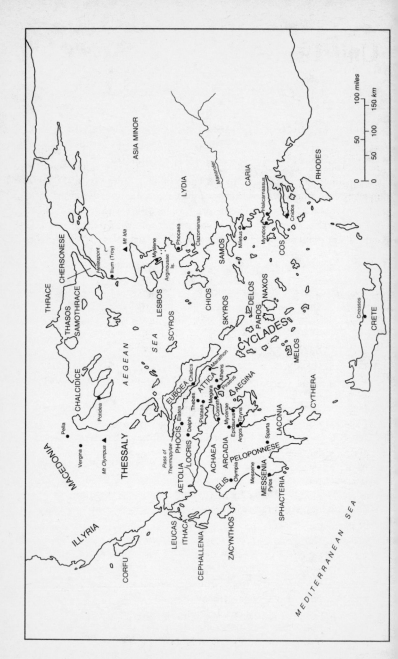

Unit 1

1.1   Grammar

1.1/1   The Greek alphabet and its pronunciation

The Greek alphabet consists of twenty-four letters, each with its traditional name. Today it is used in both upper and lower case but in antiquity it existed only in different varieties of capitals. The pronunciation given below does not in every case reflect what we know of the language of fourth century Athens (the type of Greek described here—see 1.3); because we learn Classical Greek for the purpose of reading, not of communication, we do not need to be as careful about its pronunciation as we would be with a modern language.

	NAME	PRONUNCIATION
A α	alpha	*a* (see below)
B β	beta	*b*
Γ γ	gamma	*g* (as in *game*, never as in *gesture*, but as *n* in *ink* before κ, ξ, χ or another γ; see below)
Δ δ	delta	*d*
E ε	epsilon	*e* (as in *met*)
Z ζ	zeta	*sd* (as in *wisdom*, but represented in English as *z*)
H η	eta	*ē* (like *ai* in *fairy*)
Θ θ	theta	*th* (as in *thing*; see below)
I ι	iota	*i* (see below)
K κ	kappa	*k* (but represented in English as *c*)
Λ λ	lambda	*l*
M μ	mu	*m*
N ν	nu	*n*
Ξ ξ	xi	*x* (as in *axe*)
O o	omicron	*o* (as in *lot*)
Π π	pi	*p*
P ρ	rho	*r*
C ϲ	sigma	*s* (as in *sign*) ϲ ϲ
T τ	tau	*t*
Y υ	upsilon	*u* (represented in English as *y*, except in diphthongs
Φ φ	phi	*ph* (see below)
X χ	chi	*ch* (see below)
Ψ ψ	psi	*ps* (as in *maps*)
Ω ω	omega	*ō* (like *oa* in *broad*)

In Greek words taken into English and in transcriptions of Greek proper names Greek letters are normally represented by their phonetic equivalent except where indicated above (and in some diphthongs—see note 2).

Consonants

The normal English pronunciation is recommended where no example is given. To distinguish between κ and χ the latter is pronounced as the *ch* in the Scottish pronunciation of *loch*. The letters ζ, ξ, ψ are double consonants and the equivalents of $c\delta$, κc, πc respectively, for which they must always be used: e.g. when c is added to the stem $\gamma\bar{\upsilon}\pi$- we must write $\gamma\bar{\upsilon}\psi$, never $\gamma\bar{\upsilon}\pi c$ (5.1/1). The letters θ, ϕ, χ are **not** double consonants; the pronunciation given above is that normally used today but in the Greek of our period they were pronounced as *t*, *p*, *k* with an accompanying emission of breath (i.e. something like these consonants in English when initial. Compare the difference between the English and French pronunciation of the *P* in *Paris*).

Examples of the second pronunciation of γ are: $c\pi\acute{o}\gamma\gamma oc$ (spóngos) *sponge*, $C\phi\acute{\iota}\gamma\xi$ (Sphinx) *Sphinx*, $\check{\epsilon}\lambda\epsilon\gamma\chi oc$ (élenchos) *scrutiny*.

The form of sigma given above (which dates from the Roman period) is, for reasons of convenience, the one increasingly used in modern editions. The traditional forms of lower case sigma, which date from the Middle Ages, are σ when initial or medial, ς when final, e.g. $\sigma\acute{\upsilon}\sigma\tau\alpha\sigma\iota\varsigma$ ($c\acute{\upsilon}c\tau\alpha c\iota c$) *composition*. The traditional upper case version is Σ. All three forms occur in $\Sigma\omega\sigma\iota\gamma\acute{\epsilon}\nu\eta\varsigma$ ($C\omega c\iota\gamma\acute{\epsilon}\nu\eta c$) *Sosigenes*.

Vowels

All Greek vowels have a long and short pronunciation. These pronunciations have separate symbols in the case of ϵ/η and o/ω. The other vowels have both values but only one symbol. In works of reference, but not in normal printed texts, the two values of these vowels are distinguished by marking the long form with a bar above (macron), $\bar{a}$, $\bar{\iota}$, $\bar{\upsilon}$. They are pronounced:

$\bar{a}$ as in *father*
a (i.e. short *a*) as in a shortened version of $\bar{a}$, like *u* in *but*, never as in *sat* (this sound did not exist in Greek)
$\bar{\iota}$ as *ee* in *need*
ι as *i* in *sit* (or, more accurately, as in French *petit*).
$\bar{\upsilon}$ as in French *sûr*
υ as in French *tu*

Diphthongs

Greek had two types of diphthongs:

(i)   where both elements are written normally and pronounced as follows:
   $\alpha\iota$ as *ai* in *aisle* $o\iota$ as *oi* in *oil*

αυ as *ow* in *cow*　　ου as *oo* in *cool*
ει as *ei* in *rein*　　υι as *we*
ευ/ηυ as *eu* in *feud*

When any of these combinations is not to be taken as a diphthong, the second element is marked with a diaeresis (¨): βοΐ (bo-í), Λαΐς (La-ís).

(ii) where the long vowels ᾱ, η, ω are combined with an iota. This iota is placed **below** the vowel (**iota subscript**), not after it: ᾳ, ῃ, ῳ.[1] For convenience these diphthongs are always pronounced as simple ᾱ, η, ω.

Breathings

Every word beginning with a vowel or diphthong has a rough (ʽ) or smooth (ʼ) breathing. A rough breathing denotes an initial *h*, a smooth breathing (which is something of a superfluity) the absence of initial *h*: ἡμέρα (hēméra) *day*, ἀγαθός (agathós) *good*. A breathing is placed over the second element of a category (i) diphthong: αἴνιγμα (aínigma) *riddle*, Αἰσχύλος (Aischúlos) *Aeschylus*, but when an initial vowel which does not form part of a diphthong is in upper case the breathing is placed in front: Ὅμηρος (Hómēros) *Homer*. Words beginning with υ always have a rough breathing: ὗς (hūs) *pig*, ὕψος (húpsos) *height*. Initial ρ is also given a rough breathing because it was always pronounced *rh*: ῥυθμός (rhuthmós) *rhythm*.

Notes

1　In the grammar and reference sections long α, ι, υ are marked ᾱ, ῑ, ῡ, except in the case of ᾳ, ᾶ, ῖ, ῦ, because iota subscript appears only under long vowels and in the other three cases the circumflex accent (see next subsection) shows that the vowel must be long.

2　The traditional spelling and pronunciation of Greek proper names, and also the form taken by Greek derivatives in English, almost always reflect the Roman system of transliteration (some diphthongs are modified): Αἰσχύλος (Aischúlos) *Aeschylus*, Οἰδίπους (Oidípous) *Oedipus*; κατασ-τροφή (katastrophḗ) *catastrophe*.

3　For marks of punctuation Greek uses the full stop and comma as in English but for colon and semicolon there is only one sign, which is a dot above the line (·). Our semicolon is used as a question mark in Greek (;). Inverted commas and the exclamation mark are not normally used. A capital letter is used at the beginning of a paragraph but not with each new sentence.

1.1/2　Accents

We owe the idea of visually indicating word accent to Aristophanes of Byzantium (not to be confused with the Athenian comic poet), an altruistic

---

[1] The iota is, however, placed **after** the long vowel when the latter is in upper case. The only common example is Ἅιδης *Hades*.

scholar of around 200 BC who wished to help foreigners to pronounce Greek correctly. Since the Renaissance, accents have always been employed in printed texts. While not of crucial importance in reading Greek, they are useful in distinguishing certain words and present little difficulty if correctly approached.

Accent in classical Greek was one of **pitch**, not of stress as in English. An English-speaker, when told that ἄνθρωπος *human being* is accented on its first syllable, would naturally pronounce that syllable with a heavier emphasis. A Greek, however, instead of emphasising the α, would have pronounced it at a higher pitch and so given the word what we should consider a somewhat sing-song effect. We do, of course, use pitch in spoken English, but in a totally different way. In the question *you're going to Athens?* the last word has a rising pitch, but in the statement *you're going to Athens* it has a falling pitch.

Classical Greek has three accents:

- ´ **acute**, indicating rising pitch
- ` **grave**, indicating falling pitch
- ^ **circumflex**, indicating a combined rising and falling pitch (the sign, originally ˆ, is a combination of an acute and a grave). Because the time taken by this operation was necessarily longer than that indicated by an acute or a grave, it can occur only with long vowels and diphthongs, and only on these do we find a circumflex.

The basic features of Greek accentuation are:

(a) nearly every word has an accent, which can be on the final syllable (ποταμός *river*), or the second syllable from the end (ἵππος *horse*), or on the third syllable from the end (ἱπποπόταμος *hippopotamus*). In forms of verbs the position of the accent is nearly always determined by the length of the final syllable (see **Appendix 9**, *b*); in other words whose form can change the accent is generally fixed.

(b) an acute or grave accent can stand on a diphthong or long or short vowel, but a circumflex only on a long vowel or diphthong.

(c) an acute can stand on the end syllable of a word (πειρᾱτής *pirate*), on the second from the end (μοναρχίᾱ *monarchy*), or on the third from the end (ἀκρόπολις *acropolis*).

(d) a grave can stand only on a final syllable, where it automatically replaces an acute when another word follows (ὁ πειρᾱτὴς ἀπάγει τὸν ἱπποπόταμον *the pirate is leading away the hippopotamus*). A final acute is retained, however, before a mark of punctuation (ὦ ποιητά, ἢ πῖθι ἢ ἄπιθι *O poet, either drink or go away*) or when a word so accented is quoted. (For the effect of enclitics see **Appendix 9**, *d*.)

(e) a circumflex can stand on a final syllable (τῶν ποταμῶν *of the rivers*) and, within certain limitations, on the second from the end (Μυκῆναι *Mycenae*).

The rules for accents are given in **Appendix 9**. These should be referred to and gradually mastered in the course of studying this book. For purposes of pronouncing Greek words, each of the three accents should be treated alike and given a simple stress accent as in English. The old British (and Dutch) habit of imposing the Latin system of accentuating on Greek is to be avoided. This system has prevailed in our pronunciation of nearly all Greek proper names. We say *Eurípides* (Εὐρῑπίδης), *Sócrates* (Cωκράτης), *Epidaúrus* ('Επίδαυρος) because the Romans, not unreasonably, adapted them in this way to their own language (cf. second note to last subsection). A Roman, however, who did the same in actually speaking Greek (as every educated Roman could), would have been disowned by his friends as an embarassing ignoramus.

1.2 Exercise

1 Read aloud and transliterate the following names of famous writers:

   'Αριστοτέλης, 'Αριστοφάνης, Δημοσθένης, 'Ηρόδοτος, Θεόκριτος, Καλλίμαχος, Πίνδαρος, Πλάτων.

2 Read aloud and transliterate the following words and then look up their meaning in the vocabulary:

   ἀκμή, ἀνάθεμα, ἀνάλῡcιc, ἀντίθεcιc, ἄcβεcτος, αὐτόματον, ἀφαcίᾱ, βάθος, γένεcιc, διάγνωcιc, δόγμα, δρᾶμα, ζωνή, ἦθος, ἠχώ, ἰδέᾱ, κίνημα, κλῖμαξ, κόcμος, κρίcιc, κῶλον, μέτρον, μίαcμα, νέκταρ, νέμεcιc, ὀρχήcτρᾱ, πάθος, cκηνή, cτίγμα, ὕβριc, ὑπόθεcιc, χάος, χαρακτήρ, ψῡχή.

3 For practice with capitals read aloud and identify the following proper names (accents are not used when a word is put in upper case).

   (*a*) 'ΑΓΑΜΕΜΝΩΝ, 'ΑΧΙΛΛΕΥC, 'ΕΚΤΩΡ, 'ΕΛΕΝΗ, 'ΟΔΥCCΕΥC, ΠΑΤΡΟΚΛΟC, ΠΗΝΕΛΟΠΕΙΑ.
   (*b*) 'ΑΘΗΝΑΙ, 'ΑΡΓΟC, ΘΗΒΑΙ, ΚΟΡΙΝΘΟC, CΠΑΡΤΗ, ΚΡΗΤΗ, 'ΡΟΔΟC, CΑΜΟC.

1.3 Excursus

The different forms of Greek

Greek is a member of the Indo-European family of languages, as are English, French, German and most European languages. The original Indo-European speakers lived in what is now western Russia but migration began at an early date, possibly soon after 3000 BC. The groups which we would now call Greek originally came to Greece at different times during the period 2000–1000 BC. They have lived there ever since and preserved their identity despite invasions and long periods of foreign domination. Greek settlements also existed, in some cases for over 2,500 years, in other Mediterranean countries and in Asia Minor.

The earliest records in Greek date from about 1300 BC and are written on clay tablets in a syllabic script called Linear B, which is totally different from the Greek alphabet familiar to us. The latter was taken over, with some modifications, from the Phoenicians at some time before 750–700 BC, the period to which the oldest surviving examples can be assigned.

It is possible that Greek had already split into dialects early in the second millenium BC. Certainly there is unmistakable evidence of different dialects in the oldest works of Greek literature, the *Iliad* and the *Odyssey* of Homer (25.1/1), which must have been composed before 700 BC (their exact date and manner of composition are matters of dispute). From then up to the time of Alexander the Great (died 323 BC) a large quantity of Greek texts survives and proves the existence of five major dialect groups, which show, in some instances, considerable differences from each other. By no means all dialects served as vehicles of literature and we need only concern ourselves with those which were so used. From an early stage Greek literature was clearly divided into different genres (epic, elegiac poetry, choral lyric, etc.), and often a particular dialect became so intimately associated with a literary genre that a tradition was established which, in some cases, lasted long after the dialect had ceased to be spoken. Some of these associations are mentioned in the following list:

Ionic — the language of the Aegean islands (except those on the southern fringe and Lesbos to the north) and the central area of the west coast of Asia Minor. The latter contained the most important Ionic settlements and it was there that Greek cultural and intellectual life began with Homer and the earliest philosophers. Poets of the 7th and 6th centuries BC established Ionic as the dialect of elegiac and iambic poetry. It was also the original dialect for literary prose and was used by Herodotus (a Dorian by birth) for his *Histories* (4.2.9).

Aeolic — the language of Lesbos and the adjoining Asia Minor coast. It was used by the most famous poetess of antiquity, Sappho (early 6th century BC) and her male contemporary, Alcaeus, for personal lyric poetry. Their initiative was not continued.

Homeric dialect — the language of Homer's *Iliad* and *Odyssey*. This was an artificial dialect which was never the language of a particular area or group, but had been developed over a long period by generations of poets. It was basically an older form of Ionic but with elements from other dialects, chiefly Aeolic. Homer's position as the greatest Greek poet was never disputed in antiquity, and epics which reproduced his language were still being written in the 5th century AD. The Ionic of Elegy, which survived even longer, generally had a Homeric flavour.

Doric — the language of the Peloponnesus (except the central and north-west area), Crete, and other parts of the Greek world. Choral poetry, which was sung by dancing choirs, was originally the creation of Dorians and even when written by non-Doric speakers was always given at least a Doric flavour.

Attic — the language of Athens (historically an offshoot of Ionic). With the rapid political expansion and cultural development of Athens after the final defeat of the Persians by the Greeks (479 BC) Attic became firmly established as a literary dialect despite its late start when compared with Ionic and Aeolic. By the beginning of the 4th century BC Athens had become the main cultural centre of Greece. This was in no small part brought about by the literary masterpieces that had been written and were still being written by Athenians in their own dialect. The Attic of the early and middle period of the 4th century BC, as exemplified in Plato's dialogues and Demosthenes' speeches, has always been taken as the most satisfactory form of Greek for beginners and is the type described in this book. Attic is the language of Tragedy and Comedy (except for their choral odes, which have a tinge of Doric). By the end of the 5th century BC it had superseded Ionic as the language of prose.

The conquests of Alexander had important political and linguistic consequences for the Greek world, which he enlarged considerably. Greek culture and civilisation were extended over all lands bordering on the eastern Mediterranean and a lingua franca emerged which, with a few exceptions, gradually replaced the older dialects even in Greece itself. This new language was basically a development of Attic and was called ἡ κοινὴ διάλεκτος *the common dialect* (in English the **koine**). It was the language of the Greek man in the street and for that reason was used by the writers of the New Testament, who wanted to reach as wide an audience as possible. Educated classes, imbued with the prestige of Classical Attic, regarded it as a debased form of Greek, but the koine, apart from the few survivors of the older dialects, had, by the first century of our era, become the living form of the language and is the ancestor of **Modern Greek**. The latter cannot, of course, be understood simply with a knowledge of 4th century Attic or the koine, but, because of the conservative nature of Greek, which we see at all periods, the changes that have occurred over a period of 2400 years are fewer than those which distinguish Modern English from Anglo-Saxon.

Unit 2

2.1 Grammar

2.1/1 Nouns in Greek

In English the gender of a noun is determined by its meaning; *man* is masculine, *woman* is feminine, *car* is neuter, and when referring to these we would say *he*, *she*, *it* respectively. In Greek, however, the gender of a noun is often arbitrary and does not necessarily indicate anything about what it denotes. While, for example, γυνή *woman* is feminine and ἀνήρ *man* is masculine, χώρᾱ *land* is feminine, and λόγος *speech* is masculine, though δῶρον *gift* is, understandably, neuter. More often than not we cannot see why a particular noun has a particular gender. It is, however, generally possible to tell the gender of a noun by its ending in the nominative and genitive singular, and it is also according to these endings that Greek nouns are grouped into three classes, which are called **declensions**. Each declension has a distinctive set of endings which indicate both case and number, just as in English we have *child*, *child's*, *children*, *children's*, though Greek distinguishes more cases. To go through the list of all possible forms of a noun is to **decline** it.

2.1/2 First declension (feminine nouns) and the feminine definite article

Most first declension nouns are feminine (the few masculines are declined slightly differently — 3.1/2). The feminines end in -η or -α. Those in -α change alpha to eta in the genitive and dative singular unless the alpha is preceded by a vowel or ρ. All first declension nouns have the same endings in the plural. The feminine form of the definite article is declined in the same way as the feminines in -η.

SINGULAR

Nominative	ἡ	τῑμ-ή	χώρ-ᾱ	θάλαττ-α
	the	honour	country	sea
Vocative	—	τῑμ-ή	χώρ-ᾱ	θάλαττ-α
Accusative	τήν	τῑμ-ήν	χώρ-ᾱν	θάλαττ-αν
Genitive	τῆς	τῑμ-ῆς	χώρ-ᾱς	θαλάττ-ης
Dative	τῇ	τῑμ-ῇ	χώρ-ᾳ	θαλάττ-ῃ

PLURAL

Nominative	αἱ	τῑμ-αί	χῶρ-αι	θάλαττ-αι

Vocative	—	τῑμ-αί	χώρ-αι	θάλαττ-αι
Accusative	τάς	τῑμ-άς	χώρ-ᾱς	θαλάττ-ᾱς
Genitive	τῶν	τῑμ-ῶν	χωρ-ῶν	θαλαττ-ῶν
Dative	ταῖς	τῑμ-αῖς	χώρ-αις	θαλάττ-αις

Notes

1 The definite article must agree with the noun it qualifies in number, gender and case: τῶν τῑμῶν *of the honours*, τὰς χώρᾱς *the countries* (accusative). Contexts where it is used in Greek but not in English are:

   (i) with abstract nouns, ἡ ἀλήθεια *truth*
  (ii) with nouns (usually plural) indicating a general class, αἱ κόραι *girls* (as a class)
 (iii) optionally with proper nouns with no difference in sense: ἡ Cικελίᾱ or Cικελίᾱ *Sicily*, ἡ Ἀφροδίτη *Aphrodite*.

In translating a common noun in the singular without the definite article *a* should be supplied in English: ἡ νίκη *the victory*, but νίκη *a victory*.

2 The final alpha of most nouns ending in -έα, -ία, -ρα is long.
3 Here (and in the second declension) when the final syllable bears an acute in the nominative, as in τῑμή, the accent becomes a circumflex in the genitive and dative (for the technical terms see **Appendix 9**).
4 In the genitive plural all first declension nouns have a circumflex on their final syllable.

2.1/3 Basic uses of cases

In English the only case ending in nouns is that of the genitive (as in *girl's*, *men's*, etc.). Elsewhere the function of a noun is shown by its position (the difference in meaning between *the traffic warden hit the driver* and *the driver hit the traffic warden* depends solely on the word order) or by a preposition: *the traffic warden was hit by a car* (here the part played by the car is indicated by the preposition *by*). In Greek, however, the function of a noun is indicated by its **case ending**:

(*a*) The subject of a clause must be put in the **nominative**.
(*b*) When we address a person the **vocative** is used; this is normally preceded by ὦ and followed by a mark of punctuation. For the sake of completeness the vocative is given for such nouns as τῑμή, but, of course, these forms rarely occur.
(*c*) The direct object of a verb must be put in the **accusative**.
(*d*) The **genitive** can express possession: *Kleon's horse* (in English we can also say the *horse of Kleon*). Another common use of the genitive in Greek is to express separation (20.1/4).
(*e*) With nouns denoting living things the **dative** expresses the indirect object after verbs of saying, giving and the like (23.1/2*a*). In *Socrates*

gave a drachma to Xanthippe the direct object is *drachma* (answering the question *gave what?*), which would be put into the accusative δραχμήν; the indirect object is *Xanthippe* (*gave to whom?*), which would be τῇ Ξανθίππῃ with no preposition (we may also say in English *Socrates gave Xanthippe a drachma*). The dative has other uses with nouns denoting living things and can nearly always be translated by *to* or *for*. With inanimate nouns (*Athens, arrow, boat*) different uses are possible and will be treated separately.

The accusative, genitive, and dative, are, for convenience of reference, called the **oblique cases**. They are the cases used after **prepositions**, which perform the same function in Greek as in English, i.e. they define the relation between the word they govern and the rest of the clause in which they are used. In Greek the word governed is always a noun (or noun-equivalent, see 5.1/3) or pronoun (Greek does not say *before now* because *now* is an adverb). With prepositions indicating **motion** and **rest** a pattern can be seen in the case required:

(*f*)   Prepositions indicating **motion towards** govern the accusative, e.g. εἰς τὴν χώρᾱν *into the country*, πρὸς τὴν οἰκίᾱν *towards the house*.

(*g*)   Prepositions indicating **motion away from** govern the genitive, e.g. ἀπὸ τῆς μάχης *from the battle*, ἐκ Cικελίᾱς *out of Sicily*.

(*h*)   Prepositions indicating **rest** or **fixed position** govern the dative, e.g. ἐν τῇ θαλάττῃ *in the sea*.

All the above prepositions, except πρός (3.1/5) take only the case shown.

2.1/4   Verbs in Greek

A finite form of a Greek verb (i.e. one that can function as the verb of a clause) is defined in terms of person, number, tense, mood, and voice. **Person** and **number** are determined by the subject of the verb: a finite verb must agree with its subject in person and number (just as in English we cannot say *we is*). First person is the person(s) speaking, i.e. *I* or *we*; second person is the person(s) spoken to, i.e. *you*; third person is the person(s) or thing(s) spoken about, which can be a pronoun (*he, she, it, they*) or a noun. The concept of number is the same as with nouns. **Tense** indicates the time in which the action of the verb takes place. **Mood** tells us something about the nature of the verb's action in a particular context; at the moment we are only concerned with the **indicative** mood, which is used to express facts. **Voice** shows the relation of the subject to the verb. We shall first deal with the **active**, which is the voice used when the subject is the doer of the action.

Auxiliary verbs (*shall/will, have, be*, etc.) are used to form most tenses of an English verb (*I shall teach, he has taught, we will be taught*), but in Greek are found only in certain passive forms. Elsewhere, the person, number, tense and voice (and also mood—see 14.1/1) are shown by the stem and ending. For example, we can tell by the stem and ending that λύcουcι is third person plural future indicative active of the verb λύω *loosen*, and therefore means *they will loosen*. It is superfluous to add the Greek for *they* (unless for emphasis), as this is part of the information conveyed by the ending.

Verbs in Greek belong to one of two groups (called **conjugations**). These are distinguished by the ending of the first person singular present indicative active, the form in which Greek verbs are customarily cited[1] (contrast the convention in English of referring to a verb by its present infinitive active). Those in -ω (e.g. λύω) are by far the larger class; the other consists of verbs in -μι, e.g. εἰμί *I am* (3.1/6), δίδωμι *give* (18.1/2).

2.1/5 Present and future indicative active of -ω verbs (and corresponding infinitives)

The present indicative active is formed by taking the present stem (λῡ- i.e. λύω minus ω) and adding the endings given below. For the future indicative active we make up the future stem by adding sigma to that of the present (i.e. λῡ + c > λῡc-) and we then apply the same endings. These stems are also used for the infinitives.

		PRESENT		FUTURE	
SINGULAR	1	λύ-ω	*I loosen*	λύc-ω	*I shall loosen*
	2	λύ-εις	*you* (s.) *loosen*	λύc-εις	*you* (s.) *will loosen*
	3	λύ-ει	*he, she, it loosens*	λύc-ει	*he, she, it will loosen*
PLURAL	1	λύ-ομεν	*we loosen*	λύc-ομεν	*we shall loosen*
	2	λύ-ετε	*you* (pl.) *loosen*	λύc-ετε	*you* (pl.) *will loosen*
	3	λύ-ουcι(ν)	*they loosen*	λύc-ουcι(ν)	*they will loosen*
INFINITIVE		λύ-ειν	*to loosen*	λύc-ειν	*to be going to loosen*

Notes

1   In English we have different forms of the present tense, *I loosen*, *I am loosening*, *I do loosen* and so on. There are distinctions in usage between these forms, but as Greek has only one we must decide from the context which English form we should use to translate a Greek verb in the present tense. In one context λύουcι might mean *they loosen*, in another *they are loosening* or *do they loosen*. Likewise, λύcω can also mean *I shall be loosening*.

2   The Greek second person singular is always used when addressing one person, the plural when addressing more than one person. Greek has a

[1] A sub-category called deponents is slightly different — 8.1/2.

distinction here which we no longer have in English. Greek does not, however, have familiar and polite forms of the second person as in French, German, and other languages. A slave and master would have addressed each other in the second person singular.

3 It will be noticed that in each form the stem is followed by an o- or e-sound. This indicates the presence of the so-called **thematic vowel** (o or ϵ), which is most clearly seen in the first and second persons plural. The same pattern, which marks these tenses as **thematic**, is repeated in the imperfect (4.1/1).

4 The final ν shown in brackets in the ending of the third person plural is called the movable ν. In prose it is used (without brackets) only when a word with this ending is followed by a word beginning with a vowel or diphthong or when it stands at the end of a clause (its use in verse is freer). It occurs here and in a few other endings.

5 To form the future of $\pi\acute{\epsilon}\mu\pi\omega$ *send*, the final π of the present stem is combined with c to give $\pi\acute{\epsilon}\mu\psi\text{-}\omega$ *I shall send*. Other final consonants in present stems will be treated at 6.1/4 and 11.1/3.

2.1/6 Word order and elision

(*a*) Although the order of words within a Greek sentence may often be similar to that of English, Greek word order is generally much less predictable. As mentioned in 2.1/3, there is a close link in English between the order in which words occur and their function. In Greek, however, where the grammatical function of a word is determined by its form, not by its position, word order can be varied much more than in English. This is mainly done to emphasize a particular word or phrase. If in the English sentence *Aphrodite is beautiful* we wished to emphasize *beautiful* we would, in speech, articulate it with greater weight (in writing we could underline it or put it in italics). In Greek the emphasis would be conveyed by a change in the word order; $\acute{\eta}$ $'A\phi\rho o\delta\acute{\iota}\tau\eta$ $\acute{\epsilon}c\tau\grave{\iota}$ $\kappa\alpha\lambda\acute{\eta}$ would become $\kappa\alpha\lambda\acute{\eta}$ $\acute{\epsilon}c\tau\iota\nu$ $\acute{\eta}$ $'A\phi\rho o\delta\acute{\iota}\tau\eta$. These differences will be indicated as they occur.

Emphasis apart, two further points regarding word order should be noted here:

(i) Adverbs nearly always precede the word they modify, $\tau\alpha\chi\acute{\epsilon}\omega c$ $\tau\rho\acute{\epsilon}\chi\epsilon\iota$ *he runs* ($\tau\rho\acute{\epsilon}\chi\epsilon\iota$) *quickly* ($\tau\alpha\chi\acute{\epsilon}\omega c$). This particularly applies to the negative $o\grave{v}(\kappa)$ *not*, $o\grave{v}\kappa$ $\acute{\epsilon}\chi\omega$ . . . *I do not have* . . ($o\grave{v}\kappa$ is the form used before vowels and diphthongs with a smooth breathing; it becomes $o\grave{v}\chi$ if the following vowel or diphthong has a rough breathing, e.g. $o\grave{v}\chi$ $\overset{\circ}{v}\epsilon\iota$ *it is not raining*).

(ii) Just as in English we can say *the land of Aphrodite* or *Aphrodite's land*, so in Greek we have $\acute{\eta}$ $\chi\acute{\omega}\rho\bar{a}$ $\tau\hat{\eta}c$ $'A\phi\rho o\delta\acute{\iota}\tau\eta c$ and $\acute{\eta}$ $\tau\hat{\eta}c$

'Ἀφροδίτης χώρᾱ (note that the article of χώρᾱ must be retained in the latter).

(*b*) The Greeks disliked the juxtaposition of a final vowel and an initial vowel (e.g. ἀπὸ 'Ἀθηνῶν *from Athens*). Although tolerated in prose, this is almost totally absent from most forms of verse. In the case of final short vowels (except υ) it is avoided by eliding (i.e. dropping and not pronouncing) α, ε, ι, ο before a word beginning with a vowel or diphthong, e.g. ἀπ' οἰκίᾱς (= ἀπὸ οἰκίᾱς) *from a house*; παρ' 'Ἀφρο-δίτην (= παρὰ 'Ἀ.) *to Aphrodite*. When the vowel following κ, π or τ is elided before a word beginning with a rough breathing, these conso-nants become χ, φ, θ, respectively, e.g. ὑφ' 'Ἑλένης (= ὑπὸ 'Ἑ.) *by Helen*. Elision is marked by an apostrophe as shown. It is not always applied in prose texts.

Note
The final αι of verbal endings can be elided in poetry, and occasionally even in prose (example at 21.2.2(xi)).

2.2   Greek reading

The *Odyssey* describes the return of the Greek hero Odysseus (in English we sometimes use the Latin form of his name *Ulysses*) to his homeland, Ithaca, after the sack of Troy. At a later stage we shall read some of the original, but now we shall start with a simplified version of Odysseus's landing at Scheria, possibly to be identified with the modern Corfu. The scene occurs in the sixth book of the *Odyssey*.

In reading Greek the following steps should be followed:

(*a*)   *Look up each word in the vocabulary and parse it (i.e. define it grammatically; this is particularly necessary with words which vary in form).*
(*b*)   *Mark all finite verbs as this will indicate the number of clauses.*
(*c*)   *By observing punctuation and conjunctions used to join clauses, work out where each clause begins and ends.*
(*d*)   *Take each clause separately and see how each word relates to the finite verb of its clause (subject, object, part of an adverbial phrase etc.).*
(*e*)   *See from the conjunctions how the clauses are related to each other and work out the overall meaning of the sentence.*

An analysis of sentence 13 will be found in the Key.

1   ὁ 'Ὀδυσσεὺς ἀπὸ τῆς Τροίας ἥκει, ἀλλὰ ὁ Ποσειδῶν ἐν τῇ Cχερίᾳ τὴν ναῦν (*ship*) διαφθείρει.
2   ὁ 'Ὀδυσσεὺς ἐκ τῆς θαλάττης φεύγει καὶ ὑπὸ ἐλάᾳ ἑαυτὸν (*himself* acc.) κρύπτει πρὸς τῇ ἀκτῇ.

3   ὄναρ ἡ Ἀθηνᾶ τῇ βασιλείᾳ Ναυσικάᾳ λέγει ὅτι δεῖ (*it is necessary*) τὴν
    στολὴν ἐν τῇ ἀκτῇ πλύνειν.

4   ἅμα τῇ ἡμέρᾳ ἡ Ναυσικάα τὴν στολὴν ἐκ τῆς οἰκίας ἐν ἁμάξῃ πρὸς τὴν
    θάλατταν φέρει.

5   ἐν τῇ ἁμάξῃ ἐστὶ (*there is*) καὶ (*also*) ἐδωδὴ τῇ Ναυσικάᾳ καὶ ταῖς
    ἑταίραις.

6   αἱ κόραι τάχα πλύνουσι τὴν στολὴν πρὸς τῇ ἐλάᾳ οὗ ὁ Ὀδυσσεὺς
    καθεύδει.

7   ἔπειτα αἱ κόραι τὴν στολὴν ἐπὶ τὴν ἀκτὴν ἐπιβάλλουσιν.

8   λούουσιν ἑαυτὰς (*themselves*) καὶ τὴν ἐδωδὴν ἐσθίουσιν ἥν (*which*) ἐν τῇ
    ἁμάξῃ ἔχουσιν.

9   ἕως (*while*) ἐν τῇ ἀκτῇ παίζουσιν, ἡ Ναυσικάα σφαῖραν ῥίπτει ἀλλ' ἡ
    σφαῖρα εἰς δίνην πίπτει.

10 αἱ τῶν κορῶν βοαὶ τὸν Ὀδυσσέα (acc.) ἐγείρουσι καὶ ἐκπλήττουσιν.

11 ὁ Ὀδυσσεὺς θαυμάζει ποῖ τῆς γῆς ἥκει, καὶ ἀπὸ τῆς ἐλάας ἐξαίφνης
    ἔρπει.

12 τὴν Ναυσικάαν καὶ τὰς ἑταίρας ἐκπλήττει.

13 ἀλλ' ἡ Ναυσικάα ἐν τῇ ἀκτῇ ἀναμένει διότι ἡ Ἀθηνᾶ τὴν ἀνδρείαν εἰς
    τὴν καρδίαν εἰσβάλλει.

14 ὁ Ὀδυσσεὺς τῇ Ναυσικάᾳ λέγει ὅτι ἀπὸ τῆς Ὠγυγίας ἥκει.

15 ἡ Ναυσικάα ταῖς ἑταίραις λέγει ὅτι δεῖ τῷ Ὀδυσσεῖ (dat.) ἐδωδὴν καὶ
    στολὴν παρέχειν.

16 τὸν Ὀδυσσέα πρὸς τὴν τοῦ πατρὸς (*of her father*) οἰκίαν ἄγειν ἐθέλει
    ἀλλὰ τὴν τῶν πολιτῶν (*of the citizens*) αἰτίαν δειμαίνει εἰ βλέπουσιν
    αὐτὴν (*her*) μετὰ Ὀδυσσέως (gen.).

17 ὥστε ἡ Ναυσικάα καὶ αἱ κόραι τὴν στολὴν πάλιν ἐν τῇ ἁμάξῃ πρὸς τὴν
    οἰκίαν φέρουσιν, ἀλλ' ὁ Ὀδυσσεὺς ἐκτὸς ἀναμένει.

Notes

1   ὁ nom. s. m. of the definite article (3.1/1); Ὀδυσσεύς 3rd declension
    (11.1/4); ἥκει *has come* (the subject is ὁ Ὀδυσσεύς) the present tense of
    this verb is to be translated by the perfect tense in English; τὴν ναῦν lit.
    the ship, but we would translate *his ship*; Greek normally does not
    indicate possession if this is obvious from the context (9.1/5; cf.
    sentences 4, 5, 12, 13, 15, 16).

2   ὑπὸ ἐλάᾳ *beneath an olive-tree*; as Greek does not have an indefinite
    article (*a, an* in English) this must be supplied in our translation; cf.
    below ἐν ἁμάξῃ (4) and σφαῖραν (9).

5   The datives τῇ Ναυσικάᾳ and ταῖς ἑταίραις are to be translated *for . . .*

7   ἐπὶ . . . ἐπιβάλλουσιν the repetition of ἐπί as a verbal prefix cannot be
    reproduced in English and we would simply say *they throw . . . on to the*
    shore.

9   ἀλλ'= ἀλλά (2.1/6*b*).

10 τόν acc. s. m. of the definite article; ἐκπλήττουσιν sc. *him* (Odysseus);

because the object of the second verb is the same as that of the first, no
pronoun is needed in Greek.

13 εἰς . . . εἰσβάλλει for the repetition of εἰς cf. note on 7.
15 τῷ dat. s. m. of the definite article.
16 τοῦ gen. s. m. of the definite article.

2.2/1 Vocabulary

It is normal practice in Greek dictionaries and lists of Greek words to give the
nominative singular of a noun, its genitive (usually in abbreviated form) and
the appropriate nominative singular form of the article; this information
establishes both its declension and gender, e.g. θάλαττα, -ης, ἡ (note that the
accent in the genitive — here θαλάττης — is not always on the same syllable
as in the nominative; see **Appendix 9**, *a*). Verbs are cited in the first person
singular present indicative, e.g. κρύπτω. Words already given in the
grammatical tables are not repeated below.

ἄγω   *lead, bring*
'Αθηνᾶ, -ᾶς[1], ἡ   (the goddess)
   Athena
αἰτίᾱ, -ᾱς, ἡ   *blame, censure*
ἀκτή, -ῆς, ἡ   *shore, coast*
ἀλλά (conj.)   *but*
ἅμα   *see* ἡμέρᾱ
ἅμαξα, -ης, ἡ   *wagon*
ἀναμένω   *wait, stay*
ἀνδρείᾱ, -ᾱς, ἡ   *courage*
βασίλεια, -ᾱς, ἡ   *princess*
βλέπω   *see*
βοή, -ῆς, ἡ   *shout*
γῆ, -ῆς, ἡ   *land, earth, world*
δειμαίνω (+acc.)   *be afraid of,
   fear*
διαφθείρω   *destroy*
δίνη, -ης, ἡ   *whirlpool*
διότι (conj.)   *because*
ἐγείρω   *awaken, arouse*
ἐδωδή, -ῆς, ἡ   *food*
ἐθέλω   *be willing, wish*
εἰ (conj.)   *if*
εἰς (prep.+acc.)   *into*
εἰσβάλλω   *throw into, put into*
ἐκ (prep.+gen.)   *out of*

ἐκπλήττω   *strike with panic,
   frighten*
ἐκτός (adv.)   *outside*
ἐλάᾱ, -ᾱς, ἡ   *olive-tree*
ἐν (prep.+dat.)   *in, on*
ἐξαίφνης (adv.)   *suddenly*
ἔπειτα (adv.)   *then, next*
ἐπί (prep.+acc.)   *on to*
ἐπιβάλλω   *throw upon*
ἕρπω   *creep, crawl*
ἐσθίω   *eat*
ἑταίρᾱ, -ᾱς, ἡ   *companion* (female)
ἔχω   *have*
ἥκω   *have come*
ἡμέρᾱ, -ᾱς, ἡ   *day*; ἅμα τῇ
   ἡμέρᾳ   *at day-break* or *dawn*
θαυμάζω   *wonder*
καθεύδω   *sleep*
καί (conj.)   *and*
καρδίᾱ, -ᾱς, ἡ   *heart*
κόρη, -ης, ἡ   *girl*
κρύπτω   *hide*
λέγω   *say, speak*
λούω   *wash (the body)*
μετά (prep.+gen.)   *along with, (in
   company) with*

---

[1] 'Αθηνᾶ, originally 'Αθηνάᾱ, has its genitive and dative in -ᾶς, -ᾷ (not -ῆς, -ῇ);
cf. ἐλάᾱ, -ᾱς below.

Ναυσικάα, -ᾱς, ἡ Nausicaa, the
  daughter of Alcinous, king of the
  Phaeacians
'Οδυσσεύς (3rd declension),
  ὁ Odysseus, hero of the *Odyssey*
οἰκίᾱ, -ᾱς, ἡ house
ὄναρ (adv.) *in a dream*
ὅτι (conj.) *that*
οὗ (conj.) *where*
παίζω play
πάλιν (adv.) *back*
παρέχω provide (something to
  somebody)
πίπτω fall
πλῦνω wash (clothes)
ποῖ (interrog. adv.) *(to) where?*
  ποῖ τῆς γῆς where in the world
Ποσειδῶν (3rd declension), ὁ

  Poseidon, the god who ruled the
  sea
πρός (prep.) (+acc.) towards, to;
  (+dat.) near, beside
ῥίπτω throw
στολή, -ῆς, ἡ clothes
σφαῖρα, -ᾱς, ἡ ball
Σχερίᾱ, -ᾱς, ἡ Scheria, the land
  of the Phaeacians
τάχα (adv.) quickly
Τροίᾱ, -ᾱς, ἡ Troy
ὑπό (prep.+dat.) beneath
φέρω carry, bring, take
φεύγω flee, run away
'Ωγυγίᾱ, -ᾱς, ἡ Ogygia, the
  island of Calypso
ὥστε (conj.) consequently, so

Unit 3

3.1 Grammar

3.1/1 Second declension and the masculine and neuter definite article

The second declension is divided into two groups: nouns whose nominative singular ends in -oc, which, with a few exceptions, are masculine, and those whose nominative singular ends in -ον, which are all neuter. Both groups have identical endings except for the nominative, vocative, and accusative. For these cases second declension neuter nouns observe the rule which holds for all neuter nouns in Greek:

> *The vocative and accusative of all neuter nouns are the same as the nominative, both in the singular and in the plural. In the plural the nominative, vocative and accusative of all neuter nouns end in -α (for an apparent exception see 6.1/1c).*

	ὁ ἵππος *the horse*		τὸ δῶρον *the gift*	
	SINGULAR	PLURAL	SINGULAR	PLURAL
Nom.	ὁ ἵππ-ος	οἱ ἵππ-οι	τὸ δῶρ-ον	τὰ δῶρ-α
Voc.	— ἵππ-ε	— ἵππ-οι	— δῶρ-ον	— δῶρ-α
Acc.	τὸν ἵππ-ον	τοὺς ἵππ-ους	τὸ δῶρ-ον	τὰ δῶρ-α
Gen.	τοῦ ἵππ-ου	τῶν ἵππ-ων	τοῦ δώρ-ου	τῶν δώρ-ων
Dat.	τῷ ἵππ-ῳ	τοῖς ἵππ-οις	τῷ δώρ-ῳ	τοῖς δώρ-οις

Notes

1   Feminine nouns of the second declension are declined in exactly the same way as masculines but naturally they require the feminine form of the definite article (and of adjectives; see below 3.1/3): ἡ νῆσος *the island*, τῆς νόσου *of the disease*. Only rarely can they be recognised as feminine by their meaning, e.g. παρθένος *girl*.

2   A finite verb which has a plural **neuter** noun as its subject is almost always *singular*:

> τὰ δῶρά ἐστιν ἐν τῇ οἰκίᾳ.   *The gifts are in the house* (ἐστί is the 3rd s. pres. ind. of εἰμί *I am*—see below 3.1/6).

This curious idiom, which has not been satisfactorily explained, even applies when the neuter noun denotes human beings:

> τὰ ἀνδράποδα οὐκ ἀναμένει ἐν τῇ ἀγορᾷ.   *The captives do not wait in the market-place.*

17

3   In poetry an expanded form of the dative plural of both first and second declensions, -αιcι(ν), -οιcι(ν), often occurs, e.g. τῑμαῖcι(ν), ἵπποιcι(ν) (on the movable ν see 2.1/5 note 4).

3.1/2   First declension (masculine nouns)

These nouns have borrowed the -c of the nominative singular and the -ου ending of the genitive singular from second declension masculines. They are subdivided into those ending in -ᾱc (always preceded by ε, ι or ρ) and those in -ηc.

| | νεᾱνίᾱc *young man* | | κριτήc *judge* | |
	SINGULAR	PLURAL	SINGULAR	PLURAL
Nom.	νεᾱνί-ᾱc	νεᾱνί-αι	κριτ-ήc	κριτ-αί
Voc.	νεᾱνί-ᾱ	νεᾱνί-αι	κριτ-ά	κριτ-αί
Acc.	νεᾱνί-ᾱν	νεᾱνί-ᾱc	κριτ-ήν	κριτ-ᾱ́c
Gen.	νεᾱνί-ου	νεᾱνι-ῶν	κριτ-οῦ	κριτ-ῶν
Dat.	νεᾱνί-ᾳ	νεᾱνί-αιc	κριτ-ῇ	κριτ-αῖc

Notes

1   Most nouns in this class involve male occupations; cf. also ναύτηc *sailor*, cτρατιώτηc *soldier*.
2   When used with these nouns the definite article (and adjectives) must be masculine.
3   Nouns in -τηc (as well as compounds and names of peoples) have a vocative singular in -α (not -ᾱ). All other nouns in -ηc of this declension have a vocative in -η, e.g. ὦ Ἑρμῆ *O Hermes!* Contrast third declension proper names such as Cωκράτηc (6.1/1c).
4   The patronymic suffixes -ίδηc, -ιάδηc are added to the stem of proper names to mean *son of* (Κρονίδηc *son of Κρόνοc*). In many names these suffixes have lost their original force: Θουκυδίδηc *Thucydides*, Ἀλκιβιάδηc *Alcibiades*.

3.1/3   First and second declension adjectives

Adjectives in English, apart from *this* (pl. *these*) and *that* (pl. *those*), are invariable in form. In Greek, however, adjectives must agree with the nouns they qualify (i.e. go with and describe) in case, number and gender, and consequently they are declined in the same way as nouns, e.g. ὁ κακὸc νόμοc *the wicked law*, τὴν καλὴν νίκην *the fine victory (acc.)*, λόγων δεινῶν *of clever speeches*.

The majority of Greek adjectives have their feminine form declined according to the first declension but their masculine and neuter according to the second or third. This latter feature allows us to classify them into first and second declension adjectives and first and third declension adjectives (10.1/3). First and second declension adjectives have, therefore, a feminine in -η (or -ᾱ, when preceded by ε, ι or ρ), a masculine in -ος and a neuter in -ον. καλός *handsome, beautiful, fine* is declined:

	SINGULAR			**PLURAL**		
	M.	F.	N.	M.	F.	N.
Nom.	καλ-ός	καλ-ή	καλ-όν	καλ-οί	καλ-αί	καλ-ά
Voc.	καλ-έ	καλ-ή	καλ-όν	καλ-οί	καλ-αί	καλ-ά
Acc.	καλ-όν	καλ-ήν	καλ-όν	καλ-ούς	καλ-άς	καλ-ά
Gen.	καλ-οῦ	καλ-ῆς	καλ-οῦ	καλ-ῶν	καλ-ῶν	καλ-ῶν
Dat.	καλ-ῷ	καλ-ῇ	καλ-ῷ	καλ-οῖς	καλ-αῖς	καλ-οῖς

δίκαιος *just* and αἰσχρός *ugly, disgraceful* are declined as follows in the singular:

	M.	F.	N.	M.	F.	N.
Nom.	δίκαι-ος	δικαί-ᾱ	δίκαι-ον	αἰσχρ-ός	αἰσχρ-ά	αἰσχρ-όν
Voc.	δίκαι-ε	δικαί-ᾱ	δίκαι-ον	αἰσχρ-έ	αἰσχρ-ά	αἰσχρ-όν
Acc.	δίκαι-ον	δικαί-ᾱν	δίκαι-ον	αἰσχρ-όν	αἰσχρ-άν	αἰσχρ-όν
Gen.	δικαί-ου	δικαί-ᾱς	δικαί-ου	αἰσχρ-οῦ	αἰσχρ-ᾶς	αἰσχρ-οῦ
Dat.	δικαί-ῳ	δικαί-ᾳ	δικαί-ῳ	αἰσχρ-ῷ	αἰσχρ-ᾷ	αἰσχρ-ῷ

The plural is the same as for καλός.[1]

The way in which these adjectives are given in the vocabulary (and in dictionaries) is καλός, -ή, -όν; δίκαιος, -ᾱ, -ον; αἰσχρός, -ά, -όν.

Some adjectives, however, have no separate feminine (the so-called **two termination** adjectives) but employ the -ος forms for masculine and feminine alike. These are nearly all compounds, e.g. εὔλογος *reasonable* (εὖ + λόγος *reason*), ἔμπειρος *experienced* (ἐν + πεῖρα *experience*). Many have the negative ἀ- (or ἀν- before a vowel; cf. English *in-, un-*), e.g. ἄλογος *irrational* (ἀ + λόγος *reason*); ἀνάξιος *unworthy* (ἀν + ἄξιος *worthy*). These adjectives are cited in the form εὔλογος, -ον; ἔμπειρος, -ον. Examples of them in agreement with feminine nouns are: ἡ ἄδικος νίκη *the unjust victory*, αἱ ἔμπειροι Μοῦσαι *the experienced Muses*.

Two important adjectives, πολύς *much* (pl. *many*), and μέγας *great, big*, show irregularities in the masculine and neuter nominative and accusative singular. Otherwise they are declined exactly as if their nominative singular masculine were πολλ-ός and μεγάλ-ος. So in the singular we find:

---

[1] The accent in the genitive plural feminine follows that of the masculine: δικαίων, not δικαιῶν which we would have expected on the analogy of first declension nouns (2.1/2 note 4).

	M.	F.	N.	M.	F.	N.
Nom.	**πολύς**	πολλ-ή	**πολύ**	**μέγας**	μεγάλ-η	**μέγα**
Voc.	—	—	—	μεγάλ-ε	μεγάλ-η	**μέγα**
Acc.	**πολύν**	πολλ-ήν	**πολύ**	**μέγαν**	μεγάλ-ην	**μέγα**
Gen.	πολλ-οῦ	πολλ-ῆς	πολλ-οῦ	μεγάλ-ου	μεγάλ-ης	μεγάλ-ου
Dat.	πολλ-ῷ	πολλ-ῇ	πολλ-ῷ	μεγάλ-ῳ	μεγάλ-ῃ	μεγάλ-ῳ

The plural is entirely regular.

Position of adjectives

(a) Where the definite article is absent, the adjective may appear either before or after its noun: εἰc οἰκίᾱν καλήν *into a beautiful house*, περὶ δεινοῦ λόγου *concerning a clever speech*.

(b) When a noun is used with the definite article we have several possibilities. An adjective used as a simple attribute may occupy the same position as in English: ὁ δίκαιος νεᾱνίᾱς *the just young man*. But note that Greek may achieve exactly the same effect by writing ὁ νεᾱνίᾱς ὁ δίκαιος with the article repeated. Both these positions are called **attributive**. Totally different, however, is the case where the adjective appears outside of the article-noun complex, ὁ νεᾱνίᾱς δίκαιος or δίκαιος ὁ νεᾱνίᾱς. In both these positions the adjective is considered as functioning as a predicate, and the meaning is *the young man is just* (on the omission of ἐcτί see below 3.1/6). Greek makes great use of this **predicative** position and can have a simple sentence where English would require a complex one. So whereas οἰκίᾱν ἔχει καλήν means *he has a beautiful house*, τὴν οἰκίᾱν ἔχει καλήν or καλὴν ἔχει τὴν οἰκίᾱν means *the house which he has is beautiful, it is a beautiful house which he has* (lit. *beautiful the house he has*).

3.1/4 Adverbs

Most adverbs are formed from adjectives by adding -ωc to the stem. In effect this means changing the final ν of the gen. pl. m. of the adjective to c, e.g. δίκαιος (gen. pl. m. δικαίων) *just*, adv. δικαίωc *justly*; ἄδικος (gen. pl. m. ἀδίκων) *unjust*, adv. ἀδίκωc *unjustly*.

Unlike in English, adverbs are nearly always placed immediately **before** the word they modify (2.1.6a(i)); κακῶc καθεύδουcιν *they sleep badly*. This is frequently a valuable clue in reading Greek.

3.1/5 Prepositions

We have already seen some prepositions which indicate motion or rest (2.1/

3*f,g,h*). Many prepositions govern both the accusative and genitive, some the accusative, genitive and dative. There are always, of course, differences of meaning involved, e.g. παρά + acc. = *to (wards)*; + gen. = *from*; + dat. = *at, beside* (παρά is used for persons, not places, e.g. παρὰ ἐμοί lit. *beside me*, i.e. *at my house*, cf. Fr. *chez moi*). The following prepositions are particularly common:

(*a*) **with accusative:**   διά   *on account of*
                            μετά   *after*
                            περί   *around* (time, place or number)

(*b*) **with genitive:**   ἀντί   *instead of*
                            διά   *through, by means of*
                            μετά   *(in company) with*
                            ὑπέρ   *on behalf of*
                            περί   *concerning*

Common idiomatic phrases involving παρά and another preposition κατά are: κατὰ γῆν καὶ κατὰ θάλατταν *by land and sea*; κατὰ/παρὰ τοὺς νόμους *according to/contrary to the laws*.

3.1/6   Present indicative and infinitive of εἰμί *I am*

This verb is irregular in Greek as is its equivalent in other languages. It has little in common with other -μι verbs (18.1/1).

SINGULAR	1	εἰμί	*I am*	PLURAL	ἐcμέν	*we are*
	2	εἶ	*you (s.) are*		ἐcτέ	*you (pl.) are*
	3	ἐcτί(ν)	*he, she, it is*		εἰcί(ν)	*they are*
INFINITIVE		εἶναι	*to be*			

All the above forms are enclitic (see **Appendix 9**, *d*) except εἶ and εἶναι.

εἰμί **never** governs an accusative because it does not express an action inflicted by a subject on an object. What is said about the subject in clauses such as *I am Aphrodite, wisdom is a skill, the girls are beautiful* is put into the **nominative**: Ἀφροδίτη εἰμί, ἡ cοφίᾱ τέχνη ἐcτίν, αἱ κόραι εἰcὶ καλαί. In clauses of this nature the appropriate form of εἰμί (usually ἐcτί or εἰcί) is often omitted (cf. above 3.1/3*b*): ἀθάνατοc ἡ ψῡχή *the soul [is] immortal*; ἄνθρωποc μέτρον ἁπάντων *a man [is] the measure of all things*. Sometimes the context requires that ἐcτί and εἰcί should be translated by *there is* and *there are* respectively; κόραι ἐν τῇ ἀγορᾷ εἰcιν *there are girls in the agora* (we would not normally say in English *girls are in the agora*; cf. 2.2.5).

3.2   Greek reading

An analysis of sentence 10 will be found in the Key.

Proverbs and short quotations

By the end of antiquity the Greeks had accumulated an enormous number of proverbs and pithy sayings. Some have no identifiable origin, others are quotations, generally from poets. The following, and those included in future exercises, are nearly always in their original form.

1   οὐκ εἰςὶν οἱ παμπλούςιοι (*the very rich*) ἀγαθοί.
2   ἐρημία μεγάλη ἐςτὶν ἡ μεγάλη πόλις (*city*).
3   ἡ πενία τὰς τέχνας ἐγείρει.
4   νεκρὸς οὐ δάκνει.
5   In these shorter sayings supply εἰςί in (*i*), ἐςτί in the rest: (*i*) πολλοὶ τραπέζης, οὐκ ἀληθείας, φίλοι. (*ii*) ἡ εὐτυχία πολύφιλος. (*iii*) ὁ ἄνθρωπος πολιτικὸν ζῶον. (*iv*) ἀθάνατος ὁ θάνατος. (*v*) οὐ ςχολὴ δούλοις. (*vi*) χωρὶς ὑγιείας ἄβιος βίος. (*vii*) νόςος φιλίας ἡ κολακεία. (*viii*) κακὸς ἀνὴρ (*man*) μακρόβιος.
6# τὰ μεγάλα δῶρα τῆς Τύχης ἔχει φόβον.
7# κακὸν φέρουςι καρπὸν οἱ κακοὶ φίλοι.
8# αὐθαίρετος λύπη ἐςτὶν ἡ τέκνων ςπορά.
9   δῶρα θεοὺς πείθει.
10 οὔτε ςυμπόςιον χωρὶς ὁμιλίας οὔτε πλοῦτος χωρὶς ἀρετῆς ἡδονὴν ἔχει.
11 ὁ ἀνεξέταστος βίος οὐ βιωτὸς ἀνθρώπῳ.

A fable from Aesop

Aesop was a slave on the island of Samos in the early sixth century BC who composed animal fables. These were at first transmitted orally and became widely known. The collection that survives under Aesop's name seems to have been put into its present form early in the Christian era. The following is an adaptation.

12   (*i*)   πολλοὶ βάτραχοι ἀγγέλους πέμπουςι πρὸς τὸν Κρονίδην διότι μονάρχου χρήζουςιν.

(*ii*) οἱ ἄγγελοι τῷ Κρονίδῃ ὑπὲρ τῶν βατράχων λέγουςιν· ὦ δίκαιε Κρονίδη, δεσπότης εἶ τῶν θεῶν. ἆρα ἐθέλεις τοῖς βατράχοις δεσπότην παρέχειν;

(*iii*) ὁ Κρονίδης ςφόδρα θαυμάζει καὶ μέγα ξύλον εἰς τὴν τῶν βατράχων λίμνην ῥίπτει.

(*iv*) τὸ ξύλον ἐκπλήττει τοὺς βατράχους καὶ ταχέως ἀποτρέχουςιν, ἀλλὰ ὑποπτεύειν ἄρχουςιν ἐπεὶ τὸ ξύλον ἐςτὶν ἀκίνητον.

(*v*)   ὕςτερον τῷ ξύλῳ ἄνευ φόβου ἐπιβαίνουςι καὶ λέγουςιν· ὦ ξένε, ἆρα θεὸς εἶ ἢ ἄνθρωπος ἢ ζῶον;

(*vi*) ἐπεὶ οὐ λέγει οὐδέν, νομίζουσιν ἀνάξιον εἶναι εἰ τοιοῦτον δεσπότην ἔχουσι καὶ ἀγγέλους πάλιν πρὸς τὸν Κρονίδην πέμπουσιν περὶ νέου μονάρχου.

(*vii*) οἱ ἄγγελοι τῷ Κρονίδῃ λέγουσιν· ὦ δέσποτα, δεῖ ἄλλον μόναρχον τοῖς βατράχοις πέμπειν ἐπεὶ ὁ πρῶτός ἐστιν ἀκίνητος καὶ ἀργός.

(*viii*) ὁ τῶν θεῶν δεσπότης ἐν ὀργῇ ἔχει τοὺς βατράχους καὶ μεγάλην ὕδραν πέμπει.

(*ix*) ἡ ὕδρα ἐστὶν ἀπαραίτητος καὶ τοὺς βατράχους ἐσθίει.

(*x*) ὁ μῦθος σαφηνίζει ὅτι δεῖ τοὺς ἀργοὺς δεσπότας φέρειν ἐπεὶ οἱ δραστήριοι δεσπόται ταλαιπωρίας πολλάκις φέρουσιν.

Notes

2 ἡ μεγάλη πόλις the article indicates a general class (2.1/2 note 1); in English we would say *a large city*.

3 With neither noun would we use an article in English (2.1/2 note 1). The same applies in 5(*ii*), (*iii*), (*iv*) and 7.

6 # indicates that the sentence (or passage) is in verse. Poets often vary normal prose usage (but not in 6, 7, 8). Here (and in 9) a neuter plural subject is followed by a singular verb (3.1/1 note 2).

12 (*ii*) A question which does not involve an interrogative word (*who? how?*, etc.) may be introduced by ἆρα (10.1/2*a*), which has no English equivalent; in such cases, English normally reverses subject and verb (*are you a sailor?* ἆρα ναύτης εἶ;).

(*iv*) ἄρχουσιν here *begin*.

(*v*) τῷ ξύλῳ . . . ἐπιβαίνουσι *they step on to the log*, ἐπιβαίνω here takes the dative (cf. 13.1/2*b*).

(*vi*) Certain compound negatives (here οὐδέν) **reinforce** a preceding simple negative (οὐ) and the meaning here is *it says nothing at all* (see 7.1/6); ἀνάξιον (neuter) εἶναι εἰ . . . lit. [*it*] *to be despicable if* . . . , i.e. *that it is despicable that* . . .

(*viii*) ἐν ὀργῇ ἔχει lit. *has in anger*, i.e. *is angry with*.

(*x*) Note the pun on the two meanings of φέρω, *endure* and *bring*.

3.2/1 Vocabulary

ἄβιος, -ον *unlivable, intolerable*
ἀγαθός, -ή, -όν *good*
ἄγγελος, -ου, ὁ *messenger*
ἀθάνατος, -ον *immortal*
ἀκίνητος, -ον *motionless*
ἀλήθεια, -ᾱς, ἡ *truth*
ἄλλος, -η, -ον *other, another*
ἀνάξιος, -ον *worthless, not worthwhile*
ἀνεξέταστος, -ον *without enquiry*
ἄνευ (prep.+gen.) *without*

ἄνθρωπος, -ου, ὁ *man, human being*
ἀπαραίτητος, -ον *unmoved by prayer, pitiless*
ἀποτρέχω *run away*
ἆρα (interrog. particle) *see note to 12 (ii)*
ἀργός, -όν *lazy, idle*
ἀρετή, -ῆς, ἡ *excellence, virtue*
ἄρχω *begin*

αὐθαίρετος, -ον self-chosen, self-inflicted

βάτραχος, -ου, ὁ frog

βίος, -ου, ὁ life

βιωτός, -όν worth living

δάκνω bite

δεσπότης, -ου, ὁ master

δοῦλος, -ου, ὁ slave

δραστήριος, -ον active

δῶρον, -ου, τό gift

ἐπεί (conj.) since

ἐπιβαίνω (+dat.) step on to

ἐρημίᾱ, -ᾱς, ἡ desert, wilderness

εὐτυχίᾱ, -ᾱς, ἡ good fortune

ζῷον, -ου, τό living being, animal

ἤ (conj.) or

ἡδονή, -ῆς, ἡ pleasure

θάνατος, -ου, ὁ death

θεός, -οῦ, ὁ god

κακός, -ή, -όν bad, evil

καρπός, -οῦ, ὁ fruit

κολακείᾱ, -ᾱς, ἡ flattery

Κρονίδης, -ου, ὁ son of Cronos (i.e. Zeus)

λίμνη, -ης, ἡ pool, marsh

λύπη, -ης, ἡ grief

μακρόβιος, -ον long-lived

μόναρχος, -ου, ὁ monarch

μῦθος, -ου, ὁ story, fable

νεκρός, -οῦ, ὁ corpse

νέος, -ᾱ, -ον new

νομίζω think, consider

νόσος, -ου, ἡ disease

ξένος, -ου, ὁ stranger

ξύλον, -ου, τό log

ὁμῑλίᾱ, -ᾱς, ἡ company

ὀργή, -ῆς, ἡ anger; ἐν ὀργῇ ἔχειν (+acc.) be angry with

οὐδέν (neuter pron.) nothing

οὔτε . . . οὔτε neither . . . nor

παμπλούσιος, -ον very rich

πείθω persuade

πέμπω send

πενίᾱ, -ᾱς, ἡ poverty

πλοῦτος, -ου, ὁ wealth

πολῑτικός, -ή, -όν political

πολλάκις (adv.) often

πολύφιλος, -ον having many friends

πρῶτος, -η, -ον first

σαφηνίζω make clear

σπορά, -ᾶς, ἡ sowing, begetting

συμπόσιον, -ου, τό drinking party

σφόδρα (adv.) very much, exceedingly

σχολή, -ῆς, ἡ leisure, rest

ταλαιπωρίᾱ, -ᾱς, ἡ hardship, distress

ταχέως (adv.) quickly

τέκνον, -ου, τό child

τέχνη, -ης, ἡ art, craft, skill

τοιοῦτος (adj. 21.1/3) of such a kind, such

τράπεζα, -ης, ἡ table

Τύχη, -ης, ἡ Fortune, Chance

ὑγίεια, -ᾱς, ἡ health

ὕδρᾱ, -ᾱς, ἡ hydra, water-serpent

ὑποπτεύω suspect, be suspicious

ὕστερον (adv.) later, afterwards

φέρω bear, bring

φιλίᾱ, -ᾱς, ἡ friendship

φίλος, -η, -ον dear, friendly; as a noun friend

φόβος, -ου, ὁ fear

χρήζω (+gen.) be in need of, desire

χωρίς (prep.+gen.) without, apart from

Unit 4

4.1   Grammar

4.1/1   Imperfect indicative active and weak aorist indicative and infinitive active of -ω verbs

Both the imperfect and the aorist (in the indicative) have reference to the past. The aorist has other moods, which we shall treat later, but the imperfect exists only in the indicative.

The term **weak** aorist is used to distinguish the formation of this tense in λύω (and most other -ω verbs) from that in a minority of -ω verbs which have a **strong** aorist (7.1/1). There is no difference in meaning. The weak aorist is so named because its stem requires a suffix (ϲ added to the present stem), whereas the stem of the strong aorist resembles that of the imperfect in having no suffix. The concept of verbal strength as shown in the presence (weak) or absence (strong) of suffixes is a somewhat whimsical notion of nineteenth-century grammarians.

The aorist stem of λύω is λῡϲ- (the same as for the future) while the imperfect simply uses that of the present, λῡ-. In the indicative of both the **augment** is prefixed to the stem. This, in λύω and other verbs beginning with a consonant, consists of the vowel ἐ, giving us ἐλῡ- (imperfect), ἐλῡϲ- (aorist). The two sets of endings have similarities but the vowel immediately following the stem in the aorist is α in five of the six forms, whereas in this position in the imperfect we have the same pattern of o- and e- sounds as in the present (cf. 2.1/5 note 3):

	IMPERFECT	AORIST
SINGULAR	1 ἔλῡ-ον *I was loosening, used to loosen*	ἔλῡϲ-α *I loosened*
	2 ἔλῡ-εϲ	ἔλῡϲ-αϲ
	3 ἔλῡ-ε(ν)	ἔλῡϲ-ε(ν)
PLURAL	1 ἐλῡ́-ομεν	ἐλῡ́ϲ-αμεν
	2 ἐλῡ́-ετε	ἐλῡ́ϲ-ατε
	3 ἔλῡ-ον	ἔλῡϲ-αν
INFINITIVE	——	λῦϲ-αι

The imperfect and the aorist indicative both represent actions which occurred in the past, but, whereas the aorist simply tells us that an action took place, e.g. τοὺϲ νεᾱνίᾱϲ ἐπαιδεύϲαμεν *we educated the young men*, the

25

imperfect tells us that an action was continuous or repeated, e.g. τοὺc νεᾱνίᾱc ἐπαιδεύομεν *we were educating/used to educate the young men* (the choice between continuous action *were educating* and habitual action *used to educate* will depend on the context.[1] In other words, while the aorist indicative views a past action as a simple event, the imperfect indicative views it as a process, either continuous or interrupted (repeated or habitual). The difference between the two usually depends on our perception of the nature of the action or event described. We may, in a particular context, see it simply as something that happened in the past (*it rained last summer*). In another context we may see the same event as something continuous (*it was raining last summer when Socrates visited us*) or repeated (*last summer it used to rain every time I went to the Acropolis*). Naturally, many past actions and events are not normally viewed in more than one way (*Pericles died during the plague*). The term covering distinctions of this sort is **aspect**. We say that, although both these tenses of the indicative describe something that happened in the past, the aorist indicative expresses a momentary aspect, the imperfect a continuous or habitual aspect.

This distinction in the indicative between the imperfect and the aorist also applies in the **infinitive** between the **present** and **aorist**, although there is no specific time reference (but see 8.1/3a and 21.1/1 note). The present infinitive is used for an action which is seen as going on, in the process of happening or being repeated. The aorist infinitive is used for an action which is seen simply as an event. Often both are to be translated in English simply by a present infinitive:

> ὁ Ἱππόλυτος τὸν Γλαῦκον ἐκέλευcεν αἰὲν ἀριcτεύειν. *Hippolytus ordered Glaucus to be always best* (ἀριcτεύειν *to be best* present infinitive, because the action is seen as one which is going on and continuing).
>
> ἡ Ξανθίππη τὸν δοῦλον ἐκέλευcε κροῦcαι τὴν θύραν. *Xanthippe ordered the slave to knock [on] the door* (κροῦcαι aorist infinitive, because Xanthippe envisages a simple (single) act; the present infinitive κρούειν would imply a continual action and require the translation *to keep knocking*).

The imperfect has no infinitive because the present infinitive covers the meaning it would have had (i.e. *to be loosening* in a past context). For similar reasons the imperfect has no other moods either.

Notes

1 The augment is prefixed to the indicative forms of the three **historic** tenses (the tenses whose indicative describes something in the past, viz

[1] The imperfect may also have two other meanings: *began to* (*I began to educate*, etc. **inceptive imperfect**) and *tried to* (*I tried to educate*, etc. **conative imperfect**).

imperfect, aorist, pluperfect (16.1/2)); it does **not** occur in the four **primary** tenses (the tenses whose indicative describes something in the present or future, viz present, future, perfect (15.1/1) and future perfect (16.1/4 note 2)). There is also a formal difference between the two categories in the 3rd pl. ind. act. ending. In historic tenses this has a final -ν (e.g. ἔλῡον, ἔλῡcαν), but in primary tenses ends in -cι(ν) (e.g. λῡ΄ουcι(ν), λῡ΄coucι(ν)).

2   There are two types of augment:

(i) the **syllabic** augment, as described above, where a verb begins with a consonant. An initial ρ is doubled: ῥίπτω *throw*, impf. ἔρρῑπτον. This augment is so called because it adds a syllable to the forms where it is used.

(ii) the **temporal** augment. This variety of the augment is called temporal (Latin **tempus** *time*) because it increases the time taken to pronounce (i.e. lengthens) an initial vowel according to the following table. Note that α is lengthened to η and that ι, when the second element of a diphthong, becomes subscript. As ι and υ (unlike ε/η and ο/ω) can represent both long and short vowels the temporal augment does not affect the spelling of verbs beginning with them.

$$\begin{array}{ll}
α > η & αι > ῃ \\
ε > η & αυ > ηυ \\
ι > ῑ & ει > ῃ \\
ο > ω & ευ > ηυ \\
υ > ῡ & οι > ῳ
\end{array}$$

η and ω remain unchanged

Examples are: ἀκούω *hear*, aor. ἤκουcα; ἐλπίζω *hope*, impf. ἤλπιζον; οἰκτίρω *pity*, impf. ῷκτῑρον; ὠδίνω *be in labour*, impf. ὤδῑνον (for other examples see **Principal parts of verbs**). A few verbs with initial ε take ει not η, e.g. ἔχω has impf. εἶχον (see 7.1/1 note 4). ει and ευ are often not changed, e.g. εὑρίcκω *find*, impf. εὕριcκον or ηὕριcκον.

3   The endings of the 1st s. and 3rd pl. of the imperfect indicative active are the same. The context of a particular form will always make clear which person is meant.

4   Like its present, the imperfect of εἰμί is irregular: ἦ or ἦν, ἦcθα, ἦν, ἦμεν, ἦτε, ἦcαν. This is the only past tense of εἰμί because the act of being was regarded as necessarily extending over a period of time. For all forms of εἰμί see **Appendix 3**.

4.1/2   First and second person pronouns, and αὐτόν, -ήν, -ό

As in English, so in Greek we have pronouns of the first and second persons. These are declined as follows:

	First Person		**Second Person**	
	SINGULAR			
Nom.	ἐγώ	*I*	cύ (also voc.)	*you* (s.)
Acc.	ἐμέ, με	*me*	cέ, cε	*you*
Gen.	ἐμοῦ, μου	*of me*	coῦ, coυ	*of you*
Dat.	ἐμοί, μοι	*to/for me*	coί, coι	*to/for you*
	PLURAL			
Nom.	ἡμεῖς	*we*	ὑμεῖς (also voc.)	*you* (pl.)
Acc.	ἡμᾶς	*us*	ὑμᾶς	*you*
Gen.	ἡμῶν	*of us*	ὑμῶν	*of you*
Dat.	ἡμῖν	*to/for us*	ὑμῖν	*to/for you*

The unaccented forms με, μου, μοι, cε, coυ, coι are unemphatic and enclitic (**Appendix 9**, *d*): διώκει με ἡ ᾽Αcπαcίᾱ *Aspasia is chasing me*. The other forms are emphatic: οὐ cέ, ἀλλὰ ἐμὲ διώκει ἡ ᾽Αcπαcίᾱ *it's me, not you, that Aspasia is chasing* (lit. *Aspasia is chasing not you but me*). With prepositions the emphatic forms are used, e.g. μετὰ coῦ *with you*, except in the case of πρόc: πρόc με *towards me*. Since the endings of verbs indicate the person involved, the nominative forms will occur only where emphasis is required.

Likewise, in the third person there is no need in Greek for an unemphatic form of the pronoun in the nominative since this too is supplied by the personal endings of the verb: λέγει *he/she/it speaks* (the gender of the subject will be clear from the context). The oblique cases (2.1/3), however, are supplied by αὐτόν, -ήν, -ό *him, her, it* (the nominative has another meaning—9.1/3), which is declined exactly like the corresponding forms of καλόc (3.1/3) except that the neuter accusative singular is αὐτό: ἡ ᾽Αcπαcίᾱ ἐχθὲc ἐδίωκεν αὐτόν *Aspasia was chasing him yesterday*. In the plural, whereas English has only one form (*them*), Greek distinguishes between the genders: m. αὐτούc, f. αὐτάc, n. αὐτά, etc. (for the emphatic third person pronouns, see 9.1/1).

Note

The possessive genitive of the **unemphatic** personal pronoun is placed after the noun which it qualifies, εἰc τὴν οἰκίᾱν μου *into my house* (lit. *into the house of me*); ἐκ τῆc οἰκίᾱc αὐτῶν *from their house* (lit. *from the house of them*). For the position of the genitive of the **emphatic** personal pronouns see 9.1/5*b*.

4.1/3 Connecting particles

A fundamental feature of Greek is the ubiquitous occurrence of particles. These are short, indeclinable words, many of which are **postpositive**, i.e. they cannot occur as first word in the phrase or sentence where they are used (these we shall mark here and in the vocabulary with an asterisk). Those such as καί *and* and ἀλλά *but*, which are not postpositive, are also called conjunctions.

Particles have two basic functions:

(a) to act as connectives linking grammatical elements of equal weight (words with words, phrases with phrases, sentences with sentences)

(b) to add shades of tone, colour or emphasis to individual words, phrases or sentences, which in English would simply be conveyed by a variation in the tone or emphasis of the voice.

Here we will concentrate mainly on connectives. Other particles will be explained as they occur in the reading and at 13.1/3.

With a very few well-defined exceptions, every sentence in Greek is connected to the preceding sentence by a connecting particle. The commonest of these is δέ* *and*, which is regularly used to connect a string of sentences where in English we would avoid any connecting word at all. In English it would be considered very bad style to begin sentence after sentence with *and*, but in Greek it is totally natural and acceptable. δέ* is also translatable as *but*, but when so used it denotes only a slight contrast: ὁ ᾿Αχιλλεὺς ἦν ἐν τῇ cκηνῇ· ὁ δὲ Πάτροκλοc ἔφερεν οἶνον *Achilles was in the tent but* (or *and*) *Patroclus was bringing wine*. A strongly contrasting *but* is expressed by ἀλλά, e.g. οὐ βραδέωc ἀλλὰ ταχέωc οἱ βάρβαροι ἡμᾶc ἐδίωκον *the barbarians were chasing us not slowly but quickly*. Note also γάρ* *for, as*, which introduces the **reason** for what goes before, e.g. οὐ μένομεν· οἱ γὰρ βάρβαροι ἡμᾶc διώκουcιν *we are not staying as the barbarians are chasing us*. Similarly οὖν* *therefore, so*, introduces the **result** of what goes before, e.g. οἱ βάρβαροι ἡμᾶc διώκουcιν· ταχέωc οὖν τρέχομεν *the barbarians are chasing us; therefore we are running quickly*.

καί *and* is frequently used as a simple conjunction connecting words, clauses or sentences, ἡμεῖc καὶ ὑμεῖc *you and we* (Greek gives precedence to the 1st person, English is more polite). καὶ ... καί is used to express *both ... and*, καὶ ἡ ᾿Αφροδίτη καὶ ὁ Διόνυcοc *both Aphrodite and Dionysos*, and the same sense can also be conveyed by τε* ... καί, but since τε* is postpositive (and enclitic; see **Appendix 9**, *d*), the above phrase would become ἥ τε ᾿Αφροδίτη καὶ ὁ Διόνυcοc. Less commonly τε* is used by itself as the equivalent of δέ or καί to connect a sentence to a preceding sentence.

καί may also be used **adverbially** in the sense *also, even, actually*, καὶ cύ, τέκνον *even you* (or *you too*), *[my] child*; τὸν βάρβαρον καὶ ἐδίωκον *I was actually chasing the barbarian*. In this usage καί stands immediately before the word it modifies. The negative of adverbial καί is οὐδέ, *not even*, e.g. οὐδὲ ὁ οἶνοc ἀγαθόc *not even the wine [is] good*. (As a conjunction οὐδέ also means *nor, and ... not*.)

One of the most important combinations of particles is that of μέν* followed at a distance by δέ*. μέν*, however, does **not** connect its own word group with anything preceding. For convenience, it is normally translated in dictionaries by *on the one hand*, which is somewhat too emphatic since μέν* simply introduces the first of a parallel pair of balanced or contrasted items. When we see μέν* we know to look ahead to find the corresponding δέ*. This tendency to place words in a formally balanced structure is fundamental to Greek. Any page of a Greek author will contain at least one μέν* ... δέ*.

We may think of the pair as meaning *on the one hand ... and/but on the other hand*, but in most cases such a translation would be heavy or clumsy. Thus 'Αλκιβιάδης μὲν λέγει ἐν τῇ ἀγορᾷ, ἐγὼ δὲ βαδίζω μετὰ τῆς 'Ασπασίας should not be translated by *Alcibiades on the one hand is speaking in the agora, but I on the other hand am walking with Aspasia* but by *Alcibiades is speaking ... but I am walking ...* or *whereas Alcibiades is speaking ... I am walking ...*

The two elements balanced by μὲν* ... δέ* must always be structurally parallel and the words they follow must be of equal grammatical weight. These can be nouns and pronouns (as above), or adverbs, e.g. εὖ μὲν λέγει, κακῶς δὲ πράττει *he speaks **well** but acts **badly***, or verbs, e.g. λέγει μὲν εὖ, πράττει δὲ κακῶς *he **speaks** well but **acts** badly*; here the change in the elements contrasted has meant that the adverbs εὖ and κακῶς have been placed after the words they qualify (cf. 2.1/6a). Other parts of speech can also be contrasted in this way.

4.2   Greek reading

From here on no special vocabularies will be given. An analysis of sentence 5 will be found in the Key.

1   αἱ μὲν ἡδοναὶ θνηταί, αἱ δ' ἀρεταὶ ἀθάνατοι.
2   ἄρτον οὐκ εἶχεν ὁ πτωχὸς καὶ τυρὸν ἠγόραζεν.
3   μισθὸς ἀρετῆς ἔπαινος, κακίας δὲ ψόγος.
4# δεινοὶ πλέκειν τοι μηχανὰς Αἰγύπτιοι.
5   τοῖς μὲν δούλοις ἡ ἀνάγκη νόμος, τοῖς δὲ ἐλευθέροις ἀνθρώποις ὁ νόμος ἀνάγκη.
6# πάλαι ποτ' ἦσαν ἄλκιμοι Μιλήσιοι.
7   ἀετὸς μυίας οὐ θηρεύει.
8   **Futility**
    (*i*) εἰς οὐρανὸν πτύεις. (*ii*) ἐξ ἄμμου σχοινίον πλέκεις. (*iii*) θάλατταν σπείρεις. (*iv*) ἵππον εἰς πεδίον διδάσκεις τρέχειν. (*v*) κατόπιν ἑορτῆς ἥκεις. (*vi*) νεκρὸν μαστίζεις. (*vii*) ὄνον κείρεις. (*viii*) πρὸ τῆς νίκης τὸ ἐγκώμιον ᾄδεις. (*ix*) πρὸς κέντρα λακτίζεις. (*x*) τὰς μηχανὰς μετὰ τὸν πόλεμον κομίζεις.
9   **The fall of Croesus**
    Herodotus (fifth century BC) is the earliest surviving Greek historian and

has been called the father of history. The subject of his work is the rise of the Persian empire and its fateful clash with the Greek world which culminated in the unsuccessful invasion of Greece in 480–479 BC. The following passage is based on Herodotus' description of the subjugation of Lydia (see frontispiece map), which brought the Persians into contact with the Greeks of the Asia Minor coast.

ὁ δὲ Κροῖσος ὁ τῶν Λυδῶν βασιλεὺς (king) τὴν τῶν Περςῶν ἀρχὴν
διαφθείρειν ἤθελεν· κατὰ γὰρ τὸ ἐν Δελφοῖς χρηστήριον ἀρχὴν μεγάλην
ἔμελλε παῦσαι. ἀλλὰ τέλος τὴν μὲν ἑαυτοῦ (his own) ἀρχὴν ἔπαυσεν, τὴν
δὲ τῶν Περςῶν οὔ. μετὰ δὲ τὴν τῶν Περςῶν νίκην ὁ Κῦρος ὁ τῶν
Περςῶν βασιλεὺς τὸν Κροῖσον ἐπὶ πυρὰν μεγάλην ἀνεβίβασεν   5
(made . . . go up). ὁ δὲ Κροῖσος τοὺς λόγους τοὺς τοῦ Cόλωνος (of Solon)
τοῦ Ἀθηναίου ἐφρόντιζε· οὐδεὶς (no-one) τῶν ἀνθρώπων ὄλβιος πρὸ τοῦ
θανάτου. ἥσυχος οὖν ἔμενε τὴν τελευτήν· ἀλλὰ ὁ Κῦρος, διότι ὁ Κροῖσος
καὶ ὅσιος ἦν καὶ ἀγαθός, ἐκέλευσε μὲν τοὺς στρατιώτας ἀπὸ τῆς πυρᾶς
αὐτὸν καταβιβάσαι (to bring down), ἔλεξε (spoke) δὲ ὧδε· ὦ Κροῖσε, τίς   10
(who?) ςε ἀνθρώπων ἔπεισε (persuaded) πολέμιον ἀντὶ φίλου ἐπὶ τὴν γῆν
μου στρατεῦσαι; ὁ δὲ Κροῖσος, ὦ Κῦρε, ἔφη (said), ἐγὼ μὲν ἐπὶ cὲ
ἐστράτευσα, ὁ δὲ θεὸς ὁ ἐν Δελφοῖς ἔπεισέ με στρατεῦσαι. οὐ γάρ εἰμι
ἀνόητος οὐδὲ ἐθέλω τὸν πόλεμον ἔχειν ἀντὶ τῆς εἰρήνης. ἐν μὲν γὰρ τῇ
εἰρήνῃ οἱ νεανίαι τοὺς γεραιοὺς (the old) θάπτουσιν, ἐν δὲ τῷ πολέμῳ οἱ   15
γεραιοὶ τοὺς νεανίας. ἀλλὰ τοῦτο (lit. this thing) φίλον ἦν τοῖς θεοῖς. ὁ οὖν
Κῦρος αὐτὸν ἔλυσε καὶ ἐγγὺς καθεῖσεν (made . . . sit). ὁ δὲ Κροῖσος αὖθις
ἔλεξεν· ὦ Κῦρε, τί (what?) πράττουσιν οἱ στρατιῶταί σου; τὴν πόλιν (city)
σου, ἔφη ὁ Κῦρος, ἁρπάζουσι καὶ τὸν πλοῦτόν σου ἐκφέρουσιν. οὐχ
ἁρπάζουσι τὴν πόλιν μου, ἔφη ὁ Κροῖσος, οὐδὲ τὸν πλοῦτον· οὐδὲν   20
(nothing) γὰρ ἐμοί ἐστιν. ἀλλὰ cὲ φέρουσί τε καὶ ἄγουσιν. μετὰ δὲ τοῦτο
φίλος ἦν αὐτῷ· τὴν γὰρ σοφίαν αὐτοῦ ἐν τιμῇ εἶχεν ὁ Κῦρος.

Notes

1 The appropriate part of εἰμί is to be supplied (also in 3, 4, 5).
2 Cheese (τῡρός) would have been something of a luxury to the poor.
3 Take μιςθός with the genitives ἀρετῆς and κακίας; normal prose usage would require ὁ μιςθός but the definite article is often omitted in proverbs and in verse.
4 τοι is a particle conveying emphasis, commonly employed in proverbs; it is not to be translated, as in English we would convey the emphasis by tone of voice; μηχανᾱς here used metaphorically *devices, ways and means* (in 8(*x*) below the word is used concretely).
6 Miletus, the city of the Μιλήςιοι, flourished in the seventh and sixth centuries BC; in later times it became symbolic of past greatness; Μιλήςιοι does not have an article as this is optional with proper nouns (2.1/2 note 1(ii)).
8 (*x*) μηχαναί are here *engines of war* (siege weapons and the like).
9 *l*.1 δέ connects this passage with what precedes in the original and need

not be translated. *l.2 Δελφοί* is a plural place name. There are many such names in Greek ('*Aθῆναι Athens, Θῆβαι Thebes*). *l.3 ἔμελλε was destined to, was going to.* *l.6* Solon was an Athenian statesman who had visited Croesus and, in conversation with him, had enunciated the very Greek sentiment *Call no man happy before he dies* (only then can a true and full judgement be made). *ll.7ff.* ἐφρόντιζε *began to ponder* inceptive imperfect (4.1/1 footnote); οὐδείς . . . θανάτου are Solon's actual words (inverted commas are not normally used in printing Greek—1.1/1 note 3); ἥcυχος translate by an adverb *quietly* (Greek often uses an adjective where English would have an adverb). *ll.*10–11. Take τίc . . . ἀνθρώπων together; take πολέμιον with cε, *[as an] enemy* (Greek does not here need an equivalent to the English *as*). *ll.*16f. τοῦτο refers to what has happened to Croesus; φίλον + dat. *dear to, pleasing to.* *l.*19 οὐχ 2.1/6a(i). *l.*21 φέρουcί τε καὶ ἄγουcιν lit. *are both carrying and driving*, i.e. *are plundering and carrying off* (a set expression; the τε need not be translated).

Unit 5

5.1 Grammar

5.1/1 Third declension – consonant stem nouns (1)

The third declension contains nouns of all three genders. They are divided into two classes, those with stems ending in a consonant and those with stems ending in a vowel or diphthong. Within the various sub-groups of each class masculine and feminine nouns have the same case endings but neuters always follow the rule previously given (3.1/1) for the nominative, vocative and accusative (not every sub-group has each gender). The gender of a third declension noun is only sometimes predictable from its ending.

With all consonant stem nouns we discover the stem by subtracting -ος from the genitive singular (e.g. γύψ *vulture*, gen. γῡπός, stem γῡπ-) and the other case endings are added to this. As the stem is modified, occasionally beyond recognition, in the nominative singular, both nominative and genitive singular must be learnt.

(*a*) **Stems in κ, γ, χ, (*palatals*), π, β, φ, (*labials*) and τ, δ θ, (*dentals*).**
The declension of regular masculine and feminine nouns with stems ending in these consonants is given below. Masculine and feminine nouns in these sub-groups have a nominative singular in ς, which combines with, or replaces, the final consonant of the stem as follows:

$$\kappa/\gamma/\chi + \varsigma > \xi;\ \pi/\beta/\phi + \varsigma > \psi;\ \tau/\delta/\theta + \varsigma > \varsigma$$

The same changes occur before the dative plural ending -σι (which can take a movable ν; cf. 2.1/5 note 4); they also occur in verbs with similar stems (6.1/4).

	φύλαξ (m)	γύψ (m)	ἔρως (m)	πατρίς (f)
	guard	*vulture*	*love*	*native land*
stem	φυλακ-	γῡπ-	ἐρωτ-	πατριδ-

SINGULAR

	φύλαξ (m)	γύψ (m)	ἔρως (m)	πατρίς (f)
N.V.	φύλαξ	γύψ	ἔρως	πατρίς (V. πατρί)
Acc.	φύλακ-α	γῦπ-α	ἔρωτ-α	πατρίδ-α
Gen.	φύλακ-ος	γῡπ-ός	ἔρωτ-ος	πατρίδ-ος
Dat.	φύλακ-ι	γῡπ-ί	ἔρωτ-ι	πατρίδ-ι

PLURAL

N.V.	φύλακ-ες	γῦπ-ες	ἔρωτ-ες	πατρίδ-ες
Acc.	φύλακ-ας	γῦπ-ας	ἔρωτ-ας	πατρίδ-ας
Gen.	φυλάκ-ων	γυπ-ῶν	ἐρώτ-ων	πατρίδ-ων
Dat.	φύλαξι(ν)	γῦψί(ν)	ἔρω-ςι(ν)	πατρί-ςι(ν)

Within these sub-groups the only neuters are those with a τ stem. The vast majority of these have a nominative singular in -μα and a genitive in -ματος. Of the others some have a sigma in the nominative singular (as κέρας), some do not (e.g. ἧπαρ, ἥπατος *liver*).

	cῶμα (n) *body*		κέρας (n) *horn*	
stem	cωματ-		κερᾱτ-	
	SINGULAR	PLURAL	SINGULAR	PLURAL
N.V.	cῶμα	cώματ-α	κέρας	κέρᾱτ-α
Acc.	cῶμα	cώματ-α	κέρας	κέρᾱτ-α
Gen.	cώματ-ος	cωμάτ-ων	κέρᾱτ-ος	κερᾱ́τ-ων
Dat.	cώματ-ι	cώμα-ςι(ν)	κέρᾱτ-ι	κέρᾱ-ςι(ν)

(b) Stems in ντ (*all masculine*)

These have a nominative singular in -ᾱς or -ων. Unlike nouns of the preceding sub-groups (except πατρίς), they have a separate vocative singular, which is formed by dropping τ from the stem. Their dative plural has the change ντ + ς > ς, with lengthening of the preceding α and ο to ᾱ and ου (not ω) respectively. This lengthening occurs to compensate for the reduction of three consonants to one.

	γίγᾱς (m) *giant*		λέων (m) *lion*	
stem	γιγαντ-		λεοντ-	
	SINGULAR	PLURAL	SINGULAR	PLURAL
Nom.	γίγᾱς	γίγαντ-ες	λέων	λέοντ-ες
Voc.	γίγαν	γίγαντ-ες	λέον	λέοντ-ες
Acc.	γίγαντ-α	γίγαντ-ας	λέοντ-α	λέοντ-ας
Gen.	γίγαντ-ος	γιγάντ-ων	λέοντ-ος	λεόντ-ων
Dat.	γίγαντ-ι	γίγᾱςι(ν)	λέοντ-ι	λέουςι(ν)

Notes

1 Some nouns with these stems are slightly irregular, mostly in the nominative singular. The most common are:

γόνυ	γόνατος (n)	*knee*
γυνή	γυναικός (f)	*woman* (voc. s. γύναι)
θρίξ	τριχός (f)	*hair* (dat. pl. θριξί(ν))
νύξ	νυκτός (f)	*night* (dat. pl. νυξί(ν))
ὀδούς	ὀδόντος (m)	*tooth*
οὖς	ὠτός (n)	*ear*

παῖς   παιδός (m or f)   *child* (voc. s. παῖ)
πούς   ποδός (m)   *foot*
ὕδωρ   ὕδατος (n)   *water*

2   Stems in ιδ which are **not** accented on the ι have -ιν, not -ιδα, in the acc. sing., e.g. ἔρις, ἔριδος (f) *strife*, acc. ἔριν. This also applies to χάρις, χάριτος (f) *favour*, acc. χάριν and ὄρνῑς, ὄρνῑθος (m. or f.) *bird*, acc. ὄρνῑν.
3   Third declension monosyllables are accented on their ending in the genitive and dative, both singular and plural (see γύψ above).

5.1/2   Contracted verbs

Unlike verbs with stems ending in ι and υ (ἐςθίω *eat*, λύω *loosen*), verbs whose stems end in α, ε and ο contract their stem vowel with the initial vowel of the endings in the present and imperfect. A consonantal suffix is used to form the stem of the other tenses (e.g. ς in the future and aorist—see note 2). Examples of contracted verbs are: τῑμά-ω *honour*, ποιέ-ω *do, make*, δηλό-ω *make clear, show*. Since all three types contract their stem vowels and the -ω of the 1st s. pres. ind. act. to -ῶ (τῑμῶ, ποιῶ, δηλῶ), these verbs are always cited in vocabulary lists in their **uncontracted** form to make identification immediately obvious. For the rules governing the accentuation of contracted verbs see **Appendix 9**, *b*(i). Paradigms for the three types are given in **Appendix 2**. As the endings involved are the same as for λύω, it is the rules for contraction which are our principal concern here:

(*a*)   *Stems in* **α** (*model* **τῑμάω**)

α + an e-sound (ε, η) > ᾱ: ἐτίμᾱ (ἐτίμα-ε)
α + an o-sound (ο, ου, ω) > ω: τῑμῶςι (τῑμά-ουςι); τῑμῶμεν (τῑμά--ομεν)
α + an ι-diphthong (ει, ῃ, οι) retains the iota as a subscript in the contracted form: τῑμᾷ (τῑμά-ει)

The combinations α + η/ῃ/οι occur in forms not yet treated.

(*b*)   *Stems in* **ε** (*model* **ποιέω**)

ε + ε > ει: ποιεῖτε (ποιέ-ετε)
ε + ο > ου: ἐποίουν (ἐποίε-ον)
ε disappears before a long vowel or diphthong: ποιῶ (ποιέ-ω); ποιοῦςι (ποιέ-ουςι).

(*c*)   *Stems in* **ο** (*model* **δηλόω**)

ο + ε, ο, ου > ου: ἐδήλου (ἐδήλο-ε); δηλοῦμεν (δηλό-ομεν); δηλοῦςι (δηλό-ουςι)
ο + η, ω > ω: δηλῶ (δηλό-ω)
ο + an ι-diphthong (ει, οι, ῃ) > οι: δηλοῖ (δηλό-ει)

The combinations ο + η/οι/ῃ occur in forms not yet treated.

The above contractions, which cover all forms of contracted verbs, also occur in other parts of speech, e.g. the noun νοῦς (< νόος; 6.1/2). Contraction was a regular feature of Attic Greek but was not as rigorously applied in other dialects.

Notes

1 The present infinitives of α- and o-stems contract to -ᾶν and -οῦν respectively, **not** -ᾷν and -οῖν. This is because the -ειν of the pres. inf. act. of uncontracted -ω verbs (e.g. λῡ́-ειν) is itself a contraction of ε + εν. With -αω and -οω verbs we therefore have the double contractions α + ε + εν > ᾱ + εν > ᾶν; o + ε + εν > ου + εν > ουν, which give us τῑμᾶν, δηλοῦν.

2 All tenses other than the present and imperfect are formed by lengthening the stem vowel and proceeding exactly as with uncontracted verbs (α > η (except after ε, ι, ρ where we have α > ᾱ); ε > η; o > ω). The fut. ind. act. of the model verbs is τῑμήσω, ποιήσω, δηλώσω and the aor. ind. act. ἐτῑ́μησα, ἐποίησα, ἐδήλωσα. However, γελάω *laugh* does not lengthen its α: fut. γελάσομαι (8.1/1 note 1), aor. ἐγέλασα. Likewise, καλέω *call* and τελέω *complete* do not lengthen their ε in the aorist: ἐκάλεσα, ἐτέλεσα; their future is, rather confusingly, the same as their present, καλῶ, τελῶ, because the expected καλέσω, τελέσω lost the intervocalic c and contraction resulted (cf. 6.1/1c).

3 A contracted future also occurs in most verbs in -ίζω (6.1/4b) and all verbs with stems in λ, μ, ν, ρ (11.1/3). Nearly all such futures have a stem in ε (i.e. the contraction is -ῶ, -εῖc, -εῖ, etc., exactly as the present of ποιέω). A few have a stem in α, as ἐλαύνω *drive*, fut. stem ἐλα- giving ἐλῶ, ἐλᾷc, ἐλᾷ, etc., exactly as the present of τῑμάω.

4 ζάω *be alive* contracts to η where other -άω verbs have ᾱ; pres. ind. act. ζῶ, ζῇc, ζῇ, ζῶμεν, ζῆτε, ζῶcι(ν), inf. ζῆν; impf. ind. act. ἔζων, ἔζηc, ἔζη, ἐζῶμεν, ἐζῆτε, ἔζων. So also πεινάω *be hungry* and διψάω *be thirsty*.

5 Most disyllabic verbs in -εω (as δέω *need*, πλέω *sail*, πνέω *breathe*, ῥέω *flow*) contract only when ε is followed by ε. The pres. ind. act. of πλέω is πλέω, πλεῖc, πλεῖ, πλέομεν, πλεῖτε, πλέουcι(ν); impf. ἔπλεον, ἔπλειc, ἔπλει, ἐπλέομεν, ἐπλεῖτε, ἔπλεον. The 3rd s. act of δέω *need*, pres. δεῖ, impf. ἔδει, is used impersonally in the sense of *it is/was necessary* (examples have already occurred in the reading exercises). It is construed with the **accusative** of the person involved and an infinitive: δεῖ με ἐν τῇ οἰκίᾳ μένειν, *it is necessary for me to remain in the house*, i.e. *I must remain* . . .

6 There is **no** movable ν in the 3rd s. of the impf. ind. act. of contracted verbs.

5.1/3 Further uses of the definite article

In English we can, to a limited degree, use the definite article with an adjective to form a noun-equivalent: *only the good die young*; *only the brave deserve the fair*. In Greek, however, the definite article can be used to create a noun-equivalent out of virtually any part of speech (adjective, adverb, prepositional phrase, infinitive) to which it is prefixed: ὁ coφόc *the wise [man]*; ἡ coφή *the wise [woman]*; οἱ τότε *the then [men]*, i.e. *the men of that time*; οἱ νῦν *the now [men]*, i.e. *the men of today*; οἱ ἐν τῇ οἰκίᾳ *the [men] in the house* (the last three examples can also mean *the [people]* . . ., as Greek uses the masculine article to refer to mixed groups). The neuter singular article is used with adjectives to express abstractions: τὸ καλόν *beauty*, τὸ αἰcχρόν *ugliness*. When prefixed to an infinitive (**articular infinitive**, i.e. article + infinitive) it forms an equivalent of verbal nouns in English: τὸ λέγειν *the [act of] speaking*, *speech*; τὸ φεύγειν *the [act of] fleeing*, *flight*. Each of these noun-equivalents functions exactly like any normal noun, and the case of the article (and of an accompanying adjective) varies according to a particular context:

φέρω τὸν κακόν. *I am carrying the cowardly [man]*.

περὶ τοῦ παιδεύειν ἔλεγεν. *He was speaking about the [act of] educating*, i.e. *about education*.

ἐδιώκομεν τοὺς ἐν τῇ νήcῳ. *We were chasing the [men] in the island*.

Another very common type of noun-phrase consists of the neuter plural of the definite article followed by a genitive. Here the article may be translated in a wide variety of ways. Thus τὰ τῶν ᾿Αθηναίων (lit. *the [things] of the Athenians*) can mean *the property/situation/condition/fortunes/interests*, etc., *of the Athenians*; τὰ ἐν τῇ ῾Ρώμῃ *the things/events/circumstances* etc., *in Rome*. The context must determine the most appropriate rendering.

The article can also be used as a third person pronoun when combined with the particles μέν* . . . δέ*; ὁ μέν . . . ὁ δέ *the one . . . the other* (*one man . . . another*); οἱ μέν . . . οἱ δέ *some . . . others*: ὁ μὲν διώκει τὴν δόξαν, ὁ δὲ τὸ ἀργύριον *one man chases fame, another money*; οἱ μὲν ἀπέθνῃσκον, οἱ δὲ ἔφευγον *some were dying, others running away*. ὁ δὲ *but/and he* (and οἱ δέ etc.) when used by itself refers to someone mentioned in the preceding sentence other than its subject: ὁ Cωκράτης ἐκέλευσε τὴν Ξανθίππην κροῦσαι τὴν μυῖαν· ἡ δὲ οὐκ ἤθελεν *Socrates ordered Xanthippe to swat the fly but she refused* (lit. *was not willing*). This pronominal use of the article is a survival from an earlier stage in Greek when it was employed only as a third person pronoun (cf. 25.1/3a).

We have already met three usages of the article in Greek where there is no corresponding article in English (2.1/2 note 1). There is also one important instance where the reverse holds true, viz where the noun or adjective is predicative. Thus, when Thucydides (6.2.11) is telling us that originally the Athenians called the Acropolis simply 'the polis', he writes καλεῖται (3rd s. pres. ind. passive) ἡ ᾿Ακρόπολιc ἔτι πόλιc *the Acropolis is still called 'the polis'*; but there is no article with πόλιc. In such sentences, therefore, there should be no doubt as to which word is the subject and which is the complement.

Notes

1 Adjectives without the definite article can also be used as nouns but they
 then have an indefinite sense: ἐν τῷ πολέμῳ πολλοὶ κακὰ ἔφερον *in the*
 war many [people] were suffering hardships (lit. *bad things*). When used
 indefinitely in the singular an adjective is normally accompanied by the
 indefinite pronoun τις (10.1/1).

2 In expressions such as Ἀλκιβιάδης ὁ Κλεινίου *Alcibiades, [son] of*
 Cleinias the article is followed by the genitive and the word for son or
 daughter is omitted (cf. 23.1/1*a*). As Greeks, both male and female, had
 only one name, the name of a person's father is often given in this way to
 achieve greater precision.

5.2   Greek reading

1   ὁ χρόνος παιδεύει τοὺς σοφούς.

2   πόλλ' ἔχει σιωπὴ καλά.

3# πόλλ' ἔστιν ἀνθρώποισιν, ὦ ξένοι, κακά.

4# οὐ δεῖ φέρειν τὰ πρόσθεν ἐν μνήμῃ κακά.

5   Supply ἐστί in the following: (*i*) καλὸν ἡσυχία. (*ii*) χαλεπὰ τὰ καλά. (*iii*)
 μέτρον ἄριστον. (*iv*) μέγα βιβλίον μέγα κακόν. (*v*) κοινὰ τὰ τῶν φίλων.
 (*vi*) κοινὸς Ἑρμῆς. (*vii*) μικρὸν κακὸν μέγα ἀγαθόν. (*viii*) ἄλλα ἄλλοις
 καλά. (*ix*) ἡ γλῶττα πολλῶν αἰτία κακῶν. (*x*) χαλεπὸν τὸ ποιεῖν, τὸ δὲ
 κελεῦσαι ῥάδιον. (*xi*)# κακὸν τὸ μεθύειν πημονῆς λυτήριον. (*xii*)
 παθήματα μαθήματα. (*xiii*) κακοῦ κόρακος κακὸν ᾠόν. (*xiv*) πιστὸν γῆ,
 ἄπιστον θάλαττα. (*xv*) κἂν μύρμηκι χολή.

6   (*i*) δεῖ γαμεῖν ἐκ τῶν ὁμοίων. (*ii*) μῶρος μῶρα λέγει. (*iii*) ἔξω πηλοῦ τὸν
 πόδα ἔχεις. (*iv*) ζεῖ χύτρα, ζῇ φιλία. (*v*) λέοντα ξυρεῖς. (*vi*) πρὸς σῆμα
 μητρυιᾶς κλαίεις.

7# φεῦ φεῦ, τὰ μεγάλα μεγάλα καὶ πάσχει κακά.

8# ὄνου χρείαν ἐλέγχει τραχύτης ὁδοῦ.

9# ἄνθρωπός ἐστι πνεῦμα καὶ σκιὰ μόνον.

10# τύχη τέχνην ὤρθωσεν, οὐ τέχνη τύχην.

11# πολλῶν τὰ χρήματ' αἴτι' ἀνθρώποις κακῶν.

12# γύναι, γυναιξὶ κόσμον ἡ σιγὴ φέρει.

13# καλὸν δὲ καὶ γέροντι μανθάνειν σοφά.

14 οἱ Ἀθηναῖοι Θουκυδίδην τὸν Ὀλόρου ἔπεμψαν πρὸς τὸν στρατηγὸν
 τῶν ἐν Θράκῃ.

15 οὔτε παρὰ νεκροῦ ὁμιλίαν οὔτε παρὰ φιλαργύρου χάριν δεῖ ζητεῖν.

16# ἱκανὸν τὸ νικᾶν ἐστι τοῖς ἐλευθέροις.

17# κἂν τοῖς ἀγροίκοις ἐστὶ παιδείας ἔρως.

18 ὁ λύκος τὴν τρίχα, οὐ τὴν γνώμην, ἀλλάττει.

19# τὰ χρήματ' ἀνθρώποισιν εὑρίσκει φίλους.

20 φαῦλος κριτὴς καλοῦ πράγματος ὄχλος.

21 **The Egyptians and their crocodiles** (from Herodotus).

τοῖς μὲν οὖν τῶν Αἰγυπτίων ἱεροί εἰcιν οἱ κροκόδιλοι, τοῖς δ' οὔ, ἀλλ'
ἅτε πολεμίουc περιέπουcιν. οἱ δὲ περί τε Θήβαc καὶ τὴν Μοίρεωc (*of
Moeris*) λίμνην cφόδρα νομίζουcιν αὐτοὺc εἶναι ἱερούc. ἕνα (*one*) δὲ
ἑκάτεροι τρέφουcι κροκόδιλον καὶ διδάcκουcιν, ἀρτήματα δὲ λίθινα
χυτὰ εἰc τὰ ὦτα ἐμβάλλουcι καὶ ἀμφιδέαc περὶ τοὺc ἐμπροcθίουc πόδαc 5
καὶ cιτία ἀπότακτα παρέχουcι καὶ ἱερεῖα. ἕωc μὲν οὖν ζῶcιν οἱ
κροκόδιλοι μάλ' εὖ πάcχουcιν, μετὰ δὲ τὸν θάνατον ταριχεύουcιν
αὐτοὺc οἱ Αἰγύπτιοι καὶ θάπτουcιν ἐν ἱεραῖc θήκαιc. ἀλλ' οἱ περὶ
Ἐλεφαντίνην πόλιν (*city*) καὶ ἐcθίουcιν αὐτούc· οὐ γὰρ νομίζουcιν
ἱεροὺc εἶναι.   10

Notes

2 πόλλ'= πολλά (also in 3) 2.1/6*b*.

3 ἀνθρώποιcιν dat. pl.; -οιcιν is the longer form of the ending (3.1/1 note
   3).

4 Take τὰ πρόcθεν . . . κακά together and ἐν μνήμῃ with φέρειν;
   dislocations of this sort are common in verse.

5 (*i*) καλόν is neuter because the meaning is *a fair [thing]*; we would have
   expected the definite article with ἡcυχία (2.1/2 note 1)—see note on
   4.2.3   (*iv*) here, and in some of the following proverbs, it is necessary to
   decide which is subject and which is predicate, i.e. *is a big book a big evil?*
   or *is a big evil a big book?* Obviously the former is what is meant.   (*vi*)
   An appeal to share in the luck that another is enjoying (e.g. in finding a
   coin in the street); Hermes, as god of luck, shares, or should share, his
   blessings equally.   (*viii*) ἄλλα ἄλλοιc . . . lit. *other [things] . . . to other
   [people]*, i.e. *different [things] . . . to different people.*   (*xiv*) πιcτόν,
   ἄπιcτον cf. καλόν in (*i*).   (*xv*) κἄν = καὶ ἐν (crasis 11.1/5); καί here
   means *even* (4.1/3).

6 (*iv*) ζεῖ < ζέω boil, ζῇ < ζάω live (the latter is irregular—5.1/2 note 4).

7 Prose order would be τὰ μεγάλα καὶ πάcχει μεγάλα κακά; καί is here
   adverbial *also* (4.1/3); take the second μεγάλα with κακά.

10 Translate ὤρθωcεν (< ὀρθόω) by a present; the aorist is often used to
    express general truths, particularly in proverbs (so-called **gnomic aorist**;
    cf. *faint heart never won fair lady*).

11 Supply ἐcτί (and also in 13 and 20); χρήματ' αἰτί' both have an elided α;
    the plural of χρῆμα *thing* here means *money* (a very common use).

13 δέ cf. note on 4.2.9 (there are many examples of such connectives at the
    beginning of verse and prose extracts in subsequent reading exercises);
    καί *even* 4.1/3.

14 τὸν Ὀλόρου 5.1/3 note 2.

17 κἄν see above on 5 (*xv*).

19 χρήματ(α) see on 11; ἀνθρώποιcιν see note on 3.

20 Only the sense can indicate which noun is subject and which predicate
    (cf. note on 5 (*iv*)).

21   *ll.*1f. τοῖς μὲν ... τοῖς δέ *for some ... for others* (5.1/3); οὖν connects this passage with what goes before in the original context (cf. 13 above); ἅτε πολεμίους *as enemies*; Θήβας *Thebes* not to be confused with the city of the same name in Greece. *l.*3 Take ἕνα (m. acc. of εἷς (7.1/5)) with κροκόδιλον. *l.*4 ἑκάτεροι *each of the two* (i.e. those around Thebes and those around the swamp of Moeris). *l.*6 ἕως *while*; οὖν *therefore, so* shows that what follows is a consequence of what was said in the previous sentence, while μέν functions with the δέ of the next line to contrast ἕως ζῶςιν ... *with* μετὰ τὸν θάνατον ...

Unit 6

6.1 Grammar

6.1/1 Third declension – consonant stem nouns (2)

(*a*) **Stems in ν (*masculine and, rarely, feminine*)**
These stems nearly all have a nominative singular in -ην or -ων with a
genitive -ενος/-ηνος or -ονος/-ωνος. There is no rule to determine
whether a particular word has a long or short vowel in its stem. Those
with a short vowel do not lengthen it in the dative plural because here we
have ν + c > c, not ντ + c > c (cf. 5.1/1*b*).

	λιμήν (m)	μήν (m)	δαίμων (m or f)	ἀγών (m)
	harbour	*month*	*divine being*	*contest*
stem	λιμεν-	μην-	δαιμον-	ἀγων-

SINGULAR

Nom.	λιμήν	μήν	δαίμων	ἀγών
Voc.	λιμήν	μήν	δαῖμον	ἀγών
Acc.	λιμέν-α	μῆν-α	δαίμον-α	ἀγῶν-α
Gen.	λιμέν-ος	μην-ός	δαίμον-ος	ἀγῶν-ος
Dat.	λιμέν-ι	μην-ί	δαίμον-ι	ἀγῶν-ι

PLURAL

N.V.	λιμέν-ες	μῆν-ες	δαίμον-ες	ἀγῶν-ες
Acc.	λιμέν-ας	μῆν-ας	δαίμον-ας	ἀγῶν-ας
Gen.	λιμέν-ων	μην-ῶν	δαιμόν-ων	ἀγών-ων
Dat.	λιμέ-cι(ν)	μη-cί(ν)	δαίμο-cι(ν)	ἀγῶ-cι(ν)

Notes

1 There are a few such nouns in -ῑc, -ῑνος, e.g. ῥίc, ῥῑνός (f) *nose*; δελφίc,
-ῑνος (m) *dolphin*.
2 The vocative singular of ν-stems is the same as the nominative when the
nominative is accented on the final syllable (so λιμήν, but δαῖμον).
3 κύων, κυνός (m or f) *dog* has an irregular stem κυν-.

(*b*) **Stems in ρ (*mainly masculine*)**
The majority have a nom. s. -ηρ, gen. -ηρος or nom. s. -ωρ, gen. -ορος.
Four nouns with a nom. s. in -ηρ form a special sub-group and are
declined alike: πατήρ *father*, μήτηρ *mother*, θυγάτηρ *daughter*, γαστήρ
(f) *stomach*. Also given below is the slightly irregular ἀνήρ *man, male*. Of

41

these nouns only those in -ηρ, -ηρος do not have a distinct vocative singular (cῶτερ from cωτήρ, -ῆρος (m) *saviour* is an exception).

	θήρ (m) *wild beast*	ῥήτωρ (m) *speaker*	πατήρ (m) *father*	ἀνήρ (m) *man*
stem	θηρ-	ῥητορ-	πατ(ε)ρ-	ἀνδρ-

SINGULAR

Nom.	θήρ	ῥήτωρ	πατήρ	ἀνήρ
Voc.	θήρ	ῥῆτορ	πάτερ	ἄνερ
Acc.	θῆρ-α	ῥήτορ-α	πατέρ-α	ἄνδρ-α
Gen.	θηρ-óc	ῥήτορ-ος	πατρ-óc	ἀνδρ-óc
Dat.	θηρ-í	ῥήτορ-ι	πατρ-í	ἀνδρ-í

PLURAL

N.V.	θῆρ-ες	ῥήτορ-ες	πατέρ-ες	ἄνδρ-ες
Acc.	θῆρ-ας	ῥήτορ-ας	πατέρ-ας	ἄνδρ-ας
Gen.	θηρ-ῶν	ῥητόρ-ων	πατέρ-ων	ἀνδρ-ῶν
Dat.	θηρ-cί(ν)	ῥήτορ-cι(ν)	πατρά-cι(ν)	ἀνδρά-cι(ν)

A few nouns with stems in ρ do not have a nom. sing. in -ηρ/-ωρ. Of these, χείρ, χειρóc (f) *hand* (stem χειρ-) can also have a stem χερ-, which is the more usual in the dat. pl., viz χερcί(ν); ἔαρ (n) (the season of) *spring* has gen. ἦρος, dat. ἦρι; πῦρ (n) *fire* has gen. πυρóc, dat. πυρί (see also 13.1/1c).

(c) **Stems in εc (neuters in -οc, masculine proper names in -ηc)**

Neuters in -οc, as γένοc, γένουc *race, clan* (stem γενεc-), form a large class. They appear to be irregular because they were affected by a sound change at an earlier stage of Greek whereby intervocalic sigma was lost and in Attic the two previously separated vowels were contracted (in Homeric Greek and other dialects the uncontracted forms survived).

	SINGULAR		PLURAL	
N.V.	γένοc		γένη	(< γένε(c)-α)
Acc.	γένοc		γένη	
Gen.	γένουc	(< γένε(c)-οc)	γενῶν	(< γενέ(c)-ων)
Dat.	γένει	(< γένε(c)-ι)	γένεcι(ν)	(< γένε(c)-cι)

Many masculine proper names are compounds with a stem in εc because their second element is a neuter noun of this type, e.g. Διογένηc (γένοc), Cωκράτηc (κράτοc), Ἀριστοτέληc (τέλοc). These must be distinguished from first declension masculine proper names in -ηc (see 3.1/2 notes 3 and 4). A complication arises with proper names containing the neuter κλέοc *fame* as their second element (e.g. Περικλῆc, Ἡρακλῆc, Θεμιστοκλῆc) since a further contraction is required in the

nom. voc. and dat. because of the additional ε in the stem (κλεες-).
Compare the declensions of Cωκράτης and Περικλῆς:

Nom.	Cωκράτης		Περικλῆς	(<κλέης)
Voc.	Cώκρατες		Περίκλεις	(<κλεες)
Acc.	Cωκράτη	(<-ε(c)α)	Περικλέᾱ	(<κλέε(c)α)
Gen.	Cωκράτους	(<-ε(c)ος)	Περικλέους	(<-κλέε(c)ος)
Dat.	Cωκράτει	(<-ε(c)ι)	Περικλεῖ	(<-κλέε(c)ι)

The acc. Περικλέᾱ has a final ᾱ (not η as in Cωκράτη) because of the
preceding ε (cf. ἀργυρᾶ <-εᾱ, 6.1/2 below).

One noun in -ης which belongs here but is not a masculine proper noun
is τριήρης (f) *trireme* (singular as for Cωκράτης, plural n.v.a. τριήρεις,
gen. τριήρων, dat. τριήρεσι(ν)).

6.1/2 Second declension contracted nouns and first and second declension contracted adjectives

The few second declension masculine nouns in -οος and neuters in -εον are
contracted in Attic according to the rules given for contracted verbs (5.1/2;
on ε + α, which does not occur in verbs, see below). The uncontracted forms,
which are regular, occur in other dialects. Examples are:

	νόος mind		*ὀςτέον* bone	
	CONTRACTED (Attic)	UNCONTRACTED (non-Attic)	CONTRACTED (Attic)	UNCONTRACTED (non-Attic)
SINGULAR				
Nom.	νοῦς	νό-ος	ὀςτοῦν	ὀςτέ-ον
Voc.	νοῦ	νό-ε	ὀςτοῦν	ὀςτέ-ον
Acc.	νοῦν	νό-ον	ὀςτοῦν	ὀςτέ-ον
Gen.	νοῦ	νό-ου	ὀςτοῦ	ὀςτέ-ου
Dat.	νῷ	νό-ῳ	ὀςτῷ	ὀςτέ-ῳ
PLURAL				
N.V.	νοῖ	νό-οι	ὀςτᾶ	ὀςτέ-α
Acc.	νοῦς	νό-ους	ὀςτᾶ	ὀςτέ-α
Gen.	νῶν	νό-ων	ὀςτῶν	ὀςτέ-ων
Dat.	νοῖς	νό-οις	ὀςτοῖς	ὀςτέ-οις

In the nom. voc. acc. pl. of neuters $\epsilon + \breve{\alpha} > \bar{\alpha}$ on the analogy of the α-ending of normal second declension neuters (cf. χρῡcᾶ below).

Like *νοῦc* are declined ῥοῦc *stream*, πλοῦc *voyage*, and compounds of the latter such as περίπλουc *circumnavigation*.

Most first and second declension contracted adjectives are formed from -εοc, -εα, -εον, e.g. χρῡcοῦc (< χρύ̆cεοc) *golden*, which is declined:

	M.		F.		N.	
SINGULAR						
N.V.	χρῡcοῦc	(-εοc)	χρῡcῆ	(-έᾱ)	χρῡcοῦν	(-εον)
Acc.	χρῡcοῦν	(-εον)	χρῡcῆν	(-έᾱν)	χρῡcοῦν	(-εον)
Gen.	χρῡcοῦ	(-έου)	χρῡcῆc	(-έᾱc)	χρῡcοῦ	(-έου)
Dat.	χρῡcῷ	(-έῳ)	χρῡcῇ	(-έᾳ)	χρῡcῷ	(-έῳ)
PLURAL						
N.V.	χρῡcοῖ	(-εοι)	χρῡcαῖ	(-εαι)	χρῡcᾶ	(-εα)
Acc.	χρῡcοῦc	(-έουc)	χρῡcᾶc	(-έᾱc)	χρῡcᾶ	(-εα)
Gen.	χρῡcῶν	(-έων)	χρῡcῶν	(-έων)	χρῡcῶν	(-έων)
Dat.	χρῡcοῖc	(-έοιc)	χρῡcαῖc	(-έαιc)	χρῡcοῖc	(-έοιc)

In the feminine singular $\epsilon + \bar{\alpha} > \eta$, except where ϵ is preceded by ε, ι, or ρ, e.g. ἀργυροῦc (-εοc), -ᾶ (-έᾱ), -οῦν, (-εον) *[made of] silver* whose feminine singular is: nom. ἀργυρᾶ, acc. ἀργυρᾶν, gen. ἀργυρᾶc, dat. ἀργυρᾷ (here $\epsilon + \bar{\alpha} > \bar{\alpha}$).

ἀπλοῦc, -ῆ, -οῦc *simple* is contracted from ἀπλόοc but follows χρῡcοῦc completely, even in the feminine.

6.1/3 Compound verbs formed with prepositional prefixes

Many verbs form compounds by prefixing one, or sometimes more than one, preposition (e.g. ἐπιβαίνω, 3.2.12(*v*)). This involves important sound changes when certain vowels and consonants are juxtaposed:

(*a*) With the exception of περί and πρό, prepositions ending in a vowel drop this vowel (by elision) when compounded with a verb which begins with a vowel or diphthong: ἀπάγω (ἀπό + ἄγω) *lead away*, παρέχω (παρά + ἔχω) *provide*, but προάγω *lead forward*, περιάγω *lead round* (on the meaning of these and subsequent compounds, see note 1).

(*b*) When, owing to the elision of the final vowel of the preposition, π, τ, or κ are brought into contact with an initial aspirated vowel or diphthong, these consonants must themselves adopt their aspirated forms, φ, θ and χ: ἀφαιρέω (ἀπό + αἰρέω) *take away*; καθαιρέω (κατά + αἰρέω) *destroy*.

(c) When compounded with a verb beginning with a vowel or diphthong, ἐκ becomes ἐξ: ἐξάγω (ἐκ + ἄγω) *lead out*; ἐξαιρέω (ἐκ + αἰρέω) *take out*.

(d) When compounded with a verb beginning with a consonant, the ν of ἐν and cύν is assimilated as follows:

> ν before π, β, φ, ψ and μ becomes μ: cυμβουλεύω (cύν + βουλεύω) *advise*
>
> ν before γ, κ, χ and ξ becomes nasal γ: ἐγγράφω (ἐν + γράφω) *write in/on*
>
> ν before λ becomes λ: cυλλαμβάνω (cύν + λαμβάνω) *gather together*
>
> ν of cύν is dropped before c: cυcτρατεύω (cύν + cτρατεύω) *join in an expedition*.

(e) When a verb compounded with a preposition is used in a tense which requires the augment, the augment comes between the preposition and the verb, **not** in front of the preposition: προc-έ-βαλλον *I was attacking*. If, of course, the insertion of the augment results in the clash of two vowels, e.g. κατα + έ-γίγνωcκον the same process as in (a) above will apply: so κατεγίγνωcκον *I was condemning*. In these circumstances πρό normally contracts with the augment: προὔβαλλον[1] (rather than προέβαλλον) *I was putting forward*; προὔπεμπον[1] (προέπεμπον) *I was escorting* (the contracted diphthong is generally indicated by a sign identical with a smooth breathing (11.1/5b).

(f) The assimilation of ἐν and cύν described in (d) is blocked by the syllabic augment in the augmented tenses; thus cυμβουλεύω but cυνεβούλευον.

Notes

1 The meaning of a compound verb is not always predictable from its constituent parts (cf. above παρέχω). Prepositions may retain their normal meanings (as ἀπάγω, ἐγγράφω) but some have acquired a special sense, e.g. μεταγιγνώcκω *change one's mind* (from γιγνώcκω *know*) where μετα- conveys the idea of change.

2 In the augmented tenses of compound verbs the accent never goes further back than the augment, even when the last syllable is short: παρεῖχον *they were providing*; παρῆcαν *they were present*.

3 Greek has a few compound verbs which contain no prepositional element: οἰκοδομέω *build a house* (οἶκος *house*); ναυμαχέω *fight with ships*

---

[1] On this type of contraction, which is called crasis, see 11.1/5.

(*ναῦς ship*). These compounds are augmented at the beginning, **not** between the two elements (ᾠκοδόμησα, ἐναυμάχησα).

6.1/4   -ω verbs with stems in palatals, labials, dentals

The sound changes shown by nouns with these stems (5.1/1) also occur in the corresponding verbs when c is added to form the future or weak aorist. Some resemble λύω in having a simple present stem to which this c can be attached. Others, far more numerous, have a suffix in their present stem which is not kept elsewhere.

(*a*) *Verbs of the above type with no suffix in the present stem*

πλέκω	*plait*	fut.	πλέξω	aor.	ἔπλεξα
πέμπω	*send*	fut.	πέμψω	aor.	ἔπεμψα
πείθω	*persuade*	fut.	πείcω	aor.	ἔπεισα

(*b*) *Verbs with a suffix in the present stem*

At a very early stage in its development Greek possessed a consonant which was pronounced as the *y* in the English *yes*. This sound no longer existed in the form Greek had taken by the time of the introduction of the alphabet. It had occurred in words inherited from Indo-European (1.3) and had also served as a suffix to form the present stem of many -ω verbs whose primitive or original stem ended in a consonant. In this function it combined with the preceding consonant. The combinations which concern us here are κ/γ/χ+*y* > ττ; π/β/φ+*y* > ππ; τ/δ/θ +*y* > ζ. As this suffix (and others—see below) was only used to form the present stem, the future and weak aorist are formed by applying c to the original stem. Examples are (the original stem is given in parentheses):

PALATALS

φυλάττω	*guard*	(φυλακ-)	fut.	φυλάξω	aor.	ἐφύλαξα
ἀλλάττω	*change*	(ἀλλαγ-)	fut.	ἀλλάξω	aor.	ἤλλαξα

LABIALS

κόπτω	*cut*	(κοπ-)	fut.	κόψω	aor.	ἔκοψα
βλάπτω	*harm*	(βλαβ-)	fut.	βλάψω	aor.	ἔβλαψα
κρύπτω	*hide*	(κρυφ-)	fut.	κρύψω	aor.	ἔκρυψα

DENTALS

φράζω	*tell*	(φραδ-)	fut.	φράcω	aor.	ἔφραςα

The original stem can be seen in cognate words (e.g. φυλακή *act of guarding*, βλάβη *damage*). It need not be memorized as these verbs follow the above patterns. An exception is a few verbs in -ζω which are palatals, not dentals, as e.g. *cφάζω slaughter* (*cφαγ-*), fut. *cφάξω*, aor. *ἔcφαξα* (cf. *cφαγή [act of] slaughtering*).

All dental-stem verbs in -*ίζω* of more than two syllables have a future in -*ιέω* (originally -*ιέcω*; cf. 5.1/2 note 3), which always contracts to -*ιῶ*: *νομίζω think*, fut. *νομιῶ, νομιεῖc, νομιεῖ*, etc., but *κτίζω found*, *build*, fut. *κτίcω*. A few verbs in -*ίζω* are palatals: *μαcτίζω whip* (stem *μαcτιγ-*), fut. *μαcτίξω*, aor. *ἐμάcτιξα*.

Of the other present stem suffixes belonging here we may mention *cκ* (as in *διδάcκω* (< *διδαχ+cκ-ω*) *teach*, fut. *διδάξω*, etc.) and *αν*. The latter is often accompanied by a nasal infix (i.e. a nasal inserted before the final consonant of the root); neither *αν* nor the infix occur outside the present stem, e.g. *λαμβάνω take*, aor. stem *λαβ-* (in *λα-μ-β-αν-ω* the nasal infix takes the form of the labial nasal *μ* before the following labial; cf. *μα-ν-θ-άν-ω learn*, aor. stem *μαθ-*; *λα-γ-χ-άν-ω obtain*, aor. stem *λαχ-*; see 7.1/1).

6.2 Greek reading

1 As well as translating the following give the 1st s. present indicative active of each verb:

(*i*) *οἱ φύλακες τοὺς Πέρcας ἐφύλαξαν.* (*ii*) *ἆρα ἔκρυψας τὸν χρυcοῦν ἵππον;* (*iii*) *οἱ Ἀθηναῖοι καὶ οἱ Λακεδαιμόνιοι cυνεcτράτευcαν.* (*iv*) *πολλὰ ἐν τῇ πέτρᾳ ἐνέγραψεν.* (*v*) *οἱ δαίμονες πολλὰ καὶ μεγάλα πράξουcιν.* (*vi*) *ὁ Cωκράτης ἡμᾶς ἐδίδαξεν.* (*vii*) *τὴν οἰκίαν τοῦ Περικλέους ἔβλαψαν.* (*viii*) *ἐν τῷ λιμένι ἐναυμαχήcαμεν.*

2# *κάτοπτρον εἴδους χαλκός ἐcτ', οἶνος δὲ νοῦ.*

3# *χεὶρ χεῖρα νίπτει, δάκτυλοι δὲ δακτύλους.*

4 *ἡ μὲν φωνή ἐcτιν ἀργυρᾶ, ἡ δὲ cιγὴ χρυcῆ.*

5# *ὦ δαῖμον, ὡς οὐκ ἔcτ' ἀποcτροφὴ βροτοῖς*
τῶν ἐμφύτων τε καὶ θεηλάτων κακῶν.

6 **Further futility**

(*i*) *εἰς ὕδωρ γράφεις.* (*ii*) *εἰς ψάμμον οἰκοδομεῖς.* (*iii*) *γλαῦκ' Ἀθήναζε* (*sc.* *φέρεις*). (*iv*) *κύματα μετρεῖς.* (*v*) *ὄρνιθος γάλα ζητεῖς.* (*vi*) *cίδηρον πλεῖν διδάcκεις.* (*vii*) *ἡλίῳ φῶς δανείζεις.* (*viii*) *βατράχοις οἰνοχοεῖς.* (*ix*) *τὸν ἀέρα τύπτεις.* (*x*) *ἐλέφαντα ἐκ μυίας ποιεῖς.*

7 **Other short proverbs**

(*i*) *ψυχῆς μέγας χαλινός ἐcτιν ὁ νοῦς* (*ii*) *Ἕλληνες ἀεὶ παῖδες, γέρων δὲ Ἕλλην οὐκ ἔcτιν.* (*iii*)# *εἰcὶ μητρὶ παῖδες ἄγκυραι βίου.* (*iv*) *οἴκοι λέοντες, ἐν μάχῃ δ' ἀλώπεκες.* (*v*) *νοῦς ὁρᾷ καὶ νοῦς ἀκούει.* (*vi*) *μακραὶ τυράννων χεῖρες.* (*vii*) *ψεύδεcιν Ἄρης φίλος.* (*viii*) *Ἑλλὰς*

Ἑλλάδος αἱ Ἀθῆναι. (*ix*) τέττιγι μέλιτταν συγκρίνεις. (*x*) χαλεπὸν
θυγατὴρ κτῆμα.
8 τὸ μὲν πῦρ ὁ ἄνεμος, τὸν δὲ ἔρωτα ἡ συνήθεια ἐκκαίει.
9 κατὰ τὸν Cωκράτη οὐδεὶς ἑκουσίως ἁμαρτάνει.
10 οὐ μετανοεῖν ἀλλὰ προνοεῖν χρὴ τὸν ἄνδρα τὸν σοφόν.

11 **The siege of Melos**
Thucydides, the other great historian of the fifth century BC, wrote a
history of the Peloponnesian war, which was fought between Athens
and Sparta (the major power in the Peloponnese) from 431 BC to 404 BC,
when Athens fell. Melos was an island in the southern Aegean whose
desire to stay neutral was brutally suppressed by the Athenians.
καὶ οἱ μὲν Ἀθηναίων πρέςβεις (*ambassadors*) ἀνεχώρηςαν εἰς τὸ
ςτράτευμα, οἱ δὲ ςτρατηγοὶ περιετείχιςαν τοὺς Μηλίους. καὶ ὕςτερον
φυλακὴ μὲν ὀλίγη τῶν ςυμμάχων ἐκεῖ παρέμενε καὶ ἐπολιόρκει τὸ
χωρίον, οἱ δὲ ἄλλοι ςτρατιῶται καὶ κατὰ γῆν καὶ κατὰ θάλατταν
ἀνεχώρηςαν. ἔπειτα δὲ οἱ Μήλιοι τὸ περιτείχιςμα ἀνέςπαςαν τῶν 5
Ἀθηναίων, ἐπειδὴ παρῆςαν οὐ πολλοὶ τῶν φυλάκων. ἀλλὰ ςτρατιὰν
ὕςτερον ἐκ τῶν Ἀθηνῶν ἄλλην ἐξέπεμψαν οἱ Ἀθηναῖοι, καὶ κατὰ
κράτος ἤδη ἐπολιόρκουν. προδοςία δὲ ἦν ἐν τοῖς Μηλίοις καὶ
ςυνεχώρηςαν τοῖς Ἀθηναίοις. οἱ δὲ ἔςφαξαν Μηλίων τοὺς ἄνδρας,
παῖδας δὲ καὶ γυναῖκας ἠνδραπόδιςαν. καὶ ὕςτερον ἀποίκους πολλοὺς 1
ἐξέπεμψαν καὶ τὸ χωρίον ᾤκιςαν.

Notes
1 (*v*) πολλὰ καὶ μεγάλα lit. *many and great [things]* but translate *many
great [things]*; when πολύς in the plural is combined with another
adjective καί is regularly inserted between the two.
2 Greek mirrors were made of polished bronze.
5 *l*.1 ὡς exclamatory *how . . .!* (22.1/1*a*(ii)); take ἀποςτροφή with the
genitives in the next line. *l*.2 Take κακῶν as a noun and ἐμφύτων and
θεηλάτων as adjectives; καί can be translated here by *and* or *or* because
the evils are not necessarily both *innate* and *sent by the gods*.
6 (*iii*) The Acropolis at Athens was notorious as a haunt of small brown
owls, the bird which was adopted as the Athenian emblem.
7 (*ii*) This remark of an Egyptian priest to the Athenian statesman Solon
implicitly contrasts the age of Greek civilization with that of the
Egyptians. (*iv*) A phrase of abuse, not a sentence; foxes were symbolic
of a low cunning devoid of courage. (*viii*) The Athenians liked to
regard themselves as the quintessence of Greekness. (*x*) The patriar-
chal nature of most Greek societies meant that sons were more highly
valued than daughters.
11 *l*.3 Translate the imperfects παρέμενε and ἐπολιόρκει by *stayed* and
besieged (Greek prefers to regard both events as extending over a period

of time than as single actions—4.1/1). *ll.*7f. ἐξέπεμψαν < ἐκπέμπω (6.1/3); κατὰ κράτος lit. *in accordance with [their full] strength*, i.e. *energetically*, *l.*10 παῖδας καὶ γυναῖκας the regular order in Greek for *women and children*; ἠνδραπόδισαν < ἀνδραποδίζω (4.1/1 note 2(ii)).

Unit 7

7.1 Grammar

7.1/1 Strong aorist indicative and infinitive active of -ω verbs

We have seen at 4.1/1 that -ω verbs have either a weak or a strong aorist and that the distinction between the two is solely one of form. The indicative of the strong aorist has the same endings as the imperfect; the infinitive has the same ending as the present (as do all other parts). As the strong aorist takes no suffix its stem must necessarily undergo some internal modification to differentiate it from that of the present. Any suffix attached to the latter is dropped (cf. 6.1/4b), and ει is reduced to ι, and ευ to υ. Some strong aorist stems are simply irregular and must be learnt.

The following list of the most common verbs with a strong aorist shows examples of each type. The present infinitive and the imperfect indicative are included for comparison.

PRESENT INDICATIVE	IMPERFECT INDICATIVE	AORIST INDICATIVE	PRESENT INFINITIVE	AORIST INFINITIVE
ἄγω lead, bring	ἦγον	ἤγαγον	ἄγειν	ἀγαγεῖν
αἱρέω take, capture	ᾕρουν	εἷλον (stem ἑλ-)	αἱρεῖν	ἑλεῖν
βάλλω throw	ἔβαλλον	ἔβαλον	βάλλειν	βαλεῖν
εὑρίσκω find	εὕρισκον (or ηὕ-)	εὗρον (or ηὕ-)	εὑρίσκειν	εὑρεῖν
ἔχω have	εἶχον	ἔσχον	ἔχειν	σχεῖν
λαγχάνω obtain	ἐλάγχανον	ἔλαχον	λαγχάνειν	λαχεῖν
λαμβάνω take	ἐλάμβανον	ἔλαβον	λαμβάνειν	λαβεῖν
λέγω say	ἔλεγον	εἶπον (stem εἰπ-)	λέγειν	εἰπεῖν
λείπω leave	ἔλειπον	ἔλιπον	λείπειν	λιπεῖν
μανθάνω learn	ἐμάνθανον	ἔμαθον	μανθάνειν	μαθεῖν
ὁράω see	ἑώρων	εἶδον (stem ἰδ-)	ὁρᾶν	ἰδεῖν
πάσχω suffer	ἔπασχον	ἔπαθον	πάσχειν	παθεῖν
τυγχάνω happen	ἐτύγχανον	ἔτυχον	τυγχάνειν	τυχεῖν
φέρω carry	ἔφερον	ἤνεγκον	φέρειν	ἐνεγκεῖν
φεύγω flee	ἔφευγον	ἔφυγον	φεύγειν	φυγεῖν

Notes

1　The ending of the strong aorist infinitive active always has a circumflex accent.

2　The aorists of αἱρέω, λέγω, ὁράω, φέρω come from roots entirely different from their presents (cf. English *go/went*). The unaugmented aorist stems of the first three (ἑλ-, εἰπ-, ἰδ-) require particular attention. εἶπον and ἤνεγκον quite irregularly take the **weak** aorist endings in the 2nd s. and pl.: εἶπας, εἴπατε; ἤνεγκας, ἠνέγκατε. We may sympathize with the Greeks who found εἶπον too complicated and gave λέγω a regular weak aorist ἔλεξα (good Attic but not as common). The strong aorist ἦλθον *came/went* likewise has a present tense from another root. This verb is peculiar in having an active aorist but a deponent present (ἔρχομαι 8.1/2).

3　By this stage you should be confident enough to consult the table of **Principal parts of verbs**, which sets out the principal parts of important verbs which have some irregularity. A normal transitive verb in Greek has six principal parts and from these all possible forms can be deduced (see next note for the only exceptions). These parts are:

(i)　1st s. present indicative active (λύω; 2.1/5)
(ii)　1st s. future indicative active (λύσω; 2.1/5)
(iii)　1st s. aorist indicative active (ἔλῡσα; 4.1/1; for strong aorist see above)
(iv)　1st s. perfect indicative active (λέλυκα; 15.1/1)
(v)　1st. s. perfect indicative middle and passive (λέλυμαι; 16.1/3)
(vi)　1st s. aorist indicative passive (ἐλύθην; 11.1/1).

This list is not as formidable as it might seem at first sight as some verbs do not exist in every possible part, while many (such as λύω) are completely regular and all their principal parts can be deduced from their present stem. Do not, at this stage, try to digest the **Principal parts of verbs** (in any case we have not yet dealt with principal parts (iv)–(vi)), but familiarise yourself with its arrangement and get into the habit of using it. When individual principal parts are wildly irregular (e.g. εἶπον), they are given separate entries in the **Vocabulary**.

4　A few verbs have an imperfect which cannot be predicted from their present stem. Thus ὁράω > ἑώρων, with both syllabic and temporal augment; ἔχω > εἶχον, the original form of ἔχω being ϲέχω, and ἔϲεχον losing intervocalic sigma (6.1/1c) and then contracting ε + ε (5.1/2b).

7.1/2　φημί say (see also Appendix 3)

This irregular -μι verb (2.1/4) is inflected as follows in the present and imperfect:

		PRESENT	IMPERFECT
SINGULAR	1	φημί	ἔφην
	2	φῄς	ἔφησθα or ἔφης
	3	φησί(ν)	ἔφη
PLURAL	1	φαμέν	ἔφαμεν
	2	φατέ	ἔφατε
	3	φασί(ν)	ἔφασαν
INFINITIVE		φάναι	——

Notes

1 All the forms of the present indicative are enclitic (**Appendix 9**) except the second person singular (cf. εἰμί, 3.1/6).

2 The imperfect regularly has an aorist meaning, *I said*.

3 φημί, not λέγω, is regularly used in the direct quotation of conversations (i.e. **direct speech**—see next subsection). When so used, φημί does not appear until after the beginning of the quotation:

δοκεῖς, ἔφη, ὦ Σώκρατες, εὖ λέγειν. *"You seem," he said, "to be speaking well, Socrates."*

4 The φη/φα alternation in the forms of this verb is explained at 19.1/1.

7.1/3 Indirect speech

When we wish to report what someone has said (or thought, etc.) we may do this in one of two ways. We may either give the exact words (cf. 7.1/2 note 3): "*Justice is the advantage of the stronger*," said Thrasymachus; or we may grammatically subordinate the speaker's words to a verb of saying (or thinking, etc.): *Thrasymachus said that justice was the advantage of the stronger*. The first form is called **direct speech**, the second **indirect** (or **reported) speech**.

Since speech may be conveniently divided into statement, question and command, we therefore have three corresponding forms of indirect speech:

(*a*) **Indirect statement:** *He said that he was happy*. (Direct *I am happy*.)

(*b*) **Indirect question:** *We asked if he was happy*. (Direct *Are you happy?*)

(*c*) **Indirect command:** *I told him to cheer up*. (Direct *Cheer up!*)

These examples show the adjustments in pronouns that are nearly always necessary in English. Greek does the same but does not, as we shall see, make the **tense** adjustments required by English in (*a*) and (*b*).

7.1/4 Indirect command

For this construction Greek, like English, uses an infinitive after a verb of ordering: ἐκέλευσε τὸν παῖδα τὰ γράμματα μαθεῖν *he ordered the boy to learn [his] letters.* If the infinitive is negated, the negative μή, not οὐ, is used: ὁ νόμος ἡμᾶς κελεύει μὴ ἀδικεῖν *the law orders us not to do wrong.*

The two adverbs of negation, μή and οὐ, are always to be translated by *no/not* but have quite distinct uses (see 7.1/6). The rule here is that μή is always used to negate an infinitive except in indirect statement (8.1/3).

The tense of the infinitive is a matter of aspect (4.1/1). In the above examples μαθεῖν simply conveys that the learning is to be done, whereas ἀδικεῖν indicates that we are not to do wrong on any occasion.

7.1/5 Numerals (see also Appendix 8)

There are three types of numeral:

(*a*) **Cardinals** (in English *one, two, three, four,* etc.)
In Greek, as in English, these function as adjectives. The numbers *one* to *four* are declined as follows:

	εἷς *one*			δύο *two*
	M.	F.	N.	M.F.N.
Nom.	εἷς	μία	ἕν	δύο
Acc.	ἕνα	μίαν	ἕν	δύο
Gen.	ἑνός	μιᾶς	ἑνός	δυοῖν
Dat.	ἑνί	μιᾷ	ἑνί	δυοῖν

	τρεῖς *three*		τέτταρες *four*	
	M. & F.	N.	M. & F.	N.
Nom.	τρεῖς	τρία	τέτταρες	τέτταρα
Acc.	τρεῖς	τρία	τέτταρας	τέτταρα
Gen.	τριῶν	τριῶν	τεττάρων	τεττάρων
Dat.	τρισί(ν)	τρισί(ν)	τέτταρσι(ν)	τέτταρσι(ν)

So, e.g. ἐκ μιᾶς νήσου *out of one island,* εἰς τέτταρας οἰκίας *into four houses.*

The numbers *five* to *one hundred* are indeclinable (i.e. have no variable inflections), except, of course, when they contain any of the numbers *one* to *four* (e.g. εἴκοσι τέτταρες *twenty-four,* where τέτταρες would alter its ending as required: εἴκοσι τέτταρα ἔργα *twenty-four tasks*). The words for *two hundred, three hundred,* etc. follow the plural of καλός (3.1/3): so διᾱκόσιοι, -αι, -α, *two hundred;* τρισχίλιοι, -αι, -α *three thousand.*

(*b*) **Ordinals** (in English, *first, second, third,* etc.).
These also are first and second declension adjectives (3.1/3), e.g. ἡ πρώτη γυνή *the first woman.*

(c) **Numeral adverbs** (in English, *once, twice, three times*, etc.).

In Greek all except ἅπαξ *once*, δίc *twice*, τρίc *three times*, end in -άκιc (cf. πολλάκιc *often*, lit. *many times*).

Notes

1 Like εἷc is declined the pronoun οὐδείc (< οὐδέ + εἷc *not even one*), οὐδεμία, οὐδέν, gen. οὐδενόc, οὐδεμιᾶc, οὐδενόc *no-one, nobody, none*. The neuter οὐδέν means *nothing*, but is often used adverbially in the sense *in no respect, not at all* (20.1/5). οὐδείc can also be used as an adjective meaning *no*, e.g. οὐδεμία γυνή *no woman*.

2 Compound numbers over twenty are expressed by putting the smaller number first with καί (δύο καὶ εἴκοcι *two and twenty*), or the larger number first without καί (εἴκοcι δύο *twenty-two*).

7.1/6 Negatives

Unlike English, Greek has two negatives οὐ and μή, and though we translate both by *not* their uses are quite distinct. These involve many constructions not yet described (for a summary see 24.1/2). We may, however, note:

(a) οὐ is used to negate statements and so is the negative used with a verb in the indicative in main clauses (examples at 3.2.1, 3.2.4, etc.).

(b) μή is the negative used with infinitives except in indirect statement (see above 7.1/4 and 8.1/3a).

(c) For every compound of οὐ (e.g. οὐδέ, οὐδείc) there is a corresponding compound of μή (e.g. μηδέ, μηδείc). The latter are used, where appropriate, in constructions otherwise requiring μή.

We have already seen at 3.2.12(*vi*) (see note) that the compound negative οὐδείc reinforces a simple preceding negative (οὐ λέγει οὐδέν *he says nothing*). However, when the order is reversed and a compound negative precedes a simple negative the two cancel each other to give a strong affirmative: οὐδεὶc οὐκ ἔπαθεν *no-one did not suffer*, i.e. *everyone suffered*.

7.1/7 Phrases expressing time and space

Many temporal phrases in English contain a preposition, e.g. *on Wednesday, for six days* (but cf. *I will see you next week*). In three types of temporal phrase of this sort Greek simply uses a particular case, provided that the noun involved signifies some period, point, or division of time (*dawn, day, winter, year*, etc.):

(a) **Time how long** is expressed by the **accusative**:

ἐννέα ἔτη οἱ ᾿Αχαιοὶ πρὸ τῆc Τροίαc ἐcτρατοπέδευον.　*For nine years the Achaeans were encamped before Troy.*

(b) **Time when** is expressed by the **dative**:

δεκάτῳ ἔτει ἱερὸν Ἴλιον ἐπόρθηcαν. *In the tenth year they sacked holy Ilium* (the definite article is generally omitted before ordinal numerals in this construction).

(c) **Time within which** is expressed by the **genitive**:

τριῶν ἡμερῶν ἔπλευcε Μενέλαοc εἰc τὴν Ἑλλάδα. *Within three days Menelaus sailed to Greece.*
εἴκοcι ἐτῶν Ὀδυccεὺc τὴν Ἰθάκην οὐκ εἶδεν. *For* (i.e. *within the space of*) *twenty years Odysseus did not see Ithaca.*
τέλοc εἰc τὴν πατρίδα νυκτὸc ἐνόcτηcεν. *Finally he returned to [his] native land by night.*

With nouns which do not indicate a period, point or division of time (e.g. *war* as in *during the war*) a preposition is generally used (e.g. διά + gen.).

(d) **Spatial extent** is expressed by the **accusative** (this use is similar to (a) above):

ἀπέχει τῆc Τροίαc ἡ Ἰθάκη πολλοὺc cταδίουc. *Ithaca is many stades distant from Troy.*
οἱ cτρατιῶται διὰ τοῦ πεδίου ἐβάδιcαν cταθμοὺc τέτταραc. *The soldiers walked four stages through the plain.*

7.2 Greek reading

1 ἡ παροιμία ἡμᾶc κελεύει μὴ κινεῖν ἀκίνητα.
2# εὑρεῖν τὸ δίκαιον πανταχῶc οὐ ῥᾴδιον.
3 ὁ δὲ Ἰcχόμαχοc εἶπεν, ὦ Cώκρατεc, χειμῶνοc μὲν τὴν οἰκίαν δεῖ εὐήλιον εἶναι, τοῦ δὲ θέρουc εὔcκιον.
4 οὐκ ἔχομεν οὔτε ὅπλα οὔτε ἵππουc.
5# οὐδὲν ἕρπει ψεῦδοc εἰc μῆκοc χρόνου.
6 μίαν μὲν οὖν ἡμέραν οἱ Ἀθηναῖοι αὐτοῦ ἐcτρατοπέδευcαν· τῇ δὲ ὑcτεραίᾳ Ἀλκιβιάδηc ἐκκληcίαν ἐποίηcε καὶ ἐκέλευcεν αὐτοὺc καὶ ναυμαχεῖν καὶ πεζομαχεῖν καὶ τειχομαχεῖν. οὐ γὰρ ἔcτιν, ἔφη, χρήματα ἡμῖν, τοῖc δὲ πολεμίοιc ἄφθονα.
7 οὐδεὶc ἀνθρώπων οὐκ ἀποθνῄcκει.
8 **Proverbs**
   (i) μία χελιδὼν ἔαρ οὐ ποιεῖ. (ii) δὶc παῖδεc οἱ γέροντεc. (iii) ἐν δυοῖν τρία βλέπειc. (iv) εἷc ἀνὴρ οὐδεὶc ἀνήρ. (v) μία ἡμέρα cοφὸν οὐ ποιεῖ. (vi) ἡ γλῶττα πολλοὺc εἰc ὄλεθρον ἤγαγεν. (vii) ἐν πολέμῳ οὐκ ἔνεcτι δὶc ἁμαρτεῖν. (viii) ἐξ ὀνύχων τὸν λέοντα ἔνεcτι μαθεῖν.
9 ὁ Κῦροc ἦλθε διὰ τῆc Λυδίαc cταθμοὺc τρεῖc παραcάγγαc δύο καὶ εἴκοcι ἐπὶ τὸν Μαίανδρον ποταμόν. τὸ δὲ εὖροc αὐτοῦ ἦν δύο πλέθρα.

10   ὁ κόσμος σκηνή, ὁ βίος πάροδος· ἦλθες, εἶδες, ἀπῆλθες.

11   εἶπέ τις (*someone*) τῷ Σωκράτει, κακῶς ὁ Μεγακλῆς σε λέγει· ὁ δέ,
       καλῶς γάρ, ἔφη, λέγειν οὐκ ἔμαθεν.

12   A sea battle

Thucydides did not finish his history of the Peloponnesian war but his
account was taken up and completed by Xenophon, a versatile writer
whose life straddled the fifth and fourth centuries BC. The battle
described by him below took place in 406 BC.

εἶχε δὲ τὸ δεξιὸν κέρας τῶν Πελοποννησίων Καλλικρατίδας. Ἕρμων δὲ
ὁ κυβερνήτης, καλόν ἐστιν, ἔφη, ἀποπλεῦσαι· αἱ γὰρ τριήρεις τῶν
Ἀθηναίων μάλα ἰσχυραί εἰσιν. ἀλλὰ Καλλικρατίδας, αἰσχρόν ἐστιν,
ἔφη, τὸ φεύγειν. ἐναυμάχησαν δὲ αἱ τριήρεις χρόνον πολύν, πρῶτον μὲν
ἀθρόαι, ἔπειτα δὲ σποράδες. ἐπεὶ δὲ Καλλικρατίδας τε ἀπέπεσεν εἰς τὴν   5
θάλατταν καὶ ἀπέθανε καὶ Πρωτόμαχος ὁ Ἀθηναῖος καὶ οἱ μετ' αὐτοῦ
τῷ δεξιῷ τὸ εὐώνυμον ἐνίκησαν, ἐντεῦθεν φυγὴ ἦν τῶν Πελοποννησίων
εἴς τε Χίον καὶ Φώκαιαν· οἱ δὲ Ἀθηναῖοι πάλιν εἰς τὰς Ἀργινούσας
κατέπλευσαν. τῶν μὲν οὖν Ἀθηναίων τριήρεις πέντε καὶ εἴκοσι
κατέδυσαν οἱ Λακεδαιμόνιοι, τῶν δὲ Πελοποννησίων Λακωνικὰς μὲν   10
ἐννέα οἱ Ἀθηναῖοι, τῶν δὲ ἄλλων συμμάχων ὡς ἑξήκοντα.

13   A troublesome visitor

In Athenian courts litigants were obliged to conduct their own cases, but
they could use speeches written for them by professional writers. The
following comes from such a speech composed by Lysias some time after
394 BC for a middle-aged homosexual defending himself against a charge
of assault brought against him by a fellow Athenian, Simon, who was his
rival for the affection of a young slave.

ἐπεὶ γὰρ ἐπὶ τὴν οἰκίαν μου τῆς νυκτὸς ἦλθεν ὁ Σίμων, ἐξέκοψε τὰς
θύρας καὶ εἰσῆλθεν εἰς τὴν γυναικωνῖτιν, οὗ ἦσαν ἥ τ' ἀδελφή μου καὶ αἱ
ἀδελφιδαῖ. πρῶτον μὲν οὖν οἱ ἐν τῇ οἰκίᾳ ἐκέλευσαν αὐτὸν ἀπελθεῖν, ὁ δ'
οὐκ ἤθελεν. ἔπειτα δὲ ἐξέωσαν βίᾳ. ἀλλ' ἐξηῦρεν οὗ ἐδειπνοῦμεν καὶ
πρᾶγμα σφόδρα ἄτοπον καὶ ἄπιστον ἐποίησεν· ἐξεκάλεσε γάρ με   5
ἔνδοθεν, καὶ ἐπειδὴ τάχιστα ἐξῆλθον, εὐθύς με τύπτειν ἐπεχείρησεν·
ἐπειδὴ δὲ αὐτὸν ἀπέωσα, ἔβαλλέ με λίθοις· καὶ ἐμοῦ μὲν ἁμαρτάνει,
Ἀριστόκριτον δὲ ἔβαλε λίθῳ καὶ συντρίβει τὸ μέτωπον.

Notes

2   Supply ἐστί; τὸ δίκαιον (*what is*) right (5.1/3)

3   χειμῶνος, τοῦ θέρους the definite article can be omitted in such
    expressions; τὴν οἰκίαν indicates a general class (hence the definite
    article, 2.1/2 note 1)—trans. *a house.*

5   οὐδέν is here an adjective with ψεῦδος; trans. *no falsehood* (cf. οὐδείς in
    8(*iv*)).

6   *l*.1 αὐτοῦ adv. *there, in that place* (**not** the gen. sing. m. or n. of αὐτός).
    ll.3–4 οὐ . . . ἔcτιν . . . ἡμῖν lit. *there is not to us*, i.e. *we do not have*.

8   (*vi*) The aorist is gnomic and should be translated by a present (see note
    on 5.2.10).

9   ἦλθε see 7.1/1 note 2; παραcάγγαc δύο καὶ εἴκοcι (*22 parasangs*) is in
    apposition to cταθμοὺc τρεῖc (*three days' march*) and explains how far
    Cyrus marched in three days (a parasang was a Persian measure of
    distance equal to about five kilometres); αὐτοῦ gen. sing. m. of αὐτός
    (referring back to τὸν Μαίανδρον).

10 Gnomic aorists (see note on 8 above).

11 κακῶc λέγω + acc. *speak evilly of, malign, abuse*; ὁ δέ *and he* (i.e.
    Socrates) 5.1/3; γάρ Socrates' reply sarcastically explains M's action and
    in English would be introduced by *yes, for he . . .* (see 24.1/1) or *well,
    he . . .* ; καλῶc λέγω can mean either *speak well of* or *speak properly*
    (κακῶc λέγω by itself can also mean *speak badly*)—Socrates is punning
    on the two senses.

12 *l*.1 εἶχε *had* i.e. *commanded*; the first δέ connects this sentence with the
    preceding one in the original context and need not be translated (cf. the
    beginning of 4.2.9); Καλλικρατίδᾱc (nom. s.; = Attic -ίδης—3.1/2 note
    3) was a Spartan and his name has the non-Attic (and non-Ionic) form of
    the patronymic suffix. *l*.2 τριήρειc 6.1/1*c*. *ll*.5f. cποράδεc nom. pl. f. (this
    is a third declension adj., 10.1/4*a*) *scattered* (agreeing with τριήρειc);
    Καλλικρατίδᾱc τε . . . καὶ Πρωτόμαχοc . . . lit. *both Callicratidas
    . . . and Protomachus . . .* Greek is fond of linking clauses with particles
    such as τε . . . καί (cf. 4.1/3 and φέρουcί τε καὶ ἄγουcιν in *l*.21 of 4.2.9)
    but in English we would not translate τε; notice that between this
    τε . . . καί another καί occurs to join ἀπέπεcεν (< ἀποπίπτω) and
    ἀπέθανε (< ἀποθνῄcκω) but it is the second καί which picks up τε
    because the two elements, which must be parallel, are *Callicratidas* and
    Protomachus and those with him; τῷ δεξίῳ *with their right [wing]* dat. of
    instrument (11.1/2). *l*.11 ἄλλων cannot here be translated *other* because
    the allies referred to are allies of the Spartans; the meaning is *of their
    allies as well* (cf. Ἀθῆναι καὶ αἱ ἄλλαι νῆcοι *Athens and the islands as well*
    not *Athens and the other islands* because Athens is not an island); ὡc here
    about (22.1/1*a*(vii)).

13 *ll*.1f. ἦλθεν (and εἰcῆλθεν (*l*.2) and ἀπελθεῖν (*l*.3)) 7.1/1 note 2; τὰc θύρᾱc
    i.e. the two leaves of the folding door at the house entrance; γυναικωνῖ-
    τιν in an Athenian house the women had separate quarters; ἥ τ' . . . καί
    the τε need not be translated (cf. *l*.5 of previous passage). *l*.3 μέν is
    balanced by δέ after ἔπειτα, and οὖν connects this sentence with the
    previous one (neither word would have an equivalent in idiomatic
    English). *l*.4 ἐξέωcαν < ἐξωθέω (the temporal augment in the aorist of
    this verb is irregular, cf. 4.1/1 note 2(ii). *ll*.7f. ἀπέωcα < ἀπωθέω; ἔβαλλε
    started to pelt inceptive use of the imperfect (4.1/1 footnote); λίθοιc *with
    stones* (dat. of instrument 11.1/2); ἁμαρτάνει . . . cυντρίβει Greek often
    uses the present tense in narrative for vividness (vivid present); translate
    with the English simple past (*missed . . . gashed*); take ἐμοῦ (*l*.7) with
    ἁμαρτάνει *missed me* (ἁμαρτάνω is followed by the gen., 13.1/2*a*(iv)).

Unit 8

8.1 Grammar

8.1/1 Middle and passive voices

In a clause where the verb is active the subject is the doer (*the man bit the dog*; *Alcibiades is running through the agora*). There may or may not be an object, depending on whether the verb is transitive or intransitive. In a clause with a passive verb the subject is the sufferer (*the dog was bitten by the man*; *the Athenians were defeated in Sicily*). The agent or instrument (11.1/2) may or may not be specified. The active and passive voices are used in Greek in much the same way as in English. Greek, however, has a third voice, the **middle**. This has no English equivalent because the meanings it conveys are expressed in English in different ways. These meanings are:

(*a*) to do something to oneself, e.g. λούομαι *I wash myself, I wash* (intr.); παύομαι *I stop myself, I cease, stop* (intr.)

(*b*) to do something for oneself, for one's own advantage, e.g. κομίζω (act.) *carry, convey,* κομίζομαι (mid.) *I convey for myself, recover*:

ἑκατὸν δραχμὰς ἐκομίσατο.   *He recovered a hundred drachmas.*

(*c*) to cause something to be done (naturally one's own advantage is always involved):

διδάσκομαι τοὺς παῖδας τὴν τῶν Ἑλλήνων γλῶτταν.   *I am having [my] children taught the language of the Greeks.*

Of these three uses (*a*) is restricted to verbs with an appropriate meaning, (*b*) is very common, (*c*) is somewhat rare. Very often a verb when used in the middle voice in sense (*b*) acquires a special meaning, e.g. λύω *loosen, free,* λύομαι (mid.) *free* (someone) *for one's own advantage, ransom;* αἱρέω *take, seize,* αἱρέομαι *take for oneself, choose.*

As will be seen in **Appendix 1**, the forms of the middle and passive indicative are identical in the present and imperfect (and also in the perfect and pluperfect—16.1/3). This does not create ambiguity as the context of a particular verb normally shows its voice. The future and aorist passive differ in form from the middle and will be treated separately in 11.1/1. With regard to the forms of the indicative of the present middle and passive, the imperfect middle and passive, the future middle and the aorist middle, which can now be learnt, we should note that:

(*d*) in each case the stem is the same as for the active, and the link vowel

58

between the stem and the ending proper (which is more easily distinguishable in these forms) is ο/ε in the present, imperfect (and strong aorist) and future, but α in the weak aorist (on -ω of the 2nd s., see below)

(*e*) in each tense the 2nd s. ending has undergone contraction. The present and future ending was originally -εcαι, the imperfect -εcο and the aorist -αcο. With the loss of intervocal c (cf. 6.1/1*c*) these became η (or ει), ου, ω respectively (we have already met the second and third contractions in contracted verbs—5.1/2)

(*f*) when allowance has been made for the 2nd s., the endings, except for the 1st pl. and 2nd pl. which do not vary, fall into two classes. For the primary tenses they are -μαι, -cαι, -ται, -νται and for the historic -μην, -cο, -το, -ντο (cf. 4.1/1 note 1)

(*g*) the endings of the strong aorist indicative middle are the same as those of the imperfect: αἰcθάνομαι *perceive*, impf. ἠcθανόμην, aor. ἠcθόμην; and the infinitive ending of the strong aorist is the same as that of the present: αἰcθάνεcθαι (pres.), αἰcθέcθαι (aor.).

Notes

1 Many common verbs have, for no perceptible reason, their future in the middle voice, not the active, e.g. ἀκούω *hear*, ἀκούcομαι; βοάω *shout*, βοήcομαι; διώκω *pursue*, διώξομαι; μανθάνω *learn*, μαθήcομαι. These are verbs which would not otherwise have had reason to be used in the middle. For other examples see **Principal parts of verbs**.

2 εἰμί *be* also has a middle future, which is formed with the stem ἐc-: ἔcομαι, ἔcει (-η), ἔcται, ἐcόμεθα, ἔcεcθε, ἔcονται. The original form of the 3rd s., ἔcεται, occurs in dialects other than Attic.

3 Contracted verbs form their present and imperfect middle/passive according to the rules given at 5.1/2 (see **Appendix 2**).

4 In Indo-European (1.3) there were only active and middle voices. In Greek the passive use of the middle led to the development of separate forms in the future and aorist, but even in Attic we occasionally meet the future middle used in a passive sense.

8.1/2 Deponent verbs

A linguistic peculiarity for which English offers no parallel is deponent verbs, which are **middle or passive in form** but **active in meaning**. They may be transitive (as κτάομαι *acquire*) or intransitive (as πορεύομαι *march*). In some cases the meaning of a deponent exemplifies one of the uses of the middle voice (κτάομαι originally meant *procure for oneself*), but elsewhere (as ἕπομαι *follow*) no explanation seems possible, although these verbs are among the most commonly used in Greek.

As we have seen in the previous subsections, the forms of the middle and passive voices differ only in the future and aorist. This divergence allows a classification of deponents into two groups:

(a) **middle deponents**, whose future and aorist are middle in form, as αἰνίττομαι *speak in riddles*, fut. αἰνίξομαι, aor. ἠνιξάμην. This is the larger group

(b) **passive deponents**, whose aorist is passive in form. Nearly all passive deponents, however, have a middle, not passive, future. For the aorist passive and examples of passive deponents see 11.1/1.

Examples of deponents in use are:

ἀπὸ τῶν Ἀθηνῶν ἔρχονται.   *They are coming from Athens* (ἔρχομαι *come, go*; for the aorist of this verb see 7.1/1 note 2).

τὸ ἆθλον δέχομαι.   *I accept the prize* (δέχομαι *accept, receive*).

A very common deponent is γίγνομαι which has the basic meanings *be born, become, happen*. In many contexts, however, English requires a more specific word: ἀνὴρ ἀγαθὸς ἐγένετο *he showed himself a brave man* (lit. *he became a brave man*); νὺξ ἐγένετο *night fell*.

8.1/3   Indirect statement

In English we can say, with the same meaning, *he considers that I am clever* or *he considers me to be clever*. Both constructions, a noun clause introduced by *that*, or an infinitive phrase without *that*, have their equivalents in Greek, but unlike English, Greek shows a distinct preference for the infinitive construction after most verbs of **saying**, **thinking** and the like (for verbs of **knowing** and **perceiving**, see 15.1/2a): νομίζω, οἴομαι both *think, consider*; φάσκω *state, declare*; ἡγέομαι *consider*. The first three are used virtually exclusively with the infinitive construction.

(a)   *Infinitive construction*

In this form there is no introductory word (like ὅτι *that* in the other construction—see below (b)) and the finite verb of the original statement is changed to the infinitive of the same tense (the present infinitive represents both the present and the imperfect indicative of the direct form). If the subject of the finite verb of the original direct statement is the same as the subject of the verb of saying or thinking introducing the indirect statement, it remains in the nominative, as do any words agreeing with it (**nominative and infinitive**). Such sentences are of the type *Xerxes said that he was master*. Since in the original direct statement (δεσπότης εἰμί *I am master*) there is no need to state the subject explicitly (except for emphasis: ἐγώ εἰμι δεσπότης *I am master*), so too the subject of the infinitive is normally not expressed: Ξέρξης ἔφη δεσπότης εἶναι. When the two subjects are not identical, the subject of the infinitive is put into the accusative (**accusative and infinitive**): ὁ cατράπης ἔφη Ξέρξην εἶναι δεcπότην *the satrap said that Xerxes was master* (lit. *Xerxes to be master*; original Ξέρξης ἐcτὶ δεcπότης *Xerxes is master*). If the direct statement was negated, the same negative, οὐ (see 7.1/6), will appear with the infinitive. Further examples are:

ἡ ᾿Αcπαcίᾱ νομίζει καλὴ εἶναι.   *Aspasia thinks that she is beautiful* (original καλή εἰμι *I am beautiful*).

ὁ Περικλῆς ἐνόμιζε τὴν ᾿Αcπαcίᾱν καλὴν εἶναι. *Pericles used to think that Aspasia was beautiful* (original ἡ ᾿Αcπαcίᾱ ἐcτὶ καλή. *Aspasia is beautiful*).

ἡγοῦμαι τὴν ᾿Αcπαcίᾱν οὐκ εἶναι αἰcχρᾱ́. *I consider that Aspasia is not ugly* (original ἡ ᾿Αcπαcίᾱ οὐκ ἔcτιν αἰcχρᾱ́. *Aspasia is not ugly*).

ὁ Cωκράτης ἔφη τὴν γυναῖκα χιτῶνα κτήcεcθαι. *Socrates said that [his] wife would get a chiton* (original ἡ γυνὴ χιτῶνα κτήcεται [*my*] *wife will get a chiton*).

ὑποπτεύω τὴν Ξανθίππην πέντε χιτῶνας ἐχθὲς κτήcαcθαι.   *I suspect that Xanthippe got five chitons yesterday* (original ἡ Ξανθίππη πέντε χιτῶνας ἐχθὲς ἐκτήcατο *Xanthippe got five chitons yesterday*).

Notes

1 It is only in this construction that the distinction between the present and aorist infinitives is one of time, **not** aspect (cf. 4.1/1). In the last example κτήcαcθαι means literally *to have got*. If we were to substitute the present infinitive κτᾶcθαι *to be getting* (and eliminate ἐχθέc) the meaning would be *I suspect that Xanthippe is getting* . . . (original ἡ Ξανθίππη κτᾶται . . .).

2 Since, in the accusative and infinitive construction, the infinitive of a transitive verb has both its subject and its object in the accusative, there is obviously a possibility of ambiguity. When confronted with cέ φημι ῾Ρωμαίουc νῑκήcειν (the reply of the Delphic priestess to Pyrrhus of Epirus) one might well wonder whether the meaning was *I say that you will conquer the Romans* or *I say that the Romans will conquer you*. Normal Greeks left such equivocation to oracles.

3 φημί tends to occupy an unemphatic position and so, unlike in English, does not precede the indirect statement which it reports: Πέρcης ἔφη εἶναι *he said he was a Persian* (cf. 7.1/2 note 3).

4 οὔ φημι means *I say that* . . . *not*, *I deny*: οὐκ ἔφη Πέρcης εἶναι *he denied he was a Persian*: it **never** means *I do not say that* . . . , which would require a different verb, e.g. οὐ λέγω ὅτι . . . (on ὅτι see (*b*) below).

5 Verbs of hoping (ἐλπίζω), promising (ὑπιcχνέομαι), swearing (ὄμνῡμι 20.1/1), threatening (ἀπειλέω) and the like regularly take the infinitive construction. When these verbs have a future reference, as they generally do, they can be construed with the future infinitive (a present or aorist infinitive is also possible): ἐλπίζω νῑκήcειν ἐν τῇ μάχῃ *I hope to conquer in the battle*. For a negative hope of this sort the negative μή, not οὐ, is used

because the original is really not a statement but a wish (wishes are always negated by μή—21.1/1): ἐλπίζω τοὺς Λακεδαιμονίους μὴ καύσειν τὸν ἀγρόν *I hope the Spartans won't burn the farm* (original wish *may the Spartans not burn the farm!*). This use of μή is extended to verbs of promising, swearing and threatening.

(b) *Construction with finite verb*

Indirect statements in Greek may also be expressed by a noun-clause introduced by ὅτι or ὡς, *that*. Insofar as these two conjunctions can be differentiated, ὅτι is used to introduce a fact, whereas ὡς tends to convey the suggestion that the reporter considers the statement as a mere opinion, an allegation or as untrue. As in the infinitive construction, the tense of the direct speech is retained in the indirect form even after a main verb which is in the past; in such cases we make a tense adjustment in English (see the second, third and fourth examples below).

This is the regular construction after λέγω *say* (but see note 1) and certain other verbs. Examples are:

λέγει ὡς ὑβριστής εἰμι. *He claims that I am insolent.*

εἶπον ὅτι ὁ Κῦρος διώκει. *They said that Cyrus was pursuing* (original *Cyrus is pursuing*).

ἀπεκρίναντο ὅτι στρατὸν πέμψουσιν. *They replied that they would send an army* (original *we will send an army*).

εἴπομεν ὅτι ὁ Περικλῆς ταῦτα οὐ ποιήσει. *We said that Pericles would not do this* (original *Pericles will not do this*).

Notes

1 For the impersonal English construction *it is said that* . . . Greek uses a personal construction with the infinitive: ὁ Σωκράτης λέγεται τοὺς νέους βλάψαι *it is said that Socrates harmed the young* (lit. *Socrates is said to have harmed* . . .).

2 Occasionally even a **direct** quote is introduced by ὅτι: εἶπον ὅτι ἑτοῖμοί ἐσμεν *they said, 'We are ready'*.

3 For the change of mood which may occur after a historic main verb see 14.1/4*d*.

8.1/4 Third declension nouns—stems in *ι* and *υ*

These stems differ from those in consonants (5.1/1, 6.1/1) in having *ν*, not *α*, as the acc. s. ending for masculine and feminine nouns.

Stems in *ι* consist of a large number of feminines (including many abstract nouns, mostly in -σις, e.g. φύσις *nature*), a few masculines, but no neuters in normal use. All are declined alike, with the odd anomaly that the original *ι* of the stem has been lost in most forms. The -εως of the gen. s. was originally

-ηος (as occurs in Homer); the quantity of the two vowels was interchanged but the original accent was retained, i.e. πόληος > πόλεως. This accent was extended by analogy to the genitive plural.

Masculine and feminine υ stems are divided into two sub-groups, both very small. The declension of the first (πῆχυς) is very close to πόλις, of the second (ἰχθῦς) to consonantal stems. ἄστυ, the only neuter, follows πῆχυς in the genitive and dative.

	πόλις (f) *city*	πῆχυς (m) *forearm*	ἄστυ (n) *city*	ἰχθῦς (m) *fish*
SINGULAR				
Nom.	πόλις	πῆχυς	ἄστυ	ἰχθῦς
Voc.	πόλι	πῆχυ	ἄστυ	ἰχθῦ
Acc.	πόλιν	πῆχυν	ἄστυ	ἰχθῦν
Gen.	πόλεως	πήχεως	ἄστεως	ἰχθύος
Dat.	πόλει	πήχει	ἄστει	ἰχθύϊ
PLURAL				
N.V.	πόλεις	πήχεις	ἄστη (< εα)	ἰχθύες
Acc.	πόλεις	πήχεις	ἄστη (< εα)	ἰχθῦς
Gen.	πόλεων	πήχεων	ἄστεων	ἰχθύων
Dat.	πόλεσι(ν)	πήχεσι(ν)	ἄστεσι(ν)	ἰχθύσι(ν)

The normal word for *city* is πόλις. ἄστυ means *city, town* as opposed to the country.

Note

πρέσβυς, which follows πῆχυς, is a poetical word for *old man* (prose uses γέρων or πρεσβύτης). Its plural πρέσβεις, however, is the normal prose word for *ambassadors* (the singular *ambassador* is supplied by πρεσβευτής).

8.2 Greek reading

1 ὁ θεὸς καὶ ἡ φύσις οὐδὲν μάτην ποιοῦσιν.
2# φύσιν πονηρὰν μεταβαλεῖν οὐ ῥάδιον.
3# πόλεις ὅλας ἠφάνισε διαβολὴ κακή.
4 Ἰησοῦς Χριστὸς Θεοῦ Υἱὸς Σωτήρ (*the name of an early Christian symbol is concealed in the initial letters of this formula*).
5 ὁ χρυσὸς οὐ μιαίνεται.
6 οἴεσθε ἄλλους τὴν Ἑλλάδα σώσειν, ὑμεῖς δ' ἀποδράσεσθαι;
7 ἐκ τοῦ ἐσορᾶν γίγνεται ἀνθρώποις ἐρᾶν.
8# ἀρετῆς βέβαιαί εἰσιν αἱ κτήσεις μόνης.
9# φεῦ φεῦ, παλαιὸς αἶνος ὡς καλῶς ἔχει·
   γέροντες οὐδέν ἐσμεν ἄλλο πλὴν ψόφος

καὶ cχῆμ᾽, ὀνείρων δ᾽ ἕρπομεν μιμήματα,
νοῦς δ᾽ οὐκ ἔνεστιν, οἰόμεσθα δ᾽ εὖ φρονεῖν.

10   ἐλέφας μῦν οὐ δάκνει.

11   ἀταλαίπωρος τοῖς πολλοῖς ἡ ζήτησις τῆς ἀληθείας καὶ ἐπὶ τὰ ἑτοῖμα
μᾶλλον τρέπονται.

12   οἱ Λακεδαιμόνιοι κήρυκα ἔπεμψαν καὶ τοὺς νεκροὺς διεκομίσαντο.

13   διὰ τὸ θαυμάζειν οἱ ἄνθρωποι καὶ νῦν καὶ τὸ πρῶτον ἤρξαντο
φιλοσοφεῖν.

14   ὤδινεν ὄρος, εἶτα μῦν ἔτεκεν.

15#   πολλῶν ὁ λιμὸς γίγνεται διδάσκαλος.

16   οἱ Cκύθαι οὐ λούονται ὕδατι.

17   A Greek translation of the Old Testament was prepared at Alexandria in
the third century BC. Legend tells us that the version acquired its name of
Septuagint (Latin **septuaginta** *seventy*) from the number of its trans-
lators, of whom thirty knew Greek but not Hebrew, thirty Hebrew but
not Greek, while the remaining ten had no knowledge of either. This
calumny probably arose from the colloquial nature of its language. The
following are well-known passages.

(*i*) ἐν ἀρχῇ ἐποίηcεν ὁ θεὸς τὸν οὐρανὸν καὶ τὴν γῆν. ἡ δὲ γῆ ἦν
ἀόρατος καὶ ἀκατασκεύαστος, καὶ σκότος ἐπάνω τῆς ἀβύσσου, καὶ
πνεῦμα τοῦ θεοῦ ἐπεφέρετο ἐπάνω τοῦ ὕδατος. καὶ εἶπεν ὁ θεός,
γεννηθήτω (lit. *let . . . be born*) φῶc. καὶ ἐγένετο φῶc. καὶ εἶδεν ὁ
θεὸς τὸ φῶc ὅτι καλόν. καὶ διεχώριcεν ὁ θεὸς ἀνὰ μέσον τοῦ φωτὸς   5
καὶ ἀνὰ μέσον τοῦ cκότους. καὶ ἐκάλεcεν ὁ θεὸς τὸ φῶc ἡμέραν καὶ
τὸ cκότος ἐκάλεcεν νύκτα.

(*ii*) ἐπέcτρεψα καὶ εἶδον ὑπὸ τὸν ἥλιον ὅτι οὐ τοῖς κούφοις ὁ δρόμος,
καὶ οὐ τοῖς δυνατοῖς ὁ πόλεμος, καὶ οὐ τοῖς σοφοῖς ἄρτος, καὶ οὐ
τοῖς cυνετοῖς πλοῦτος.

18   Crime does not pay

Hegestratus, a rascally owner-captain, had hired his ship to an Athenian
who wished to import grain from Syracuse. After the grain had been
loaded, Hegestratus, with Zenothemis, an accomplice in crime, went
round Syracuse borrowing money against the cargo as though it were
his. This type of loan (bottomry) was made to enable merchants to meet
costs of transportation by sea, and was not recoverable if the ship sank.

Ζηνόθεμις δ᾽ ἀδίκημα κακὸν μεθ᾽ Ἡγεστράτου cυνεσκευάσατο.
χρήματα γὰρ ἐν ταῖς Cυρακούcαις ἐδανείζοντο. ὡς δὲ ἐλάμβανον τὰ
χρήματα, οἴκαδε ἀπέστελλον εἰς τὴν Μασσαλίαν, καὶ οὐδὲν εἰς τὸ
πλοῖον εἰσέφερον. ἐπειδὴ δὲ ἦσαν αἱ cυγγραφαὶ ἀποδοῦναι (*to repay*) τὰ
χρήματα μετὰ τὸν τοῦ πλοίου κατάπλουν, καταδῦσαι ἐβουλεύσαντο τὸ
πλοῖον· ἐβούλοντο γὰρ τοὺς δανειστὰς ἀποστερῆσαι. ὁ μὲν οὖν
Ἡγέστρατος, ὡς ἀπὸ τῆς γῆς ἀπῆραν δυοῖν ἢ τριῶν ἡμερῶν πλοῦν, τῆς

νυκτὸς διέκοπτε τοῦ πλοίου τὸ ἔδαφος, ὁ δὲ Ζηνόθεμις ἄνω μετὰ τῶν
ἄλλων ἐπιβατῶν διέτριβεν. ἀλλὰ ἐπεὶ ψόφος ἐγένετο, αἰcθάνονται οἱ ἐν
τῷ πλοίῳ ὅτι κακόν τι (*some mischief*) κάτω γίγνεται, καὶ βοηθοῦcιν.   10
ὡς δ' ἡλίcκετο ὁ Ἡγέcτρατος καὶ κακῶς πείcεcθαι ὑπελάμβανε,
φεύγει καὶ πηδᾷ εἰς τὴν θάλατταν. οὕτως οὖν, ὥσπερ ἄξιος ἦν, κακὸς
κακῶς ἀπέθανεν.

Notes

2 ῥᾴδιον (sc. ἐcτί) *it is easy*—when impersonal expressions involve an
adjective the neuter singular form is used.

3 ἠφάνιcε < ἀφανίζω (4.1/1 note 2(ii)), the aorist is gnomic (see note on
5.2.10).

6 ἄλλους . . . cώcειν acc. and inf., ὑμεῖς . . . ἀποδράcεcθαι nom and inf.;
ἀποδράcεcθαι < ἀποδιδράcκω, which has a middle future (8.1/1 note 1).

7 ἐρᾶν is the subject of γίγνεται.

8 κτήcεις should be translated by a singular.

9 *l.*1 *how right the old saying is* (ὡc is exclamatory, 22.1/1*a*(ii)); Greek uses
ἔχω + an adverb (here καλῶc) to express a state where English has the
verb *to be* + an adjective.   *l.*3 μιμήματα is in apposition to the subject of
ἕρπομεν *we crawl [along] [as] copies* . . .   *l.*4 -μεcθα (in οἰόμεcθα) is an
alternative ending used in verse for -μεθα (1st pl.) of the middle and
passive; εὖ φρονεῖν *think rightly*, i.e. *be sane, be of right mind.*

11 τοῖc πολλοῖc lit. *for the many*, i.e. *for the majority, for most people*;
τρέπονται lit. *they turn themselves* (use (*a*) of the middle in 8.1/1).
Whereas the English verb *turn* can be either transitive (*I turned my car
towards him*) or intransitive (*I turned towards him*), τρέπω in the active is
transitive only (i.e. must always be followed by an object), and the
middle (τρέπομαι lit. *I turn myself*, i.e. *I turn*) is employed for the
intransitive use of the English *turn*. Here we would translate *they turn*.

12 διεκομίcαντο could represent use (*b*) or (*c*) as given in 8.1/1.

14 ὠδῖνεν impf. (or aorist) of ὠδίνω (4.1/1 note 2(ii)).

16 λούονται *wash*; just as with τρέπω and *turn* (above 11), λούω is transitive
only, whereas *wash* in English can be transitive (*I washed the baby five
times*) or intransitive (*I washed five times*).

17 (*i*) *l.*1 ἐν ἀρχῇ the absence of the article gives the phrase a poetical ring.
*ll.*4f. εἶδεν . . . τὸ φῶς ὅτι καλόν lit. *saw the light that [it was] beautiful*,
i.e. *saw that the light was* . . .   *ll.*5f. ἀνὰ μέcον (+gen. *between*) need
only be translated once
(*ii*) ἐπέcτρεψα *I turned* (unlike τρέπω this verb can be either transitive or
intransitive in the active mood)—the author, who was of a rather
pessimistic nature, *turned* from one depressing observation to another;
ὑπὸ τὸν ἥλιον, i.e. here on earth.

18 *l.*1 cυνεcκευάcατο < cυcκευάζομαι (6.1/3).   *ll.*2ff. ὡc *when, as* as also
in *ll.*7 and 11 below (22.1/1*b*(iv)); ἐλάμβανον . . . ἀπέcτελλον . . .
εἰcέφερον the imperfect indicates that they did these things on several
occasions.   *l.*4 αἱ cυγγραφαί *the contracts*—the infinitive phrase begin-

ning with ἀποδοῦναι defines them.　*l.7* ἀπῆραν < ἀπαίρω *sail away*;
πλοῦν acc. of extent (7.1/7*d*).　*l.8* διέκοπτε *began to cut through*
(inceptive imperfect 4.1/1 footnote). *ll.*9f. αἰcθάνονται . . . γίγνεται . . .
βοηθοῦcιν vivid presents (cf. note on 7.2.13 *ll.*7f.).　*l.11* ἡλίcκετο . . .
ὑπελάμβανε imperfect because these two actions were going on when
Hegestratus escaped; the two following verbs are in the vivid present,
which is more commonly used in main clauses than in subordinate
clauses.

Unit 9

9.1 Grammar

9.1/1 Demonstrative Pronouns

Demonstratives in Greek draw our attention to persons and things and are used not only as pronouns but also as adjectives. The English *this* and *that* have similar functions although their use as pronouns is restricted; *this* in *this temple* is an adjective, *that* in *I do not like that* is a pronoun. Greek has three demonstratives, each with a special shade of meaning. The basic differences between them when used as adjectives are:

ὅδε   *this near me* (the speaker); normally to be translated *this*
οὗτος   *this* or *that near you* (the person spoken to); normally to be translated *this* or *that*
ἐκεῖνος   *that over there* (i.e. away from both speaker and person spoken to); normally to be translated *that*.

When used as pronouns ὅδε will literally mean *this man near me*, οὗτος *this or that man near you*, ἐκεῖνος *that man over there*, but the first can generally be translated by *this man*, the third by *that man*, while the translation of οὗτος by *this man* or *that man* will depend on the context.

ὅδε is simply a compound of the definite article and -δε. In this combination even the unaccented forms of the article bear an accent: ὅδε, ἥδε, οἵδε, αἵδε (cf. 2.1/2; 3.1/1). ἐκεῖνος is declined as a first and second declension adjective (3.1/3), except that the neuter nom. and acc. s. is ἐκεῖνο (for other words with the ending -ο see 9.1/3). οὗτος is similarly declined but the first syllable undergoes changes according to the following rules:

(*a*)   an initial vowel with a rough breathing occurs in the same forms as in the definite article (2.1/2, 3.1/1)
(*b*)   an initial τ occurs in the same forms as in the definite article
(*c*)   where the ending contains α or η the diphthong of the first syllable changes from ου to αυ.

	SINGULAR			PLURAL		
	M.	F.	N.	M.	F.	N.
Nom.	οὗτος	αὕτη	τοῦτο	οὗτοι	αὗται	ταῦτα
Acc.	τοῦτον	ταύτην	τοῦτο	τούτους	ταύτᾱς	ταῦτα
Gen.	τούτου	ταύτης	τούτου	τούτων	τούτων	τούτων
Dat.	τούτῳ	ταύτῃ	τούτῳ	τούτοις	ταύταις	τούτοις

67

In prose, when a demonstrative is used as an adjective, the noun which it qualifies must retain the definite article and the demonstrative must appear in the predicative position (3.1/3*b*): ἐκεῖνος ὁ νεανίας *that young man*; ἡ γυνὴ ἥδε *this woman*.

Notes

1 In certain contexts οὗτος refers to what precedes, ὅδε to what follows: ταῦτα ἔλεξεν *he said this* (as already reported), but τάδε ἔλεξεν *he spoke as follows*.

2 ἐκεῖνος ... οὗτος can mean *the former ... the latter*.

9.1/2   The relative pronoun ὅς and adjectival clauses

Adjectival clauses qualify nouns or pronouns and so perform the same function as adjectives. They are introduced by a relative pronoun, which in English is *who, which* etc.

> I am the man **who** dedicated a bronze tripod at Delphi.
>
> The tripod **which** you dedicated is inferior.

An adjectival clause normally has an antecedent, i.e. a noun or pronoun to which the clause refers and which it qualifies (in the above examples *man* and *tripod*). In English the forms of the relative pronoun are not interchangeable but are influenced by the antecedent (*the man which* or *the tripod who* are clearly impossible). Further, we cannot say *I know the man whom visited Delos* because, although *man*, the antecedent of the adjectival clause, is the object of *know* (and so would be in the accusative in Greek), the relative pronoun is the subject of the clause it introduces and must take the nominative form *who*, not the accusative form *whom*. The same holds for Greek, where the rule is **a relative pronoun takes its number and gender from its antecedent but its case from the function it performs in its own clause** (but see note 2 below). Greek cannot, moreover, omit the relative pronoun as we so often do in English (*the man Apollo cursed cannot come into my house*; Greek must say *the man whom*).

The normal relative pronoun in Greek is ὅς, which is declined as a first and second declension adjective (3.1/3) except that the neuter s. nom. and acc. is ὅ without ν (for other words with this ending see 9.1/3):

	SINGULAR			PLURAL		
	M.	F.	N.	M.	F.	N.
Nom.	ὅς	ἥ	ὅ	οἵ	αἵ	ἅ
Acc.	ὅν	ἥν	ὅ	οὕς	ἅς	ἅ
Gen.	οὗ	ἧς	οὗ	ὧν	ὧν	ὧν
Dat.	ᾧ	ᾗ	ᾧ	οἷς	αἷς	οἷς

Unlike *who, which*, etc. in English, which can also be used as interrogatives (*which is your tripod?*), the Greek relative pronoun has no other functions in prose. Examples of adjectival clauses are:

> Θάνατον εἰcορῶ ὃc Ἄλκηcτιν εἰc Ἅιδου δόμον μέλλει κατάξειν.   *I see Death who is going to* (μέλλει) *take Alcestis down to the house of Hades.*
>
> ὁρᾷc τὸν μόρον τοῦ Ἀκταίωνοc ὃν οἱ κύνεc οὓc ἐθρέψατο διεcπάcαντο.   *You know* (lit. *see*) *the fate of Actaeon whom the dogs whom he [had] reared tore apart.*
>
> οἱ cτρατιῶται οἷc ταῦτα εἶπε Ξενοφῶν ἐπανῆλθον πρὸc τοὺc Πέρcᾱc.   *The soldiers to whom Xenophon said this* (lit. *these things*) *returned to the Persians.*

Notes

1   The antecedent of an adjectival clause, if a pronoun, is often omitted: ὃν οἱ θεοὶ φιλοῦcιν ἀποθνῄcκει νέοc *[he] whom the gods love dies young.*
2   Contrary to the rule given above, the Greek relative pronoun is often put into the same case as its antecedent. This quite illogical attraction is most frequent when a relative pronoun in the accusative case has an antecedent in the genitive or dative: ἤγαγεν cτρατὸν ἀπὸ τῶν πόλεων ὧν (for ᾱ̔c) ἔπειcεν *he led an army from the cities which he [had] persuaded.* Sometimes the antecedent, if a pronoun, is omitted (cf. note 1); ἐπαινῶ cε ἐφ᾽ οἷc (for ἐπὶ τούτοιc ἃ) λέγειc *I praise you for what you are saying.*
3   Sometimes when both the relative and its antecedent are in the accusative the latter is put into the adjectival clause: οὐκ ἀπεκρύπτετο ἣν εἶχε γνώμην *he did not conceal the opinion which he had* (= τὴν γνώμην ἣν εἶχε); here the relative is used as an adjective.

9.1/3   αὐτόc and its uses

For the terms **attributive position** *and* **predicative position** *see 3.1/3b.*

αὐτόc is a pronoun which, like demonstratives (9.1/1), is also used as an adjective. αὐτόc is declined like καλόc (3.1/3) except that in the neuter its nom. and acc. s. is αὐτό (the expected αὐτόν only occurs in ταὐτόν—see below). The -ο ending for the nom. and acc. neuter singular also occurs in the definite article (τό), the relative pronoun (ὅ), τοῦτο, ἐκεῖνο (9.1/1), and ἄλλο *other.*

αὐτόc is used in three ways:

(*a*)   as an **emphasizing adjective** meaning *self.* Greek has no separate words corresponding to the English emphatic *myself, yourself*, etc. (as opposed to the **reflexive** *myself, yourself*, etc., see 9.1/4) and instead uses αὐτόc for all persons. When used with a noun it stands in the **predicative** position: αὐτὸc ὁ ἀνήρ *the man himself*, περὶ τῆc γυναικὸc αὐτῆc *concerning the woman herself.* αὐτός can also be used by itself in the nominative and agree with the understood subject: αὐτὸς ἥκεις *you yourself have come.*

Two idioms involving this use of αὐτός are:

(i) with ordinal numbers: πρεσβευτὴς ἦλθε δέκατος αὐτός *he came as ambassador with nine others* (lit. *himself the tenth*).

(ii) with a dative to express the idea of accompaniment (23.1/2*k*), especially in connection with the loss or destruction of something: τῶν τριήρων μίαν κατέδυσαν αὐτοῖς ἀνδράσιν *they sank one of the triremes crew and all* (lit. *[with] men themselves*).

(b) ὁ αὐτός means *the same.* In the **attributive** position (i.e. between the article and the noun) αὐτός **always** has this meaning: τοὺς αὐτοὺς δεσπότᾱς εἴχομεν, *we had the same masters*; ἐγὼ μὲν ὁ αὐτός εἰμι, ὑμεῖς δὲ μεταβάλλετε, *I am the same, [it is] you [who] change. The same as* is expressed either by ὁ αὐτὸς καί or, more commonly, by ὁ αὐτός plus the dative: τὰ αὐτὰ φρονεῖ ἐμοί *he thinks the same as I do*; τὰ αὐτὰ καὶ ὁ Ἀλκιβιάδης πείθουσιν, *they give the same advice as Alcibiades* (lit. *they persuade the same [things] . . .*).

In this use αὐτός may coalesce with those parts of the article ending in a vowel (**crasis**—11.1/5), and where this is possible both contracted and uncontracted forms are found in normal use. The following table shows all possible variations.

SINGULAR

	M.	F.	N.
Nom.	ὁ αὐτός, αὑτός	ἡ αὐτή, αὑτή	τὸ αὐτό, ταὐτό, ταὐτόν
Acc.	τὸν αὐτόν	τὴν αὐτήν	τὸ αὐτό, ταὐτό, ταὐτόν
Gen.	τοῦ αὐτοῦ, ταὐτοῦ	τῆς αὐτῆς	τοῦ αὐτοῦ, ταὐτοῦ
Dat.	τῷ αὐτῷ, ταὐτῷ	τῇ αὐτῇ, ταὐτῇ	τῷ αὐτῷ, ταὐτῷ

PLURAL

	M.	F.	N.
Nom.	οἱ αὐτοί, αὑτοί	αἱ αὐταί, αὑταί	τὰ αὐτά, ταὐτά
Acc.	τοὺς αὐτούς	τὰς αὐτάς	τὰ αὐτά, ταὐτά
Gen.	τῶν αὐτῶν	τῶν αὐτῶν	τῶν αὐτῶν
Dat.	τοῖς αὐτοῖς	ταῖς αὐταῖς	τοῖς αὐτοῖς

The alternative neuter in -ον occurs only in the contracted form.

The shorter forms bear a confusing resemblance to the corresponding parts of οὗτος, e.g. αὑτή *the same woman*, αὕτη *this/that woman*; ταὐτά *the same things*, ταῦτα *these/those things.* The accent will always show which word is involved.

(c) The **oblique cases** (2.1/3) of αὐτός are used to express **the personal pronoun of the third person,** *him, her, it, them* (4.1/2). In this use αὐτόν, αὐτήν etc. are unemphatic and postpositive (just as are με, cε, etc., cf. 4.1/2): ἐκέλευcεν αὐτὴν μένειν *they ordered her to remain.* As an **emphatic** third person pronoun, Greek uses the demonstratives οὗτος or ἐκεῖνος:

οὗτος μὲν τοὺς Ἀθηναίους φιλεῖ, αὕτη δὲ τοὺς Λακεδαιμονίους. **He** *likes the Athenians, but* **she** *likes the Spartans.*
ἐκεῖνον φιλοῦμεν. *We like* **him**.

Greek has no word which functions as an unemphatic third person pronoun in the nominative since the verbal inflections themselves already indicate the person involved.

To illustrate all three principal uses of αὐτός learn the following sentence:
ὁ cτρατηγὸς αὐτὸς τῷ αὐτῷ ξίφει αὐτοὺς ἔcφαξεν *the general himself killed them with the same sword.*

9.1/4 Reflexive and reciprocal pronouns

(*a*) A **reflexive pronoun** is one which refers back to the subject of a sentence or clause, as in the sentence *he killed himself.* In English all reflexive pronouns end in *-self* (*myself, yourself, himself, themselves,* etc.) and are to be carefully distinguished from the emphatic adjectives of the same form, e.g. *he himself killed the soldier.*

In the singular the reflexives of the first and second persons are formed by joining the stems of the personal pronouns (4.1/2) to the appropriate parts of αὐτός; in the plural the two components are written and declined separately. The normal third person reflexive is formed from the stem of the indirect third person reflexive ἕ (see below) plus αὐτός. Reflexive pronouns can occur only in the oblique cases and the possibility of a neuter exists only in the direct third person forms.

	First Person		**Second Person**	
	M.	F.	M.	F.
		SINGULAR		
Acc.	ἐμαυτόν	ἐμαυτήν	cεαυτόν, cαυτόν	cεαυτήν, cαυτήν
Gen.	ἐμαυτοῦ	ἐμαυτῆς	cεαυτοῦ, cαυτοῦ	cεαυτῆς, cαυτῆς
Dat.	ἐμαυτῷ	ἐμαυτῇ	cεαυτῷ, cαυτῷ	cεαυτῇ, cαυτῇ
		PLURAL		
Acc.	ἡμᾶς αὐτούς	ἡμᾶς αὐτάς	ὑμᾶς αὐτούς	ὑμᾶς αὐτάς
Gen.	ἡμῶν αὐτῶν	ἡμῶν αὐτῶν	ὑμῶν αὐτῶν	ὑμῶν αὐτῶν
Dat.	ἡμῖν αὐτοῖς	ἡμῖν αὐταῖς	ὑμῖν αὐτοῖς	ὑμῖν αὐταῖς

Third Person

	Direct			**Indirect**
M.	F.	N.		M. & F.

SINGULAR

	M.	F.	N.	M. & F.
Acc.	ἑαυτόν, αὑτόν	ἑαυτήν, αὑτήν	ἑαυτό, αὑτό	ἕ
Gen.	ἑαυτοῦ, αὑτοῦ	ἑαυτῆς, αὑτῆς	ἑαυτοῦ, αὑτοῦ	οὗ
Dat.	ἑαυτῷ, αὑτῷ	ἑαυτῇ, αὑτῇ	ἑαυτῷ, αὑτῷ	οἷ

PLURAL

	M.	F.	N.	M. & F.
Acc.	ἑαυτούς, αὑτούς	ἑαυτάς, αὑτάς	ἑαυτά, αὑτά	σφᾶς
Gen.	ἑαυτῶν, αὑτῶν	ἑαυτῶν, αὑτῶν	ἑαυτῶν, αὑτῶν	σφῶν
Dat.	ἑαυτοῖς, αὑτοῖς	ἑαυταῖς, αὑταῖς	ἑαυτοῖς, αὑτοῖς	σφίσι(ν)

The contracted forms of the second and third person reflexives are more common than the uncontracted ones. ἕ, οὗ and οἷ are usually enclitic.

Examples of these pronouns in use are:

βούλομαι ἐμαυτὸν μὲν ἀποκτείνειν, ὑμᾶς δ' οὔ.   *I want to kill myself, not you.*

ἑαυτοὺς μὲν φιλοῦσιν οἱ κακοί, τοὺς δ' ἄλλους οἱ ἀγαθοί.   *Wicked people love themselves, good people [love] others.*

ὁρᾷς σαυτὸν ἐν τῷ κατόπτρῳ.   *You see yourself in the mirror.*

The third person **direct** reflexive is used as above. The third person **indirect** reflexive is used only in subordinate constructions referring back to the subject of the main clause, κελεύουσιν ἡμᾶς κοινῇ μετὰ σφῶν πολεμεῖν *they urge us to make war in common with them* (ἡμᾶς is the subject of the infinitive πολεμεῖν but σφῶν refers back to the subject of the main verb, κελεύουσιν). Direct reflexive forms are, however, often substituted, Ὀρέστης ἔπεισεν τοὺς Ἀθηναίους ἑαυτὸν κατάγειν *Orestes persuaded the Athenians to restore him(self)*.

(b)   For **reciprocal** action the reflexive pronoun can be used: ἡμῖν αὐτοῖς διαλεξόμεθα *we shall converse with ourselves*, i.e. *each other*. Greek does, however, have a special reciprocal pronoun which was originally formed by doubling the stem of ἄλλος *other*: ἀλλήλους, ἀλλήλᾱς, ἄλληλα *one another, each other*. It is declined like καλός (3.1/3) except that its meaning excludes a nominative case and a singular number. With ἀλλήλους no ambiguity is possible: ἀλλήλους σφάζουσιν *they are killing each other*. It is used for all three persons.

9.1/5   Possessive adjectives and pronouns

*For the terms **attributive position** and **predicative position** see 3.1/3b.*

Possessive adjectives are of two types in English, attributive (*my*, *your*, *his*, *her*, *its*; *our*, *your*, *their*, which occur in phrases such as *my house*) and predicative (*mine*, *yours*, *his*, *hers*; *ours*, *yours*, *theirs*, which occur in clauses such as *the house is mine*). Greek has similar possessive adjectives for the first and second persons only, and these may be used either attributively or predicatively. For the third person it uses the genitive of the personal and demonstrative pronouns. Significantly, however, where the context leaves no doubt as to who the possessor is and there is no need for emphasis, the definite article alone suffices in Greek: ὠφέλησα τὸν πατέρα *I helped my father*; εὖ ἐποίησε τὴν πόλιν *he benefited his city* (cf. note on 2.2.1). In these cases no personal pronoun or possessive adjective is employed.

In cases where it is desirable to clarify the reference, Greek proceeds as follows:

(*a*) Where no emphasis is intended the genitive of the unemphatic personal pronouns (μου, σου, αὐτοῦ, αὐτῆς; ἡμῶν, ὑμῶν, αὐτῶν) is employed in the **predicative** position:

φιλεῖ τὴν μητέρα μου. *He loves my mother* (lit. *the mother of me*).
εἰς τὴν οἰκίαν αὐτοῦ εἰσήλθομεν. *We entered his house* (*the house of him*).
θαυμάζω τὸ κάλλος αὐτῆς. *I admire her beauty* (*the beauty of her*).

(*b*) Where some degree of emphasis is desired:

(i) For the first and second persons Greek uses the adjectives ἐμός, -ή, -όν (*my*, *mine*); σός, σή, σόν (*your* when referring to one person); ἡμέτερος, -ᾱ, -ον (*our*); ὑμέτερος, -ᾱ, -ον (*your* when referring to more than one person), in the **attributive** position:

εἰς τὰς ὑμετέρᾱς οἰκίᾱς ἦλθον. *They went into **your** houses*.
ὁ σός, Αἰσχίνη, κοινωνός, οὐχ ὁ ἐμός. ***Your** partner, Aeschines, not **mine***.

Note carefully that Greek requires both the definite article and the possessive adjective.[1]

(ii) For the third person Greek uses the genitive of a demonstrative pronoun, e.g. τούτου *of this/that man*; ἐκείνης *of that woman*, again in the **attributive** position:

περὶ τῶν τούτου λόγων. *Concerning **his** words*.
ἀφικνοῦνται παρ᾽ Ἀριαῖον καὶ τὴν ἐκείνου στρατιάν. *They come up to Ariaeus and **his** army*.

(*c*) When a **reflexive** sense is involved (i.e. when the reference is to the subject of the clause to which the noun-group containing the possessive belongs), the genitive of the reflexive pronouns is used, again in the **attributive** position:

---

[1] But contrast ὁ ἐμὸς δοῦλος *my slave* and ἐμὸς ὁ δοῦλος (or ὁ δοῦλος ἐμός) *the slave [is] mine* (predicative). The latter has **no** article immediately before the possessive.

τὸν ἐμαυτοῦ ἀδελφὸν ἔπεμψα.   *I sent my own brother.*
τὴν ἑαυτοῦ γυναῖκα ὑβρίζει.   *He misuses his own wife.*
ἀγαπῶσι τοὺς ἑαυτῶν ἵππους.   *They love their own horses.*

In less emphatic contexts, however, the ordinary first and second person possessives, ἐμός, σός, ἡμέτερος, ὑμέτερος (above *b*(i)), may also be used:

τοὺς ὑμετέρους παῖδας ἀγαπᾶτε.   *You love your children.*

9.2   Greek reading

1# καλὸν τὸ θνήσκειν οἷς ὕβριν τὸ ζῆν φέρει.

2 ὁ σοφὸς ἐν αὑτῷ περιφέρει τὴν οὐσίαν.

3# καρτερὸς ἐν πολέμοις Τιμόκριτος οὗ τόδε σῆμα·
  Ἄρης δ' οὐκ ἀγαθῶν φείδεται, ἀλλὰ κακῶν.

4 ὁ Κλέων οὐκ ἔφη αὐτὸς ἀλλ' ἐκεῖνον στρατηγεῖν.

5 οἱ αὐτοὶ περὶ τῶν αὐτῶν τοῖς αὐτοῖς τὰ αὐτά (*sc.* λέγουσιν).

6 τὸ ἐμὸν ἐμοὶ λέγεις ὄναρ.

7 ἔπειτα ἐκεῖνος ὁ ἀνὴρ εἶπεν, ἀλλ' εἰ ἄλλου δεῖ πρὸς τούτοις οἷς λέγει
  Ξενοφῶν, αὐτίκα ἔξεστι ποιεῖν. μετὰ δὲ ταῦτα Ξενοφῶν εἶπε τάδε·
  δῆλον ὅτι πορεύεσθαι ἡμᾶς δεῖ ὅπου ἕξομεν τὰ ἐπιτήδεια· ἀκούω δὲ
  κώμας εἶναι καλὰς αἳ εἴκοσι στάδια ἀπέχουσιν.

8 ὁ φίλος ἐστὶν ἄλλος αὐτός.

9 φιλοσοφίαν πρῶτος ὠνόμασε Πυθαγόρας καὶ ἑαυτὸν φιλόσοφον.

10 παραβαλεῖν δεῖ αὐτοὺς παρ' ἀλλήλους· οὕτω γὰρ σκεψόμεθα εἰ
  διοίσουσιν ἀλλήλων.

11 ἀπίστως ἔχουσι πρὸς αὐτοὺς οἱ Ἕλληνες.

12 The Persian empire was founded in the sixth century BC by Cyrus the
  Great (559–529 BC). His achievements were such that in the following
  century Xenophon (7.2.12) wrote an account of his life (the earliest
  surviving biography). The following is an extract:

  μετὰ δὲ δεῖπνον ἐπήρετο ὁ Κῦρος, ὦ Τιγράνη, ποῦ δὴ ἐκεῖνός ἐστιν ὁ
  ἀνὴρ ὃς συνεθήρα ἡμῖν; σὺ γάρ μοι μάλα ἐδόκεις θαυμάζειν αὐτόν.
  ἐφόνευσεν αὐτόν, ἔφη, οὗτος ὁ ἐμὸς πατήρ. διαφθείρειν γὰρ αὐτὸν ἔφη
  ἐμέ. καίτοι, ὦ Κῦρε, καλὸς κἀγαθὸς ἐκεῖνος ἦν· ὅτε γὰρ ἀποθνήσκειν
  ἔμελλε προσεκάλεσέ με καὶ εἶπε, οὐ δεῖ σέ, ὦ Τιγράνη, χαλεπαίνειν ὅτι   5
  ὁ σὸς πατὴρ ἀποκτείνει με· οὐ γὰρ διὰ κακόνοιαν τοῦτο ποιεῖ, ἀλλὰ δι'
  ἄγνοιαν· ἃ δὲ δι' ἄγνοιαν οἱ ἄνθρωποι ἐξαμαρτάνουσιν, ἀκούσια ταῦτ'
  ἔγωγε νομίζω.

13 Δημοσθένης δέ, ὃς ἑώρα τοὺς Λακεδαιμονίους μέλλειν προσβάλλειν
  ναυσί τε ἅμα καὶ πεζῷ, παρεσκευάζετο καὶ αὐτός, καὶ τὰς τριήρεις αἳ
  περιῆσαν αὐτῷ ἀνέσπασε ὑπὸ τὸ τείχισμα, καὶ τοὺς ναύτας ἐξ αὐτῶν
  ὥπλισεν ἀσπίσι φαύλαις καὶ οἰσυΐναις ταῖς πολλαῖς· οὐ γὰρ ἦν ὅπλα ἐν
  χωρίῳ ἐρήμῳ πορίσασθαι, ἀλλὰ καὶ ταῦτα ἐκ λῃστρικῆς Μεσσηνίων   5

τριακοντέρου καὶ κέλητος ἔλαβον, οἳ παρεγίγνοντο. ὁπλῖταί τε τῶν
Μεςςηνίων τούτων ὡς τετταράκοντα ἐγένοντο. τοὺς μὲν οὖν πολλοὺς
τῶν ϲτρατιωτῶν ἐπὶ τὰ ἐχυρὰ τοῦ χωρίου πρὸς τὴν ἤπειρον ἔταξε,
αὐτὸς δὲ ἀπελέξατο ἑξήκοντα ὁπλίτας καὶ τοξότας ὀλίγους καὶ ἐχώρει
ἔξω τοῦ τείχους ἐπὶ τὴν θάλατταν, ᾗ μάλιϲτα ἐκείνους προϲεδέχετο   10
πειράϲεϲθαι ἀποβαίνειν. κατὰ τοῦτο οὖν πρὸς αὐτὴν τὴν θάλατταν
ἔταξε τοὺς ὁπλίτας.

Notes

1 τὸ θνῄϲκειν (supply ἐϲτί) and τὸ ζῆν are both articular infinitives (5.1/
3); understand τούτοις as the antecedent of οἷϲ.

3 Translate πολέμοις by a singular; supply ἦν with Τιμόκριτος and ἐϲτί
with ϲῆμα. *l.*2 φείδεται *is sparing of, spares* takes the genitive (cf.
13.1/2).

4 οὐκ ἔφη 8.1/3*a* note 4; after ἔφη we have a combination of a nominative
(αὐτός) + infinitive and accusative (ἐκεῖνον) + infinitive (8.1/3*a*).

7 *l.*1 δεῖ + gen. *there is need of* (21.1/4*b* and note 3); both ἄλλου (*another
thing*) and τούτοις (*those things*) are neuter; οἷϲ (= ἅ) has been attracted
into the case of its antecedent (τούτοις)—9.1/2 note 2. *l.*2 ἔξεϲτι an
impersonal verb (cf. δεῖ, χρή) meaning *it is possible* (21.1/4*a*). *l.*3 δῆλον
supply ἐϲτί, *[it is] clear*; ἕξομεν (note rough breathing) fut. of ἔχω.

10 As this sentence comes from a conversation we can supply ἡμᾶς (*us*, i.e.
the speaker and his audience) with δεῖ; διοίϲω (< διαφέρω *differ from*) is
accompanied by the genitive.

11 ἀπίϲτως ἔχουϲι = ἄπιϲτοί εἰϲι (cf. note on 8.2.9).

12 *l.*1 ἐπήρετο < ἐπερωτάω. *ll.*3f. οὗτος ὁ ἐμὸς πατήρ *my father here*; we
must tell from the context that αὐτόν is the subject of διαφθείρειν and
ἐμέ its object; καλὸς κἀγαθός (= καὶ ἀγαθός) a set expression meaning
fine fellow, gentleman (cf. 13.3(ii) *l.*14). *l.*5 οὐ δεῖ ϲέ . . . i.e. **you** must
not . . . *ll.*7f. The relative clause ἃ . . . precedes its antecedent ταῦτ'(α);
νομίζω here has the acc. and inf. construction (8.1/3*a*) but the inf. εἶναι
is understood; ἔγωγε = ἐγώ + γε lit. *I at any rate* (13.1/3*b*).

13 *l.*2 ναυϲί . . . πεζῷ dat. of instrument (11.1/2) lit. *with both ships and
infantry at the same time* (ἅμα, which is here an adverb). *l.*3 αὐτῷ (*to/
for him*) is dative with περιῆϲαν (< περίειμι). *l.*4 ἀϲπίϲι . . . πολλαῖϲ
lit. *with shields* (dat. of instrument—see above) *inferior and the many
made of wickerwork*, i.e. *inferior shields mostly made of wickerwork* (οἱ
πολλοί can mean *the majority* as it does in *l.*7). *l.*4 ἦν = ἐξῆν *it was
possible* (ἔϲτι used in the sense of the impersonal ἔξεϲτι (21.1/4*a*) is
common). *ll.*5f. Μεϲϲηνίων, which is to be taken with both τριακοντέρου and κέλητος in the sense *belonging to [some] Messenians*, is the
antecedent of οἵ. *l.*7 ὡς *about* (cf. 7.2.12 *l.*11). *l.*8 τὰ ἐχυρά *the strong
[points]*; πρός *towards*, i.e. *facing*. *l.*10 ᾗ is here the relative adverb
where, not the relative pronoun; ἐκείνους, i.e. *the enemy*. *l.*11 κατὰ
τοῦτο *at this [point]* (κατά is used here of *place where*); πρός . . . τὴν
θάλατταν Greek regularly uses prepositions appropriate to **motion**

towards ($\pi\rho\acute{o}c$ + acc., $\epsilon\acute{\iota}c$ etc.) with verbs logically requiring a preposition indicating **position at**, when some previous motion is to be understood (Demosthenes must have moved his troops **to** the seaside before drawing them up there). Consequently $\pi\rho\grave{o}c \ldots \tau\grave{\eta}\nu \ \theta\acute{a}\lambda\alpha\tau\tau\alpha\nu$ must be translated *by the sea*. This **pregnant** use of prepositions is so termed because the idea of motion towards is implied by (i.e. contained within) the preposition.

Unit 10

10.1 Grammar

10.1/1 Interrogative τίc and indefinite τιc

The interrogative and indefinite pronouns belong to the third declension and have identical forms except for the accent. The interrogative pronoun τίc *who?*, τί *what?* is easily identifiable, since it always retains an acute accent on the first syllable (see **Appendix 9**, note 2). The indefinite pronoun τιc *someone, anyone*, τι *something, anything*, is enclitic and postpositive.

		Interrogative		**Indefinite**	
		M. & F.	N.	M. & F.	N
SINGULAR	Nom.	τίc	τί	τιc	τι
	Acc.	τίνα	τί	τινά	τι
	Gen.	τίνοc, τοῦ	τίνοc, τοῦ	τινόc, του	τινόc, του
	Dat.	τίνι, τῷ	τίνι, τῷ	τινί, τῳ	τινί, τῳ
PLURAL	Nom.	τίνεc	τίνα	τινέc	τινά
	Acc.	τίναc	τίνα	τινάc	τινά
	Gen.	τίνων	τίνων	τινῶν	τινῶν
	Dat.	τίcι(ν)	τίcι(ν)	τιcί(ν)	τιcί(ν)

In the genitive and dative singular the shorter forms coincide with the corresponding masculine and neuter forms of the definite article (3.1/1; the indefinite forms have no accent). Both the interrogative and the indefinite pronouns may also be used as adjectives: τίc (τίc ἀνὴρ) τοῦτο ἐποίηcεν; *who (what man) did this?* λέγει τιc τοῦτο *someone says this*; κλέπτηc τιc τοῦτο ἐποίηcεν *some thief did this*. Used in this way, indefinite τιc is often little more than the equivalent of the English indefinite article.

Notes

1 The acc. sing. neuter τί (or, more fully, διὰ τί, lit. *on account of what?*) means *why* (cf. 20.1/5).

2 ἄττα, which is **not** enclitic, sometimes replaces the indefinite neuter pl. τινά.

10.1/2 Questions, direct and indirect

(*a*) **Direct questions** are those which are directly asked of someone else. In Greek, as in English, they are, where appropriate, introduced by an interrogative pronoun or adjective (10.1/1) or adverb (e.g. πότε *when?*). Where there is no interrogative word and English uses inversion (*are you sick?*) Greek, as we have seen (e.g. 3.2.12(ii)), uses the interrogative particle ἆρα (ἆρα νοϲεῖϲ;), which has no English equivalent. However, a question of this sort may simply be indicated by a different tone of voice without ἆρα: ταῦτα εἶπαϲ; *you said this?* (lit. *these things*).

This latter type of direct question may also be framed in such a way as to invite (but not necessarily receive) a negative answer: *you didn't say this, did you?* or *surely you didn't say this?* In Greek such a question is prefixed with μῶν (< μὴ οὖν) or μή: μῶν (or μὴ) ταῦτα εἶπαϲ; We may also invite a positive answer by saying *you did say this, didn't you?* or *surely you said this?* In Greek we begin with ἆρα οὐ (ἆρ' οὐ) or οὐ: ἆρα οὐ ταῦτα εἶπαϲ;

For alternative questions Greek uses an introductory word for which English has no equivalent, πότερον or πότερα (there is no distinction between the two[1]): πότερον ταῦτα εἶπαϲ ἢ ἐκεῖνα; *did you say this or that?* (lit. *these things or those things*). As with ἆρα, the introductory word can be omitted.

(b) **Indirect questions** are another form of indirect speech (7.1/3) and are expressed in Greek by a subordinate clause, just as in English: ἐρωτᾷ εἰ Περικλῆϲ πρὸϲ τὸν Πειραιᾶ ἦλθεν *he is asking if Pericles went to Piraeus* (direct question: ἆρα Περικλῆϲ πρὸϲ τὸν Πειραιᾶ ἦλθεν; *did Pericles go to Piraeus?*).

The Greek interrogative pronouns, adjectives and adverbs, which, where appropriate, introduce questions, can have a direct form (τίϲ, πότε, ποῦ, etc.) or an indirect form:

DIRECT	INDIRECT	DIRECT	INDIRECT
τίϲ, *who? which?*	ὅϲτιϲ	ποῦ, *(at) where?*	ὅπου
ποῖοϲ, *of what kind?*	ὁποῖοϲ	ποῖ *(to) where?*	ὅποι
πόϲοϲ, *how big? how much?*	ὁπόϲοϲ	πόθεν, *from where?*	ὁπόθεν
pl. *how many?*		πότε, *when?*	ὁπότε
πότεροϲ, *which (of two)?*	ὁπότεροϲ	πῶϲ, *how?*	ὅπωϲ

(The forms ending in -οϲ are declined as first and second declension adjectives (3.1/3); for the declension of ὅϲτιϲ see note 1.)

The difference between direct and indirect forms is one of use, not meaning. The indirect are used in indirect questions only, as ἐρωτᾷ ὅϲτιϲ εἶ *he is asking who you are* (but see also note 2). The direct forms can be used in direct questions (τίϲ εἶ *who are you?*) or in indirect ones (ἐρωτᾷ

---

[1] They are respectively the n. acc. s. and n. acc. pl. of πότεροϲ *which (of two)?* The accusative is here used adverbially (20.1/5).

τίϲ εἶ *he is asking who you are*). When used in the latter context they give a touch of immediacy and vividness.

Where the original question begins with ἆρα (ἆρα εὐωχεῖ; *are you holding a party?*) or has no interrogative word at all (εὐωχεῖ;) the indirect version is introduced by εἰ *if, whether*: ἐρωτᾷ εἰ εὐωχεῖ *he is asking if* (or *whether*) *you are holding a party*).

As in indirect statements (8.1/3), the tense of the original direct question is retained in the indirect form.[1] As will be seen in the third example below, an indirect question is not always preceded by a verb of asking.

τούτων ἕκαϲτον ἠρόμην εἴ τινέϲ εἰϲι μάρτυρεϲ. *I asked each of them if there were any witnesses* (direct: ἆρα μάρτυρέϲ τινέϲ εἰϲιν; *Are there any witnesses?*)

ὁ κῆρυξ ἠρώτᾱ τίϲ (or ὅϲτιϲ) ἀγορεύειν βούλεται. *The herald used to ask who wanted to speak* (direct τίϲ ἀγορεύειν βούλεται;).

οὐ δεῖ ϲε εἰπεῖν πόϲουϲ (or ὁπόϲουϲ) πόνουϲ ἔχειϲ. *You don't have to say how many troubles you have* (implying a direct question πόϲουϲ πόνουϲ ἔχω; in the mind of the person addressed).

Notes

1 ὅϲτιϲ is a combination of the relative pronoun ὅϲ (9.1/2) and the indefinite τιϲ (10.1/1). There are some alternative forms:

		M.	F.	N.
SINGULAR	*Nom.*	ὅϲτιϲ	ἥτιϲ	ὅτι
	Acc.	ὅντινα	ἥντινα	ὅτι
	Gen.	οὗτινοϲ, ὅτου	ἧϲτινοϲ	οὗτινοϲ, ὅτου
	Dat.	ᾧτινι, ὅτῳ	ᾗτινι	ᾧτινι, ὅτῳ
PLURAL	*Nom.*	οἵτινεϲ	αἵτινεϲ	ἅτινα, ἅττα
	Acc.	οὕϲτιναϲ	ἅϲτιναϲ	ἅτινα, ἅττα
	Gen.	ὧντινων, ὅτων	ὧντινων, ὅτων	ὧντινων, ὅτων
	Dat.	οἷϲτιϲι(ν), ὅτοιϲ	αἷϲτιϲι(ν)	οἷϲτιϲι(ν), ὅτοιϲ

The neuter singular ὅτι is sometimes printed ὅ τι in modern texts to avoid confusion with the conjunction ὅτι *that, because*. This distinction is not employed in this book; the context should show which is being used.

2 The indirect interrogative ὅϲτιϲ is also used as an **indefinite relative** with the meaning *whoever*; ὅϲτιϲ γαμεῖ πονηρᾱ́ν, μῶρόϲ ἐϲτιν *whoever marries an evil woman is stupid*. The other indirect interrogatives are similarly used (ὅπου *wherever*, etc.). For ὅπωϲ, which has additional meanings, see the **Vocabulary**.

---

[1] For the change of mood which may occur after an introductory historic verb, see 14.1/4*d*.

3 Just as the interrogative τίϲ becomes, with a change in accentuation, the
   indefinite τιϲ (10.1/1), so the other direct interrogatives can be converted
   to indefinite pronouns and adverbs. Very common are που *somewhere*,
   ποτέ *at some time, once (upon a time)*, πωϲ *somehow* (all enclitic).

10.1/3 First and third declension adjectives

The masculine and neuter of adjectives in this category belong to the third
declension, but their feminine to the first. There are two types:

(*a*) *Stems in υ*
       In this large class the nom. s. ends in -ύϲ, -εῖα, -ύ (always so accented).
       ἡδύϲ *sweet* is declined:

| | SINGULAR | | | PLURAL | | |
	M.	F.	N.	M.	F.	N.
Nom.	ἡδύϲ	ἡδεῖα	ἡδύ	ἡδεῖϲ	ἡδεῖαι	ἡδέα
Voc.	ἡδύ	ἡδεῖα	ἡδύ	ἡδεῖϲ	ἡδεῖαι	ἡδέα
Acc.	ἡδύν	ἡδεῖαν	ἡδύ	ἡδεῖϲ	ἡδείᾱϲ	ἡδέα
Gen.	ἡδέοϲ	ἡδείᾱϲ	ἡδέοϲ	ἡδέων	ἡδειῶν	ἡδέων
Dat.	ἡδεῖ	ἡδείᾳ	ἡδεῖ	ἡδέϲι(ν)	ἡδείαιϲ	ἡδέϲι(ν)

(*b*) *Stems in ντ*
       This class contains only a few adjectives but very many participles (12.1/
       1). The ντ of the stem is lost in all feminine forms and in the masculine
       and neuter dat. pl. (cf. γίγᾱϲ 5.1/1*b*). πᾶϲ *all* is declined:

| | SINGULAR | | | PLURAL | | |
	M.	F.	N.	M.	F.	N.
N.V.	πᾶϲ	πᾶϲα	πᾶν	πάντεϲ	πᾶϲαι	πάντα
Acc.	πάντα	πᾶϲαν	πᾶν	πάντας	πᾱ́ϲᾱϲ	πάντα
Gen.	παντόϲ	πᾱ́ϲηϲ	παντόϲ	πάντων	πᾱϲῶν	πάντων
Dat.	παντί	πᾱ́ϲῃ	παντί	πᾶϲι(ν)	πᾱ́ϲαιϲ	πᾶϲι(ν)

Like πᾶϲ are declined its emphatic forms ἅπᾱϲ and ϲύμπᾱϲ (which we
must also translate by *all*). The only other adjectives in this group end in
-ειϲ (gen. -εντοϲ), -εϲϲα, -εν, e.g. χαρίειϲ, χαρίεϲϲα, χαρίεν *graceful*,
gen. s. χαρίεντοϲ, χαριέϲϲηϲ, χαρίεντοϲ, dat. pl. χαρίεϲι(ν), χαριέϲϲαιϲ,
χαρίεϲι(ν).

Notes
1 In the predicative position πᾶϲ means *all*: περὶ πάντας τοὺς θεοὺς
   ἀϲεβοῦϲιν *they commit impiety with respect to all the gods*. In the
   attributive position it means *whole*: ἡ πᾶϲα Ϲικελίᾱ *the whole of Sicily*.

Without the article it means *every* in the singular, but *all* in the plural: πᾶca πόλιc *every city;* πάντεc πολῖται *all citizens.*

2 μέλᾱc, μέλαινα, μέλαν *black* has a stem in ν (not ντ); gen. s. μέλανοc, μελαίνηc, μέλανοc; dat. pl. μέλαcι(ν), μελαίναιc, μέλαcι(ν). Exactly similar is τάλᾱc *miserable.*

10.1/4 Third declension adjectives

These adjectives are declined wholly within the third declension and fall into two main groups. In both, the masculine and feminine have the same form.

(*a*) *Stems in* ον

These are declined like δαίμων (6.1/1*a*), except that the nom. voc. and acc. neuter end in -ον in the singular and -ονα in the plural. An example is ἄφρων *senseless:*

	SINGULAR			PLURAL	
	M. & F.	N.		M. & F.	N.
Nom.	ἄφρων	ἄφρον		ἄφρον-εc	ἄφρον-α
Voc.	ἄφρον	ἄφρον		ἄφρον-εc	ἄφρον-α
Acc.	ἄφρον-α	ἄφρον		ἄφρον-αc	ἄφρον-α
Gen.	ἄφρον-οc	ἄφρον-οc		ἀφρόν-ων	ἀφρόν-ων
Dat.	ἄφρον-ι	ἄφρον-ι		ἄφρο-cι(ν)	ἄφρο-cι(ν)

Comparative adjectives in -ων (17.1/2*b*) are similarly declined.

(*b*) *Stems in* εc
These belong to the same type as neuter nouns in εc (6.1/1*c*). This is most obvious in the genitive and dative, where we find similar endings. ἀληθήc *true* (stem ἀληθεc-) is declined:

	SINGULAR			PLURAL	
	M. & F.	N.		M. & F.	N.
Nom.	ἀληθήc	ἀληθέc		ἀληθεῖc	ἀληθῆ
Voc.	ἀληθέc	ἀληθέc		ἀληθεῖc	ἀληθῆ
Acc.	ἀληθῆ	ἀληθέc		ἀληθεῖc	ἀληθῆ
Gen.	ἀληθοῦc	ἀληθοῦc		ἀληθῶν	ἀληθῶν
Dat.	ἀληθεῖ	ἀληθεῖ		ἀληθέcι(ν)	ἀληθέcι(ν)

ἀληθῆ, ἀληθεῖc are contractions of ἀληθέ(c)α, ἀληθέ(c)εc. ἀληθεῖc as acc. pl. (m. and f.) is irregular; we would have expected ἀληθῆc (< -ε(c)αc). The n. pl. nom. voc. and acc. ἀληθῆ are only an apparent exception to the rule given at 3.1/1 (cf. γένοc: pl. γένη < γένεc-α).

The few adjectives with other stems are mostly compounds whose second element is a third declension noun, e.g. εὔχαρις (εὖ + χάρις) *charming*, stem εὐχαριτ-; εὔελπις (εὖ + ἐλπίς) *hopeful*, stem εὐελπιδ-.

10.2   Greek reading

1# παχεῖα γαστὴρ λεπτὸν οὐ τίκτει νόον.

2# ὡς ἡδὺ τὴν θάλατταν ἀπὸ τῆς γῆς ὁρᾶν.

3# ὁ χρόνος ἅπαντα τοῖσιν ὕστερον φράσει.

4   ἡ εὐδαιμονία ἐστὶν ἐνέργειά τις τῆς ψυχῆς.

5   ὦ Μένανδρε καὶ βίε, πότερος ἄρ᾽ ὑμῶν πότερον ἀπεμιμήσατο;

6# τίς δ᾽ οἶδεν (*knows*) εἰ τὸ ζῆν μέν ἐστι κατθανεῖν,
   τὸ κατθανεῖν δὲ ζῆν κάτω νομίζεται;

7   ὁ βίος βραχύς, ἡ δὲ τέχνη μακρή, ὁ δὲ καιρὸς ὀξύς, ἡ δὲ πεῖρα σφαλερή,
   ἡ δὲ κρίσις χαλεπή.

8   σύντομος ἡ πονηρία, βραδεῖα ἡ ἀρετή.

9   ὅπου εὖ πράττει τις, ἐνταῦθα πατρίς.

10# ὅστις δὲ θνητῶν βούλεται δυσώνυμον
    εἰς γῆρας ἐλθεῖν, οὐ λογίζεται καλῶς·
    μακρὸς γὰρ αἰὼν μυρίους τίκτει πόνους.

11# ὡς ἡδὺ δούλοις δεσπότας χρηστοὺς λαβεῖν
    καὶ δεσπόταισι δοῦλον εὐμενῆ δόμοις.

12# ἅπαντ᾽ ἐπαχθῆ πλὴν θεοῖσι κοιρανεῖν·
    ἐλεύθερος γὰρ οὔτις ἐστὶ πλὴν Διός.

13   οἱ ἀμαθεῖς ὥσπερ ἐν πελάγει καὶ νυκτὶ φέρονται ἐν τῷ βίῳ.

14   ἡ γυνὴ ἔφη ὅτι αὐτάρκης κόσμος μοι ἡ τοῦ ἀνδρὸς ἀρετή.

15# ὅπου τις ἀλγεῖ, κεῖσε καὶ τὸν νοῦν ἔχει.

16   **Other proverbs**

(*i*) μισῶ μνήμονα συμπότην.   (*ii*) δυσμενὴς ὁ τῶν γειτόνων ὀφθαλμός.
(*iii*) τὸν ἀτυχῆ καὶ πρόβατον δάκνει.   (*iv*) ἀνὴρ ἄτεχνος τοῖς πᾶσίν ἐστι δοῦλος.   (*v*) γλυκὺς ἀπείρῳ πόλεμος.   (*vi*) χρόνῳ τὰ πάντα κρίνεται.
(*vii*) ἐν νυκτὶ λαμπρός, ἐν φάει δ᾽ ἀνωφελής.   (*viii*) ἀλλήλας νίπτουσι χεῖρες.   (*ix*) ὑπὸ παντὶ λίθῳ σκόρπιος καθεύδει.   (*x*) ῥᾴδια πάντα θεῷ.   (*xi*) ἅπας ἐχῖνος τραχύς.   (*xii*) ὃν ἡ τύχη μέλανα γράψει τοῦτον ὁ πᾶς χρόνος οὐ δύναται λευκάναι.

17   **Stories about Diogenes**
The Greeks were fond of short, pithy anecdotes ending in a *bon mot*. Diogenes, the philosopher of the fourth century BC whose eccentric lifestyle made him a tourist attraction in the Athens of his day, is the subject of a large collection.

(*i*) ὁ Διογένης ᾔτει ποτὲ ἀνδριάντα· ἐρωτηθεὶς (*having been asked*) δὲ διὰ τί τοῦτο ποιεῖ, μελετῶ, εἶπεν, ἀποτυγχάνειν.

(*ii*) ἐρωτηθεὶς ποῖον οἶνον ἡδέως πίνει, ἔφη, τὸν ἀλλότριον.

(*iii*) φιλάργυρον ᾔτει· ὅτε δὲ ἐβράδυνεν, ὁ Διογένης, ἄνθρωπε, εἶπεν, εἰς τροφήν ϲε αἰτῶ, οὐκ εἰς ταφήν.

(*iv*) ἐρωτηθεὶς πόθεν ἐϲτίν, κοσμοπολίτης, ἔφη.

(*v*) ὅτε εἶπέ τις κακὸν εἶναι τὸ ζῆν, οὐ τὸ ζῆν, ἔφη, ἀλλὰ τὸ κακῶς ζῆν.

Notes

1   The uncontracted νόον (= νοῦν, 6.1/2) shows that this is Ionic Greek (1.3).

3   τοῖϲιν = τοῖϲ (3.1/1 note 3).

5   Menander was famous for his faithful representation of everyday life; πότερος ἄρ' lit. *which of you two then . . .?* (ἄρ'= ἄρα an inferential particle which must be distinguished from ἆρα, 10.1/2*a*).

6   κατθανεῖν shortened form of καταθανεῖν (aor. inf. act. of καταθνήϲκειν). *l*.2. δέ is postponed for metrical reasons (prose order would be τὸ δὲ κατθανεῖν); κάτω *below*, i.e. in Hades.

7   The well-known aphorism of Hippocrates, the famous doctor of the 5th century BC. He wrote in Ionic Greek and the η of μακρή and ϲφαλερή would be ᾱ in Attic. By τέχνη Hippocrates meant the art of medicine.

9   ὅπου here (and in 15 below) is the relative adverb *where*, not the interrogative.

10 Take δυϲώνυμον with γῆρας *old age* (acc. s., 13.1/1*b*(iii)).

11 *1*.2 λαβεῖν is to be understood; δεϲπόταιϲι has the longer form of the dat. pl. ending (3.1/1 note 1; cf. θεοῖϲι in the next sentence); δόμοιϲ dat. without preposition to express place where (23.1/2*n*)—translate by a singular.

12 κοιρανεῖν here takes the dative, not the genitive as is normal after verbs of ruling (13.1/2*a*); Διός gen. of Ζεύς (11.1/4).

14 For ὅτι introducing a **direct** statement see 8.1/3*b* note 2.

16 (*iv*) τοῖϲ πᾶϲιν the article is added for emphasis (as also in (*vi*)). (*vi*) χρόνῳ *by time* dat. of instrument (11.1/2); τὰ πάντα cf. (*iv*) above. (*vii*) A phrase of abuse, not a sentence (cf. 6.2.7 (*iv*)). (*xii*) Although ὅν comes first its antecedent is τοῦτον; δύναται *is able* from δύναμαι (on verbs with -αμαι instead of -ομαι see 19.1/3*b*).

17 (*i*) ᾔτει (< αἰτέω) *was begging [alms from]* + acc.; ποιεῖ on the tense see 10.1/2*b* (this also applies to πίνει (*ii*) and ἐϲτίν (*iv*)). (*ii*) with τὸν ἀλλότριον supply ἡδέως πίνω. (*iii*) ᾔτει see (*i*); εἰϲ *with regard to*, i.e. *for*.

10.3   Extra reading

From this point extra reading will be included with certain units. Because it will consist of longer passages it will necessarily be somewhat harder than the other exercises. If you do not feel confident enough to tackle it when working your way through the book for the first time, it may conveniently be left until later.

The wisdom of Socrates

Socrates (469–399 B.C.) was to philosophy what Herodotus was to history. Previous thinkers had speculated on the physical nature of the world, but Socrates was the first to concern himself with moral and ethical problems. His uncompromising pursuit of truth made him so unpopular with his fellow citizens at Athens that, when he was brought to trial on a trumped-up charge of corrupting the young, he was convicted and executed. The following is from his defence in court, as reported by his pupil Plato; here Socrates explains the origin of his reputation (ὄνομα) for exceptional wisdom, which, he claims, is unjustified.

ἐγὼ γάρ, ὦ ἄνδρες ᾿Αθηναῖοι, δι᾿ οὐδὲν ἄλλ᾿ ἢ διὰ ϲοφίαν τινὰ τοῦτο τὸ ὄνομα ἔχω. ποίαν δὴ ϲοφίαν ταύτην; ἥπερ ἐϲτὶν ἴϲωϲ ἀνθρωπίνη ϲοφία· τῷ ὄντι γὰρ κινδυνεύω ταύτην εἶναι ϲοφόϲ. οὗτοι δέ, οὓϲ ἄρτι ἔλεγον, δαιμονίαν τινὰ ϲοφίαν ϲοφοί εἰϲιν, ἣν οὐκ ἔχω διηγεῖϲθαι· οὐ γὰρ δὴ ἔγωγε αὐτὴν ἐπίϲταμαι, ἀλλ᾿ ὅϲτιϲ φηϲί, ψεύδεταί τε καὶ ἐπὶ διαβολῇ τῇ ἐμῇ λέγει. καὶ 5 ἐλπίζω ὑμᾶϲ, ὦ ἄνδρεϲ ᾿Αθηναῖοι, μὴ θορυβήϲειν μοι, μηδ᾿ εἰ δοκῶ τι ὑμῖν μέγα λέγειν· οὐ γὰρ ἐμὸν ἐρῶ τὸν λόγον ὃν λέγω, ἀλλ᾿ εἰϲ ἀξιόπιϲτόν τινα ἀνοίϲω. τῆϲ γὰρ ἐμῆϲ, εἰ δή τίϲ ἐϲτι ϲοφία καὶ οἵα, μάρτυρα ὑμῖν παρέξομαι τὸν θεὸν τὸν ἐν Δελφοῖϲ. γνώριμοϲ γάρ που ὑμῖν ἦν Χαιρεφῶν. οὗτοϲ ἐμόϲ τε ἑταῖροϲ ἦν ἐκ νέου καὶ ὑμῶν τῷ πλήθει. καὶ εὔγνωϲτον ὑμῖν ἐϲτιν οἷοϲ ἦν Χαιρεφῶν, ὡϲ παντάπαϲι ϲφοδρόϲ. καὶ δή ποτε καὶ εἰϲ Δελφοὺϲ ἦλθε καὶ ἐτόλμηϲε μαντεύεϲθαι, εἴ τίϲ ἐϲτι ϲοφώτεροϲ ἢ (*wiser than*) ἐγώ. ἀνεῖλεν οὖν ἡ Πυθία οὐδένα ϲοφώτερον εἶναι.

Notes

l.1 ἄλλ᾿=ἄλλο; ἤ *than*. *ll*.2f ποίαν etc. supply λέγω; ἥπερ *[the one] which*, the suffix περ is added to the relative pronoun for emphasis; τῷ ὄντι *in reality*, *really* (12.1/1 note 1); ταύτην (sc. τὴν ϲοφίαν) accusative of respect (20.1/5) with ϲοφόϲ, lit. *wise in respect of this [wisdom]*, i.e. *possessed of this wisdom*—the same construction occurs with ϲοφοί (*l*.4). *l*.4 οὐκ ἔχω *I am not able*; ἔγωγε see note on 9.2.12 *l*.8. *l*.5 ἐπίϲταμαι has -αμαι instead of -ομαι (19.1/3*b*); φηϲί sc. *that this is so*; ἐπί *with a view to*, i.e. *to arouse*; διαβολῇ τῇ ἐμῇ not *my prejudice* but *prejudice against me*; this use of the possessive adjective is the same as that of the objective genitive (23.1/1*c*). *l*.6 μή is used after ἐλπίζω (8.1/3*a* note 5) and consequently we also have μηδ᾿(μηδέ) (7.1/6*c*), which here means *not even*, but, as we would not normally repeat the negative in such a construction in English, simply translate by *even*; θορυβήϲειν μοι lit. *to be going to make a noise for me*, i.e. *to be going to interrupt me*. *l*.7 ἐμόν predicative with τὸν λόγον, lit. *not [as] mine shall I tell the story which I am telling*. *l*.8 ἀνοίϲω < ἀναφέρω; τῆϲ . . . ἐμῆϲ (sc. ϲοφίαϲ) with μάρτυρα *a witness of my [wisdom]*; εἰ . . . οἵα two indirect questions to be taken with μάρτυρα *[as to] whether it is some sort of* (τιc) *wisdom and what sort of [wisdom it is]* (the indefinite τιc has an acute accent because of the following ἐcτιν (see **Appendix 9**, *d*(ix)); it is **not** the interrogative τίc). *l.*9f. τὸν θεόν, i.e. Apollo; που *I suppose, think*; the original meaning, which is also common, is *somewhere* (10.1/2*b* note 3); τε . . . καί (*both . . . and* but trans. simply by *and*) joins ἐμόc and ὑμῶν; ἐκ νέου lit. *from [being] young*, i.e. *from youth*; ὑμῶν τῷ πλήθει lit. *to the people of you*, i.e. *to the [Athenian] democracy* (to be taken with ἕταιροc, which may be here translated by one word and by another word with ἐμόc). *l.*11 ὡc . . . cφοδρόc *how [he was] completely impetuous*. Chaerephon had died before the trial (hence ἦν in the previous clause); καὶ δή *and indeed, and as a matter of fact*; ποτε καί . . . *once even/actually* (*he actually went to Delphi once*). *l.*12 ἀνεῖλεν < ἀναιρέω.

Unit 11

11.1 Grammar

11.1/1 Root aorist, aorist passive and future passive

A few -ω verbs form their aorist active by adding endings directly to their basic stem or root without a suffix (such as c in the weak aorist—4.1/1) or a link vowel (such as o/ε of the strong aorist endings—7.1/1). The roots of all such verbs end in the long vowels ᾱ, η, ῡ or ω, and the endings applied to form the root aorist are -ν, -c, -, -μεν, -τε, -cαν. As an example we may take the aorist of βαίνω *go* (root βη-).

	SINGULAR	PLURAL
1	ἔβην *I went*	ἔβημεν
2	ἔβης	ἔβητε
3	ἔβη	ἔβηcαν
INFINITIVE	βῆναι	

Some other common verbs with root aorists are given below. Note that the form of the root cannot be predicted from the present stem.

	PRESENT STEM	ROOT	ROOT AORIST
(ἀπο)διδράcκω[1] *run away*	διδραcκ-	δρᾱ-	-έδρᾱν
φύω *cause to grow, produce*	φῡ-	φῡ-	ἔφῡν
γιγνώcκω *get to know*	γιγνωcκ-	γνω-	ἔγνων
βιόω *live*	βιο-	βιω-	ἐβίων

φύω also has a regularly formed weak aorist active: ἔφῡcα. In such cases where a verb has two sets of aorist active forms, the root aorist is intransitive: ἔφῡν (*I grew* intr.), and the weak aorist transitive: ἔφῡcα (*I caused to grow, I produced*); cf. καταδύω *cause to sink*; κατέδῡcα *I caused to sink*, κατέδῡν *I sank*.[2] Examples are:

αἱ τρίχες ἔρρεον ἃς πρὶν ἔφῡcε τὸ φάρμακον. *The hairs fell out which the drug previously made grow.*
ἐλάᾱ ἐντὸς τῆς αὐλῆς ἔφῡ. *An olive tree grew inside the courtyard.*

---

[1] This verb occurs only in compounds.

[2] In these verbs the 3rd plural of the root aorist and of the weak aorist active are identical: ἔφῡcαν (from ἔφῡ-cαν or ἔφῡc-αν).

Another important verb with two aorists and a similar distinction between them is ἵστημι (19.1/1).

Only a few verbs, however, have a root aorist with an active meaning. Elsewhere the root aorist has developed a passive meaning and is normally classified as an aorist passive. An example is πνίγω *strangle, choke* (tr.), which, like φύω, has a weak aorist ἔπνῖξα *I strangled, choked* (tr., e.g. ἐχθὲς ἔπνῖξα τὸν τοῦ γείτονος κύνα *yesterday I choked the neighbour's dog*) and what is really a root aorist ἐπνίγην *I choked* (intr., e.g. ὁ còc κύων, ἔφην, ἐπνίγη ἐν τῷ τοῦ πυρὸς καπνῷ "*Your dog," I said, "choked in the smoke of the fire*"). The original contrast between the transitive and intransitive aorists in verbs of this sort developed into one of active/passive, and forms such as ἐπνίγην were used in contexts where they must be interpreted as passive (ὁ ἐμὸς κύων, ἔφη, οὐκ ἐπνίγη καπνῷ "*My dog," he said, "was not choked by smoke*"—on this use of the dative see 11.1/2 below). Consequently, most root aorists in -ην, (but not in -ᾱν, ῡν, or, with one exception, -ων) which could be interpreted as passive came to be so regarded and classified. This could not happen with intransitive verbs, such as βαίνω, whose meaning precludes any passive sense.

The total number of aorist passives in -ην is also small, but they formed the model for the vast majority of transitive verbs, where a special aorist passive stem is created by attaching the suffix θη to the root.[1] To this are added the same endings as for the root aorist. For this reason **all** aorist passive endings are of the **active** type; the aorist passive **never** has the passive endings of the other historic tenses (-μην, -cο, -το etc., 8.1/1*f*).

The aorist passive indicative (and corresponding infinitive) of λύω will be found in **Appendix 1**. This tense is included in the principal parts of verbs which show some irregularity (7.1/1 note 3) as the form it takes is not always predictable. We may, however, note:

(*a*) Most verbs whose present stem ends in a vowel or diphthong form their aorist passive stem regularly. In a few cases the suffix is enlarged to cθη on the analogy of dental stems (see below), e.g. ἠκούcθην *I was heard* (ἀκούω); ἐκελεύcθην *I was ordered* (κελεύω). In regular contracted verbs the final vowel of the present stem is lengthened in the same way as in the aorist active (5.1/2 note 2), e.g. ἐτῑμήθην (τῑμάω); ἐποιήθην (ποιέω); ἐδηλώθην (δηλόω).

(*b*) In palatal and labial stems (6.1/4*b*) final κ and γ become χ, final π and β become φ (i.e. they are assimilated to the following θ by becoming aspirates), e.g. ἐφυλάχθην *I was guarded* (φυλάττω, stem φυλακ-); ἐπέμφθην *I was sent* (πέμπω, stem πεμπ-). In dental stems the final

---

[1] The η of the suffix undergoes change in some forms other than the indicative, e.g. the aor. pass. pple. λυθείc (12.1/1).

consonant becomes ς, e.g. ἐπείςθην *I was persuaded* (πείθω, stem πειθ-).

Occasionally (and unpredictably) a verb has a root aorist passive, e.g. ἐπνίγην (see above); ἐκόπην *I was cut* (κόπτω), sometimes both, e.g. ἐβλάβην, ἐβλάφθην *I was hurt* (βλάπτω; there is no difference in meaning).

The stem of the **future passive** is that of the aorist passive with an added ς (λυθης-, τῑμηθης-, κοπης-). The endings are those of the present middle and passive: λυθήςομαι *I shall be loosened*; τῑμηθήςομαι *I shall be honoured*; κοπήςομαι *I shall be cut*. For the full future passive of λύω see **Appendix 1**.

Note
As mentioned in 8.1/2 some deponents are classified as **passive** because their aorist is passive, not middle, in form (most, however, have a **middle future**). Among the most common passive deponents are:

βούλομαι *wish*; fut. βουλήςομαι; aor. ἐβουλήθην
δύναμαι *be able*; fut. δυνήςομαι; aor. ἐδυνήθην
πορεύομαι *march*; fut. πορεύςομαι; aor. ἐπορεύθην

In the future and aorist of the first two η is inserted. δύναμαι has -αμαι, -αςαι, -αται etc., not -ομαι -ῃ, -εται etc. in the present (see 19.1/3*b*).

The difference between middle and passive deponents is simply one of **form**; both are active in **meaning**.

11.1/2 Agent and instrument

In English we can say *the policeman was hit **by** a demonstrator* and *the policeman was hit **by** a placard* but Greek makes a distinction between agent (*demonstrator*) and instrument (*placard*). An agent is a living being and is normally expressed by ὑπό with the genitive. An instrument is nearly always inanimate and is expressed by the dative without a preposition (examples have already occurred at 7.2.13 *l*.7, 9.2.13 *l*.4, 10.2.16(vi)); in English we use either *by* or *with*.

Ἀσπασίᾱ με τύπτει μήλοις. *Aspasia is hitting me with apples* (instrument).
ἡ Τροίᾱ ὑπὸ τῶν Ἑλλήνων ἐπορθήθη. *Troy was sacked by the Greeks* (agent).

11.1/3 -ω verbs with stems in λ, μ, ν, ρ

Most verbs with these stems originally formed their present with a *y* suffix (6.1/4*b*). This combined with a preceding λ to give λλ, but disappeared after μ, ν, ρ, although, by way of compensation, a preceding ε, ι, υ was lengthened and a preceding α became αι. The future of these verbs is of the contracted type (-ῶ < -έω; 5.1/2 note 3); where a *y* suffix has been used in the present the future reverts to the original stem. In the weak aorist (which occurs in all common verbs of this group, except βάλλω *throw*) the sigma is dropped and the preceding vowel lengthened (note that here we have α > η except after vowels and ρ, where α becomes ᾱ; also ε becomes ει). The following table shows the different possibilities:

PRESENT			FUTURE	AORIST
βάλλω	throw	(< βάλ-yω)	βαλῶ	ἔβαλον
στέλλω	send	(< στέλ-yω)	στελῶ	ἔστειλα
νέμω	apportion	(no *y* suffix)	νεμῶ	ἔνειμα
μένω	wait	(no *y* suffix)	μενῶ	ἔμεινα
cημαίνω	indicate	(< cημάν-yω)	cημανῶ	ἐcήμηνα
μιαίνω	stain	(< μιάν-yω)	μιανῶ	ἐμίᾱνα
αἰcχῡ́νω	dishonour	(< αἰcχύν-yω)	αἰcχυνῶ	ᾔcχῡνα
αἴρω	lift	(< ἄρ-yω)	ἀρῶ	ἦρα
οἰκτίρω	pity	(< οἰκτίρ-yω)	οἰκτιρῶ	ᾤκτῑρα

For the principal parts of ἐλαύνω *drive* and φέρω *carry*, which are irregular, see the **Principal parts of verbs**.

The aorist passive of verbs in -αίνω and -ῡ́νω ends in -άνθην and -ύνθην, e.g. ἐcημάνθην (cημαίνω); ᾐcχύνθην (αἰcχῡ́νω). Likewise, we have ἤρθην from αἴρω, but the other verbs listed above which have an aorist passive are irregular.

11.1/4 Third declension nouns—stems in εὐ, αυ, ου

A large number of masculine nouns end in -εύc (always so accented). Most common nouns of this type involve male occupations, e.g. ἱερεύc *priest*, ἱππεύc *horseman*. The names of some Homeric heroes are also of this type, as Ὀδυccεύc, Ἀχιλλεύc. The genitive and dative singular endings are the same as for stems in ι (8.1/4).

The only examples of stems in αυ and ου are those given below:

	βαcιλεύc (m) *king*	ναῦc (f) *ship*	γραῦc (f) *old woman*	βοῦc (m or f) *ox, cow*
	SINGULAR			
Nom.	βαcιλεύ-c	ναῦ-c	γραῦ-c	βοῦ-c
Voc.	βαcιλεῦ	ναῦ	γραῦ	βοῦ
Acc.	βαcιλέ-ᾱ	ναῦ-ν	γραῦ-ν	βοῦ-ν
Gen.	βαcιλέ-ωc	νε-ώc	γρᾱ-όc	βο-όc
Dat.	βαcιλεῖ	νη-ΐ	γρᾱ-ΐ	βο-ΐ

PLURAL

N.V.	βαcιλῆc (or -εῖc)	νῆ-ες	γρᾶ-ες	βόες
Acc.	βαcιλέ-ᾱc	ναῦc	γραῦc	βοῦc
Gen.	βαcιλέ-ων	νε-ῶν	γρᾱ-ῶν	βο-ῶν
Dat.	βαcιλεῦ-cι(ν)	ναυ-cί(ν)	γραυ-cί(ν)	βου-cί(ν)

Note also *Ζεύc Zeus*, which is irregular: voc. *Ζεῦ*, acc. *Δία*, gen. *Διός*, dat. *Διί* (in poetry there is an alternative stem, *Ζην-*, for the oblique cases, giving *Ζῆνα, Ζηνός, Ζηνί*).

11.1/5 Crasis

Crasis (*κρᾶcιc mixing, blending*) is the contraction of a vowel or diphthong at the end of one word with a vowel or diphthong at the beginning of the following word. It is found chiefly in poetry but is not uncommon in the orators.

Only a very small number of words occur as the first element of crasis, viz the relevant parts of the definite article, *καί* and a few others. Examples we have already met are *κἄν* (= *καὶ ἐν* 5.2.17) and *αὑτός* (= *ὁ αὐτός*), *ταὐτοῦ* etc. (9.1/3*b*). In all such cases elision (2.1/6*b*), even if theoretically possible, is never used in preference to crasis.

The rules for crasis are:

(*a*) The first word loses its accent, if any.

(*b*) A vowel (always long) or diphthong resulting from crasis is marked with ᾽ (technically called **coronis** but identical in form with a smooth breathing), e.g. *τοὔνομα* (*τὸ ὄνομα*). When the second word begins with a rough breathing, a consonant preceding it in crasis (always *κ* or *τ*) is aspirated, e.g. *θοἰμάτιον* (*τὸ ἱμάτιον*). When, however, the first word is simply an aspirated vowel or diphthong (*ὁ, οἱ* etc.), the rough breathing is kept in crasis, e.g. *οὑν* (*ὁ ἐν*).

(*c*) The rules that apply for internal contraction in verbs (5.1/2) are generally followed, as in the above examples. There are, however, some combinations which do not occur in verbs, as well as some exceptions. We should note:

(i) When the definite article is combined with a word beginning with *α*, this *α* is always kept, e.g. *ἅνθρωπος* (*ὁ ἄνθρωπος*), *αὑτός* (*ὁ αὐτός*, 9.1/3*b*).

(ii) The *αι* of *καί* is dropped in certain combinations, e.g. *κοὐ* (*καὶ οὐ*), *χἠ* (*καὶ ἡ*).

11.2   Greek reading

1 ἡ τυραννὶς ἀδικίας μήτηρ ἔφυ.

2 ἀεὶ εὖ πίπτουσιν οἱ Διὸς κύβοι.

3# ἔστι τι κἂν κακοῖσιν ἡδονῆς μέτρον.

4# κοὐκ ἐμὸς ὁ μῦθος, ἀλλ' ἐμῆς μητρὸς πάρα,
ὡς οὐρανός τε γαῖά τ' ἦν μορφὴ μία·
ἐπεὶ δ' ἐχωρίσθησαν ἀλλήλων δίχα
τίκτουσι πάντα κἀνέδωκαν (sent up) εἰς φάος
δένδρη, πετεινά, θῆρας, οὕς θ' ἅλμη τρέφει   5
γένος τε θνητῶν.

5# κακὸν τὸ κεύθειν κοὐ πρὸς ἀνδρὸς εὐγενοῦς.

6 εἶπέ τις τῷ Cωκράτει, θάνατον σοῦ κατέγνωσαν οἱ Ἀθηναῖοι, ὁ δὲ
εἶπεν, κἀκείνων ἡ φύσις (sc. θάνατον καταγιγνώσκει).

7 ἅμαξα τὸν βοῦν ἕλκει.

8 **Advanced futility**

(*i*) γραῦς χορεύει.   (*ii*) τυφλῷ κάτοπτρον χαρίζῃ.   (*iii*) ἄνεμον δικτύῳ
θηρᾷς.   (*iv*) λίθοις τὸν ἥλιον βάλλεις.   (*v*) καλεῖ χελώνη τοὺς βοῦς
βραδύποδας.   (*vi*) σπόγγῳ πάτταλον κρούεις.   (*vii*) πάτταλον
ἐξέκρουσας παττάλῳ.   (*viii*) τὴν ἀμίδα σανδάλῳ ἐπιφράττεις.   (*ix*)
οἴνῳ οἶνον ἐξελαύνεις.   (*x*) αὐτὸς τὴν σαυτοῦ θύραν κρούεις λίθῳ.

9# πᾶσιν γὰρ ἀνθρώποισιν, οὐχ ἡμῖν μόνον,
ἢ καὶ παραυτίκ' ἢ χρόνῳ δαίμων βίον
ἔσφηλε, κοὐδεὶς διὰ τέλους εὐδαιμονεῖ.

10# Odysseus explains to Neoptolemus that they must obtain the bow of
Philoctetes if Troy is to be captured.

τούτων γὰρ οὐδὲν ἀλγυνεῖ μ'· εἰ δ' ἐργάσῃ
μὴ ταῦτα, λύπην πᾶσιν Ἀργείοις βαλεῖς.
εἰ γὰρ τὰ τοῦδε τόξα μὴ ληφθήσεται,
οὐκ ἔστι (= ἔξεστι) πέρσαι σοι τὸ Δαρδάνου πέδον.

11 In 525 BC Egypt was conquered and permanently occupied by the
Persians, whose power in the eastern Mediterranean continued to
increase until their unsuccessful invasion of Greece (480–479 BC). The
subsequent rise of Athens encouraged the Athenians to invade Egypt
(c.461 BC), with disastrous results, as Thucydides tells us in the
introduction to his history.

οὕτω μὲν τὰ τῶν Ἑλλήνων πράγματα ἐφθάρη· καὶ ὀλίγοι ἀπὸ πολλῶν
διὰ τῆς Λιβύης ἐς Κυρήνην ἐπορεύθησαν καὶ ἐσώθησαν, οἱ δὲ πλεῖστοι
ἀπέθανον. Αἴγυπτος δὲ πάλιν ὑπὸ βασιλέα ἐγένετο πλὴν Ἀμυρταίου
τοῦ ἐν τοῖς ἕλεσι βασιλέως· τοῦτον δὲ διὰ μέγεθός τε τοῦ ἕλους οὐκ
ἐδύναντο ἑλεῖν καὶ ἅμα σφόδρα μάχιμοί εἰσιν οἱ ἕλειοι. Ἴναρως δὲ ὁ   5
Λιβύων βασιλεύς, ὃς τὰ πάντα ἔπραξε περὶ τῆς Αἰγύπτου, προδοσίᾳ
ἐλήφθη καὶ ἀνεσταυρώθη. ἐκ δὲ τῶν Ἀθηνῶν καὶ τῆς ἄλλης

ξυμμαχίδος πεντήκοντα τριήρεις διάδοχοι ἔπλευσαν ἐς Αἴγυπτον καὶ
ἔσχον κατὰ τὸ Μενδήσιον κέρας. ἀλλ' αὐτοῖς ἔκ τε γῆς ἐπέπεσον πεζοὶ
καὶ ἐκ θαλάσσης Φοινίκων ναυτικὸν καὶ διέφθειραν τὰς πολλὰς τῶν 1⁰
νεῶν. τὰ οὖν κατὰ τὴν μεγάλην στρατείαν 'Αθηναίων καὶ τῶν
ξυμμάχων ἐς Αἴγυπτον οὕτως ἐτελεύτησεν.

12 Euxitheos and Herodes were fellow passengers on a voyage to Thrace.
In the process of changing ships at Lesbos Herodes disappeared and
Euxitheos was subsequently charged with his murder. His speech of
defence was written by Antiphon.

ἐπειδὴ δὲ μετεξέβημεν εἰς τὸ ἕτερον πλοῖον, ἐπίνομεν. καὶ φανερὸν μέν
ἐστιν ὅτι ὁ Ἡρώδης ἐξέβη ἐκ τοῦ πλοίου καὶ οὐκ εἰσέβη πάλιν· ἐγὼ δὲ
τὸ παράπαν οὐκ ἐξέβην ἐκ τοῦ πλοίου τῆς νυκτὸς ἐκείνης. τῇ δὲ
ὑστεραίᾳ, ἐπειδὴ ἀφανὴς ἦν ὁ ἀνήρ, ἐζητεῖτο οὐδέν τι μᾶλλον ὑπὸ τῶν
ἄλλων ἢ καὶ ὑπ' ἐμοῦ· καὶ εἴ τῳ τῶν ἄλλων ἐδόκει δεινὸν εἶναι, καὶ ἐμοὶ 5
ὁμοίως. καὶ εἴς τε τὴν Μυτιλήνην ἐγὼ αἴτιος ἢ πεμφθῆναι ἄγγελον, καὶ
ἐπεὶ ἄλλος οὐδεὶς ἤθελε βαδίζειν, οὔτε τῶν ἀπὸ τοῦ πλοίου οὔτε τῶν
αὐτοῦ τοῦ Ἡρώδου ἑταίρων, ἐγὼ τὸν ἀκόλουθον τὸν ἐμαυτοῦ πέμπειν
ἕτοιμος ἦ. ἐπειδὴ δὲ ὁ ἀνὴρ οὔτε ἐν τῇ Μυτιλήνῃ ἐφαίνετο οὔτ' ἄλλοθι
οὐδαμοῦ, πλοῦς τε ἡμῖν ἐγίγνετο, καὶ τἆλλ' ἀνήγετο πλοῖα ἅπαντα, 1
ᾠχόμην κἀγώ.

Notes

1 ἔφῡ < φύω (11.1/1) the primary meaning of this root aorist is *was born*
but often, as here, it has the present sense *is*.

2 Διός gen. of Ζεύς (11.1/4).

3 τι with μέτρον; κακοῖσιν = κακοῖς (3.1/1 note 3).

4 *l*.1 κοὔκ = καὶ οὐκ (11.1/5); πάρα some disyllabic prepositions can, in
verse, be placed after the noun they govern, cf. δίχα in *l*.3; when they are
normally accented on the final syllable (as with παρά, but not with δίχα),
the accent is then thrown back on to the first syllable. *l*.2 With a double
subject (οὐρανός and γαῖα) the verb sometimes agrees only with the
nearer, hence ἦν; τε . . . τ(ε) lit. *both . . . and* but simply trans. by
and. *l*.4 τίκτουσι vivid present, trans. *brought forth* (τίκτω can be used
of either parent); κἀνέδωκαν = καὶ ἀνέδωκαν (ἔδωκαν is the 3rd pl. aor.
ind. act. of δίδωμι *give*, 18.1/2 note 3). *l*.5 δένδρη acc. pl. of δένδρον
(13.1/1*c*); οὕς an antecedent meaning *creatures* is to be understood; θ'
i.e. τε, after the ε is elided, τ' becomes θ' because of the rough breathing
of ἄλμη.

6 καταγιγνώσκω *condemn* takes the gen. of the person condemned and the
accusative of what he is condemned to (23.1/1*k*(i)); κἀκείνων = καὶ
ἐκείνων.

8 (*iv*) λίθοις instrumental dat. (11.1/2); βάλλεις here *pelt*. (*vii*) ἐξέκρουσας < ἐκκρούω.

9 *l*.1 The datives should be translated by *for*. *l*.2 καί is here adverbial and
emphasizes the following word; it need not be translated; βίον English

idiom requires the plural. *l*.3 ἔϲφηλε gnomic aorist (see note on 5.2.10); ϲφάλλω *trip up, cause to fall* (as in wrestling) is here (and often elsewhere) used metaphorically; κοὐδείϲ = καὶ οὐδείϲ.

10 The future tense in εἰ clauses (*l*.1 ἐργάϲῃ and *l*.3 ληφθήϲεται) is to be translated in English by a present; μή (as in *ll*.2 and 3) is the negative used in εἰ clauses (18.1/5) but in *l*.2 it is somewhat unusually placed after the verb it negates (cf. 2.1/6*a*(i)). *l*.3 Translate τὰ τόξα by a singular (the plural is often used for the singular in verse). *l*.4 On ἔϲτι = ἔξεϲτι see 21.1/4 note 1.

11 Thucydides uses the non-Attic spelling ϲϲ for ττ (*l*.10 θαλάϲϲηϲ), the old Attic form ξύν (ξυμ- etc. in compounds) for the normal ϲύν (*l*.8 ξυμμαχίδοϲ, *l*.12 ξυμμάχων), and the old Attic ἐϲ for εἰϲ (*ll*.2, 8, 12). *l*.1 ἐφθάρη < φθείρω. *l*.3 ὑπό lit. *under*, i.e. *under the control of*; βαϲιλέᾱ at this period the Persian king was a figure of supreme importance and the Greeks referred to him simply as βαϲιλεύϲ. *ll*.4f. τε . . . καί join the two reasons why Amyrtaeus could not be captured and in English we would supply *because* after ἅμα. *l*.6 τὰ πάντα see note on 10.2.16(iv). *l*.7 ἐλήφθη < λαμβάνω. *ll*.8f. διάδοχοι lit. *[as] relieving*, i.e. *as a relieving force*; ἔϲχον *put in*; τὸ Μενδήϲιον κέραϲ the north-east arm of the Nile delta; take αὐτοῖϲ with ἐπέπεϲον (< ἐπιπίπτω), lit. *fell upon them*. *l*.10 τὰϲ πολλάϲ *the majority of, most of*. *l*.11 τὰ . . . κατὰ τὴν . . . cf. 5.1/3, lit. *the [things] with respect to the* . . .

12 *l*.1 Translate μετεξέβημεν (< μετεκβαίνω) by a pluperfect *had trans-ferred* (16.1/2); ἐπίνομεν *we began to drink* (inceptive imperfect 4.1/1). *l*.3 τὸ παράπαν οὐκ *not . . . at all*; the adverb παράπαν is converted by τό to a noun equivalent (5.1/3), which functions here as an accusative of respect (20.1/5), lit. *[with respect to] the altogether*. *ll*.4f. οὐδέν τι μᾶλλον ὑπό . . . ἢ . . . ὑπό lit. *nothing more by . . . than by* (οὐδέν τι *not at all* is also an accusative of respect); τῳ = τινι (indefinite, 10.1/1). *ll*.6ff. The καὶ of καὶ εἷϲ τε joins this sentence to the preceding one; τε is to be taken with the καί before ἐπεί (*l*.7) and the two link ἐγὼ αἴτιοϲ ἦ . . . with ἐγὼ . . . ἕτοιμοϲ ἦ; τε . . . καί literally mean *both . . . and* but translate here *not only . . . but also* to give the necessary emphasis; πεμφθῆναι ἄγγελον accusative and infinitive (8.1/3*a*) after αἴτιοϲ ἦ; οὔτε . . . οὔτε continue the preceding negative οὐδείϲ, lit. *no-one . . . neither from . . . nor of*, but in English we would say *either . . . or* (the rule given at 7.1/6 does not apply because οὔτε . . . οὔτε do not negate the verb of this clause; cf. 10.3, *l*.6). *ll*.9ff. ἐπειδή is followed by three clauses with the second joined to the first by τε (*l*.10) and the third to the second by καί (*l*.10); πλοῦϲ *[the time for] sailing*; ἐγίγνετο lit. *was coming into being*, i.e. *was starting*; τἆλλ᾽ = τὰ ἄλλα; κἀγώ = καὶ ἐγώ (11.1/5); ἀνήγετο impf. of ἀνάγομαι.

Unit 12

12.1 Grammar

12.1/1 Participles

Participles are those parts of verbs which function as adjectives. They have tense (*killing* is present, *going to kill* future) and voice (*killing* is active, *being killed* passive). In Greek there are participles for all three voices in the present, future, and aorist (and also the perfect, 15.1/1) and they use the same stem as the corresponding indicatives (but the augment is dropped in the historic tenses). For the sake of completeness the following table includes perfect participles, which can be ignored until we treat these in 16.1/4.

ACTIVE

Present m. λύ-ων (gen. λύ-οντος), f. λύ-ουσα, n. λῦ-ον *loosening*
Future m. λύς-ων (gen. λύς-οντος), f. λύς-ουσα, n. λῦς-ον *going to loosen, about to loosen*
Aorist m. λύς-ᾱς (gen. λύς-αντος), f. λύς-ᾱσα, n. λῦς-αν *having loosened, after loosening*
Perfect m. λελυκ-ώς (gen. λελυκ-ότος), f. λελυκ-υῖα, n. λελυκ-ός (*in a state of*) *having loosened*

MIDDLE

Present λῡ-όμενος, -ομένη, -όμενον *ransoming*
Future λῡς-όμενος, -ομένη, -όμενον *going to ransom, about to ransom*
Aorist λῡς-άμενος, -αμένη, -άμενον *having ransomed, after ransoming*
Perfect λελυ-μένος, -μένη, -μένον (*in a state of*) *having ransomed*

PASSIVE

Present λῡ-όμενος, -ομένη, -όμενον *being loosened*
Future λυθης-όμενος, -ομένη, -όμενον *going to be loosened, about to be loosened*
Aorist m. λυθ-είς (gen. λυθ-έντος), f. λυθεῖσα, n. λυθέν *having been loosened, after being loosened*
Perfect λελυ-μένος, -μένη, -μένον (*in a state of*) *having been loosened*

All active participles, together with that of the aorist passive, are declined like first and third declension adjectives (10.1/3). The declension of the aorist active participle is identical with that of πᾶς (10.1/3b). The present active and aorist passive are declined as follows:

SINGULAR

	M.	F.	N.	M.	F.	N.
N.V.	λύων	λύουσα	λῦον	λυθείς	λυθεῖσα	λυθέν
Acc.	λύοντα	λύουσαν	λῦον	λυθέντα	λυθεῖσαν	λυθέν
Gen.	λύοντος	λυούςης	λύοντος	λυθέντος	λυθείςης	λυθέντος
Dat.	λύοντι	λυούςῃ	λύοντι	λυθέντι	λυθείςῃ	λυθέντι

PLURAL

	M.	F.	N.	M.	F.	N.
N.V.	λύοντες	λύουςαι	λύοντα	λυθέντες	λυθεῖςαι	λυθέντα
Acc.	λύοντας	λυούςᾱς	λύοντα	λυθέντας	λυθείςᾱς	λυθέντα
Gen.	λυόντων	λυουςῶν	λυόντων	λυθέντων	λυθεις ῶν	λυθέντων
Dat.	λύουςι(ν)	λυούςαις	λύουςι(ν)	λυθεῖςι(ν)	λυθείςαις	λυθεῖςι(ν)

The future active participle follows λύων. All middle participles and that of the future passive follow καλός (3.1/3). The present (and perfect) participle passive has the same form as the middle.

The meanings given above for the present and aorist participles simply reflect the temporal distinction between their corresponding indicatives: λύων *loosening*, λύςᾱς *having loosened*. This difference of time occurs in a sentence such as ἐργαζόμενοι μὲν ἠρίςτων, ἐργαςάμενοι δὲ ἐδείπνουν *they used to have breakfast while they were working* (lit. *working*), *but used to dine after they finished work* (lit. *having worked*), but the distinction is sometimes one of aspect (4.1/1), i.e. the present participle conveys the idea of continuation, the aorist of simple occurrence. An aorist participle so used can denote an action which happens **at the same time** as that of the finite verb of its clause (**coincidental** use), e.g. εὖ ἐποίηςας ἀναμνήςᾱς με *you did well to remind me* (lit. *reminding*, not *having reminded*); ὑπολαβὼν ἔφη *he said in reply* (lit. *replying*, not *having replied*).

Notes

1 The present participle of εἰμί (*I am*) is ὤν, οὖςα, ὄν *being*; gen. s. ὄντος, οὔςης, ὄντος; dat. pl. οὖςι(ν), οὔςαις, οὖςι(ν). Its future participle is ἐςόμενος, -η, -ον (cf. 8.1/1 note 2); it has no others. The idiomatic expression τὸ ὄν (lit. *the [really] existing [thing]*) has the meaning *reality*; τῷ ὄντι is used in the sense *in reality*, *in truth* (on this use of the dative see 23.1/2*j*).

2 In tenses where they differ from λύω, contracted verbs, verbs with a contracted future, and verbs with stems in λ, μ, ν, ρ form their participles according to the rules already given for those tenses, e.g. the future active and aorist active participles of ςτέλλω are ςτελῶν (< έ + ων), ςτελοῦςα (< έ + ουςα), ςτελοῦν (< έ + ον) and ςτείλ-ᾱς, -ᾱςα, -αν.

3 Strong aorists take the participial endings of the present (cf. 7.1/1), e.g. active λαβών, -οῦςα, -όν;[1] middle λαβόμενος, -η, -ον (< λαμβάνω).

[1] Unlike the present active participle, the strong aorist active participle is always accented on the first syllable of its ending, hence λαμβάνων (pres.) but λαβών (aor.).

4   The participles of root aorists are similar to those of the weak aorist active or the aorist passive, as the following examples show:

(*a*) ἔγνων (γιγνώϲκω): m. γνούϲ (gen. γνόντοϲ), f. γνοῦϲα, n. γνόν.
(*b*) ἔφῦν (φύω): m. φύϲ (gen. φύντοϲ), f. φῦϲα, n. φύν.
(*c*) -ἔδρᾶν (-διδράϲκω, which occurs only in compounds): m. -δράϲ (gen. -δράντοϲ), f. -δρᾶϲα, n. -δράν.
(*d*) ἐπνίγην (πνῑ́γω): m. πνιγείϲ (gen. πνιγέντοϲ), f. πνιγεῖϲα, n. πνιγέν.
(*e*) ἔβην (βαίνω) follows -ἔδρᾶν: m. βάϲ (gen. βάντοϲ), f. βᾶϲα, n. βάν (cf. ἔϲτην 19.1/1).

12.1/2   Uses of participles

(*a*)   A participle in Greek can often be rendered by the same in English, but Greek regularly uses a participle and finite verb where English would more naturally have two verbs joined by *and*: τοῦτο ποιήϲαϲ ἀπῆλθεν *he did this and went away* (lit. *having done this he went away*). In many other cases a subordinate clause should be used to translate a participle, particularly when it expresses one of the following senses (the negative, when required, varies as indicated):

(i)   The **temporal** relation between two actions (negated by οὐ):

ἀφικόμενοι εἰϲ τὰϲ ᾿Αθήνᾱϲ ἔλεξαν τάδε.   *When they arrived* (lit. *having arrived*) *at Athens, they spoke as follows.*

Sometimes the temporal relation is made more precise by qualifying the participle with adverbs such ἅμα *together with*, εὐθύϲ *immediately*, μεταξύ *in the middle of*:

μεταξὺ θύων ληκύθιον ἀπώλεϲεν; *Did he lose his little oil-flask while* (lit. *in the middle of*) *sacrificing?* (on ἀπώλεϲεν see 20.1/1 note 2).
ἅμα φεύγοντεϲ τοὺϲ ῞Ελληναϲ ἐτίτρωϲκον. *While* (lit. *together with, at the same time as*) *fleeing they kept wounding the Greeks.*

(ii)   **Cause** (negated by οὐ). A participle used in this sense is often preceded by ἅτε *because* for a reason the writer or speaker sees as valid, or by ὡϲ *as* for a reason he does not vouch for. ὡϲ (which has many other uses— 22.1/1) here, and elsewhere, marks what follows as the subjective opinion of the person described and must often be translated by *thinking that, on the grounds that.* ἅτε is used only with phrases (with or without a participle):

ὁ Κῦροϲ, ἅτε τὸν χρῡϲὸν ἔχων πάντα, ἐπικούρουϲ ἐμιϲθώϲατο. *Cyrus hired mercenaries because he had all the gold.*

ὁ βαϲιλεὺϲ τοὺϲ Πέρϲᾱϲ εἶρξεν ὡϲ καταϲκόπουϲ ὄνταϲ.   *The king imprisoned the Persians on the ground that they were spies.*

οὐχ ἡγεμόναϲ ἔχων πλανᾷ ἀνὰ τὰ ὄρη.   *Because you have no guides you are wandering over the mountains.*

(iii) **Concession** (negated by οὐ). The participle is often preceded by καίπερ *although*, which, like ἅτε, is used only with phrases:

ταῦτα φέρειν ἀνάγκη καίπερ ὄντα δύcφορα. *It is necessary* (lit. *[there is] necessity*) *to endure these things although they are* (lit. *although being*) *hard to bear.*

δόξω γυναῖκα, καίπερ οὐκ ἔχων, ἔχειν. *I shall seem to have [my] wife, although I do not have [her]* (lit. *although not having*).

καί and καὶ ταῦτα (*and that [too]*) are used as equivalents of καίπερ:

ἐν τῇ Ἰλιάδι οἱ ἥρωες ἰχθῦc οὐκ ἐcθίουcι καὶ ταῦτα ἐπὶ τῇ θαλάττῃ ὄντεc. *In the Iliad the heroes do not eat fish although they are* (lit. *and that being*) *by the sea.*

(iv) **Condition** (negated by μή, as in conditional clauses, 18.1/5). No introductory word is required:

ἁμαρτήσῃ μὴ δράcαc τάδε. *You will make a mistake if you do not do this* (lit. *not having done these things*).

(v) **Purpose** (negated by οὐ). With verbs of motion a future participle can be used by itself:

ἥκομεν τοὺc coὺc ἄθλουc, Προμηθεῦ, ὀψόμενοι (< ὁράω). *We have come to see your ordeals, Prometheus.*

Elsewhere the future participle is preceded by ὡc (cf. (ii) above; in both cases ὡc presents the attitude of the subject of the participle):

cυλλαμβάνει Κῦρον ὡc ἀποκτενῶν. *He seizes Cyrus in order to kill [him].*

In these examples English uses an infinitive phrase to express purpose (for clauses expressing purpose see 14.1/4c(i)).

(vi) **A noun equivalent.** If preceded by the definite article, adjectives may function as nouns, as ὁ κακόc *the evil man* (5.1/3). Since participles are adjectives, they can be treated in the same way. οἱ μανθάνοντεc literally means *the learning [ones]* and, depending on the context, could be translated *those who are learning* or *(the) learners* (in English the article is dropped if a general class is meant—2.1/2 note 1):

ὡc ἡδὺ λεύccειν τὸ φῶc τοῖc τε καλῶc πράττουcι καὶ τοῖc δυcτυχοῦcιν. *How sweet [it is] both for those who are faring well and for those who are unfortunate to look upon the light* (i.e. *be alive*).

This use is negated by μή if a general class meant, but by οὐ if the reference is to a specific person or group:

οἱ μὴ εὐτυχοῦντεc lit. *the [class of] people who are not fortunate*, i.e. *the unfortunate.*

οἱ οὐκ εὐτυχοῦντεc *those [particular] people who are not fortunate.*

Note

ἄγων *leading*, ἔχων *having*, φέρων *carrying* are often to be translated simply
by *with*: ἦλθεν ἔχων ξίφος *he came with a sword* (lit. *having a sword*).

(b)   Another common use of participles is in the **genitive absolute**. This
construction (*absolute* here means *independent*), in its simplest form,
involves a noun or pronoun and a participle which are both in the
genitive case and which stand apart from (i.e. are **grammatically**
independent of) the rest of the sentence; there is, of course, a connection
in **sense** as otherwise there would be no point in putting the two
together. We have an absolute construction (the nominative absolute)
in English. Although it is a little clumsy, we can say *the Persians having
sailed away, Miltiades returned to Athens*. In Greek this becomes τῶν
Περσῶν ἀποπλευσάντων, ὁ Μιλτιάδης ἐπανῆλθεν εἰς τὰς ᾿Αθήνᾱς. The
genitive absolute is employed in uses (i)–(iv) as detailed above and can
be accompanied by ἅτε, ὡς, καίπερ when appropriate. It is negated by
οὐ except when it expresses a condition (above (iv)).

ταῦτ᾽ ἐπράχθη Κόνωνος στρατηγοῦντος.   *These things were done when
Conon was general* (lit. *Conon being general*) (**temporal relation**).

ἅτε πυκνοῦ ὄντος τοῦ ἄλσους οὐκ εἶδον οἱ ἐντὸς τοὺς ἐκτός.   *Because
the grove was thick those inside did not see those outside* (lit. *inasmuch
as the grove being thick*) (**cause**).

ἀποπλεῖ οἴκαδε καίπερ μέσου χειμῶνος ὄντος.   *He sails home although
it is midwinter* (lit. *although [it] being midwinter*) (**concession**).

ἀνέβη ἐπὶ τὰ ὄρη τῶν πολεμίων οὐ κωλυόντων.   *He went up on to the
mountains as the enemy did not prevent [him]* (lit. *the enemy not
preventing*) (**cause**, hence οὐ).

ὡς ἡδὺ τὸ ζῆν μὴ φθονούσης τῆς τύχης.   *How sweet [is] life if fortune
is not jealous* (lit. *fortune not being jealous*) (**condition**, hence μή).

12.2   Greek reading

1# ἀνὴρ ὁ φεύγων καὶ πάλιν μαχήσεται.
2   ἄρκτου παρούσης οὐ δεῖ ἴχνη ζητεῖν.
3# λίαν φιλῶν σεαυτὸν οὐχ ἕξεις φίλον.
4   ἑαυτὸν οὐ τρέφων κύνας τρέφει.
5# ὁ μὴ γαμῶν ἄνθρωπος οὐχ ἔχει κακά.
6   καπνὸν φεύγων εἰς τὸ πῦρ ἐνέπεσες.
7   ἀνὴρ φεύγων οὐ μένει λύρας κτύπον.
8   οἱ κύνες ἅπαξ δὴ καυθέντες λέγονται φοβεῖσθαι τὸ πῦρ.
9# θάψων γὰρ ἥκω Καίσαρ᾽, οὐκ ἐπαινέσων.
10   οὐδεὶς πεινῶν καλὰ ᾄδει.

11   ἄγροικός εἰμι τὴν σκάφην σκάφην λέγων;

12   ὁ δηχθεὶς ὑπὸ ὄφεως καὶ σχοινίον φοβεῖται.

13# ὁ γραμμάτων ἄπειρος οὐ βλέπει βλέπων.

14   χαλεπόν ἐστι πρὸς γαστέρα λέγειν ὦτα οὐκ ἔχουσαν.

15# *ΠΡΟΜΗΘΕΥΣ*

δέρκῃ θέαμα, τόνδε τὸν Διὸς φίλον,
οἵαις ὑπ' αὐτοῦ πημοναῖσι κάμπτομαι.

ΩΚΕΑΝΟΣ

ὁρῶ, Προμηθεῦ, καὶ παραινέσαι γέ σοι
θέλω τὰ λῷστα καίπερ ὄντι ποικίλῳ.

16   ὁ Κῦρος ἐντεῦθεν ἐξελαύνει διὰ τῆς Λυκαονίας σταθμοὺς πέντε,
παρασάγγας τριάκοντα, ταύτην δὲ τὴν χώραν ἐπέτρεψε διαρπάσαι τοῖς
Ἕλλησιν ὡς πολεμίαν οὖσαν.

17# Ἡσιόδου ποτὲ βίβλον ἐμαῖς ὑπὸ χερσὶν ἑλίσσων
          Πύρρην ἐξαπίνης εἶδον ἐπερχομένην·
      βίβλον δὲ ῥίψας ἐπὶ γῆν χερί, τοῦτ' ἐβόησα·
          ἔργα τί μοι παρέχεις, ὦ γέρον Ἡσίοδε;

18# In this fragment from a lost play of Euripides the leader of a band of
mystics greets Minos, the king of Cnossus in Crete whose wife, Pasiphae,
after an unfortunate experience with a bull, will give birth to the
Minotaur.

Φοινικογενοῦς τέκνον Εὐρώπης
καὶ τοῦ μεγάλου Ζηνός, ἀνάσσων
Κρήτης ἑκατομπτολιέθρου,
ἥκω ζαθέους ναοὺς προλιπών . . .
ἁγνὸν δὲ βίον τείνομεν ἐξ οὗ   5
Διὸς Ἰδαίου μύστης γενόμην (= ἐγεν-),
καὶ νυκτιπόλου Ζαγρέως βούτης
τὰς ὠμοφάγους δαῖτας τελέσας
μητρί τ' ὀρείᾳ δᾷδας ἀνασχὼν
μετὰ Κουρήτων,   10
βάκχος ἐκλήθην ὁσιωθείς.

Notes

2 ἄρκτου παρούσης gen. absolute (12.1/2*b*).

3 φιλῶν < φιλέων (pres. pple. m. nom. s. of φιλέω).

5 μή because a general class is meant (12.1/2*a*(vi)).

6 ἐνέπεσες < ἐμπίπτω.

8 δή emphasises ἅπαξ.

9 A translation of a line of Shakespeare, not a piece of original Greek;
θάψων, ἐπαινέσων 12.1/2*a*(v).

10 καλά (n. pl.) trans. by an adverb.

13 βλέπων is used here concessively, *[though] seeing*.

14 ὦτα < οὖς.

15   *l.1* τόνδε τὸν Διὸς φίλον *this friend of Zeus* (i.e. me, Prometheus) is in apposition to θέαμα (lit. *spectacle*). *l.2* οἴαις (with πημοναῖς) lit. *with what sort of* dat. of instrument (11.1/2). *l.3* παραινέω takes the dative (13.1/2*b*(i)); γε (lit. *at any rate* (13.1/3*b*)) need not be translated.

16   ἐξελαύνει vivid present (see note on 7.2.13*ll.*7f.); on the relation between σταθμούς and παρασάγγας see note on 7.2.9.

17   Hesiod, an early poet, wrote the Ἔργα καὶ Ἡμέραι (traditionally translated *Works and Days* but the real meaning is *Fields and Days [for ploughing them]*), which is the book referred to here; *l.*1 Books in antiquity were written on papyrus rolls and the reader kept his hands on top of a roll to manipulate it (hence ἐμαῖς ὑπὸ χερσίν *under my hands*) *l.*2 ἐπερχομένην *coming* (for this use of a participle see 15.1/2). *l.*4 ἔργα here *troubles*, but trans. by a singular—the author is punning on the title of the book he is reading (and wilfully misinterpreting the sense of ἔργα).

18   Europa, the daughter of Agenor, king of Tyre in Phoenicia (hence Φοινικογενής) was carried off by Zeus to Crete after the latter had taken the form of a bull (not related to the bull loved by Pasiphae); she subsequently gave birth to Minos. *ll.*1f. τέκνον vocative—with it we must take ἀνάσσων; the m. pple. (ἀνάσσων) is used because τέκνον, although neuter, refers to a male being, viz Minos—slight violations of strict grammatical agreement on this pattern are not rare (agreement according to the sense); Ζηνός see 11.1/4; ἀνάσσω *be king of*, *rule over* takes the genitive (13.1/2*a*(i)). *l.*4 προλιπών < προλείπω. *l.*5 τείνομεν lit. *we lead* but as ἐξ οὗ (*from what [time]*, i.e. *since*) follows, English idiom requires *have led*. *l.*6 Διός see 11.1/4. *l.*7 νυκτιπόλου Ζαγρέως βούτης *[as] a herdsman of night-roaming Zagreus*. *l.*8 ὠμοφάγους δαῖτας *meals of raw flesh* were a regular feature of Dionysiac orgies (the beast was torn apart by the participants). *l.*9 μητρὶ ὀρείᾳ, i.e. Cybele, another divinity worshipped with nocturnal orgies. *l.*11 ἐκλήθην < καλέω.

12.3   Extra reading – Epigrams

For the Greeks an epigram was a short poem of two to twelve lines (we have already met examples at 9.2.3 and 12.2.17). The genre formed a sub-division of elegiac poetry because it was written in the elegiac metre (see **Appendix 10**; particular metres had, from an early stage in Greek literature, become the hallmarks of most poetical genres). Authors of epigrams used, although not very consistently, forms of words from Ionic and Homeric Greek (examples in 1, 3, 4, 8, 9). There was virtually no restriction on subject matter.

1# χρυσὸν ἀνὴρ εὑρὼν ἔλιπεν βρόχον· αὐτὰρ ὁ χρυσὸν
  ὃν λίπεν οὐχ εὑρὼν ἦψεν ὃν εὗρε βρόχον.

2# ἡ Κύπρις τὴν Κύπριν ἐνὶ Κνίδῳ εἶπεν ἰδοῦσα,
  φεῦ, φεῦ, ποῦ γυμνὴν εἶδέ με Πραξιτέλης;

3# πάντες μὲν Κίλικες κακοὶ ἀνέρες· ἐν δὲ Κίλιξιν
  εἷς ἀγαθὸς Κινύρης, καὶ Κινύρης δὲ Κίλιξ.

4# εἴςιδεν Ἀντίοχος τὴν Λυςιμάχου ποτὲ τύλην
  κοὐκέτι τὴν τύλην εἴςιδε Λυςίμαχος.

5# εἴκοςι γεννήςας ὁ ζωγράφος Εὔτυχος υἱοὺς
  οὐδ' ἀπὸ τῶν τέκνων οὐδὲν ὅμοιον ἔχει.

6# ἡ τὰ ῥόδα, ῥοδόεσσαν ἔχεις χάριν· ἀλλὰ τί πωλεῖς,
  cαυτὴν, ἢ τὰ ῥόδα, ἠὲ cυναμφότερα;

7# τὴν ψυχὴν, Ἀγάθωνα φιλῶν, ἐπὶ χείλεςιν ἔςχον·
  ἦλθε γὰρ ἡ τλήμων ὡς διαβηcομένη.

8# ἡ cοβαρὸν γελάcαcα καθ' Ἑλλάδος, ἡ τὸν ἐραcτῶν
  ἑcμὸν ἐπὶ προθύροιc Λαῒς ἔχουcα νέων,
  τῇ Παφίῃ τὸ κάτοπτρον· ἐπεὶ τοίη μὲν ὁρᾶcθαι
  οὐκ ἐθέλω, οἵη δ' ἦν πάρος οὐ δύναμαι.

9# They told me, Heraclitus, they told me you were dead . . .
  εἶπέ τις, Ἡράκλειτε, τεὸν μόρον, ἐc δέ με δάκρυ
  ἤγαγεν, ἐμνήcθην δ' ὁccάκις ἀμφότεροι
  ἥλιον ἐν λέcχῃ κατεδύcαμεν· ἀλλὰ cὺ μέν που,
  ξεῖν' Ἁλικαρνηcεῦ, τετράπαλαι cποδιή·
  αἱ δὲ τεαὶ ζώουcιν ἀηδόνες, ἧcιν ὁ πάντων   5
  ἁρπακτὴc Ἀΐδης οὐκ ἐπὶ χεῖρα βαλεῖ.

Notes

1 λίπεν = ἔλιπεν (aorist of λείπω) in Homer the augment is optional in the
   imperfect and aorist, and unaugmented forms of these tenses are often
   found in literary genres which use features of Homeric language, cf.
   below 4.
2 *Κύπρις* another name for Aphrodite because of her association with
   Cyprus (*Κύπρος*).
3 ἄνερες (Homeric) = ἄνδρες.
4 εἴcιδεν = εἰcεῖδεν (< εἰcοράω) the augment is dropped as in λίπεν (above
   1); κοὐκέτι = καὶ οὐκέτι (11.1/5).
5 Eutychus apparently was a bad painter with an unfaithful wife; οὐδ'(ἐ)
   not even, but trans. *even*.
6 ἡ τὰ ῥόδα (sc. ἔχουcα) *[you] the [woman having*, i.e. *with* (12.1/2a note)*]
   the roses*, a concise form of address towards someone whose name the
   speaker does not know.
7 *l*.1 φιλῶν *kissing* (despite some restrictions, male homosexuality was
   common in Greek society, cf. 7.2.13).   *l*.2 As the future participle is used
   by itself to express purpose (12.1/2a(v)) ὡς διαβηcομένη means *thinking
   that it was going to cross over* (i.e. *with the idea of* . . . cf. 12.1/2a(ii)).
8 Lais (4th century BC), a beautiful courtesan now past her prime, dedicates
   her mirror to Aphrodite because she has no further use for it. The
   epigram consists of a single sentence and a main verb meaning *I dedicate*
   is to be supplied (the first two lines are in apposition to *I*, i.e. *I, the one*

who . . .). *l*.1 ϲοβαρόν the n. acc. s. of the adjective is used adverbially, trans. *haughtily*; καθ', i.e. κατά with elision and aspiration before the following initial aspirate; καθ' Ἑλλάδοϲ lit. (*laughing*) *against Greece*, i.e. *at Greece*. *l*.2 Trans. προθύροιϲ as singular (the plural is often used for the singular in verse); take νέων (< νέοϲ) with ἐραϲτῶν in the previous line. *l*.3 τῇ Παφίῃ, i.e. to Aphrodite, whose temple at Paphos in Cyprus was famous; τοίη (= Attic τοιαύτη (21.1/3)) *of such a sort [as I am now]*, translate simple by *as I am now*; ὁρᾶϲθαι middle voice *see myself* (8.1/1*a*). *l*.4 οἵη (= Attic οἵα) lit. *of what sort I was before*, trans. *as I was before*; with δύναμαι (on deponents in -αμαι see 19.1/3*b*) supply ὁρᾶϲθαι from the previous line.

9 An epigram of Callimachus (3rd century BC), well known in its English translation (see **Appendix 10**). The person addressed is not the philosopher Heraclitus. *l*.1 τεόϲ is the Homeric form of ϲόϲ (cf. τεαί in *l*.5). *l*.2 ἐμνήϲθην (aor. of μέμνημαι 19.1/3*a*) *I remembered*. *l*.3 *We sank the sun in conversation*, i.e. we talked into the night. *l*.5 ζώουϲιν Homeric for ζῶϲιν (< ζάω); Heraclitus' nightingales were his poems, which, ironically, have not survived; ᾗϲιν = αἷϲιν (i.e. αἷϲ)—the dat. is governed by ἐπὶ . . . βαλεῖ, *on to which*. *l*.6 ἐπὶ χεῖρα βαλεῖ = χεῖρα ἐπιβαλεῖ; in Homer when the first element of a compound verb (as ἐπιβάλλω) is a prepositional prefix (ἐπί), it can be separated from the verbal element (βάλλω) by one or more words (**tmesis** lit. *a cutting*).

Unit 13

13.1 Grammar

13.1/1 Oddities of declension

As we have now covered all regular nouns and adjectives, a few remaining oddities can be conveniently listed here. Only a very small number of nouns exist in each group.

(a) *Attic declension*

This subdivision of the second declension contains nouns which in Attic (and sometimes Ionic) end in -ως, but which in other dialects preserve the original -ος. Hence Homeric νᾱός (m) *temple* became first νηός (in Attic ᾱ > η except after a vowel or ρ) and then νεώς (cf. the gen. s. of πόλις, 8.1/4). νεώς is declined:

	SINGULAR	PLURAL
N.V.	νεώς	νεώ
Acc.	νεών	νεώς
Gen.	νεώ	νεών
Dat.	νεώ	νεώς

Other nouns of this class are λεώς (m; Homeric λᾱός) *people*, Μενέλεως (Homeric Μενέλᾱος) *Menelaus*, λαγώς (m) *hare*, ἕως (f) *dawn* (singular only; the accusative is ἕω). The adjective ἵλεως *propitious* also belongs here (m.f. ἵλεως, n. ἵλεων; n. pl. ἵλεα). The masculine and neuter of πλέως *full* follow ἵλεως but its feminine, πλέᾱ, follows δικαίᾱ (3.1/3).

(b) *Third declension nouns in -ως, -ω and -ας*

(i) ἥρως (m) *hero* is declined:

	SINGULAR	PLURAL
N.V.	ἥρως	ἥρω-ες
Acc.	ἥρω-α or ἥρω	ἥρω-ας
Gen.	ἥρω-ος	ἡρώ-ων
Dat.	ἥρω-ι or ἥρῳ	ἥρω-σι(ν)

Similarly declined are δμώς (m) *slave* and Τρῶες (m.pl.) *Trojans*. αἰδώς

(f) *shame* is irregular: n.v. αἰδώς; acc. αἰδῶ; gen. αἰδοῦς; dat. αἰδοῖ (no plural).

(ii) πειθώ (f) *persuasion* has affinities with αἰδώς and is declined: n. πειθώ; v. πειθοῖ; acc. πειθώ; gen. πειθοῦς; dat. πειθοῖ (no plural). So also ἠχώ (f) *echo* and women's names such as Σαπφώ and Καλυψώ.

(iii) In addition to neuter dental stems with a nominative in -ας (as κέρας *horn*, gen. κέρατος, 5.1/1*a*), there are a few neuter nouns in -ας whose declension is parallel to neuters in -ος (6.1/1*c*, i.e. contraction has taken place after the loss of intervocalic sigma). γέρας (n) *prize* is declined:

	SINGULAR		PLURAL	
N.V.	γέρας		γέρᾱ	(< α(ς)-α)
Acc.	γέρας		γέρᾱ	
Gen.	γέρως	(< α(ς)-ος)	γερῶν	(< ά(ς)-ων)
Dat.	γέραι	(< α(ς)-ι)	γέρασι(ν)	(< α(ς)-σι)

Similarly declined are γῆρας *old age*, κρέας *meat*, and also κέρας when it means *wing of an army* (cf. 5.1/1*a*).

(c) Nouns declined in two ways

In English *brothers* and *brethren* are both plural forms of *brother*, even though we attach a broader meaning to the second. In Greek, anomalies of this sort sometimes reflect dialectal differences (as, e.g., between Homeric and Attic Greek), but some examples exist entirely within Attic. These may involve alternative forms (as in υἱός), or an apparent irregularity (as in δένδρον). The main examples are

δάκρυον, -ου (n) *tear*; alternative n.v.a. in the singular: δάκρυ (as in 12.3.9 *l*.1).

δένδρον, -ου (n) *tree* has an irregular dat. pl. δένδρεσι(ν). δένδρε(α) in 13.2.22 *l*.2 is the Homeric and old Ionic form of the n.v.a. plural, which can be contracted to δένδρη (11.2.4 *l*.5).

πῦρ, πυρός (n) *fire* (6.1/1*b*); the plural πυρά is second declension (πυρῶν, πυροῖς) and means *watch-fires*.

σῖτος, -ου (m) *grain* (i.e. wheat or barley); the plural is neuter: σῖτα.

υἱός, -οῦ (m) *son* can be declined in the second declension throughout but also has the following third declension forms from an original nom.s. υἱύς (declined like ἡδύς—10.1/3): gen.s. υἱέος; dat.s. υἱεῖ; nom. voc. and acc.pl. υἱεῖς; gen.pl. υἱέων; dat.pl. υἱέσι(ν).

13.1/2 Verbs used with the genitive or dative

A transitive verb is defined as one that can be followed by the accusative case.

Both the Greek πέμπω and the English *send* are transitive, and in the sentences Περικλῆς δῶρον ἔπεμψεν *Pericles sent a gift* both δῶρον and *gift* are direct objects and therefore accusative. We might at first assume that if a verb is transitive in English its Greek equivalent will be the same. However, although this is true for the greater number of verbs, there are some which are transitive in one language but intransitive in the other.

The verb δειπνέω (*dine*) is transitive in Greek and so we can say ἄρτον δειπνῶ *I am dining [on] bread*, but we cannot say in English *I dine bread* because *dine* is an intransitive verb and must be followed by a preposition, not a direct object (in *I am dining on bread, bread* is accusative after the preposition *on*). Similarly there are verbs which are transitive in English but not in Greek, but, whereas in English the logical object of an intransitive verb is preceded by a preposition (*dine on bread*), in Greek it is put into the genitive or dative. Greek verbs of this type can, to a large extent, be classified according to their meaning. The following are the main groups:

(a) **Verbs followed by the genitive** (see also 23.1/1k)

(i) Verbs of **ruling**, e.g. ἄρχω *rule*; κρατέω lit. *have power* (κράτος) *over*; βασιλεύω lit. *be king* (βασιλεύς) *of* (all three are normally translated by *rule*).

ἐν ἀμφιάλῳ Ἰθάκῃ βασιλεύσει Ἀχαιῶν.   *He will rule the Achaeans in sea-girt Ithaca.*

(ii) Verbs of **desiring, needing, caring for**, e.g. ἐπιθῡμέω *desire*; ἐράω *love, desire* (sexually); δέομαι *need*; ἐπιμελέομαι *care for*.

οὐκ ἐρᾷ ἀδελφὸς ἀδελφῆς οὐδὲ πατὴρ θυγατρός.   *A brother does not desire his sister, nor a father his daughter.*

(iii) Verbs of **perceiving, remembering, forgetting**, e.g. αἰσθάνομαι *perceive* (also + acc.); πυνθάνομαι *ascertain* (+ acc. of thing ascertained and gen. of informant); ἀκούω *hear, listen to* (+ acc. of thing heard, gen. of person heard); μέμνημαι (19.1/3a) *remember*; ἐπιλανθάνομαι *forget* (also + acc.).

ταῦτα Κίρκης ἤκουσα.   *I heard this from Circe* (but Κίρκης ἤκουσα *I heard* (or *listened to*) *Circe*).

(iv) Verbs of **reaching, obtaining, missing**, e.g. τυγχάνω *hit the mark, succeed, obtain*; ἁμαρτάνω *miss, fail to achieve*.

τίνος πότμου ἔτυχεν; *What fate did he meet* (lit. *obtain*)?
τῶν ἐλπίδων ἡμάρτομεν. *We did not realize* (lit. *missed*) *our hopes.*

(v) Verbs of **sharing**, e.g. μετέχω *share, have a share in.*

πάντες οἱ πολῖται μετέχουσι τῆς ἑορτῆς.   *All the citizens take part in* (lit. *share*) *the festival.*

(b) **Verbs followed by the dative**

(i) Verbs indicating that **the subject is asserting himself in some way over someone else**, e.g. παραινέω *advise*; βοηθέω (*run to*) *help, assist*; ὀργίζομαι *become angry with*; ἀπειλέω *threaten*; φθονέω *feel ill-will against, grudge*.

φθονεῖν φασι μητρυιᾶς τέκνοις. *They say that step-mothers feel ill-will against their children.*

(ii) Verbs indicating that **the subject is submitting himself in some way to somebody else**, e.g. πείθομαι (middle of πείθω) *obey*; πιστεύω *trust*; εἴκω *yield*.

πατρὶ πείθεσθαι χρὴ τέκνα. *Children must obey their father.*

(iii) Verbs indicating **association of some sort**, e.g. ἕπομαι *follow*; ἐντυγχάνω *fall in with*; ἀπαντάω *meet*; πλησιάζω *approach, associate with*; μάχομαι *fight*; χράομαι *associate with* (people), *use* (things).

οὐδεὶς ἔτι ἡμῖν μάχεται. *No-one is fighting us any longer.*
τῷ δεσπότῃ ἑσπόμην (< ἕπομαι). *I followed my master.*

(iv) Verbs indicating **likeness**, e.g. ὁμοιόομαι, ἔοικα (19.1/3a) both *be like, resemble*.

οὐ χρή σε ὁμοιοῦσθαι κακοῖς. *You should not be like bad men.*

Not all verbs which, by virtue of their meaning, we would expect to belong to these groups do in fact take the genitive or dative, e.g. φιλέω *love* and ὠφελέω *help* both take the accusative (we would have expected the genitive and dative respectively). Some of the verbs listed above (e.g. ἐπιλανθάνομαι) also take the accusative with no difference in meaning. Full details will be found in the vocabulary.

13.1/3 Further particles

The fundamental importance of particles (see 4.1/3) should now be clear. Their use, especially as connectives, has been widely illustrated in the reading exercises, and we have now met ἀλλά *but*; ἄρα* *then, so*; γάρ* *for, because*; δέ* *and, but*; δήπου* *I presume, I should hope, doubtless*; καί *and, even*; οὐδέ *and not, nor, not even*; οὖν* *therefore, so, then*; τοι* *in truth, be assured, you know*; and που* *perhaps, I suppose*, as well as the combinations μέν* ... δέ* *on the one hand ... and/but on the other hand*, τε* ... καί and καὶ ... καί *both ... and*, and καὶ δή *and moreover*.

Some other particles of common occurrence are listed below:

(a) Particles with a **connective** function
    δῆτα*: (i) in answers, particularly emphatic negative answers, οὐ δῆτα *no indeed*.

(ii) in questions, πῶс δῆτα; *how then?*, τί δῆτα; *what* (or *why*) *then?*, e.g. τί δῆτά με ζῆν δεῖ; *why then* (or *in that case*) *should I live?*

μήν* may also be used to enliven a question, often in combination with ἀλλά, e.g. ἀλλὰ τί μὴν δοκεῖс; *but* (or *well*) *what then do you think?* By itself, τί μήν; has the meaning *of course*:

A. μιсθωτῷ μᾶλλον ἐπιτρέπουсιν ἢ соὶ τοὺс ἵππουс; B. ἀλλὰ τί μήν; *A. Do they entrust the horses to a hireling rather than to you? B. But of course* (lit. *But what then* sc. *if not that?*).

τοίνυν*: the temporal adverb νῦν (so accented) means *now, at present*. Unaccented νυν* is an inferential particle, *now* in the sense *then, therefore*, especially with imperatives (17.1/1): сπεῦδέ νυν *hurry up then*. τοίνυν, a strengthened form of νυν, likewise has a transitional or inferential force, *now then, furthermore, well now*, e.g. ἐπειδὴ τοίνυν ἐποιήсατο τὴν εἰρήνην ἡ πόλιс ... *well now, since the city made peace* ...

(*b*) Particles which do not connect but convey **shades of tone, colour or emphasis**

γε* is an intensive and restrictive particle which affects the preceding word. Its literal meaning is *at least, at any rate, certainly, indeed*, e.g. ἔγωγε[1] *I for my part* (examples have already occurred at 9.2.12 *l*.8 and 10.3 *l*.4), but in English we would often simply use an emphatic tone of voice rather than an equivalent word, e.g. οἵδε κρινοῦсί γε εἰ χρή сε μίμνειν *they shall **judge** if you are to remain*; сυγχωρεῖс τοῦτό γε καὶ сύ *even you admit **this***. It is also extremely common in replies to previous remarks, especially to questions, and is often to be rendered as *yes*:

A. ἆρα сτενάζει; B. κλαίει γε. *A. Is he groaning? B. Yes, he is weeping.*
A. κενὸν τόδ᾽ ἄγγοс ἢ сτέγει τι; B. сά γ᾽ ἔνδυτα. *A. [Is] this vessel empty, or does it hold something? B. Yes, your garments.*

Sometimes it re-enforces a negative and must be translated by *no*:

A. ἔсτι τιс λόγοс; B. οὐδείс γε. *A. Is there some explanation? B. No, none.*

(On ways of saying *yes* and *no* in Greek see 24.1/1.)

δή* emphasizes the preceding word. *Indeed, certainly* are only approximate translations; the force of the particle would normally be conveyed to the hearer in English by the loudness of the voice or some accompanying emphatic gesture. δή is particularly common with adjectives or adverbs, e.g. ἅπαντεс δή *absolutely everyone*; μόνοс δή *quite alone*; πολλάκιс δή *very often*. It may also convey irony or sarcasm,

---

[1] ἐγώ and γε are combined to form one word (with a different accent). Cf. below μέντοι (μέν+τοι), καίτοι (καί+τοι).

Cωκράτης ὁ cοφὸς δή *Socrates the **wise*** (the tone of voice in English will indicate whether *wise* is complimentary or ironical).

(c) Frequent **combinations** of particles

καὶ δή: as well as being used as a lively connective, *and moreover* (e.g. καὶ δὴ τὸ μέγιστον *and moreover the principal point*) καὶ δή is common in replies to a command:

A. οὔκουν ἐπείξει τῷδε δεcμὰ περιβαλεῖν; B. καὶ δὴ πρόχειρα ψάλια
   A. *Hasten* (lit. *won't you hasten*) *then to cast fetters round this man?*
   B. *There you are* (lit. *actually indeed*), *the chains [are] ready to hand.*

It is also used in making assumptions: καὶ δὴ πολέμιοί εἰcιν *and suppose they are hostile.*

Note that καὶ δὴ καί means *and especially, and in particular*; in this combination the stress is laid on the word following the second καί:

καὶ δὴ καὶ τότε ἅμ' ἡμέρᾳ cυνελέγημεν. *And on that particular occasion* (lit. *and then in particular*) *we gathered at dawn.*

Combinations with οὖν*

(i) οὐκοῦν is merely a synonym for οὖν*, *therefore, accordingly, well then*:

ἢ τοὺς ἀμῡ́νεcθαι κελεύοντας πόλεμον ποιεῖν φήcομεν; οὐκοῦν ὑπόλοιπον δουλεύειν. *Or shall we say that those who urge [us] to defend ourselves are making war? Then* (or *in that case*) *it remains [for us] to be slaves.*

It is to be distinguished from οὔκουν (so accented), in which the negative retains its full force:

οὔκουν, Προμηθεῦ, τοῦτο γιγνώcκειν, ὅτι ὀργῆς νοcούcης εἰcὶν ἰατροὶ λόγοι; *Do you not know this then, Prometheus, that when a temperament is sick* (lit. *a temperament being sick* gen. absolute, 12.1/2b) *there are words [to act as] healers?* (see also second example given in (c) above).

(ii) δ' οὖν* has a resumptive force, *be that as it may*, used in dismissing a subject:

εἰ δὴ δίκαια ποιήcω, οὐ γιγνώcκω· αἱρήcομαι δ' οὖν ὑμᾶc. *If indeed I shall do what is right* (lit. *just things*) *I do not know; however that may be, I shall choose you.*

(iii) μὲν οὖν*: this combination sometimes has no other force than the value of its two constituent parts (μέν looking forward to δέ, and οὖν *therefore*), but it can also be used to correct a previous statement, with the sense *no, on the contrary*:

A. ἢ cὺ οὐδὲν ἡγῇ πράττειν τὸν γραμματιcτήν; B. ἔγωγε ἡγοῦμαι μὲν οὖν. A. *Or do you think that the schoolmaster does nothing?* B. *On the contrary, I do think* (sc. *that he does something*).

Combinations with τοι*

(iv) καίτοι means *and yet, however*:

καίτοι τί φημι; *And yet what am I saying?*

(v) μέντοι* is used either to emphasize, e.g. A. ἐγώ; B. σὺ μέντοι. A. *Me?* (lit. *I*) B. *Yes, you.*

or in an adversative sense, *however, yet,* often with an added γε:

οὐ μέντοι οἵ γε Cκύθαι ταύτῃ εἰσέβαλον. *Yet the Scythians did not invade by this route.*

It is impossible, of course, to give a complete survey of all the nuances of Greek particles in a few pages. Other uses will be explained as they occur in the reading. Meanwhile, keep your eyes open for the occurrence of particles and try to assess in each instance just what they contribute to a given utterance.

13.2   Greek reading

1# καλόν γε γαστρὸς κἀπιθυμίας κρατεῖν.
2#   τῷ γήρᾳ φιλεῖ
χὠ νοῦς ὁμαρτεῖν καὶ τὸ βουλεύειν ἃ δεῖ.
3 τοῦτό τοι τἀνδρεῖον, ἡ προμηθία.
4# πανταχοῦ γε πατρὶς ἡ βόσκουσα γῆ.
5# σοφόν γέ τοί τι πρὸς τὸ βουλεύειν ἔχει
τὸ γῆρας, ὡς δὴ πόλλ' ἰδόν τε καὶ παθόν.
6# ὦ τλῆμον ἀρετή, λόγος ἄρ' ἦσθ'· ἐγὼ δέ σε
ὡς ἔργον ἤσκουν· σὺ δ' ἄρ' ἐδούλευες τύχῃ.
7# πατὴρ μὲν ἡμῖν Οἰδίπους ὁ Λαΐου,
ἔτικτε δ' Ἰοκάστη με, παῖς Μενοικέως·
καλεῖ δὲ Πολυνείκη με Θηβαῖος λεώς.
8# οὐκ ἔστι Πειθοῦς ἱερὸν ἄλλο πλὴν λόγος,
καὶ βωμὸς αὐτῆς ἔστ' ἐν ἀνθρώπου φύσει.
9 ὁ δύο λαγὼς διώκων οὐδέτερον καταλαμβάνει.
10 ὁ Κῦρος ἅτε παῖς ὢν καὶ φιλόκαλος καὶ φιλότιμος ἤδετο τῇ στολῇ.
11 ἀνάγκῃ οὐδὲ οἱ θεοὶ μάχονται.
12 κακὸν ἀναγκαῖον τὸ πείθεσθαι γαστρί.
13 τὴν Χάρυβδιν ἐκφυγὼν τῇ Cκύλλῃ περιέπεσες.
14 ὄνος πεινῶν οὐ φροντίζει ῥοπάλου.
15# τοῦ ζῆν γὰρ οὐδεὶς ὡς ὁ γηράσκων ἐρᾷ.

16# μόνος θεῶν θάνατος οὐ δώρων ἐρᾷ.

17# ὁ μηδὲν ἀδικῶν οὐδενὸς δεῖται νόμου.

18   τέτταρας δακτύλους θανάτου οἱ πλέοντες ἀπέχουσιν.

19   ἦρος χρήζεις ἐπειδὴ παλαιὸν χιτῶνα ἔχεις.

20   Γοργὼ ἡ Λάκαινα, ἐρωτηθεῖσα ὑπό τινος Ἀττικῆς, διὰ τί ὑμεῖς ἄρχετε
     μόναι τῶν ἀνδρῶν αἱ Λάκαιναι; ὅτι, ἔφη, καὶ τίκτομεν μόναι ἄνδρας.

21   **A noteworthy pun**

     Ἀντισθένης ὁ φιλόσοφος, πρὸς μειράκιόν τι μέλλον φοιτᾶν παρὰ αὐτὸν
     καὶ πυθόμενον τίνων αὐτῷ δεῖ, ἔφη, βιβλίου καινοῦ καὶ γραφείου
     καινοῦ καὶ πινακιδίου καινοῦ, τὸν νοῦν παρεμφαίνων.

22# ἡ γῆ μέλαινα πίνει,
     πίνει δὲ δένδρε᾽ αὐτήν·
     πίνει θάλασσα κρουνούς,
     ὁ δ᾽ ἥλιος θάλασσαν,
     τὸν δ᾽ ἥλιον σελήνη.   5
     τί μοι μάχεσθ᾽, ἑταῖροι,
     καὐτῷ θέλοντι πίνειν;

Notes

1   κἀπιθῡμίᾱς = καὶ ἐπιθῡμίᾱς (11.1/5).

2   φιλέω + infinitive *be accustomed to*; φιλεῖ is singular because it agrees
    with the closer of the two subjects; χὠ = καὶ ὁ (11.1/5); ἃ δεῖ is the object
    of βουλεύειν.

3   The subject τοῦτο (sc. ἐστί) anticipates ἡ προμηθίᾱ; τἀνδρεῖον = τὸ
    ἀνδρεῖον (11.1/5).

5   Take σοφόν ... τι together as the object of ἔχει (the subject is τὸ γῆρας);
    ὡς + participle to give a supposed reason (12.1/2a(ii)); πόλλ᾽, i.e. πολλά;
    ἰδόν < ὁράω; παθόν < πάσχω (both aorist participles are neuter nom. s.
    agreeing with γῆρας).

6   ἀρετή *virtue* was the philosophical ideal of the Stoics. These lines, whose
    exact source is unknown, were the last words of the Roman Brutus
    before committing suicide; ἆρ᾽ = ἆρα (distinguish from ἆρα);
    ἦσθ᾽ = ἦσθα; ὡς *as* (22.1/1a(i)).

7   *l.*1 ἡμῖν trans. by a singular (royal plural—Polyneices in fact continues
    in the singular).   *l.*2 ἔτικτε trans. as though aorist, *bore* (τίκτω is used
    idiomatically to mean *be parent of*).

9   λαγώς acc. pl. (13.1/1a).

12 τὸ πείθεσθαι is the subject; κακόν is used as a noun *an evil*.

15 ὡς *as* (cf. 6 above).

17 μηδέν, not οὐδέν, because a general class is meant (12.1/2a(vi)), lit. *the
    [person] doing wrong not at all* (adverbial acc., 20.1/5), i.e. *those who do
    no wrong*.

18 τέτταρας δακτύλους acc. of extent of space (7.1/7d); the width of four
    fingers was the normal thickness of the sides of an ancient ship.

19 ἦρος < ἔαρ (6.1/1b).

20 Spartan men prided themselves on manly virtues; they were not,
however, male chauvinists, as the story shows; ὅτι *because*.

21 μέλλον acc. n. s. of the pres. act. pple. of μέλλω (here *intend*), to be taken
with μειράκιον; δεῖ *there is need of* + gen. of thing needed and dat. of the
person in need (cf. 21.1/4*b* and note 3); in Antisthenes' reply the genitives
depend on an understood δεῖ (i.e. *you need . . .*).

22 A poem in imitation of Anacreon (22.3). It is written in Ionic Greek as is
shown by the forms θάλαccα and θέλοντι. *l*.1 the prose order would be
ἡ μέλαινα γῆ. *l*.2 πίνει, i.e. *draws nourishment from*; δένδρε', i.e.
δένδρεα. *l*.6 μάχεcθ' i.e. μάχεcθε. *l*.7 καὐτῷ = καὶ αὐτῷ.

13.3   Extra reading – Plato (*c*. 429–347 BC)

All Plato's philosophical writings (except the *Apology*) are in the form of
discussions and arguments which are supposed to have taken place on a
particular occasion between various contemporaries. For this reason they are
called dialogues, but we have no way of telling where factual reporting stops
and Plato's imagination (or his desire to expound his own ideas) begins.
Some dialogues are in simple dramatic form, whereas in others the
conversation is reported by one of the characters (the second extract is an
example of the former, the first of the latter). In all his dialogues (except the
Laws) Plato introduces his master, Socrates (10.3), as a protagonist, but
nowhere does he introduce himself.

(i) *CΩKPATHC*

ἐπορευόμην μὲν ἐξ 'Ακαδημείας εὐθὺ Λυκείου τὴν ἔξω τείχους ὑπ' αὐτὸ τὸ
τεῖχος· ἐπειδὴ δ' ἐγενόμην κατὰ τὴν πυλίδα ᾗ ἡ Πάνοπος κρήνη, ἐνταῦθα
cυνέτυχον 'Ιπποθάλει τε τῷ 'Ιερωνύμου καὶ Κτηcίππῳ τῷ Παιανιεῖ καὶ
ἄλλοιc μετὰ τούτων νεανίκοιc. καί με προcιόντα (*approaching*) ὁ 'Ιππο-
θάληc ἰδών, ὦ Cώκρατεc, ἔφη, ποῖ δὴ πορεύῃ καὶ πόθεν;   5
ἐξ' 'Ακαδημείας, ἦν δ' ἐγώ, πορεύομαι εὐθὺ Λυκείου.
δεῦρο δή, ἦ δ' ὅc, εὐθὺ ἡμῶν. οὐ παραβάλλειc; ἄξιον μέντοι.
ποῖ, ἔφην ἐγώ, λέγειc, καὶ παρὰ τίναc τοὺc ὑμᾶc;
δεῦρο, ἔφη, δείξαc (*showing*) μοι ἐν τῷ καταντικρὺ τοῦ τείχους περίβολόν τέ
τινα καὶ θύραν. διατρίβομεν δέ, ἦ δ' ὅc, αὐτόθι ἡμεῖc τε αὐτοὶ καὶ ἄλλοι   10
πάνυ πολλοὶ καὶ καλοί.
ἔcτιν δὲ δὴ τί τοῦτο, καὶ τίc ἡ διατριβή;
παλαίcτρα, ἔφη, νέα· ἡ δὲ διατριβὴ τὰ πολλὰ ἐν λόγοιc ὧν cε μετέχειν
ἐθέλομεν.
καλῶc γε, ἦν δ' ἐγώ, ποιοῦντεc· διδάcκει δὲ τίc αὐτόθι;   15
còc ἑταῖρόc γε, ἦ δ' ὅc, καὶ ἐπαινέτηc, Μίκκοc.
μὰ Δία, ἦν δ' ἐγώ, οὐ φαῦλόc γε ἀνήρ, ἀλλ' ἱκανὸc cοφιcτήc.
βούλει οὖν ἕπεcθαι, ἔφη, καὶ ὁρᾶν τοὺc ὄνταc αὐτόθι;

112   *Unit Thirteen*

(ii)   *ΕΥΚΛΕΙΔΗC—ΤΕΡΨΙΩΝ*

ΕΥ. ἄρτι, ὦ Τερψίων, ἢ πάλαι ἐξ ἀγροῦ;

ΤΕΡ. ἐπιεικῶς πάλαι. καὶ cέ γε ἐζήτουν κατ᾽ ἀγορὰν καὶ ἐθαύμαζον ὅτι οὐχ οἷός τ᾽ ἦ εὑρεῖν.

ΕΥ. οὐ γὰρ ἦ κατὰ πόλιν.

ΤΕΡ. ποῦ μήν;

ΕΥ. εἰς λιμένα καταβαίνων Θεαιτήτῳ ἐνέτυχον φερομένῳ ἐκ Κορίνθου ἀπὸ τοῦ στρατοπέδου Ἀθήναζε.

ΤΕΡ. πότερον ζῶντι ἢ οὔ;

ΕΥ. ζῶντι καὶ μάλα μόλις· χαλεπῶς μὲν γὰρ ἔχει καὶ ὑπὸ τραυμάτων τινῶν, μᾶλλον μὴν αὐτὸν αἱρεῖ τὸ νόσημα τὸ ἐν τῷ στρατεύματι.

ΤΕΡ. μῶν ἡ δυcεντερία;

ΕΥ. ναί.

ΤΕΡ. οἷον ἄνδρα λέγεις ἐν κινδύνῳ εἶναι.

ΕΥ. καλόν τε καὶ ἀγαθόν, ὦ Τερψίων, ἐπεί τοι καὶ νῦν ἤκουόν τινων μάλα ἐγκωμιαζόντων αὐτὸν περὶ τὴν μάχην.

ΤΕΡ. καὶ οὐδέν γ᾽ ἄτοπον. ἀτὰρ πῶς οὐκ αὐτοῦ Μεγαροῖ κατέλυεν;

ΕΥ. ἠπείγετο οἴκαδε· ἐπεὶ ἔγωγ᾽ ἐδεόμην καὶ cυνεβούλευον, ἀλλ᾽ οὐκ ἤθελεν. καὶ δῆτα προπέμψας αὐτόν, ἀνεμνήσθην καὶ ἐθαύμασα Cωκράτους ὡς μαντικῶς ἄλλα τε δὴ εἶπε καὶ περὶ τούτου. δοκεῖ γάρ μοι ὀλίγον πρὸ τοῦ θανάτου ἐντυχεῖν αὐτῷ μειρακίῳ ὄντι, καὶ cυγγενόμενός τε καὶ διαλεχθεὶς πάνυ ἀγαcθῆναι αὐτοῦ τὴν φύσιν.

Notes

(i)

The speaker is Socrates, who is going from the Academy, a park with sporting facilities (i.e. a γυμνάcιον) lying north-west of ancient Athens, to the Lyceum, a similar establishment to the east. The road between the two skirted the north wall.   *l*.1 τὴν ἔξω τείχους sc. ὁδόν *on/along the [road] outside the wall*, this use of the accusative without a preposition is classified as an acc. of spatial extent (7.1/7*d*).   *l*.2. ᾗ *where* (sc. ἐcτί).   *l*.3 Παιανιεῖ (< Παιανιεύc) an adjective meaning *of the deme Paeania*; as the Athenians had only one personal name (cf. 5.1/3 note 2) they were officially distinguished by the *deme* (local administrative unit) to which they belonged.   *l*.6 ἦν δ᾽ ἐγώ *said I* a stereotyped formula, often used by Plato, which employs the nearly defunct verb ἠμί *say* (18.1/1*a*) (δ᾽ is part of the formula and should not be translated).   *l*.7 δεῦρο often used as an order *[come] over here*; ἦ δ᾽ ὅc *said he* the same formula as above but in its third person singular version (the use of the relative ὅc as a demonstrative pronoun is archaic).   *l*.8 λέγεις *do you mean*; παρὰ τίναc τοὺς ὑμᾶς sc. ὄντας *to whom the [group of] you being [am I to come]?*, i.e. *who are you to whom*, etc.   *l*.9 δείξαc *showing* coincidental use of aor. pple. (12.1/1).   *l*.12 Supply ἐcτί with ἡ διατριβή.   *l*.13 τὰ πολλά lit. *for the many [times]*, i.e. *usually* (adverbial acc. 20.1/5); ὧν has λόγοιc as its antecedent and is governed by μετέχειν, which takes the genitive of what is shared (13.1/2*a*(v)).   *l*.15 καλῶc γε . . . ποιοῦντεc (sc. ἐθέλετε, to be supplied from ἐθέλομεν in the previous line) *doing well at any rate [you wish this]*, an expression of gratitude for their invitation.

(ii)

The speakers are Eucleides and Terpsion. *l*.1 sc. ἦλθες the omission is typical of Plato's colloquial style. *l*.3 οἷός τ᾽ εἰμί an idiom meaning *I am able* (τ᾽ is not to be translated; on οἷος see 21.1/3)). *l*.4 Terpsion has not been able to find Eucleides in the agora; in English the latter's reply would be *No, you couldn't, for I was not in the city*, but Greek omits the words *No, you couldn't* (which confirm the previous statement) and simply gives the reason *for I was not*, etc. (24.1/1). *l*.8 πότερον introduces two alternative questions (10.1/2*a*) but is not to be translated; with ζῶντι supply ἐνέτυχες from ἐνέτυχον in *l*.6. *l*.9 ἔχω + adv. to express a state (cf. note on 8.2.9 *l*.1). *l*.10 μήν has an adversative sense (*but*) and balances the preceding μέν; the combination gives a stronger contrast than μέν . . . δέ. *l*.11 μῶν (10.1/2*a*) in his anxiety Terpsion is hoping for a negative answer. *l*.13 οἷον . . . exclamatory *what a man . . .!* (21.1/3) *l*.14 The Athenian male ideal was summed up in the phrase καλὸς κἀγαθός (here slightly varied), which can be translated *gentleman* (cf. 9.2.12 *l*.4). *l*.17 ἐπεί *since* introduces proof for the fact that Theaetetus was hurrying home, and governs the following three finite verbs; we would omit it in English; ἐδεόμην καὶ συνεβούλευον sc. *him to stay*. *l*.18 καὶ δῆτα *in fact* (lit. *and indeed* but more emphatic than καὶ δή); translate προπέμψας by a finite verb and supply *and* before the next clause; Σωκράτους is genitive with ἀνεμνήσθην and ἐθαύμασα lit. *remembered and admired Socrates, how prophetically he spoke . . .* but English idiom requires *how prophetically Socrates spoke . . .* (where appropriate, Greek often anticipates the subject of an indirect question in this way). *l*.19 ἄλλα τε . . . καὶ περὶ τούτου lit. *both other [things] and about him*, i.e. *in particular about him*; ἄλλος τε καί is often used in the sense *particularly, especially* (see note on 20.3 *l*.1); δοκεῖ the subject is *he* (i.e. Socrates). *ll*.20f. διαλεχθείς < διαλέγομαι; ἀγασθῆναι < ἄγαμαι.

Unit 14

14.1 Grammar

14.1/1 Moods of the Greek verb

Mood is a characteristic of all finite forms[1] of the Greek verb (i.e. those that can stand alone in a clause). Up to now we have dealt only with the indicative, the mood used for facts. There are three other moods, the imperative, which expresses commands (17.1/1), and the subjunctive and optative. In a main clause the subjunctive can express the will of the subject, e.g. λύcωμεν (aor. subj. act.) τοὺς δούλους *let us free the slaves*, while the optative can express the wish of the speaker, e.g. μὴ γένοιτο (aor. opt. mid.) *may it not happen!* These uses illustrate, in part, an original distinction between what is **willed** or **expected** (subjunctive) and what is **desired** or considered **possible** (optative), but the functions of both moods have been expanded to such a degree that neither can be brought under a single definition.

In English we still possess some single-word subjunctive forms (*be that as it may*; *if I were you*) but the optative disappeared in the Germanic branch of Indo-European (1.3) before the evolution of English. Apart from the few relics of the subjunctive, we use auxiliary verbs (*let, may, would,* etc.) for uses covered by these moods in Greek.

The subjunctive and optative exist in the present and aorist (and perfect, 16.1/4 note 1). There is also a future optative, but **no** future subjunctive. The distinction between the present and aorist forms of these moods is one of aspect (4.1/1) **not** time (for an exception see 14.1/4*d*). As with infinitives, the present subjunctive or optative is used for an action which is seen as going on, in the process of happening, or being repeated; the aorist subjunctive or optative is used for an action which is seen as a simple event (cf. 4.1/1).

14.1/2 Subjunctive mood

For complete table of λύω see **Appendix 1**.

The subjunctive has only one set of endings, which are applied to the present and aorist stems (the latter without the augment). The endings are formed by lengthening all the initial short vowels (even when the first element of a diphthong) of the indicative endings:

---

[1] The non-finite forms of verbs (participles and infinitives) are not considered as belonging to any mood.

Active: -ω, -ης, -ῃ, -ωμεν, -ητε, -ωςι(ν).

Middle and passive: -ωμαι, -ῃ, -ηται, -ωμεθα, -ηςθε, -ωνται.

Note that ει becomes η but in ου > ω (3rd pl. act.) the second element of the diphthong disappears. As the aorist passive takes active endings (11.1/1), for the aorist passive subjunctive of λύω we have λυθῶ,[1] λυθῇς, etc.

In the present subjunctive of contracted verbs the rules of contraction apply as for the indicative (5.1/2). Paradigms will be found in **Appendix 2**.

The endings for the subjunctive are classified as **primary** (4.1/1 note 1 and 8.1/1*f*.; we have -ςι(ν) in the 3rd pl. act., -μαι in the 1st s. mid./pass., etc.). This classification is relevant to the use of the subjunctive in certain subordinate clauses (14.1/4*c*).

Notes

1 The indicative and subjunctive coincide in a few forms, e.g. λύω, τῑμῶ, τῑμᾷς.
2 Strong aorists and root aorists have the normal subjunctive endings (i.e. -ω, -ης, -ῃ etc), except for a few root aorists in -ων, which have -ω, -ῳς, -ῳ, -ωμεν, -ωτε, -ωςι(ν). An example is ἔγνων (γιγνώςκω), subj. γνῶ, γνῷς, γνῷ, γνῶμεν, γνῶτε, γνῶςι(ν); cf. the present and aorist subjunctive active of δίδωμι (18.1/2 note 1).
3 The subjunctive of εἰμί is identical with the endings of the present subjunctive of λύω, viz ὦ, ᾖς, ᾖ, ὦμεν, ἦτε, ὦςι(ν).

14.1/3 Optative mood

For complete table of λύω *see* **Appendix 1**.

The optative, like the subjunctive, uses the same stems as the indicative, but its endings show some variety between tenses. For λύω and other uncontracted -ω verbs we have:

(*a*) **present and future active**: -οιμι, -οις, -οι, -οιμεν, -οιτε, -οιεν; e.g. λύοιμι, λύοις etc. (present); λύςοιμι, λύςοις, etc. (future).
(*b*) **present and future, middle and passive**: -οιμην, -οιο, -οιτο, -οιμεθα, -οιςθε, -οιντο; e.g. λῡοίμην (pres. mid./pass.), λῡςοίμην (fut. mid.), λυθηςοίμην (fut. pass.).
(*c*) **weak aorist active**: -αιμι, -ειας (or -αις), -ειε(ν) (or -αι), -αιμεν, -αιτε, -ειαν (or -αιεν); e.g. λύςαιμι, λύςειας, etc. The bracketed forms are less common.
(*d*) **weak aorist middle**: -αιμην, -αιο, -αιτο, -αιμεθα, -αιςθε, -αιντο; e.g. λῡςαίμην, λύςαιο, etc.

---

[1] The aorist passive subjunctive is always accented with a circumflex on the first syllable of the ending (the circumflex indicates contraction, λυθῶ < λυθέω, etc.).

(*e*) in the **aorist passive** the final η of the stem is dropped (λυθη > λυθ) and to this are added: -ειην, -ειης, -ειη, -ειμεν, -ειτε, -ειεν; e.g. λυθείην, λυθείης, etc.

Contracted -ω verbs have different endings for the singular of the present optative active: -οιην, -οιης, -οιη. These, and the other present endings, contract according to the rules given at 5.1/2 (for paradigms see **Appendix 2**).

Present active	**Present middle/passive**
τῑμῴην (τῑμα-οίην), τῑμῴης, etc.	τῑμῴμην (τῑμα-οίμην), τῑμῷο, etc.
ποιοίην (ποιε-οίην), ποιοίης, etc.	ποιοίμην (ποιε-οίμην), ποιοῖο, etc.
δηλοίην (δηλο-οίην), δηλοίης, etc.	δηλοίμην (δηλο-οίμην), δηλοῖο, etc.

In the future, aorist and perfect of contracted verbs the optative is formed by taking the appropriate stem and adding the normal endings.

The endings of the optative are classified as **historic** (4.1/1 note 1 and 8.1/1*f*; we have -ν in the 3rd pl. act., -μην in the 1st s. mid./pass., etc.). This classification is relevant to the use of the optative in certain subordinate clauses (14.1/4*c*).

Notes

1 The optative of the strong aorist has the same endings as the present; e.g. the aorist optative active of μανθάνω is μάθοιμι, μάθοις, μάθοι, μάθοιμεν, μάθοιτε, μάθοιεν.
2 The root aorist ἔβην (βαίνω) has an optative βαίην, βαίης, βαίη, βαῖμεν, βαῖτε, βαῖεν (cf. the optative of -έδρᾱν which is -δραίην, -δραίης, etc.) but other root aorists in -ην have an optative in -ειην, -ειης etc., just as that of the aorist passive. The optative of root aorists in -ων has the endings -οιην, -οιης, etc., and so from ἔγνων (γιγνώςκω) we have γνοίην, γνοίης, γνοίη, γνοῖμεν, γνοῖτε, γνοῖεν. The optative of root aorists in -υν is extremely rare.
3 The present optative of εἰμί is εἴην, εἴης, εἴη, εἶμεν, εἶτε, εἶεν. The future optative is ἐςοίμην, ἔςοιο, ἔςοιτο, etc.

14.1/4 Uses of the subjunctive and optative

The subjective and optative complement each other in several types of subordinate clauses, but in main clauses their uses are quite distinct.

(*a*) *Subjunctive in main clauses*

(i) The **jussive** subjunctive (negated by μή) is used for giving orders but, because we also have the imperative (17.1/1), its use is limited. In the first person plural (the singular is possible but not as common) it expresses self-exhortation or self-encouragement: μή, πρὸς θεῶν, μαινώμεθα *in the name of* (πρός) *the gods, let us not be mad!* The use of the second and third persons of the jussive subjunctive complements the imperative mood in the aorist. Both are treated at 17.1/1.

(ii) The **deliberative** subjunctive (negated by μή) is used exclusively in questions and indicates the uncertainty of the speaker about the future and what must be done (in English we use the verb *to be* followed by an infinitive):

εἴπωμεν ἢ σῑγῶμεν; *Are we to speak or keep silent?*
ποῖ φύγω μητρὸς χέρας; *Where am I to escape my mother's hands?*

(b) *Optative in main clauses*

The two uses of the optative in main clauses, to express a future wish and to express a future potential, are complemented by the indicative, which is used for both constructions in the present and past. For this reason we shall treat all forms of wishes at 21.1/1, of conditions at 18.1/5 and of potentials at 19.1/2.

(c) *Subordinate clauses where the subjunctive and optative complement each other*

In three types of subordinate clause the subjunctive is used after a main verb in a primary tense (4.1/1 note 1), the optative after a main verb in a historic tense. This reflects the fact that the subjunctive has primary endings (14.1/2) and the optative has historic endings (14.1/3).

In uses (i) and (ii) both subjunctive and optative can be literally translated by *may* or *might*. In (iii) both are to be translated by an indicative in English:

(i) **Purpose clauses** (negated by μή)
These can be introduced by ἵνα or ὅπως (both conjunctions meaning *in order that*, *so that*). The negative is μή, but a negated purpose clause can also be introduced by μή alone.

ἀποφεύγομεν ἵνα (or ὅπως) οἱ βάρβαροι μὴ ἕλωσιν ἡμᾶς. *We are fleeing so that the barbarians may not capture us.*
ἀπεφύγομεν ἵνα (or ὅπως) οἱ βάρβαροι μὴ ἕλοιεν ἡμᾶς. *We fled so that the barbarians might not capture us.*

In both cases ἵνα/ὅπως . . . μή could be replaced by μή alone at the beginning of the purpose clause (μὴ οἱ βάρβαροι ἕλωσιν/ἕλοιεν ἡμᾶς).

However, the subjunctive is often retained after a historic main verb, as this was regarded as producing a vivid effect (cf. vivid present, see note on 7.2.13 *ll*.7f.). The second of the above examples would then become: ἀπεφύγομεν ἵνα (or ὅπως) οἱ βάρβαροι μὴ ἕλωσιν ἡμᾶς. As English has no way of bringing out the force of the subjunctive here, we must translate as previously.

(ii) **Noun clauses after verbs of fearing** (negated by οὐ)

The most common verb meaning *to fear* is φοβέομαι, which functions as a passive deponent with a middle future (11.1/1 note; it is not a true deponent as we also have an active φοβέω *terrify*). φοβέομαι and other verbs of fearing can be followed by a noun in the accusative: τὸν λέοντα φοβοῦμαι *I fear* (or *am afraid of*) *the lion*. They may also be followed by a clause which performs the same function as a noun (and hence is called a noun clause): *I am afraid that the lion may eat me*. Most (but not all) clauses of this sort have reference to a time subsequent to that of the main verb and in Greek are introduced by μή, which here, and elsewhere when used as a conjunction, can be literally translated by *lest*. The verb in the μή clause is put into the subjunctive after a main verb in a primary tense or into the optative after a main verb in a historic tense. As with purpose clauses, the subjunctive can be retained after a historic tense for a vivid effect.

φοβοῦμαι μὴ ὁ λέων με φάγῃ.   *I am afraid that* (lit. *lest*) *the lion may* (or *will*) *eat me.*

ἐφοβήθην μὴ ὁ λέων με φάγοι (or φάγῃ).   *I was afraid that the lion might* (or *would*) *eat me.*

If the μή clause is negated, the negative is οὐ:

ὁ λέων φοβεῖται μὴ τροφὴν οὐχ εὕρῃ.   *The lion is afraid that he may not find food.*

The noun clause can also have reference to the same time as, or a time anterior to, the verb of fearing. Here μή is followed by the indicative because what is feared either is happening or has happened:

φοβοῦμαι μὴ ὁ λέων τὸν ἐμὸν φίλον νῦν ἐσθίει/τὴν ἐμὴν γυναῖκα ἐχθὲς ἔφαγεν.   *I am afraid that the lion is now eating my friend/ate my wife yesterday.*

Where in English a verb of fearing is followed by an infinitive, Greek has the same construction:

αἱ ψύλλαι οὐ φοβοῦνται φαγεῖν τὸν λέοντα.   *The fleas are not afraid to eat the lion* (or *of eating the lion*).

(iii) **Indefinite subordinate clauses** (negated by μή)

Certain temporal conjunctions (e.g. ἐπεί, ὅτε) may introduce a subordinate clause referring to the present or past and be followed by the indicative. Greek idiom here is very similar to that of English and we have already met examples (e.g. at 7.2.12). These clauses refer to single definite events.

Another type of subordinate clause is that with an indefinite sense and is expressed in English by the addition of *ever*. In *I dislike what he is doing* the subordinate clause refers to a specific thing (viz the thing that he is doing), but in *I dislike whatever he does* the subordinate clause refers to a general class of thing (viz whatever thing he does), and so is called **indefinite**. Such clauses may be adjectival (as above), or adverbial, e.g. *I am going wherever my sister goes* (contrast *I am going to where my sister lives* where the adverbial clause refers to a definite place).

In Greek the construction used for these clauses in **primary sequence** (i.e. when the main verb is in a primary tense) is similar. The particle ἄν, which here[1] is the equivalent of *ever*, is added to the subordinate clause but in addition its verb is put into the subjunctive. ἄν coalesces with certain conjunctions, e.g. ὅταν (= ὅτε + ἄν) *whenever*, ἐπειδάν (= ἐπειδή + ἄν) *whenever*. Examples of indefinite clauses in primary sequence are:

ὅταν τις κλέπτῃ, ζημιοῦται. *Whenever anyone steals he is punished.*
πράττουσιν ἃ ἂν βούλωνται. *They do whatever they want [to do].*

Compare the above with the definite relative clause in the following:

πράττουσιν ἃ βούλονται. *They are doing [the things] which they want [to do].*

Because we can never be completely certain of what is going to happen in the future, the construction of ἄν + subjunctive is very common in subordinate temporal clauses with a future reference (cf. 18.1/5). Often English idiom does not require us to translate ἄν:

ἡ Δίκη μάρψει τοὺς κακοὺς ὅταν τύχῃ. *Justice will seize the wicked men when* (lit. *whenever*) *she finds [them].*

For indefinite subordinate clauses in **historic sequence** the optative **without** ἄν is used (we do **not** have the option of the primary construction as in (i) and (ii) above):

ὁ Κῦρος ἐθήρευεν ἀπὸ ἵππου ὁπότε γυμνάσαι βούλοιτο ἑαυτὸν καὶ τοὺς ἵππους. *Cyrus used to hunt from horseback whenever* (or simply *when*) *he wanted to exercise himself and his horses.*

The negative for all indefinite clauses is μή:

ὁ μῶρος γελᾷ καὶ ὅταν τι μὴ γέλοιον ᾖ. *Fools laugh* (lit. *the fool laughs*) *even when something is not funny.*

(d) Optative in indirect speech

The optative has two further uses in subordinate clauses, one of which we shall deal with here (for the other see 18.1/5).

In indirect speech which is introduced by a verb in a historic tense (*he said that . . . ; he asked if . . .* etc.) all finite verbs **may** be put into the optative. There is no change in sense, and optatives of this sort are translated as indicatives:

---

[1] ἄν has an entirely different force when used in a main clause (18.1/5).

ὁ Κλέανδρος εἶπεν ὅτι Δέξιππον οὐκ ἐπαινοίη (or ind. ἐπαινεῖ). *Cleander said that he did not commend Dexippus* (original: Δέξιππον οὐκ ἐπαινῶ *I do not commend Dexippus*).

εἶπεν ὅτι κατίδοι (or κατεῖδε, < καθοράω) στράτευμα. *He said that he had caught sight of an army* (original: κατεῖδον στράτευμα *I caught sight of an army*; on the use of the English pluperfect *had caught* see 16.1/2).

Ξενοφῶν οὐκ ἤρετο τί τὸ πάθος εἴη (or ἐστίν). *Xenophon did not ask what the misfortune was* (original: τί ἐστι τὸ πάθος; *what is the misfortune?*).

Finite verbs in indirect speech always retain the tense of the original direct speech (8.1/3*b*), and consequently the distinction between the present and aorist optative here involves time, **not** aspect, as the above examples show.

A verb in a future tense in direct speech can be put into the future optative when reported in historic sequence:

εἶπον ὅτι τοῦτο ποιήσοιμι (or ποιήσω). *I said that I would do this* (original: τοῦτο ποιήσω *I shall do this*).

The future optative has no other uses.

Notes

1 When an adverbial clause of reason (introduced by ὅτι *because*, ἐπεί *since*, etc.) occurs after a historic tense its verb is put into the optative if the speaker or writer wishes to ascribe a reason or motive to the subject of the main verb but does not vouch for it himself. This type of expression is called **virtual indirect speech** as no verb of saying, thinking, etc. is actually used. The subordinating conjunction is to be translated by *on the grounds that*, *thinking/saying that*:

οἱ Ἀθηναῖοι τὸν Περικλέᾱ ἐκάκιζον ὅτι στρατηγὸς ὢν οὐκ ἐπεξάγοι. *The Athenians abused Pericles on the grounds that, [though] being general, he did not lead [them] out.*

2 When a deliberative question (τί ποιῶμεν; *what are we to do?*) is reported after a verb in a historic tense its verb may be put into the optative: ἠποροῦμεν τί (or ὅτι) ποιοῖμεν *we were at a loss [as to] what we should do.* The subjunctive may, however, be retained.

14.2 Greek reading

In addition to translating, define each use of the subjunctive and optative.

1# ἔνεστι γάρ τις καὶ λόγοισιν ἡδονή,
   λήθην ὅταν ποιῶσι τῶν ὄντων κακῶν.

2# πῶς οὖν μάχωμαι θνητὸς ὢν θείᾳ τύχῃ;

3# νοῦν χρὴ θεᾶσθαι, νοῦν· τί τῆς εὐμορφίας
   ὄφελος, ὅταν τις μὴ καλὰς φρένας ἔχῃ;

4 ὃς ἂν δὶς ναυαγήσῃ, μάτην μέμφεται Ποσειδῶνα.

5 Cωκράτης ἔφη τοὺς μὲν πολλοὺς ἀνθρώπους ζῆν ἵνα ἐςθίωςιν, αὐτὸς δὲ ἐςθίειν ἵνα ζῇ.

6 φάγωμεν καὶ πίωμεν· αὔριον γὰρ ἀποθνήκομεν.

7# θεὸς αἰτίαν φύει βροτοῖς ὅταν κακῶσαι δῶμα παμπήδην θέλῃ.

8# ὡς χαρίεν ἐςτὶ ἄνθρωπος ὅταν ἄνθρωπος ᾖ.

9# Α. τίς ἐςθ' οὗτος; Β. ἰατρός. Α. ὡς κακῶς ἔχει ἅπας ἰατρός, ἐὰν κακῶς μηδεὶς ἔχῃ.

10# σφόδρ' ἐςτὶν ἡμῶν ὁ βίος οἴνῳ προσφερής· ὅταν ᾖ τὸ λοιπὸν μικρόν, ὄξος γίγνεται.

11 οἱ μὲν φοβούμενοι μὴ φύγωςι πατρίδα καὶ οἱ μέλλοντες μάχεςθαι φοβούμενοι μὴ ἡττηθῶςιν οὔτε ςίτου οὔτε ὕπνου δύνανται λαγχάνειν διὰ τὸν φόβον· οἱ δὲ ἤδη φυγάδες, ἤδη δὲ ἡττηθέντες δύνανται καὶ μᾶλλον τῶν εὐδαιμόνων ἐςθίειν καὶ καθεύδειν.

12 πίθηκος ὁ πίθηκος κἂν (= καὶ ἐὰν) χρυςᾶ ἔχῃ ςάνδαλα.

13 ἐφοβήθηςαν οἱ Ἕλληνες μὴ προςάγοιεν οἱ Πέρςαι πρὸς τὸ κέρας καὶ περιπτύξαντες ἀμφοτέρωθεν αὐτοὺς κατακόψειαν.

14 ὁ δὲ ἀνήρ, ὃν ςυνέλαβον, ἐρωτώμενος ποδαπὸς εἴη, Πέρςης μὲν ἔφη εἶναι, πορεύεςθαι δ' ἀπὸ τοῦ Τιριβάζου στρατεύματος ὅπως ἐπιτήδεια λάβοι.

15 ὁ Διογένης, ἰδὼν τοξότην ἀφυῆ, παρὰ τὸν σκοπὸν ἐκάθιςεν εἰπών, ἵνα μὴ πληγῶ.

16# τοῦ θανεῖν ἀπειρίᾳ πᾶς τις φοβεῖται φῶς λιπεῖν τόδ' ἡλίου.

17 ἔτρεχέ τις μὴ βρεχθείη καὶ εἰς βόθρον ἀπεπνίγη.

18 ἅμα δὲ τῇ ἡμέρᾳ ςυνελθόντες οἱ στρατηγοὶ ἐθαύμαζον ὅτι Κῦρος οὔτε ἄλλον πέμποι ςημανοῦντα ὅτι χρὴ ποιεῖν, οὔτε αὐτὸς φαίνοιτο. ἔδοξεν οὖν αὐτοῖς ςυσκευαςαμένοις ἃ εἶχον καὶ ἐξοπλιςαμένοις ἰέναι (to go) εἰς τὸ πρόςθεν. ἤδη δὲ ἐν ὁρμῇ ὄντων, ἅμα ἡλίῳ ἀνέχοντι ἦλθε Προκλῆς ὁ Τευθρανίας ἄρχων καὶ Γλοῦς ὁ Ταμῶ. οὗτοι δὲ εἶπον ὅτι Κῦρος μὲν 5 ἀποθάνοι, Ἀριαῖος δὲ ἐν τῷ σταθμῷ εἴη μετὰ τῶν ἄλλων βαρβάρων καὶ λέγοι ὅτι ταύτην τὴν ἡμέραν περιμενοῖεν αὐτούς.

19 εἴ ποτε τοὺς στρατιώτας εὐτάκτως βαδίζοντας ἴδοι, ἐπῄνει.

20# νόμον φοβηθεὶς οὐ ταραχθήςῃ νόμῳ.

Notes

1 *l*.1 ἔνεστι *is in* is followed by the dat. λόγοιςιν. *l*.2 The first two words would be in reverse order in prose; ὄντων (< ὤν) lit. *being*, i.e. *existing*.

3 The pl. φρένες is very often used with the meaning of the singular (here *mind*).

5 τοὺς πολλοὺς ἀνθρώπους *most people, the majority of people* (cf. note on ποῖς πολλοῖς in 8.2.11 and on τὰ πολλά in 13.3(i)*l*.13).

7   φύει here *plant*; βροτοῖс *in mortals* (dat. to express place where, 23.1/2*n*); take παμπήδην with κακῶсαι (*ruin completely*).

8   ὡс exclamatory *how* (also in 9, see 22.1/1*a*(ii)); χαρίεν (n.) lit. *charming thing*; ἄνθρωποс crasis for ὁ ἄνθρωποс, 11.1/5 (the general class is meant); ἄνθρωποс, i.e. *a [real] human being*.

9   A and B hold this conversation on seeing a destitute doctor; A's second remark plays on two possible meanings of κακῶс ἔχω (*a*) *I am destitute*, (*b*) *I am sick* (on ἔχω+adv. to express a state see note on 8.2.9 *l*. 1).

11   φεύγω+acc. here means *go/be in exile from* (17.1/5); λαγχάνειν (+gen., lit. *get*) should be translated *take* (the men spoken of can obtain food and have time for sleep, but their fear prevents them from taking either); δύνανται on deponents in -αμαι see 19.1/3*b*; μᾶλλον+gen. *more than* (genitive of comparison 17.1/4*a*).

13   προсάγω is here used intransitively, *advance*.

14   сυνέλαβον (< сυλλαμβάνω) take as 3rd pl., not as 1st s.

15   εἰπών coincidental use of the aorist pple. (12.1/1); πληγῶ 1st s. aor. subj. pass. of πλήττω.

17   The pass. of βρέχω means *to get wet*; εἰс illustrates the pregnant use of prepositions (see on 9.2.13 *l*.11)—the person must have fallen **into** the hole before drowning **in** it. Consequently εἰс βόθρον is to be translated by *in a hole*.

18   *ll*.2f. πέμποι and φαίνοιτο opt. in indirect speech 14.1/4*d*; сημανοῦντα fut. pple. to express purpose, 12.1/2*a*(v); ὅτι here the indirect interrogative pronoun (10.1/2*b* note 1), trans. *what*; ἔδοξεν (< δοκέω) αὐτοῖс *it seemed good to them*, i.e. *they decided* (21.1/4*a*).   *ll*.3f. εἰс τὸ πρόсθεν *to the in front [place]*, i.e. *forward*; ὄντων is the pple. of a genitive absolute in which the subject (αὐτῶν) is omitted, lit. *[they] being already at the point of starting* (ὁρμῇ); ἦλθε is singular because it agrees with the nearer subject (Προκλῆс) only.   *l*.5 ὁ Ταμῶ *the son of Tamos* (Ταμώс, which is declined like νεώс 13.1/1*a*), for this use of the definite article see 5.1/3 note 2.   *l*.7 περιμενοῖεν the fut. opt. represents a fut. ind. in direct speech (14.1/4*d*).

19   As the optative in itself makes the εἰ clause indefinite (14.1/4*c*(iii)), ποτέ is really superfluous.

20   ταραχθήсῃ 2nd s. fut. ind. pass. of ταράττω.

Unit 15

15.1 Grammar

15.1/1 Perfect indicative active

The perfect tense in both Greek and English expresses a present state resulting from an action in the past. κέκλεικα τὴν θύραν *I have closed the door* means that the door is now closed as a result of my past action of closing it. The aorist ἔκλεισα τὴν θύραν *I closed the door* describes a single past action, but tells us nothing about the present state of the door, not even whether it is still in existence. Because the perfect tense describes a present state it is classified as a **primary** tense (4.1/1 note 1). The perfect is by no means as common as the aorist and does not exist in every Greek verb.

There are two types of the perfect active, called **weak** and **strong**; only in the few verbs with both is there a difference in meaning (see note 2). There is a common set of endings (in the indicative -α, -ας, -ε(ν), -αμεν, -ατε, -ᾱσι(ν)), but, whereas the strong perfect, like the strong aorist, has no suffix, the weak perfect has a suffixed κ which is attached in a way similar to that of the ς of the weak aorist (see below).

The stem of the perfect is normally modified by **reduplication**. Thus if a verb begins with a single consonant (except ρ) or with two consonants of which the second is λ, μ, ν, or ρ, the initial consonant is doubled with the insertion of ε; hence **weak** λέλυκα (λύω) *I have loosened*; πεπίστευκα (πιστεύω) *I have trusted*; κέκλεικα (κλείω) *I have closed*; **strong** γέγραφα (γράφω) *I have written*. When, however, the initial consonant is an aspirate (θ, φ, χ), it is reduplicated in its unaspirated form; τεθήρᾱκα (θηράω) *I have hunted*; πεφόνευκα (φονεύω) *I have murdered*; κεχόρευκα (χορεύω) *I have danced*.

In other cases the perfect stem is not reduplicated but simply augmented by the **temporal augment** (4.1/1 note 2(ii)) for verbs with an initial vowel or diphthong: ἦχα (ἄγω) *I have led*; ᾕρηκα (αἱρέω) *I have captured* (see also note 3); or by the **syllabic augment** (4.1/2 note 2(i)) for verbs beginning with ρ, a double consonant (ζ, ξ, ψ), or two consonants (the second not being λ, μ, ν, ρ): ἔρρῑφα (ῥίπτω) *I have thrown*; ἐζήτηκα (ζητέω) *I have sought*; ἔκτικα (κτίζω) *I have founded*.

The conjugation of λέλυκα (perf. ind. act. of λύω) will be found in **Appendix 1**. An example of a strong perfect is ἔρρῑφα (ῥίπτω *throw*), which is conjugated: ἔρρῑφα, ἔρρῑφας, ἔρρῑφε(ν), ἐρρίφαμεν, ἐρρίφατε, ἐρρίφᾱσι(ν).

The weak perfect occurs mostly in:

(a) stems ending in vowels or diphthongs. Here the κ suffix is added to the present stem: κέκλεικα (κλείω). As in the aorist, the final vowel of most contracted verbs is lengthened: δεδήλωκα (δηλόω)

(b) stems ending in λ and ρ, where the κ suffix must be added to the original stem (i.e. the present stem stripped of any suffix, cf. 11.1/3): ἤγγελκα (ἀγγέλλω, i.e. ἀγγέλ-yω); ἦρκα (αἴρω, i.e. ἄρ-yω)

(c) dental stems (6.1/4), where the final dental is lost before the κ suffix: πέπεικα (πείθω); κεκόμικα (κομίζω, stem κομιδ-).

The strong perfect occurs in palatal and labial stems: πέφευγα (φεύγω); γέγραφα (γράφω). Often a final unaspirated consonant is aspirated (i.e. γ/κ > χ; β/π > φ): πέπρᾱχα (πρᾱ́ττω stem πραγ-); τέτριφα (τρῑ́βω *rub*, stem τριβ-). In many strong perfects an ε in the present stem is changed to ο: λέλοιπα (λείπω); πέπομφα (πέμπω). A few verbs with stems in other consonants have a strong perfect, e.g. γέγονα (γίγνομαι—note change in voice; the verb has another perfect, γεγένημαι, which has the same meaning as γέγονα). For other examples of all types see **Principal parts of verbs**.

Notes

1 The strong perfect of some otherwise transitive verbs has an intransitive sense: ἐγείρω *I wake* (*somebody*) *up* (tr.), ἐγρήγορα (on this form see below note 3) *I have woken up* (intr.), i.e. *I am awake*.

2 πείθω and πρᾱ́ττω each have both a transitive and an intransitive perfect (cf. also ἵστημι 19.1/1):

   transitive: πέπεικα *I have persuaded*; πέπρᾱχα *I have done*.
   intransitive: πέποιθα *I have confidence in* (+dat.), i.e. *I trust*; πέπρᾱγα *I have fared*.

   Note that πέποιθα can be translated by a present tense in English (*I trust*; cf. ἐγρήγορα above). A few other verbs (e.g. ὄλλῡμι, 20.1/1 note 2) follow πείθω and πρᾱ́ττω in having a transitive weak perfect and an intransitive strong perfect.

3 Some verbs which begin with α, ε, ο reduplicate their entire initial syllable in addition to lengthening their original initial vowel:

   ἀκήκοα (ἀκούω—the only common verb in a vowel stem which has a strong perfect)
   ἐγρήγορα (ἐγείρω—the reduplicated syllable ἐγρ- also contains the ρ of the stem).

4 Many perfects are slightly irregular, e.g. βέβληκα (βάλλω); κέκληκα (καλέω); πέπτωκα (πῑ́πτω).

15.1/2 Verbs used with participles

In the sentence Περικλέᾱ εἶδον ἐν τῇ ἀγορᾷ βαδίζοντα *I saw Pericles walking in the agora* the participle is not used in any of the ways mentioned in 12.1/2, where participles qualify either the finite verb of their clause or the clause itself. Here βαδίζοντα gives us further information (*I not only saw Pericles—I saw him **walking***; cf. ex. in 12.2.17 *l*.2) and is called a **supplementary participle**. Participles can only be used in this way with verbs whose meaning permits it (as ὁράω in Greek and *see* in English). Such verbs can generally be classified according to their meaning. With some the accompanying participle may occur in a case other than the accusative.

(*a*) Verbs of **knowing** and **perceiving**, e.g. ἐπίσταμαι (present tense as for δύναμαι, 19.1/3*b*) *know*; γιγνώσκω *recognise*; ὁράω *see*; αἰσθάνομαι *perceive*; πυνθάνομαι *ascertain*; ἀκούω *hear*; μανθάνω *learn*.

τῶν στρατιωτῶν τις εἶδε Κλέαρχον διελαύνοντα. *One of the soldiers saw Clearchus riding through.*

ἤκουσαν αὐτοῦ βοῶντος. *They heard him shouting* (genitive because ἀκούω is followed by the genitive of the person heard—13.1/2*a*(iii)).

These verbs can also be followed by a noun clause introduced by ὅτι (8.1/3*b*):

ὁ Δωριεὺς εὖ ἠπίστατο ὅτι (αὐτὸς) σχήσει τὴν βασιλείᾱν. *Dorieus knew well that he (himself) would obtain the kingship.*

All such ὅτι clauses can, however, be converted to a participial phrase. When the subject of the participle is the same as the subject of the finite verb (as in the converted form of the above example), the participle is naturally put into the nominative; the subject itself will only be expressed if emphasis is required (normally some form of αὐτός; cf. nominative and infinitive, 8.1/3*a*):

ὁ Δωριεὺς εὖ ἠπίστατο (αὐτὸς) σχήσων τὴν βασιλείᾱν (the meaning is the same as above).

When the subject of the participle is **not** the same as that of the finite verb both the participle and its subject are put into the accusative:

ἔμαθε τὴν Χερρόνησον πόλεις ἕνδεκα ἢ δώδεκα ἔχουσαν. *He learnt that the Chersonese had eleven or twelve cities* (= ὅτι ἡ Χερρόνησος ἔχει . . .)

Verbs of **knowing** and **learning** can also be followed by an **infinitive**, but in the sense of *know/learn how to* . . .

ἐπίσταμαι νεῖν. *I know how to swim.*

(*b*) Verbs of **beginning, stopping, continuing**, e.g. ἄρχομαι (mid.) *begin* (doing something; the middle is more common the active in this use); παύω *stop* (someone doing something); παύομαι (mid.) *stop* (doing something oneself); διατελέω *continue*. With such verbs in English we have sometimes a participle, sometimes an infinitive.

ὁ ἄνεμος ἐπαύσατο θύων.   *The wind stopped raging.*

μόνοι Θρᾳκῶν διατελοῦσιν ὄντες ἐλεύθεροι.   *Alone of the Thracians they continue to be free.*

γελῶντας ἐχθροὺς παύσομεν τῇ νῦν ὁδῷ.   *With our present journey we will stop our enemies laughing.*

ἄρχομαι regularly takes a participle: ἄρξομαι διδάσκων *I shall begin teaching*. However, as with the English *begin*, an infinitive is also found: ἦρξαντο οἰκοδομεῖν *they began to build*.

(c) Verbs of **emotion**, e.g. ἥδομαι, χαίρω both *be pleased, take pleasure*; ἄχθομαι *be vexed*; αἰσχύνομαι *be ashamed*.

ἥδομαι ἀκούων σου φρονίμους λόγους. *I am pleased to hear wise words from you.*

οὐκ αἰσχύνῃ εἰς τοιαῦτα ἄγων τοὺς λόγους; *Aren't you ashamed at bringing the argument to such a point?* (lit. *to such things*).

αἰσχύνομαι may also be followed by an infinitive in the sense *be ashamed to* do something (and therefore not do it):

αἰσχύνομαί σε προσβλέπειν ἐναντίον. *I am ashamed to look at you straight in the face.*

Verbs of emotion may be followed by ὅτι and a finite verb with the same sense as their use with a participle. The first example above could be ἥδομαι ὅτι ἀκούω ... (lit. *I am pleased that I hear ...*). They are followed by the dative in clauses such as Πηνελοπείᾳ ἄχθομαι *I am annoyed with Penelope*.

(d) φαίνομαι *seem, be seen, be obvious*. Although φαίνομαι with an infinitive has the expected meaning *seem* (to be doing something), with a participle it means the same as δῆλός/φανερός εἰμι + participle, viz *I am obviously* (doing something).

φαίνονται οὐδὲν λέγειν.   *They seem to be speaking nonsense* (lit. *saying nothing*).

φαίνονται οὐδὲν λέγοντες.   *They are obviously speaking nonsense* (lit. *they, saying nothing, are obvious*).

(e) τυγχάνω *chance, happen* (to be doing something, i.e. *by chance I am [doing something]*; there is an etymological connection with τύχη *chance, fortune*). τυγχάνω is often used with a participle to express the idea that something has occurred fortuitously.[1]

ἔτυχε τότε ἐλθών.   *He happened to have come then* (lit. *he chanced having come then*).

δηλώσω τὸ πᾶν ὃ παρὰ τοῦδε τυγχάνω μαθών.   *I shall reveal the whole [matter] which I happen to have learnt from this man.*

---

[1] This verb must be distinguished from γίγνομαι, which means *happen* in the sense of *take place* (for its range of meanings see 8.1/2).

(*f*) λανθάνω *escape the notice of* (+acc.) and φθάνω *anticipate, be beforehand* can also be accompanied by a participle agreeing with their subject (in this construction they generally, but not always, have an object). As the main idea is contained in the participle, this will become the finite verb of the clause in an idiomatic translation.

πάντας λανθάνει δάκρυα λείβων.   *He sheds tears without anyone knowing* (lit. *he [in] shedding tears escapes the notice of all*).

Μενέλεως ἡμᾶς ἔλαθε παρών.   *Menelaus was present without us knowing* (lit. *Menelaus [in] being present escaped the notice of us*).

ἔφθασαν τὸν χειμῶνα ἀνασπάσαντες τὰς ναῦς.   *They hauled up their ships before winter* (lit. *they [in] hauling up their ships anticipated the winter*).

ἔφθασαν οἱ Cκύθαι τοὺς Πέρcᾱς ἐπὶ τὴν γέφῡραν ἀφικόμενοι.   *The Scythians arrived at the bridge before the Persians* (lit. *The Scythians [in] arriving at the bridge anticipated the Persians*).

The difference here between the present and aorist participle is one of **aspect**, not of time. A present participle indicates a **condition** or **process** (first and second examples), an aorist participle indicates an **event** (third and fourth examples). Cf. 12.1/1 and, for a similar distinction between the present and aorist infinitive, 4.1/1.

In sentences of this type it is, in fact, immaterial whether λανθάνω/φθάνω appear as the finite verb with an accompanying participle (as above), or as the participle (always aorist; the participle here has no temporal force) with an accompanying finite verb. Thus in the first and third examples we could have, with identical meanings:

πάντας λαθὼν δάκρυα λείβει (lit. *escaping the notice of all, he sheds tears*).

φθάσαντες οἱ Cκύθαι τοὺς Πέρcᾱς ἐπὶ τὴν γέφῡραν ἀφίκοντο (lit. *the Scythians, anticipating the Persians, arrived at the bridge*).

15.2   Greek reading

1   cποδὸν φεύγων εἰς πῦρ ἐμπέπτωκα.

2   οὐδεὶς λανθάνει θεοὺς πονηρὰ ποιῶν.

3   καρκίνος ὀρθὰ βαδίζειν οὐ μεμάθηκεν.

4# ἅπαντές ἐcμεν εἰς τὸ νουθετεῖν cοφοί,
   αὐτοὶ δ' ἁμαρτάνοντες οὐ γιγνώcκομεν.

5   εἴληφεν ἡ παγὶς τὸν μῦν.

6# ἀνὴρ γὰρ ὅcτις ἥδεται λέγων ἀεί,
   ἔλαθεν ἑαυτὸν τοῖς cυνοῦcιν ὢν βαρύς.

7   cκορπίους βέβρωκεν.

8# ὅcτις καθ' ἑτέρου δόλια μηχανεύεται,
   αὐτὸς καθ' αὑτοῦ λανθάνει ποιῶν.

9 ἔτυχον ἐν τῇ ἀγορᾷ οἱ ὁπλῖται καθεύδοντες.

10 Μένων δῆλος ἦν ἐπιθυμῶν πλουτεῖν ἰσχυρῶς.

11 **The crucifixion of Jesus**

παρέλαβον οὖν τὸν Ἰησοῦν· καὶ βαστάζων ἑαυτῷ τὸν σταυρὸν ἐξῆλθεν εἰς τὸν λεγόμενον Κρανίου Τόπον, ὃ λέγεται ἑβραϊστὶ Γολγοθα, ὅπου αὐτὸν ἐσταύρωσαν, καὶ μετ' αὐτοῦ ἄλλους δύο ἐντεῦθεν καὶ ἐντεῦθεν, μέσον δὲ τὸν Ἰησοῦν. ἔγραψεν δὲ καὶ τίτλον ὁ Πιλᾶτος καὶ ἔθηκεν (placed [it]) ἐπὶ τοῦ σταυροῦ, ΊΗϹΟΥϹ Ὁ ΝΑΖΩΡΑΙΟϹ Ὁ ΒΑϹΙΛΕΥϹ ΤΩΝ ἸΟΥΔΑΙΩΝ. τοῦτον οὖν τὸν τίτλον πολλοὶ ἀνέγνωσαν τῶν Ἰουδαίων, ὅτι ἐγγὺς ὁ τόπος τῆς πόλεως ὅπου ἐσταυρώθη ὁ Ἰησοῦς. ἔλεγον οὖν τῷ Πιλάτῳ οἱ ἀρχιερεῖς τῶν Ἰουδαίων, μὴ γράφε (do not write), ὁ βασιλεὺς τῶν Ἰουδαίων, ἀλλ' ὅτι ἐκεῖνος εἶπεν, βασιλεύς εἰμι τῶν Ἰουδαίων. ἀπεκρίθη ὁ Πιλᾶτος, ὃ γέγραφα γέγραφα.

12 ἑπτὰ ἡμέρας, ἃς ἐπορεύοντο διὰ τῶν Καρδούχων, πάσας μαχόμενοι διετέλεσαν.

13 Κλέαρετος, παρακαλέσας τοὺς στρατιώτας, ἦγεν ἐπὶ τὸ χωρίον· πορευόμενον δ' αὐτὸν ἔφθασεν ἡμέρα γενομένη.

14 According to Plutarch intellectual pleasures are much superior to those of the body and therefore our reactions to the former are much more enthusiastic.

ὁ Ἀρχιμήδης λουόμενος, ὥς φασιν, ἐκ τῆς ὑπερχύσεως ἐννοήσας τὴν τοῦ στεφάνου μέτρησιν, οἷον ἔκ τινος κατοχῆς ἢ ἐπιπνοίας, ἐξήλατο βοῶν, εὕρηκα, καὶ τοῦτο πολλάκις φθεγγόμενος ἐβάδιζεν. οὐδενὸς δ' ἀκηκόαμεν οὔτε γαστριμάργου οὕτως περιπαθῶς βοῶντος, βέβρωκα, οὔτε ἐρωτικοῦ, πεφίληκα, μυρίων ἀκολάστων γενομένων καὶ ὄντων.

15# A. γεγάμηκε δήπου. B. τί σὺ λέγεις; ἀληθινῶς γεγάμηκεν, ὃν ἐγὼ ζῶντα περιπατοῦντά τε κατέλιπον;

16 τὸ δὲ μέγα τεῖχος ἐπαύσαντο οἰκοδομοῦντες φοβούμενοι μὴ οὐχ ἱκανὸν εἴη ἀντέχειν.

17# ὁρῶ δὲ τοῖς πολλοῖσιν ἀνθρώποις ἐγὼ τίκτουσαν ὕβριν τὴν πάροιθ' εὐπραξίαν.

Notes

3 ὀρθά acc. n. pl. used adverbially (= ὀρθῶς, cf. 20.1/5).

4 εἰς with respect to.

6 ἀνὴρ . . . ὅστις lit. whatever man (ὅστις is here the indefinite relative—10.1/2b note 2) but translate the man who; ἔλαθεν gnomic aor.; translate by present; συνοῦσι dat. pl. m. of the pres. pple. of σύνειμι.

9 As the subject is plural ἔτυχον must be 3rd pl.

10 δῆλος ἦν ἐπιθυμῶν lit. was obvious desiring, i.e. it was obvious/clear that M. desired.

11 *l*.2. Γολγοθα has no accent because it is not a Greek word. *l*.3 ἐντεῦθεν
καὶ ἐντεῦθεν lit. *from here and from there*, i.e. *on each side*. *ll*.6f. Take
πολλοί with τῶν Ἰουδαίων and ἐγγύς with τῆς πόλεως. *l*.8 ἔλεγον *said*
the imperfect is used because the subject is an unspecified number of
individuals. *l*.9 ὅτι is used redundantly to introduce what the chief
priests tell Pilate he should write (cf. 8.1/3*b* note 2).

13 ἦγεν inceptive imperfect *began to lead*.

14 The famous story of Archimedes' discovery of the principle of
displacement (when two bodies of the same weight are submerged they
will displace the same amount of liquid only if they are of identical
composition). Using this he was able to establish that his patron, Hiero
of Syracuse, had been cheated by a jeweller who had been commissioned
to make a crown of pure gold (the crown did not displace the same
volume of water as the amount of gold of exactly equal weight). *ll*.3ff.
ἐβάδιζεν impf. to express repeated action *went about*; οὐδενὸς . . .
οὔτε . . . οὔτε lit. *of no-one . . . neither . . . nor* but translate *neither of
any . . . nor of any . . .*; ἀκηκόαμεν royal (or author's) plural. *l*.5
ἀκολάστων the adj. (*unrestrained, licentious*) is here used as a noun
(*sensualist*).

16 φοβούμενοι μὴ οὐχ . . . see 14.1/4*c*(ii).

17 τοῖς πολλοῖς *for the majority* (cf. 8.2.11); ὕβριν is governed by τίκτουσαν,
which agrees with εὐπρᾱξίᾱν; πάροιθ'(ε) is an adv. but translate by an
adj. *former*.

15.3 Extra reading –
Prometheus Bound (1)

This is the first of two passages from *Prometheus Bound*, a play of the first
great Attic tragedian, Aeschylus (525–456 BC). Its plot, like that of nearly all
tragedies, is taken from mythology.

Prometheus, who belonged to an older but minor order of divinities called
Titans, had helped Zeus wrestle supreme control of heaven from his father
Cronus. At this stage mankind lived in primitive squalor, but Prometheus
took pity on them and gave them fire. This he was obliged to steal from
heaven as it had been the exclusive possession of the gods. Zeus, incensed by
the theft, ordered that Prometheus be fastened to a rock at the ends of the
earth. In the following scene, with which the play opens, Zeus' henchman
Κράτος (*Might*), who with his fellow lackey Βία (*Violence*) has escorted
Prometheus to the rock, tells Hephaestus to execute Zeus' command.

ΚΡΑΤΟΣ

    χθονὸς μὲν εἰς τηλουρὸν ἥκομεν πέδον,
    Σκύθην ἐς οἶμον, ἄβροτον εἰς ἐρημίαν.
    Ἥφαιστε, σοὶ δὲ χρὴ μέλειν ἐπιστολὰς

130   *Unit Fifteen*

ἅς σοι πατὴρ ἐφεῖτο (*enjoined on*), τόνδε πρὸς πέτραις
ὑψηλοκρήμνοις τὸν λεωργὸν ὀχμάσαι   5
ἀδαμαντίνων δεσμῶν ἐν ἀρρήκτοις πέδαις.
τὸ σὸν γὰρ ἄνθος, παντέχνου πυρὸς σέλας,
θνητοῖς κλέψας ὤπασεν. τοιᾶςδέ τοι
ἁμαρτίας ςφε δεῖ θεοῖς δοῦναι (*to give*, i.e. *to pay*) δίκην,
ὡς ἂν διδαχθῇ τὴν Διὸς τυραννίδα   10
στέργειν, φιλανθρώπου δὲ παύεςθαι τρόπου.

ἩΦΑΙϹΤΟϹ

Κράτος Βία τε, ϲφῶν μὲν ἐντολὴ Διὸς
ἔχει τέλος δὴ κοὐδὲν ἐμποδὼν ἔτι,
ἐγὼ δ' ἄτολμός εἰμι ϲυγγενῆ θεὸν
δῆσαι βίᾳ φάραγγι πρὸς δυϲχειμέρῳ.   15
πάντως δ' ἀνάγκη τῶνδέ μοι τόλμαν ϲχεθεῖν·
εὐωριάζειν γὰρ πατρὸς λόγους βαρύ.
τῆς ὀρθοβούλου Θέμιδος αἰπυμῆτα παῖ,
ἄκοντά ϲ' ἄκων δυϲλύτοις χαλκεύμαϲι
προσπαϲϲαλεύϲω τῷδ' ἀπανθρώπῳ πάγῳ,   20
ἵν' οὔτε φωνὴν οὔτε του μορφὴν βροτῶν
ὄψῃ, σταθευτὸς δ' ἡλίου φοίβῃ φλογὶ
χροιᾶς ἀμείψεις ἄνθος· ἀϲμένῳ δέ ϲοι
ἡ ποικιλείμων νὺξ ἀποκρύψει φάος
πάχνην θ' ἑῴαν ἥλιος ϲκεδᾷ (*will scatter*) πάλιν·   25
ἀεὶ δὲ τοῦ παρόντος ἀχθηδὼν κακοῦ
τρύϲει ϲ', ὁ λωφήϲων γὰρ οὐ πέφυκέ πω.

Notes

*ll.*1f. In poetry the demonstrative adjective, as well as the definite article, can
be omitted, and in English we would supply *this* with πέδον, οἶμον and
ἐρημίαν; take Ϲκύθην with οἶμον and ἄβροτον with ἐρημίᾶν.   *l.*3 δέ is here
used idiomatically in a clause following a vocative and should not be
translated; ἐπιϲτολᾱς is the subject of μέλειν (which governs the dative
ϲοί).   *l.*4 πατήρ, i.e. Zeus, whom Homer calls *father of gods and men.   l.*5
ὀχμάϲαι aor. inf., to be taken after ἐπιϲτολᾱς which it explains.   *l.*7 ἄνθος
flower but here metaphorically *glory, pride*; παντέχνου lit. *[required] for all
arts* because fire was seen as necessary for any technological progress.   *ll.*8f.
θνητοῖϲι = θνητοῖϲ (3.1/1 note 3); κλέψᾱς ὤπαϲεν lit. *having stolen . . . he
gave [it]*; τοιᾶςδέ . . . ἁμαρτίᾱς gen. with δίκην (*penalty for such a wrong*);
ϲφε = αὐτόν, i.e. Prometheus.   *l.*10 ὡς ἄν + subj. expresses purpose
(= ἵνα + subj. 14.1/4*c*(i)).   *l.*11 παύεϲθαι is followed by a gen. (φιλανθρώπου
. . . τρόπου).   *l.*12 ϲφῶν *for you two* (24.1/4).   *l.*13 κοὐδέν = καὶ οὐδέν
(11.1/5).   *l.*15 δῆϲαι aor. inf. act. of δέω bind.   *ll.*16f. supply ἐϲτί with both
ἀνάγκη and βαρύ.   *l.*19 ϲ' = ϲε (also in *l.*27); δυϲλύτοις χαλκεύμαϲι dat. of
instrument (11.1/2).   *l.*20 τῷδ'(ε) ἀπανθρώπῳ πάγῳ *to this . . . the* dat. is

governed by the προς- of προςπαςςαλεύω. *l.*21 ἵν'(α) (+ind.) *where*; του = τινός (10.1/1). *l.*22 ὄψη (< ὁράω) lit. *you will see* is appropriate to μορφήν but not to φωνήν although it governs both—trans. *you will perceive.* *l.*23 χροιᾶς ἀμείψεις ἄνθος *you will alter* (i.e. *lose*) *the bloom* (lit. *flower*) *of [your] skin* (through constant exposure to the sun Prometheus' skin will become tanned and rough); ἀςμένῳ ... ςοι *for you [being] glad* dat. of reference (23.1/2*e*). *l.*25 θ' i.e. τε. *l.*27 ὁ λωφήςων lit. *the [one] going to relieve*; γάρ can be placed after the first phrase rather than the first word; πέφῡκε (perf. of φύω is always intransitive) *has been born.*

Unit 16

16.1 Grammar

16.1/1 Phrases and clauses of result

Result in English is usually expressed by a subordinate clause of the type (*he was so poor*) *that he couldn't buy food*, although in English we may omit *that* and say *he was so poor he couldn't buy food*. In Greek the corresponding conjunction, ὥϲτε *that, so that*, is always expressed. As in English, there is usually an anticipatory word in the main clause such as οὕτωϲ *so, to such an extent*; τοιοῦτοϲ *of this kind, of such a kind*; τοϲοῦτοϲ *so much*, pl. *so many* (on the declension of the last two see note 1 below).

ὥϲτε is usually followed by an **infinitive**, particularly where the result is to be marked as merely contemplated or in prospect and not stressed as a fact (here ὥϲτε is to be translated *as*—see first example). Where the subject of the infinitive is the same as the subject of the main verb, it is normally not expressed; where it is different, it is in the accusative (just as in the infinitive construction of indirect statement (8.1/3)). If the infinitive is negated, the negative is μή:

> οὕτω ϲκαιὸϲ εἶ ὥϲτε μὴ δύναϲθαι μανθάνειν. *You are so stupid as not to be able to understand.*
>
> τοϲαύτην κραυγὴν ἐποίηϲαν ὥϲτε τοὺϲ ταξιάρχουϲ ἐλθεῖν. *They made such a din that the taxiarchs came* (i.e. *such a din as to cause the taxiarchs to come*).

ὥϲτε + infinitive may also express an **intended** result. The distinction between this and a purpose clause can be tenuous:

> τοῦτο ποιοῦϲιν ὥϲτε μὴ ἀποθανεῖν. *They are doing this so as not to die.*

ὥϲτε may also be followed by a finite verb in the **indicative** (negated by οὐ) but only where there is emphasis on the actual occurrence of the result: so οὕτω ϲκαιὸϲ εἶ ὥϲτε οὐ δύναϲαι μανθάνειν would mean *you are so stupid that you [actually] cannot understand*; ἐπέπεϲε χιὼν ἄπλετοϲ ὥϲτε ἀπέκρυψε καὶ τὰ ὅπλα καὶ τοὺϲ ἀνθρώπουϲ *an immense amount of* (lit. *boundless*) *snow fell so that it [actually] covered both the weapons and the men.*

Notes

1 τοιοῦτοϲ and τοϲοῦτοϲ are compounds of οὗτοϲ (9.1/1) and are inflected in the same way, except that the initial τ which οὗτοϲ has in most forms is

dropped: τοιοῦτος, τοιαύτη, τοιοῦτο(ν); τοσοῦτος, τοσαύτη, τοσοῦτο(ν) (unlike τοῦτο, the neuter s. nom. and acc. can end in ν).

2 ὥστε may be used to introduce an independent sentence, with much the same force as οὖν, i.e. *and so, therefore, consequently*:

οὐχ ἧκεν· ὥστε οἱ Ἕλληνες ἐφρόντιζον. *He had not come; consequently, the Greeks were worried.*

3 The English phrase *to such a pitch/point/degree of x* is expressed in Greek by εἰς τοῦτο or εἰς τοσοῦτο(ν)+genitive (cf. 23.1/1*d*):

εἰς τοσοῦτον ὕβρεως ἦλθον ὥστε ἔπεισαν ὑμᾶς ἐλαύνειν αὐτόν. *They reached such a pitch of insolence that they persuaded you to drive him out.*

4 ὥστε may also be used in the sense *on the condition that* to express a condition or proviso:

ὑπέσχοντο ὥστε ἐκπλεῖν. *They made a promise on condition that they should sail away.*

However, *on condition that* is more usually expressed by ἐφ' ᾧ or ἐφ' ᾧτε followed by the infinitive or, less frequently, by the future indicative:

ἐποιήσαντο εἰρήνην ἐφ' ᾧ τὰ μακρὰ τείχη καθελόντες τοῖς Λακεδαιμο-νίοις ἕπεσθαι (or ἕψονται). *They made peace on condition that after taking down the long walls they would follow the Spartans.*

Both the infinitive and future indicative in conditions of this type are negated by μή.

5 For the use of a comparative+ἢ ὥστε, see 17.1/4*c*.

16.1/2 Pluperfect indicative active

The Greek pluperfect exists only in the indicative mood. It is normally to be translated by the same tense in English (*I had washed* before you came) but its use is much more restricted (see below).

The pluperfect is a **historic** tense (4.1/1 note 1) and its active stem is formed from that of the perfect active. Where the latter contains reduplication (15.1/1), the pluperfect active stem is formed by adding the augment, e.g.

PERFECT ACTIVE STEM		PLUPERFECT ACTIVE STEM
λελυκ-	(λύ̄ω)	ἐλελυκ-
γεγραφ-	(γράφω)	ἐγεγραφ-
πεπομφ-	(πέμπω)	ἐπεπομφ-

Where, however, the perfect active stem is already augmented it is also used for the pluperfect without change, e.g. ἦχ- (ἄγω).

The pluperfect active endings are: -η, -ης, -ει(ν), -εμεν, -ετε, -εσαν. For the conjugation of ἐλελύκη *I had loosened* see **Appendix 1**.

The pluperfect is the past version of the perfect and thus expresses a state that existed in the past (cf. 15.1/1):

> ἔθυον πρότερον οἱ Πελασγοὶ τοῖς θεοῖς, ὄνομα δὲ ἐποιοῦντο οὐδενὶ αὐτῶν· οὐ γὰρ ἀκηκόεσάν πω. *Formerly the Pelasgians used to sacrifice to the gods but gave a name to none of them; for they had not yet (πω) heard [their names]* (i.e. they were in a state of ignorance about the names of the gods).

The pluperfect is not common in Greek. In English we often use the pluperfect in subordinate clauses to denote an action which happened two stages back in the past, e.g. *when the soldiers had assembled, Cyrus spoke as follows* (if we regard Cyrus' speaking as one stage back in the past, then the soldiers' assembling, which happened before Cyrus' speaking, is two stages back in the past). Greek, however, normally regards both actions as simple past events and uses two aorists: ἐπεὶ οἱ στρατιῶται cυνῆλθον, Κῦρος ἔλεξε τάδε (lit. *when the soldiers assembled . . .*, which we can also say in English). It would be possible to regard the soldiers as being in a state of having assembled and so justify a Greek pluperfect, but in subordinate clauses of time and reason (and also relative clauses) this is rarely done.

16.1/3 Perfect and pluperfect indicative middle/passive

In both the perfect and pluperfect the middle and passive voices have the same forms.

PERFECT

The stem of the strong perfect active is retained in the middle/passive, but that of the weak perfect active loses its κ. Consequently the distinction between strong and weak perfects is not maintained. As, however, the stem of the perfect middle/passive is not always predictable, the first person perfect indicative middle/passive is included in the principal parts of irregular verbs (7.1/1 note 4 and **Principal parts of verbs**).

When a perfect middle/passive stem ends in a vowel or diphthong,[1] e.g. λέλυ-, νενίκη-, the endings -μαι, -cαι, -ται, -μεθα, -cθε, -νται are added (for the conjugation of λέλυμαι *I have ransomed* (mid.), *I have been loosened* (pass.) see **Appendix 1**).

When a perfect middle/passive stem ends in a consonant, a sound change is necessary in certain cases to assimilate the final consonant of the stem to the initial consonant of the ending. With all consonant stems a succession of three consonants in the second and third plural is avoided; in the second

---

[1] This occurs only in verbs with a weak perfect active where the κ of the stem is preceded by a vowel or diphthong; the strong perfect ἀκήκοα (ἀκούω) has no passive in Classical Greek.

plural the c of the ending (-cθε) is dropped, but in the third plural Attic Greek sidesteps the difficulty by using a two-word periphrasis consisting of the perfect middle/passive participle (see 16.1/4) and the third plural present of εἰμί.

Consonant stems are classified in the same way as for the present tense (6.1/4 and 11.1/3):

(a) Palatal stems

The final palatal of the stem appears as γ before -μαι and -μεθα (and -μένοι of the participle), and as κ before -cαι (giving -ξαι) and -ται. In the second pl. κ + cθε > κθε > χθε (the κ is aspirated to assimilate it to θ). From φυλάττω guard (perf. mid./pass. stem πεφυλακ-) we have:

	S.		PL.	
	1	πεφύλαγμαι		πεφυλάγμεθα
	2	πεφύλαξαι		πεφύλαχθε
	3	πεφύλακται		πεφυλαγμένοι εἰcί(ν)

When these forms are used as passives they mean *I have been guarded, you have been guarded*, etc. When they are used as middles their sense depends on the use of the middle involved in a particular context (8.1/1), i.e. *I have guarded myself*, etc., or *I have guarded for myself*, etc., or *I have had (something) guarded*, etc. The participle used in the third plural varies, of course, in gender according to the subject. This applies to all forms of this type.

(b) Labial stems

The final labial of the stem appears as μ before -μαι and -μεθα (and -μένοι of the participle), and as π before -cαι (giving -ψαι) and -ται. In the second pl. π + cθε > πθε > φθε. From κρύπτω hide (perf. mid./pass. stem κεκρυπ-) we have:

	S.		PL.	
	1	κέκρυμμαι		κεκρύμμεθα
	2	κέκρυψαι		κέκρυφθε
	3	κέκρυπται		κεκρυμμένοι εἰcί(ν)

The passive meaning is *I have been hidden*, etc.

(c) Dental stems

The final dental of the stem becomes c before all endings. In the second person s. and pl. cc > c. From πείθω persuade (perf. mid./pass. stem πεπειθ-) we have:

	S.		PL.	
	1	πέπεισμαι		πεπείσμεθα
	2	πέπεισαι		πέπεισθε
	3	πέπεισται		πεπεισμένοι εἰcί(ν)

The passive meaning is *I have been persuaded*, etc.

(d) Stems in λ, μ, ν, ρ

The final consonant of λ and ρ stems remains unchanged. ἀγγέλλω *announce*, cπείρω *sow* (perf. mid./pass. stems ἤγγελ-, ἔcπαρ-; the α of the latter is irregular) have ἤγγελμαι, ἤγγελcαι etc. and ἔcπαρμαι, ἔcπαρcαι, etc. The final consonant of ν stems is dropped in some verbs, but in others becomes c before -μαι, -μεθα (and -μένοι). From κρίνω *judge*, φαίνω *show* (perf. mid./pass. stems κεκρι-, πεφαν-) we have:

s.	1	κέκριμαι	πέφαcμαι
	2	κέκριcαι	πέφανcαι
	3	κέκριται	πέφανται
PL.	1	κεκρίμεθα	πεφάcμεθα
	2	κέκριcθε	πέφανθε
	3	κεκριμένοι εἰcί(ν)	πεφαcμένοι εἰcί(ν)

The passive meaning is *I have been judged*, etc., *I have been shown*, etc.

η is added to the few μ stems both in the perfect active and in the perfect middle/passive, e.g. νέμω *apportion*, νενέμηκα (act.), νενέμημαι (mid./pass.), 3 pl. νενέμηνται.

PLUPERFECT

The pluperfect indicative middle/passive uses the perfect middle/passive stem except that the syllabic augment is added when the latter is reduplicated, e.g. ἐλελυ- (λύω), ἐπεφυλακ- (φυλάττω); but ἔcπαρ- (cπείρω) is used for both perfect and pluperfect (cf. 16.1/2). The historic middle/passive endings are -μην, -cο, -το, -μεθα, -cθε, -ντο (cf. 8.1/1f). For the conjugation of ἐλελύμην *I had ransomed* (mid.), *I had been loosened* (pass.) see **Appendix 1**. With stems ending in a consonant the same sound changes are involved as with the perfect indicative middle/passive, and the perfect middle/passive participle with ἦcαν is used for the third plural, e.g.

s.	1	ἐπεφυλάγμην	PL.	ἐπεφυλάγμεθα
	2	ἐπεφύλαξο		ἐπεφύλαχθε
	3	ἐπεφύλακτο		πεφυλαγμένοι ἦcαν

The passive meaning is *I had been guarded*, etc.

Note

Third **plural** endings in -αται (< νται) and -ατο (< ντο) occur in early Attic and other dialects, e.g. πεφυλάχαται (perf.—its passive meaning is *they have been guarded*), ἐπεφυλάχατο (plpf.—its passive meaning is *they had been guarded*). These endings must be carefully distinguished from third **singular** endings in -ται and -το.

16.1/4 Other parts of the perfect tense

The perfect infinitives and participles are formed from the same stems as the corresponding indicatives (the reduplication or the temporal/syllabic augment of the perfect indicative stem is **not** dropped). The infinitive endings are -έναι (act.) and -cθαι (mid./pass.; with consonantal stems this ending undergoes the same changes as -cθε). The active participle is a first and third declension adjective (10.1/3) in -ώc, -υῖα, -όc (see below), and the middle/passive participle is a first and second declension adjective (3.1/3) in -μένοc, -μένη, -μένον.[1] In the following table for λύω, φυλάττω, κρύπτω, πείθω, κρῑνω only the masculine forms of the participles are given.

Infinitives		**Participles**	
ACTIVE	MIDDLE/PASSIVE	ACTIVE	MIDDLE/PASSIVE
λελυκέναι	λελύcθαι	λελυκώc	λελυμένοc
to have	mid. *to have*	*having*	mid. *having*
loosened	*ransomed*	*loosened*	*ransomed*
	pass. *to have been*		pass. *having been*
	loosened		*loosened*
πεφυλαχέναι	πεφυλάχθαι	πεφυλαχώc	πεφυλαγμένοc
κεκρυφέναι	κεκρύφθαι	κεκρυφώc	κεκρυμμένοc
πεποιθέναι ⎫		πεποιθώc ⎫	
⎬ πεπεῖcθαι		⎬ πεπειcμένοc[2]	
πεπεικέναι ⎭		πεπεικώc ⎭	
κεκρικέναι	κεκρίcθαι	κεκρικώc	κεκριμένοc

The corresponding forms of the aorist are sometimes to be translated in the same way as those of the perfect, but the meanings and uses of the two tenses are quite distinct. The perfect always expresses a state (on the meaning of the aorist see 4.1/1, 12.1/1).

λελυκώc is declined:

	SINGULAR			PLURAL		
	M.	F.	N.	M.	F.	N.
N.V.	λελυκώc	λελυκυῖα	λελυκόc	λελυκότεс	λελυκυῖαι	λελυκότα
Acc.	λελυκότα	λελυκυῖαν	λελυκόc	λελυκότας	λελυκυῑᾱс	λελυκότα
Gen.	λελυκότοс	λελυκυῑᾱс	λελυκότοс	λελυκότων	λελυκυιῶν	λελυκότων
Dat.	λελυκότι	λελυκυίᾳ	λελυκότι	λελυκόcι(ν)	λελυκυίαιс	λελυκόcι(ν)

Notes
1 A perfect subjunctive and perfect optative exist but are rare. The active is formed by adding to the active stem the endings -ω, -ηс, -η, -ωμεν, -ητε,

[1] The accent of all forms of the perfect middle/passive participle is on the second syllable from the end (paroxytone, see **Appendix 9**, b(v)).
[2] On the two perfect stems of πείθω see 15.1/1 note 2.

-ωσι(ν) (subj., giving λελύκω, etc.) and -οιμι, -οις, -οι, -οιμεν, -οιτε, -οιεν (opt., giving λελύκοιμι, etc.). There are alternative active forms consisting of the perfect active participle and the appropriate part of εἰμί: λελυκὼς ὦ, etc. (subj.); λελυκὼς εἴην, etc. (opt.). In the middle/passive the subjunctive and optative follow the latter pattern (subj. λελυμένος ὦ, etc., opt. λελυμένος εἴην, etc.). For tables see **Appendix 1**.

2 Greek has also a future perfect tense, which expresses a future state. For most verbs it exists only in the passive and is not common. Its stem is formed by adding ς to the perfect middle/passive stem (e.g. λελῦς-), and to this are added the present middle/passive endings, viz λελύςομαι *I shall have been loosened*, λελύςῃ (-ει), λελύςεται, λελυςόμεθα, λελύςεςθε, λελύςονται. The future perfect occurs mostly with verbs whose perfect has a present meaning (19.1/3*a*) and for this reason is not included in **Appendix 1**.

16.2 Greek reading

1 ἐπεὶ δὲ ἐπὶ τὰς ςκηνὰς ἦλθον, οἱ μὲν ἄλλοι περὶ τὰ ἐπιτήδεια ἦςαν, ςτρατηγοὶ δὲ καὶ λοχαγοὶ ςυνῆλθον. καὶ ἐνταῦθα πολλὴ ἀπορία ἦν. ἔνθεν μὲν γὰρ ὄρη ἦν ὑπερύψηλα, ἔνθεν δὲ ὁ ποταμὸς τοςοῦτος ὥςτε μηδὲ τὰ δόρατα ὑπερέχειν πειρωμένοις τοῦ βάθους.

2 ὁ Διογένης, ἐρωτηθεὶς διὰ τί οἱ ἀθληταὶ ἀναίςθητοί εἰςιν, ἔφη ὅτι κρέαςιν ὑείοις καὶ βοείοις ἀνῳκοδόμηνται.

3 γαμεῖν κεκρικότα δεῖ.

4 πάντα τὸν βίον ἐν κινδύνοις διατελοῦμεν ὄντες, ὥςτε οἱ περὶ ἀςφαλείας διαλεγόμενοι λελήθαςιν αὑτοὺς τὸν πόλεμον εἰς ἅπαντα τὸν χρόνον καταςκευάζοντες.

5 κύνα δέρεις δεδαρμένην.

6 οἱ Ποτειδεᾶται προςδεχόμενοι τοὺς Ἀθηναίους ἐςτρατοπεδεύοντο πρὸς Ὀλύνθου ἐν τῷ ἰςθμῷ, καὶ ἀγορὰν ἔξω τῆς πόλεως ἐπεποίηντο. καὶ ςτρατηγὸν μὲν τοῦ πεζοῦ παντὸς οἱ ξύμμαχοι ᾕρηντο Ἀριςτέα, τῆς δὲ ἵππου Περδίκκαν.

7 ἐπεὶ οἱ βάρβαροι ἐκ τῆς χώρας ἀπῆλθον, οἱ Ἀθηναῖοι τὴν ἑαυτῶν πόλιν ἀνοικοδομεῖν παρεςκευάζοντο. τῶν γὰρ οἰκιῶν αἱ μὲν πολλαὶ ἐπεπτώκεςαν, ὀλίγαι δὲ περιῆςαν, ἐν αἷς αὐτοὶ ἐςκήνωςαν οἱ δυνατοὶ τῶν Περςῶν.

8 εἰς ἠκονημένας μαχαίρας ἡ αἴξ ἥκει.

9 καὶ τὴν μὲν νύκτα ἐνταῦθα διήγαγον· ἐπεὶ δ᾽ ἡμέρα ὑπέφαινεν, ἐπορεύοντο ςιγῇ ςυντεταγμένοι ἐπὶ τοὺς πολεμίους· καὶ γὰρ ὁμίχλη ἐγένετο, ὥςτε ἔλαθον ἐγγὺς προςελθόντες.

10 ἔπειτα δὲ καὶ πρὸς ἅπαντας τοὺς μετὰ Δημοςθένους ὁμολογία γίγνεται, ἐφ᾽ ᾧτε μὴ ἀποθανεῖν μηδένα, μήτε βιαίως, μήτε δεςμοῖς, μήτε ςίτου ἐνδείᾳ.

11 Τιρίβαζος εἶπεν ὅτι cπείcαcθαι βούλοιτο ἐφ᾽ ᾧ μήτε αὐτὸс τοὺс
"Ελληνας ἀδικεῖν, μήτ᾽ ἐκείνους καίειν τὰς οἰκίας, λαμβάνειν τε τὰ
ἐπιτήδεια ὧν δέοιντο. ἔδοξε ταῦτα τοῖς στρατηγοῖς καὶ ἐσπείcαντο ἐπὶ
τούτοις.

12 οὐδὲ βουλεύεcθαι ἔτι ὥρα, ὦ Cώκρατες, ἀλλὰ βεβουλεῦcθαι. μία δὲ
βουλή· τῆσδε γὰρ τῆς νυκτὸς πάντα ταῦτα δεῖ πεπρᾶχθαι.

13 οὕτως οὖν οὐ ταὐτόν ἐcτι θάρcος τε καὶ ἀνδρεία· ὥcτε cυμβαίνει τοὺς
μὲν ἀνδρείους θαρραλέους εἶναι, μὴ μέντοι τούς γε θαρραλέους
ἀνδρείους πάντας· θάρcος μὲν γὰρ καὶ ἀπὸ τέχνης γίγνεται ἀνθρώποις
καὶ ἀπὸ θυμοῦ καὶ ἀπὸ μανίας, ὥσπερ ἡ δύναμις, ἀνδρεία δ᾽ ἀπὸ φύσεως
καὶ εὐτροφίας τῶν ψυχῶν γίγνεται.   5

14 οἱ Λακεδαιμόνιοι τὰς σπονδὰς προτέρους λελυκέναι τοὺς Ἀθηναίους
ἡγοῦντο.

15 ἡ αἴξ οὔπω τέτοκεν.

16 Φίλιππος, ὁ πατὴρ τοῦ μεγάλου Ἀλεξάνδρου, φρούριόν τι βουλόμενος
λαβεῖν ὀχυρόν, ὡς ἀπήγγειλαν οἱ κατάσκοποι χαλεπὸν εἶναι παντάπαcι
καὶ ἀνάλωτον, ἠρώτησεν εἰ χαλεπὸν οὕτως ἐcτὶν ὥcτε μηδὲ ὄνον
προσελθεῖν χρυσίον κομίζοντα.

Notes

1 ἦλθον had come (16.1/2); περὶ ... ἦcαν were busy with; πειρωμένοις τοῦ
βάθους lit. *for [them] testing the depth*.

2 ὅτι here *because*; ἀνῳκοδόμηνται < ἀνοικοδόμεω.

3 κεκρικότα agrees with ἄνδρα understood, lit. *it is necessary for a man* ...

4 εἰς + acc. is used here instead of the plain acc. for emphasis (cf. 7.1/7*a*).

6 ᾕρηντο < αἱρέομαι choose (18.1/4); ἡ ἵππος the cavalry.

7 ἐπεπτώκεcαν < πίπτω; αἱ πολλαί the majority, most (cf. 8.2.11 and
15.2.17).

8 ἠκονημένᾱς < ἀκονάω.

9 ὑπέφαινεν, ἐπορεύοντο inceptive imperfects (*began to* . . .).

11 βούλοιτο (and later δέοιντο) opt. in reported speech in historic sequence
(14.1/4*d*); μήτε . . . μήτ᾽ introduce the negated conditions (*that neither
he . . . nor they* . . .); the subject of λαμβάνειν is ἐκείνους from the
previous phrase but note that it is **not** negated; ἔδοξε ταῦτα these things
seemed good.

12 οὐδὲ . . . ἔτι ὥρα supply ἐcτί nor [is it] still [the] time; βεβουλεῦcθαι,
i.e. to have finished deliberating.

13 *l*.1 ταὐτόν the same [thing]; the subject of ἐcτί is θάρcος and ἀνδρείᾱ
(with double subjects the verb may agree only with the nearer one).

14 Take προτέρους with τοὺς Ἀθηναίους, which is the subject of
λελυκέναι.

16 ὡς when; ἐcτίν present tense because in indirect speech Greek always
retains the tense of the original direct speech (7.1/3); Philip cynically
implies that any fort can be captured if a sufficient bribe is offered to a
potential traitor; προcελθεῖν the infinitive here denotes a **possible** result,
could approach.

16.3   Extra reading – Heracles

After an attack of madness, Heracles wakes up to find himself tied to a pillar and surrounded by destruction which he himself has unwittingly perpetrated. The passage is from the *Heracles* of Euripides (485–406 BC), the third of the great Attic tragedians.

> ἔμπνους μέν εἰμι καὶ δέδορχ᾽ ἅπερ με δεῖ,
> αἰθέρα τε καὶ γῆν τόξα θ᾽ ἡλίου τάδε.
> ὡς δ᾽ ἐν κλύδωνι καὶ φρενῶν ταράγματι
> πέπτωκα δεινῷ καὶ πνοὰς θερμὰς πνέω
> μετάρσι᾽, οὐ βέβαια πλευμόνων ἄπο.   5
> ἰδού, τί δεσμοῖς ναῦς ὅπως ὡρμισμένος
> νεανίαν θώρακα καὶ βραχίονα
> πρὸς ἡμιθραύστῳ λαΐνῳ τυκίσματι
> ἧμαι, νεκροῖσι γείτονας θάκους ἔχων;
> πτερωτὰ δ᾽ ἔγχη τόξα τ᾽ ἔσπαρται πέδῳ,   10
> ἃ πρὶν παρασπίζοντ᾽ ἐμοῖς βραχίοσιν
> ἔσῳζε πλευρὰς ἐξ ἐμοῦ τ᾽ ἐσῴζετο.
> οὔ που κατῆλθον αὖθις εἰς Ἅιδου πάλιν,
> Εὐρυσθέως δίαυλον ἐξ Ἅιδου μολών;
> ἀλλ᾽ οὔτε Cισύφειον εἰσορῶ πέτρον   15
> Πλούτωνά τ᾽ οὐδὲ σκῆπτρα Δήμητρος κόρης.
> ἔκ τοι πέπληγμαι· ποῦ ποτ᾽ ὢν ἀμηχανῶ;
> ὠή, τίς ἐγγὺς ἢ πρόσω φίλων ἐμῶν
> δύσγνοιαν ὅστις τὴν ἐμὴν ἰάσεται;

Notes

l.1 δέδορχ᾽ (=-κα) the perfect here is virtually an emphatic present *I really see*.   *ll*.3ff. ὡς ... exclamatory, lit. *how I have fallen in a terrible wave* ... i.e. *into what a terrible wave* ...; μετάρσι᾽(α) ... βέβαια n. acc. pl. used adverbially (20.1/5), lit. *how* (ὡς *l*.3) ... *I breathe warm breaths shallowly, not steadily from my lungs* (Heracles is panting but does not know why); ἄπο on the accent of disyllabic prepositions when they follow the word they govern see note on 11.2.4. *ll*.6f. Take ναῦς ὅπως together *like a ship*; ὡρμισμένος (< ὁρμίζω) *anchored*; νεανίαν here used adjectivally in the sense *sturdy* (not *youthful*, Heracles being no longer young); θώρακα καὶ βραχίονα lit. *with respect to arms and chest* this use of the accusative (called *accusative of respect*, 20.1/5) is used to clarify verbs and adjectives; here the accusatives tell where (i.e. with respect to what parts of his body) Heracles is anchored (ὡρμισμένος).   *l*.9 ἧμαι (19.1/3*b*) *I sit*; θάκους trans. by a singular *seat* (the plural is often used for the singular in verse; cf. τόξα in *l*.10 and σκῆπτρα in *l*.16).   *l*.10 The *winged weapons* (πτερωτὰ ἔγχη) are arrows; ἔσπαρται 3rd s. perf. ind. pass. of σπείρω.   *l*.11 πρίν (here an adverb) *previously, formerly*; παρασπίζοντ᾽(α) governs the following dative, lit. *shielding my arms*.   *l*.12

ἐξ = ὑπό *by.* *l.*14 Eurystheus was the king of Mycenae for whom Heracles had to complete his twelve labours (one of them, the descent to Hades to bring back Cerberus, is referred to here); Εὐρυσθέως δίαυλον lit. *the double course* (i.e. the descent and return) *of* (i.e. *prescribed by*) *Eurystheus*; μολών (aor. pple. of βλώσκω) to be taken with δίαυλον *going [on] the double course* (acc. of spatial extent, 7.1/7*d*). *ll.*15f. Sisyphus was one of the sights of Hades. For his sins on earth he had to push a rock to the top of a hill, but when he reached the summit the rock invariably rolled down and he had to start afresh; οὔτε . . . τ᾽(ε) . . . οὐδέ *neither . . . or* (lit. *and*) *. . . nor yet* (οὐδέ indicates a slight climax). *l.*16 The daughter of Demeter was Persephone, who was the wife of Pluto (= Hades). *l.*17 ἐκ . . . πέπληγμαι = ἐκπέπληγμαι (tmesis, see 12.3.9 *l.*6); ποῦ, etc. lit. *wherever being am I helpless?* but the emphasis is on ὤν and we must translate *wherever am I in my helplessness?*

Unit 17

17.1 Grammar

17.1/1 Imperative mood: commands and prohibitions

The imperative mood is used for **commands**. In Greek it exists in the present and aorist tenses (and also the perfect—see note 4). The stem used is the same as that of the corresponding indicative. As well as second person imperatives (which we have in English), Greek also has imperatives in the **third** person with the meanings given below.

The imperative of λύω is:

Present

		ACTIVE		MIDDLE/PASSIVE		
s.	2	λῦε	*loosen!*	λύου	mid.	*ransom!*
					pass.	*be loosened!*
	3	λῡέτω	*let him loosen!*	λῡέcθω	mid.	*let him ransom!*
					pass.	*let him be loosened!*
PL.	2	λύετε	*loosen!*	λύεcθε	mid.	*ransom!*
					pass.	*be loosened!*
	3	λῡόντων[1]	*let them loosen!*	λῡέcθων	mid.	*let them ransom!*
					pass.	*let them be loosened!*

Aorist

		ACTIVE	MIDDLE	PASSIVE
s.	2	λῦcον	λῦcαι	λύθητι
	3	λῡcάτω	λῡcάcθω	λυθήτω
PL.	2	λύcατε	λύcαcθε	λύθητε
	3	λῡcάντων[1]	λῡcάcθων	λυθέντων[1]

The aorist is usually to be translated in the same way as the present but the two are not interchangeable. The difference, as elsewhere, is one of aspect. The present is used for an action which is seen as going on, in the process of happening or being repeated, the aorist for an action which is seen simply as an event. Sometimes this distinction can be brought out in English by using a verbal periphrasis:

κροῦcον (aor.) ἐκείνην τὴν μυῖαν. *Swat that fly!*
κροῦε (pres.) ἐκείνην τὴν μυῖαν. *Keep swatting that fly!*

[1] Note that these forms can also be the gen. pl. masculine and neuter of the corresponding participles.

Generally the present imperative is used with verbs which in themselves imply continual action, e.g. ϲπεῦδε βραδέωϲ *hasten slowly*, while the aorist imperative is used with verbs which usually (but not necessarily) indicate a single act, e.g. καῦϲον πῦρ ἐν τῇ ἑϲτίᾳ *light a fire in the hearth*.

Prohibitions (negative commands) are expressed with μή, e.g. μὴ πᾶϲι πίϲτευε *do not trust everyone*; μηδεὶϲ τοῦτο ἀγνοείτω *let no-one be unaware of this*, but if the **aorist** aspect is appropriate the mood employed is always the **subjunctive**, not the imperative:

μὴ ἐπὶ δουλείᾱν ἑκὼν ἔλθῃϲ.   *Do not go willingly to slavery.*
μηδεὶϲ θαυμάϲῃ.   *Let no-one be surprised.*

For the other use of this (jussive) subjunctive see 14.1/4a(i).

To express a very strong prohibition οὐ μή and the future indicative is used, e.g. τί ποιεῖϲ; οὐ μὴ καταβήϲει.   *What are you doing? You shall* (or *must*) *not come down.*

Notes
1 The imperative of the strong aorist has the same endings as the present. From μανθάνω (aor. ἔμαθον) the aor. imp. act. is μάθε, μαθέτω, μάθετε, μαθόντων. However, five strong aorist imperatives are irregularly accented on the last syllable in the second person singular: εἰπέ (λέγω), ἐλθέ (ἔρχομαι), εὑρέ (εὑρίϲκω), ἰδέ (ὁράω), λαβέ (λαμβάνω).
2 The imperative of the root aorist (11.1/1) follows that of the aorist passive except that the ending for the 2nd s. is -θι, not -τι: from ἔγνων (γιγνώϲκω) we have γνῶθι, γνώτω, γνῶτε, γνόντων.
3 The present imperative of contracted verbs is regular but, because of contraction, the 2nd s. forms are easily confused:

Active   τίμᾱ (τίμαε)   ποίει (ποίεε)   δήλου (δήλοε)
Mid./pass. τῑμῶ (τῑμάου)   ποιοῦ (ποιέου)   δηλοῦ (δηλόου)

The position of the accent can be important for distinguishing between different forms, e.g. ποίει (imp.), ποιεῖ (ind.).
4 In addition to the present and aorist there is also a perfect imperative. The perfect imperative active consists of the perfect active participle and the imperative of εἰμί (see below note 6), e.g. λελυκὼϲ ἴϲθι (lit. *be in a state of having loosened*); but the perfect imperative middle/passive has single-word forms, e.g. λέλυϲο (lit. *be in a state of having been loosened*). The perfect imperative is rare except in verbs whose perfect has a present meaning (19.1/3a), e.g. μέμνηϲο *remember!* (< μέμνημαι). For these forms of λύ̄ω see **Appendix 1**.
5 The **infinitive** is sometimes used instead of the second person imperative (cf. English *Not to worry*, i.e. *do not worry*): πάντωϲ, ὦ Κριτόβουλε, ἀπαληθεῦϲαι πρὸϲ ἡμᾶϲ. *At any rate, Critobulus, tell the truth to us.*
6 The imperative of εἰμί is ἴϲθι *be!*, ἔϲτω, ἔϲτε, ἔϲτων (or ὄντων). ἴϲθι is also the 2nd s. imperative active of οἶδα (19.1/3a), with the meaning *know!*

7 Some imperatives have a fixed use:

χαῖρε, χαίρετε *hello* or *goodbye* (χαίρω *rejoice*)
ἔρρε, ἔρρετε *be damned! go to hell!* ἐρρέτω *let him/her/it be damned!* (ἔρρω
  go to one's harm)
ἄγε, ἄγετε; φέρε, φέρετε *come on! come now!* (by way of encouragement).

17.1/2 Comparison of adjectives and adverbs

Adjectives (and adverbs) have three degrees: **positive** *bad, sick, wonderful*;
comparative *worse, sicker, more wonderful*; **superlative** *worst, sickest, most
wonderful*. To give the three degrees of an adjective is to **compare** it. Some
adjectives in English are compared regularly (*sick, wonderful*), some
irregularly (*bad*). The same applies in Greek. By far the greater number of
adjectives are compared by the addition of suffixes, and of these Greek has
two sets:

(*a*) **Comparative in -τερος, superlative in -τατος.**
   In this type both the comparative in -τερος (f. -τερᾱ, n. -τερον) and the
   superlative in -τατος (f.-τατη, n.-τατον) are first and second declension
   adjectives (3.1/3). All regularly compared adjectives belong here. The
   way in which -τερος and -τατος are attached to the stem of an adjective
   depends on the class of its positive form:

   (i) First and second declension adjectives (3.1/3) add -οτερος, -οτατος
      if the last syllable of their stem is long, but -ωτερος, -ωτατος if this
      is short (the stem is obtained by subtracting -ος from the nom. m.
      s., e.g. σοφός, stem σοφ-). A syllable is long if it contains either a
      long vowel, or a diphthong, or a short vowel followed by two
      consonants (the second not being λ, μ, ν, or ρ); a syllable is short if
      it contains a short vowel followed by a single consonant (for
      further details see **Appendix 10**). Examples are:

POSITIVE	STEM	COMPARATIVE	SUPERLATIVE
σοφός *wise*	σοφ-	σοφώτερος *wiser*	σοφώτατος *wisest*
δίκαιος *just*	δικαι-	δικαιότερος *more just*	δικαιότατος *most just*
ἐρῆμος *desolate*	ἐρημ-	ἐρημότερος *more desolate*	ἐρημότατος *most desolate*

   Some 1st and 2nd declension adjectives belong to class (*b*) below. A
   few others belong to class (*a*) but are irregular, e.g. φίλος *dear*,
   compar. φιλαίτερος, supl. φιλαίτατος or φίλτατος.
   (ii) Third declension adjectives (10.1/4) with a stem in ον add -εστερος,
      -εστατος, e.g. ἄφρων (stem ἀφρον-) *stupid*, ἀφρονέστερος *more*

stupid, ἀφρονέϲτατοϲ *most stupid.* Those with a stem in εϲ add -τεροϲ, -τατοϲ, e.g. ἀληθήϲ (stem ἀληθεϲ-) *true,* ἀληθέϲτεροϲ, ἀληθέϲτατοϲ.

(iii) First and third declension adjectives (10.1/3) in -ειϲ follow χαρίειϲ, *charming,* χαριέϲτεροϲ, χαριέϲτατοϲ. Some in -υϲ follow γλυκύϲ, *sweet,* γλυκύτεροϲ, γλυκύτατοϲ but most are irregular (see below).

(b) **Comparative in -(ῑ)ων, superlative in -ιϲτοϲ.**

This group, which is much smaller, contains irregular adjectives from all classes. The stem of the positive form is sometimes changed for the other degrees of comparison. The following are the most common examples:

POSITIVE		COMPARATIVE	SUPERLATIVE
ἀγαθόϲ	*good*	ἀμείνων	ἄριϲτοϲ
		βελτίων	βέλτιϲτοϲ
		κρείττων	κράτιϲτοϲ
αἰϲχρόϲ	*ugly*	αἰϲχίων	αἴϲχιϲτοϲ
ἀλγεινόϲ	*painful*	ἀλγίων	ἄλγιϲτοϲ
ἐχθρόϲ	*hostile*	ἐχθίων	ἔχθιϲτοϲ
ἡδύϲ	*sweet*	ἡδίων	ἥδιϲτοϲ
κακόϲ	*bad*	κακίων	κάκιϲτοϲ
		χείρων	χείριϲτοϲ
καλόϲ	*beautiful*	καλλίων	κάλλιϲτοϲ
μέγαϲ	*great*	μείζων	μέγιϲτοϲ
ὀλίγοϲ	*small, few*	ἐλάττων	ἐλάχιϲτοϲ
πολύϲ	*much*	πλείων	πλεῖϲτοϲ
ῥᾴδιοϲ	*easy*	ῥᾴων	ῥᾷϲτοϲ
ταχύϲ	*swift*	θάττων	τάχιϲτοϲ

Two adjectives (ἀγαθόϲ and κακόϲ) are compared in more than one way; κρείττων, κράτιϲτοϲ (from ἀγαθόϲ) can also mean *stronger, strongest* (cf. κράτοϲ *power*).

Comparatives in this class are declined as third declension adjectives with stems in ον (10.1/4a), but with some very important alternative forms (we can ignore the vocative, which is rare), e.g.

	SINGULAR		PLURAL	
	M. & F.	N.	M. & F.	N.
Nom.	μείζων	μεῖζον	μείζονεϲ/μείζουϲ	μείζονα/μείζω
Acc.	μείζονα/μείζω	μεῖζον	μείζοναϲ/μείζουϲ	μείζονα/μείζω
Gen.	μείζονοϲ	μείζονοϲ	μειζόνων	μειζόνων
Dat.	μείζονι	μείζονι	μείζοϲι(ν)	μείζοϲι(ν)

The alternatives are contracted versions of forms without ν (μείζω < μείζοα). The acc. pl. μείζουϲ (< μείζοαϲ) has an irregular contraction (ο + α normally produces ω, as in the singular). It is important to note that the forms in -ους may be **nom**. pl. as well as acc. pl.

πλείων *larger*, (pl.) *more*, has a stem πλει- before ω/ου but πλει- or πλε- before ο (but always πλέον):

	SINGULAR		PLURAL	
	M. & F.	N.	M. & F.	N.
Nom.	πλείων	πλέον	πλείονες	πλείονα
			πλέονες	πλέονα
			πλείους	πλείω
Acc.	πλείονα	πλέον	πλείονας	πλείονα
	πλέονα		πλέονας	πλέονα
	πλείω		πλείους	πλείω
Gen.	πλείονος		πλειόνων	
	πλέονος		πλεόνων	
Dat.	πλείονι		πλείοσι(ν)	
	πλέονι		πλέοσι(ν)	

Adverbs formed from adjectives (e.g. cοφῶc *wisely*) have as their comparative the neuter **singular** nom./acc. of the comparative of the adjective (cοφώτερον *more wisely*), and as their superlative the neuter **plural** nom./acc. of the superlative (cοφώτατα *most wisely*). Of the few adverbs not formed from adjectives we may note μάλα *very*, μᾶλλον *more*, μάλιστα *most*.

Notes

1 The meaning of some adjectives (e.g. πᾶc *all*) precludes a comparative or superlative.
2 The adverbs μᾶλλον *more* and μάλιστα *most* are sometimes used to compare adjectives: μᾶλλον φίλοc *more dear*, *dearer*; μάλιστα φίλοc *most dear*, *dearest*.
3 ἥττων *lesser*, *weaker*, *inferior* has no positive. Its superlative (ἥκιστοc) is common only as an adverb, ἥκιστα *least of all*, *not at all*.

17.1/3　Meaning of the comparative and superlative

Comparatives and superlatives in Greek are not always to be understood in the sense *more X* and *most X*. A comparative adjective is sometimes used where no comparison is expressed, and indicates a higher degree than the positive. English here uses *rather* or *too* (cf. also 17.1/4).

ὁ Κῦρος ἦν πολυλογώτερος.　*Cyrus was rather talkative.*
αἱ ἐμαὶ διατριβαὶ ὑμῖν βαρύτεραι γεγόνασι καὶ ἐπιφθονώτεραι.　*My discourses have become too burdensome and odious for you.*

Likewise, the superlative (without the definite article) is often used to express a very high degree:

καί ποτε ὄντος πάγου δεινοτάτου Cωκράτης ἐξῆλθεν ἱμάτιον ἔχων.
And once when there was a very terrible frost Socrates went out wearing
(lit. *having*) *[only] a cloak.*

As in English, a superlative adjective is preceded by the definite article
when it means *the most x*: ὁ δεινότατος πάγος *the most terrible frost.*
The article is omitted, however, when a superlative adjective is used as a predicate, e.g. ὁ Cωκράτης coφώτατος πάντων ἐστίν *Socrates is the wisest of all*
(cf. 5.1/3).

17.1/4 Constructions involving the comparative and superlative

(*a*) In comparisons in English a comparative adjective or adverb is followed
by *than*. In Greek ἤ *than* (which may elsewhere mean *or*) is used in the
same way:

ἐν τοῖς ὄχλοις πιθανώτεροι οἱ ἀπαίδευτοι ἤ οἱ πεπαιδευμένοι. *Among
crowds the uneducated [are] more persuasive than the educated* (lit. *the
having been educated [people]*).
τὸ μὴ εἶναι κρεῖττον ἤ τὸ ζῆν κακῶς. *Not existing [is] better than
living badly.*

ἤ is here a conjunction and what follows must be in the same case as
what precedes. Whereas in English we can nowadays say *Socrates is
wiser than me*, in Greek we must have Cωκράτης coφώτερός ἐστιν ἤ
ἐγώ; the first member of the comparison (Cωκράτης) is nominative and
therefore the second member must also be nominative (hence ἐγώ).
There is, however, another construction, the **genitive of comparison**, in
which the second member of the comparison is put in the genitive and ἤ
is omitted:

ὁ χρῡσὸς κρείττων μῡρίων λόγων βροτοῖς. *For mortals gold [is]
stronger than countless words.*
οὐδὲν cιωπῆς ἐστι χρησιμώτερον. *Nothing is more useful than silence.*

(*b*) A comparative may be accompanied by a dative of **measure of
difference**:

κεφαλῇ ἐλάττων. *Shorter by a head.*
τέχνη ἀνάγκης ἀσθενεστέρᾱ μακρῷ. *Art [is] weaker by far* (or *far
weaker*) *than necessity.*

(*c*) In sentences of the type *he is too weak to help, it is too hot to sleep* Greek
uses a comparative adjective followed by ἤ ὥστε and an infinitive (ὥστε
here introduces a phrase of result—16.1/1):

μεῖζόν ἐστι τὸ κακὸν ἤ ὥστε φέρειν. *The evil is too great to bear* (lit.
greater than so as to . . .).

(*d*) A superlative adjective or adverb is preceded by ὡς or ὅτι (both used here adverbially) for expressions such as ὡς (ὅτι) πλεῖcτοι *as many as possible*; ὡς (ὅτι) τάχιcτα *as quickly as possible*.

17.1/5   Active verbs used in a passive sense

The verb ἀποκτείνω does not occur in the passive. Instead, Greek uses the active forms of ἀποθνήͺcκω (literally *die*, but in this context *be killed*):

> οἱ αἰχμάλωτοι ἀπέθανον ὑπὸ τῶν βαρβάρων.   *The captives were killed by the barbarians.*

The passive sense of ἀπέθανον is here made clear by the agent construction ὑπό + gen. (11.1/2). Some indication of this sort is normally present.

Similarly, φεύγω (literally *flee*) and ἐκπίπτω (literally *fall out*) are used as the passive of ἐκβάλλω *banish, send into exile*:

> ἐκ Νάξου ἔφυγον πλούcιοί τινες ὑπὸ τοῦ δήμου.   *Some wealthy men were exiled from Naxos by the people.*
> ἐκ γὰρ τῆς ἄλλης Ἑλλάδος οἱ πολέμῳ ἢ cτάcει ἐκπίπτοντες παρ᾽ Ἀθηναίους οἱ δυνατώτατοι ἀνεχώρουν.   *For when the most influential men were driven out of the rest of Greece by war or sedition, they used to withdraw to the Athenians* (lit. *those exiled by war . . ., the most influential . . . used to . . .*).

εὖ/κακῶς λέγω (+acc.) *speak well/badly/of* has the passive εὖ/κακῶς ἀκούω *be well/badly spoken of* (lit. *hear well/badly*):

> ἐμὲ κακῶς ἀκούcαντα ὑπὸ cοῦ μεγάλη ἔδακε λύπη.   *I was deeply grieved when you spoke badly of me* (lit. *great grief bit me being badly spoken of by you*).

Likewise, εὖ/κακῶς ποιέω (+acc.) *treat well/badly* has the passive εὖ/κακῶς πάcχω *be treated well/badly* (lit. *suffer well/badly*):

> οὐκ ἀεικὲς κακῶς πάcχειν ὑπὸ ἐχθρῶν.   *[It is] not shameful to be badly treated by enemies.*

17.2   Greek reading

1   A large number of pithy maxims current in antiquity were said to be inscribed on the columns of the temple of Apollo at Delphi. The following is a selection from surviving lists (the columns themselves no longer exist). The most famous are (*v*) and (*x*).

(*i*) ἀδικούμενος διαλλάττου.   (*ii*) ἀλλοτρίων ἀπέχου.   (*iii*) βραδέως ἐγχείρει.   (*iv*) γαμεῖν μέλλε.   (*v*) γνῶθι cεαυτόν.   (*vi*) γονέας αἰδοῦ.

(*vii*) φρόνει θνητά. (*viii*) ἐπὶ νεκρῷ μὴ γέλα. (*ix*) καιρὸν γνῶθι. (*x*) μηδὲν ἄγαν. (*xi*) πίνων μὴ πολλὰ λάλει. (*xii*) πλούτει δικαίως. (*xiii*) τύχην νόμιζε. (*xiv*) ὑβριζόμενος τιμωροῦ. (*xv*) υἱοῖς μὴ καταρῶ.

2# γύμναζε παῖδας· ἄνδρας οὐ γὰρ γυμνάσεις.

3 φοβερώτερόν ἐστι στρατόπεδον ἐλάφων ἡγουμένου λέοντος ἢ στρατόπεδον λεόντων ἡγουμένου ἐλάφου.

4# φοβοῦ τὸ γῆρας· οὐ γὰρ ἔρχεται μόνον.

5# καλῶς ἀκούειν μᾶλλον ἢ πλουτεῖν θέλε.

6# ῥόδον παρελθὼν μηκέτι ζήτει πάλιν.

7 δύο ὦτα ἔχομεν, στόμα δὲ ἕν, ἵνα πλείω μὲν ἀκούωμεν, ἥττω δὲ λέγωμεν.

8 **Shorter proverbs**

(*i*) ὀξύτερον οἱ γείτονες βλέπουσι τῶν ἀλωπέκων. (*ii*) πεζῇ βαδίζων μὴ φοβοῦ τὰ κύματα. (*iii*) φαγέτω με λέων καὶ μὴ ἀλώπηξ. (*iv*) ἴσθι καὶ λέων ὅπου χρὴ καὶ πίθηκος ἐν μέρει. (*v*) ἤν τις ἔμαξε μᾶζαν, ταύτην καὶ ἐσθιέτω. (*vi*) στρατηγοῦ παρόντος πᾶσα ἀρχὴ παυσάσθω. (*vii*) ὁ πλεόνων ἐρῶν καὶ τῶν παρόντων ἀποστερεῖται. (*viii*) σιτίον εἰς ἀμίδα μὴ ἐμβάλλειν. (*ix*) ξένος ὢν ἀκολούθει τοῖς ἐπιχωρίοις νόμοις. (*x*) τὸν φίλον κακῶς μὴ λέγε, μηδ' εὖ τὸν ἐχθρόν. (*xi*) μὴ καταφρονήσῃς τοῦ πένητος εὐτυχῶν. (*xii*) μὴ κρίνετε ἵνα μὴ κριθῆτε. (*xiii*) αἱ δεύτεραί πως φροντίδες σοφώτεραι. (*xiv*) οἱ πλεῖστοι κακοί. (*xv*) ἀεὶ τὰ πέρυσι βελτίω.

9# ἀσπίδι μὲν Σαΐων τις ἀγάλλεται, ἣν παρὰ θάμνῳ,
    ἔντος ἀμώμητον, κάλλιπον (= κατέλιπον) οὐκ ἐθέλων·
αὐτὸς δ' ἐξέφυγον θανάτου τέλος· ἀσπὶς ἐκείνη
ἐρρέτω· ἐξαῦτις κτήσομαι οὐ κακίω.

10 ὁ βασίλειος πῆχυς τοῦ μετρίου ἐστὶ πήχεως μείζων τρισὶ δακτύλοις.

11 The Spartans (οἱ Λάκωνες/Λακεδαιμόνιοι) were men of few words (hence our *laconic*) and had a reputation for a blunt, dry humour. Most of the following stories are about Spartan kings.

(*i*) Εὐδαμίδας ἰδὼν ἐν Ἀκαδαμείᾳ Ξενοκράτη ἤδη πρεσβύτερον μετὰ τῶν μαθητῶν φιλοσοφοῦντα καὶ πυθόμενος ὅτι τὴν ἀρετὴν ζητεῖ, πότε οὖν, εἶπεν, αὐτῇ χρήσεται;

(*ii*) Ἀργείου δέ τινος λέγοντος, ὡς φαυλότεροι γίγνονται κατὰ τὰς ἀποδημίας οἱ Λάκωνες, ἀλλ' οὐχ ὑμεῖς γε, ἔφη, εἰς τὴν Σπάρτην ἐλθόντες χείρονες ἀλλὰ βελτίονες γίγνεσθε.

(*iii*) Ἆγις πρὸς ἄνθρωπον πονηρὸν ἐρωτῶντα τίς ἄριστος εἴη Σπαρτιάτης, εἶπεν, ὁ σοὶ ἀνομοιότατος.

(*iv*) Ἀνταλκίδας, σοφιστοῦ μέλλοντος ἀναγιγνώσκειν ἐγκώμιον Ἡρακλέους, τίς γὰρ αὐτόν, ἔφη, ψέγει;

(*v*) Θεαρίδας ξίφος ἀκονῶν ἠρωτήθη, εἰ ὀξύ ἐστιν, καὶ εἶπεν, ὀξύτερον διαβολῆς.

(*vi*) Ἀρχέλαος, ἀδολέσχου κουρέως ἐρωτήσαντος αὐτόν, πῶς ϲε
κείρω, ὦ βασιλεῦ; σιωπῶν, ἔφη.

12 ὁ Ἀριστοτέλης ἀκούσας ὑπό τινος λοιδορεῖσθαι, ἀπόντα με, ἔφη, καὶ
μαστιγούτω.

13 οἱ σοφισταί, τἆλλα σοφοὶ ὄντες, τοῦτο ἄτοπον ἐργάζονται πρᾶγμα·
φάσκοντες γὰρ ἀρετῆς διδάσκαλοι εἶναι πολλάκις κατηγοροῦσιν τῶν
μαθητῶν ὡς ἀδικοῦσι ϲφᾶς, τοὺς μισθοὺς ἀποστεροῦντες καίπερ εὖ
παθόντες ὑπ' αὐτῶν.

14 πολλὴ ἔχθρα καὶ μῖσος ἀλλήλων τοῖς πολίταις ἐγγίγνεται, δι' ἃ ἔγωγε
μάλα φοβοῦμαι ἀεὶ μή τι μεῖζον ἢ ὥστε φέρειν κακὸν τῇ πόλει συμβῇ.

15 οἱ Λακεδαιμόνιοι ἐπρεσβεύοντο πρὸς τοὺς Ἀθηναίους ἐγκλήματα
ποιούμενοι, ὅπως ϲφίσιν ὅτι μεγίστη πρόφασις εἴη τοῦ πολεμεῖν, ἢν
(= ἐὰν) μή τι ἐσακούωσιν.

16 Κλέανδρος ἐτυράννευσε μὲν Γέλας ἑπτὰ ἔτη, ἀπέθανε δὲ ὑπὸ Ϲαβύλλου
ἀνδρὸς Γελῴου.

17# Ἐλπὶς καὶ ϲὺ Τύχη, μέγα χαίρετε· τὸν λιμέν' ηὗρον·
οὐδὲν ἐμοὶ χ' ὑμῖν· παίζετε τοὺς μετ' ἐμέ.

Notes

1 (*ii*) ἀπέχομαι is followed by the gen. (20.1/4).   (*x*) Supply an imperative such as ποίει.   (*xiii*) νομίζω+acc. *believe in*.   (*xiv*) τῑμωροῦ <
τῑμωρέου.   (*xv*) καταρῶ < καταράου.

2 γάρ is here placed 3rd word in its clause (cf. 15.3 *l*.27).

3 ἡγουμένου λέοντος and ἡγουμένου ἐλάφου are both genitive absolutes
(12.1/2*b*).

8 (*iv*) ἴϲθι is here the 2nd s. imp. of εἰμί (17.1/1 note 6).   (*v*) ἢν . . . μάζαν
lit. *which bread* (ἢν is here the relative adjective, 9.1/2 note 3);
ἔμαξα < μάττω.   (*vi*) ἀρχή as an abstract noun can mean *magistracy*
but is used here concretely in the sense *officer*.   (*vii*) Both ἐράω *desire*
(13.1/2*a*(ii)) and ἀποστερέομαι *be deprived of* (20.1/4) are followed by
the genitive, cf. ἀπέχου in 1(ii) above.   (*viii*) ἐμβάλλειν infinitive for
imperative (17.1/1 note 5).   (*xv*) Supply ἢν.

9 A poem of Archilochus (7th cent. BC), the earliest figure in Greek
literature about whom we have any reliable information. *l*.2 ἔντος
ἀμώμητον is in apposition to ἢν in the previous line *which, a blameless
weapon,* . . . *l*.3 θανάτου τέλος *[the] doom of death* (a Homeric
phrase). *l*.4 κακίω f. acc. s. to agree with ἀϲπίδα understood.

10 The *royal cubit* was that used by the Persians, the other was standard in
the Greek world.

11 (*i*) πυθόμενος *ascertaining*; Xenocrates was *looking for virtue* in the sense
that he was investigating its nature from a philosophical point of
view.   (*ii*) This story is also about Eudamidas, who is the subject of ἔφη;
γε emphasizes ὑμεῖς.   (*iii*) ἄριστος . . . Ϲπαρτιάτης *[the] best Spartan*
the article is not used with a predicate (5.1/3).   (*iv*) For a down-to-earth

Spartan, praising Heracles would have seemed as superfluous as praising motherhood; γάρ here introduces an ironical question "*Well, who . . .?*" (*vi*) κείρω aor. subj. in a deliberative question (14.1/4a(ii)) "*How am I to cut . . .?*"

12 After ἀκούσᾱς we have the infinitive construction for reported speech (8.1/3a), lit. *having heard [himself] to be abused . . .*; ἀπόντα < ἄπειμι.

13 τᾆλλα (= τὰ ἄλλα) adverbial accusative (20.1/5), *in other respects*; τοῦτο refers to what follows (9.1/1 note 1) but the meaning is not *this extraordinary thing* (there is no definite article with ἄτοπον . . . πρᾶγμα), but *an extraordinary thing [viz] this*; γάρ explains what precedes, but we would omit it in English; σφᾶς i.e. the sophists (9.1/4a); both ἀποστεροῦντες and παθόντες agree with the subject of ἀδικοῦσι (3rd pl. pres. ind. act., **not** a pple.), i.e. the students; αὐτῶν also refers back to the sophists and is used instead of σφῶν for variety.

14 μῖσος ἀλλήλων *hatred of each other* (9.1/4b), i.e. *mutual hatred*.

15 ἐπρεσβεύοντο impf. to express repeated action (4.1/1); ποιούμενοι *making* the middle of ποιέω is used with nouns to indicate the involvement of the subject, cf. πόλεμον ποιεῖσθαι *to wage war*; εἰρήνην ποιεῖσθαι *to keep peace* but πόλεμον ποιεῖν *to cause a war* (but not necessarily be involved in it); εἰρήνην ποιεῖν *to impose peace* (on belligerents); ὅπως (= ἵνα) + opt. to express purpose after a historic tense (14.1/4c(i)); ἐς- = εἰς-.

17 χαίρετε (17.1/1 note 7) is qualified by μέγα (here an adverb), lit. *farewell greatly* (the author is pleased to be rid of them); χ' ὑμῖν elision for καὶ ὑμῖν (English idiom reverses the order, *you and me*—the clause means *there is nothing for* (i.e. *between*) *you and me*; παίζετε (here imp.) + acc. *play with*.

17.3   Extra reading –
Prometheus Bound (2)

Prometheus has revealed that he alone can save Zeus from a marriage which
will rob him of his divine kingship. In the scene below Hermes, the messenger
of the gods, has come to force Prometheus to disclose his secret. Shortly after,
the play ends with Prometheus persisting in his refusal.

ʹΕΡΜΗϹ

ϲὲ τὸν ϲοφιϲτήν, τὸν πικρῶϲ ὑπέρπικρον,
τὸν ἐξαμαρτόντ' εἰϲ θεοὺϲ ἐφημέροιϲ
πορόντα τιμάϲ, τὸν πυρὸϲ κλέπτην λέγω·
πατὴρ ἄνωγέ ϲ' οὕϲτιναϲ κομπεῖϲ γάμουϲ
αὐδᾶν, πρὸϲ ὧν τ' ἐκεῖνοϲ ἐκπίπτει κράτουϲ·   5
καὶ ταῦτα μέντοι μηδὲν αἰνικτηρίωϲ,
ἀλλ' αὔθ' ἕκαϲτα φράζε, μηδέ μοι διπλᾶϲ
ὁδούϲ, Προμηθεῦ, προϲβάλῃϲ. ὁρᾷϲ δ' ὅτι
Ζεὺϲ τοῖϲ τοιούτοιϲ οὐχὶ μαλθακίζεται.

ΠΡΟΜΗΘΕΥϹ

ϲεμνόϲτομόϲ γε καὶ φρονήματοϲ πλέωϲ   10
ὁ μῦθόϲ ἐϲτιν, ὡϲ θεῶν ὑπηρέτου.
νέον νέοι κρατεῖτε, καὶ δοκεῖτε δὴ
ναίειν ἀπενθῆ πέργαμ'· οὐκ ἐκ τῶνδ' ἐγὼ
διϲϲοὺϲ τυράννουϲ ἐκπεϲόνταϲ ᾐϲθόμην;
τρίτον δὲ τὸν νῦν κοιρανοῦντ' ἐπόψομαι   15
αἴϲχιϲτα καὶ τάχιϲτα. μή τί ϲοι δοκῶ
ταρβεῖν ὑποπτήϲϲειν τε τοὺϲ νέουϲ θεούϲ;
πολλοῦ γε καὶ τοῦ παντὸϲ ἐλλείπω. ϲὺ δὲ
κέλευθον ἥνπερ ἦλθεϲ ἐγκόνει πάλιν·
πεύϲῃ γὰρ οὐδὲν ὧν ἀνιϲτορεῖϲ ἐμέ.   20

Notes

*l.*1 Hermes' words are aggressive and rude. This shows itself in the omission
of the verb governing ϲέ (καλῶ *I am addressing*), trans. *you there, the clever
one* . . .   *ll.*2f. τὸν ἐξαμαρτόντ'(α) . . . πορόντα lit. *the one who offended
. . . [by] giving* (πορόντα aor. pple. of a defective verb which only exists in the
aor. and perf. and is listed under the aor. ind. ἔπορον); take ἐφημέροιϲ with
πορόντα *giving . . . to mortals*; λέγω *I mean*.   *l.*4 πατήρ, i.e. Zeus; ἄνωγέ
orders from ἄνωγα a verb perfect in form but present in meaning (cf. 19.1/3*a*);
οὕϲτιναϲ (indirect interrogative, 10.1/2*b*) . . . γάμουϲ plural for singular.   *l.*5
πρόϲ (= ὑπό) ὧν *by which*; ἐκπίπτει for vividness the present is used for the
future in prophecies; κράτουϲ (gen.) is governed by ἐκ-.   *l.*6 Understand

φράζε from the next line; καὶ . . . μέντοι *and indeed, and what is more*; μηδέν adverbial acc. (20.1/5) *in no way*. *ll.*7f. αὔθ' (= αὐτά) ἕκαστα, i.e. *each thing, every detail*; μηδέ . . . προςβάλῃς negative command (17.1/1). *l.*9 τοῖς τοιούτοις lit. *by such things* (i.e. *behaviour*). *l.*10 πλέως 13.1/1*a*. *l.*11 ὡς *for [the talk] of a lackey*, on this restrictive use of ὡς see 22.1/1*a*(vi). *l.*12 νέον is n. acc. s. used adverbially (20.1/5) and to be taken with κρατεῖτε, lit. *you rule newly*, i.e. *you have only just come to power*; δοκεῖτε *you think, expect*; δή adds a note of sarcasm *indeed*. *l.*14 διccoὺς (= διττούς the non-Attic form is used in Tragedy) τυράννους Uranus, the first king of the gods, had been dethroned by his son Cronus, who in turn was dethroned by Zeus (Prometheus sarcastically calls them τύραννοι). *l.*15 Supply ἐκπίπτοντα from ἐκπεσόντας in the previous line; ἐπόψομαι < ἐφοράω. *l.*16 μή . . . coι δοκῶ is a question expecting a negative answer (10.1/2*a*), lit. *surely I do not seem to you* (μή here = *surely not*); τί (the accent is from the enclitic coι, see **Appendix 9**, *d*(ix)) acc. s. n. of the indefinite τις, here used as an adverbial acc. (20.1/5) *to some extent*. *l.*18 ἐλλείπω takes the gen. *I lack much* (πολλοῦ, i.e. of such behaviour), *in fact* (καί) *all* (lit. *the whole*, i.e. of such behaviour)— Prometheus is strongly emphasizing that he is not frightened of the new rulers of heaven. *l.*19 κέλευθον acc. of space traversed *along the road*, after ἐγκόνει (2nd s. pres. imp. of ἐγκονέω); ἥνπερ (< ὅςπερ, i.e. ὅς + περ) is an emphatic form of the relative. *l.*20 ὧν = τούτων ἅ *of those things which* the relative pronoun has been attracted into the case of the antecedent, and the latter then omitted (9.1/2 note 2).

Unit 18

18.1 Grammar

18.1/1 -μι verbs

-μι verbs fall into two groups:

(a) The suffixless class, where the endings of the present and imperfect are added directly to the stem without any suffix or link vowel, e.g. εἶ-μί (3.1/6) and φη-μί (7.1/2). There are nine other common verbs in this class:

δίδωμι	give and τίθημι put, place (18.1/2)
εἶμι	I shall go (18.1/3; distinguish from εἰμί I am)
ἵστημι	make to stand (19.1/1)
ἵημι	let go, send forth (20.1/2)
δύναμαι	be able and ἐπίσταμαι know (19.1/3b; the only common deponents of this type)
πίμπλημι	fill and πίμπρημι burn (19.1/1 note 2)

From another such verb, ἠμί say (obsolescent in Attic) Plato often uses the forms ἦν I said, ἦ he/she said (13.3(i)l.6; both forms were originally imperfect).

(b) The -νῡμι class, where the stem of the present and imperfect has a νυ suffix (20.1/1).

Both classes differ from -ω verbs in the present and imperfect; of class (a) δίδωμι, τίθημι, ἵστημι, ἵημι also differ in the aorist active and middle (ἵστημι in the perfect and pluperfect as well). Elsewhere -μι verbs take the same suffixes and endings as -ω verbs.

18.1/2 δίδωμι give, τίθημι put, place

These two -μι verbs are closely parallel. In nearly all their forms an ο/ω in δίδωμι corresponds to an ε/η in τίθημι; and also οι to ει in optative forms, and ου to ει in forms other than those of the optative; the only exceptions are the 1st s. impf. (ἐδίδουν/ἐτίθην), the present and aorist subjunctive (see note 1) and the perfect mid./pass. (δέδομαι etc. but τέθειμαι etc.). Both verbs form their present stem by reduplication with iota (cf. γιγνώσκω); as in the perfect tense (15.1/1), an aspirated consonant is reduplicated with the corresponding non-aspirate, hence τιθη- (not θιθη-). In both, the aorist active is weak in the singular, with κ (not ς) added to the long-vowel form of the root (δω-/θη-); in the plural the endings are added directly to the short-vowel form of the root (δο-/θε-; this is really a type of root aorist).

Their principal parts are:

PRESENT	FUTURE	AOR. ACT.	PERF. ACT.	PERF. MID./PASS.	AOR. PASS.
δίδωμι	δώcω	ἔδωκα	δέδωκα	δέδομαι	ἐδόθην
τίθημι	θήcω	ἔθηκα	τέθηκα	κεῖμαι (note 4)	ἐτέθην
				(τέθειμαι)	

The future, perfect (act. and mid./pass.) and aorist passive are regular (see above, 18.1/1). The present, imperfect and aorist active forms, which require the greatest attention and should be mastered first, are set out here. The middle and passive forms are easily recognised from their endings (for full tables see **Appendix 5**).

		PRESENT		AORIST	
INDICATIVE					
S.	1	δίδωμι	τίθημι	ἔδωκα	ἔθηκα
	2	δίδως	τίθης	ἔδωκας	ἔθηκας
	3	δίδωcι(ν)	τίθηcι(ν)	ἔδωκε(ν)	ἔθηκε(ν)
PL.	1	δίδομεν	τίθεμεν	ἔδομεν	ἔθεμεν
	2	δίδοτε	τίθετε	ἔδοτε	ἔθετε
	3	διδόᾱcι(ν)	τιθέᾱcι(ν)	ἔδοcαν	ἔθεcαν
INFINITIVE					
		διδόναι	τιθέναι	δοῦναι	θεῖναι
PARTICIPLE					
	m.	διδούς, -όντος	τιθείς, -έντος	δούς, δόντος	θείς, θέντος
	f.	διδοῦcα, -ούcης	τιθεῖcα, -είcης	δοῦcα, δούcης	θεῖcα, θείcης
	n.	διδόν, -όντος	τιθέν, -έντος	δόν, δόντος	θέν, θέντος
IMPERATIVE					
S.	2	δίδου	τίθει	δός	θές
	3	διδότω	τιθέτω	δότω	θέτω
PL.	2	δίδοτε	τίθετε	δότε	θέτε
	3	διδόντων	τιθέντων	δόντων	θέντων
SUBJUNCTIVE (see note 1)					
S.	1	διδῶ	τιθῶ	δῶ	θῶ
	2	διδῷc etc.	τιθῇc etc.	δῷc etc.	θῇc etc.
OPTATIVE					
S.	1	διδοίην	τιθείην	δοίην	θείην
	2	διδοίης	τιθείης	δοίης	θείης
	3	διδοίη	τιθείη	δοίη	θείη
PL.	1	διδοῖμεν	τιθεῖμεν	δοῖμεν	θεῖμεν
	2	διδοῖτε	τιθεῖτε	δοῖτε	θεῖτε
	3	διδοῖεν	τιθεῖεν	δοῖεν	θεῖεν

IMPERFECT ACTIVE

ἐδίδουν, ἐδίδους, ἐδίδου, ἐδίδομεν, ἐδίδοτε, ἐδίδοσαν
ἐτίθην, ἐτίθεις, ἐτίθει, ἐτίθεμεν, ἐτίθετε, ἐτίθεσαν

Notes

1   The present and aorist subjunctive active of δίδωμι have the endings -ῶ, -ῷς, -ῷ, -ῶμεν, -ῶτε, -ῶσι(ν) (cf. 14.1/2 note 2). τίθημι has the regular endings (-ῶ, -ῇς, -ῇ etc.) but in both verbs the first syllable of the subjunctive endings has a circumflex as a result of contraction (διδῶ < διδόω, τιθῶ < τιθέω).

2   The present and imperfect active of δίδωμι can also mean *offer*.

3   The aorist active also has weak forms for the 3rd pl.: ἔδωκαν (= ἔδοσαν), ἔθηκαν (= ἔθεσαν); weak forms may also occur in the 1st and 2nd pl. (ἐδώκαμεν etc.) but are rare.

4   The **present** tense of the deponent κεῖμαι *lie* (19.1/3b) is generally used instead of the **perfect passive** of τίθημι in the sense *to have been put, placed, established*, e.g. οἱ νόμοι οἱ ὑπὸ τῶν βασιλέων κείμενοι (= τεθειμένοι) *the laws established by the kings*. Likewise ἐκείμην, the **imperfect** of κεῖμαι, is used for the **pluperfect passive** of τίθημι.

18.1/3   εἶμι *I shall come/go*

In Attic Greek prose the verb ἔρχομαι *come/go* occurs only in the present indicative. The remainder of its present tense (subjunctive, optative, imperative, infinitive, participle), and its future and imperfect are supplied by εἶμι which, though present in form, has in the indicative the future meaning *I shall come/go* (to be distinguished from εἰμί *I am*):

PRESENT

IND.	SUBJ.	OPT.	IMP.	INF.	PPLE.
ἔρχομαι	ἴω	ἴοιμι	ἴθι	ἰέναι	ἰών
I come/go					

FUTURE

εἶμι	—	ἴοιμι	—	ἰέναι	ἰών
I shall come/go					

IMPERFECT

ᾖα
I was coming/going, used to come/go

For a complete table of forms see **Appendix 3**.

Note that ἴοιμι, ἰέναι and ἰών can be either present or future (the context will normally show which tense is meant). The aorist of ἔρχομαι is ἦλθον (7.1/1 note 2), and the perfect ἐλήλυθα.

18.1/4 Other verbs with principal parts from different roots

The English verb *to be* is a combination of separate and etymologically distinct words (*be, am, was*, etc.). We have already seen the same in Greek with αἱρέω, λέγω, ὁράω, φέρω (7.1/1 note 2) as well as ἔρχομαι; other examples are ἐσθίω *eat*, πωλέω *sell*, ὠνέομαι *buy* (see **Principal parts of verbs**; the principal parts of all eight should now be learnt).

A particularly troublesome set is that associated with αἱρέω *take*, *capture*, whose passive is normally supplied by another verb, ἁλίσκομαι *be captured*, and whose middle αἱροῦμαι has the special sense *choose*. When used as a passive αἱροῦμαι normally means *be chosen*. These variations can be set out as follows:

PRESENT		FUTURE	AORIST	PERFECT
αἱρέω	I take, capture	αἱρήσω	εἷλον (stem ἑλ-)	ᾕρηκα
ἁλίσκομαι (pass.)	I am being taken, am being captured	ἁλώσομαι	ἑάλων	ἑάλωκα
αἱροῦμαι (mid.)	I choose	αἱρήσομαι	εἱλόμην	ᾕρημαι
αἱροῦμαι (pass.)	I am being chosen	αἱρεθήσομαι	ᾑρέθην	ᾕρημαι

The moods, infinitives and participles of εἷλον *I took, captured* (stem ἑλ-, cf. 7.1/1 note 2) and of the root aorist ἑάλων *I was taken, was captured* are as follows:

IND.	SUBJ.	OPT.	IMP.	INF.	PPLE.
εἷλον	ἕλω	ἕλοιμι	ἕλε	ἑλεῖν	ἑλών
ἑάλων	ἁλῶ	ἁλοίην	ἅλωθι	ἁλῶναι	ἁλούς

ἑάλων is exactly parallel to ἔγνων (11.1/1), e.g. ind. ἑάλων, ἑάλως, ἑάλω, etc.

Notes
1 Most **compounds** of λέγω have the meaning *pick up*, *gather*, e.g. ἐκλέγω *pick out*, συλλέγω *collect*, καταλέγω *pick, choose* (and also *recount*). These compounds have principal parts from the stem λεγ- only, e.g. ἐκλέγω, ἐκλέξω, ἐξέλεξα etc.
2 The alternative principal parts of λέγω (ἐρῶ, εἷπον, etc.) are, however, used in the compounds of ἀγορεύω *speak in public*, e.g. ἀπαγορεύω *forbid* (fut. ἀπερῶ, aor. ἀπεῖπον), προαγορεύω *proclaim*.

18.1/5 Conditional sentences

Conditional sentences contain at least one main clause and one adverbial clause of condition; the latter is introduced by εἰ *if*. They fall into two clearly defined categories which, in both English and Greek, are distinguished by the form of the main clause:

Category 1

In the main clause English has the auxiliary verb *would* or *should* (or occasionally *could*), and Greek has the particle ἄν (see below). An English example is: *I would be sorry if you were not to persist with Greek.*

Category 2

In the main clause English does **not** have the auxiliary *would* or *should*, and Greek does **not** have the particle ἄν. An English example is: *I am sorry if you find Greek verbs difficult.*

There is a clear distinction between the two categories. The first is used in cases where something could have happened in the past, could be happening now, or could happen in the future. The cases covered by the second are also hypothetical (as all conditional sentences must be), but here, by not using *would* or *should* in English or ἄν in Greek, we express ourselves in a more positive and confident way.

We have already seen that the particle ἄν, when used with the subjunctive in subordinate clauses (14.1/4c(iii)), can be represented in English by *ever*. Here, however, it has no semantic equivalent. When in English we wish to express potentiality (as in the main clause of first category conditional sentences) we use an auxiliary verb (generally *would* or *should*), e.g. *I would have liked to see you.* ἄν, however, which expresses potentiality in Greek, is an adverbial particle and modifies the verb to which it is attached: οὐκ ἐγένετο means *it did not happen*; οὐκ ἄν ἐγένετο means *it would not have happened.*

Conditional clauses of both categories refer either to the future, present, or past. οὐ is used to negate main clauses[1] but the negative in the εἰ clause is μή. ἄν is postpositive and therefore never stands as first word in the main clause of conditional clauses of the first category.

The three time frames of each category are given below:

---

[1] Unless, of course, these are in the form of a command (17.1/1) or wish (21.1/1).

CATEGORY 1

English
would/should in the main clause

Greek
ἄν in the main clause

CATEGORY 2

verb without *would/should* in the
main clause

no ἄν in the main clause

FUTURE

Conditional clause
εἰ + optative (pres. or aor.)

ἐάν (see note 2) + subjunctive (pres.
or aor.)

Main clause
optative (pres. or aor.) + ἄν

εἰ τοῦτο πράξειας, ἁμάρτοις ἄν.
*If you were to do this you
would be wrong.*

future indicative

ἐὰν τοῦτο πράξῃς, ἁμαρτήσει.
If you do this you will be wrong.

PRESENT

Conditional clause
εἰ + imperfect indicative

εἰ + present indicative

Main clause
imperfect indicative + ἄν

εἰ τοῦτο ἔπραττες, ἡμάρτανες ἄν.
*If you were [now] doing this
you would be wrong.*

present indicative

εἰ τοῦτο πράττεις, ἁμαρτάνεις.
*If you are doing this you are
wrong*

PAST

Conditional clause
εἰ + aorist indicative

εἰ + imperfect or aorist indicative

Main clause
aorist indicative + ἄν

εἰ τοῦτο ἔπραξας, ἥμαρτες ἄν.
*If you had done this you
would have been wrong.*

imperfect or aorist indicative

εἰ τοῦτο ἔπραττες, ἡμάρτανες.
*If you used to do this you were
(used to be) wrong.*
εἰ τοῦτο ἔπραξας, ἥμαρτες.
If you did this you were wrong.

Notes

1 The meaning of εἰ . . . ἔπραττες/ἔπραξας depends on what follows, i.e.
on whether it is in a category 1 or category 2 sentence.

2   The conjunction ἐάν of the future time-frame of category 2 is a contraction of εἰ + ἄν (cf. ὅταν < ὅτε + ἄν, 14.1/4c(iii)). It may also be written as ἄν (to be distinguished from the particle ἄν—the latter has a short vowel) or ἤν in some dialects.

3   It is, of course, possible to combine certain time references within one sentence:

   εἰ τοῦτο ἔπραξας, ἐκινδύνευες ἄν.   *If you had done that you would [now] be in danger.*

   εἰ τοῦτο ἔπραξας, κινδῦνεύεις.   *If you did that you are in danger.*

4   In category 2 sentences with a future reference εἰ + fut. ind. is substituted for ἐάν + subj. where a **threat** or **warning** is implied:

   ἀποκτενεῖς εἴ με γῆς ἔξω βαλεῖς.   *You will kill [me] if you throw me out of the country.*

18.1/6   ἄκρος, μέσος, ἔσχατος

These three adjectives vary in meaning according to whether they are used in the attributive or predicative position (3.1/1b):

τὸ ἄκρον ὄρος *the high mountain*   ἄκρον τὸ ὄρος *the top of the mountain*
τὸ μέσον ὄρος *the middle mountain*   μέσον τὸ ὄρος *the middle of the mountain*
τὸ ἔσχατον ὄρος *the furthest mountain*   ἔσχατον τὸ ὄρος *the furthest part of the mountain*

For the predicative position we may also, of course, have τὸ ὄρος ἄκρον, etc.

18.2   Greek reading

1   Κυμαῖός τις μέλι ἐπώλει. γευσαμένου δέ τινος καὶ εἰπόντος, πάνυ καλόν ἐστιν, εἰ μὴ γάρ, ἔφη, μῦς ἐνέπεσεν εἰς αὐτὸ οὐκ ἂν ἐπώλουν.

2   Λάκαινά τις πρὸς τὸν υἱὸν λέγοντα μικρὸν ἔχειν τὸ ξίφος εἶπε, καὶ βῆμα πρόσθες.

3   **Proverbs**

   (i) ἐὰν ἡ λεοντῆ μὴ ἐξίκηται, τὴν ἀλωπεκῆν πρόσαψον.   (ii) κυνὶ δίδως ἄχυρα, ὄνῳ δὲ ὀστᾶ.   (iii) ἐπ' ἄκρᾳ τῇ γλώττῃ τὸ φιλεῖν ἔχεις.   (iv) ἄν (= ἐὰν) τοὺς φίλους μισῶμεν, τί ποιήσομεν τοὺς μισοῦντας;   (v) εἰ τυρὸν εἶχον, οὐκ ἂν ἐδεόμην ὄψου.   (vi)# φίλον δι' ὀργὴν ἐν κακοῖσι μὴ προδῷς.   (vii)# τὸ κέρδος ἡδύ, κἂν ἀπὸ ψευδῶν ἴῃ.   (viii) δός τι καὶ λαβέ τι.   (ix)# πλάνη βίον τίθησι σωφρονέστερον.   (x) αἰσχρὸν εὐεργέτας προδοῦναι.   (xi) ἐὰν ἔχωμεν χρήματα, ἕξομεν φίλους.   (xii) ἴτω τὰ πράγματα ὅπῃ τῷ θεῷ φίλον.

4#   εἰς Ῥόδον εἰ πλεῖν δεῖ, τις Ὀλυμπικὸν ἦλθεν ἐρωτῶν τὸν μάντιν, καὶ πῶς πλεύσεται ἀσφαλέως·

χὠ μάντις, πρῶτον μέν, ἔφη, καινὴν ἔχε τὴν ναῦν,
καὶ μὴ χειμῶνος, τοῦ δὲ θέρους ἀνάγου·
ταῦτα γὰρ ἦν ποιῇς, ἥξεις κἀκεῖσε καὶ ὧδε,   5
ἢν μὴ πειρατὴς ἐν πελάγει σε λάβῃ.

5   γέρων ποτὲ ξύλα κόψας καὶ ταῦτα φέρων πολλὴν ὁδὸν ἐβάδιζε. διὰ δὲ
τὸν κόπον ἀποθέμενος τὸ φορτίον τὸν Θάνατον ἐπεκαλεῖτο. τοῦ δὲ
Θανάτου φανέντος καὶ πυνθανομένου διὰ τίνα αἰτίαν ἐπεκαλεῖτο, ὁ
γέρων ἔφη, ἵνα τὸ φορτίον τοῦτο ἄρας ἐπιθῇς μοι.

6# ἄπαν διδόμενον δῶρον, ἂν καὶ μικρὸν ᾖ,
μέγιστόν ἐστιν, ἂν μετ' εὐνοίας δοθῇ.

7   ὄφις, ἢν μὴ φάγῃ ὄφιν, δράκων οὐ γενήσεται.

8# γῆς ἐπέβην γυμνός, γυμνός θ' ὑπὸ γαῖαν ἄπειμι·
καὶ τί μάτην μοχθῶ, γυμνὸν ὁρῶν τὸ τέλος;

9   **More stories about Diogenes**

    (*i*) θαυμάζοντός τινος τὰ ἐν Σαμοθράκῃ ἀναθήματα ἔφη, πολλῷ ἂν ἦν
πλείω εἰ καὶ οἱ μὴ σωθέντες ἀνετίθεσαν.

    (*ii*) εἰς Μύνδον ἐλθὼν καὶ θεασάμενος μεγάλας τὰς πύλας, μικρὰν δὲ
τὴν πόλιν, ἄνδρες Μύνδιοι, ἔφη, κλείσατε τὰς πύλας μὴ ἡ πόλις
ὑμῶν ἐξέλθῃ.

    (*iii*) δύσκολον ᾔτει· τοῦ δ' εἰπόντος, ἐάν με πείσῃς, ἔφη, εἴ σε ἐδυνάμην
πεῖσαι, ἔπεισα ἄν σε ἀπάγξασθαι.

    (*iv*) λύχνον μεθ' ἡμέραν ἅψας περιῄει λέγων, ἄνθρωπον ζητῶ.

10   In order to lure the Syracusan army away from Syracuse, the Athenians
sent an agent who persuaded the Syracusans that they could surprise the
Athenians at a neighbouring city, Catana. The ruse was totally
successful. The passage is from Thucydides' account of the disastrous
Athenian expedition to Sicily (415–413 BC).

    οἱ δὲ στρατηγοὶ τῶν Συρακοσίων ἐπίστευσαν τῷ ἀνθρώπῳ πολλῷ
ἀπερισκεπτότερον, καὶ εὐθὺς ἡμέραν ξυνθέμενοι ᾗ παρέσονται ἀπέστει-
λαν αὐτόν, καὶ αὐτοὶ προεῖπον πανδημεὶ πᾶσιν ἐξιέναι Συρακοσίοις.
ἐπεὶ δὲ ἑτοῖμα αὐτοῖς τὰ τῆς παρασκευῆς ἦν καὶ αἱ ἡμέραι ἐν αἷς
ξυνέθεντο ἥξειν ἐγγὺς ἦσαν, πορευόμενοι ἐπὶ Κατάνης ηὐλίσαντο ἐπὶ   5
τῷ Συμαίθῳ ποταμῷ. οἱ δ' Ἀθηναῖοι, ὡς ᾔσθοντο αὐτοὺς προσιόντας,
ἀναλαβόντες τὸ στράτευμα ἅπαν τὸ ἑαυτῶν καὶ ἐπιβιβάσαντες ἐπὶ τὰς
ναῦς καὶ τὰ πλοῖα ὑπὸ νύκτα ἔπλεον ἐπὶ τὰς Συρακούσας.

Notes

1   γάρ *yes, for* Greek has no word which corresponds exactly to the English
yes and often the assent of a speaker is implied by particles (24.1/1).

2   μῑκρόν is in the predicative position (3.1/3*b*), i.e. *that he had his sword
short*, i.e. *that the sword he had was short*; καί is adverbial (*as well*) but
need not be translated; πρόσθες < προστίθημι.

3 (*i*) πρόcαψον < προcάπτω. (*iv*) ποιέω + two accusatives *do [some-thing] to/with* (22.1/2*f* (ii)). (*vii*) κἄν = καὶ ἐάν; ψευδῶν < ψεῦδος. (*ix*) τίθηcι here *render*. (*xi*) ἕξομεν < ἔχω. (*xii*) ἴτω 3rd s. imp. of ἔρχομαι (18.1/3 and **Appendix 3**); τῷ θεῷ φίλον (neuter s.) sc. ἐcτί *it is dear to God.*

4 *l*.1 εἰ *if* would be first word of its clause in prose. *l*.2 πλεύcεται lit. *he will sail*, but translate *he would sail* (Greek retains the original tense in reported speech (8.1/3 and 10.1/2*b*)); ἀcφαλέωc, i.e. ἀcφαλῶc the uncontracted form is Ionic (on Ionic forms in poetry see 1.3). *l*.3 χῶ = καὶ ὁ; καινήν predicative as in (2) above, lit. *have the ship [which you sail in] new*, i.e. *get a new ship*. *l*.4 χειμῶνος . . . θέρους gen. of time within which (7.1/7*c*). *l*.5 ἤν = ἐάν (also in next line and in 7 below). *l*.5 κἀκεῖcε (= καὶ ἐκεῖcε) καὶ ὧδε lit. *both thither and hither*, i.e. *both there and back*.

5 ἀποθέμενος aor. mid. pple. of ἀποτίθημι; φανέντος gen. m. s. of the aor. pple. of φαίνομαι; πυνθανομένου *asking*; ἄρᾱς nom. m. s. of the aor. act. pple. of αἴρω; ἐπιθῇς 2nd s. aor. subj. act. of ἐπιτίθημι.

6 In both lines ἄν = ἐάν; ἐὰν (or εἰ) καί normally *although* but here obviously *even if* (which is usually καὶ εἰ/ἐάν); δοθῇ 3rd s. aor. subj. pass. of δίδωμι.

7 φάγῃ 3rd s. aor. subj. act. of ἐcθίω.

8 θ' i.e. τε.

9 (*i*) Samothrace, an island in the northern Aegean, was notorious for shipwrecks; the subject of ἔφη (and in (*ii*) and (*iii*)) is Diogenes; πολλῷ dat. of measure of difference (17.1/4*b*); take καί *also* with what follows; οἱ μὴ cωθέντες (aor. pass. pple. of cῴζω) the negative μή is used because Diogenes is referring to a general class (12.1/2*a*(vi)); ἀνετίθεcαν *had dedicated* the imperfect, not the aorist, is used because the verb refers to **repeated** action in the past. (*ii*) μεγάλᾱς . . . μῑκράν both adjectives are predicative as in (2) above; μή introducing a negative purpose clause (14.1/4*c*(i)). (*iii*) τοῦ refers to the δύcκολος; ἀπάγξαcθαι aor. inf. of ἀπάγχομαι. (*iv*) περιῄει 3rd s. impf. of περιέρχομαι (18.1/3); μεθ' ἡμέρᾱν *after day[break]*, i.e. *by day*, cf. ἅμα τῇ ἡμέρᾳ.

10 *l*.1 πολλῷ (dat. of measure of difference, 17.1/4*b*) is to be taken with the following word. *l*.2 παρέcονται (< πάρειμι) on the future see note on πλεύcεται in 4 *l*.2 above (cf. ἥξειν in *l*.5). *l*.3 Take πᾶcιν . . . Cυρακοcίοιc with προεῖπον (< προαγορεύω, 18.1/4 note 2). *l*.4 τὰ τῆc παραcκευῆc lit. *the [things] of their preparation* but trans. *their preparations*. *l*.5 ηὐλίcαντο < αὐλίζομαι. *l*.8 τὰ πλοῖα is acc. after ἐπί.

18.3 Extra reading –
The sea, the sea!

The *Anabasis* of Xenophon (7.2.1) tells how an army of Greek mercenaries, after becoming embroiled in a dispute between rivals for the Persian throne, had to make their way back from Persia to Greece. The following passage describes their elation when, after many months of hardship, they finally reached the Black Sea.

καὶ ἀφικνοῦνται ἐπὶ τὸ ὄρος τῇ πέμπτῃ ἡμέρᾳ· ὄνομα δὲ τῷ ὄρει ἦν
Θήχης. ἐπεὶ δὲ οἱ πρῶτοι ἐγένοντο ἐπὶ τοῦ ὄρους καὶ κατεῖδον τὴν
θάλατταν, κραυγὴ πολλὴ ἐγένετο. ἀκούσας δὲ ὁ Ξενοφῶν καὶ οἱ
ὀπισθοφύλακες ᾠήθησαν ἔμπροσθεν ἄλλους ἐπιτίθεσθαι πολεμίους·
ἐπειδὴ δ' ἡ βοὴ πλείων τε ἐγίγνετο καὶ ἐγγύτερον καὶ οἱ ἀεὶ ἐπιόντες   5
ἔθεον δρόμῳ ἐπὶ τοὺς ἀεὶ βοῶντας καὶ πολλῷ μείζων ἐγίγνετο ἡ βοὴ ὅσῳ
δὴ πλείους ἐγίγνοντο, ἐδόκει δὴ μεῖζόν τι εἶναι τῷ Ξενοφῶντι, καὶ
ἀναβὰς ἐφ' ἵππον καὶ τοὺς ἱππέας ἀναλαβὼν παρεβοήθει· καὶ τάχα δὴ
ἀκούουσι βοώντων τῶν στρατιωτῶν, θάλαττα θάλαττα, καὶ παρεγ-
γυώντων. ἔνθα δὴ ἔθεον πάντες καὶ οἱ ὀπισθοφύλακες, καὶ τὰ ὑποζύγια   10
ἠλαύνετο καὶ οἱ ἵπποι. ἐπεὶ δὲ ἀφίκοντο πάντες ἐπὶ τὸ ἄκρον, ἐνταῦθα δὴ
περιέβαλλον ἀλλήλους καὶ στρατηγοὺς καὶ λοχαγοὺς δακρύοντες.

Notes

l.1 ἀφῑκνοῦνται vivid present (see note on 7.2.13 *l*.7; cf. ἀκούουσι in *l*.9).   *l*.4 ᾠήθησαν < οἴομαι.   *ll*.5f. οἱ ἀεὶ ἐπιόντες (< ἐπέρχομαι) *those who kept coming up* refers to the different groups who went up the hill, but τοὺς ἀεὶ βοῶντας *those who kept shouting* refers to the ever-increasing group which could see the sea; δρόμῳ *at a run* is redundant after ἔθεον (inceptive imperfect *began to run* 4.1/1 footnote).   *ll*.6f. ὅσῳ etc. lit. *by how much they became more [numerous]*; on ὅσος see 21.1/3; ἐδόκει . . . τῷ Ξενοφῶντι lit. *it seemed to Xenophon*; μεῖζόν τι *something more serious*.   *l*.8 παρεβοήθει and the imperfects in the following lines are inceptive (see above on ἔθεον).   *ll*.10f. ἠλαύνετο has τὰ ὑποζύγια and οἱ ἵπποι as its subjects but it agrees with the nearer one, τὰ ὑποζύγια, which as a neuter plural takes a singular verb (3.1/1 note 2; for another example of a double subject see 16.2.13 *l*.1).

Unit 19

19.1 Grammar

19.1/1 ἵστημι and its compounds

ἵστημι *make to stand, set up* was originally σίστᾱμι with a present stem of the same formation as δίδωμι and τίθημι (i.e. reduplication with iota and no suffix). At an early stage in the history of Greek the initial sigma developed into a rough breathing; the resulting ἵστᾱμι (the form in most dialects) became ἵστημι in Attic with the regular change of ᾱ > η.[1] Consequently, where the alternation δω/δο occurs in δίδωμι and θη/θε in τίθημι we have στη/στα in ἵστημι; the alternation φη/φα in φημί (7.1/2) has the same explanation (the original form of the first person singular is φᾱμί).

The present and imperfect of ἵστημι are roughly parallel to δίδωμι and τίθημι. In the active we have:

PRESENT

		IND.	IMP.	SUBJ.	OPT.
S.	1	ἵστημι		ἱστῶ	ἱσταίην
	2	ἵστης	ἵστη	ἱστῇς	ἱσταίης
	3	ἵστησι(ν)	ἱστάτω	ἱστῇ	ἱσταίη
PL.	1	ἵσταμεν		ἱστῶμεν	ἱσταῖμεν
	2	ἵστατε	ἵστατε	ἱστῆτε	ἱσταῖτε
	3	ἱστᾶσι(ν)	ἱστάντων	ἱστῶσι(ν)	ἱσταῖεν

INFINITIVE ἱστάναι
PARTICIPLE ἱστάς, ἱστᾶσα, ἱστάν; gen. ἱστάντος, ἱστάσης, ἱστάντος
IMPERFECT ἵστην, ἵστης, ἵστη, ἵσταμεν, ἵστατε, ἵστασαν

The future στήσω *I shall make to stand, shall set up* is also parallel, but we meet a divergence in the aorist. ἵστημι has two sets of forms (cf. the two aorists of φύω, 11.1/1):

(a) A weak aorist ἔστησα, which is transitive and means *I made to stand, set up*.

(b) A root aorist ἔστην (conjugated as ἔβην, 11.1/1), which is intransitive and means *I stood*.

---

[1] This change, which occurs when ᾱ is not preceded by ε, ι or ρ, is one of the more striking differences between Attic and most other dialects.

Examples of these two aorists are:

ἔγχος ἔστησε πρὸς κίονα. *He stood his spear against a pillar* (transitive).

'Ἀλκμήνης τόκος ἔστη σιωπῇ. *The son of Alcmene stood in silence* (intransitive).

The two aorists have identical forms in the 3rd pl. indicative active ἔστησαν (ἔστης-αν from ἔστησα; ἔστη-σαν from ἔστην). Where this form occurs, only the context will show whether it is transitive or intransitive.

ἵστημι is also irregular in its perfect and pluperfect. Both tenses have a κ suffix in the singular of the indicative but elsewhere a stem without κ (ἑστα-) is normally used (see below). Because these tenses are intransitive (see below) they occur only in the active voice:

PERFECT

		IND.	IMP.	SUBJ.	OPT.
S.	1	ἕστηκα		ἑστῶ	ἑσταίην
	2	ἕστηκας	ἕσταθι	ἑστῇς	ἑσταίης
	3	ἕστηκε(ν)	ἑστάτω	ἑστῇ	ἑσταίη
PL.	1	ἕσταμεν		ἑστῶμεν	ἑσταῖμεν
	2	ἕστατε	ἕστατε	ἑστῆτε	ἑσταῖτε
	3	ἑστᾶσι(ν)	ἑστάντων	ἑστῶσι(ν)	ἑσταῖεν

INFINITIVE ἑστάναι
PARTICIPLE ἑστώς, ἑστῶσα, ἑστός; gen. ἑστῶτος, ἑστώσης, ἑστῶτος
PLUPERFECT εἱστήκη, εἱστήκης, εἱστήκει(ν), ἕσταμεν, ἕστατε, ἕστασαν

Except for the imperative, forms with the stem ἑστα- have alternatives in ἑστηκ- (e.g. 3rd pl. ind. ἑστήκāσι(ν), inf. ἑστηκέναι) but these are less common.

The first syllable of the perfect stem was originally σεστ- with reduplication of σ, but, as in the present stem, the initial σ developed into a rough breathing, giving ἑστ-. Because ἑ is in fact the reduplication it is kept in **all** forms of the perfect (16.1/4). The initial εἱστ- of the singular of the pluperfect was originally ἐσεστ- with the syllabic augment and reduplication (quite irregularly the augment does not occur in the plural and hence the 1st and 2nd pl. forms are identical with those of the perfect).

Both perfect and pluperfect are intransitive and they are used as a **present** and **imperfect** tense respectively: ἕστηκα *I am standing* and εἱστήκη *I was standing*. The future perfect ἑστήξω *I shall stand* (cf. 16.1/4 note 2) is also intransitive.

We may summarise these forms as follows:

	Transitive		**Intransitive**
PRESENT	ἵστημι *I am making to stand*	PERFECT	ἕστηκα *I am standing*
FUTURE	cτήcω *I shall make to stand*	FUT. PERF.	ἑcτήξω *I shall stand*
IMPERFECT	ἵcτην *I was making to stand*	PLUPERFECT	εἱcτήκη *I was standing*
WEAK AORIST	ἕcτηcα *I made to stand*	ROOT AORIST	ἕcτην *I stood*

A comprehensive table of ἵcτημι is given in **Appendix 5**. The present middle ἵcταμαι is intransitive and literally means *I am in the process of making myself stand*, i.e. it represents a present **act** as opposed to the perfect, which represents a present **state** (*I am in a standing position*). The imperfect middle (ἱcτάμην) and future middle (cτήcομαι) are also intransitive but the weak aorist middle (ἐcτηcάμην) is transitive and means *I made (something) stand for myself*.

ἵcτημι has many compounds and these retain the same distinctions between transitive and intransitive tenses. Among the most common are:

TRANSITIVE TENSES

ἀνίcτημι (ἀνά *up*) *raise up; restore; cause to migrate, expel, uproot*

ἀφίcτημι (ἀπό *away*) *remove; cause to revolt*

καθίcτημι (κατά *down*) *set down; put in a certain state; appoint; establish (laws*, etc.)

INTRANSITIVE TENSES

rise up; be expelled; migrate

go away from; revolt

settle down; come into a certain state; be appointed; be established

The middle voice of compounds of ἵcτημι follows the pattern of the simple verb: οἱ βάρβαροι ἀφίcτανται *the barbarians are in [the act of] revolt* (cf. οἱ βάρβαροι ἀφεcτᾶcιν (perfect) *the barbarians are in [a state of] revolt*).

Examples of the above compounds are:

ἀνέcτηcαν καὶ Αἰγῑνήτᾱc τῷ αὐτῷ θέρει τούτῳ ἐξ Αἰγίνηc Ἀθηναῖοι. *In this same summer the Athenians also expelled the Aeginetans from Aegina.*

Βοιωτοὶ οἱ νῦν ἑξηκοcτῷ ἔτει μετὰ Ἰλίου ἅλωcιν ἐξ Ἄρνηc ἀναcτάντεc ὑπὸ Θεccαλῶν τὴν Βοιωτίᾱν ᾤκιcαν. *In the sixtieth year after the capture of Troy the present Boeotians, after being expelled from Arne by the Thessalians, colonised Boeotia.*

εἰ τοὺc ξυμμάχουc αὐτῶν ἀφιcτάναι πειρᾱcόμεθα, δεήcει καὶ τούτοιc ναυcὶ βοηθεῖν τὸ πλέον οὖcι νηcιώταιc. *If we try* (lit. *shall try*) *to make their allies revolt, we shall have to come to their assistance as well* with a fleet because they are for the most part islanders (lit. *it will be necessary to assist them also with ships, being [for] the greater [part] islanders*).

πρῶτοι ἀπ' αὐτῶν Μῆδοι ἤρξαντο ἀφίϲταϲθαι.   *The Medes were the first to start to revolt from them* (lit. *the Medes first started . . .*).

κατέϲτηϲε τύραννον εἶναι παῖδα τὸν ἑαυτοῦ.   *He appointed his own son to be tyrant.*

ἐϲ φόβον καταϲτάντων διαφθείρονται πολλοὶ Χαόνων.   *When they were reduced to a state of panic many of the Chaonians were killed* (vivid present).

Notes

1   To distinguish the different forms of ἵϲτημι it is essential to remember that:

(i)   ἱϲτ- occurs in all forms of the present and imperfect but nowhere else.

(ii)   ἐϲτ- occurs only in the aorist indicative.

(iii)   ἑϲτ- occurs in all forms of the perfect and in the pluperfect plural but nowhere else.

(iv)   εἱϲτ- occurs only in the pluperfect singular.

2   πίμπλημι *fill* and πίμπρημι *burn* (tr.) follow ἵϲτημι in the present and imperfect, e.g. the pres. ind. act. of the first is: πίμπλημι, πίμπληϲ, πίμπληϲι(ν), πίμπλαμεν, πίμπλατε, πιμπλᾶϲι(ν).

19.1/2   Potential clauses

Potential clauses express an action or state which has or had the potentiality of happening: *I wouldn't like to meet him on a dark night*; *Alcibiades would have been a disaster at our last party*. In Greek the construction is the same as for main clauses in category 1 conditional sentences (18.1/5; for the only complication see note 1 below); and the same is true in English, which uses *would* or *could* (although other auxiliaries such as *might* are also possible). As with conditional sentences (18.1/5) we have three time-frames:

Future the optative (present or aorist as appropriate) with ἄν:

τοῦτο οὐκ ἂν γένοιτο.   *That would not happen.*

Present the imperfect indicative with ἄν:

τοῦτο οὐκ ἂν ἐγίγνετο.   *That would not be happening* or *happen [now—* to make a distinction between future and present English may need to add an adverb*]*.

Past the aorist indicative with ἄν:

τοῦτο οὐκ ἂν ἐγένετο.   *That would not have happened.*

Notes

1 A future potential can be used as a form of politeness to make a statement or request less blunt, e.g. βουλοίμην ἄν *I should like* (cf. βούλομαι *I want*). ἐβουλόμην ἄν *I could wish* (*sc.* that something were now the case) is also frequently used with a past reference *I could have wished*; this is a relic of older use.

2 In a particular context it is sometimes possible to translate a present or future potential by *can*, instead of *could/would*; the above examples would then be translated *that can not happen/be happening*.

19.1/3 Oddities in verbs

(a) Perfects with a present meaning

As we have seen (15.1.1), the perfect expresses a state in the present resulting from an action in the past. The perfect of some Greek verbs is best expressed in English by the present tense of verbs which in themselves indicate a state. The most common examples are:

> δέδοικα *I am afraid* (lit. *I have become alarmed*) from δείδω *become alarmed*. The aorist ἔδεισα is common and has the meaning *I was afraid*.

> ἔγνωκα *I know* (lit. *I have recognized*) from γιγνώσκω *recognize*.

> ἔοικα *I resemble*, *I seem* exists only in a few forms outside the perfect. Poetical forms in εἰκ- occur in the infinitive (εἰκέναι, otherwise ἐοικέναι) and participle (εἰκώς, εἰκυῖα, εἰκός, otherwise ἐοικώς etc.).

> κέκτημαι,[1] lit. *I have acquired* or *I am in a state of having acquired* (< κτάμαι *acquire*), is normally to be translated by *I possess*, *own* (plpf. ἐκεκτήμην *I possessed*, *owned*; fut. perf. κεκτήσομαι *I shall possess*, *own*).

> μέμνημαι *I remember* (lit. *I have reminded myself*) from μιμνήσκομαι *remind oneself*. The aorist passive ἐμνήσθην means *I remembered* (ex. at 12.3.9 *l*.2).

> οἶδα *I know* exists only in the perfect, pluperfect and future—see **Appendix 3**.

> τέθνηκα *I am dead* (lit. *I have died*) from ἀποθνήσκω *die* (the perfect is exceptional in never having the prefix ἀπο-, whereas the other tenses of the uncompounded verb are normally restricted to poetry). As with the perfect of ἵστημι (19.1/1) shorter forms occur, e.g. inf. τεθνάναι (for τεθνηκέναι), pple. τεθνεώς (for τεθνηκώς), opt. τεθναίην.

---

[1] This reduplication is an exception to the rule given at 15.1/1 (we would have expected ἐκτη-).

(b) Eccentric -μαι verbs

A few deponents end in -αμαι, not -ομαι, because they belong to the -μι class of verbs (18.1/1; cf. ἵcταμαι pres. mid./pass. of ἵcτημι, 19.1/1). The only common examples are δύναμαι *be able* and ἐπίcταμαι *know how to, understand* (both passive deponents with a middle future—see **Principal parts of verbs**; we have already met some forms, e.g. 10.3 *l.*5). These differ from -ω verbs only in the present and imperfect. In these tenses δύναμαι is conjugated:

PRESENT

    INDICATIVE   δύναμαι, δύναcαι, δύναται, δυνάμεθα, δύναcθε, δύνανται
    INFINITIVE   δύναcθαι   PARTICIPLE   δυνάμενος, -η, -ον

IMPERFECT

    ἐδυνάμην, ἐδύνω (< -αcο), ἐδύνατο, ἐδυνάμεθα, ἐδύναcθε, ἐδύναντο.

For ἐδυν- we may also have ἠδυν-. The other moods of the present, where they occur, follow ἵcτημι (19.1/1). The forms of ἐπίcταμαι are parallel.

Two similar verbs are κεῖμαι *lie, be laid down* and κάθημαι *be seated, sit*[1] which, because they both describe a continuous action, exist only in the present, imperfect and future. κεῖμαι is conjugated:

PRESENT

    INDICATIVE   κεῖμαι, κεῖcαι, κεῖται, κείμεθα, κεῖcθε, κεῖνται
    INFINITIVE   κεῖcθαι   PARTICIPLE   κείμενος, -η, -ον

IMPERFECT   ἐκείμην, ἔκειcο, ἔκειτο, ἐκείμεθα, ἔκειcθε, ἔκειντο
FUTURE INDICATIVE   κείcομαι, κείcῃ, etc.

The forms of κάθημαι follow the same pattern. The other moods of the present of both verbs are rare. On the use of κεῖμαι for the perfect passive of τίθημι see 18.1/2 note 4.

19.2   Greek reading

1 λέγει που Ἡράκλειτος ὅτι πάντα χωρεῖ καὶ οὐδὲν μένει, καὶ ποταμοῦ
    ῥοῇ ἀπεικάζων τὰ ὄντα λέγει ὡς δὶς εἰς τὸν αὐτὸν ποταμὸν οὐκ ἂν
    ἐμβαίης.

2# νῆφε καὶ μέμνης᾽ (=-cο) ἀπιστεῖν· ἄρθρα ταῦτα τῶν φρενῶν.

3 Πύρρων οὐδὲν ἔφη διαφέρειν ζῆν ἢ τεθνάναι. εἰπόντος δέ τινος, τί οὖν
    οὐκ ἀποθνῄcκεις; ὅτι, ἔφη, οὐδὲν διαφέρει.

4# δοκεῖτε πηδᾶν τἀδικήματ᾽ εἰς θεοὺς
    πτεροῖcι, κἄπειτ᾽ ἐν Διὸς δέλτου πτυχαῖς
    γράφειν τιν᾽ αὐτά, Ζῆνα δ᾽ εἰcορῶντά νιν
    θνητοῖc δικάζειν; οὐδ᾽ ὁ πᾶc ἂν οὐρανός,

---

[1] κάθημαι is used in prose but the uncompounded verb, ἧμαι, is found in verse (e.g. 16.3 *l.*9).

Διὸς γράφοντος τὰς βροτῶν ἁμαρτίας,   5
ἐξαρκέσειεν οὐδ' ἐκεῖνος ἂν σκοπῶν
πέμπειν ἑκάστῳ ζημίαν· ἀλλ' ἡ Δίκη
ἐνταῦθά ποὐστιν ἐγγύς, εἰ βούλεσθ' ὁρᾶν.

5 Proverbs and famous sayings

(*i*) ἐὰν δύνῃ ὁδεῦσαι, μὴ πλεύσῃς.   (*ii*) τοῖς σεαυτοῦ πτεροῖς ἑάλως.   (*iii*) ἐκ παντὸς ξύλου Ἑρμῆς οὐκ ἂν γένοιτο.   (*iv*) ὕδωρ πίνων οὐδὲν ἂν τέκοις σοφόν.   (*v*)# ὁ χρῄσιμ' εἰδώς, οὐχ ὁ πόλλ' εἰδώς, σοφός.   (*vi*)# θεοῦ διδόντος οὐκ ἂν ἐκφύγοις κακά.   (*vii*) πάντες ἄνθρωποι τοῦ εἰδέναι ὀρέγονται φύσει.   (*viii*) ὅταν εὐπλοῇς, μάλιστα μέμνησο ζάλης.   (*ix*) δός μοι ποῦ στῶ καὶ κινήσω τὴν γῆν.   (*x*) πολυμαθίη (= -ία) νόον ἔχειν οὐ διδάσκει· Ἡσίοδον γὰρ ἂν ἐδίδαξε καὶ Πυθαγόρην (= -αν).   (*xi*) τὸ φύσει πεφυκὸς οὐ μεθίσταται.   (*xii*) κούφως φέρειν δεῖ τὰς παρεστώσας τύχας.   (*xiii*) ἀθυμοῦντες ἄνδρες οὔπω τροπαῖον ἔστησαν.   (*xiv*) ἄνθρωπος ὢν μέμνησο.   (*xv*) πάγην ἱστὰς ἐν πάγῃ ληφθήσῃ.   (*xvi*) πόρρω ἑστὼς ὁ θεὸς ἐγγύθεν βλέπει.   (*xvii*) ἐπὶ ξυροῦ ἵσταται.

6#   ὡς τοῖς κακῶς πράσσουσιν ἡδὺ καὶ βραχὺν
χρόνον λαθέσθαι τῶν παρεστώτων κακῶν.

7   One of the most famous Spartan kings was Leonidas, who died with three hundred Spartan soldiers at Thermopylae in an attempt to defend the pass against the invading Persians (480 BC). The following are stories about him:

(*i*) Λεωνίδας πρός τινα εἰπόντα, πλὴν τοῦ βασιλεύειν ἡμῶν οὐδὲν διαφέρεις, ἀλλ' οὐκ ἄν, ἔφη, εἰ μὴ βελτίων ὑμῶν ἦν, ἐβασίλευον.

(*ii*) γενόμενος ἐν Θερμοπύλαις πρός τινα εἰπόντα, ἀπὸ τῶν ὀϊστευμάτων τῶν βαρβάρων οὐδὲ τὸν ἥλιον ἰδεῖν ἔξεστιν, οὐκοῦν, ἔφη, χαρίεν, εἰ ὑπὸ σκιᾷ αὐτοῖς μαχούμεθα.

(*iii*) Ξέρξου δὲ γράψαντος αὐτῷ, ἔξεστί σοι μὴ θεομαχοῦντι, μετ' ἐμοῦ δὲ ταττομένῳ, τῆς Ἑλλάδος μοναρχεῖν, ἀντέγραψεν, εἰ τὰ καλὰ τοῦ βίου ἐγίγνωσκες, ἀπέστης ἂν τῆς τῶν ἀλλοτρίων ἐπιθυμίας· ἐμοὶ δὲ κρείττων ὁ ὑπὲρ τῆς Ἑλλάδος θάνατος τοῦ μοναρχεῖν τῶν ὁμοφύλων.

(*iv*) πάλιν δὲ τοῦ Ξέρξου γράψαντος, πέμψον τὰ ὅπλα, ἀντέγραψε, μολὼν λαβέ.

The following epitaph for Leonidas and his men was written by Simonides:

(*v*)# ὦ ξεῖν', ἀγγέλλειν Λακεδαιμονίοις ὅτι τῇδε
κείμεθα, τοῖς κείνων ῥήμασι πειθόμενοι.

8   The normal way of publishing an official document in the Greek world was to cut the text on stone (usually marble) and display it in a prominent place. Many thousands of such inscriptions have survived. The following is an extract from the record of the Athenian settlement with the Euboean city of Chalcis after the Euboean revolt from the Athenian empire in

446 BC, and gives the wording of the oath to be sworn by all adult males in Chalcis.

οὐκ ἀποστήσομαι ἀπὸ τοῦ δήμου τοῦ Ἀθηναίων οὔτε τέχνῃ οὔτε μηχανῇ
οὐδεμιᾷ οὐδ᾽ ἔπει οὐδὲ ἔργῳ, οὐδὲ τῷ ἀφισταμένῳ πείσομαι, καὶ ἐὰν
ἀφιστῇ τις, κατερῶ Ἀθηναίοις, καὶ τὸν φόρον ὑποτελῶ Ἀθηναίοις ὃν ἂν
πείθω Ἀθηναίους, καὶ ξύμμαχος ἔσομαι οἷος ἂν δύνωμαι ἄριστος καὶ
δικαιότατος, καὶ τῷ δήμῳ τῷ Ἀθηναίων βοηθήσω καὶ ἀμυνῶ, ἐάν τις   5
ἀδικῇ τὸν δῆμον τὸν Ἀθηναίων, καὶ πείσομαι τῷ δήμῳ τῷ Ἀθηναίων.

Notes

1 τὰ ὄντα neuter pl., lit. *the being [things]*, i.e. *existing things*; ὡς = ὅτι (8.1/3*b*).

2 ταῦτα is subject and ἄρθρα predicate.

3 οὐδὲν ἔφη cf. οὔ φημι (8.1/3*a* note 4); οὐδέν *in no respect*, *not at all* (20.1/5); ζῆν and τεθνάναι (19.1/3*a*) are the subjects of διαφέρειν; εἰπόντος . . . τινος gen. absolute (12.1/2*b*).

4 *l*.1 δοκεῖτε *do you think*; τἀδικήματ᾽(α) (= τὰ ἀδ-) is the subject of πηδᾶν. *l*.3 τιν᾽(α) *someone* is the subject of γράφειν and αὐτά the object; νιν an obsolete pronoun used solely in verse; it exists only in this form, which can function as the accusative of either the singular or plural of any gender of the 3rd person unemphatic pronoun (i.e. it can mean *him, her, it, them*); here it is the equivalent of αὐτά (acc.), i.e. the ἀδικήματα. *l*.4 Take ἄν with ἐξαρκέσειεν. *l*.6 ἐξαρκέσειεν (< ἐξαρκέω—the ε is not lengthened, cf. 5.1/2 note 2) is to be supplied after οὐδ᾽. *l*.8 ποῦστιν crasis (11.1/5) for ποῦ ἐστιν; βούλεσθ᾽, i.e. βούλεσθε.

5 (*i*) δύνῃ 2nd s. pres. subj. of δύναμαι (the subjunctive is required after ἐάν—14.1/4*c*(iii)). (*ii*) ἑάλως < ἁλίσκομαι (18.1/4). (*iii*) Not the god himself but a statue of him. (*iv*) ὕδωρ πίνων is the equivalent of a conditional clause (*if you drink water*—12.1/2*a*(iv)); τέκοις 2nd s. aor. opt. act. of τίκτω. (*v*) εἰδώς < οἶδα (19.1/3*a* and **Appendix 3**). (*vii*) τοῦ εἰδέναι articular infinitive (5.1/3—other examples below in 7(*i*) and (*iii*)); ὀρέγομαι is followed by the genitive (13.1/2*a*(ii)). (*viii*) μέμνησο, cf. 17.1/1 note 4. (*ix*) δός 2nd s. aor. imp. act. of δίδωμι; στῶ (1st s. intrans. aor. subj. of ἵστημι) deliberative subjunctive in indirect speech (14.1/4*a*(ii)), *where I am to stand*. (*x*) Written in Ionic (1.3); γάρ *for [otherwise]*. (*xi*) πεφυκός < φύω. (*xii*) παρεστώσας f. perf. pple. of παρίστημι. (*xiii*) ἔστησαν gnomic aor. (see note on 5.2.10). (*xiv*) μέμνημαι is followed, where appropriate, by a participle, not an infinitive (cf. 15.1/2*a*). (*xv*) ληφθήσῃ 2nd s. fut. ind. pass. of λαμβάνω.

6 παρεστώτων n. perf. pple. of παρίστημι.

7 (*i*) Take ἡμῶν with διαφέρεις, not with βασιλεύειν. (*ii*) οὐδέ *not even*; χαρίεν sc. ἔσται; ἔξεστιν (also in (*iii*)) an impersonal verb meaning *it is possible* (21.1/4*a*). (*iii*) Take ταττομένῳ (mid. of τάττω, *drawing yourself up* (*with me*)) with σοι; τοῦ μοναρχεῖν gen. of comparison (17.1/4*a*). (*iv*) μολών aor. pple. of βλώσκω. (*v*) ξεῖν᾽(ε) = ξένε; ἀγγέλλειν infinitive used as imperative (17.1/1 note 5); κείνων = ἐκείνων.

8   *ll*.1f. The first negative, οὐκ, is reinforced by οὔτε . . . οὔτε . . . οὐδεμιᾷ
and οὐδ᾽ . . . οὐδέ, lit. *I will not . . . neither in no . . . nor*, etc. but trans. *I
will not . . . either in any . . . or*, etc. (οὐδεμιᾷ goes with both τέχνῃ and
μηχανῇ); the fut. mid. ἀποστήσομαι (< ἀφίστημι) is intransitive; τοῦ
δήμου τοῦ ᾿Αθηναίων *the people [i.e.] the [people] of [the] Athenians*, a
regular formula in inscriptions, trans. *the people of Athens*; ἔπει dat. s. of
ἔπος; πείσομαι fut. of πείθομαι, not πάσχω.   *ll*.3ff. ἀφιστῇ 3rd s. pres.
subj. act., this is a transitive tense (19.1/1) but the verb here has no object
expressed—lit. *causes [others] to revolt*; i.e. *tries to stir up revolt;*
κατερῶ < καταγορεύω (18.1/4 note 2); ὑποτελῶ fut. (5.1/2 note 2); τὸν
φόρον . . . ὃν ἂν πείθω ᾿Αθηναίους lit. *the tribute whatever I persuade the
Athenians*, i.e. *whatever tribute I persuade the Athenians* (sc. *is appropriate*); οἷος *of what sort* (21.1/3) is given a general reference (*of whatever
sort*) because it is followed by ἄν and the subj. (14.1/4c(iii)), lit. *of
whatever sort best and most just I am able [to be]*.   *ll*.5f. The phrase ὁ
δῆμος ὁ ᾿Αθηναίων is repeated to avoid any misunderstanding
whatsoever.

Unit 20

20.1 Grammar

20.1/1 Verbs in -νῦμι

The -νῦμι class (18.1/1) constitutes the more numerous subdivision of -μι verbs but presents no especial difficulty. All forms of the present and imperfect contain the suffix νῦ or νῠ; the present indicative, infinitive and participle, and the imperfect have endings without the o/e characteristic of -ω verbs (cf. 2.1/5 note 3), but the present subjunctive and optative have the same endings as λύω. The other tenses, which do not keep the νῦ/νῠ suffix, are formed in the same way as those of -ω verbs. An example is δείκνῡμι *show*, which has the principal parts δείκνῡμι, fut. δείξω, aor. act. ἔδειξα, perf. act. δέδειχα, perf. mid./pass. δέδειγμαι, aor. pass. ἐδείχθην. The present and imperfect of this verb are given in full in **Appendix 6**.

Notes

1 A number of verbs in this class end in -ννῡμι rather than -νῡμι, e.g. κεράννῡμι *mix*, σκεδάννῡμι *scatter*, κρεμάννῡμι *hang* (tr.; the intransitive meaning of this verb is supplied by the passive κρέμαμαι, which is conjugated like ἴσταμαι (19.1/1)).

2 ὄλλῡμι (originally ὄλ-νῡμι) *destroy, ruin, lose* (fut. ὀλῶ) has two aorist and two perfects. The weak forms of both are transitive and the strong intransitive (cf. 15.1/1 note 2):

AORIST	(weak)	ὤλεσα	*I destroyed/ruined/lost*
	(strong)	ὠλόμην	*I perished* (middle voice, not active!)
PERFECT	(weak)	ὀλώλεκα	*I have destroyed/ruined/lost*
	(strong)	ὄλωλα	*I have perished, am ruined* or *lost*

ὄλλῡμι in its uncompounded form occurs only in verse. In prose we find the compound ἀπόλλῡμι, which has the same meaning. Cf. the use of θνήσκω in verse but ἀποθνήσκω in prose (19.1/3a).

20.1/2 ἵημι and its compounds

ἵημι *let go, send forth* is another -μι verb of group (a) (18.1/1). Its present stem was originally σισ η- (root ση/σε; cf. δίδωμι and τίθημι) but with the change of the initial sigma to a rough breathing (cf. ἵστημι 19.1/1) and the loss of intervocal sigma (cf. 6.1/1c) this was reduced to ἱη- (root ἡ/ἑ).

The principal parts of ἵημι are: pres. ἵημι, fut. ἥcω, aor. act ἧκα, perf. act. εἷκα, perf. pass. εἷμαι, aor. pass. εἵθην.

As will be seen from **Appendix 5** its present and imperfect tenses are exactly parallel to those of τίθημι except in the 3rd pl. pres. ind. act., where contraction has taken place (ἱᾶcι < ἱέᾱcι). The parallelism extends to nearly every other form, although it is obscured in some cases by contraction. Note that the sing. aor. act. ind. has a κ suffix as in τίθημι.

Almost all forms of ἵημι, except those of the present and imperfect, exist only in compounds. The following are the most common:

ἀφίημι	*send forth*; *discharge*; *let go*
ἐφίημι	*send*; *set on, send against*; (mid.) *aim at, desire*
μεθίημι	*let go, release*; *give up*
παρίημι	*pass over*; *let pass*

Examples of each of these compounds are:

πρέπει cοι τὴν ὀργὴν ἀφιέναι εἰc τὸν τοῦτον τὸν τρόπον cε θρέψαντα. *It is fitting for you to vent your anger on the man who brought you up in this way* (on the construction of τοῦτον τὸν τρόπον see below 20.1/5).

ἐὰν ἑλών τίc τινα ἀκουcίου φόνου καὶ cαφῶc ἐπιδείξᾱc μὴ καθαρόν, μετὰ ταῦτ' αἰδέcηται καὶ ἀφῇ, οὐκέτ' ἐκβαλεῖν κύριοc τὸν αὐτόν ἐcτιν. *If anyone convicts a man of involuntary homicide and clearly shows him to be polluted* (lit. *not pure*), *and then feels pity for him and releases him, he no longer has the power to cast the same person into exile.*

ἐφῆκε τὴν ἵππον ἐπὶ τοὺc Ἕλληναc. *He sent the cavalry against the Greeks.*

οὐ γὰρ τοῖc ἔθνεcιν τοῦ ἑτέρου ἔχθει ἐπιᾶcιν, ἀλλὰ τῶν ἐν τῇ Cικελίᾳ ἀγαθῶν ἐφϊέμενοι. *For they will not attack the races because of hatred of one of them but because they are aiming at the good things of Sicily.*

ἐλευθέρᾱν δέ μ', ὡc ἐλευθέρᾱ θάνω, πρὸc θεῶν μεθέντεc κτείνατε. *In the name of the gods, release me [to be] free, so that I may die free, and [then] kill me* (a woman is speaking).

εἰ μεθήcει τὴν ἀρχήν, ἄλλοc τιc ἀντ' αὐτοῦ τύραννοc καταcτήcεται. *If he gives up his power, someone else will set himself up as tyrant in his stead.*

μὴ τοίνυν γιγνώcκοντέc γε παρῶμεν αὐτὸ ἄρρητον. *Let us not then, since we know [it], pass it over unmentioned.*

χρὴ ἡμᾶc καταcκόπουc μὴ πέμπειν μηδὲ διαμέλλειν καιρὸν παρϊένταc. *We ought not to send inspectors or to delay, letting an opportunity pass.*

20.1/3   Genitive of price or value

The genitive is used to express price or value with verbs and adjectives denoting buying, selling, valuing and the like:

ὅταν δέῃ ἀργυρίου πρίαϲθαι ἢ ἀποδόϲθαι ἵππον ... *Whenever it is*
necessary to buy or sell a horse for money ...
τοῦτο δ᾽ ἐϲτὶν ὃ τῶν ἀναλιϲκομένων χρημάτων πάντων Φίλιππος
ὠνεῖται. *This is what Philip is buying with all the money which is*
being spent.
A. πόϲου διδάϲκει; B. πέντε μνῶν. *A. What is his fee for teaching?* (lit.
for how much does he teach?) *B. Five minae* (lit. *for five minae*).
ἡμᾶϲ οὐδενὸϲ λόγου ἀξιοῖ. *He thinks us of no account.*
ϲμῑκρὰ καὶ ὀλίγου ἄξια ἀνερωτᾷ. *He asks petty, insignificant questions*
(lit. *things small and worth little*).

To *value highly/little/not at all*, etc. is commonly expressed by ποιεῖϲθαι
and a genitive governed by περί: περὶ πολλοῦ (πλέονος, πλείϲτου) /ὀλίγου
(ἐλάττονος, ἐλαχίϲτου)/ οὐδενὸϲ ποιεῖϲθαι. Examples are:

τὰ πλείϲτου ἄξια περὶ ἐλαχίϲτου ποιεῖται, τὰ δὲ φαυλότερα περὶ
πλέονος. *He values least what is worth most, and [values] more*
highly what is more trivial.
ἀναγκαῖον ἐδόκει εἶναι τὸ θεοῦ περὶ πλείϲτου ποιεῖϲθαι. *It seemed to*
be essential to value most highly the god's [word].
οὗτος ἅπαντας τοὺς πολίτᾱς περὶ οὐδενὸϲ ἐποιήϲατο. *He valued all*
the citizens at nothing.

20.1/4   Genitive of separation

The genitive is used with verbs and adjectives denoting separation, cessation,
prevention, hindrance, difference etc. It is common with verbs compounded
with ἀπό and ἐκ:

ἀπέχει τῶν Ἐπιπολῶν ἓξ ἢ ἑπτὰ ϲταδίουϲ. *It is six or seven stades*
distant from Epipolae.
ἔπαυϲαν αὐτὸν τῆϲ ϲτρατηγίᾱϲ. *They deposed him from his general-*
ship.
ἐκώλῡον τῆϲ πορείᾱϲ αὐτόν. *They prevented him from passing* (lit. *from*
the passage).
ἐψηφίϲαϲθε ῡμεῖϲ αὐτὸν εἴργεϲθαι τῆϲ ἀγορᾶϲ καὶ τῶν ἱερῶν. *You*
voted that he be excluded from the agora and the temples.
οὐ διοίϲειϲ Χαιρεφῶντος. *You will be no different from Chaerephon.*
ἔργων πονηρῶν χεῖρ᾽ ἐλευθέρᾱν ἔχε. *Keep your hand free from wicked*
deeds.

20.1/5   Accusative of respect or specification

The accusative may be used with a verb (usually intransitive) or an adjective
to denote a thing with respect to which that verb or adjective is limited. A
literal translation may be obtained by employing the words *with respect to*

before the noun involved, but, to produce an idiomatic translation, it will often be necessary to recast the expression somewhat in English:

τὰς γνάθους ἀλγήσετε. *You will have a pain with respect to your jaws,* i.e. *you'll have sore jaws.*

πόδας ὠκὺς Ἀχιλλεύς. *Swift-footed* (lit. *swift with respect to feet) Achilles.*

τυφλὸς τά τ' ὦτα τόν τε νοῦν τά τ' ὄμματ' εἶ. *You are blind both in* (lit. *with respect to) ears and mind and eyes.*

τεῖχος πεντήκοντα μὲν πήχεων τὸ εὖρος, ὕψος δὲ διᾱκοσίων πήχεων. *A wall fifty cubits wide and two hundred cubits high* (lit. *of fifty cubits with respect to the width, and of two hundred with respect to height).*

λέξον ὅστις εἶ γένος. *Tell [me] who you are by race.*

Under this heading may also be included the so-called **adverbial accusatives**, e.g.

οὐδέν   *in no respect, not at all*
τι   *to some extent*
τί   *why* (lit. *with respect to what?*)
πολύ   *much, by far*
τὰ ἄλλα, τἆλλα   *in other respects*
τοῦτον τὸν τρόπον   *in this way*
τίνα τρόπον . . .;   *in what way . . .? how . . .?*

Examples of some of the above have already occurred. We have also met the neuter accusative (both singular and plural) of adjectives employed in this way, e.g. ὀρθὰ βαδίζειν *to walk straight* (15.2.3, see also 16.3 *l*.5, 17.3 *ll*.12 and 16). Adjectives so used are the equivalent of adverbs.

20.2   Greek reading

1   νεανίας τίς ποτε νοσήσας εἶπε τῷ ἰατρῷ οὕτως ἀλγεῖν ὥστε μὴ δύνασθαι μήτε καθῆσθαι μήτε κεῖσθαι μήτε ἑστάναι· ὁ δὲ ἰατρός, ὦ φίλε, ἔφη, οὐδὲν ἄλλο σοι λοιπόν ἐστιν ἢ κρέμασθαι.

2# τίς δ' οἶδεν εἰ ζῆν τοῦθ' ὃ κέκληται θανεῖν,
    τὸ ζῆν δὲ θνήσκειν ἐστί; πλὴν ὅμως βροτῶν
    νοσοῦσιν οἱ βλέποντες, οἱ δ' ὀλωλότες
    οὐδὲν νοσοῦσιν οὐδὲ κέκτηνται κακά.

3   **Proverbs and famous sayings**

   (*i*) δραχμῆς μὲν ηὔλει, τεττάρων δὲ παύεται.   (*ii*) ἡ κάμηλος ἐπιθυμή-σασα κεράτων καὶ τὰ ὦτα προσαπώλεσεν.   (*iii*)# οὐκ ἔστιν ὅστις πάντ' ἀνὴρ εὐδαιμονεῖ.   (*iv*) πολλοὶ στρατηγοὶ Καρίαν ἀπώλεσαν.   (*v*) ἀφεὶς τὰ φανερὰ μὴ δίωκε τὰ ἀφανῆ.   (*vi*)# χρόνος δίκαιον ἄνδρα δείκνυσιν μόνος.   (*vii*) ἐλέφαντος διαφέρεις οὐδέν.   (*viii*)# ἀπάτης δικαίας οὐκ

ἀποστατεῖ θεός. (ix) πολλῶν ἰατρῶν εἴcοδός μ' ἀπώλεcεν. (x) λέων
εἶ τὴν τρίχα, ὄνος δὲ τὸν βίον.

4# An epic nose

τοῦ γρυποῦ Νίκωνος ὁρῶ τὴν ῥῖνα, Μένιππε,
  αὐτὸς δ' οὖν μακρὰν φαίνεται εἶναι ἔτι·
ἀλλ' ἥξει, μείνωμεν ὅμως· εἰ γὰρ πολύ, πέντε
  τῆς ῥινὸς cταδίους, οἶμαι, οὐκ ἀπέχει.
ἀλλ' αὐτὴ μέν, ὁρᾷς, προπορεύεται· ἢν δ' ἐπὶ βουνὸν   5
  ὑψηλὸν cτῶμεν, καὐτὸν ἐcοψόμεθα.

5# τὴν κεφαλὴν βάπτων τις ἀπώλεcε τὰς τρίχας αὐτάς,
  καὶ δαcὺς ὢν λίαν ᾠὸν ἅπας γέγονεν.

6 ἐπὶ τούτῳ Κλεάνωρ ἀνέcτη καὶ ἔλεξεν ὧδε· ἀλλ' ὁρᾶτε μέν, ὦ ἄνδρες,
τὴν βαcιλέως ἐπιορκίαν καὶ ἀcέβειαν, ὁρᾶτε δὲ τὴν Τιccαφέρνους
ἀπιcτίαν, ὅcτις, λέγων ὡς γείτων τε εἴη τῆς Ἑλλάδος καὶ περὶ
πλείcτου ἂν ποιήcαιτο cῶcαι ἡμᾶς, καὶ ἐπὶ τούτοις αὐτὸς ὀμόcας ἡμῖν,
αὐτὸς δεξιὰς δούς, αὐτὸς ἐξαπατήcας cυνέλαβε τοὺς cτρατηγούς, καὶ 5
οὐδὲ Δία ξένιον ᾐδέcθη, ἀλλὰ Κλεάρχῳ καὶ ὁμοτράπεζος γενόμενος
αὐτοῖς τούτοις ἐξαπατήcας τοὺς ἄνδρας ἀπολώλεκεν.

7 ἀλλ', ὦ Cώκρατες, πειθόμενος τοῖς νόμοις μήτε παῖδας περὶ πλείονος
ποιοῦ μήτε τὸ ζῆν μήτε ἄλλο μηδὲν πρὸ τοῦ δικαίου, ἵνα εἰς Ἅιδου
ἐλθὼν ἔχῃς πάντα ταῦτα ἀπολογήcαcθαι τοῖς ἐκεῖ ἄρχουcιν.

8 ὁ Cωκράτης φανερὸς ἦν οὐ τῶν τὰ cώματα πρὸς ὥραν, ἀλλὰ τῶν τὰς
ψυχὰς πρὸς ἀρετὴν εὖ πεφυκότων ἐφιέμενος.

9# γραμματικοῦ θυγάτηρ ἔτεκεν φιλότητι μιγεῖcα
  παιδίον ἀρcενικόν, θηλυκόν, οὐδέτερον.

10# Ζεὺς γὰρ τὰ μὲν μέγιcτα φροντίζει βροτῶν,
  τὰ μικρὰ δ' ἄλλοις δαίμοcιν παρεὶς ἐᾷ.

11 οἱ δ' ἐν τῇ Χίῳ μετὰ τοῦ Ἐτεονίκου cτρατιῶται ὄντες, ἕως μὲν θέρος
ἦν, ἀπό τε τῆς ὥρας ἐτρέφοντο καὶ ἐργαζόμενοι μιcθοῦ κατὰ τὴν
χώραν· ἐπεὶ δὲ χειμὼν ἐγένετο καὶ τροφὴν οὐκ εἶχον γυμνοί τε ἦcαν καὶ
ἀνυπόδητοι, cυνίcταντο ἀλλήλοις ὡς τῇ Χίῳ ἐπιθηcόμενοι.

12# Polymnestor, who has been blinded by Hecuba, screams for vengeance
but is restrained by Agamemnon.

  ΠΟ. ὤμοι, τί λέξεις; ἦ γὰρ ἐγγύς ἐcτί που;
      cήμηνον, εἰπὲ ποῦ 'cθ', ἵν' ἁρπάcας χεροῖν
      διαcπάcωμαι καὶ καθαιμάξω χρόα.
  ΑΓ. οὗτος, τί πάcχεις; ΠΟ. πρὸς θεῶν cε λίccομαι,
      μέθες μ' ἐφεῖναι τῇδε μαργῶcαν χέρα.   5
  ΑΓ. ἴcχ'· ἐκβαλὼν δὲ καρδίας τὸ βάρβαρον
      λέγ', ὡς ἀκούcας cοῦ τε τῇcδέ τ' ἐν μέρει
      κρίνω δικαίως ἀνθ' ὅτου πάcχεις τάδε.

Notes

1 νοcήcᾱc *having fallen sick*, **not** *having been sick*, as is shown by the context (technically called an **ingressive** aorist); μὴ δύναcθαι . . . lit. *not to be able neither to . . . nor to*, i.e. *not to be able either to . . . or to*.

2 *l*.1 τοῦθ' (τοῦτο) is the subject of the first clause after εἰ (supply ἐcτί from the next line). *l*.2 πλὴν ὅμωc *except however* (lit. *except nevertheless*). *l*.3 οἱ βλέποντεc sc. the light of day, a regular expression for the living; οἱ ὀλωλότεc (20.1/1 note 2), i.e. the dead.

3 (*i*) ηὔλει inceptive imperfect (4.1/1 footnote) *started to play the pipe*. (*ii*) καί adv. *also*. (*iii*) Lit. *there is not whatever man* . . . i.e. *there is no man who* . . . (on ὅcτιc, which is here used adjectivally, see 10.1/2*b* note 2). (*v*) μή negates the whole sentence, i.e. ἀφείc (aor. pple. of ἀφίημι) and δίωκε. (*x*) εἶ (< εἰμί) *you are*.

4 *l*.2 δ' οὖν (13.1/3*c*(ii)) introduces a contrast *but/however* (οὖν does not have its normal meaning here). *ll*.3f. μείνωμεν jussive subj. (14.1/4*a*(i)); with εἰ γὰρ πολύ supply ἀπέχει from next line, lit. *for [even] if he is far away*; πέντε cταδίουc acc. of spatial extent (7.1/7*d*); τῆc ῥῑνόc *from his nose* gen. of separation (20.1/4). *l*.5 ἤν = ἐάν (18.1/5 note 2), which is followed by the subj. *l*.6 cτῶμεν intr. aor. subj. of ἵcτημι (19.1/1); καὐτόν (= καὶ αὐτόν) *him too*.

5 The participle ὤν has a concessive force *though being* (we might have expected an accompanying καίπερ (12.1/2*a*(iii)) but cf. λέγων, ὀμόcαc, δούc in the next passage, which are used in the same way); take λίαν with δαcύc (this unusual word order is dictated by metre).

6 *l*.1 ἀνέcτη < ἀνίcτημι. *ll*.3f. The indefinite relative ὅcτιc (10.1/2 note 2) is also used to introduce an adjectival clause which gives a **reason**, trans. *since he*; εἴη . . . ποιήcαιτο opt. in indirect speech in historic sequence (14.1/4*d*); ὀμόcαc < ὄμνῡμι. *l*.6 οὐδέ *not even*; ᾐδέcθη < αἰδέομαι; Κλεάρχῳ dat. with ὁμοτράπεζοc (to share a meal automatically involved permanent ties of friendship and a violation of these was an offence against Ζεὺc ξένιοc); καί *actually*. *l*.7 αὐτοῖc τούτοιc (instrumental dat., 11.1/2) *by these very means*.

7 μήτε ἄλλο μηδέν *nor anything else* (7.1/6); πρό lit. *in preference to* but trans. *than*; εἰc is used with the gen. to mean *to the place/house of*—the *house of Hades* is the Underworld, to which all souls (ψῡχαί) went after death; ἔχῃc *you may be able* (ἔχω + an infinitive means *be able*).

8 φανερὸc ἦν + pple. lit. *was clear(ly)* . . . (cf. 15.2/10); εὖ πεφῡκότων must be taken with both phrases beginning with τῶν; εὖ πεφῡκέναι (< φύω, the pple. is used here) means *to be well-endowed by nature, to be naturally sound*; τὰ cώματα and τὰc ψῡχᾱc are acc. of respect (20.1/5), but trans. *in body* . . . *in soul* and trans. πρόc (lit. *towards*) by *with respect to*.

9 μιγεῖcα f. aor. pass. pple. of μείγνῡμι; the lady gave birth to triplets, whose gender reflected her father's professional interests.

10 παρείc aor. act. pple. of παρίημι.

11 ὥρᾱ *[produce of] the season*; γυμνοί lit. *naked* but here to be understood simply as *badly clothed*.

12   *l.*1 ἦ γάρ introduces a surprised question *is she really . . .?* (ἦ = ἆρα).   *l.*2 'cθ' i.e. ἐcτί; χεροῖν is dat. dual (24.1/4), lit. *with two hands.*   *l.*3 καθαιμάξω aor. subj. (as is διαcπάcωμαι) after ἵνα (14.1/4c(i)); χρόα acc. s. of χρώc.   *l.*4 The nom. οὗτοc (which does not, in any case, have a voc.) expresses an impatient demand for the attention of the person addressed (here Polymnestor), trans. *you there!* or *what's this?*; τί πάcχειc lit. *what are you suffering?*, i.e. *what's wrong with you?*   *l.*5 μέθεc 2nd s. aor. imp. act. of μεθίημι; ἐφεῖναι aor. inf. of ἐφίημι;   *l.*6 τὸ βάρβαρον *the barbarous [element]*, i.e. *savagery.*   *ll.*7f. ὡc (here = ἵνα) introduces a purpose clause (22.1/1b(ii)), and consequently κρίνω is subjunctive.

Unit 21

21.1 Grammar

21.1/1 Wishes

Like potential clauses (19.1/2) and conditional sentences (18.1/5), wishes can have reference to the present, past or future. The negative used in wishes is always μή.

(*a*) Wishes for the **future** are expressed by the optative (present or aorist, according to the aspect involved—14.1/1) and **may** be introduced by εἴθε or εἰ γάρ (*if only . . .!*):

> ὑμῖν θεοὶ δοῖεν ἐκπέρσαι Πριάμου πόλιν. *May the gods grant that you sack* (lit. *give to you to sack*) *the city of Priam.*

> εἴθε γράψειεν ὡς χρή. *I wish that he would write as he should* (lit. *would that he would write as is necessary* or *if only he would . . .*).

(*b*) Wishes for the **present** are expressed by the imperfect indicative and **must** be introduced by εἴθε or εἰ γάρ:

> εἰ γὰρ τοσαύτην δύναμιν εἶχον. *I wish I had so much power* (lit. *would that I had . . .* or *if only I had . . .*)

> εἴθ' εἶχες βελτίους φρένας. *I wish you had better thoughts.*

(*c*) Wishes for the **past** are expressed by the aorist indicative, also with an obligatory εἴθε/εἰ γάρ:

> εἴθ' εὕρομέν c', ὦ Ἄδμητε, μὴ λυπούμενον. *I wish we had not found you grieving, Admetus.*

> εἴθε coι, ὦ Περίκλεις, τότε cυνεγενόμην. *I wish I had been with you then, Pericles.*

In the nature of things only wishes for the future can be fulfilled (and then not always). Wishes for the present and past are futile protests against what is happening or has happened.

Note
A present or past wish may also be expressed by ὤφελον (an aorist of ὀφείλω *owe, be obliged to*) which has the meaning *ought*. It is followed by a present or aorist infinitive, depending on whether the wish is for the present or past. εἴθε/εἰ γάρ is optional:

> ὤφελε Κῦρος ζῆν. *I wish Cyrus were alive* (lit. *Cyrus ought to be alive*).

> μήποτ' ὤφελον λιπεῖν τὴν Cκῦρον. *I wish I had never left Scyrus* (lit. *I ought never to have left . . .*).

21.1/2 Further temporal conjunctions (ἕως, μέχρι, πρίν)

Each of these three words has more than one use, but all can be employed as subordinating conjunctions with the meaning *until*.

ἕως and μέχρι both take the same construction as certain other temporal conjunctions (ὅτε, ἐπειδή, etc., see 14.1/4c (iii)). They are followed by the indicative when the clause they introduce refers to a definite event:

ταῦτα ἐποίουν μέχρι cκότος ἐγένετο.   *They were doing these things until darkness fell* (lit. *came into being*).

When the reference is to something anticipated (but we do not know if it eventuates or not), the indefinite construction is used (14.1/4c (iii)):

περιμένετε ἕως ἂν ἔλθω.   *Wait until I come* (or *for me to come*).
ἔδοξεν αὐτοῖς προϊέναι ἕως Κύρῳ cυμμείξειαν.   *They decided* (lit. *it seemed good to them*, 21.1/4a) *to advance until they should meet Cyrus*.

With these conjunctions the indefinite construction can also refer to repeated action:

περιεμένομεν ἑκάστοτε ἕως ἀνοιχθείη τὸ δεcμωτήριον.   *On each occasion we used to wait until the prison opened*.

πρίν has a wider range of constructions:

(a) When the main verb is **affirmative**, πρίν is followed by an infinitive (usually aorist) and has the meaning *before*:

ἐπὶ τὸ ἄκρον ἀνέβη Χειρίcοφος πρίν τινα αἰcθέcθαι τῶν πολεμίων.   *Cheirisophus went up to the peak before any of the enemy noticed*.
λέγεται Ἀλκιβιάδης, πρὶν εἴκοcιν ἐτῶν εἶναι, Περικλεῖ διαλεχθῆναι περὶ νόμων.   *Alcibiades is said to have conversed with Pericles about laws before he was twenty years old* (lit. *of twenty years*).

The rules governing the case of the subject of the infinitive are exactly the same as in the infinitive construction in indirect statement (8.1/3a); in the first example above, the subject (τινά) of the infinitive is not the same as the subject of the main verb and so is in the accusative.

(b) When the main verb is **negated** and πρίν can be translated by *until* or *before*, it has the same construction as ἕως and μέχρι:

οὐκ ἦν γένος ἀθανάτων πρὶν Ἔρως ξυνέμειξεν ἅπαντα.   *There was not a race of immortals until* (or *before*) *Love mixed everything together*.
μὴ ἀπέλθετε πρὶν ἄν μου ἀκούcητε.   *Do not go away before* (or *until*) *you hear me*.

(c) When the main verb is **negated** and πρίν must be translated by *before*, it has the same construction as in (a):

οὐδὲ πρὶν νικηθῆναι ἐθάρρει ὁ cτρατηγός.   *Not even before being defeated was the general confident* (πρίν cannot here be translated by *until*).

Notes

1 ἕως (and occasionally μέχρι) with the indicative can also mean *while, as long as*:

Κλέαρχος, ἕως πόλεμος ἦν τοῖς Λακεδαιμονίοις πρὸς τοὺς ᾽Αθηναίους, παρέμενεν. *As long as the Spartans were at war* (lit. *there was war for the Spartans*) *with the Athenians, Clearchus remained loyal.*

2 μέχρι may also function as a **preposition** (with gen.) with the meaning *until, up to, as far as* (with reference to time or space):

μέχρι τοῦ γόνατος *up to the knee*; μέχρι τούτου *up to this [time]*.

3 πρίν can also be used as an **adverb** meaning *before, formerly*: ἐν τῷ πρὶν χρόνῳ *in the previous time*.

4 οὐ is used to negate the indicative in the subordinate clauses described above, μή to negate the indefinite construction and also the infinitive after πρίν.

21.1/3 Further demonstrative and relative adjectives/pronouns

Greek possesses two series of adjectives, each containing a demonstrative, relative (and exclamatory) and interrogative form. One series, with the element -oc-, refers to **quantity**, the other, with the element -oι-, refers to **quality**:

DEMONSTRATIVE	RELATIVE/EXCLAMATORY	INTERROGATIVE
τοσοῦτος, τοσόςδε *so much/many*	ὅσος *as much/many as, how much/many!*	πόσος *how big?* pl. *how many?*
τοιοῦτος, τοιόςδε *of this sort, such*	οἷος *of what sort, what a ...!*	ποῖος *of what sort?*

The relative/exclamatory and interrogative forms are first and second declension adjectives (3.1/3). On the declension of τοσοῦτος, τοιοῦτος see 16.1/1 note 1. τοσόςδε and τοιόςδε are compounds of τος/τοι + ος (declined as καλός, 3.1/3) + δε. All can function as pronouns as well as adjectives.

We have already dealt with the interrogatives (10.1/2) and the use of τοσοῦτος and τοιοῦτος to anticipate an adverbial clause or phrase of result (16.1/1). We must also note that:

(*a*) τοιοῦτος is used with reference to what precedes in a narrative, τοιόςδε with reference to what follows. This is the principal use of the latter, e.g. οἱ μὲν τοιαῦτα εἶπον, οἱ δὲ ᾽Αθηναῖοι τοιάδε ἀπεκρίναντο *they said this* (lit. *such things as precede*) *and the Athenians replied as follows* (lit. *such things as follow*). οὗτος and ὅδε are used in the same way (9.1/1 note 1).

(*b*) τοcόcδε, like τοιόcδε, can refer to what follows but is generally the equivalent of τοcοῦτοc.

(*c*) ὅcοc and οἷοc can introduce exclamations:

ὅcα πράγματα ἔχειc. *How much trouble* (lit. *how many things*) *you have!*

οἷα δράᾱc οἷα λαγχάνει κακά. *After what deeds what sufferings are his!* (lit. *what things having done what evil things he obtains!*).

(*d*) πάντεc ὅcοι is used in the sense *all who* (lit. *all as many as*) instead of the expected πάντεc οἵ:

πάνταc ἐχθαίρω θεοὺc ὅcοι κακοῦcί μ' ἐκδίκωc. *I hate all the gods who unjustly wrong me.*

Very often ὅcοc is used by itself in this sense:

οἱ Καδμεῖοι ὅcουc κακοὺc εὗρον . . . *All the Cadmeans whom I found wicked . . .* (lit. *the Cadmeans as many as I found . . .*).

(*e*) τοcοῦτοc/ὅcοc and τοιοῦτοc/οἷοc are used in sentences where ὅcοc and οἷοc introduce a comparison. As English does not have relatives of this sort some change is needed in translation:

οἷοc ὁ πατήρ ἐcτιν, τοιοῦτοc καὶ ὁ υἱόc. *Like father, like son* (lit. *of what sort the father is, of that sort [is] the son too*).

ἔχετε τοcούτουc cτρατιώτᾱc ὅcουc οἱ Πέρcαι. *You have as many soldiers as the Persians* (sc. *have*; lit. *you have so many soldiers as many as the Persians*).

The relatives alone, without the corresponding demonstratives, may be used in this way:

οὔ μοι ἡ δύναμίc ἐcτιν οἵᾱ πάροc ἦν. *I have not the same strength as I previously had* (lit. *there is not to me the strength of what sort (= of the sort which) there was previously*).

Notes

1 In verse τόcοc and τοῖοc often occur as the equivalents of τοcοῦτοc and τοιοῦτοc respectively.

2 οἷόc τ' εἰμί *I am able* is a stereotyped formula (example in 13.3(ii) *l*.3); τε here is purely idiomatic and is not to be translated, and οἷοc has no relative force.

21.1/4 Further impersonal verbs

Impersonal verbs have no real subject. In English they are given a grammatical subject *it*, which is purely idiomatic and does not refer to anything. In Greek impersonal verbs are simply put in the 3rd singular. We have already met δεῖ and χρή *it is necessary*, which are followed by an infinitive whose subject, if expressed, is put into the accusative (examples at 3.2.12(*x*), 5.2.15, etc.). Other impersonals can be classified as follows:

(*a*) **Impersonals followed by the dative and infinitive**

δοκεῖ	it seems good	πρέπει	it is fitting
ἔξεςτι	it is allowed/possible	προςήκει	it concerns/is fitting
λῡ̄ςιτελεῖ	it is profitable	ϲυμφέρει	it is expedient
πάρεςτι	it is possible		

Examples of ἔξεςτι occur at 9.2.7 and 19.2.7(ii). Of the others we may cite:

ταῦτα πρέπει μᾶλλον βαρβάροιϲ ποιεῖν ἢ Ἕλληϲιν.   *It is more fitting for barbarians than Greeks to do these things.*

οὔ ϲοι προϲήκει φωνεῖν.   *You have no business speaking* (lit. *it does not concern you to speak*).

δοκεῖ is usually to be translated by *think, intend, decide*, e.g. ὡϲ ἐμοὶ δοκεῖ *as I think* (lit. *as it seems good to me*); δοκεῖ αὐτῷ ἀπιέναι *he intends to leave*; ἔδοξε τοῖϲ Ἀθηναίοιϲ μάχεϲθαι *the Athenians decided to fight* (another example at 14.2.18 *l.*2).

Some of the above verbs can be used personally, sometimes with a different meaning, e.g. πάρειμι *I am present*.

(*b*) **Impersonals followed by the dative of the person involved and the genitive of the thing**

μέτεϲτι μοι τούτου	there is a share to me of this
	i.e. *I have a share in this*
μέλει μοι τούτου	there is a concern to me of this,
	i.e. *I am concerned about this*
μεταμέλει μοι τούτου	there is repentance to me of this,
	i.e. *I repent of this*

Examples are:

τοῖϲ θεοῖϲ δίκηϲ μέλει.   *The gods are concerned with justice.*

τί τοῦδέ ϲοι μέτεϲτι πρᾱ́γματοϲ; *What concern* (lit. *share*) *have you in this business?*

ὑμῖν μεταμεληϲάτω τῶν πεπρᾱγμένων   *Repent of your deeds!* (lit. *let there be repentance* [3rd s. aor. imp. act.] *to you of the things done*).

(*c*) **Weather impersonals**

The various verbs for expressing weather conditions, as ὕ̈ει *it is raining*, νείφει *it is snowing*, are not strictly impersonals because Zeus, in his capacity as sky god, is their understood subject. We should, however, translate them by the impersonal English expression.

Notes

1 ἔϲτι (always so accented) is often used in the sense of ἔξεϲτι (examples at
9.2.13 *l*.4 and 11.2.10 *l*.4). For other cases of this accentuation see
Appendix 9, *d*(x).

2 πάρα, μέτα (note accent!) are often used for πάρεϲτι, μέτεϲτι respectively.

3 When the impersonal δεῖ means *there is need of* it takes the same
construction as class (*b*) (example in 13.2.21); in the sense *it is necessary* it
is always followed by the infinitive.

21.1/5 Accusative absolute

The **participle** of an impersonal verb stands in the **accusative**, in the neuter
singular, in circumstances where other verbs would be placed in the genitive
absolute (cf. 12.1/2*b*); it has **no** subject. Such accusative absolutes are δέον *it
being necessary*; ἐξόν, παρόν, παρέχον *it being possible*; μέλον *it being a care*;
προϲῆκον, πρέπον *it being fitting*; δόξαν *it having been decided*. Examples are:

ἐξὸν εἰρήνην ἔχειν, αἱρεῖται πολεμεῖν.   *Although he can live in peace*
(lit. *it being possible to have peace*), *he chooses to make war*.
δῆλον γὰρ ὅτι οἶϲθα, μέλον γέ ϲοι.   *For it [is] clear that you know, since
you are interested [in the subject]* (lit. *it being a care to you*).
ϲυνδόξαν τῷ πατρὶ καὶ τῇ μητρί, γαμεῖ τὴν Κυαξάρου θυγατέρα.
Since his father and mother approved (lit. *it having seemed good also
to . . .*) *he married* (vivid present) *the daughter of Cyaxares*.

The accusative absolute is also found with expressions consisting of a
neuter adjective and ὄν, such as ἀδύνατον ὄν *it being impossible*, αἰϲχρὸν ὄν *it
being disgraceful*, ἄδηλον ὄν *it being unclear*, e.g.

παρεκελεύοντο ἀλλήλοιϲ κραυγῇ οὐκ ὀλίγῃ χρώμενοι, ἀδύνατον ὂν ἐν
νυκτὶ ἄλλῳ τῳ ϲημῆναι.   *They encouraged each other with* (lit. *using*)
no little shouting, since it was impossible (lit. *it being impossible*) *by
night to signal by any other [means]*.

21.2   Greek reading

1 Ϲπαρτιάτηϲ τιϲ εἰϲ ᾿Αθήναϲ ἐλθὼν καὶ ἰδὼν ἐν ἀποχωρήϲει θακοῦνταϲ
ἐπὶ δίφρων ἀνθρώπουϲ, μή μοι γένοιτο, εἶπεν, ἐνταῦθα καθίϲαι ὅθεν
οὐκ ἔϲτιν ἐξαναϲτῆναι πρεϲβυτέρῳ.

2 **Proverbs**

(*i*) πρὶν τοὺϲ ἰχθῦϲ ἑλεῖν τὴν ἅλμην κυκᾷϲ.   (*ii*) οὐ μέλει τῇ χελώνῃ
μυιῶν.   (*iii*) ἀεί με τοιοῦτοι πολέμιοι διώκοιεν.   (*iv*) προϲήκει τοῖϲ
τέκνοιϲ ἐντὸϲ θυρῶν λοιδορεῖϲθαι.   (*v*) οἷοϲ ὁ τρόποϲ τοιοῦτοϲ ὁ
λόγοϲ.   (*vi*)# μηδένα νομίζετε εὐτυχεῖν πρὶν ἂν θάνῃ.   (*vii*) οἷάπερ ἡ

δέσποινα τοία χἠ κύων. (viii)# νέῳ δὲ ϲιγᾶν μᾶλλον ἢ λαλεῖν
πρέπει. (ix) ὦ οἶα κεφαλή, καὶ ἐγκέφαλον οὐκ ἔχει. (x) μέτεϲτι τοῖϲ
δούλοιϲιν δεϲποτῶν νόϲου. (xi)# μή μοι γένοιθ' ἃ βούλομ', ἀλλ' ἃ
ϲυμφέρει. (xii) Ἅιδου πρωκτῷ περιπέϲοιϲ. (xiii)# εἴθ' ἦν ἄφωνον
ϲπέρμα δυϲτήνων βροτῶν.

3# ὅϲτιϲ δὲ θνητῶν θάνατον ὀρρωδεῖ λίαν,
μῶροϲ πέφυκε· τῇ τύχῃ τῶνδε μέλει.
ὅταν δ' ὁ καιρὸϲ τοῦ θανεῖν ἐλθὼν τύχῃ,
οὐδ' ἂν πρὸϲ αὐλὰϲ Ζηνὸϲ ἐκφύγοι μολών.

4 ὅϲοι γαμοῦϲι γένει κρείττουϲ γάμουϲ οὐκ ἐπίϲτανται γαμεῖν.

5 οἴῳ τιϲ ἂν τὸ πλεῖϲτον τῆϲ ἡμέραϲ ϲυνῇ, τοιοῦτον ἀνάγκη γενέϲθαι καὶ
αὐτὸν τοὺϲ τρόπουϲ.

6 ἀναϲτὰϲ αὖθιϲ Θώραξ ὁ Βοιώτιοϲ, ὃϲ περὶ ϲτρατηγίαϲ Ξενοφῶντι
ἐμάχετο, ἔφη, εἰ ἐξέλθοιεν ἐκ τοῦ Πόντου, ἔϲεϲθαι αὐτοῖϲ Χερρόνηϲον,
χώραν καλὴν καὶ εὐδαίμονα, ὥϲτε ἐξεῖναι τῷ βουλομένῳ ἐνοικεῖν, τῷ
δὲ μὴ βουλομένῳ ἀπιέναι οἴκαδε. γελοῖον δὲ εἶναι, ἐν τῇ Ἑλλάδι οὔϲηϲ
χώραϲ πολλῆϲ καὶ ἀφθόνου, ἐν τῇ βαρβάρων μαϲτεύειν. ἕωϲ δ' ἄν, ἔφη,   5
ἐκεῖ γένηϲθε, κἀγὼ ὑπιϲχνοῦμαι ὑμῖν τὸν μιϲθόν.

7 Διογένηϲ ἰδών ποτε γυναῖκαϲ ἀπ' ἐλάαϲ ἀπηγχονιϲμέναϲ, εἴθε γάρ,
ἔφη, πάντα τὰ δένδρα τοιοῦτον καρπὸν ἤνεγκεν.

8# ὅϲτιϲ δὲ πράϲϲει πολλά, μὴ πράϲϲειν παρόν,
μῶροϲ, παρὸν ζῆν ἡδέωϲ ἀπράγμονα.

9 βουλευομένοιϲ τοῖϲ ϲτρατιώταιϲ ἔδοξεν ἀποκρίναϲθαι τάδε· καὶ ἔλεξε
Χειρίϲοφοϲ· ἡμῖν δοκεῖ, εἰ μέν τιϲ ἐᾷ ἡμᾶϲ ἀπιέναι οἴκαδε, διαπορεύ-
εϲθαι τὴν χώραν ὡϲ ἂν δυνώμεθα ἀϲινέϲτατα· ἢν δέ τιϲ ἡμᾶϲ τῆϲ ὁδοῦ
ἀποκωλύῃ, διαπολεμεῖν τούτῳ ὡϲ ἂν δυνώμεθα κράτιϲτα.

10# *Prometheus laments his lot*
ἦ δυϲπετῶϲ ἂν τοὺϲ ἐμοὺϲ ἄθλουϲ φέροιϲ,
ὅτῳ θανεῖν μέν ἐϲτιν οὐ πεπρωμένον·
αὕτη γὰρ ἦν ἂν πημάτων ἀπαλλαγή·
νῦν δ' οὐδέν ἐϲτι τέρμα μοι προκείμενον
μόχθων πρὶν ἂν Ζεὺϲ ἐκπέϲῃ τυραννίδοϲ.   5

11 καὶ ὁ Κῦροϲ ἀκούϲαϲ τοῦ Γωβρύα τοιαῦτα τοιάδε πρὸϲ αὐτὸν ἔλεξεν.

12# *Medea resolves to murder her children*
εἶεν· τί δράϲειϲ, θυμέ; βούλευϲαι καλῶϲ
πρὶν ἐξαμαρτεῖν καὶ τὰ προϲφιλέϲτατα
ἔχθιϲτα θέϲθαι. ποῖ ποτ' ἐξῆξαϲ τάλαϲ;
κάτιϲχε λῆμα καὶ ϲθένοϲ θεοϲτυγέϲ.
καὶ πρὸϲ τί ταῦτα δύρομαι, ψυχὴν ἐμὴν   5
ὁρῶϲ' ἔρημον καὶ παρημελημένην
πρὸϲ ὧν ἐχρῆν ἥκιϲτα; μαλθακοὶ δὲ δὴ
τοιαῦτα γιγνόμεϲθα πάϲχοντεϲ κακά;
οὐ μὴ προδώϲειϲ, θυμέ, ϲαυτὸν ἐν κακοῖϲ.

οἴμοι δέδοκται· παῖδες, ἐκτὸς ὀμμάτων 10
ἀπέλθετ'· ἤδη γάρ με φοίνιον νέα
δέδυκε λύccα θυμόν. ὦ χέρες χέρες,
πρὸς οἷον ἔργον ἐξοπλιζόμεcθα· φεῦ
τάλαινα τόλμης, ἣ πολὺν πόνον βραχεῖ
διαφθεροῦca τὸν ἐμὸν ἔρχομαι χρόνῳ. 15

13 εἰc Λακεδαίμονα παραγενόμενόc τιc καὶ τὴν πρὸς τοὺς πρεσβύτας τῶν
νέων τιμὴν θεαcάμενος, ἐν Cπάρτῃ μόνῃ, εἶπε, λυcιτελεῖ γηράcκειν.

14# ἐχρῆν γὰρ ἡμᾶς cύλλογον ποιουμένους
τὸν φύντα θρηνεῖν εἰc ὅc' ἔρχεται κακά,
τὸν δ'αὖ θανόντα καὶ πόνων πεπαυμένον
χαίροντας εὐφημοῦντας ἐκπέμπειν δόμων.

Notes

1 The Spartans, as well as living in a primitive simplicity where a public toilet would have been unheard of, prided themselves on old-fashioned virtues such as respect for people older than oneself (cf. 13 below); ἔcτιν = ἔξεcτιν; ἐξαναcτῆναι intr. root aor. inf of ἐξανίcτημι.

2 (*i*) The brine is to boil the fish. (*iv*) Take τέκνοιc with λοιδορεῖcθαι, not with προcήκει. (*v*) Supply ἐcτί with οἷοc and with τοιοῦτος (cf. (*vii*) below). (*ix*) οἷᾶ exclamatory. (*x*) Take δεcποτῶν with νόcου, and νόcου with μέτεcτι. (*xi*) γένοιθ' = γένοιτο; βούλομ' = βούλομαι (2.1/6*b* note); cυμφέρει is not here impersonal but has ἅ as its subject.

3 *l*.2 τῶνδε neuter *these things*. *l*.3 ἐλθὼν τύχῃ (3rd s. aor. subj. of τυγχάνω) *chances to come* (15.1/2*a*).

4 γένει *in race* (dat. of respect, 23.1/2*m*).

5 cυνῇ 3rd s. pres. subj. of cύνειμι, which takes a dative (here οἴῳ); ἀνάγκη sc. ἐcτί; τοὺς τρόπους acc. of respect (20.1/5) with τοιοῦτον.

6 After ἔφη in *l*.2 we have a passage of indirect speech, but the last sentence of the passage is in direct speech with an extra ἔφη inserted (cf. 8.1/3*a* and 7.1/2 note 3). *l*.2 εἰ ἐξέλθοιεν represents in historic sequence ἐὰν ἐξέλθωcι of the original direct speech (14.1/4*c*(iii)); ἔcεcθαι αὐτοῖc lit. *there to be going to be for them*, i.e. *they would have*. *ll*.3f. τῷ . . . μὴ βουλομένῳ the negative is μή because a general class is meant (12.1/2*a*(vi)), trans. *anyone who [so] wished*. *l*.6 ἐκεῖ γένηcθε, i.e. *you get there*.

7 ἀπηγχονιcμένᾱc f. acc. pl. of the perf. pass. pple. of ἀπαγχονίζω; εἴθε + aor. expresses a wish for the past (21.1/1*c*).

8 The old Athenian aristocratic ideal was a life of leisure. In both lines παρόν is an acc. absolute (21.1/5). *l*.1 μή negates πράccειν.

9 ἀπιέναι < ἀπέρχομαι (18.1/3); ὡς . . . ἀcινέcτατα lit. *in whatever way* (ὡς ἄν) *we can most harmlessly*, i.e. *doing the least possible harm*.

10 *l*.2 ὅτῳ the relative ὅcτιc can be used to introduce an adjectival clause which gives a **reason** (cf. note on 20.2.6 *l*.3). *l*.3 αὕτη *this* refers to what has just been mentioned (i.e. death), but is attracted into the gender of ἀπαλλαγή. *ll*.4f. νῦν δέ *but as it is*; take μόχθων with τέρμα; ἐκπίπτω

is here acting as the pass. of ἐκβάλλω *throw out* (cf. 17.1/5); τυραννίδος gen. of separation (20.1/4).

11   Take τοιαῦτα with ἀκούσας, τοιάδε with ἔλεξεν; Γωβρύᾱς (1st declension) has the non-Attic gen. s. Γωβρύᾱ.

12   *l.*1 βούλευσαι 2nd s. aor. imp. mid. of βουλεύω.   *l.*3 θέσθαι (< τίθημι) here *make*; ἐξῆξας 2nd s. aor. ind. act. of ἐξαΐσσω; τάλᾱς (10.1/3 note 2) is voc. (Medea is still addressing her θῡμός).   *l.*5 πρὸς τί lit. *with a view to what*, i.e. *why*.   *l.*6 ἔρημον is f. and agrees with ψῡχήν (ἔρημος is one of the few two termination adjectives (3.1/3) which are not compounds); παρημελημένην perf. pass. pple. of παραμελέω. *ll.*7f. πρὸς ὧν, i.e. πρὸς (= ὑπὸ) τούτων οὕς (9.1/2 note 2); δὲ δή here introduces an emphatic question *And so . . .?, Then . . .?*; when a woman is using the royal plural, as with γιγνόμεσθα (= -μεθα, cf. 8.2.9 and ἐξοπλιζόμεσθα in *l.*13 below), she refers to herself with masculine pl. adjectives and participles, hence μαλθακοί and πάσχοντες; take τοιαῦτα . . . κακά after πάσχοντες.   *l.*9 οὐ μή + fut. ind. expresses a strong prohibition (17.1/1).   *l.*10 δέδοκται *it is decided* (i.e. *by me*, lit. *it is in a state of seeming good [to me]*) the impers. δοκεῖ (21.1/4a) is mid./pass. in the perfect; παῖδες voc. *ll.*11f. ἀπέλθετ᾽(ε) 2nd pl. aor. imp.; με . . . δέδῡκε . . . θῡμόν lit. *has entered me [with respect to] my heart*, i.e. *has entered my heart* (acc. of respect 20.1/5).   *l.*14 τόλμης gen. of cause (23.1/1k(ii)) with τάλαινα *wretched [that I am] because of my daring*, Medea is talking about herself; πόνον, i.e. the labour of bearing and raising her children.   *l.*15 διαφθεροῦσα fut. pple. to express purpose (12.1/2a(v)).

14   *l.*1 ἐχρῆν = ἐχρῆν ἄν a common idiom which means *it should be necessary*, not *it was necessary*, because it expresses something which should be happening now (present potential, 19.1/2), trans. *we should . . . l.*2 κακά is acc. of respect (20.1/5) after θρηνεῖν and the antecedent of εἰς ὅσ᾽(α) ἔρχεται, lit. *with respect to the troubles to how many he is coming*, i.e. *for all the troubles he is coming to* (21.1/3d).   *ll.*3f. δ᾽(ὲ) αὖ *and in turn*; πόνων, δόμων gen. of separation (20.1/4); δόμων is also an example of the singular used for the plural, *from [his*, i.e. the dead man's*] house.

21.3   Extra reading – Love poetry

Love poetry had a long history in Greek. The first example below is from Mimnermus (7th century BC) but the others are much later (2 and 3 are attributed to Plato, whether correctly or not we have no means of telling; the authors of 4 and 5 are unknown). All are written in elegiacs (**Appendix 10**), the metre most associated with this genre.

1   τίς δὲ βίος, τί δὲ τερπνὸν ἄτερ χρυσῆς Ἀφροδίτης;
      τεθναίην, ὅτε μοι μηκέτι ταῦτα μέλοι,
   κρυπταδίη φιλότης καὶ μείλιχα δῶρα καὶ εὐνή,
      οἷ᾽ ἥβης ἄνθεα γίγνεται ἁρπαλέα

ἀνδράςιν ἠδὲ γυναιξίν· ἐπεὶ δ' ὀδυνηρὸν ἐπέλθῃ   5
   γῆρας, ὅ τ' αἰςχρὸν ὁμῶς καὶ κακὸν ἄνδρα τιθεῖ,
αἰεί μιν φρένας ἀμφὶ κακαὶ τείρουςι μέριμναι
   οὐδ' αὐγὰς προςορῶν τέρπεται ἠελίου,
ἀλλ' ἐχθρὸς μὲν παιςίν, ἀτίμαστος δὲ γυναιξίν·
   οὕτως ἀργαλέον γῆρας ἔθηκε θεός.   10
2 ἀςτέρας εἰςαθρεῖς ἀςτὴρ ἐμός· εἴθε γενοίμην
   οὐρανός, ὡς πολλοῖς ὄμμαςιν εἰς ςὲ βλέπω.
3 ἀςτὴρ πρὶν ἔλαμπες ἐνὶ ζωοῖςιν Ἑῶος·
   νῦν δὲ θανὼν λάμπεις Ἕςπερος ἐν φθιμένοις.
4 πέμπω ςοι μύρον ἡδύ, μύρῳ παρέχων χάριν, οὐ ςοί·
   αὐτὴ γὰρ μυρίςαι καὶ τὸ μύρον δύναςαι.
5 Ἠοῦς ἄγγελε, χαῖρε, Φαεςφόρε, καὶ ταχὺς ἔλθοις
   Ἕςπερος, ἣν ἀπάγεις, λάθριος αὖθις ἄγων.

Notes

1 All deviations from Attic in this poem are Ionic (1.3). *l.*2 τεθναίην the
   shorter form of the perf. opt. of θνῄςκω (19.1/3a)—the opt. is used here to
   express a wish for the future (21.1/1a); ταῦτα (referring to the nouns in
   *l.*3) is the subject of μέλοι, which is not impersonal here and should be
   translated as though ind. (the verb has been assimilated to the mood of
   τεθναίην). *l.*3 κρυπταδίη = -ία. *l.*4 οἷ'(α) . . . γίγνεται lit. *of what sort
   are*, i.e. *the sorts of things which*; ἄνθεα = ἄνθη (< ἄνθος). *l.*5 ἐπεί . . .
   ἐπέλθῃ in this indefinite construction Attic would require ἄν (14.1/
   4c(iii)). *l.*6 αἰςχρόν and κακόν (here *lowly, base*) are predicative after
   ἄνδρα τιθεῖ (= τίθηςι), *makes a man both* (ὁμῶς) *ugly and base*—note here
   that we have ὁμῶς, **not** ὅμως *nevertheless*. *l.*7 φρένας ἀμφί = ἀμφὶ
   φρένας.
2 *l.*1 ἀςτὴρ ἐμός is in apposition to *you*, the subject of εἰςαθρεῖς. *l.*2 ὡς = ἵνα
   (βλέπω is subj., 14.1/4c(i)).
3 *l.*1 πρίν here an adverb *formerly*; ἀςτήρ . . . Ἑῶος *the Morning Star*. *l.*2
   Ἕςπερος *the Evening Star*; the Greeks knew that both were in fact the
   planet Venus (see 5 below), which makes the poet's fanciful identification
   of his lover with them all the more appropriate.
4 *l.*1 παρέχων χάριν *doing a favour*. *l.*2 καί *even* (μύρον has a very strong
   scent).
5 The poet, who supposes that the planet Venus in its guise as the Morning
   Star is taking away his girl friend, expresses the wish that it return quickly
   as the Evening Star and bring her back. *l.*1 Ἠοῦς gen. of Ἠώς. *l.*2
   Ἕςπερος, i.e. *[as] the Evening Star*; ἣν ἀπάγει . . . ἄγων *bringing [the
   girl] whom you are [now] leading away*.

Unit 22

22.1 Grammar

22.1/1 Summary of the uses of ὡϲ

ὡϲ, originally an adverb of manner meaning *in which way, how,* came to have various uses as an adverb or as a conjunction. It may also occur as a preposition.

(*a*) **ὡϲ *as an adverb***

 (*i*) **ὡϲ with participles and prepositional phrases**
   We have already seen how ὡϲ is used with participles of **cause** (12.1/2*a*(ii)) and **purpose** (12.1/2*a*(v)), reflecting the attitude (thought, opinion, intention, hope) of the subject of the participle without any implication about the belief of the writer or speaker. In this use, which also occurs with phrases introduced by a preposition, ὡϲ expresses an alleged reason or assumed motive, and may be translated *as if, in the opinion that, under the impression that, with the (avowed) intention of,* etc.:

   ϲυλλαμβάνει Κῦρον ὡϲ ἀποκτενῶν. *He seized* (vivid present) *Cyrus with the intention of putting him to death.*
   ἀγανακτοῦϲιν ὡϲ μεγάλων τινῶν ἀπεϲτερημένοι. *They are annoyed in the belief that they have been deprived of some very great [benefits].*
   ἀνήγοντο ὡϲ ἐπὶ ναυμαχίᾱν. *They put out to sea with the intention of fighting* (lit. *as for a sea-battle*).
   ἀπέπλεον ὡϲ εἰϲ τὰ̄ϲ Ἀθήνᾱϲ. *They sailed away as if for Athens.*

 (*ii*) **ὡϲ exclamatory**
   ὡϲ *how . . .!* is used in exclamations with adjectives, adverbs and verbs:
   ὡϲ ἀϲτεῖοϲ ὁ ἄνθρωποϲ. *How charming the man is!*
   ὡϲ ἀδεῶϲ καὶ γενναίωϲ ἐτελεύτᾱ. *How fearlessly and nobly he died!*
   ὥϲ μ' ἀπώλεϲαϲ, γύναι. *How you have destroyed me, woman!*
   βλέψον πρὸϲ τὰ ὄρη καὶ ἰδὲ ὡϲ ἄβατα πάντα ἐϲτίν. *Look at the mountains and see how impassable they all are* (the exclamation here is indirect).

 (*iii*) **ὡϲ with positive adverbs**
   ὡϲ may be used to emphasise positive adverbs: ὡϲ ἀληθῶϲ *in very truth;* ὡϲ ἑτέρωϲ *quite otherwise;* ὡϲ αὔτωϲ (often written ὡϲαύτωϲ) *in the same way, just so.*

Note too the common idiom where ὡς is added to the adverbs θαυμασίως and θαυμαστῶς (lit. *marvellously, wonderfully*) to express emphasis:

νῦν δὲ θαυμασίως ὡς ἄθλιος γέγονεν. *But now he has become prodigiously wretched.*

εὖ λέγει θαυμαστῶς ὡς σφόδρα. *He speaks marvellously well* (lit. *he speaks well marvellously very*).

(*iv*) **ὡς with superlative adjectives and adverbs** (see 17.1/4*d*)

(*v*) **ὡς ἕκαστος/ἑκάτερος**
ὡς is often combined with ἕκαστος (or ἑκάτερος) in the sense *each by himself, each severally* or *individually*:

ἄλλοι παριόντες ἐγκλήματα ἐποιοῦντο ὡς ἕκαστοι. *Others came forward and made their separate complaints* (lit. *each [group] by themselves*).

παυσάμενοι τῆς μάχης ὡς ἑκάτεροι ἡσυχάσαντες τὴν νύκτα ἐν φυλακῇ ἦσαν. *They ceased from fighting and on either side* (lit. *each side by themselves*) *remained quiet [but] on guard for the night.*

(*vi*) **ὡς restrictive**
ὡς may also be used to limit the validity of a statement, with the meaning *for*:

ἦν δὲ οὐδὲ ἀδύνατος, ὡς Λακεδαιμόνιος, εἰπεῖν. *He was not a bad speaker* (lit. *not unable to speak*) *either, for a Spartan* (or *considering that he was a Spartan*).

μακρὰ ὡς γέροντι ὁδός. *A long road, for an old man.*

φρονεῖ ὡς γυνὴ μέγα. *She has proud thoughts* (lit. *thinks big*), *for a woman.*

Restrictive ὡς is also found with the **infinitive** in certain idiomatic expressions which stand independent of the overall grammatical construction and which express some limitation or qualification of the sentence as a whole. This use is particularly common in the phrase ὡς ἔπος εἰπεῖν (or ὡς εἰπεῖν) *so to speak*, which usually modifies a sweeping statement with πᾶς or οὐδείς (or the like); occasionally it apologies for a metaphor:

ἀληθές γε ὡς ἔπος εἰπεῖν οὐδὲν εἰρήκᾱσιν. *They have spoken virtually no word of truth* (lit. *nothing true so to speak*).

Ἱππόλυτος οὐκέτ᾽ ἔστιν, ὡς ἔπος εἰπεῖν. *Hippolytus is as good as dead* (lit. *is no longer alive, so to speak*).

ἰδιῶται ὡς εἰπεῖν χειροτέχναις ἀνταγωνισάμενοι. *Laymen, as it were, pitted against craftsmen* (the metaphorical use of ἀνταγωνισάμενοι is toned down).

(*vii*) **ὡς with numerals**

ὡς is used with numerals in the sense *about, nearly*:

διέσχον ἀλλήλων βασιλεύς τε καὶ οἱ Ἕλληνες ὡς τριάκοντα στάδια. *The King and the Greeks were about thirty stades distant from each other.*

ὡς is similarly used in the common phrase ὡς ἐπὶ τὸ πολύ for the most part (lit. *nearly so far as regards the much*).

(*b*) **ὡς as a conjunction**

(*i*) **In indirect speech**, *that* (see 8.1/3*b*)

(*ii*) **In purpose clauses**, *in order that* (see 14.1/4*c*(i))

Purpose clauses are generally introduced by ἵνα or ὅπως, but ὡς may also be used, especially in poetry and in Xenophon:

διανοεῖται τὴν γέφυραν λῦσαι ὡς μὴ διαβῆτε. *He intends to break up the bridge in order that you may not cross.*

(*iii*) **In clauses of reason**, *as, since, because*

Causal clauses are regularly introduced by ὅτι, διότι *because, as*, ἐπεί, ἐπειδή *since*, but may also be introduced by ὡς. As in its use with the participle (see *a*(i) above), ὡς sometimes carries the implication that the reason given is the subjective opinion of the person described:

ἔπειτα δὲ ξύμβασιν ποιησάμενοι πρὸς τὸν Περδίκκαν, ὡς αὐτοὺς κατήπειγεν ἡ Ποτείδαια, ἀπανίστανται ἐκ τῆς Μακεδονίας. *Then, when they had made an agreement with Perdiccas because (in their opinion) [the situation in] Potidaea was pressing them, they withdrew* (vivid present) *from Macedonia.*

(*iv*) **In temporal clauses**, *when, after*

ὡς may be used like ἐπεί (cf. 14.1/4*c*(iii))

ὡς ᾔσθετο Κῦρον πεπτωκότα ἔφυγεν. *When he perceived that Cyrus had fallen, he fled.*

ὡς τάχιστα may be used in place of ἐπειδὴ τάχιστα in the sense *as soon as*:

ὡς τάχιστα ἥκομεν εἰς Μακεδονίαν, συνετάξαμεν τὸν πρεσβύτατον πρῶτον λέγειν. *As soon as we had come to Macedonia, we arranged for the eldest man to speak first.*

(*v*) **ὡς in clauses of manner**

ὡς may be used to introduce adverbial clauses of manner in the sense *as, according as, in which way*, often coupled with οὕτω(ς) *thus, so* in the principal clause. In such clauses the verb in the subordinate clause will be in the indicative mood if the action is marked as a fact:

ἐκέλευσε τοὺς Ἕλληνας, ὡς νόμος αὐτοῖς (*sc.* ἦν) εἰς μάχην, οὕτω ταχθῆναι. *He ordered the Greeks to be drawn up as was their custom for battle* (lit. *as was their custom, so . . . to be drawn up*).

But if the action has a future reference or is indefinite, the mood of the verb will follow the rules for indefinite clauses (cf. 14.1/4c(iii)), i.e. subjunctive with ἄν in primary sequence, optative without ἄν in historic sequence:

τὸ πέρας ὡς ἂν ὁ δαίμων βουληθῇ πάντων γίγνεται.   *The end of all things comes about in whatever way God wishes.*

ξυνετίθεσαν ὡς ἕκαστόν τι ξυμβαίνοι.   *They put [them] together as each [piece] fitted.*

The verb in the ὡς clause is often omitted, e.g. εἴθε πάντες σε φιλοῖεν ὡς ἐγώ. *Would that all loved you as I* (sc. *do*). Other examples occur at 13.2.6 and 15.

ὡς is likewise frequently used to introduce clauses which are parenthetical: ὡς ἔοικε *as it seems*; ὡς ἐγᾦμαι (= ἐγὼ οἶμαι) *as I think*; ὡς ἐμοὶ δοκεῖ *in my opinion* (lit. *as it seems to me*).

(c) **ὡς *as a preposition***

ὡς as a preposition governs the accusative case and has the sense *to, towards*. It is so used only with **persons**:

νῦν δὴ ἄπειμι ὡς βασιλέα.   *Now I shall go off to the King.*

ὡς Περδίκκᾱν ἔπεμψαν ἀμφότεροι πρέσβεις.   *Both sides sent ambassadors to Perdiccas.*

22.1/2   Uses of cases (1) – accusative

Apart from its use as the case of the direct object of transitive verbs (2.1/3c) and after certain prepositions (2.1/3f; 3.1/5a), the accusative can function in a number of ways, some of which require rephrasing to be turned into normal English.

(a) *Accusative and infinitive* (see 8.1/3a, and cf. 16.1/1)

(b) *Accusative to express time how long* (see 7.1/7a)

(c) *Accusative to express spatial extent* (see 7.1/7d)

(d) *Accusative of respect or specification* (see 20.1/5)

(e) *Accusative absolute* (see 21.1/5)

(f) *Verbs taking two accusatives*
These occur in Greek as in English (*we chose him leader*; *they asked us our opinion*) and can be divided into two categories:

  (i) Verbs of **making, considering, naming, choosing, appointing**, etc.

(factive verbs), which take a direct object and an object complement (also called a predicate):

οἱ Θετταλοὶ καὶ οἱ Θηβαῖοι φίλον, εὐεργέτην, cωτῆρα τὸν Φίλιππον ἡγοῦντο.   *The Thessalians and Thebans considered Philip* (direct object) *a friend, benefactor and saviour* (object complement).

τρεῖc τῶν ἐμῶν ἐχθρῶν νεκροὺc θήcω.   *I shall make three of my enemies corpses.*

When such expressions are put into the passive, both accusatives become nominative:

Λαcθένηc φίλοc ὠνομάζετο Φιλίππου.   *Lasthenes was called the friend of Philip.*

(*ii*) Verbs of **asking for** (αἰτέω), **teaching** (διδάcκω), **concealing** (κρύπτω), **depriving** (ἀποcτερέω), **taking away** (ἀφαιρέομαι) and a few others, which may take two accusatives (one accusative of the person and the other of the thing involved). The construction of the corresponding verbs in English is not always the same:

ὁ πόλεμοc ἀείμνηcτον παιδείᾱν αὐτοὺc ἐπαίδευcεν.   *The war taught them a lesson never to be forgotten.*

ἀποcτερεῖ με τὴν τῑμήν.   *He takes the honour from me.*

τὴν θυγατέρα ἔκρυπτε τὸν θάνατον τοῦ ἀνδρόc.   *He concealed her husband's death from his daughter.*

When such expressions are put into the passive, the thing involved remains in the accusative (**retained accusative**):

ἐκεῖνοι τοὺc ἵππουc ἀπεcτέρηνται.   *Those men have been deprived of their horses.*

οὐδὲν ἄλλο διδάcκεται ἄνθρωποc ἢ ἐπιcτήμην.   *A man is taught nothing else except knowledge.*

Under this heading also belong the phrases ἀγαθά (κακά etc.) λέγειν τινά *to speak well* (*ill*, etc.) *of someone*, and ἀγαθά (κακά etc.) ποιεῖν τινα *to do good* (*evil* etc.) *to someone* and the like:

τοὺc Κορινθίουc πολλά τε καὶ κακὰ ἔλεγεν.   *He said many bad things about the Corinthians.*

Instead of the neuter pl. acc. of the adjective, however, we often find the adverbs εὖ/κακῶc, etc.:

τὸν μέντοι καὶ λόγῳ καὶ ἔργῳ πειρώμενον ἐμὲ ἀνιᾶν οὐκ ἂν δυναίμην οὔτ᾽ εὖ λέγειν οὔτ᾽ εὖ ποιεῖν.   *However I would be able neither to speak well of nor to do good to the man who tries to vex me both in word and in deed.*

For the passive of expressions using λέγω and ποιέω see 17.1/5.

(g) **Cognate accusative**

This describes an expression in which a noun and the verb (usually otherwise intransitive) by which it is governed are both derived from the same root (as in English *sing a song*): νοϲεῖ νόϲον ἀγρίᾱν *he is ill with a cruel disease*; ἑωρᾶτε Ϲωκράτη πολλὴν φλυᾱρίᾱν φλυᾱροῦντα *you used to see Socrates talking much nonsense*. Except in poetry, the cognate accusative is usually accompanied by an adjective or other attribute.

Also included under this heading are accusatives used exactly in the same way with nouns not actually derived from the same root as the verb: ἠϲθένηϲε ταύτην τὴν νόϲον *he fell sick with this disease*.

Instead of a cognate noun in the accusative we may also find the neuter of an adjective used as an equivalent: Ὀλύμπια (acc. pl. n.) νῑκᾶν *to win an Olympic victory* (lit. *Olympic things*).

(h) **Accusative in oaths**

The accusative is regularly found in oaths, especially after the particles μά and νή. νή conveys strong affirmation; νὴ τὸν Δία *yes, by Zeus!*, but μά may be either affirmative or negative, the choice being determined either simply by the context (as, e.g., in 23.2.5 *l*.4) or by the prefixing of ναί or οὐ: ναὶ μὰ τὸν Δία *yes, by Zeus!*; μὰ τὸν Ἀπόλλω, οὔκ *no, by Apollo!* (cf. 24.1/1c).

In these expressions we must understand the verb ὄμνῡμι *swear*, which can also be used with the accusative of the god's name in the sense *I swear by*: ὄμνῡμι θεοὺς καὶ θεᾱ́ϲ *I swear by [all the] gods and goddesses*.

(i) **Accusative to express motion towards** (see 2.1/3*f*)

In poetry the accusative can be used with verbs of motion **without any preposition**: Μήδεια πύργους γῆς ἔπλευϲ' Ἰωλκίᾱϲ. *Medea sailed to the towers of the Iolcian land.*

22.2 Greek reading

1# ϲὺ δ' ὦ θεῶν τύραννε κἀνθρώπων Ἔρωϲ,
ἢ μὴ δίδαϲκε τὰ καλὰ φαίνεϲθαι καλά,
ἢ τοῖϲ ἐρῶϲιν εὐτυχῶϲ ϲυνεκπόνει
μοχθοῦϲι μόχθουϲ ὧν ϲὺ δημιουργὸϲ εἶ.

2 ἑϲπέρα μὲν γὰρ ἦν, ἧκε δ' ἀγγέλλων τιϲ ὡϲ τοὺϲ πρυτάνειϲ ὡϲ Ἐλάτεια κατείληπται. καὶ μετὰ ταῦτα οἱ μὲν εὐθὺϲ ἐξαναϲτάντεϲ μεταξὺ δειπνοῦντεϲ τούϲ τ' ἐκ τῶν ϲκηνῶν τῶν κατὰ τὴν ἀγορὰν ἐξεῖργον καὶ τὰ γέρρα ἐνεπίμπραϲαν, οἱ δὲ τοὺϲ ϲτρατηγοὺϲ μετεπέμποντο καὶ τὸν ϲαλπικτὴν ἐκάλουν· καὶ θορύβου πλήρηϲ ἦν ἡ πόλιϲ. τῇ δ' ὑϲτεραίᾳ ἅμα   5
τῇ ἡμέρᾳ οἱ μὲν πρυτάνειϲ τὴν βουλὴν ἐκάλουν εἰϲ τὸ βουλευτήριον,

ὑμεῖς δ᾽ εἰς τὴν ἐκκλησίαν ἐπορεύεςθε, καί, πρὶν ἐκείνην χρηματίςαι καὶ
προβουλεῦςαι, πᾶς ὁ δῆμος ἄνω καθῆτο. καὶ μετὰ ταῦτα ὡς ἦλθεν ἡ
βουλὴ καὶ ἀπήγγειλαν οἱ πρυτάνεις τὰ προςηγγελμέν᾽ ἑαυτοῖς καὶ τὸν
ἥκοντα παρήγαγον κἀκεῖνος εἶπεν, ἠρώτα μὲν ὁ κῆρυξ, τίς ἀγορεύειν   10
βούλεται; παρήει δ᾽ οὐδείς.

3   In addition to translating, define each use of the accusative:

(*i*) αἴτει καὶ τοὺς ἀνδρίαντας ἄλφιτα.   (*ii*) ἔςτιν τις Cωκράτης ςοφὸς
ἀνήρ, τά τε μετέωρα φροντιςτὴς καὶ τὰ ὑπὸ γῆς πάντα
ἀνεζητηκώς.   (*iii*) ἥκει καὶ τὰ τοῦ πάππου χρήματα ἡμᾶς ἀποςτερήςων.
(*iv*)# ἦλθε πατρὸς ἀρχαῖον τάφον.   (*v*)# πολλὰ διδάςκει μ᾽ ὁ πολὺς
βίοτος.   (*vi*) Μέλητός με ἐγράψατο τὴν γραφὴν ταύτην.   (*vii*) ὁ Κῦρος
ἦν εἶδος μὲν κάλλιστος, ψυχὴν δὲ φιλανθρωπότατος.   (*viii*) μὰ Δία, οὐκ
εἶδον ἐμαυτοῦ ἀμείνω ὑλοτόμον.   (*ix*) ςπονδὰς καὶ ξυμμαχίαν ἐποιή-
ςαντο ἑκατὸν ἔτη.   (*x*)# ὄμνυμι δ᾽ ἱερὸν αἰθέρ᾽, οἴκηςιν Διός.

4   As well as translating the following define each use of ὡς:

(*i*) ὡς ἡδὺ τῷ μιςοῦντι τοὺς φαύλους ἐρημία.   (*ii*)# κρύπτε μηδέν, ὡς
πάνθ᾽ ὁρῶν πάντ᾽ ἀναπτύςςει χρόνος.   (*iii*)# τέκνα τοῦδ᾽ ἔκατι
τίκτομεν, ὡς θεῶν τε βωμοὺς πατρίδα τε ῥυώμεθα.   (*iv*) κατέλαβε τὴν
ἀκρόπολιν ὡς ἐπὶ τυραννίδι.   (*v*) πειρᾶςθαι δὲ χρὴ ὡς ῥᾶςτα τἀναγκαῖα
(= τὰ ἀν-) τοῦ βίου φέρειν.   (*vi*)# πόνος γάρ, ὡς λέγουςιν, εὐκλείας
πατήρ.   (*vii*)# φεῦ, φεῦ, τὸ νικᾶν τἄνδιχ᾽ (= τὰ ἔνδικα) ὡς καλὸν γέρας,
τὰ μὴ δίκαια δ᾽ ὡς πανταχοῦ κακόν.   (*viii*)# ὡς ἡδὺς ὁ βίος, ἄν τις αὐτὸν
μὴ μάθῃ.   (*ix*)# δίδου πένηςιν ὡς λάβῃς θεὸν δότην.   (*x*)# κρίνει φίλους
ὁ καιρός, ὡς χρυςὸν τὸ πῦρ.   (*xi*)# μέμνηςο νέος ὢν ὡς γέρων ἔςῃ
ποτέ.   (*xii*)# οὐ ζῶμεν ὡς ἥδιςτα μὴ λυπούμενοι;   (*xiii*) ἀπέπλευςαν ἐξ
Ἑλληςπόντου ὡς ἕκαςτοι κατὰ πόλεις.   (*xiv*) ἄνδρες ςοφοὶ ὡς ἀληθῶς.

5#   ἦν Οἰδίπους τὸ πρῶτον εὐτυχὴς ἀνήρ,
εἶτ᾽ ἐγένετ᾽ αὖθις ἀθλιώτατος βροτῶν.

6#   Deianeira laments the absence of her husband Heracles.
πάθη μὲν οὖν δὴ πόλλ᾽ ἔγωγ᾽ ἐκλαυςάμην·
ἓν δ᾽, οἷον οὔπω πρόςθεν, αὐτίκ᾽ ἐξερῶ.
ὁδὸν γὰρ ἦμος τὴν τελευταίαν ἄναξ
ὡρμᾶτ᾽ ἀπ᾽ οἴκων Ἡρακλῆς, τότ᾽ ἐν δόμοις
λείπει παλαιὰν δέλτον ἐγγεγραμμένην   5
ξυνθήμαθ᾽, ἁμοὶ (= ἃ ἐμοὶ) πρόςθεν οὐκ ἔτλη ποτέ,
πολλοὺς ἀγῶνας ἐξιών, οὕτω φράςαι,
ἀλλ᾽ ὥς τι δράςων εἷρπε κοὐ θανούμενος.

7   καὶ πρῶτον πρὸς τοὺς Θρᾷκας ἐπολέμηςα, ἐκ τῆς Χερρονήςου αὐτοὺς
ἐξελαύνων βουλομένους ἀφαιρεῖςθαι τοὺς Ἕλληνας τὴν γῆν.

8#   ὦ γῆρας, οἵαν ἐλπίδ᾽ ἡδονῆς ἔχεις,
καὶ πᾶς τις εἰς ςὲ βούλετ᾽ ἀνθρώπων μολεῖν·
λαβὼν δὲ πεῖραν, μεταμέλειαν λαμβάνει,
ὡς οὐδέν ἐςτι χεῖρον ἐν θνητῷ γένει.

9 ἐγὼ γάρ, ὦ Κέβης, νέος ὢν θαυμαστῶς ὡς ἐπεθύμησα ταύτης τῆς σοφίας ἣν δὴ καλοῦσι περὶ φύσεως ἱστορίαν.

Notes

1 *l*.1 κἄν- = καὶ ἄν-. *ll*.3f. ϲυνεκπόνει 2nd s. pres. imp. act., as the accent indicates (the 3rd s. pres. ind. act would be ϲυνεκπονεῖ); ἐρῶϲι and μοχθοῦϲι (the latter agrees with the former) are m. dat. pl. of the pres. act. pples. of ἐράω and μοχθέω respectively.

2 A famous passage of the orator Demosthenes in which he describes how the Athenians in 339 BC received the news that their enemy Philip of Macedon (father of Alexander the Great) had captured a town only three days march from Athens. *ll*.1f. ὡς τοὺς πρυτάνεις to (22.1/1*c*) *the prytaneis* (a committee of the Council in charge of day-to-day administration); take ὡς (= ὅτι) Ἐλάτεια κατείληπται with ἀγγέλλων; κατείληπται 3rd s. perf. ind. pass. of καταλαμβάνω (the tense used in the original direct speech is kept, 8.1/3). *ll*.2ff. μεταξὺ δειπνοῦντες 12.1/2*a*(i); τοὺς ἐκ τῶν ϲκηνῶν lit. *those from the stalls* but trans. *those in the stalls*; in this pregnant use of ἐκ (cf. note on 9.2.13 *l*.11 where the use is somewhat different) the choice of preposition has been influenced by ἐξεῖργον; the imperfect is often used for vivid effect in narrative, hence ἐξεῖργον, ἐνεπίμπρασαν (< ἐμπίμπρημι) etc.—trans. by the simple past (*cleared out, set fire to,* etc.); the γέρρα (wicker-work of some kind) were set on fire to inform the Athenians of the emergency. *l*.7 ὑμεῖς, i.e. the people (referred to as ὁ δῆμος in *l*.8). *l*.8 ἄνω *above,* i.e. on the Pnyx, a hill to the south-west of the Athenian agora which was used for meetings of the Assembly; καθῆτο impf. (19.1/3*b*); ὡς *when* (22.1/1*b*(iv)). *ll*.9f. τὰ προϲηγγελμέν'(α) ἑαυτοῖς *the things reported* (perf.) *to them* (refl. because it refers back to the subject of the clause οἱ πρυτάνεις); τὸν ἥκοντα the person mentioned in the first line as having brought the message. *l*.11 παρῄει < παρέρχομαι (cf. 18.1/3).

3 (i) αἴτει 2nd s. pres. imp. act. (ii) ἔϲτιν here *there is*; ἀνεζητηκώς perf. act. pple. of ἀναζητέω. (x) Zeus dwelt in the heavens or upper air (αἰθήρ).

4 Supply ἐϲτί in (i), (vi), (vii), (viii). (ii) πάνθ', i.e. πάντα. (iii) Take τοῦδ' ἕκατι together—the phrase anticipates the ὡς clause. (vii) δ'(ἐ) is placed here after the first phrase, not the first word; with τὰ μὴ δίκαια supply τὸ νῑκᾶν. (viii) ἄν = ἐάν. (xi) ἔϲῃ 2nd s. fut. ind. of εἰμί. (xii) μή with a pple. to express a condition (12.1/2*a*(iv)). (xiv) A phrase, not a sentence.

5 τὸ πρῶτον acc. of respect (20.1/5), *with respect to the first [period],* i.e. *at first.*

6 *ll*.1f. μέν and δέ contrast πάθη . . . πόλλ' (= πολλά) and ἕν (sc. πάθος); οὖν δή *so then, well as you know*; with οἷον οὔπω πρόϲθεν supply ἐκλαυϲάμην; ἐξερῶ fut. of ἐξαγορεύω (cf. 18.1/4 note 2). *ll*.3f. γάρ begins the explanation of the previous line and need not be translated; take ὁδὸν . . . τὴν τελευταίαν as virtual cognate acc. (22.1/2*g*) with ὡρμᾶτ'(ο) *was setting out on . . .*; οἴκων . . . δόμοις plural for singular (a common use in poetry). *l*.6 ξυνθήμαθ'(= -τα) a type of retained acc.

(22.1/2*f*(ii)) with ἐγγεγραμμένην (*l*.5), *inscribed with signs* (ἐγγράφει ξυνθήματα δέλτῳ means *he inscribes signs on a tablet*; this can, somewhat illogically, be put into the passive δέλτος ἐγγράφεται ξυνθήματα with the original accusative retained, but we must translate *a tablet is inscribed with signs*—this differs from the examples in 22.1/2*f*(ii) in that ἐγγράφω takes an acc. and dat., not two accusatives); ἔτλη aor. of τλάω.   *l*.7 πολλοὺς ἀγῶνας ἐξιών *going out on many exploits* virtual cognate acc. (22.1/2*g*); οὕτω *thus, like this* as Deianeira goes on to explain later.   *l*.8 ὡς ... *under the impression of going to do something, as [one] going to do something* (see note on 12.3.7).

8   *l*.2 πᾶς τις emphatic for πᾶς, lit. *every single one*; βούλετ᾽, i.e. βούλεται *l*.4 ὡς to introduce a clause of reason (22.1/1*b*(iii)).

9   θαυμαστῶς ὡς 22.1/1*a*(iii).

22.3   Extra reading – Anacreontea

Anacreon was an Ionic poet of the sixth century BC. His personal poetry was famous but very little has survived. It attracted many imitators in antiquity and some of their poems (as 1 below) have come down under his name. The second poem is certainly genuine.

1   μακαρίζομέν σε, τέττιξ,
ὅτε δενδρέων ἐπ᾽ ἄκρων
ὀλίγην δρόσον πεπωκὼς
βασιλεὺς ὅπως ἀείδεις·
cὰ γάρ ἐστι κεῖνα πάντα,   5
ὁπόσα βλέπεις ἐν ἀγροῖς,
ὁπόσα τρέφουσιν ὗλαι.
cὺ δὲ τίμιος βροτοῖσιν,

θέρεος γλυκὺς προφήτης.
φιλέουσι μέν σε Μοῦσαι,   10
φιλέει δὲ Φοῖβος αὐτός,
λιγυρὴν δ᾽ ἔδωκεν οἴμην.
τὸ δὲ γῆρας οὔ σε τείρει,
σοφέ, γηγενές, φίλυμνε,
ἀπαθὴς δ᾽, ἀναιμόσαρκε,   15
cχεδὸν εἶ θεοῖς ὅμοιος.

2   πολιοὶ μὲν ἡμῖν ἤδη
κρόταφοι, κάρη τε λευκόν,
χαρίεσσα δ᾽ οὐκέτι ἥβη
πάρα, γηράλεοι δ᾽ ὀδόντες.
γλυκεροῦ δ᾽ οὐκέτι πολλὸς   5
βίοτου χρόνος λέλειπται·

διὰ ταῦτ᾽ ἀνασταλύζω
θαμὰ Τάρταρον δεδοικώς.
Ἀΐδεω γάρ ἐστι δεινὸς
μυχός, ἀργαλέη δ᾽ ἐς αὐτὸν   10
κάθοδος· καὶ γὰρ ἑτοῖμον
καταβάντι μὴ ἀναβῆναι.

Notes

1   *l*.2 δενδρέων (Ionic for δένδρων, cf. 13.1/1*c*) ἐπ᾽ ἄκρων *on the tops of trees* (18.1/6).   *l*.4 βασιλεὺς ὅπως = ὅπως (*like*) βασιλεύς.   *ll*.5f. πάντα, ὁπόσα (= ὅσα, as also in *l*.7) 21.1/3*d*.   *l*.8 Supply εἶ (< εἰμί); βροτοῖσιν *among mortals* (dat. of reference, 23.1/2*e*).   *ll*.9ff. Three examples of the use of uncontracted forms in Ionic, θέρεος (= θέρους, cf. 6.1/1*c*), φιλέουσι (= φιλοῦσι), φιλέει (= φιλεῖ).   *l*.12 λιγυρήν = -άν.

2   *l*.1 Supply εἰςί; ἡμῖν plural for singular (the dative is one of possession, 23.1/2*c*). *l*.2 κάρη, an irregular noun, is neuter, hence λευκόν. *l*.4 πάρα = πάρεςτι (cf. 21.1/4 note 2 but here it is not used impersonally). *ll*.7f. Take θαμά with ἀναςταλύζω; δεδοικώς 19.1/3*a*. *l*.9. Ἀΐδεω = Attic Ἄιδου (gen. of Ἄιδης), on the ending cf. 25.1/2*b*(i). *l*.10 ἀργαλέη = -έᾱ. *l*.11 ἑτοῖμον *[it is] fixed* the neuter singular adj. is used in impersonal expressions.

Unit 23

23.1 Grammar

23.1/1 Uses of cases (2) – genitive

Apart from its use as the case of possession (2.1/3*d*) and after certain prepositions (2.1/3*g*, 3.1/5*b*), the genitive can function in a number of ways with another noun, verb, adjective or even adverb. Although the genitive is often to be translated by *of*, in some of its uses a different rendering in English is required.

(*a*) *Possessive genitive* (see 2.1/3*d*)

In this use the genitive denotes ownership, possession or some looser association: ἡ τοῦ Δημοσθένους οἰκίᾱ *the house of Demosthenes* (or *Demosthenes' house*); οἱ Σόλωνος νόμοι *the laws of (made by) Solon*; τὰ τῆς πόλεως *the [affairs] of the city*. In certain very restricted contexts a possessive genitive qualifies a missing noun, which can easily be supplied; the most common are *wife*, *son/daughter* (cf. 5.1/3 note 2), *place of abode*: Ἀλέξανδρος ὁ Φιλίππου *Alexander, [son] of Philip*; Ἄρτεμις ἡ Διός *Artemis, [daughter] of Zeus*; ἐν Ἀρίφρονος *at Ariphron's* (*in [the house] of Ariphron*); ἐν Διονῡ́σου *at [the shrine] of Dionysus* (cf. *at St. Paul's*).

(*b*) *Genitive of characteristic*

In English we may say *it is the part/duty/nature/characteristic*, etc. *of someone to do something*. In Greek this is expressed simply by the use of the third singular of εἰμί plus the genitive. In translation from Greek the appropriate English word to be supplied must be gauged from the context: οὔτοι γυναικός ἐστιν ῑ̔μείρειν μάχης *It is indeed not a woman's part to long for battle*; δοκεῖ δικαίου τοῦτ' εἶναι πολῑ́του *this seems to be the duty of a just citizen*.

(*c*) *Subjective and objective genitive*

An **objective** genitive stands in the same relation to a noun or adjective as an object does to a transitive verb. In *Socrates' love of truth dominated his life*, the genitive *of truth* is objective because the sense connection between *truth* and *love* is the same as between an object and a verb (we could say, with the same meaning, *Socrates loved the truth*; *this dominated his life*). Examples in Greek are: φόβος τοῦ γήρως *fear of old age*, τὸ κράτος τῆς θαλάττης *the command of the sea*, ἔρως τῆς ἀρετῆς *love of virtue*. Because this use is more extensive in Greek than in English we must sometimes translate it by a different preposition: ὁ τοῦ κυνὸς λόγος *the story about the dog*, νίκη τῶν ἡδονῶν *victory over pleasures*. A **subjective** genitive, on the other hand, stands in the same relation to a noun as a subject does to a verb: νίκη τῶν βαρβάρων *victory of the barbarians* (i.e. οἱ βάρβαροι νῑκῶσιν *the barbarians are victorious*). This use is only a variety of the possessive genitive.

Sometimes, however, we must decide from the context whether a genitive is subjective or objective. ὁ τῶν Ἑλλήνων φόβος can mean *the Greeks' fear* (i.e. *the fear felt by the Greeks*) (subjective), as well as *the fear of the Greeks* (i.e. *fear inspired by the Greeks*) (objective). A possessive adjective (9.1/5*b*) usually represents a subjective genitive, but may on occasion be the equivalent of an objective genitive: φιλίᾳ τῇ ἐμῇ can mean *through friendship for me* as well as *through my friendship*. Cf. ἐπὶ διαβολῇ τῇ ἐμῇ in 10.3 *l*.5.

(*d*) *Partitive genitive*

In this construction the genitive denotes the whole and the noun or pronoun on which it depends denotes a part of that whole: μέρος τι τῶν βαρβάρων *a part of the barbarians*; οἱ ἄδικοι τῶν ἀνθρώπων *the unjust among men*; ὀλίγοι αὐτῶν *few of them*; οἱ πρεσβύτατοι τῶν στρατηγῶν *the oldest of the generals*. The partitive genitive may also occur by itself as the object of a verb: τῆς γῆς ἔτεμον *they ravaged [part] of the land* (τὴν γῆν ἔτεμον would mean *they ravaged the [whole] land*). It can also be used predicatively: Σόλων τῶν ἑπτὰ σοφιστῶν ἐκλήθη *Solon was called [one] of the Seven Sages*.

This use of the genitive also occurs in abstract nouns after the phrase εἰς τοῦτο (τοσοῦτο) ἀφικνεῖσθαι (ἥκειν etc.) *to reach this (such a) pitch/ point/stage of* (cf. 16.1/1 note 3): εἰς τοῦτο θράσους καὶ ἀναιδείας ἀφίκετο *he reached such a pitch of boldness and shamelessness*; εἰς τοῦθ' ὕβρεως ἥκει *he has come to such a pitch of insolence*.

Under this heading also belongs the **chorographic** genitive, or genitive of **geographic definition**: ἔπλευσαν τῆς Ἰταλίᾱς εἰς Τάραντα *they sailed to Tarentum in Italy* (lit. *[a part] of Italy*); τῆς Σικελίᾱς οἱ Σῡρᾱκόσιοι *the Syracusans in Sicily*. Compare the use of the genitive with adverbs of place, e.g. εἰδέναι ὅπου γῆς ἐστιν *to know where in the world he is* (cf. 2.2.11).

(*e*) *Genitive of explanation*

The genitive may be used as the equivalent of a noun in apposition which gives an explanation or definition of the preceding noun. The construction in English is generally the same: ὦ πόλι Θηβῶν *O city of Thebes* (i.e. *O city, viz Thebes*); τέλος θανάτου *the end of death* (i.e. *the end that is death*); ὕπνου δῶρον *the gift of sleep*.

(*f*) **Genitive of price or value** (see 20.1/3)

(*g*) **Genitive of time within which** (see 7.1/7*c*)

(*h*) **Genitive absolute** (see 12.1/2*b*)

(*i*) **Genitive of comparison** (see 17.1/4*a*)

(*j*) **Genitive of separation** (see 20.1/4)

(*k*) **Genitive with verbs** (see 13.1/2*a*)
At 13.1/2*a* we considered certain intransitive verbs which take the genitive. Two other groups are followed by an accusative and a genitive:

  (*i*) Verbs of **accusing**, **acquitting**, **condemning**, **prosecuting** and the like are generally followed by an accusative of the person involved and a genitive of the crime or charge. Such verbs are αἰτιάομαι *accuse*, γράφομαι *indict*, διώκω *prosecute*:

  ὁ Μέλητος ἀσεβείᾱς ἐμὲ ἐγράψατο. *Meletus indicted me for impiety.*
  διώξομαί σε δειλίᾱς. *I shall prosecute you for cowardice.*

  However, verbs of accusing and condemning which are compounded with κατά (such as κατηγορέω *accuse*, καταγιγνώσκω *give judgement against, condemn*, κατακρῑ́νω *give sentence against*, καταψηφίζομαι *vote against*) reverse the normal construction, and so take a genitive of the person and an accusative of the crime or penalty:

  ἐγὼ δ᾽ ῡ̔μῶν δέομαι μὴ καταγνῶναι δωροδοκίᾱν ἐμοῦ. *I request you not to condemn me for bribery.*
  ἐμοῦ Φιλιππισμὸν κατηγορεῖ. *He accuses me of siding with Philip.*

  (*ii*) A genitive of **cause** can follow verbs of **emotion**. Such verbs are θαυμάζω *wonder at*, ζηλόω *admire*, οἰκτῑ́ρω *pity*, etc.: τούτους τῆς τόλμης θαυμάζω *I wonder at these men for* (or *because of*) *their boldness*; τοῦ πάθους ᾤκτῑρεν αὐτόν *he pitied him for his suffering*.
  A genitive of cause can also occur with adjectives: εὐδαίμων τοῦ τρόπου *happy in his way of life.*

(*l*) **Genitive of exclamation**
This genitive, which is often coupled with an interjection (φεῦ *alas* (of grief); *ah, oh* (of astonishment), οἴμοι *alas*), is akin to the genitive of cause as it gives the reason for the speaker's astonishment or grief: οἴμοι ταλαίνης τῆσδε συμφορᾶς *alas for this wretched plight!*; φεῦ φεῦ τῆς ὥρᾱς, τοῦ κάλλους *ah, what youthful bloom, what beauty!*; εἶπε πρὸς αὑτόν, τῆς τύχης *he said to himself, "What luck!"*

23.1/2 Uses of cases (3) – dative

The Greek dative is an amalgam of three cases:

the **dative proper**, generally to be translated *to* or *for*, indicating the person (or thing) involved in an action (the recipient, the person advantaged or disadvantaged, etc.);

the old **instrumental** case, denoting that *by* which or *with* which an action is done or accompanied;

the original **locative** case, which expressed *place where* and *time when*.

Some of these uses are distinguished and made more precise by the use of prepositions (cf. 2.1/3*h*, 3.1/5).

DATIVE PROPER

(*a*) **Verbs governing the dative**

(i) Verbs followed by a direct object (accusative) and an indirect object (dative—2.1/3*e*), such as verbs of **giving, saying, promising**: *Κῦρος δίδωσιν αὐτῷ μυρίους δαρεικούς Cyrus gives him 10,000 darics*; *ὑπιϲχνοῦμαί ϲοι δέκα τάλαντα I promise you ten talents.* However, many verbs of **reproaching, blaming** and the like, which in English take a direct object of the person involved, in Greek take a **dative** of the person and an accusative of the thing (when expressed): *μὴ πάθωμεν ὃ ἄλλοιϲ ἐπιτῑμῶμεν let us not get into a situation for which we censure others* (lit. *let us not experience [the thing] which we censure in others*); *αἰϲχῡνομαί ϲοι τοῦτ' ὀνειδίϲαι I am ashamed to reproach you with this*; *τί ἄν μοι μέμφοιο; what would you blame me for?*

The English construction which allows the indirect object of a verb in the active voice to be made the subject of the same verb in the passive (*I was given this land*) is generally impossible in Greek. *ταύτην τὴν χώρᾱν μοι ἔδωκε he gave me this land* becomes *αὕτη ἡ χώρᾱ μοι ὑπ' αὐτοῦ ἐδόθη this land was given to me by him.* *ἐδόθην* would mean *I was given* in the sense *I was handed over.* For an exception see note on 22.2.6 *l.*6.

(ii) **Intransitive verbs** followed by the dative (see 13.1/2*b*).

(iii) **Impersonal verbs** followed by the dative (see 21.1/4).

(*b*) **Dative with adjectives, adverbs and nouns**

The dative is used with certain **adjectives** whose English equivalent is usually followed by *to* or *for*. These include *φίλος dear, friendly*; *ἐχθρός hateful, hostile*; *ἴϲος equal*; *ὅμοιος like, resembling*; *ἀνόμοιος unlike, dissimilar*: *τύραννος ἅπᾱς ἐχθρὸς ἐλευθερίᾳ καὶ νόμοις ἐναντίος every tyrant [is] hostile to freedom and opposed to laws*; *ποιεῖτε ὅμοια τοῖϲ* λόγοιc *you are acting in accordance with* (lit. *doing things like*) *your words.* Compare ὁ αὐτόc with the dative *the same as* (9.1/3*b*).

A similar use of the dative is found after some **adverbs**: ἀκολούθωc τοῖc νόμοιc *in accordance with the laws*; ὁμολογουμένωc τῆ φύcει ζῆν *to live in agreement with nature*; as well as with some **nouns**, especially those related to verbs of similar meaning which take the dative: ἐπιβουλὴ ἐμοί *a plot against me*; κοινωνία τοῖc ἀνδράcι *association with men.*

(*c*) **Dative of possession**
The dative is used with εἶναι (and verbs of similar meaning such as ὑπάρχειν and γίγνεcθαι) to denote the owner or possessor: οἰκεῖοί μοί εἰcι καὶ υἱεῖc *I have relatives and sons* (lit. *relatives and sons are to me*); τῷ δικαίῳ παρὰ θεῶν δῶρα γίγνεται *the just man has gifts* (lit. *gifts come into being for the just man*) *from the gods.*

(*d*) **Dative of advantage and disadvantage**
The dative is used to indicate the person or thing for whose advantage or disadvantage something is done: πᾶc ἀνὴρ αὐτῷ πονεῖ *every man works for himself* (advantage); ἄλλο cτράτευμα αὐτῷ cυνελέγετο *another army was being gathered for him* (advantage); ἥδε ἡ ἡμέρᾱ τοῖc Ἕλληcι μεγάλων κακῶν ἄρξει *this day will be the beginning of great troubles for the Greeks* (disadvantage). Sometimes this use cannot be translated by *for*: cῖτον αὐτοῖc ἀφεῖλεν *he took food away from them* (lit. *he took food away to their disadvantage*; for the other construction used with verbs meaning *take away* see 22.1/2*f*(ii)).

(*e*) **Dative of reference or relation**
Similarly, the dative may be used to denote a person or thing to whose case a statement is limited: τριήρει ἐcτὶν εἰc Ἡράκλειαν ἡμέρᾱc μακρᾶc πλοῦc *for a trireme it is a long day's voyage to Heraclea.* This dative is often used to denote *in the eyes of* or *in the judgement of*: ἡμῖν Ἀχιλλεὺc ἄξιοc τῑμῆc *in our eyes* (lit. *for us*) *Achilles [is] worthy of honour*; ἀνάξιοι πᾶcίν ἐcτε δυcτυχεῖν *in the eyes of all* (lit. *for all*) *you are unworthy to suffer misfortune.*

A participle in the dative singular is used in this way with an indefinite reference: Ἐπίδαμνοc ἐν δεξιᾷ ἐcτιν εἰcπλέοντι ἐc τὸν Ἰόνιον κόλπον *Epidamnus is on the right as one sails into* (lit. *in relation to one sailing into*) *the Ionian Gulf*; ἔλεγον ὅτι ἡ ὁδὸc διαβάντι τὸν ποταμὸν ἐπὶ Λῡδίᾱν φέροι *they said that, when one had crossed the river, the road led to Lydia.* Compare also the phrase ὡc cυνελόντι εἰπεῖν *to speak concisely, in a word* (lit. *so to speak for one having brought [the matter] together*).

(*f*) **Ethic dative** (a purely conventional term, with no connection with ethics)

The dative of the first or second person pronouns can be used simply to attract the attention of the person addressed. There is no grammatical connection with the surrounding words. This so-called ethic dative is usually to be represented in English by *I beg you, please, let me tell you, you know*, and the like: καί μοι μὴ θορυβήϲητε and, *I beg you, don't make a clamour*; Ἀρταφέρνηϲ ὑμῖν Ὑϲτάϲπου ἐϲτὶ παῖϲ *Artaphernes, you know, is Hystaspes' son*.

(g) **Dative of the agent**

This use, replaced in most contexts by ὑπό + gen., is found with the perfect and pluperfect passive (very rarely with other tenses): πάνθ᾽ ἡμῖν πεποίηται *everything has been done by us*; ἐπειδὴ αὐτοῖϲ παρεϲκεύαϲτο *when they had made their preparations* (lit. *it had been prepared by them*).

For the dative of the agent with verbal adjectives, see 24.1/5b.

INSTRUMENTAL DATIVE

(h) **Dative of instrument** (see 11.1/2)

(i) **Dative of cause**

The dative may denote cause: ῥίγει ἀπωλλύμεθα *we were perishing from* (or *because of*) *cold*. Often the noun in the dative denotes an emotional or mental condition:

ὕβρει καὶ οὐκ οἴνῳ τοῦτο ποιεῖ. *He does this through insolence and not because he is drunk* (lit. *because of wine*).
ἠπείγοντο πρὸϲ τὸν ποταμὸν τοῦ πιεῖν ἐπιθυμίᾳ. *They were hurrying towards the river because of their desire to drink* (lit. *because of a desire for drinking*).

Occasionally cause may also be expressed by ὑπό with the genitive: οὐκ ἐδύνατο καθεύδειν ὑπὸ λύπηϲ *he could not sleep because of* (or *for*) *grief*.

(j) **Dative of manner and attendant circumstances**

The dative may be used to denote the manner in which something is done or the circumstances accompanying an action; οἱ Ἀθηναῖοι παντὶ ϲθένει ἐπεκούρηϲαν *the Athenians helped with all their strength* (manner); ἀτελεῖ τῇ νίκῃ ἀπῆλθον *they went away with their victory incomplete* (accompanying circumstance).

Normally a noun used in this way is qualified by an adjective (as above). Some nouns, however, are regularly employed by themselves as datives of manner and are virtually the equivalent of adverbs: βίᾳ *by force, forcibly*; δρόμῳ *at a run*; ἔργῳ *in fact, in deed*; λόγῳ *in word, in theory*; ϲιγῇ *in silence*; ϲπουδῇ *hastily*; φύϲει . . . νόμῳ *by nature . . . by convention*; compare also τῷ ὄντι *in reality* (see 12.1/1 note 1); τούτῳ τῷ τρόπῳ *in this way*.

Under this category are also included the datives of feminine adjectives with a noun understood: ταύτῃ *in this way*; ἰδίᾳ *privately*; δημοσίᾳ *publicly*; πεζῇ *on foot*.

(k)　*Dative of accompaniment*
We have already met this use of the dative with αὐτός (see 9.1/3*a*(ii)). The dative by itself is particularly common in military contexts (the **military dative**) to denote the forces with which a journey or expedition is made: ᾿Αθηναῖοι ἐφ᾿ ἡμᾶς πολλῇ στρατιᾷ ὥρμηνται *the Athenians have made an expedition against us with a large force.*

(l)　*Dative of measure of difference* (see 17.1/4*b*)

(m)　*Dative of respect*
As well as an accusative of respect (20.1/5) we may also find the dative used in a similar way: ἀνὴρ ἡλικίᾳ ἔτι νέος *a man still young in age*; ὀνόματι σπονδαί *a truce in name [alone].*

LOCATIVE DATIVE

(n)　*Dative of place where*
In poetry **place where** may be expressed by the dative **without a preposition**: Κρονίδης αἰθέρι ναίων *the son of Cronos living in the sky*. In Attic prose, however, a preposition is generally required (2.1/3*h*), except with some place names, e.g. Μαραθῶνι *at Marathon*. Traces of the old locative endings remain in such forms such as: ᾿Αθήνησι (= ἐν ᾿Αθήναις) *at Athens*; Φαληροῖ (=ἐν Φαλήρῳ) *at Phalerum*; cf. οἴκοι *at home*. These words are usually classified as adverbs.

(o)　*Dative of time when* (see 7.1/7*b*)

23.2　Greek reading

1　*In addition to translating, define each use of the genitive and dative:*

(*i*)# ὦ φίλον ὕπνου θέλγητρον, ἐπίκουρον νόσου. (*ii*) ἤθελε τῶν μενόντων εἶναι. (*iii*) ὦ Πόσειδον, τῆς τέχνης. (*iv*) πενίαν φέρειν οὐ παντός, ἀλλ᾿ ἀνδρὸς σοφοῦ. (*v*) τούτῳ πάνυ μοι προσέχετε τὸν νοῦν. (*vi*) πολλαὶ θεραπεῖαι τοῖς ἰατροῖς εὕρηνται. (*vii*) ὕπνος πέφυκε σωμάτων σωτηρία. (*viii*) τὸν αὐτὸν αἰνεῖν καὶ ψέγειν ἀνδρὸς κακοῦ. (*ix*) τοιοῦτο ὑμῖν ἐστιν ἡ τυραννίς, ὦ Λακεδαιμόνιοι. (*x*) ταῦτα Ζεὺς οἶδεν ᾿Ολύμπιος, αἰθέρι ναίων. (*xi*) αἰτιῶνται αὐτὸν κλοπῆς. (*xii*) οἱ ἄνθρωποι διὰ τὸ αὐτῶν δέος τοῦ θανάτου ψεύδονται. (*xiii*) ἐφοβοῦντο μὴ οἱ ᾿Αθηναῖοι μείζονι παρασκευῇ ἐπέλθωσιν. (*xiv*) κραυγῇ πολλῇ ἐπίασιν. (*xv*) ὄνομα τῷ μειρακίῳ ἦν Πλάτων. (*xvi*)# τέχνη ἀνάγκης ἀσθενεστέρα μακρῷ. (*xvii*)# ζηλῶ σε τοῦ νοῦ, τῆς δὲ δειλίας

ϲτυγῶ. (xviii) ἐγὼ τῶν κρεῶν ἔκλεπτον. (xix)# ἆρ' ὑμῖν οὗτος ταῦτ'
ἔδραϲεν ἔνδικα; (xx) θεοῖϲ ταῦτα ἐποίηϲαν. (xxi) ϲτυγνὸϲ ἦν καὶ τῇ
φωνῇ τραχύϲ. (xxii) ὁ ϲτρατὸϲ ἀφίκετο τῆϲ Ἀττικῆϲ ἐϲ Οἰνόην. (xxiii)
ὁρᾶτε τὴν βαϲιλέωϲ ἐπιορκίαν. (xxiv) οὐκ εἰμὶ τοῖϲ πεπραγμένοιϲ
δύϲθυμοϲ.

2 ὁ Διογένηϲ, Ἀναξιμένει τῷ ῥήτορι παχεῖ ὄντι προϲελθών, ἐπίδοϲ καὶ
ἡμῖν, ἔφη, τοῖϲ πτωχοῖϲ τῆϲ γαϲτρόϲ· καὶ γὰρ αὐτὸϲ κουφιϲθήϲει καὶ
ἡμᾶϲ ὠφελήϲειϲ.

3# ἦν γάρ τιϲ αἶνοϲ ὡϲ γυναιξὶ μὲν τέχναι
μέλουϲι, λόγχῃ δ' ἄνδρεϲ εὐϲτοχώτεροι.
εἰ γὰρ δόλοιϲιν ἦν τὸ νικητήριον,
ἡμεῖϲ ἂν ἀνδρῶν εἴχομεν τυραννίδα.

4# καὶ νῦν παραινῶ πᾶϲι τοῖϲ νεωτέροιϲ
μὴ πρὸϲ τὸ γῆραϲ ἀναβολὰϲ ποιουμένουϲ
ϲχολῇ τεκνοῦϲθαι παῖδαϲ· οὐ γὰρ ἡδονή,
γυναικί τ' ἐχθρὸν χρῆμα πρεϲβύτηϲ ἀνήρ·
ἀλλ' ὡϲ τάχιϲτα. καὶ γὰρ ἐκτροφαὶ καλαὶ   5
καὶ ϲυννεάζων ἡδὺ παῖϲ νέῳ πατρί.

5 One of the accusations brought against Socrates (10.3) was that he did not
believe in the traditional gods. In the *Apology* of Plato (see 13.3), which is
an account of his trial, he is represented as interrogating one of his
accusers on this charge.

ΜΕΛΗΤΟϹ—ϹΩΚΡΑΤΗϹ

ΜΕ. ταῦτα λέγω, ὡϲ τὸ παράπαν οὐ νομίζειϲ θεούϲ.

ϹΩ. ὦ θαύμαϲιε Μέλητε, τί ταῦτα λέγειϲ; οὐδὲ ἥλιον οὐδὲ ϲελήνην ἄρα
νομίζω θεοὺϲ εἶναι, ὥϲπερ οἱ ἄλλοι ἄνθρωποι;

ΜΕ. μὰ Δί', ὦ ἄνδρεϲ δικαϲταί, ἐπεὶ τὸν μὲν ἥλιον λίθον φηϲὶν εἶναι, τὴν
δὲ ϲελήνην γῆν.   5

ϹΩ. Ἀναξαγόρου οἴει κατηγορεῖν, ὦ φίλε Μέλητε; καὶ οὕτω καταφρονεῖϲ
τῶνδε καὶ οἴει αὐτοὺϲ ἀπείρουϲ γραμμάτων εἶναι ὥϲτε οὐκ εἰδέναι ὅτι τὰ
Ἀναξαγόρου βιβλία τοῦ Κλαζομενίου γέμει τούτων τῶν λόγων; καὶ δὴ
καὶ οἱ νέοι ταῦτα παρ' ἐμοῦ μανθάνουϲιν, ἃ ἔξεϲτιν δραχμῆϲ ἐκ τῆϲ
ὀρχήϲτραϲ πριαμένοιϲ Ϲωκράτουϲ καταγελᾶν, ἐὰν προϲποιῆται ἑαυτοῦ   10
εἶναι, ἄλλωϲ τε καὶ οὕτωϲ ἄτοπα ὄντα; ἀλλ', ὦ πρὸϲ Διόϲ, οὑτωϲί ϲοι
δοκῶ; οὐδένα νομίζω θεὸν εἶναι;

ΜΕ. οὐ μέντοι μὰ Δία οὐδ' ὁπωϲτιοῦν.

ϹΩ. ἄπιϲτόϲ γ' εἶ, ὦ Μέλητε, καὶ ταῦτα μέντοι, ὡϲ ἐμοὶ δοκεῖϲ, ϲαυτῷ.
ἐμοὶ γὰρ δοκεῖ οὑτοϲί, ὦ ἄνδρεϲ Ἀθηναῖοι, πάνυ εἶναι ὑβριϲτὴϲ καὶ   15
ἀκόλαϲτοϲ, καὶ ἀτεχνῶϲ τὴν γραφὴν ὕβρει τινὶ καὶ ἀκολαϲίᾳ καὶ νεότητι
γράψαϲθαι. ἔοικεν γὰρ ὥϲπερ αἴνιγμα ϲυντιθέντι διαπειρωμένῳ, ἆρα
γνώϲεται Ϲωκράτηϲ ὁ ϲοφὸϲ δὴ ἐμοῦ χαριεντιζομένου καὶ ἐναντί'
ἐμαυτῷ λέγοντοϲ, ἢ ἐξαπατήϲω αὐτὸν καὶ τοὺϲ ἄλλουϲ τοὺϲ ἀκούονταϲ;

οὗτος γὰρ ἐμοὶ φαίνεται τὰ ἐναντία λέγειν αὐτὸς ἑαυτῷ ἐν τῇ γραφῇ   20
ὥσπερ ἂν εἰ εἴποι· ἀδικεῖ Cωκράτης θεοὺς οὐ νομίζων, ἀλλὰ θεοὺς
νομίζων. καίτοι τοῦτό ἐστι παίζοντος.

Notes

1 (i) ὕπνου θέλγητρον 23.1/1e.   (iv) Supply ἐστί; cf. (viii) and (xvi).
2 ἐπίδος 2nd s. aor. imp. act. of ἐπιδίδωμι; τῆς γαστρός 23.1/1d;
   κουφισθήσει 2nd s. fut. ind. pass.
3 l.2 Supply εἰσί with ἄνδρες.   l.3 Lit. *for if the prize of victory were through
   guiles* (dat. of instrument), i.e. *were [won] by guiles.*
4 ll.2f. ἀναβολὰς ποιοῦμαι (mid.) *I make delays,* i.e. for myself—the active
   would mean *I make delays (for others),* cf. 8.1/1b; the middle is used in the
   same way with τεκνοῦσθαι; οὐ . . . ἡδονή (ἐστι), i.e. in producing children
   in old age.   l.5 ὡς τάχιστα is contrasted with cχολῇ (l.3), i.e. have
   children as quickly as possible; ἐκτροφαί (plural for singular) *the rearing
   [of children],* i.e. *rearing children.*   l.6 The neuter adj. ἡδύ is predicate
   [is] a pleasant [thing] (ἐστί is understood), cf. 5.2.5(i).
5 l.1 ταῦτα trans. *this* (the neuter plural is often used where we would have
   the singular in English); τὸ παράπαν οὐ *not at all,* cf. note on 11.2.12 l.3;
   νομίζεις *believe in.*   l.2 οὐδὲ . . . οὐδέ *not even . . . nor* (**not** *neither-
   . . . nor* which is οὔτε . . . οὔτε)—note that this question is **not** marked by
   any introductory word (the same applies to all the questions in what
   Socrates says next).   l.4 μὰ Δί'(α) here *no, by Zeus* (22.1/2h).   l.6
   Anaxagoras of Clazomenae was a philosopher of the generation before
   Socrates who taught that the sun and moon were material bodies
   suspended in the sky (the sun was a burning rock about the size of the
   Peloponnese); the traditional belief was that they were divinities.   l.7
   τῶνδε i.e. the jurymen; αὐτοὺς . . . ὥστε lit. *them to be inexperienced in
   letters with the result . . . ,* i.e. *that they are [so] illiterate that . . .;* οὐκ
   εἰδέναι an exception to the rule given at 24.1/2e—ὥστε + inf. is often
   negated by οὐ when it follows the inf. construction of indirect speech (here
   αὐτοὺς . . . εἶναι);   ll.9ff. ἅ is the object of πριαμένοις, lit. *which having
   bought . . . it is allowed* (ἔξεστιν) *[to them] to mock* (καταγελᾶν) . . ., i.e.
   which they can buy . . . and [then] laugh at . . .; δραχμῆς gen. of price
   (20.1/3); ἐκ τῆς ὀρχήστρᾶς lit. *from the orchestra* (a part of the Athenian
   agora where books were sold) but English idiom requires *in the orchestra;*
   ἑαυτοῦ εἶναι *[them,* i.e. the doctrines of Anaxagoras] *to be his* (lit. *of
   himself* possessive gen., 23.1/1a); ἄλλως τε καί *especially;* ἄτοπα ὄντα
   agrees with the understood subject of εἶναι.   l.14 καὶ ταῦτα μέντοι *and
   that* (cf. note on l.1) *too* (ταῦτα refers to the clause ἄπιστός γ' εἶ *you are
   not to be believed*).   l.16 ὕβρει τινί, ἀκολασίᾳ datives of cause (23.1/
   2i).   l.17 ὥσπερ (lit. *as if*) tones down the metaphor (cf. 22.1/1a(vi) for
   ὡς used in the same way) and need not be translated; αἴνιγμα object of
   cυντιθέντι which agrees with διαπειρωμένῳ *[a man] composing a riddle
   making trial [of me],* i.e. *[a man] making trial [of me] [by] composing
   . . .* (the actual riddle is ἆρα . . . ἀκούοντας;).   ll.18f. δή adds a note of
   sarcasm to ὁ σοφός; ἐμοῦ . . . ἐναντί'(α) ἐμαυτῷ λέγοντος (*saying*

[things] opposite to myself, i.e. *contradicting myself*) gen. absol. with two
participles (*will S. realise when I . . .?*). l.21 ὥϲπερ ἄν εἰ (=ὥϲπερ εἰ)
εἴποι *as if he were to say.* l.22 παίζοντοϲ gen. of characteristic (23.1/1*b*).

23.3 Extra reading –
Further elegaic poetry

Of the following, 1–5 are epitaphs, which were nearly always written in
elegiac couplets (**Appendix 10**). Other examples of epitaphs occur at 9.2.3 and
19.2.7(*v*).

1   ναυηγοῦ τάφοϲ εἰμί· ὁ δ' ἀντίον ἐϲτὶ γεωργοῦ·
      ὡϲ ἁλὶ καὶ γαίῃ ξυνὸϲ ὕπεϲτ' Ἀΐδηϲ.

2   τῇδε Ϲάων ὁ Δίκωνοϲ Ἀκάνθιοϲ ἱερὸν ὕπνον
      κοιμᾶται· θνήϲκειν μὴ λέγε τοὺϲ ἀγαθούϲ.

3   δωδεκετῆ τὸν παῖδα πατὴρ ἀπέθηκε Φίλιπποϲ
      ἐνθάδε, τὴν πολλὴν ἐλπίδα, Νικοτέλην.

4   *On the Spartans who died fighting the Persians at Plataea*
    ἄϲβεϲτον κλέοϲ οἵδε φίλῃ περὶ πατρίδι θέντεϲ
      κυάνεον θανάτου ἀμφιβάλοντο νέφοϲ·
    οὐδὲ τεθνᾶϲι θανόντεϲ, ἐπεί ϲφ' ἀρετὴ καθύπερθεν
      κυδαίνουϲ' ἀνάγει δώματοϲ ἐξ Ἀΐδεω.

5   Αἰϲχύλον Εὐφορίωνοϲ Ἀθηναῖον τόδε κεύθει
      μνῆμα καταφθίμενον πυροφόροιο Γέλαϲ·
    ἀλκὴν δ' εὐδόκιμον Μαραθώνιον ἄλϲοϲ ἂν εἴποι
      καὶ βαθυχαιτήειϲ Μῆδοϲ ἐπιϲτάμενοϲ.

6   δάκρυα ϲοὶ καὶ νέρθε διὰ χθονόϲ, Ἡλιοδώρα,
      δωροῦμαι ϲτοργᾶϲ λείψανον εἰϲ Ἀΐδαν,
    δάκρυα δυϲδάκρυτα· πολυκλαύτῳ δ' ἐπὶ τύμβῳ
      ϲπένδω νᾶμα πόθων, μνᾶμα φιλοφροϲύναϲ·
    οἰκτρὰ γὰρ οἰκτρὰ φίλαν ϲε καὶ ἐν φθιμένοιϲ Μελέαγροϲ   5
      αἰάζω, κενεὰν εἰϲ Ἀχέροντα χάριν.
    αἰαῖ, ποῦ τὸ ποθεινὸν ἐμοὶ θάλοϲ; ἅρπαϲεν Ἀΐδαϲ
      ἅρπαϲεν, ἀκμαῖον δ' ἄνθοϲ ἔφυρε κόνιϲ.
    ἀλλά ϲε γουνοῦμαι, γᾶ παντρόφε, τὰν πανόδυρτον
      ἠρέμα ϲοῖϲ κόλποιϲ, μᾶτερ, ἐναγκάλιϲαι.   10

Notes

1 l.1 ὁ *sc.* τάφοϲ.   l.2 ὡϲ exclamatory (22.1/1*a*(ii)); ὕπεϲτ'(ι) < ὕπειμι.
2 ὁ Δίκωνοϲ 23.1/1*a*; ἱερὸν ὕπνον cognate acc. (22.1/2*g*) with κοιμᾶται.
3 l.1 ἀπέθηκε < ἀποτίθημι.   l.2 τὴν πολλὴν ἐλπίδα is in apposition to
  παῖδα.

4　*l*.1 περὶ . . . θέντες tmesis (12.3.9 *l*.6 note) for περιθέντες (the image is from putting a wreath on a person's head). *l*.2 ἀμφιβάλοντο (= ἀμφεβάλοντο) a Homeric form without the augment (25.1/2*d*(i))—the image here is of putting on a mantle. *l*.3 τεθνᾶσι shorter form of τεθνήκᾱσι (19.1/3*a*); cφ᾽(ε) here *them*. *l*.4 κυδαίνουσ᾽(α) f. nom. pple.; in prose the order of the last three words would be ἐκ δώματος Ἀΐδεω (= Ἄιδου, cf. 22.3.2 *l*.9 and 25.1/2*b*(i)).

5　*l*.1 Εὐφορίωνος *[son] of E*., 23.1/1*a* (the article can be omitted). *l*.2 καταφθίμενον (Homeric aorist mid. pple.) *dead* (trans. *who died*); πῡροφόροιο (=-ου, 25.1/2*b*(ii)) Γέλᾱς Homeric use of gen. to denote place where. *ll*.3f. Μαραθώνιον ἄλσος the grove at Marathon (a village to the north of Athens) which celebrated the Athenian victory over an invading Persian force in 490 BC. Aeschylus had distinguished himself in the battle and set more value on this than on any literary achievements, if the tradition assigning the epitaph to him is correct. The subject of εἴποι is both ἄλσος and Μῆδος (with double subjects of this sort the verb may agree with the closer noun). *l*.4 ἐπιστάμενος sc. *it*, i.e. Aeschylus' ἀλκή.

6　The poem has a smattering of Doric forms, which are sometimes used in elegiac poetry; these involve ᾱ for Attic η: στοργᾶς, Ἀΐδᾶν (= Ἄιδην) (*l*.2); μνᾶμα, φιλοφροσύνᾱς (*l*.4); Ἄιδᾱς (*l*.7); γᾶ, τᾱ́ν (*l*.9); μᾶτερ (*l*.10). *ll*.1f. Take στοργᾶς with λείψανον, which is in apposition to δάκρυα. *l*.4 μνᾶμα is in apposition to νᾶμα. *l*.5 οἰκτρὰ . . . οἰκτρά; n. pl. acc. used adverbially (20.1/5), *piteously*. *l*.6 κενεὰν . . . χάριν is in apposition to the whole of the preceding clause; Acheron, one of the rivers of the Underworld, is used here to mean the Underworld itself. *l*.7 ἐμοί indicates possession (23.1/2*c*); ἅρπασεν = ἥρπασεν (cf. ἀμφιβάλοντο in 4 *l*.2 above). *l*.10 ἐναγκάλισαι 2nd s. aor. imp. mid. of ἐναγκαλίζομαι.

Unit 24

24.1   Grammar

24.1/1   *Yes* and *no*

Greek has four ways of answering questions where in English we would use
yes or *no*. In answer to the question ἆρα τοῦτο εἶπας; *Did you say this?* we
may have:

(*a*)   the key word of the question repeated either affirmatively or negatively:
εἶπον *yes* (lit. *I said [it]*); οὐκ εἶπον *no* (lit. *I did not say [it]*)

(*b*)   the personal pronoun with γε: ἔγωγε *yes* (lit. *I at any rate [said it]*); οὐκ
ἔγωγε *no*

(*c*)   by ναί *yes* and οὔ *no*; or by a phrase such as πάνυ μὲν οὖν *certainly*;
οὐδαμῶς *certainly not*. This can take the form of an abbreviated
question, e.g. πῶς γὰρ οὔ; *of course* (lit. *for how not?*); or of an oath
(22.1/2*h*)

(*d*)   a short clause such as ἀληθῆ λέγεις *you speak [the] truth* (lit. *true
things*).

Sometimes one speaker in a conversation makes a comment on what the
other speaker has said (which may or may not have been a question), and we
must infer from his words whether he is agreeing or not:

> A. σύ γ᾽ οὔπω σωφρονεῖν ἐπίστασαι. B. σὲ γὰρ προσηύδων οὐκ ἄν. A.
> *You do not yet know prudence* (lit. *how to be prudent*). B. *[No], for I
> would not be speaking to you* (sc. *if I did*).

Other examples have already occurred at 13.3(ii) *l*.4 and 18.2.1.

24.1/2   Summary of uses of οὐ and μή

Both οὐ and μή are to be translated by *not*. Their uses, which involve
distinctions which we do not make in English, can be classified as follows:

(*a*)   In **main clauses**, οὐ is used as the negative in statements of fact and in
suppositions (i.e. in the main clause of a category 1 conditional sentence
(18.1/5) and in potential clauses (19.1/2)); μή is used in constructions
expressing an order or desire, i.e. prohibitions (17.1/1), exhortations
(14.1/4*a*(i)), and wishes (21.1/1).

Also, οὐ is used in direct questions expecting the answer *yes*, μή in direct questions expecting the answer *no* (10.1/2*a*) and in deliberative questions (14.1/4*a*(ii)).

(*b*) When the verb of an **adverbial clause** is negated, μή is used in clauses of purpose (14.1/4*c*(i)), condition (18.1/5), and for indefinite adverbial clauses (14.1/4*c*(iii) and 21.1/2 note 4); elsewhere the negative is οὐ.

(*c*) When the verb of an **adjectival clause** is negated, μή is used if the clause has an indefinite or general sense whether the indefinite construction (14.1/4*c*(iii)) is used or not, e.g.

οὐ γὰρ ἃ πράττουσιν οἱ δίκαιοι, ἀλλ' ἃ μὴ πράττουσι, ταῦτα λέγεις. *You are speaking not of those things which the just do, but [of those things] which they do not do.*

(*d*) οὐ is used to negate the verb of a **noun clause**, i.e. in indirect statements when expressed by a ὅτι/ὡc clause (8.1/3*b*), indirect questions (10.1/2*b*), and clauses following verbs of fearing (14.1/4*c*(ii)).

(*e*) **Infinitives** are always negated by μή, except in the infinitive construction for indirect statement after verbs of saying and thinking (8.1/3*a*).

(*f*) **Participles** are negated by οὐ except:

  (i) when used with the article to denote a general class (12.1/2*a*(vi)); this also applies to adjectives, e.g. οἱ μὴ ἀγαθοί *the [general class of] people who are not good*, but οἱ οὐκ ἀγαθοί *the [particular] people who are not good*

  (ii) when used conditionally (12.1/2*a*(iv)).

(*g*) οὐ μή with the fut. ind. expresses a strong prohibition (17.1/1).

(*h*) οὐ μή with the aor. subj. expresses a strong denial: οὐ μὴ παύcωμαι φιλοcοφῶν *I shall certainly not stop studying philosophy.*

(*i*) *Or not* as an alternative question in indirect speech is either ἢ οὔ or ἢ μή: ὑμῶν δέομαι cκοπεῖν εἰ δίκαια λέγω ἢ μή (or ἢ οὔ). *I ask you to examine whether I am speaking justly or not.*

24.1/3 Diminutives

Nouns can be modified by the addition of a suffix to indicate something smaller, e.g. *booklet* (< *book*), *islet* (< *isle*). The modified form is called a **diminutive**. Greek has a number of diminutive suffixes but the most common is -ιον, e.g. παιδίον *little child* (παῖc, stem παιδ-). All diminutives in -ιον (including those from proper names) are 2nd declension neuters, even when they denote living beings.

Very often diminutives are used to indicate affection and familiarity without any real connotation of smallness, e.g. πατρ-ίδιον *daddy* (< πατήρ, with the suffix -ίδιον), Cωκρατίδιον *dear little/old Socrates*. Occasionally a diminutive has lost any special meaning and simply replaced the original noun, e.g. θηρίον *wild beast* (< θήρ, which has the same meaning but is used mainly in verse).

Diminutives were a feature of the colloquial language, and consequently are not found in literary genres such as tragedy, which are written in an elevated style. They are, however, very common in comedy, and in the dialogues of Plato, who aimed at reproducing the everyday speech of educated Athenians. An amusing example occurs in Aristophanes' *Clouds* where Strepsiades wakes his adult son by coaxing him with the diminutive of his name:

> πῶς δῆτ' ἂν ἥδιcτ' αὐτὸν ἐπεγείραιμι; πῶς; Φειδιππίδη, Φειδιππίδιον.
> *How could I wake him most gently? How? Pheidippides, dear little Pheidippides.*

24.1/4 Dual number

In addition to the singular and plural, Indo-European (1.3) also had a dual number, which was used for two persons or objects. In Homer it is still frequent, but in Attic Greek of the fifth and fourth centuries BC its use is generally confined to two persons or things closely associated or normally considered to form a pair, e.g. two brothers, sisters, hands, eyes, but even here it is optional. Its endings do not show anything like the same variety as either the singular or plural.

In **verbs** the same stems are used as elsewhere. There is **no** first person dual. In the second person the dual endings are identical for the primary and historic tenses but in the third person endings there is a distinction between primary and historic forms (cf. 4.1/1 note 1 and 8.1/1*f*):

	ACTIVE		MIDDLE/PASSIVE	
	Primary	*Historic*	*Primary*	*Historic*
2	-τον	-τον	-cθον	-cθον
3	-τον	-την	-cθον	-cθην

The link vowel (cf. 8.1/1*d*) is the same in the singular and plural. For λύω in the **indicative** we have:

	ACTIVE	MIDDLE/PASSIVE	
PRESENT	2 λΰ-ετον *you two loosen*	λΰ-εϲθον	
	3 λΰ-ετον *two (people) loosen*	λΰ-εϲθον	
FUTURE	2 λΰϲ-ετον	mid. λΰϲ-εϲθον	pass. λυθήϲ-εϲθον
	3 λΰϲ-ετον	λΰϲ-εϲθον	λυθήϲ-εϲθον
IMPERFECT	2 ἐλΰ-ετον	ἐλΰ-εϲθον	
	3 ἐλῡ-έτην	ἐλῡ-έϲθην	
AORIST	2 ἐλΰϲ-ατον	mid. ἐλΰϲ-αϲθον	pass. ἐλΰθη-τον
	3 ἐλῡϲ-άτην	ἐλῡϲ-άϲθην	ἐλυθή-την
PERFECT	2 λελύκ-ατον	λέλυ-ϲθον	
	3 λελύκ-ατον	λέλυ-ϲθον	
PLUPERFECT	2 ἐλελύκ-ετον	ἐλέλυ-ϲθον	
	3 ἐλελυκ-έτην	ἐλελύ-ϲθην	

The **subjunctive** mood takes the primary endings (cf. 14.1/2), giving for both second and third persons λΰ-ητον (pres. act.) and λΰ-ηϲθον (pres. mid./pass.) etc. (the η represents the lengthening of ε in λΰ-ε-τον, λΰ-ε-ϲθον of the indicative).

The **optative** takes the historic endings (cf. 14.1/3) with the same preceding diphthong as occurs in the singular and plural of the tenses which have an optative (i.e. οι/αι/ει), e.g. pres. act. 2 λΰ-οιτον, 3 λῡ-οίτην; aor. act. 2 λΰϲ-αιτον, 3 λῡϲ-αίτην; aor. pass. 2 λυθ-εῖτον, 3 λυθ-είτην.

The 2nd person dual of the **imperative** is the same as in the indicative. The 3rd person dual of the imperative is rare.

The dual endings for **nouns** and the dual forms of the **article** and **personal pronouns** are:

	NOUNS (Declension)			ARTICLE M.F.N.	PERSONAL PRONOUNS	
	1st	2nd	3rd			
N.V.A.	-ᾱ	-ω	-ε	τώ	νώ *we two*	ϲφώ *you two*
Gen. Dat.	-αιν	-οιν	-οιν	τοῖν	νῷν	ϲφῷν

The article has the same forms for al! genders, and the demonstrative pronouns follow the same pattern (τούτω/τούτοιν from οὗτος; τώδε/τοῖνδε from ὅδε). First and second declension **adjectives** (and αὐτός) take the endings given above for nouns.

Because the dual is not obligatory we often find dual and plural forms used indiscriminately:

δύο ἄνδρες προσελθόντε ᾿Αγιδι διελεγέςθην. *Two men came forward and*
(lit. *having come forward*) *were talking with Agis* (we might have
expected ἄνδρε instead of δύο ἄνδρες).

24.1/5 Verbal adjectives in -τος/-τός and -τέος

(*a*) We have already met many verbal adjectives in -τος/-τός. Most have a
prefix, in many cases the negative ἀ-/ἀν-, e.g. ἔμφυτος (ἐν + φυτος),
ἄβατος (ἀ + βατος), but some have none, e.g. χυτός. They can be either:

  (i) the equivalent of a perfect passive participle, e.g. εὔγνωςτος *well-
      known,* ἔμφυτος *inborn,* χυτός *melted.*
 (ii) the equivalent of a present participle active, e.g. ἀνόητος *stupid* (lit.
      not perceiving)
(iii) an adjective denoting possibility, e.g. ἄβατος *impassable,* βιωτός
      livable.

Some can be either (i) or (iii), e.g. ἀόρᾱτος *unseen/invisible.*

(*b*) The verbal adjective in -τέος differs from the above in being considered
a normal part of a verb, although, in its neuter singular form, it is given a
separate listing in dictionaries. It is formed by replacing θη of the aorist
passive stem with -τέος, e.g. φιλητέος (< φιλέω, aor. pass ἐφιλήθην),
κελευστέος (< κελεύω, aor. pass. ἐκελεύςθην); and has the meaning of a
present passive participle but with the added idea of necessity. The
literal translation of φιλητέος εἰμί is *I am needing-to-be-loved,* i.e. *I must
be loved.* The agent is expressed by the dative (23.1/2g), not by
ὑπό + gen.: ὁ ποταμὸς ἡμῖν ἐςτι διαβατέος *the river is needing-to-be-
crossed-over by us,* i.e. *we must cross over the river;* ἐκείνη coι οὐ φιλητέᾱ
that woman [is] not needing-to-be-loved by you, i.e. *you must not love that
woman.*

The neuter singular (and occasionally the neuter plural) of the verbal
adjective can be used **impersonally**: διαβατέον ἡμῖν ἐςτιν *it is needing-to-
be-crossed-over (there must be a crossing over) by us,* i.e. *we must cross
over.* The verbal adjective of a transitive verb can, when used
impersonally, take an object: τὸν ποταμὸν ἡμῖν ἐςτι διαβατέον *it is
needing-to-be-crossed-over the river (there must be a crossing over the
river) by us,* i.e. *we must cross over the river.* There is no difference in
meaning between ὁ ποταμός ἐςτι διαβατέος and τὸν ποταμόν ἐςτι
διαβατέον.

Sometimes a literal translation of an impersonal verbal adjective is
impossible:

τῷ ἀδικοῦντι δοτέον ἐςτὶ δίκην. *The [person] doing wrong must pay
  the penalty* (the closest translation is *there must-be-a-paying of the
  penalty . . .*)

The neuter plural of the verbal adjective has exactly the same meaning. We may equally well have τὸν ποταμόν ἐςτι διαβατέα or τὸν ποταμόν ἐςτι διαβατέον.

24.1/6 Verbs of precaution and striving

When these verbs, which include ἐπιμελέομαι, εὐλαβέομαι both *take care*, ϲπουδάζω *be eager/busy*, ϲκοπέω *consider, take heed*, are followed by a clause (*take care that . . .*, *be eager that . . .*, etc.), this is expressed by ὅπωϲ with the future indicative. The future indicative is retained even after main verbs in a historic tense. The ὅπωϲ clause is negated by μή:

ὅπωϲ ἀμυνούμεθα, οὐδεὶϲ παραϲκευάζεται οὐδὲ ἐπιμελεῖται. *No-one is making preparations or taking care that we should defend ourselves.*

δεῖ ϲκοπεῖν ὅπωϲ τὰ παρόντ' ἐπανορθωθήϲεται. *We must take heed that the present state of affairs be remedied.*

ἐϲκόπουν ὅπωϲ αὐτὸϲ ἀπολυθήϲομαι τῆϲ ἐγγύηϲ. *I was taking heed that I myself be freed from the pledge.*

Less often ὅπωϲ is followed by the subjunctive or optative, as in purpose clauses (14.1/4*c*(i)):

οὐ φυλάξεϲθε ὅπωϲ μὴ δεϲπότην εὕρητε; *Will you not be on your guard that you do not find a master?*

ἐπεμελεῖτο ὁ Κῦροϲ ὅπωϲ μήποτε οἱ ϲτρατιῶται ἀνίδρωτοι γενόμενοι ἐπὶ τὸ ἄριϲτον εἰϲίοιεν. *Cyrus took care that the soldiers should never come to lunch without working up a sweat* (lit. *being without a sweat*).

Note

Sometimes a main verb in the imperative such as ϲκόπει/ϲκοπεῖτε *see to it* is omitted and we are left with nothing but ὅπωϲ and the future indicative:

ὅπωϲ ἔϲεϲθε ἄνδρεϲ ἄξιοι τῆϲ ἐλευθερίαϲ. *[See to it] that you show yourselves* (lit. *will be*) *men worthy of freedom!*

24.1/7 Verbs of hindering, preventing, forbidding, denying

In English, verbs with these and similar meanings take various constructions (*I prevented him from entering, we forbid you to do this*). In Greek they are always followed by an infinitive which is accompanied by the negative μή; the latter is redundant from an English point of view: εἴργω ὑμᾶϲ μὴ μάχεϲθαι *I hinder you from fighting*; ἀπαγορεύομεν αὐτὸν μὴ οἰκοδομεῖν *we forbid him to build*. When the main verb is itself negated, the infinitive is accompanied by a double redundant negative μὴ οὐ: οὐκ εἴργω ὑμᾶϲ μὴ οὐ μάχεϲθαι *I do not hinder you from fighting*.

However, κωλύω *prevent* is usually followed by a simple infinitive without μή or μὴ οὐ: κωλύω αὐτὸν ἱππεύειν *I prevent him from riding*; οὐ κωλύω αὐτὸν βαδίζειν *I do not prevent him from walking*.

24.2 Greek reading

1 *In addition to translating, explain each use of a negative.*
(*i*) ὁ μηδὲν εἰδὼς οὐδὲν ἐξαμαρτάνει. (*ii*) μηδένα φίλον ποιοῦ πρὶν ἂν
ἐξετάσῃς πῶς κέχρηται τοῖς πρότερον φίλοις. (*iii*) πᾶν ποιοῦσιν ὥστε
μὴ δοῦναι δίκην. (*iv*) οὐδὲν ἐπράχθη διὰ τὸ μὴ τὸν ἄρχοντα
παρεῖναι. (*v*) οὐκ οἶδα πότερον πορευθῶ ἢ μή. (*vi*) δέδοικα μὴ οὐχ
ἱκανοὺς ἔχω οἷς τὸν χρυσὸν δῶ. (*vii*) θάρρει, ὦ Κῦρε, οὐ μή σε κρύψω
πρὸς ὄντινα βούλομαι ἀφικέσθαι. (*viii*) οἱ δ᾽ ἔφασαν ἀποδώσειν τοὺς
νεκροὺς ἐφ᾽ ᾧ μὴ καίειν τὰς κώμας. (*ix*)# τὸ μὴ δίκαιον ἔργον οὐ
λήθει θεούς. (*x*) τί ἐμποδὼν μὴ οὐκ ἀποθανεῖν αὐτούς; (*xi*) φίλος
ἐβούλετο εἶναι τοῖς μέγιστα δυναμένοις ἵνα ἀδικῶν μὴ διδοίη δίκην.
(*xii*)# εἰ μὴ καθέξεις γλῶτταν, ἔσται σοι κακά. (*xiii*)# οὐκ ἂν δύναιο μὴ
καμὼν εὐδαιμονεῖν. (*xiv*)# οὐ μὴ δυσμενὴς ἔσει φίλοις. (*xv*) εἰπὼν ἃ
θέλεις, ἀντάκου᾽ ἃ μὴ θέλεις. (*xvi*) ἢ δεῖ χελώνης κρέα φαγεῖν ἢ μὴ
φαγεῖν. (*xvii*) δύναcαί μοι λέγειν εἰ διδακτὸν ἡ ἀρετὴ ἢ οὔ; (*xviii*)
οὐδείς ἀπαρνήσεται μὴ οὐχὶ ἐπίστασθαι τὰ δίκαια. (*xix*) ἐφοβεῖτο μὴ
οὐ δύναιτο ἐκ τῆς χώρας ἐξελθεῖν. (*xx*) μὴ ἀπέλθητε πρὶν ἂν
ἀκούσητε.

2 θεραπευτέον τοὺς θεούς, τοὺς φίλους εὐεργετητέον, τὴν πόλιν
ὠφελητέον, τὴν Ἑλλάδα πειρατέον εὖ ποιεῖν, τὴν γῆν θεραπευτέον,
τῶν βοσκημάτων ἐπιμελητέον, τὰς πολεμικὰς τέχνας μαθητέον.

3# ὁ φόβος, ὅταν τις αἵματος μέλλῃ πέρι
λέγειν καταστὰς εἰς ἀγῶν᾽ ἐναντίον,
τό τε στόμ᾽ εἰς ἔκπληξιν ἀνθρώπων ἄγει
τὸν νοῦν τ᾽ ἀπείργει μὴ λέγειν ἃ βούλεται.

4 ὑμᾶς εὐλαβεῖσθαι δεῖ ὅπως μηδὲν ὧν ἰδίᾳ φυλάξαισθ᾽ ἄν, τοῦτο δημοσίᾳ
ποιοῦντες φανήσεσθε.

5 οὗτοι πάντες οἱ νόμοι κεῖνται πολὺν ἤδη χρόνον, ὦ ἄνδρες δικασταί, καὶ
οὐδεὶς πώποτ᾽ ἀντεῖπεν μὴ οὐ καλῶς ἔχειν αὐτούς.

6 εὐλαβοῦ μὴ φανῇς κακὸς γεγώς.

7 ἠσπαζόμην οὖν αὐτὼ ἅτε διὰ χρόνου ἑωρακώς· μετὰ δὲ τοῦτο εἶπον
πρὸς τὸν Κλεινίαν· ὦ Κλεινία, τώδε μέντοι τὼ ἄνδρε σοφώ, Εὐθύδημός
τε καὶ Διονυσόδωρος, οὐ τὰ σμικρὰ ἀλλὰ τὰ μεγάλα· τὰ γὰρ περὶ τὸν
πόλεμον ἐπίστασθον.
εἰπὼν οὖν ταῦτα κατεφρονήθην ὑπ᾽ αὐτοῖν· ἐγελασάτην οὖν ἄμφω 5
βλέψαντε εἰς ἀλλήλω, καὶ ὁ Εὐθύδημος εἶπεν· οὗτοι ἔτι ταῦτα, ὦ
Σώκρατες, σπουδάζομεν, ἀλλὰ παρέργοις αὐτοῖς χρώμεθα.
κἀγὼ θαυμάσας εἶπον· καλὸν ἄν που τὸ ἔργον ὑμῶν εἴη, εἰ τηλικαῦτα
πράγματα πάρεργα ὑμῖν τυγχάνει ὄντα, καὶ πρὸς θεῶν εἴπετόν μοι τί
ἐστι τοῦτο τὸ καλόν; 10
ἀρετήν, ἔφη, ὦ Σώκρατες, οἰόμεθα οἵω τ᾽ εἶναι παραδοῦναι κάλλιστ᾽
ἀνθρώπων καὶ τάχιστα.

ὦ Ζεῦ, οἷον, ἦν δ' ἐγώ, λέγετον πρᾶγμα· πόθεν τοῦτο τὸ ἕρμαιον
ηὕρετον; ἐγὼ δὲ περὶ ὑμῶν διενοούμην ἔτι, ὥσπερ νυνδὴ ἔλεγον, ὡς τὸ
πολὺ τοῦτο δεινοῖν ὄντοιν, ἐν ὅπλοις μάχεσθαι, καὶ ταῦτα ἔλεγον περὶ   1.
σφῷν· ὅτε γὰρ τὸ πρότερον ἐπεδημήσατον, τοῦτο μέμνημαι σφὼ
ἐπαγγελλομένω.

8   μετὰ τοῦτον Ξενοφῶν εἶπεν· ἐγὼ δ' οὕτω γιγνώσκω. εἰ μὲν ἀνάγκη
μάχεσθαι, τοῦτο δεῖ παρασκευάσασθαι ὅπως ὡς κράτιστα μαχούμεθα.
εἰ δὲ βουλόμεθα ὡς ῥᾷστα ὑπερβάλλειν, τοῦτό μοι δοκεῖ σκεπτέον εἶναι
ὅπως ὡς ἐλάχιστα μὲν τραύματα λάβωμεν, ὡς ἐλάχιστα δὲ σώματα
ἀποβάλωμεν.

9   σκεπτέον πότερον δίκαιον ἐμὲ ἐνθένδε πειρᾶσθαι ἐξιέναι μὴ ἀφιέντων
Ἀθηναίων ἢ οὐ δίκαιον.

10   Α. εἰπέ μοι, ἔστι σοι ἀγρός; Β. οὐκ ἔμοιγε.

11   καὶ μὴν εἰ ὑφησόμεθα καὶ ἐπὶ βασιλεῖ γενησόμεθα, τί οἰόμεθα πείσεσθαι;
ὃς καὶ τοῦ ὁμομητρίου ἀδελφοῦ καὶ τεθνηκότος ἤδη ἀποτεμὼν τὴν
κεφαλὴν καὶ τὴν χεῖρα ἀνεσταύρωσεν· ἡμᾶς δέ, οἷς κηδεμὼν μὲν οὐδεὶς
πάρεστιν, ἐστρατεύσαμεν δὲ ἐπ' αὐτὸν ὡς δοῦλον ἀντὶ βασιλέως
ποιήσοντες καὶ ἀποκτενοῦντες εἰ δυναίμεθα, τί ἂν οἰόμεθα παθεῖν; ἆρ'   5
οὐκ ἂν ἐπὶ πᾶν ἔλθοι ὡς ἡμᾶς τὰ ἔσχατα αἰκισάμενος πᾶσιν ἀνθρώποις
φόβον παράσχῃ τοῦ στρατεῦσαί ποτε ἐπ' αὐτόν; ἀλλ' ὅπως τοι μὴ ἐπ'
ἐκείνῳ γενησόμεθα πάντα ποιητέον.

Notes

1   (*i*) οὐδέν adverbial acc. (20.1/5).   (*ii*) ποιοῦ 2nd s. pres. imp. mid.;
κέχρηται < χράομαι; πρότερον here an adverb (cf. οἱ νῦν, 5.1/3) but
trans. by an adjective.   (*v*) πορευθῶ (aor. subj. pass. of πορεύομαι)
deliberative subj. (14.1/4*a*(ii)) in indirect speech (cf. δῶ in (*vi*)).   (*vii*)
θάρρει (< θάρρε-ε) pres. imp.; κρύψω is here aor. subj. (24.1/2*h*).   (*viii*)
ἐφ' ᾧ 16.1/1 note 4.   (*x*) ἐμποδών *sc.* ἐστί; because the construction
appropriate after a negated verb of hindering, preventing etc. (μὴ οὐ) is
used here, we know that the question expects the answer *nothing* and so
counts as a virtual negation.   (*xi*) μέγιστα adverb (17.1/2).   (*xii*)
καθέξεις < κατέχω.   (*xiv*) οὐ μή+fut. ind., 17.1/1   (*xv*) ἀντάκου'(ε)
imp.   (*xvi*) κρέᾱ acc. pl. of κρέας (13.1/1*b*(iii)).

2   ἐστί is very often omitted with verbal adjectives and must be supplied
with each example here.

3   A murder trial is being described.   *l*.1 ὁ φόβος is the subject of ἄγει (*l*.3);
take πέρι with αἵματος (see note on 11.2.4 *l*.1).   *l*.2 καταστάς intrans.
aor. pple. of καθίστημι.   *ll*.3f. Take ἀνθρώπων with στόμ'(α) and νοῦν.

4   ὅπως . . . φανήσεσθε (2nd pl. fut. pass. of φαίνω) see 24.1/6; φυλά-
ξαισθ'(ε) ἄν potential optative (19.1/2).

5   κεῖνται is used here as the perf. pass of τίθημι (18.1/2 note 4); ἕξειν fut.
act. inf. of ἔχω.

6   μή = ὅπως μή.

7   Socrates tells of his encounter with two sophists whom he has previously

met. The passage has many dual forms (24.1/4). *l*.1 ἑωρᾱκώc perf. act. pple. of ὁράω.   *l*.2 μέντοι emphatic, not adversative (13.1/3*c*(v)).   *l*.3 τὰ cμῑκρὰ . . . τὰ μεγάλα acc. of respect with cοφώ in *l*.2 (20.1/5).   *l*.7 παρέργοιc here predicative with αὐτοῖc, *them* (αὐτοῖc) *[as] subordinate issues*.   *l*.8 θαυμάcᾱc coincidental use of the aor. pple. (12.1/1), *marvelling*; ἂν . . . εἴη potential opt. (19.1/2), lit. *would be*, but trans. *must be*.   *l*.9 εἴπετόν 2nd dual aor. imp. act.   *ll*.11f. κάλλιcτ᾽(α) ἀνθρώπων καὶ τάχιcτα lit. *most excellently and speedily of men*, i.e. *as excellently and speedily as is humanly possible*.   *l*.13 οἷον exclamatory (21.1/3); ἦν δ᾽ ἐγώ *said I* (18.1.1*a*).   *ll*.14f. ὡc τὸ πολύ (= ὡc ἐπὶ τὸ πολύ) *for the most part*, 22.1/1*a*(vii); τοῦτο (acc. of respect with δεινῶν (20.1/5)) anticipates ἐν . . . μάχεcθαι; δεινοῖν ὄντοιν agrees with ῡ̔μῶν in *l*.14, although the latter is plural, not dual (note that Socrates somewhat illogically goes on to use the dual pronoun cφῷν).

8   οὕτω anticipates the following sentence, lit. *I think* (γιγνώcκω) *thus*; each τοῦτο anticipates the ὅπωc clause which follows it and need not be translated; ὡc + supl. 17.1/4*d*.

9   Supply ἐcτί with both cκεπτέον (see note on 2 above) and δίκαιον; ἀφῑέντων gen. pl. of the pres. act. pple. of ἀφῑημι.

10   ἔμοιγε 24.1/1*b*.

11   *ll*.1f. καὶ μήν *and further*; ὑφηcόμεθα fut. mid. of ὑφῑημι; τί etc. *what do we think we shall suffer* (cf. 8.1/3*a*); ὅc lit. *who* (the antecedent is βαcιλεῖ) but trans. *he* (the relative pronoun is often used to join a sentence with what precedes); καί (before τοῦ and before τεθνηκότοc) *even*, but trans. the second by *and that too* for variety; take ἤδη with τεθνηκότοc.   *ll*.3ff. ἡμᾶc is the subject of παθεῖν in *l*.5; οἷc . . . πάρεcτιν lit. *for whom there is no protector at hand*; before ἐcτρατεύcαμεν we must supply the relative οἵ from the preceding οἷc, and the two adjectival clauses can be translated *who have no protector at hand but* (δέ) *who campaigned against him* (ἐπ᾽ αὐτόν); ὡc + fut. pple. (12.1/2*a*(v)); εἰ δυναίμεθα indefinite construction in historic sequence (14.1/4*c*(iii)), lit. *if ever we could*; ἂν . . . παθεῖν represents ἂν πάθοιμεν in direct speech (potential opt., 19.1/2), and the subject of the infinitive (ἡμᾶc in *l*.3) is, quite irregularly, inserted in the acc. although it is the same as the subject of οἰόμεθα— trans. *what do we think we would suffer*.   *ll*.5ff. ἆρ᾽ οὐκ (10.1/2*a*); ἐπὶ πᾶν lit. *to everything*, i.e. *to any lengths*; ὡc introduces a purpose clause (22.1/ 1*b*(ii)); τὰ ἔcχατα acc. of respect (20.1/5), lit. *in respect of the worst things*, i.e. *in the worst [possible] ways*; take τοῦ cτρατεῦcαι . . . as objective gen. (23.1/1*c*) with φόβον, *fear of campaigning*; the clause ὅπωc . . . γενηcόμεθα is governed by ποιητέον (ἐcτίν)—ὅπωc + fut. is used to express purpose (the normal construction with ὅπωc in this context would be the subjunctive, 14.1/4*c*(i)).

24.3   Extra reading –
The Think Tank

Old Comedy is the term given to the form of comic drama which flourished in Athens during the fifth century BC. Two of its main characteristics, comic situations and unbridled criticism of contemporaries, can be seen in the following passage from Aristophanes' *Clouds*, which was a stinging attack on Socrates and what were popularly supposed to be his intellectual interests. In this scene Strepsiades, a stupid and uneducated Athenian of the older generation, has just gained admittance to Socrates' Φροντιστήριον (*Think Tank*) in order to improve himself.

ΣΤΡΕΨΙΑΔΗΣ—ΜΑΘΗΤΗΣ

ΣΤ.   πρὸς τῶν θεῶν, τί γὰρ τάδ' ἐςτίν; εἰπέ μοι.
ΜΑ.   ἀςτρονομία μὲν αὐτή. ΣΤ. τουτὶ δὲ τί;
ΜΑ.   γεωμετρία. ΣΤ. τοῦτ' οὖν τί ἐςτι χρήςιμον;
ΜΑ.   γῆν ἀναμετρεῖςθαι. ΣΤ. πότερα τὴν κληρουχικήν;
ΜΑ.   οὔκ, ἀλλὰ τὴν ςύμπαςαν. ΣΤ. ἀςτεῖον λέγεις.   5
      τὸ γὰρ ςόφιςμα δημοτικὸν καὶ χρήςιμον.
ΜΑ.   αὕτη δέ ςοι γῆς περίοδος πάςης. ὁρᾶς;
      αἵδε μὲν 'Αθῆναι. ΣΤ. τί ςὺ λέγεις; οὐ πείθομαι,
      ἐπεὶ δικαςτὰς οὐχ ὁρῶ καθημένους.
ΜΑ.   ὡς τοῦτ' ἀληθῶς 'Αττικὸν τὸ χωρίον.   10
ΣΤ.   φέρε τίς γὰρ οὗτος οὑπὶ τῆς κρεμάθρας ἀνήρ;
ΜΑ.   αὐτός. ΣΤ. τίς αὐτός; ΜΑ. Σωκράτης. ΣΤ. ὦ Σωκράτης.
      ἴθ' οὗτος, ἀναβόηςον αὐτόν μοι μέγα.
ΜΑ.   αὐτὸς μὲν οὖν ςὺ κάλεςον· οὐ γάρ μοι ςχολή.
ΣΤ.   ὦ Σώκρατες,
      ὦ Σωκρατίδιον.

ΣΩΚΡΑΤΗΣ

                τί με καλεῖς, ὦ 'φήμερε;   15
ΣΤ.   πρῶτον μὲν ὅτι δρᾷς, ἀντιβολῶ, κάτειπέ μοι.
ΣΩ.   ἀεροβατῶ καὶ περιφρονῶ τὸν ἥλιον.
ΣΤ.   ἔπειτ' ἀπὸ ταρροῦ τοὺς θεοὺς ὑπερφρονεῖς,
      ἀλλ' οὐκ ἀπὸ τῆς γῆς, εἴπερ; ΣΩ. οὐ γὰρ ἄν ποτε
      ἐξηῦρον ὀρθῶς τὰ μετέωρα πράγματα,   20
      εἰ μὴ κρεμάςας τὸ νόημα καὶ τὴν φροντίδα.

Notes

The Φροντιστήριον of Aristophanes' play (he seems to have coined the word himself) was a school where various sciences were both investigated and taught. In the opening lines a pupil shows Strepsiades pieces of equipment, which, for humorous effect, are given the names of the sciences (astronomy and geometry) for which they are used. *l*.1 γάρ explains why Strepsiades has used the exclamation πρὸϲ τῶν θεῶν (*in the name of the gods*) but should not be translated. *l*.2 αὑτηί, τουτί emphatic forms of αὕτη, τοῦτο with the suffix ί, before which a final short vowel is dropped. *l*.3 οὖν *well, so*; τί lit. *in what respect*. *l*.4 When the pupil replies that the purpose of geometry is to measure land, Strepsiades, who is unable to rise above self-interested parochialism, asks if the land involved is for κλῆροι, which were allotments of foreign land confiscated by the state and given to poorer Athenian citizens. The term for this allocation was κληρουχίᾱ *cleruchy*. πότερα introduces alternative questions (10.1/2*a*) but the second, ἢ οὔ *or not*, is omitted; κληρουχικήν sc. γῆν *land for cleruchies*. *ll*.5f. Strepsiades finds the idea of measuring the whole earth attractive because he supposes that this would mean distributing it to needy Athenians. *l*.7 coι ethic dat. (23.1/2f). *l*.9 Large juries were a prominent feature of the Athenian legal system, which was often the butt of Aristophanes' humour. *l*.10 A main clause meaning *I assure you* must be supplied. *l*.11 At this point Socrates appears overhead suspended from the end of a crane (see note on *l*.18); φέρε 17.1/1 note 7; οὑπί = ὁ ἐπί. *l*.12 αὐτόc was used to mean *the master* (cf. Irish use of *himself*); ὦ Cωκράτηϲ (nom. **not** voc.) an exclamation *Ah, [it's] Socrates*. *l*.13 ἴθ'(ι) 2nd s. pres. imp. of ἔρχομαι (18.1/3); οὗτοc *you there!* (see note on 20.2.12 *l*.4). *l*.15 Cωκρατίδιον 24.1/3; ὦ 'φήμερε, i.e. ὦ ἐφ- initial elision of this type (prodelision) is poetical. *l*.16 ὅτι indirect form of τί, 10.1/2*b* note 1. *ll*.17f. Socrates, who is comically represented as some sort of divine being, says he is thinking about (περιφρονῶ) the sun but Strepsiades perversely takes περιφρονῶ in its other meaning *despise* and replies with the unequivocal ὑπερφρονεῖc; ἀπὸ ταρροῦ *from your mat* although Strepsiades speaks of a basket in *l*.11—Socrates is apparently sitting on a mat which is suspended from each corner to the gib of the crane and so resembles a basket. *l*.19 ἀλλ'(ά) trans. *and* as there is no strong contrast; εἴπερ *if indeed [that's what you're really doing]* Strepsiades expresses himself cautiously because he cannot understand what Socrates is up to; οὐ γὰρ ἄν . . . lit. *for I would not . . .*, i.e. *yes, for I would not . . .* (24.1/1). *l*.21 εἰ μὴ κρεμάcᾱc *except by* (lit. *if not*) *suspending* (εἰ is here followed by a phrase, not a clause).

Unit 25

25.1 Grammar

25.1/1 Homeric Greek

The language of the *Iliad* and *Odyssey* is an older version of Ionic (1.3) with elements from other dialects. It differs to some extent from Attic in **phonology** (the individual sounds of words), **morphology** (the different forms which some words can take), and **syntax** (grammatical constructions and uses). Listed below are the main differences which occur in the passages in 25.2, together with examples from them.

A good introduction to Homer is G.S.Kirk *Homer and the Epic* (Cambridge U.P.).

25.1/2 Differences in phonology and morphology

(*a*) *Vowels and diphthongs*

    (i) Contraction is not always observed, e.g. αἰδέομαι (1 *l*.3 in 25.2).

    (ii) ᾱ becomes η after ε, ι and ρ, e.g. κρατερή (1 *l*.19).

    (iii) Diphthongs are sometimes broken up into two vowels, e.g. ἐϋμμελίω (1 *l*.10, = εὐ-); χήτεϊ (1 *l*.24, = χήτει).

    (iv) Homeric Greek sometimes has cc where the Attic has c, e.g. ὄccον (1 *l*.15).

(*b*) *Case endings*

    (i) -εω, -ω (= Attic -ου) for the gen. s. of first declension masculines, e.g. ἐϋμμελίω (1 *l*.10).

    (ii) -οιο (= Attic -ου) for the gen. s. of the second declension, e.g. πολέμοιο (1 *l*.4).

    (iii) -άων (= Attic -ῶν) for the gen. pl. of the first declension, e.g. ῥοάων (2 *l*.8).

    (iv) -εccι (= Attic -cι) for the dat. pl. of some third declension nouns, e.g. Τρώεccι 1 *l*.6).

    (v) -ῃcι (= Attic -αιc) for the dat. pl. of the first declension, e.g. κονίῃcι (1 *l*.14).

    (vi) πολύc has an irregular nom. pl. m. πολέεc (1 *l*.13).

    (vii) The gen. s. of cύ is cεῦ (1 *l*.15).

(c) **Verbal endings**

    (i) -ῃcι(ν) (=Attic -ῃ) for the 3rd s. subj. act., e.g. εἴπῃcιν (1 *l*.20).

    (ii) -ατο (=Attic -ντο) for the 3rd pl. mid./pass. of certain tenses (cf. 16.1/3 note), e.g. ἥατο (2 *l*.2).

    (iii) -εν (=Attic -ηcαν) for the 3rd pl. of the aor. ind. pass. and root aorists in -ην, e.g. ἔφανεν (2 *l*.5).

    (iv) -έμεν (=Attic -ειν) for the pres. (and strong aor.) inf. act., e.g. μενέμεν (4 *l*.16).

    (v) The pres. inf. of εἰμί is ἔμμεναι (1 *l*.5), not εἶναι.

(d) **Verbal stems**

    (i) The augment is frequently omitted, e.g. μάθον (1 *l*.5, =ἔμαθον).

    (ii) The aor. ind. stem of εἶπον (<λέγω) is given a syllabic augment, προcέειπε (1 *l*.1, =προcεῖπε).

    (iii) The pres. pple. of εἰμί is ἐών, ἐοῦcα, ἐόν (1 *l*.17).

(e) Words with a different form, e.g. αἰ (1 *l*.4, =εἰ *if*); ἦμαρ (1 *l*.9, =ἡμέρᾱ).

25.1/3   Differences in syntax

(a) What became the definite article in Attic is a third person pronoun in Homer, e.g. τήν (1 *l*.1) *her* (=αὐτήν). A relic of this use survives in Attic in the idiom οἱ μὲν ... οἱ δέ (5.1/3).

(b) The future tense exists in Homer (e.g. ἔccεται 1 *l*.9), but the future can also be expressed by the subjunctive with or without ἄν or κε (an equivalent of ἄν which Homer often uses), e.g. κέν ... ἄγηται (1 *ll*.15f.) *will lead*; ἄν ὀλώλῃ (1 *l*.9) *will be destroyed* (the perfect expresses a future state, lit. *will be in a state of having perished*); εἴπῃcιν (1 *l*.20) *will say*. Further, the optative with ἄν (or κε) does not always have a strong future potential sense as in Attic, and is sometimes to be translated by a simple future, e.g. κεν ... ὑφαίνοιc *you will weave* (1 *l*.17).

25.2   Readings from Homer

The Attic equivalent of certain Homeric words and endings is given in the right-hand margin. The Homeric forms so explained (e.g. ἱρή, 1 *l*.9) are not listed separately in the vocabulary.

    The Homeric poems are written in hexameters (**Appendix 10**).

1   **Hector talks with his wife Andromache**

    τὴν δ' αὖτε προcέειπε μέγας κορυθαίολος Ἕκτωρ·   -εῖπε
    ἦ καὶ ἐμοὶ τάδε πάντα μέλει, γύναι· ἀλλὰ μάλ' αἰνῶc
    αἰδέομαι Τρῶας καὶ Τρῳάδας ἑλκεcιπέπλους,

αἴ κε κακὸς ὣς νόσφιν ἀλυσκάζω πολέμοιο·   -ου
οὐδέ με θυμὸς ἄνωγεν, ἐπεὶ μάθον ἔμμεναι ἐσθλὸς 5 ἔμαθον, εἶναι
αἰεὶ καὶ πρώτοισι μετὰ Τρώεσσι μάχεσθαι,   Τρωσί
ἀρνύμενος πατρός τε μέγα κλέος ἠδ᾽ ἐμὸν αὐτοῦ.
εὖ γὰρ ἐγὼ τόδε οἶδα κατὰ φρένα καὶ κατὰ θυμόν·
ἔσσεται ἦμαρ ὅτ᾽ ἄν ποτ᾽ ὀλώλῃ Ἴλιος ἱρὴ   ἔσται, ἱερή (=-ά)
καὶ Πρίαμος καὶ λαὸς ἐϋμμελίω Πριάμοιο. 10 -ίου, -ου
ἀλλ᾽ οὔ μοι Τρώων τόσσον μέλει ἄλγος ὀπίσσω,   τόσον, ὀπίσω
οὔτ᾽ αὐτῆς Ἑκάβης οὔτε Πριάμοιο ἄνακτος   -ου
οὔτε κασιγνήτων, οἵ κεν πολέες τε καὶ ἐσθλοὶ   πολλοί
ἐν κονίῃσι πέσοιεν ὑπ᾽ ἀνδράσι δυσμενέεσσιν,   -ίαις, δυσμενέσιν
ὅσσον σεῦ, ὅτε κέν τις Ἀχαιῶν χαλκοχιτώνων 15 ὅσον, σοῦ
δακρυόεσσαν ἄγηται, ἐλεύθερον ἦμαρ ἀπούρας·
καί κεν ἐν Ἄργει ἐοῦσα πρὸς ἄλλης ἱστὸν ὑφαίνοις,   οὖσα
καί κεν ὕδωρ φορέοις Μεσσηΐδος ἢ Ὑπερείης   φοροίης (=φέροις)
πόλλ᾽ ἀεκαζομένη, κρατερὴ δ᾽ ἐπικείσετ᾽ ἀνάγκη.
καί ποτέ τις εἴπῃσιν ἰδὼν κατὰ δάκρυ χέουσαν· 20 εἴπῃ
Ἕκτορος ἥδε γυνή, ὃς ἀριστεύεσκε μάχεσθαι
Τρώων ἱπποδάμων, ὅτε Ἴλιον ἀμφιμάχοντο.   ἀμφεμάχοντο
ὥς ποτέ τις ἐρέει· σοὶ δ᾽ αὖ νέον ἔσσεται ἄλγος   ἐρεῖ, ἔσται
χήτεϊ τοιοῦδ᾽ ἀνδρὸς ἀμύνειν δούλιον ἦμαρ.
ἀλλά με τεθνηῶτα χυτὴ κατὰ γαῖα καλύπτοι, 25 τεθνεῶτα
πρίν γέ τι σῆς τε βοῆς σοῦ θ᾽ ἑλκηθμοῖο πυθέσθαι.   -ου

2 The Trojans camp on the plain outside Troy

οἱ δὲ μέγα φρονέοντες ἐπὶ πτολέμοιο γεφύρας   -οῦντες, πολέμου
ἥατο παννύχιοι, πυρὰ δέ σφισι καίετο πολλά.   ἦντο, ἐκαίετο
ὡς δ᾽ ὅτ᾽ ἐν οὐρανῷ ἄστρα φαεινὴν ἀμφὶ σελήνην
φαίνετ᾽ ἀριπρεπέα, ὅτε τ᾽ ἔπλετο νήνεμος αἰθήρ·   -ῆ
ἔκ τ᾽ ἔφανεν πᾶσαι σκοπιαὶ καὶ πρώονες ἄκροι 5 ἐφάνησαν
καὶ νάπαι· οὐρανόθεν δ᾽ ἄρ᾽ ὑπερράγη ἄσπετος αἰθήρ,
πάντα δὲ εἴδεται ἄστρα, γέγηθε δέ τε φρένα ποιμήν·
τόσσα μεσηγὺ νεῶν ἠδὲ Ξάνθοιο ῥοάων   τόσα, -ου, ῥοῶν
Τρώων καιόντων πυρὰ φαίνετο Ἰλιόθι πρό.   ἐφαίνετο, Ἰλίου
χίλι᾽ ἄρ᾽ ἐν πεδίῳ πυρὰ καίετο, πὰρ δὲ ἑκάστῳ 10 ἐκαίετο, παρά
ἥατο πεντήκοντα σέλᾳ πυρὸς αἰθομένοιο.   ἦντο, -ου
ἵπποι δὲ κρῖ λευκὸν ἐρεπτόμενοι καὶ ὀλύρας
ἑσταότες παρ᾽ ὄχεσφιν ἐΰθρονον Ἠῶ μίμνον.   ἑστῶτες, ὄχεσιν,
                                               ἔμιμνον

3 The beginning of the *Odyssey*

ἄνδρα μοι ἔννεπε, Μοῦσα, πολύτροπον, ὃς μάλα πολλὰ
πλάγχθη, ἐπεὶ Τροίης ἱερὸν πτολίεθρον ἔπερσε·   ἐπλάγχθη, -ᾱς
πολλῶν δ᾽ ἀνθρώπων ἴδεν ἄστεα καὶ νόον ἔγνω,   εἶδεν, ἄστη, νοῦν
πολλὰ δ᾽ ὅ γ᾽ ἐν πόντῳ πάθεν ἄλγεα ὃν κατὰ θυμόν,   ἔπαθεν, ἄλγη
ἀρνύμενος ἥν τε ψυχὴν καὶ νόστον ἑταίρων. 5
ἀλλ᾽ οὐδ᾽ ὣς ἑτάρους ἐρρύσατο, ἱέμενός περ·   καίπερ

αὐτῶν γὰρ σφετέρηισιν ἀτασθαλίηισιν ὄλοντο,   -αις, -αις, ὤλοντο
νήπιοι, οἳ κατὰ βοῦς Ὑπερίονος Ἠελίοιο   Ἡλίου
ἤσθιον· αὐτὰρ ὁ τοῖσιν ἀφείλετο νόστιμον ἦμαρ.

4 The Lotus-eaters

ἔνθεν δ' ἐννῆμαρ φερόμην ὀλοοῖς ἀνέμοισι   ἐφερόμην
πόντον ἐπ' ἰχθυόεντα· ἀτὰρ δεκάτηι ἐπέβημεν
γαίης Λωτοφάγων, οἵ τ' ἄνθινον εἶδαρ ἔδουσιν.   γῆς
ἔνθα δ' ἐπ' ἠπείρου βῆμεν καὶ ἀφυσσάμεθ' ὕδωρ,   ἔβημεν, ἠφυσάμεθα
αἶψα δὲ δεῖπνον ἕλοντο θοῆς παρὰ νηυσὶν ἑταῖροι.   5 εἵλοντο, -αις, ναυσίν
αὐτὰρ ἐπεὶ σίτοιό τ' ἐπασσάμεθ' ἠδὲ ποτῆτος,   -ου, ἐπασάμεθα
δὴ τότ' ἐγὼν ἑτάρους προΐειν πεύθεσθαι ἰόντας
οἵτινες ἀνέρες εἶεν ἐπὶ χθονὶ σῖτον ἔδοντες,   ἄνδρες
ἄνδρε δύω κρίνας, τρίτατον κήρυχ' ἅμ' ὀπάσσας.   ὀπάσας
οἱ δ' αἶψ' οἰχόμενοι μίγεν ἀνδράσι Λωτοφάγοισιν·   10 ἐμίγησαν
οὐδ' ἄρα Λωτοφάγοι μήδονθ' ἑτάροισιν ὄλεθρον   ἐμήδοντο
ἡμετέροις, ἀλλά σφι δόσαν λωτοῖο πάσασθαι.   ἔδοσαν, -οῦ
τῶν δ' ὅστις λωτοῖο φάγοι μελιηδέα καρπόν,   -οῦ, μελιηδῆ
οὐκέτ' ἀπαγγεῖλαι πάλιν ἤθελεν οὐδὲ νέεσθαι,   νεῖσθαι
ἀλλ' αὐτοῦ βούλοντο μετ' ἀνδράσι Λωτοφάγοισι   15 ἐβούλοντο
λωτὸν ἐρεπτόμενοι μενέμεν νόστου τε λαθέσθαι.   μένειν
τοὺς μὲν ἐγὼν ἐπὶ νῆας ἄγον κλαίοντας ἀνάγκηι,   ἦγον
νηυσὶ δ' ἐνὶ γλαφυρῆισιν ὑπὸ ζυγὰ δῆσα ἐρύσσας.   ναυσί, -αῖς,
    ἔδησα, ἐρύσας

αὐτὰρ τοὺς ἄλλους κελόμην ἐρίηρας ἑταίρους   ἐκελόμην
σπερχομένους νηῶν ἐπιβαινέμεν ὠκειάων,   20 νεῶν, -βαίνειν, -ῶν
μή πώς τις λωτοῖο φαγὼν νόστοιο λάθηται.   -οῦ, -ου
οἱ δ' αἶψ' εἴσβαινον καὶ ἐπὶ κληῖσι καθῖζον,   εἰσέβαινον
ἑξῆς δ' ἑζόμενοι πολιὴν ἅλα τύπτον ἐρετμοῖς.   πολιὰν, ἔτυπτον

Notes

1

l.1 τήν = αὐτήν (25.1/3a). *l*.2 ἦ *indeed*; τάδε is the subject of μέλει. *l*.4 αἵ κε = ἐάν (ἀλυσκάζω is subj.); κακὸς ὣς *like a coward* (ὡς is accented when it follows the word to which it belongs); take νόσφιν with πολέμοιο. *l*.5 με ... ἄνωγεν *orders me [to do this]*. *l*.7 The genitives are to be translated *for*; ἐμὸν αὐτοῦ = ἐμοῦ αὐτοῦ, lit. *of me myself*. *l*.9 ὅτ'(ε) *when*; translate ἄν ... ὀλώλη (strong perf. subj. of ὄλλῡμι) as a future (25.1/3b). *l*.11 τόσσον (= normal Attic τοσοῦτο) agrees with ἄλγος (which is the subject of μέλει) and is balanced by ὅσσον in *l*.15 (21.1/3e). *l*.12 Ἑκάβης, Πριάμοιο (together with κασιγνήτων (*l*.13) and σεῦ (*l*.15)) are objective genitives (23.1/1c) with ἄλγος (*l*.11), *grief for* ... *ll*.13f. κεν ... πέσοιεν fut. potential (19.1/2) but trans. *may fall*; ὑπ'(ό) + dat. (= gen. in Attic) *by, at the hands of*. *l*.15f. κέν ... ἄγηται lit. *will lead for himself* (25.1/3b); ἐλεύθερον ἦμαρ lit. *free day* a regular Homeric expression for *freedom*, trans. *day of liberty* (similar expressions occur in *l*.24 below and in 3 *l*.9). *ll*.17f. The two examples of κε + opt. are potential (Hector is stating something that may possibly happen), but are better translated *will weave . . . and carry* (25.1/3*b*); πρός *at the command of*; Μεccηΐδος ἢ Ὑπερείης gen. of separation (20.1/4) *from M. or H. l.*19 πόλλ' (i.e. πολλά) adverbial acc. (20.1/5) *much*; ἐπικείcετ'(αι). *l.*20 εἴπῃcι (subj., 25.1/2*c*(i)) *will say* (25.1/3*b*); κατὰ δάκρυ χέουcαν = καταχέουcαν δάκρυ (tmesis, 12.3.9 *l.*6 note). *l.*21f. Take Τρώων ἱπποδάμων with ἀριcτεύεcκε (=ἠρίcτευε) *was best of the* etc. *l.*23 ὧc (= οὕτωc) *thus*. *l.*24 χήτεϊ (= χήτει) + gen. *because of the lack* (dat. of cause 23.1/2*i*); δούλιον ἦμαρ cf. ἐλεύθερον ἦμαρ (*l.*16). *l.*25 κατὰ . . . καλύπτοι tmesis as in *l.*20—the opt. expresses a wish for the future (21.1/1).

2

*l.*1 *The embankments of war* apparently means the places where battles were normally fought. *l.*2 παννύχιοι is an adj. (*staying all night*) but trans. *all night long*; cφιcι (= αὐτοῖc) is not here reflexive. *l.*3 ὧc . . . ὅτ'(ε) *as when* introduces a simile. *ll.*4f. φαίνετ'(αι); aorists such as ἔπλετο and ἔφανεν are often interspersed among presents in Homeric similes and should be translated by the present; ἔκ . . . ἔφανεν tmesis (see on 1 *l.*20 above). *l.*6 ὑπερράγη root aor. of ὑπορρήγνῡμι. *l.*7 τε is often used to mark similes and has no connective force; φρένα acc. of respect (20.1/5). *l.*8 τόccα agrees with πυρά (*l.*9) and brings out the point of the simile. *l.*9 Τρώων καιόντων gen. abs. (12.1/2*b*); Ἰλιόθι πρό = πρὸ Ἰλίου (the suffix -θι, which denotes *place where*, is used as the equivalent of the genitive ending). *l.*11 cέλᾳ = cέλαι dat. s. of cέλαc (cf. 13.1/1*b*(iii)). *l.*14 The ending of ὄχεcφιν (< ὄχοc) is peculiar to Homer and is generally the equivalent of the dat. pl., as here.

3

*l.*1 πολλά *much* (20.1/5). *l.*2 πλάγχθη 3rd s. aor. ind. (without augment) of πλάζομαι. *l.*4 ὅ γ'(ε) *he* (25.1/3*a*; γε is often added to ὁ in this use and is not to be translated); ὅν **not** the relative but a 3rd person reflexive possessive adjective, ὅc, ἥ, ὅν (*his, her, its*), which did not survive in Attic—take with θῡμόν, lit. *his own heart* but trans. simply by *his heart* (but ἥν . . . ψῡχήν (*l.*5) *his own life* because of the contrast with νόcτον ἑταίρων). *l.*5 ἀρνύμενοc *trying to win*. *l.*6 ὧc *so, thus* (cf. 1 *l.*23 above); ἱέμενόc (< ἵημι) περ lit. *although striving*. *l.*7 αὐτῶν . . . cφετέρῃcιν *their own* (αὐτῶν lit. *of them* is added for particular emphasis); ἀταcθαλίῃcιν plural for singular. *ll.*8f. νήπιοι *fools* in apposition to the subject of ὄλοντο (*l.*7); κατὰ . . . ἤcθιον tmesis; ὁ *he*, i.e. Helios; τοῖcιν (= αὐτοῖc) *from them*, dat. of disadvantage (23.1/2*d*).

4

*l.*2 δεκάτῃ sc. ἡμέρᾳ. *l.*3 οἵ τ'(ε) *who*, **not** *and who*—in Homer τε is added to the relative when the antecedent is a class (here the Lotus-eaters). *l.*5 ἕλοντο lit. *took for themselves* (the mid. of αἱρέω does not here have the meaning *choose*). *l.*6 ἐπαccάμεθ'(α) < πατέομαι. *l.*7 δή here not postpositive as in Attic; προΐειν 1st s. impf. ind. act. of προΐημι; ἰόντας (< εἶμι) here **fut.** pple. (18.1/3) to express purpose (12.1/2*a*(v)). *l.*8 οἵτινεc indirect interrogative

(10.1/2*b* note 1); εἶεν opt. in historic sequence (14.1/4*d*).   *l.*9 ἄνδρε acc. dual, 24.1/4; τρίτατον κήρυχ᾽ ἅμ᾽ (= κήρυκα ἅμα) lit. *a third together* (i.e. *with them*) *[as] herald.*   *l.*12 cφι = αὐτοῖc; λωτοῖο partitive gen. (23.1/1*d*) with δόcαν, lit. *gave of lotus*, i.e. *gave some lotus* (cf. λωτοῖο φαγών *eating some lotus l.*21 below).   *l.*13 τῶν = αὐτῶν; ὅcτιc . . . φάγοι indefinite clause (14.1/4*c*(iii), *whoever ate.*   *l.*15 αὐτοῦ (adv.) *there.*   *l.*17 ἄγον . . . ἀνάγκῃ *I brought by force* (the impf. here and in the following lines is used for vividness and should be translated by a simple past).   *l.*21 μή πώc τιc . . . *lest somehow* (πωc) *anyone* . . .

Revision Exercises

Units 2–4 1 Give the following: (i) gen. pl. of ἀκτή (ii) acc. pl. of δῶρον (iii) dat. s. of νεανίας (iv) dat. pl. of λόγος (v) voc. s. of ποιητής (vi) gen. s. of Κρονίδης (vii) gen. s. of τράπεζα (viii) acc. s. of τέκνον (ix) acc. pl. of ὕδρα (x) dat. pl. of βασίλεια. 2 Decline in the s. and pl.: δοῦλος, δεσπότης, γλῶττα, ζῷον, βοή. 3 Conjugate the following: (i) pres. ind. act. of πίπτω (ii) fut. ind. act. of κελεύω (iii) impf. ind. act. of φροντίζω (iv) aor. ind. act. of παύω. 4 Give the pres., fut., and aor. inf. act. of στρατεύω and πέμπω.

Units 5–7 1 Decline the following in the s. and pl. (where necessary consult the vocabulary to discover the stem): χρῆμα, μήτηρ, κόραξ, γέρων, ψεῦδος, ὄρνις, παῖς, κρατήρ, Ἕλλην. 2 Conjugate the following: (i) aor. ind. act. of φυλάττω, ἄγω, ποιέω, γράφω, νομίζω (ii) impf. ind. act. of φιλέω, δουλόω, τιμάω (iii) fut. ind. act. of ἐλπίζω, κόπτω, ἄγω (iv) pres. ind. act. of ὁράω, ὀρθόω, καλέω. 3 Give the following forms: (i) 2nd pl. aor. ind. act. of συλλαμβάνω (ii) 1st s. aor. ind. act. of περιφέρω (iii) 1st s. impf. ind. act. of συστρατεύω (iv) 3rd pl. aor. ind. act. of ἐξαιρέω (v) 3rd s. impf. ind. act. of ἐγγράφω.

Units 8–10 1 Conjugate the following: (i) pres. ind. mid. of παύω (ii) impf. ind. pass. of κομίζω (iii) aor. ind. mid. of διδάσκω (iv) fut. ind. mid. of λούω (v) pres. ind. pass. of δουλόω (vi) impf. ind. mid. of πολεμέω. 2 Decline in the s. and pl.: (i) οὗτος ὁ χαρίεις μῦς (ii) ὅδε ὁ ἀμαθής (iii) ἐκεῖνος ὁ ὀξύς (iv) ὁ ὄφις αὐτός. 3 Parse and distinguish between: (i) αὐτή, αὑτή, αὕτη, ταύτῃ (ii) ταῦτα, ταὐτά (iii) ταὐτοῦ, τούτου, αὐτοῦ (iv) αὐτῷ, τούτῳ, ταὐτῷ. 4 Translate and distinguish between: (i) ἥδε/ἐκείνη ἡ κόρη (ii) αὕτη/αὐτὴ ἡ γυνή (iii) οὗτος/ὅδε ὁ ἀνήρ (iv) οὗτος ὁ παῖς, αὐτὸς παῖς.

Units 11–13 1 Conjugate the following: (i) aor. ind. act. of γιγνώσκω (ii) aor. ind. mid. of ἀμύνω (iii) fut. ind. act. of ἀγγέλλω (iv) aor. ind. act. of ἀποδιδράσκω (v) fut. ind. pass. of μιαίνω (vi) aor. ind. pass. of δουλόω (vii) fut. ind. act. of ἀπαίρω (viii) aor. ind. pass. of τάττω. 2 Give the nom. s. m. and f. forms of the participle of the following: (i) fut. act. of βουλεύω (ii) aor. mid. of διδάσκω (iii) pres. pass. of ἀποφαίνω (iv) fut. act. of βάλλω (v) aor. pass. of φιλέω (vi) aor. act. of σημαίνω (vii) pres. mid. of οἰκοδομέω (viii) aor. act. of τυγχάνω (ix) fut. mid. of ἀλγύνω (x) aor. act. of γιγνώσκω. 3 Decline in the s. and pl.: ἥρως, λαγώς, υἱός (give all possible forms).

Units 14–16 1 Conjugate the following: (i) aor. opt. act. of κρίνω (ii) perf. ind. act. of γράφω (iii) pres. subj. of πορεύομαι (with intransitive verbs it is unnecessary to give the voice) (iv) plpf. ind. act. of δουλόω (v) aor. subj. of βαίνω (vi) plpf. ind. mid./pass. of ἀλλάττω (vii) pres. subj. act. of ὀρθόω (viii) perf. ind. mid./pass. of κλέπτω (ix) pres. opt. act. of ὁράω (x) aor. opt. of φεύγω (xi) perf. ind. mid./pass of κρούω (xii) pres. subj. mid./pass of φιλέω. 2 Parse the following: (i) βεβληκότος (ii) μεμαθηκέναι (iii) πεπεικυίας (iv) πεφοβῆσθαι (v) λελυμένης (vi) γραφεῖς (vii) κεκρύφθαι (viii) ἐγνωκότας (ix) εἰληφέναι (x) πεπομφός. 3 Give the mid. forms corresponding to the following act. ones: ἁρπάσητε, βάλλοι, ἅψωσι, πράξειε, δηλοῖ (subj.), βεβουλεύκαμεν, λάβοιμεν, ἐπεποιήκη, τιμῴη, εὕρηκε.

Units 17–19 1 Parse the following: (i) δοίη (ii) ἑστῶτος (iii) ἱέναι (iv) διδόναι (v) ἔστησαν (vi) ἰοῦσι (vii) στῆτε (viii) ἐτίθεσαν (ix) ἵω (x) θέντι (xi) ἵοιεν (xii) ἔστασαν (xiii) θές (xiv) στῆναι (xv) θεῖμεν (xvi) ἴθι (xvii) δοῦσι (xviii) ἷασι. 2 Conjugate the following: (i) aor. subj. act. of δίδωμι (ii) pres. opt. act. of τίθημι (iii) impf. mid. of ἵστημι (iv) perf. ind. of ἵϲτημι (v) impf. act. of δίδωμι (vi) perf. opt. of ἵϲτημι (vii) aor. imp. act. of δίδωμι (viii) pres. ind. pass. of τίθημι. 3 Translate into English and give the time reference of each clause: (i) εἰ τοῦτο ἐποιήϲατε, οὐδὲν ἂν ἐπάθετε. (ii) εἰ τοῦτο ἐποιεῖτε, οὐδὲν ἂν ἐπάϲχετε. (iii) ἐὰν τοῦτο ποιήϲητε, οὐδὲν πείϲεϲθε. (iv) εἰ τοῦτο ποιήϲαιτε, οὐδὲν ἂν πάθοιτε. (v) εἰ τοῦτο ἐποιήϲατε, οὐδὲν ἐπάθετε. (vi) εἰ τοῦτο ποιεῖτε, οὐδὲν πάϲχετε. (vii) εἰ τοῦτο ἐποιεῖτε, οὐδὲν ἐπάϲχετε. (viii) εἰ τοῦτο ἐποιήϲατε, οὐδὲν ἂν ἐπάϲχετε. 4 Give the compar. and supl. (m. s. only) of: ἀρχαῖος, ἀϲθενήϲ, ἐχθρόϲ, κακόϲ, κενόϲ, ῥᾴδιοϲ, ϲώφρων, ταχύϲ. 5 Parse the following: πλέονι, πλειόνων, πλείουϲ, πλείω, πλεόνων.

Units 20–22 1 Conjugate the following: (i) pres. ind. mid. of ἐφίημι (ii) aor. ind. act. of ἀφίημι (iii) pres. ind. act. of ἀνοίγνυμι (iv) impf. pass. of μεθίημι (v) aor. opt. act. of παρίημι (vi) impf. mid. of ἀπόλλυμι (vii) aor. imp. act. of ἀφίημι (viii) pres. subj. act. of παρίημι. 2 Parse and distinguish between the following: (i) ὤλεϲε, ὤλετο (ii) ἀπολώλαμεν, ἀπολωλέκαμεν (iii) ἀπωλώλει, ἀπωλωλέκει (iv) ὄλοιο, ὀλέϲειαϲ (v) ἵᾱϲι, ἵωϲι, ἱεῖϲι (vi) δεικνῦϲι, δεικνύαϲι (vii) ἵεμεν, ἵμεν (viii) ἱῶ, ἵω (ix) ὦ, ὤ (x) δεικνύναι, δείκνυται.

Suggestions for further study

Editions of Greek texts with notes and a vocabulary

Euripides, *Hecuba*, ed. M. Tierney.

Homer, *Iliad III*, ed. J. T. Hooker.

Homer, *Odyssey vi & vii*, ed. G. M. Edmonds.

Plato, *The Martyrdom of Socrates* (*Apology*, *Crito* and selections from *Phaedo*), ed. F. Doherty.

Plato, *The Atlantis Story* (*Timaeus 17–27* and *Critias*), ed. C. Gill.

Xenophon, *The Fall of Athens* (selections from *Hellenica I & II*), ed. T. Horn.

Xenophon, *The Persian Expedition* (selections from the *Anabasis*), ed. J. Antrich & S. Usher.

All the above are published and distributed by the Bristol Classical Press (University of Bristol, Wills Memorial Building, Queens Road, Bristol BS8 1RJ, England).

Bilingual editions of these authors (and of nearly every other Greek writer) exist in the series *The Loeb Classical Library*, published by Heinemann and Harvard University Press. A number of other elementary editions are available from the Bristol Classical Press and from Bolchazy-Carducci Publishers (8 South Michigan Ave., Chicago, IL 60603, U.S.A.).

Dictionaries

H. G. Liddell and R. Scott, *Abridged Greek Lexicon*, Oxford U.P. (the best dictionary available for those who have finished this book and wish to read authors in editions which do not have a vocabulary).

H. G. Liddell and R. Scott, *Greek–English Lexicon*, 9th ed., Oxford U.P. (the largest Greek-English dictionary).

S. G. Woodhouse, *English–Greek Dictionary*, Routledge & Kegan Paul.

Grammars and books on language

E. Abbott and E. D. Mansfield, *A Primer of Greek Grammar*, Duckworth (uses much the same terminology as the present work and contains a certain amount of additional information).

H. W. Smyth, *Greek Grammar*, Harvard U.P. (a full treatment of all aspects of Greek grammar).

L. R. Palmer, *The Greek Language*, Faber and Faber (an advanced account of ancient Greek and its history).

W. S. Allen, *Vox Graeca: A Guide to the Pronunciation of Classical Greek*, Cambridge U.P.

Other works of reference

K. J. Dover (ed.) *Ancient Greek Literature*, Oxford U.P.

H. D. F. Kitto, *The Greeks*, Penguin.

Oxford Companion to Classical Literature, Oxford U.P.

Oxford Classical Dictionary, Oxford U.P.

H. J. Rose, *Handbook of Greek Mythology*, Methuen.

The World of Athens, an introduction to classical Athenian culture, J.A.C.T.,
    Cambridge U.P.

Appendix 1

Conjugation of λύω *loosen*

ACTIVE

		Pres.	Impf.	Future	Aorist	Perfect	Pluperfect
Indicative							
s.	1	λΰ-ω	ἔλῡ-ον	λΰc-ω	ἔλῡc-α	λέλυκ-α	ἐλελύκ-η
		I loosen, etc.	*I was loosening,* etc.	*I shall loosen,* etc.	*I loosened*	*I have loosened*	*I had loosened*
	2	λΰ-εις	ἔλῡ-ες	λΰc-εις	ἔλῡc-ας	λέλυκ-ας	ἐλελύκ-ης
	3	λΰ-ει	ἔλῡ-ε(ν)	λΰc-ει	ἔλῡc-ε(ν)	λέλυκ-ε(ν)	ἐλελύκ-ει(ν)
pl.	1	λΰ-ομεν	ἐλΰ-ομεν	λΰc-ομεν	ἐλΰc-αμεν	λελύκ-αμεν	ἐλελύκ-εμεν
	2	λΰ-ετε	ἐλΰ-ετε	λΰc-ετε	ἐλΰc-ατε	λελύκ-ατε	ἐλελύκ-ετε
	3	λΰ-ουcι(ν)	ἔλῡ-ον	λΰc-ουcι(ν)	ἔλῡc-αν	λελύκ-ᾱcι(ν)	ἐλελύκ-εcαν

Subjunctive					
s.	1	λΰ-ω		λΰc-ω	λελύκ-ω[1]
	2	λΰ-ῃς		λΰc-ῃς	λελύκ-ῃς
	3	λΰ-ῃ		λΰc-ῃ	λελύκ-ῃ
pl.	1	λΰ-ωμεν		λΰc-ωμεν	λελύκ-ωμεν
	2	λΰ-ητε		λΰc-ητε	λελύκ-ητε
	3	λΰ-ωcι(ν)		λΰc-ωcι(ν)	λελύκ-ωcι(ν)

Optative					
s.	1	λΰ-οιμι	λΰc-οιμι	λΰc-αιμι	λελύκ-οιμι[1]
	2	λΰ-οις	λΰc-οις	λΰc-ειας (λΰc-αις)	λελύκ-οις
	3	λΰ-οι	λΰc-οι	λΰc-ειε(ν) (λΰc-αι)	λελύκ-οι
pl.	1	λΰ-οιμεν	λΰc-οιμεν	λΰc-αιμεν	λελύκ-οιμεν
	2	λΰ-οιτε	λΰc-οιτε	λΰc-αιτε	λελύκ-οιτε
	3	λΰ-οιεν	λΰc-οιεν	λΰc-ειαν (λΰc-αιεν)	λελύκ-οιεν

Imperative				
s.	2	λῦ-ε		λῦc-ον	λελυκὼς ἴcθι
	3	λῡ-έτω		λῡc-άτω	λελυκὼς ἔcτω
pl.	2	λΰ-ετε		λΰc-ατε	λελυκότες ἔcτε
	3	λῡ-όντων		λῡc-άντων	λελυκότες ἔcτων

Infinitive			
λΰ-ειν	λΰc-ειν	λῦc-αι	λελυκ-έναι

Participle			
λΰ-ων	λΰc-ων	λΰc-ᾱc	λελυκ-ώς
λΰ-ουcα	λΰc-ουcα	λΰc-ᾱcα	λελυκ-υῖα
λῦ-ον	λῦc-ον	λῦc-αν	λελυκ-όc

[1] See also 16.1/4 note 1.

MIDDLE

	Pres.	Impf.	Future	Aorist	Perfect	Pluperfect
Indicative						
s. 1	λῡ́-ομαι	ἐλῡ-όμην	λῡ́ς-ομαι	ἐλῡς-άμην	λέλυ-μαι	ἐλελύ-μην
2	λῡ́-ῃ(-ει)	ἐλῡ́-ου	λῡ́ς-ῃ(ει)	ἐλῡ́ς-ω	λέλυ-cαι	ἐλέλυ-co
3	λῡ́-εται	ἐλῡ́-ετο	λῡ́ς-εται	ἐλῡ́ς-ατο	λέλυ-ται	ἐλέλυ-το
pl. 1	λῡ-όμεθα	ἐλῡ-όμεθα	λῡς-όμεθα	ἐλῡς-άμεθα	λελύ-μεθα	ἐλελύ-μεθα
2	λῡ́-εcθε	ἐλῡ́-εcθε	λῡ́ς-εcθε	ἐλῡ́ς-αcθε	λέλυ-cθε	ἐλέλυ-cθε
3	λῡ́-ονται	ἐλῡ́-οντο	λῡ́ς-ονται	ἐλῡ́ς-αντο	λέλυ-νται	ἐλέλυ-ντο

Subjunctive					
s. 1	λῡ́-ωμαι			λῡ́ς-ωμαι	λελυμένος ὦ
2	λῡ́-ῃ			λῡ́ς-ῃ	λελυμένος ᾖc
3	λῡ́-ηται			λῡ́ς-ηται	λελυμένος ᾖ
pl. 1	λῡ-ώμεθα			λῡς-ώμεθα	λελυμένοι ὦμεν
2	λῡ́-ηcθε			λῡ́ς-ηcθε	λελυμένοι ἦτε
3	λῡ́-ωνται			λῡ́ς-ωνται	λελυμένοι ὦcι(ν)

Optative					
s. 1	λῡ-οίμην		λῡς-οίμην	λῡς-αίμην	λελυμένος εἴην
2	λῡ́-οιο		λῡ́ς-οιο	λῡ́ς-αιο	λελυμένος εἴηc
3	λῡ́-οιτο		λῡ́ς-οιτο	λῡ́ς-αιτο	λελυμένος εἴη
pl. 1	λῡ-οίμεθα		λῡς-οίμεθα	λῡς-αίμεθα	λελυμένοι εἶμεν
2	λῡ́-οιcθε		λῡ́ς-οιcθε	λῡ́ς-αιcθε	λελυμένοι εἶτε
3	λῡ́-οιντο		λῡ́ς-οιντο	λῡ́ς-αιντο	λελυμένοι εἶεν

Imperative					
s. 2	λῡ́-ου			λῦς-αι	λέλυ-co
3	λῡ-έcθω			λῡς-άcθω	λελύ-cθω
pl. 2	λῡ́-εcθε			λῡ́ς-αcθε	λέλυ-cθε
3	λῡ-έcθων			λῡς-άcθων	λελύ-cθων

Infinitive					
	λῡ́-εcθαι		λῡ́ς-εcθαι	λῡ́ς-αcθαι	λελύ-cθαι

Participle					
	λῡ-όμενος,		λῡς-όμενος,	λῡς-άμενος,	λελυ-μένος,
	-η, -ον		-η, -ον	-η, -ον	-η, -ον

PASSIVE

The forms for the present, imperfect, perfect and pluperfect are the same as for the middle; for the future perfect passive see 16.1/4 note 2.

Future

		Indicative	Optative	
s.	*1*	λυθήc-ομαι	λυθηc-οίμην	
	2	λυθήc-η(-ει)	λυθήc-οιο	**Infinitive** λυθήc-εcθαι
	3	λυθήc-εται	λυθήc-οιτο	**Participle** λυθηc-όμενοc, -η, -ον
pl.	*1*	λυθηc-όμεθα	λυθηc-οίμεθα	
	2	λυθήc-εcθε	λυθήc-οιcθε	
	3	λυθήc-ονται	λυθήc-οιντο	

Aorist

		Indicative	Subjunctive	Optative	Imperative
s.	*1*	ἐλύθη-ν	λυθ-ῶ	λυθ-είην	
	2	ἐλύθη-c	λυθ-ῇc	λυθ-είηc	λύθη-τι
	3	ἐλύθη	λυθ-ῇ	λυθ-είη	λυθή-τω
pl.	*1*	ἐλύθη-μεν	λυθ-ῶμεν	λυθ-εῖμεν	
	2	ἐλύθη-τε	λυθ-ῆτε	λυθ-εῖτε	λύθη-τε
	3	ἐλύθη-cαν	λυθ-ῶcι(ν)	λυθ-εῖεν	λυθέ-ντων

Infinitive λυθῆ-ναι   **Participle** λυθ-είc, λυθ-εῖcα, λυθ-έν

Note

In all forms of the perfect which are made up of a perfect participle and εἰμί the participle must agree with the subject of the verb in number and gender.

Appendix 2

Conjugation of contracted verbs (present and imperfect)

τῑμάω *honour*

		ACTIVE		MIDDLE/PASSIVE	
		Present	**Imperfect**	**Present**	**Imperfect**

Indicative

		Present	Imperfect	Present	Imperfect
s.	1	τῑμῶ	ἐτῑμων	τῑμῶμαι	ἐτῑμώμην
	2	τῑμᾷς	ἐτῑμᾱς	τῑμᾷ	ἐτῑμῶ
	3	τῑμᾷ	ἐτῑμᾱ	τῑμᾶται	ἐτῑμᾶτο
pl.	1	τῑμῶμεν	ἐτῑμῶμεν	τῑμώμεθα	ἐτῑμώμεθα
	2	τῑμᾶτε	ἐτῑμᾶτε	τῑμᾶσθε	ἐτῑμᾶσθε
	3	τῑμῶσι(ν)	ἐτῑμων	τῑμῶνται	ἐτῑμῶντο

Subjunctive

s.	1	τῑμῶ		τῑμῶμαι
	2	τῑμᾷς		τῑμᾷ
	3	τῑμᾷ		τῑμᾶται
pl.	1	τῑμῶμεν		τῑμώμεθα
	2	τῑμᾶτε		τῑμᾶσθε
	3	τῑμῶσι(ν)		τῑμῶνται

Optative

s.	1	τῑμῴην		τῑμῴμην
	2	τῑμῴης		τῑμῷο
	3	τῑμῴη		τῑμῷτο
pl.	1	τῑμῷμεν		τῑμώμεθα
	2	τῑμῷτε		τῑμῷσθε
	3	τῑμῷεν		τῑμῷντο

Imperative

s.	2	τῑμᾱ		τῑμῶ
	3	τῑμᾱτω		τῑμάσθω
pl.	2	τῑμᾶτε		τῑμᾶσθε
	3	τῑμώντων		τῑμάσθων

Infinitive

	τῑμᾶν	τῑμᾶσθαι

Participle

τῑμῶν, τῑμῶσα, τῑμῶν	τῑμώμεν-ος, -η, -ον

ποιέω   *make, do*

		ACTIVE		MIDDLE/PASSIVE	
		Present	Imperfect	Present	Imperfect

Indicative

s.	1	ποιῶ	ἐποίουν	ποιοῦμαι	ἐποιούμην
	2	ποιεῖc	ἐποίεις	ποιῇ(-εῖ)	ἐποιοῦ
	3	ποιεῖ	ἐποίει	ποιεῖται	ἐποιεῖτο
pl.	1	ποιοῦμεν	ἐποιοῦμεν	ποιούμεθα	ἐποιούμεθα
	2	ποιεῖτε	ἐποιεῖτε	ποιεῖcθε	ἐποιεῖcθε
	3	ποιοῦcι(ν)	ἐποίουν	ποιοῦνται	ἐποιοῦντο

Subjunctive

s.	1	ποιῶ		ποιῶμαι	
	2	ποιῇς		ποιῇ	
	3	ποιῇ		ποιῆται	
pl.	1	ποιῶμεν		ποιώμεθα	
	2	ποιῆτε		ποιῆcθε	
	3	ποιῶcι(ν)		ποιῶνται	

Optative

s.	1	ποιοίην		ποιοίμην	
	2	ποιοίης		ποιοῖο	
	3	ποιοίη		ποιοῖτο	
pl.	1	ποιοῖμεν		ποιοίμεθα	
	2	ποιοῖτε		ποιοῖcθε	
	3	ποιοῖεν		ποιοῖντο	

Imperative

s.	2	ποίει		ποιοῦ	
	3	ποιείτω		ποιείcθω	
pl.	2	ποιεῖτε		ποιεῖcθε	
	3	ποιούντων		ποιείcθων	

Infinitive

	ποιεῖν		ποιεῖcθαι	

Participle

	ποιῶν, ποιοῦcα, ποιοῦν		ποιούμεν-ος, -η, -ον	

δηλόω   *make clear, show*

		ACTIVE		MIDDLE/PASSIVE	
		Present	**Imperfect**	**Present**	**Imperfect**
		Indicative			
s.	*1*	δηλῶ	ἐδήλουν	δηλοῦμαι	ἐδηλούμην
	2	δηλοῖc	ἐδήλους	δηλοῖ	ἐδηλοῦ
	3	δηλοῖ	ἐδήλου	δηλοῦται	ἐδηλοῦτο
pl.	*1*	δηλοῦμεν	ἐδηλοῦμεν	δηλούμεθα	ἐδηλούμεθα
	2	δηλοῦτε	ἐδηλοῦτε	δηλοῦcθε	ἐδηλοῦcθε
	3	δηλοῦcι(ν)	ἐδήλουν	δηλοῦνται	ἐδηλοῦντο
		Subjunctive			
s.	*1*	δηλῶ		δηλῶμαι	
	2	δηλοῖc		δηλοῖ	
	3	δηλοῖ		δηλῶται	
pl.	*1*	δηλῶμεν		δηλώμεθα	
	2	δηλῶτε		δηλῶcθε	
	3	δηλῶcι(ν)		δηλῶνται	
		Optative			
s.	*1*	δηλοίην		δηλοίμην	
	2	δηλοίηc		δηλοῖο	
	3	δηλοίη		δηλοῖτο	
pl.	*1*	δηλοῖμεν		δηλοίμεθα	
	2	δηλοῖτε		δηλοῖcθε	
	3	δηλοῖεν		δηλοῖντο	
		Imperative			
s.	*2*	δήλου		δηλοῦ	
	3	δηλούτω		δηλούcθω	
pl.	*2*	δηλοῦτε		δηλοῦcθε	
	3	δηλούντων		δηλούcθων	
		Infinitive			
		δηλοῦν		δηλοῦcθαι	
		Participle			
		δηλῶν, δηλοῦcα, δηλοῦν		δηλούμεν-ος, -η, -ον	

Appendix 3

Conjugation of *εἰμί be,* *ἔρχομαι* (and *εἶμι*) *come/go,* *φημί say,* *οἶδα know* (the last is perfect in form but present in meaning; it has been classified below according to its meaning)

		εἰμί *be*	*ἔρχομαι* *come/go* (18.1/3)	*φημί* *say*	*οἶδα* *know* (19.1/3*a*)
Present indicative					
s.	*1*	εἰμί	ἔρχομαι	φημί	οἶδα
	2	εἶ	ἔρχῃ(-ει)	φῄς	οἶϲθα
	3	ἐϲτί(ν)	ἔρχεται	φηϲί(ν)	οἶδε(ν)
pl.	*1*	ἐϲμέν	ἐρχόμεθα	φαμέν	ἴϲμεν
	2	ἐϲτέ	ἔρχεϲθε	φατέ	ἴϲτε
	3	εἰϲί(ν)	ἔρχονται	φαϲί(ν)	ἴϲᾱϲι(ν)
Present subjunctive					
s.	*1*	ὦ	ἴω	φῶ	εἰδῶ
	2	ᾖϲ	ἴῃϲ	φῇϲ	εἰδῇϲ
	3	ᾖ	ἴῃ	φῇ	εἰδῇ
pl.	*1*	ὦμεν	ἴωμεν	φῶμεν	εἰδῶμεν
	2	ἦτε	ἴητε	φῆτε	εἰδῆτε
	3	ὦϲι(ν)	ἴωϲι(ν)	φῶϲι(ν)	εἰδῶϲι(ν)
Present optative					
s.	*1*	εἴην	ἴοιμι	φαίην	εἰδείην
	2	εἴηϲ	ἴοιϲ	φαίηϲ	εἰδείηϲ
	3	εἴη	ἴοι	φαίη	εἰδείη
pl.	*1*	εἶμεν	ἴοιμεν	φαῖμεν	εἰδεῖμεν
	2	εἶτε	ἴοιτε	φαῖτε	εἰδεῖτε
	3	εἶεν	ἴοιεν	φαῖεν	εἰδεῖεν
Present imperative					
s.	*2*	ἴϲθι	ἴθι	φαθί	ἴϲθι
	3	ἔϲτω	ἴτω	φάτω	ἴϲτω
pl.	*2*	ἔϲτε	ἴτε	φάτε	ἴϲτε
	3	ἔϲτων (or ὄντων)	ἰόντων	φάντων	ἴϲτων
Present infinitive					
		εἶναι	ἰέναι	φάναι	εἰδέναι
Present participle					
		ὤν, οὖϲα, ὄν	ἰών, ἰοῦϲα, ἰόν	#φάϲ, φᾶϲα, φάν	εἰδώϲ, εἰδυῖα, εἰδόϲ

238

Imperfect indicative

s.	1	ἦ or ἦν	ἦα	ἔφην	ᾔδη
	2	ἦϲθα	ἤειϲθα	ἔφηϲθα or ἔφηϲ	ᾔδηϲθα
	3	ἦν	ᾔει(ν)	ἔφη	ᾔδει(ν)
pl.	1	ἦμεν	ᾖμεν	ἔφαμεν	ᾖϲμεν
	2	ἦτε	ᾖτε	ἔφατε	ᾖϲτε
	3	ἦϲαν	ᾖϲαν or ᾖϲαν	ἔφαϲαν	ᾔδεϲαν or ᾖϲαν

Future indicative

s.	1	ἔϲομαι	εἶμι	φήϲω	εἴϲομαι
	2	ἔϲῃ(-ει)	εἶ	φήϲεις	εἴϲῃ(-ει)
	3	ἔϲται	εἶϲι(ν)	φήϲει	εἴϲεται
pl.	1	ἐϲόμεθα	ἴμεν	φήϲομεν	εἰϲόμεθα
	2	ἔϲεϲθε	ἴτε	φήϲετε	εἴϲεϲθε
	3	ἔϲονται	ἴαϲι(ν)	φήϲουϲι(ν)	εἴϲονται

The other parts of the future are regular. εἰμί, φημί and οἶδα do not exist in other tenses. For the other parts of ἔρχομαι see **Principal parts of verbs**. The optative, infinitive and participle of εἶμι may also have a future meaning (18.1/3).

Appendix 4

Root aorists (11.1/1).

ἔβην (βαίνω) and **ἔγνων** (γιγνώϲκω) are conjugated:

		Ind.	Subj.	Opt.	Imp.	
s.	1	ἔβην	βῶ	βαίην		
	2	ἔβης	βῇς	βαίης	βῆθι	**Infinitive** βῆναι
	3	ἔβη	βῇ	βαίη	βήτω	
pl.	1	ἔβημεν	βῶμεν	βαῖμεν		
	2	ἔβητε	βῆτε	βαῖτε	βῆτε	**Participle** βάϲ, βᾶϲα, βάν
	3	ἔβηϲαν	βῶϲι(ν)	βαῖεν	βάντων	

s.	1	ἔγνων	γνῶ	γνοίην		
	2	ἔγνωϲ	γνῷς	γνοίης	γνῶθι	**Infinitive** γνῶναι
	3	ἔγνω	γνῷ	γνοίη	γνώτω	
pl.	1	ἔγνωμεν	γνῶμεν	γνοῖμεν		
	2	ἔγνωτε	γνῶτε	γνοῖτε	γνῶτε	**Participle** γνούς,
	3	ἔγνωϲαν	γνῶϲι(ν)	γνοῖεν	γνόντων	γνοῦϲα, γνόν

Appendix 5

Conjugation of δίδωμι *give,* τίθημι *put, place,* ἵημι *let go,* **send forth,** ἵστημι *make stand* (for full details of which tenses of ἵστημι are transitive and which are intransitive see 19.1/1). Many of the forms of ἵημι occur only in compounds.

	δίδωμι	τίθημι	ἵημι	ἵστημι

ACTIVE

Present indicative

		δίδωμι	τίθημι	ἵημι	ἵστημι
s.	1	δίδωμι	τίθημι	ἵημι	ἵστημι
	2	δίδως	τίθης	ἵης	ἵστης
	3	δίδωcι(ν)	τίθηcι(ν)	ἵηcι(ν)	ἵστηcι(ν)
pl.	1	δίδομεν	τίθεμεν	ἵεμεν	ἵσταμεν
	2	δίδοτε	τίθετε	ἵετε	ἵστατε
	3	διδόαcι(ν)	τιθέᾱcι(ν)	ἱᾶcι(ν)	ἱστᾶcι(ν)

Present subjunctive

s.	1	διδῶ	τιθῶ	ἱῶ	ἱστῶ
	2	διδῷς	τιθῇς	ἱῇς	ἱστῇς
	3	διδῷ	τιθῇ	ἱῇ	ἱστῇ
pl.	1	διδῶμεν	τιθῶμεν	ἱῶμεν	ἱστῶμεν
	2	διδῶτε	τιθῆτε	ἱῆτε	ἱστῆτε
	3	διδῶcι(ν)	τιθῶcι(ν)	ἱῶcι(ν)	ἱστῶcι(ν)

Present optative

s.	1	διδοίην	τιθείην	ἱείην	ἱσταίην
	2	διδοίης	τιθείης	ἱείης	ἱσταίης
	3	διδοίη	τιθείη	ἱείη	ἱσταίη
pl.	1	διδοῖμεν	τιθεῖμεν	ἱεῖμεν	ἱσταῖμεν
	2	διδοῖτε	τιθεῖτε	ἱεῖτε	ἱσταῖτε
	3	διδοῖεν	τιθεῖεν	ἱεῖεν	ἱσταῖεν

Present imperative

s.	2	δίδου	τίθει	ἵει	ἵστη
	3	διδότω	τιθέτω	ἱέτω	ἱστάτω
pl.	2	δίδοτε	τίθετε	ἵετε	ἵστατε
	3	διδόντων	τιθέντων	ἱέντων	ἱστάντων

Present infinitive

	διδόναι	τιθέναι	ἱέναι	ἱστάναι

Present participle

	διδούς	τιθείς	ἱείς	ἱστάς
	διδοῦcα	τιθεῖcα	ἱεῖcα	ἱστᾶcα
	διδόν	τιθέν	ἱέν	ἱστάν

Imperfect indicative

s.	1	ἐδίδουν	ἐτίθην	ἵην	ἵcτην
	2	ἐδίδους	ἐτίθεις	ἵεις	ἵcτης
	3	ἐδίδου	ἐτίθει	ἵει	ἵcτη
pl.	1	ἐδίδομεν	ἐτίθεμεν	ἵεμεν	ἵcταμεν
	2	ἐδίδοτε	ἐτίθετε	ἵετε	ἵcτατε
	3	ἐδίδοcαν	ἐτίθεcαν	ἵεcαν	ἵcταcαν

Future indicative

s.   *1* δώcω etc.   θήcω etc.   ἥcω etc.   cτήcω etc.

The other parts of the future active are formed regularly with the same stems (δωc-, θηc-, ἡc-, cτηc-).

Aorist indicative

					Transitive	*Intransitive*
s.	1	ἔδωκα	ἔθηκα	ἧκα	ἔcτηcα	ἔcτην
	2	ἔδωκας	ἔθηκας	ἧκας	ἔcτηcας	ἔcτης
	3	ἔδωκε(ν)	ἔθηκε(ν)	ἧκε(ν)	ἔcτηcε(ν)	ἔcτη
pl.	1	ἔδομεν	ἔθεμεν	εἷμεν	ἐcτήcαμεν	ἔcτημεν
	2	ἔδοτε	ἔθετε	εἷτε	ἐcτήcατε	ἔcτητε
	3	ἔδοcαν	ἔθεcαν	εἷcαν	ἔcτηcαν	ἔcτηcαν

On the alternative forms for the plural of ἔδωκα and ἔθηκα see 18.1/2 note 3.

Aorist subjunctive

s.	1	δῶ	θῶ	ὧ	cτήcω	cτῶ
	2	δῷc	θῇc	ἧ̓c	cτήcῃc	cτῇc
	3	δῷ	θῇ	ἧ̓	cτήcῃ	cτῇ
pl.	1	δῶμεν	θῶμεν	ὧμεν	cτήcωμεν	cτῶμεν
	2	δῶτε	θῆτε	ἧτε	cτήcητε	cτῆτε
	3	δῶcι(ν)	θῶcι(ν)	ὧcι(ν)	cτήcωcι(ν)	cτῶcι(ν)

Aorist optative

s.	1	δοίην	θείην	εἵην	cτήcαιμι	cταίην
	2	δοίης	θείης	εἵης	cτήcειας(-αιc)	cταίης
	3	δοίη	θείη	εἵη	cτήcειε(ν) (-αι)	cταίη
pl.	1	δοῖμεν	θεῖμεν	εἷμεν	cτήcαιμεν	cταῖμεν
	2	δοῖτε	θεῖτε	εἷτε	cτήcαιτε	cταῖτε
	3	δοῖεν	θεῖεν	εἷεν	cτήcειαν(-αιεν)	cταῖεν

Aorist imperative

s.	2	δόc	θέc	ἕc	cτῆcον	cτῆθι
	3	δότω	θέτω	ἕτω	cτηcάτω	cτήτω
pl.	2	δότε	θέτε	ἕτε	cτήcατε	cτῆτε
	3	δόντων	θέντων	ἕντων	cτηcάντων	cτάντων

Aorist infinitive

δοῦναι	θεῖναι	εἷναι	cτῆcαι	cτῆναι

Aorist participle

δούc	θείc	εἷc	cτήcᾱc	cτάc
δοῦcα	θεῖcα	εἷcα	cτήcᾱcα	cτᾶcα
δόν	θέν	ἕν	cτῆcαν	cτάν

Perfect and pluperfect

The perfect and pluperfect active of δίδωμι, τίθημι, ἵημι are formed regularly from the stems δεδωκ-, τεθηκ-, εἱκ-.

The perfect and pluperfect active of ἵστημι (which are intransitive—see 19.1/1) are conjugated as follows:

Perfect

		Indicative	Subjunctive	Optative	Imperative
s.	1	ἕστηκα	ἑστῶ	ἑσταίην	
	2	ἕστηκας	ἑστῇς	ἑσταίης	ἕσταθι
	3	ἕστηκε(ν)	ἑστῇ	ἑσταίη	ἑστάτω
pl.	1	ἕσταμεν	ἑστῶμεν	ἑσταῖμεν	
	2	ἕστατε	ἑστῆτε	ἑσταῖτε	ἕστατε
	3	ἑστᾶσι(ν)	ἑστῶσι(ν)	ἑσταῖεν	ἑστάντων

Infinitive ἑστάναι   **Participle** ἑστώς, ἑστῶσα, ἑστός

Pluperfect *s.* εἱστήκη (*I stood*), εἱστήκης, εἱστήκει, *pl.* ἕσταμεν, ἕστατε, ἕστασαν. (On alternatives for forms in ἑστα- see 19.1/1.)

MIDDLE

Present indicative

s.	1	δίδομαι	τίθεμαι	ἵεμαι	ἵσταμαι
	2	δίδοσαι	τίθεσαι	ἵεσαι	ἵστασαι
	3	δίδοται	τίθεται	ἵεται	ἵσταται
pl.	1	διδόμεθα	τιθέμεθα	ἱέμεθα	ἱστάμεθα
	2	δίδοσθε	τίθεσθε	ἵεσθε	ἵστασθε
	3	δίδονται	τίθενται	ἵενται	ἵστανται

Present subjunctive

s.	1	διδῶμαι	τιθῶμαι	ἱῶμαι	ἱστῶμαι
	2	διδῷ	τιθῇ	ἱῇ	ἱστῇ
	3	διδῶται	τιθῆται	ἱῆται	ἱστῆται
pl.	1	διδώμεθα	τιθώμεθα	ἱώμεθα	ἱστώμεθα
	2	διδῶσθε	τιθῆσθε	ἱῆσθε	ἱστῆσθε
	3	διδῶνται	τιθῶνται	ἱῶνται	ἱστῶνται

Present optative

s.	1	διδοίμην	τιθείμην	ἱείμην	ἱσταίμην
	2	διδοῖο	τιθεῖο	ἱεῖο	ἱσταῖο
	3	διδοῖτο	τιθεῖτο	ἱεῖτο	ἱσταῖτο
pl.	1	διδοίμεθα	τιθείμεθα	ἱείμεθα	ἱσταίμεθα
	2	διδοῖσθε	τιθεῖσθε	ἱεῖσθε	ἱσταῖσθε
	3	διδοῖντο	τιθεῖντο	ἱεῖντο	ἱσταῖντο

Present imperative

s.	2	δίδοσο	τίθεσο	ἵεσο	ἵστασο
	3	διδόσθω	τιθέσθω	ἱέσθω	ἱστάσθω
pl.	2	δίδοσθε	τίθεσθε	ἵεσθε	ἵστασθε
	3	διδόσθων	τιθέσθων	ἱέσθων	ἱστάσθων

Present infinitive

δίδοϲθαι   τίθεϲθαι   ἵεϲθαι   ἵϲταϲθαι

Present participle

διδόμεν-οϲ, -η, -ον τιθέμεν-οϲ, -η, -ον ἱέμεν-οϲ, -η, -ον ἱϲτάμεν-οϲ, -η, -ον

Imperfect indicative

s.	1	ἐδιδόμην	ἐτιθέμην	ἱέμην	ἱϲτάμην
	2	ἐδίδοϲο	ἐτίθεϲο	ἵεϲο	ἵϲταϲο
	3	ἐδίδοτο	ἐτίθετο	ἵετο	ἵϲτατο
pl.	1	ἐδιδόμεθα	ἐτιθέμεθα	ἱέμεθα	ἱϲτάμεθα
	2	ἐδίδοϲθε	ἐτίθεϲθε	ἵεϲθε	ἵϲταϲθε
	3	ἐδίδοντο	ἐτίθεντο	ἵεντο	ἵϲταντο

Future indicative

s. 1 δώϲομαι etc.   θήϲομαι etc.   ἥϲομαι etc.   ϲτήϲομαι etc.

The other parts of the future middle are formed regularly with the same stems (δωϲ-, θηϲ-, ἡϲ-, ϲτηϲ-).

Aorist

The only aorist middle of ἵϲτημι is weak (and transitive), ἐϲτηϲάμην, conjugated in exactly the same way as ἐλῡϲάμην (see **Appendix 1**). The aorists middle of the other verbs are conjugated as follows:

Aorist indicative

s.	1	ἐδόμην	ἐθέμην	εἵμην
	2	ἔδου	ἔθου	εἷϲο
	3	ἔδοτο	ἔθετο	εἷτο
pl.	1	ἐδόμεθα	ἐθέμεθα	εἵμεθα
	2	ἔδοϲθε	ἔθεϲθε	εἷϲθε
	3	ἔδοντο	ἔθεντο	εἷντο

Aorist subjunctive

s.	1	δῶμαι	θῶμαι	ὧμαι
	2	δῷ	θῇ	ᾗ
	3	δῶται	θῆται	ἧται
pl.	1	δώμεθα	θώμεθα	ὥμεθα
	2	δῶϲθε	θῆϲθε	ἧϲθε
	3	δῶνται	θῶνται	ὧνται

Aorist optative

s.	1	δοίμην	θείμην	εἵμην
	2	δοῖο	θεῖο	εἷο
	3	δοῖτο	θεῖτο	εἷτο
pl.	1	δοίμεθα	θείμεθα	εἵμεθα
	2	δοῖϲθε	θεῖϲθε	εἷϲθε
	3	δοῖντο	θεῖντο	εἷντο

Aorist imperative

s.	2	δοῦ	θοῦ	οὗ
	3	δόϲθω	θέϲθω	ἔϲθω
pl.	2	δόϲθε	θέϲθε	ἔϲθε
	3	δόϲθων	θέϲθων	ἔϲθων

Aorist infinitive

δόϲθαι   θέϲθαι   ἕϲθαι

Aorist participle

δόμεν-οϲ, -η, -ον   θέμεν-οϲ, -η, -ον   ἕμεν-οϲ, -η, -ον

Perfect and pluperfect

The perfect and pluperfect middle/passive of δίδωμι and ἵημι are formed regularly from the stems δεδο- and εἱ- (e.g. perfect middle/passive indicative δέδομαι, δέδοϲαι etc., εἷμαι, εἷϲαι etc.). Similar forms exist for τίθημι (τέθειμαι, τέθειϲαι etc.) but on the perfect passive of this verb see 18.1/2 note 4. The perfect middle/passive forms of ἵϲτημι are rare.

PASSIVE

As with other verbs, the forms for the present, imperfect, perfect and pluperfect are the same as for the middle. The future and aorist passive follow λύω (see **Appendix 1**):

Future indicative

δοθήϲομαι   τεθήϲομαι   ἑθήϲομαι   ϲταθήϲομαι

Aorist indicative

ἐδόθην   ἐτέθην   εἵθην   ἐϲτάθην

Appendix 6

Conjugation of δείκνῡμι (present and imperfect).

For the other tenses of δείκνῡμι see 20.1/1.

		ACTIVE		**MIDDLE/PASSIVE**	
		Present	Imperfect	Present	Imperfect

Indicative

		ACTIVE Present	ACTIVE Imperfect	M/P Present	M/P Imperfect
s.	1	δείκνῡμι	ἐδείκνῡν	δείκνυμαι	ἐδεικνύμην
	2	δείκνῡc	ἐδείκνῡν	δείκνυcαι	ἐδείκνυcο
	3	δείκνῡcι(ν)	ἐδείκνῡ	δείκνυται	ἐδείκνυτο
pl.	1	δείκνυμεν	ἐδείκνυμεν	δεικνύμεθα	ἐδεικνύμεθα
	2	δείκνυτε	ἐδείκνυτε	δείκνυcθε	ἐδείκνυcθε
	3	δεικνύᾱcι(ν)	ἐδείκνυcαν	δείκνυνται	ἐδείκνυντο

Subjunctive

		Active		Middle/Passive
s.	1	δεικνύω		δεικνύωμαι
	2	δεικνύῃc		δεικνύῃ
	3	δεικνύῃ		δεικνύηται
pl.	1	δεικνύωμεν		δεικνυώμεθα
	3	δεικνύητε		δεικνύηcθε
	3	δεικνύωcι(ν)		δεικνύωνται

Optative

		Active		Middle/Passive
s.	1	δεικνύοιμι		δεικνυοίμην
	2	δεικνύοιc		δεικνύοιο
	3	δεικνύοι		δεικνύοιτο
pl.	1	δεικνύοιμεν		δεικνυοίμεθα
	2	δεικνύοιτε		δεικνύοιcθε
	3	δεικνύοιεν		δεικνύοιντο

Imperative

		Active		Middle/Passive
s.	2	δείκνῡ		δείκνυcο
	3	δεικνύτω		δεικνύcθω
pl.	2	δείκνυτε		δείκνυcθε
	3	δεικνύντων		δεικνύcθων

Infinitive

	Active	Middle/Passive
	δεικνύναι	δείκνυcθαι

Participle

	Active	Middle/Passive
	δεικνύc, δεικνῦcα, δεικνύν	δεικνύμεν-οc, -η, -ον

Appendix 7

Table of nouns

SINGULAR

nom./voc.	acc.	gen.	dat.

First declension

nom./voc.	acc.	gen.	dat.
τῑμ-ή	τῑμ-ήν	τῑμ-ῆς	τῑμ-ῇ
χώρ-ᾱ	χώρ-ᾱν	χώρ-ᾱς	χώρ-ᾳ
θάλαττ-α	θάλαττ-αν	θαλάττ-ης	θαλάττ-ῃ
κριτ-ής (v. -ά)	κριτ-ήν	κριτ-οῦ	κριτ-ῇ
νεᾱνί-ᾱς (v. -ᾱ)	νεᾱνί-ᾱν	νεᾱνί-ου	νεᾱνί-ᾳ

Second declension

nom./voc.	acc.	gen.	dat.
ἵππ-ος (v. -ε)	ἵππ-ον	ἵππ-ου	ἵππ-ῳ
δῶρ-ον	δῶρ-ον	δώρ-ου	δώρ-ῳ
νοῦς (v. νοῦ)	νοῦν	νοῦ	νῷ
νεώς	νεών	νεώ	νεῴ

Third declension

nom./voc.	acc.	gen.	dat.
φύλαξ	φύλακ-α	φύλακ-ος	φύλακ-ι
γύψ	γῦπ-α	γῦπ-ός	γῦπ-ί
πατρίς (v. -ί)	πατρίδ-α	πατρίδ-ος	πατρίδ-ι
σῶμα	σῶμα	σώματ-ος	σώματ-ι
γίγᾱς (v. -αν)	γίγαντ-α	γίγαντ-ος	γίγαντ-ι
λέων (v. -ον)	λέοντ-α	λέοντ-ος	λέοντ-ι
λιμήν	λιμέν-α	λιμέν-ος	λιμέν-ι
μήν	μῆν-α	μην-ός	μην-ί
δαίμων (v. -ον)	δαίμον-α	δαίμον-ος	δαίμον-ι
ἀγών	ἀγῶν-α	ἀγῶν-ος	ἀγῶν-ι
θήρ	θῆρ-α	θηρ-ός	θηρ-ί
ῥήτωρ (v. -ορ)	ῥήτορ-α	ῥήτορ-ος	ῥήτορ-ι
πατήρ (v. -ερ)	πατέρ-α	πατρ-ός	πατρ-ί
ἀνήρ (v. -ερ)	ἄνδρ-α	ἀνδρ-ός	ἀνδρ-ί
γένος	γένος	γένους	γένει
Cωκράτης (v. -ες)	Cωκράτη	Cωκράτους	Cωκράτει
Περικλῆς (v. -κλεις)	Περικλέᾱ	Περικλέους	Περικλεῖ
πόλις (v. -ι)	πόλιν	πόλεως	πόλει
πῆχυς (v. -υ)	πῆχυν	πήχεως	πήχει
ἄστυ	ἄστυ	ἄστεως	ἄστει
ἰχθῦς (v. -ύ)	ἰχθῦν	ἰχθύος	ἰχθύϊ
βασιλεύ-ς (v. -εῦ)	βασιλέ-ᾱ	βασιλέ-ως	βασιλεῖ
ναῦ-ς (v. ναῦ)	ναῦ-ν	νε-ώς	νη-ΐ

PLURAL

nom./voc.	acc.	gen.	dat.
τῑμ-αί	τῑμ-ᾱ́ς	τῑμ-ῶν	τῑμ-αῖς
χῶρ-αι	χώρ-ᾱς	χωρ-ῶν	χώρ-αις
θάλαττ-αι	θαλάττ-ᾱς	θαλαττ-ῶν	θαλάττ-αις
κριτ-αί	κριτ-ᾱ́ς	κριτ-ῶν	κριτ-αῖς
νεᾱνί-αι	νεᾱνί-ᾱς	νεᾱνι-ῶν	νεᾱνί-αις
ἵππ-οι	ἵππ-ους	ἵππ-ων	ἵππ-οις
δῶρ-α	δῶρ-α	δώρ-ων	δώρ-οις
νοῖ	νοῦς	νῶν	νοῖς
νεῴ	νεώς	νεών	νεῴς
φύλακ-ες	φύλακ-ας	φυλάκ-ων	φύλαξι(ν)
γῦπ-ες	γῦπ-ας	γῡπ-ῶν	γῦψί(ν)
πατρίδ-ες	πατρίδ-ας	πατρίδ-ων	πατρί-ςι(ν)
σώματ-α	σώματ-α	σωμάτ-ων	σώμα-ςι(ν)
γίγαντ-ες	γίγαντ-ας	γιγάντ-ων	γίγᾱςι(ν)
λέοντ-ες	λέοντ-ας	λεόντ-ων	λέουςι(ν)
λιμέν-ες	λιμέν-ας	λιμέν-ων	λιμέ-ςι(ν)
μῆν-ες	μῆν-ας	μην-ῶν	μη-ςί(ν)
δαίμον-ες	δαίμον-ας	δαιμόν-ων	δαίμο-ςι(ν)
ἀγῶν-ες	ἀγῶν-ας	ἀγών-ων	ἀγῶ-ςι(ν)
θῆρ-ες	θῆρ-ας	θηρ-ῶν	θηρ-ςί(ν)
ῥήτορ-ες	ῥήτορ-ας	ῥητόρ-ων	ῥήτορ-ςι(ν)
πατέρ-ες	πατέρ-ας	πατέρ-ων	πατρά-ςι(ν)
ἄνδρ-ες	ἄνδρ-ας	ἀνδρ-ῶν	ἀνδρά-ςι(ν)
γένη	γένη	γενῶν	γένεςι(ν)
—	—	—	—
πόλεις	πόλεις	πόλεων	πόλεςι(ν)
πήχεις	πήχεις	πήχεων	πήχεςι(ν)
ἄστη	ἄστη	ἄστεων	ἄστεςι(ν)
ἰχθύες	ἰχθῦς	ἰχθύων	ἰχθύςι(ν)
βασιλῆς (or -εῖς)	βασιλέ-ᾱς	βασιλέ-ων	βασιλεῦ-ςι(ν)
νῆ-ες	ναῦς	νε-ῶν	ναυ-ςί(ν)

Appendix 8

Numerals

Cardinals

For the declension of εἷς, δύο, τρεῖς, τέτταρες see 7.1/5a. διᾱκόσιοι, τριᾱκόσιοι etc. follow the plural of καλός (3.1/3).

1	εἷς	20	εἴκοσι(ν)
2	δύο	30	τριάκοντα
3	τρεῖς	40	τετταράκοντα
4	τέτταρες	50	πεντήκοντα
5	πέντε	60	ἑξήκοντα
6	ἕξ	70	ἑβδομήκοντα
7	ἑπτά	80	ὀγδοήκοντα
8	ὀκτώ	90	ἐνενήκοντα
9	ἐννέα	100	ἑκατόν
10	δέκα	200	διᾱκόσιοι
11	ἕνδεκα	300	τριᾱκόσιοι
12	δώδεκα	400	τετρακόσιοι
13	τρεῖς καὶ δέκα	500	πεντακόσιοι
14	τέτταρες καὶ δέκα	600	ἑξακόσιοι
15	πεντεκαίδεκα	700	ἑπτακόσιοι
16	ἑκκαίδεκα	800	ὀκτακόσιοι
17	ἑπτακαίδεκα	900	ἐνακόσιοι
18	ὀκτωκαίδεκα	1,000	χίλιοι
19	ἐννεακαίδεκα	10,000	μύριοι

The cardinals *two thousand, three thousand* etc. are compounds of the appropriate numeral adverbs and χίλιοι, e.g. δισχίλιοι, τρισχίλιοι etc.; likewise we have δισμύριοι *twenty thousand*, τρισμύριοι *thirty thousand* etc.

	Ordinals	Adverbs
1	πρῶτος	ἅπαξ
2	δεύτερος	δίς
3	τρίτος	τρίς
4	τέταρτος	τετράκις
5	πέμπτος	πεντάκις
6	ἕκτος	ἑξάκις
7	ἕβδομος	ἑπτάκις
8	ὄγδοος	ὀκτάκις
9	ἔνατος	ἐνάκις
10	δέκατος	δεκάκις

The ordinals are normal first and second declension adjectives (3.1/3), except that the feminine of ὄγδοος is ὀγδόη (not -ᾱ).

Appendix 9

Accentuation

The basic features of Greek accentuation are described at 1.1/2, and information given there is not repeated below.

The following terms are used to describe words according to their accent:

Oxytone – a word with an acute on its final syllable, e.g. ποταμός.

Paroxytone – a word with an acute on its penultimate (i.e. last syllable but one), e.g. λόγος.

Proparoxytone – a word with an acute on its last syllable but two, e.g. ἄνθρωπος.

Perispomenon – a word with a circumflex on its final syllable, e.g. ποταμοῦ.

Properispomenon – a word with a circumflex on its penultimate, e.g. δῶρον.

Barytone – a word with a grave on its final syllable, e.g. ποταμὸν εἶδον *I saw a river*.

These are the only places in which each accent can occur (we cannot, for example, have an acute on the last syllable but three, or a circumflex on the last syllable but two).

For purposes of accentuation a syllable is long if it contains a long vowel or diphthong (1.1/1*b,c*), and short if it contains a short vowel, except that **all endings in -αι and -οι, apart from those of the optative, are counted as short.**[1]

The length of the final syllable of a word and, to a lesser extent, of its penultimate is important for accentuation because:

a word can only be proparoxytone if its final syllable is short, e.g. ἄνθρωπος;

a word can only be properispomenon if its final syllable is short; as a circumflex must in any case stand on a long vowel or diphthong, a word so accented must end in – ◡, or be a disyllable consisting of – ◡, e.g. πολῖται, γλῶττα. Conversely, if such a word is accented on its penultimate, the accent must be a circumflex, and this is why we get the change of accent from πολῑ́της to πολῖται (the reverse in γλῶττα/γλώττης).

For purposes of accentuation words are divided into five categories:

(a) *Nouns, adjectives and pronouns*

There are no overall rules about the position of the accent in the nominative singular of nouns or in the nominative masculine singular of adjectives and pronouns, and we must simply learn that ποταμός is oxytone but λόγος is paroxytone. There are some rules for certain small groups which can be learnt by observation, e.g. nouns in -ευς are always oxytone (as βασιλεύς); the

---

[1] The rules in verse are different; see Appendix 10.

accent of comparative and superlative adjectives is always as far from the end of the word as possible (σοφός but σοφώτερος, σοφώτατος).

Once, however, we know where a noun, adjective or pronoun is accented in the nominative (masculine) singular it is easy to deduce how its other forms will be accented because the accent stays on the same syllable as far as this is allowed by the rules given above for proparoxytones and perispomenons. In λόγος, for example, the accent remains unchanged (λόγε, λόγον, λόγου, λόγῳ, λόγοι, λόγους, λόγων, λόγοις), but in ἄνθρωπος the accent must become paroxytone when the ending is long: ἄνθρωπε, ἄνθρωπον, ἀνθρώπου, ἀνθρώπῳ, ἄνθρωποι, ἀνθρώπους, ἀνθρώπων, ἀνθρώποις (ἄνθρωποι because -οι does **not** count as long—see above).

In many third declension nouns the genitive singular is a syllable longer than the nominative singular, e.g. σῶμα (properispomenon, not paroxytone, because it is a disyllable of the form – ◡; see above): σώματος, σώματι, σώματα (the accent must change to an acute because the added short syllable makes all three forms proparoxytone), σωμάτων (the added syllable is long and therefore the accent must become paroxytone), σώμασι.

We must, however, note:

(i)   Where a first or second declension word has an acute on its final syllable in the nominative singular, this becomes a circumflex in the genitive and dative (in both singular and plural, cf. 2.1/2 note 3), e.g. from ποταμός we have ποταμέ, ποταμόν, ποταμοῦ, ποταμῷ, ποταμοί, ποταμούς, ποταμῶν, ποταμοῖς.[1] For an example of an adjective so accented see καλός (3.1/3).

(ii) All first declension nouns are perispomenon in the genitive plural (2.1/2 note 4), e.g. χωρῶν (< χώρα), νεᾱνιῶν (< νεᾱνίᾱς). This does **not** apply to the gen. f. pl. of adjectives when this form would not otherwise differ from the masculine, e.g. μεγάλων is both gen. m. pl. and gen. f. pl. of μέγας. Where, however, the masculine and feminine forms differ, the rule holds, e.g. χαρίεις, gen. m. pl. χαριέντων, gen. f. pl. χαριεσσῶν.

(iii) In the third declension monosyllabic nouns are accented on the final syllable of the genitive and dative, in both singular and plural, e.g. αἴξ, αἶγα, αἰγός, αἰγί, αἶγες, αἶγας, αἰγῶν, αἰξί. An exception is the gen. pl. of παῖς (παίδων). Of polysyllabic nouns γυνή also follows this pattern: γυνή, γύναι (5.1/1 note 1), γυναῖκα, γυναικός, γυναικί, γυναῖκες, γυναῖκας, γυναικῶν, γυναιξί, and ἀνήρ, μήτηρ and πατήρ follow it in the gen. s., dat. s. and gen. pl. (6.1/1b). For the accentuation of πᾶς see 10.1/3b.

(iv) The accent in the genitive (s. and pl.) of third declension nouns with stems in ι and of some with stems in υ (8.1/4) is quite irregular: πόλεως, πόλεων (< πόλις); πήχεως, πήχεων (< πῆχυς).

(v)   Contracted nouns and adjectives (6.1/2) follow the same rules as for contracted verbs (below b(i)).

---

[1] The Attic declension (13.1/1a) is an exception.

(b) Verbs

With verbs the accent falls as far from the end of a word as possible (here too final -αι and -οι count as short, **except in optative endings**). In forms such as ἀκουετε, ἀκουουσι, κελευεcθαι, ἐκελευcαν the final short syllable shows that they must be proparoxytone: ἀκούετε, ἀκούουσι, κελεύεcθαι, ἐκέλευcαν (in disyllabic forms such as ἑλε and λῦε the accent goes back to the penultimate but becomes properispomenon in λῦε because of its long ῡ: ἕλε but λῦε). In κελευω, προφερει, ἐλυθην, where the final syllable is long, the accent is paroxytone: κελεύω, προφέρει, ἐλύθην.

We must, however, note:

(i) In the forms of contracted verbs where contraction occurs, the accent follows that of the original uncontracted form according to the following rules:

> If the accent is on neither of the syllables to be contracted it remains unchanged, e.g. ἐποίει (< ἐποίε-ε).
>
> If the accent is on the first of the two syllables to be contracted it becomes a circumflex on the contracted syllable, e.g. ποιεῖ (< ποιέ-ει); νῑκῶμεν (< νῑκά-ομεν).
>
> If the accent is on the second of the two syllables to be contracted it stays as an acute on the contracted syllable, e.g. ἐτῑμώμεθα (< ἐτῑμα-όμεθα); τῑμῴην (< τῑμα-οίην).

(ii) Certain forms of uncontracted -ω verbs and of -μι verbs are in origin contracted and for this reason the first syllable of their endings is always accented. These are:

> the aorist subjunctive passive of all verbs, e.g. λυθῶ, λυθῇc, λυθῇ, λυθῶμεν, λυθῆτε, λυθῶcι;
>
> the subjunctive and optative of both present (act. mid./pass.) and aorist (act., mid.) of δίδωμι, τίθημι, ἵημι and their compounds, e.g. διδῶ, διδοῖμεν, ἀποδῶ, ἀποδοῖμεν.

(iii) In all strong aorists the first syllable of the ending always carries the accent in the active participle (e.g. λαβών, λαβοῦcα, λαβόν), the active and middle infinitives (λαβεῖν, λαβέcθαι), and the 2nd s. imperative middle (λαβοῦ).

(iv) The first syllable of the ending also carries the accent in participles in -εις, -ουc and -ωc, e.g. λυθείc, λυθεῖcα, λυθέν; τιθείc, τιθεῖcα, τιθέν; διδούc, διδοῦcα, διδόν; λελυκώc, λελυκυῖα, λελυκόc.

(v) In certain participles and infinitives the accent is always either paroxytone or properispomenon, depending on whether it stands on a short or long syllable. These are:

> infinitives in -cαι (weak aorist active), e.g. λῦcαι, νῑκῆcαι, αἰνέcαι.
>
> infinitives in -ναι (perf. act., aor. pass., root aor. act., and certain active infinitives of -μι verbs), e.g. λελυκέναι, λυθῆναι, γνῶναι, διδόναι.
>
> the infinitive and participle of the perf. mid./pass., e.g. νενῑκῆcθαι, λελυμένοc.

(vi)   In compound verbs the accent cannot fall further back than the augment, e.g. ἀπῆγον (<ἀπάγω), παρέσχον (<παρέχω), or the last vowel of a prepositional prefix, e.g. παράδος (<παραδίδωμι).

(c)   *Adverbs, conjunctions, interjections, particles, prepositions*

These have only one form and therefore their accent does not vary, e.g. σοφῶς *wisely*, ὅταν *whenever*, εὖ *well*, except for oxytones becoming barytones (1.1/2). A few words which would otherwise be included here are enclitic or atonic and so come under categories (*d*) or (*e*).

(d)   *Enclitics*

An enclitic combines with the preceding word for pronunciation, and can affect its accentuation. Monosyllabic enclitics are listed with no accent (e.g. γε), disyllabics as oxytone (e.g. ποτέ), except for τινῶν.

The total number of enclitics is small and consists of:

(i)   The present indicative of εἰμί *I am* and φημί *say*, with the exception in both cases of the 2nd singular.
(ii)   The unemphatic forms of the personal pronouns, viz με, μου, μοι; σε, σου, σοι; ἑ, οὑ, οἱ.
(iii)   All forms of the indefinite τις (10.1/1).
(iv)   The indefinite adverbs ποτέ, που, πω, πως.
(v)   The particles γε, νυν, περ, τε.

The rules for enclitics are:

(vi)   An enclitic has no accent when it follows a word accented on its final syllable, e.g. ποταμῶν τινων. If this word has a final acute (i.e. is oxytone), this accent is kept, e.g. ποταμός τις.
(vii)   If the preceding word is paroxytone a monosyllabic enclitic has no accent but a disyllabic enclitic keeps the accent on its final syllable, e.g. ἵππος τις, ἵπποι τινές.
(viii)   If the preceding word is proparoxytone or properispomenon, an enclitic, whether monosyllabic or disyllabic, has the effect of adding an acute to the final syllable, e.g. ἄνθρωπός τις, ἄνθρωποί τινες, δῶρόν τι, δῶρά τινα.
(ix)   In groups of two or more enclitics all are accented except the last, e.g. ἡμεῖς γέ ποτέ πού τι εἴδομεν *we at any rate once saw something somewhere*.
(x)   ἐστί is accented on its first syllable (ἔστι) when:
    it denotes existence, e.g. Ἱππόλυτος οὐκέτ' ἔστιν *Hippolytus is no longer alive*;
    it stands for ἔξεστι (21.1/4 note 1);
    it follows ἀλλά, εἰ, καί, οὐκ, μή, τοῦτο, ὡς;
    it begins a clause.

(e) *Atonics*

Atonics are monosyllables which have no accent unless followed by an enclitic. These are:

the nom. m. and f. (s. and pl.) of the article (ὁ, ἡ, οἱ, αἱ), εἰ, οὐ, ὡς; the prepositions εἰς, ἐκ, ἐν.

Of these, however, οὐ is accented if it occurs as last word of a clause (example at 5.2.21 *l*.1).

Notes

1 A few words which we would expect to be properispomenon are in fact paroxytone: εἴθε, ὥστε and compound demonstratives and relatives whose second element is -δε, -περ and -τις (οἴδε, αἴπερ, ἥτις etc.).
2 τίς and τί never become barytone (10.1/1).
3 Certain disyllabic prepositions throw their accent back on to their first syllable when they follow the noun they govern (example at 11.2.4 *l*.1).

Appendix 10

Greek verse

(a) The nature of Greek verse; long and short syllables

Greek poetry was composed on an entirely different principle from that employed in English. It was not constructed by arranging stressed syllables in patterns, nor with a system of rhymes. Greek poets employed a number of different metres, all of which consist of certain fixed arrangements of **long and short syllables**. In English verse, whether rhymed or not, the length and rhythm of a line is determined by the number and arrangement of its stressed syllables:

> They tóld me, Heraclítus, they tóld me yoú were déad;
> They broúght me bitter néws to heár and bitter teárs to shéd.
> I wépt, as I remémbered how óften yoú and Í
> Had tired the sún with tálking and sént him down the sky.
> And nów that thou art lying, my deár old Cárian guést,
> A hándful of gréy áshes, long lóng ago at rést,
> Still are thy pleásant voices, thy nightingales, awáke,
> For deáth he taketh áll away, but thém he cánnot táke.

In this translation of a poem of Callimachus (12.3.9) the poet, William Johnston Cary, has changed the position of stressed syllables in some lines for purposes of rhythm and emphasis. No comparable variation is possible in Greek poetry because its structure is much more formal. Every line of verse consists of a succession of long and short syllables whose number and order are prescribed by the metre used; word accent, which in any case is different from that of English (1.1/2), plays no part. To scan a line (i.e. indicate its metre) syllables are marked with a macron (–) when long and a micron (‿) when short (to avoid a confusion of signs and letters, accents and breathings are omitted and capitals are not used for vowels):

$$εἰπέ̆ τῐς ἡ̄ρᾱκλεῖτε̆ τεό̄ν μό̆ρο̆ν ἐ̄ς δέ̆ μὲ̆ δᾱκρῠ$$

The rules for determining the length of syllables are:

(i)   Vowels are classified as short (α, ε, ι, ο, υ) or long (ᾱ, η, ῑ, ῡ, ω). For metrical purposes all diphthongs are long (this is not true for accentuation—see **Appendix 9**).

(ii) A short syllable must contain a short vowel followed by either a single consonant or no consonant at all.

(iii) A syllable is long if it contains:

> **either** a long vowel or diphthong. When, however, either occurs at the end of a word and the following word does not begin with a

consonant, the long vowel or diphthong is shortened, μοῐ
ἔννĕπĕ;[1]

or   a short vowel followed by two consonants (ζ, ξ, ψ count as
double consonants but θ, φ, χ do not; breathings have no
metrical value). When a short vowel occurs before certain
combinations of two consonants where the second is λ, μ, ν, ρ,
the syllable may be long or short.

(iv)   In counting consonants after a final short vowel no account is taken of
word division, hence τεŏν μορον, τō cχημα.

(b) *Metrical feet, the hexameter, pentameter and iambic trimeter*

A metrical foot is made up of certain combinations of long and short
syllables. Of the numerous possibilities only the following need concern us:

Dactyl	— ∪ ∪	Iamb	∪ —
Spondee	— —	Trochee	— ∪

The metre used for epic and pastoral was the hexameter; the combination
of one hexameter and one pentameter forms an elegiac couplet (see below).

The **hexameter** (< ἕξ + μέτρον) consists of six feet. The first four can be
either dactyls or spondees, the fifth is almost always a dactyl and the sixth can
be either a spondee or trochee. This can be represented as follows:

$$— \smile\smile \mid — \smile\smile \mid — \smile\smile \mid — \smile\smile \mid — \smile\smile \mid — \smile$$

The upright lines show the syllable division between one foot and the next.
They do **not** necessarily coincide with word division. The first two lines of the
Odyssey (25.2.3) are scanned:

ᾱν-δρᾰ μοῐ | ἔν-νĕ-πĕ | Μοῦ-cᾰ ‖ πŏ- | λῡτ-ρŏ-πŏν | ōc μᾰ-λᾰ | πōλ-λᾰ

πλᾱγ-χθῄ ĕ- | πεῑ Τροῑ- | ῃc ‖ ῐ-ĕ | ρōν πτŏ-λῐ- | ēθ-ρŏν ĕ- | πēρ-cĕ.

It was felt that the rhythm of a hexameter would be impaired if there were a
break between words at the end of the third foot as a line so composed would
fall into two equal halves. To avoid this, there is always a break between
words (**caesura** *cut* or *break*) either (*a*) after the first syllable of the third foot
(as in the second line above), or (*b*) after the second syllable of the third foot
when a dactyl (as in the first line above), or (*c*) after the first syllable of the
fourth foot. The caesura is marked by two vertical lines, as in the above
examples.

A pentameter following a hexameter makes up an **elegiac couplet**, and is by
convention indented (see e.g. 12.3). It does not occur by itself. The elegiac
couplet was the metre of elegiac poetry, a broad literary genre which included
epigram and certain narrative, didactic, and occasional poetry. The penta-

---

[1] Epic correption (i.e. shortening). It occurs in hexameters and pentameters but is
completely avoided in iambic trimeters (on these terms see below).

meter consists of two halves of two and a half feet each; the division between the two is marked by a break between words (here called **diaeresis**, not **caesura** because it occurs at the end, not in the middle, of a metrical unit; it also is marked by two vertical lines). The metrical pattern of the **pentameter** is:

$$\_\,\underline{\smile\smile}\,|\,\_\,\underline{\smile\smile}\,|\,\_\,\|\,\_\,\smile\smile\,|\,\_\,\smile\smile\,|\,\underline{\smile}$$

Examples (from 12.3.1 and 3) are:

$ὃν\ λῐ\text{-}πὲν\ |\ οὐχ\ εὐ\text{-}\ |\ ρῶν\ \|\ ῆ\text{-}ψὲν\ ὃν\ |\ εὐ\text{-}ρὲ\ βρὄ\text{-}\ |\ χὸν$

$εἷς\ ἄ\text{-}γᾰ\text{-}\ |\ θὸς\ Κῐ\text{-}νῠ\text{-}\ |\ ρῆς\ \|\ καῖ\ Κῐ\text{-}νῠ\text{-}\ |\ ρῆς\ δὲ\ Κῐ\text{-}\ |\ λῐξ$

The **iambic trimeter** is the chief metre used for dialogue and speeches in drama because it was considered to come closest to the rhythm of normal speech. It consists of three pairs of iambs but more variation was allowed than in the hexameter or pentameter. Its basic form is:

$$\underline{\smile}\,\_\,\smile\,\_\,|\,\underline{\smile}\,\_\,\smile\,\_\,|\,\underline{\smile}\,\_\,\smile\,\underline{\smile}$$

A caesura occurs after either the fifth or seventh syllables in the above schema:

Examples (15.2.4) are:

$ᾰ\text{-}πᾶν\text{-}τὲς\ ἒς\text{-}\ |\ μὲν\ \|\ εἷς\ τὸ\ νοῦ\text{-}\ |\ θὲ\text{-}τεῖν\ cὄ\text{-}φοῖ$

$αῦ\text{-}τοῖ\ δ\ ᾰ\text{-}μᾱρ\text{-}\ |\ τᾰ\text{-}νὸν\text{-}\ τὲς\ \|\ οῦ\ |\ γῑγ\text{-}νῶς\text{-}\ κὄ\text{-}μὲν$

Included in the reading are poems in some of the many other metres used by Greek poets (an example occurs at 12.2.18, which is written in anapaests, $\smile\smile\_$).

Key to Exercises

Explanations and more literal interpretations are given in round brackets. Some words which have no specific equivalent in the Greek original but which must be supplied in English are enclosed in square brackets. Translations from Greek authors are generally as literal as possible and should not be taken as reflecting the style of the original.

References are given for longer prose passages, for whole poems and for extracts from verse of more than two lines. In these references Roman numerals refer to books (e.g. of Thucydides), Arabic to chapters and sections in prose works but in poetry to lines. Fragments of the Greek tragedians are given the number assigned to them in Nauck's edition (*Fragmenta Tragicorum Graecorum*). *A.P.* is the abbreviation of *Anthologia Palatina*, an enormous collection of shorter Greek poems whose present form dates from Byzantine times; it has a supplement entitled *App(endix) Plan(udea)*. In both the latter works the reference is first to book (Roman), then to poem number (Arabic).

Greek reading exercises

1.2

1 Aristotelēs (Aristotle), Aristophanēs, Dēmosthenēs, Hērodotos (Herodotus), Theokritos (Theocritus), Kallimachos (Callimachus), Pindaros (Pindar), Platōn (Plato).
2 akmē, anathema, analūsis, antithesis, asbestos, automaton, aphasiā, bathos, genesis, diagnōsis, dogma, drāma, zōnē, ēthos, ēchō, ideā, kīnēma, klīmax, kosmos, krisis, kōlon, metron, miasma, nektar, nemesis, orchēstrā, pathos, skēnē, stigma, hubris, hupothesis, chaos, charaktēr, psūchē.
3 (a) Agamemnōn, Achilleus (Achilles), Hektōr (Hector), Helenē (Helen), Odusseus (Odysseus), Patroklos (Patroclus), Pēnelopeia (Penelope) (*all are characters in Homer*).
   (b) Athēnai (Athens), Argos, Thēbai (Thebes), Korinthos (Corinth), Spartē (Sparta), Krētē (Crete), Rhodos (Rhodes), Samos (*all are places in Greece*).

2.2

(1) Odysseus has come from Troy, but Poseidon destroys his ship on (*or* at) Scheria. (2) Odysseus flees out of (*or* from) the sea and hides himself beneath [an] olive-tree near the shore. (3) In a dream Athena says to (*or* tells) the princess Nausicaa that she must (it is necessary [for her] to) wash the clothes on the shore. (4) At daybreak (*or* dawn) Nausicaa brings the clothes in [a] wagon from her house to the sea. (5) In the wagon there is also food for Nausicaa and her companions. (6) The girls quickly wash the clothes near the olive-tree where Odysseus is sleeping. (7) Then (*or* next) the girls throw the clothes on to the shore. (8) They wash themselves and eat the food which they have in the wagon. (9) While they are playing on the shore, Nausicaa throws [a] ball but the ball falls into [a] whirlpool. (10) The girls' shouts (the shouts of the girls) awaken Odysseus and frighten him. (11) Odysseus wonders where in the world he has come to, and suddenly creeps from the olive-tree. (12) He

257

frightens Naucisaa and her companions.   (13) But Nausicaa stays on the shore because Athena puts courage into her heart.   (14) Odysseus says to (*or* tells) Nausicaa that he has come from Ogygia.   (15) Nausicaa says to (*or* tells) her companions that they must (it is necessary [for them] to) provide Odysseus with food and clothes (provide food and clothes to Odysseus).   (16) She wishes (*or* is willing) to bring Odysseus to her father's house (the house of her father) but she fears (*or* is afraid of) the citizens' blame (the blame of the citizens) if they see her with Odysseus.   (17) So Nausicaa and the girls bring the clothes back to the house in the wagon, but Odysseus waits outside.

In 2, 4 and 9 the indefinite article, which does not exist in Greek, has to be supplied in the English.

Analysis of sentence 13 (according to the steps given in 2.2)

ἀλλ' ἡ Ναυσικάα ἐν τῇ ἀκτῇ ἀναμένει διότι ἡ ᾿Αθηνᾶ τὴν ἀνδρείᾱν εἰς τὴν καρδίᾱν εἰσβάλλει.

(*a*)   ἀλλ' (= ἀλλά) conjunction *but*; ἡ feminine nominative singular of the definite article (2.1/2); Ναυσικάα can be either nominative or vocative singular but, as ἡ precedes, it must be the former (the voc. would normally be preceded by ὦ (2.1/3), **never** by the article)—note that the article **must** agree in number, gender and case with the noun it qualifies (2.1/2 note 1; cf. τῇ ἀκτῇ, ἡ ᾿Αθηνᾶ, τὴν ἀνδρείᾱν, τὴν καρδίᾱν); ἐν preposition governing the dative *in*, *on*, *among*, and we would expect the following words to be in this case, which they are: τῇ ἀκτῇ dative singular of ἡ ἀκτή *the shore*; ἀναμένει 3rd person singular present indicative active of ἀναμένω *wait*, *stay* (the corresponding form of λύω would be λύει); διότι conjunction *because*; ἡ ᾿Αθηνᾶ nominative singular (the same reasoning applies as for ἡ Ναυσικάα); τὴν ἀνδρείᾱν accusative singular of ἡ ἀνδρείᾱ lit. *the courage*; εἰς preposition governing the accusative *to*, *into*, and we would expect the following words to be in this case, which they are: τὴν καρδίᾱν accusative singular of ἡ καρδίᾱ *the heart*; εἰσβάλλει 3rd person present indicative active of εἰσβάλλω *throw into*, *put into*.

(*b*)   There are two finite verbs, ἀναμένει and εἰσβάλλει; therefore we have two clauses.

(*c*)   Because ἀλλ'(ά) stands as first word it must link this sentence with the previous one. As we have two clauses and διότι comes after the first finite verb, this conjunction must introduce the second clause.

(*d*)   In the first clause ἡ Ναυσικάα is nominative and therefore must be the subject of ἀναμένει (we note that the verb agrees with ἡ Ναυσικάα in the way prescribed at the beginning of 2.1/4). ἐν τῇ ἀκτῇ *on the shore* (*on* seems more appropriate with *shore* than *in* or *among*) must be an adverbial phrase qualifying the verb. The clause therefore means *but Nausicaa* (the definite article can be used with proper names in Greek (2.1/2 note 1(iii)), but is never so employed in English) *stays* (or *waits*) *on the shore*. In the second clause ἡ ᾿Αθηνᾶ, which is nominative, must be the subject of εἰσβάλλει (note the agreement as in the previous clause). τὴν ἀνδρείᾱν is accusative and is **not** preceded by a preposition; therefore it must be the object of the verb as it can have no other grammatical function in the clause. We may translate *because Athena throws courage* (the definite article is not to be translated—2.1/2 note 1(i)) *into*; the other meaning of εἰσβάλλω, *invade*, makes no sense in this context. εἰς τὴν καρδίᾱν *into the heart* must be an adverbial phrase qualifying the verb but we have one too many *in/into*—the problem is solved by reference to the note on (7) and we can translate *because Athena throws courage into the heart* (*to*, the other meaning of εἰς, does not seem appropriate here).

(*e*)   The conjunction διότι shows that the second clause gives the reason for the first and we can put both together as *but Nausicaa stays on the shore because Athena throws courage into the heart*. English idiom requires that we specify whose heart is involved (obviously Nausicaa's, as otherwise the reason introduced by διότι would have no point—on this use of the Greek definite article see note on (1)). Also *put* seems more in accordance with English idiom than *throw* (all possible translations of some words cannot be given in either vocabularies or dictionaries). We now have: *But Nausicaa stays on the shore because Athena puts courage into her heart.*

3.2

(1) Millionaires (the very rich) are not good.   (2) A large city is [a] large desert (*or* wilderness).   (3) Poverty stimulates skills (*i.e.* necessity is the mother of invention).   (4) [A] corpse does not bite (*i.e.* dead men tell no tales).   (5) (*i*) Many [are] friends of [the] table, not of truth. (*ii*) Good fortune has many friends ([is] many-friended). (*iii*) Man [is] [a] political animal. (*iv*) Death [is] immortal (*or* deathless). (*v*) Slaves have no leisure ([there is] not leisure to/for slaves). (*vi*) Without health life [is] no life (*or* unlivable). (*vii*) Flattery [is a] disease of friendship. (*viii*) [A] wicked man [is] long-lived.   (6) Fortune's great gifts involve (have) fear.   (7) Wicked friends bear wicked fruit.   (8) The sowing (procreation) of children is a self-inflicted (self-chosen) grief.   (9) Gifts persuade [the] gods.   (10) Neither [a] drinking-party without company nor wealth without virtue is pleasurable (*lit.* has pleasure).   (11) For [a] human being the unexamined life [is] not worth living.   (12) (*i*) A large number of (*lit.* many) frogs send messengers to the son of Cronos (*i.e.* Zeus) because they desire [a] monarch. (*ii*) The messengers say to the son of Cronos on behalf of the frogs, "Just son of Cronos, you are master of the gods. Are you willing to provide the frogs with [a] master?" (*lit.* provide [a] master to the frogs). (*iii*) The son of Cronos is very surprised and hurls [a] large log into the frogs' marsh. (*iv*) The log frightens the frogs and they quickly run away, but they begin to be suspicious, since the log does not move (*lit.* is motionless). (*v*) Later they step on to the log without fear and say "Stranger, are you [a] god or [a] human being or [an] animal?" (*vi*) Since it says nothing at all, they consider that it is despicable that they have such a master and they send messengers again to the son of Cronos about [a] new monarch. (*vii*) The messengers say to the son of Cronos, "Master, you must (it is necessary [for you] to) send the frogs (to the frogs) another monarch since the first is motionless and idle." (*viii*) The master of the gods is angry with the frogs and sends [a] great hydra. (*ix*) The hydra is pitiless and eats the frogs. (*x*) The fable makes [it] clear that one (*or* we) must (it is necessary [for one/us] to) bear (*i.e.* put up with) idle masters since active masters often bear (*i.e.* bring) hardships.

Analysis of sentence 10 (according to the steps given in 2.2)

οὔτε cυμπόcιον χωρὶc ὁμῑλίᾱc οὔτε πλοῦτος χωρὶc ἀρετῆc ἡδονὴν ἔχει.

(*a*) οὔτε . . . οὔτε conjunctions *neither . . . nor*; cυμπόcιον, which is neuter, could be either nominative or accusative singular (the vocative is virtually ruled out by the meaning of the word, *drinking-party*); χωρίc preposition governing the genitive *without*; ὁμῑλίᾱc could be either genitive singular or accusative plural of ὁμῑλίᾱ *company, companionship*, but as it is preceded by a preposition governing the genitive it must be the former; πλοῦτος nominative singular *wealth*; χωρίc as before; ἀρετῆc genitive singular of ἀρετή *courage, excellence, virtue*; ἡδονήν accusative singular of ἡδονή *pleasure*; ἔχει 3rd person singular present indicative active of ἔχω *have*.

(*b*) and (*c*) The one finite verb, ἔχει, indicates that we have only one clause.

(*d*) and (*e*) οὔτε . . . οὔτε (like *neither . . . nor* in English) join elements of equal grammatical weight. Therefore, since πλοῦτος is nominative, cυμπόciον is also nominative, and both are the subject of ἔχει (the verb is singular just as it would be in a similar construction in English, e.g. *neither my wife nor my dog was waiting for me*). As the accusative ἡδονήν is not preceded by a preposition it must be the object of ἔχει. We may now translate: *neither drinking-party without company nor wealth without virtue has pleasure* (of the possible meanings of ἀρετή *courage* and *excellence* are not appropriate as a combination of either with wealth would hardly seem to produce pleasure). English, however, would normally put the indefinite article (which does not exist in Greek) before *drinking-party*. Also *is pleasurable* or *is enjoyable* would be more idiomatic than *has pleasure*. Our final version then could be: *neither a drinking-party without company nor wealth without virtue is pleasurable*.

4.2

(1) Pleasures [are] mortal, virtues immortal. (2) The beggar did not have bread, and was buying cheese. (3) Praise [is the] reward of virtue, and (*or* but) censure of wickedness. (4) [The] Egyptians [are] clever at contriving ways and means. (5) Necessity [is] law for slaves, but law [is] necessity for free men. (6) Once long ago [the] Milesians were brave. (7) [An] eagle does not hunt flies. (8) (*i*) You are spitting into [the] sky. (*ii*) You are plaiting [a] rope out of sand. (*iii*) You are sowing [the] sea. (*iv*) You are teaching [a] horse to run on to [a] plain. (*v*) You have come after [the] feast. (*vi*) You are whipping [a] corpse. (*vii*) You are shearing [an] ass. (*viii*) You are singing the victory-song before the victory. (*ix*) You are kicking against [the] pricks (*i.e.* of a goad). (*x*) You are bringing the war-engines after the war. (9) Croesus, the Lydian king (king of the Lydians), wanted to destroy the Persian empire (empire of the Persians). For, according to the Delphic oracle (*lit.* oracle at Delphi), he was destined to put an end to a mighty empire. But finally he put an end to his own empire, but not that (*lit.* the [empire]) of the Persians. After the Persians' victory Cyrus, the Persian king (*lit.* king of the Persians), made Croesus go up on to [a] great pyre, and Croesus began to consider the words of Solon the Athenian: no-one of men [is, *i.e.* can be considered] happy before his death. So he quietly awaited his death. But because Croesus was both pious and good, Cyrus ordered his soldiers to bring him down from the pyre and spoke as follows, "Croesus, who among (*lit.* of) men persuaded you to make an expedition [as an] enemy instead of [as a] friend against my land?" But Croesus said, "Cyrus, I (*lit.* I on the one hand) made an expedition against you, but the god (*lit.* but on the other hand the god) at Delphi persuaded me to make the expedition. For I am not foolish nor do I wish to have war instead of peace. For in peace-time the young men bury the old, but in war-time the old [bury] the young. But this was the god's pleasure (*lit.* this thing was dear to the gods)." So Cyrus set him free and made [him] sit nearby. And Croesus spoke once more, "Cyrus, what are your soldiers doing?" "They are plundering your city," said Cyrus, "and carrying off your wealth." "They are not plundering my city," said Croesus, "nor my wealth. For I have nothing (*lit.* nothing is to me). [It is] **you** [whom] they are plundering." After this he (*i.e.* Croesus) was dear to him; for Cyrus respected his wisdom. (Based on Herodotus i. 86–88).

Analysis of sentence 5 (according to the steps given in 2.2)

τοῖς μὲν δούλοις ἡ ἀνάγκη νόμος, τοῖς δὲ ἐλευθέροις ἀνθρώποις ὁ νόμος ἀνάγκη.

(*a*) μὲν . . . δέ *on the one hand . . . and/but on the other hand* indicate that we have two balanced grammatical elements (4.1/3); τοῖς . . . δούλοις dative plural *to/for the slaves* (on the meaning of the dative with living things see 2.1/3*e*); ἡ ἀνάγκη nominative singular *the necessity* but to be translated *necessity* in view of 2.1/2 note 1(i); νόμος nominative singular *law*; τοῖς ... ἐλευθέροις ἀνθρώποις dative plural *to/for the free men*; ὁ νόμος nominative singular *the law*; ἀνάγκη nominative singular *necessity*.

(*b*)   There are no finite verbs! However, even without the hint given in the note on (1), we learn from 3.1/3*b* and 3.1/6 that εἰμί is often omitted in clauses where something is predicated of something else. The fact that in each half of the sentence we have two nominatives suggests that this is what we have here. Since we have two balanced elements the appropriate part of εἰμί (viz ἐστί) is to be supplied in each. Therefore we have two clauses.

(*c*)   The comma after νόμος shows the division between clauses.

(*d*)   In τοῖς ... νόμος the definite article with ἀνάγκη shows that this is the subject; the absence of the definite article with νόμος shows that it is the predicate. The basic meaning (leaving aside μέν) is therefore *for the slaves* (the other meaning of the dative, *to*, is not appropriate) *necessity is law*. In τοῖς ... ἀνάγκη we realise that ὁ νόμος must be translated by *law* and not *the law* because it is parallel with ἀνάγκη and must mean the abstract concept of law, not a particular law. We then have *for the free men law is necessity*.

(*e*)   We can translate μέν ... δέ by *but* with the second clause. However, when we put both halves together we realise that we are dealing with a proverb and that the general class of slaves and the general class of free men are meant. We must, therefore, omit the definite article with each in English (2.1/2 note 1(ii)), and we have: *Necessity is law for slaves, but law is necessity for free men.*

5.2

(1) Time educates the wise. (2) Silence has many fine [things] (*i.e.* silence is golden). (3) Human beings have many troubles, strangers (*lit.* there are many troubles to human beings). (4) [One] must not (it is not necessary to) keep former evils in mind (*lit.* bear ... in memory). (5) (*i*) Quietness (*or* peace and quiet) [is] a fine [thing]. (*ii*) Fine [things] [are] difficult. (*iii*) Moderation [is] best. (*iv*) [A] big book [is] [a] big evil. (*v*) The property (*lit.* the [things]) of friends [is] shared. (*vi*) Hermes [is] shared. (*vii*) [A] small evil [is] [a] big blessing. (*viii*) Different [things] [are] beautiful to different [people] (*i.e.* some people like one thing, others another). (*ix*) The tongue [is] [the] cause of (*or* responsible for) many troubles. (*x*) Doing [is] difficult, giving the order (*sc.* to do it) [is] easy. (*xi*) Getting drunk (*or* drunkenness) [is] [a] bad remedy for (*i.e.* way to get rid of) woe. (*xii*) One learns by experience (*lit.* sufferings [are] lessons). (*xiii*) [A] bad egg comes from (*lit.* [is] of) [a] bad crow. (*xiv*) Trust the land, mistrust the sea (*lit.* [the] land [is] [a] trustworthy [thing], [the] sea [an] untrustworthy [thing]). (*xv*) Even an ant can get angry (*lit.* [there is] bile (anger) even in [an] ant). 6 (*i*) One must find a wife amongst one's own class (*lit.* it is necessary [*sc.* for a person] to marry from among those who are similar). (*ii*) [A] fool speaks foolish [things]. (*iii*) You have your feet out of trouble (*lit.* foot outside mud). (*iv*) [The] pot boils, friendship lives. (*v*) You are shaving (*or* bearding) [a] lion. (*vi*) You are weeping on [your] step-mother's tomb (*i.e.* being hypocritical). (7) Alas, alas, greatness (*lit.* great things) also suffers great evils. (8) [The] roughness of [the] road tests [the] serviceability of [the] ass. (9) Man is only (*or* nothing but) breath and shadow. (10) Fortune guides art, not art fortune. (11) Money [is] responsible for many evils for men. (12) Woman, silence is becoming (*lit.* brings decoration) for women. (13) Even for [an] old man, [it is] [a] fine [thing] to learn wisdom (*lit.* wise things). (14) The Athenians sent Thucydides the [son] of

Olorus to the general of those in Thrace. (15) One should seek neither companionship (*or* company) from [a] corpse nor [a] favour from [a] miser. (16) Victory is sufficient for the free. (17) Even among rustics there is love of culture. (18) The wolf changes his coat (*lit.* hair), not his mind. (19) Money finds friends for men. (20) [A] mob [is] [a] poor judge of [a] fine matter. (21) To some of the Egyptians, therefore, crocodiles are sacred, to others [they are] not, but they treat [them] as enemies. Those around Thebes and [those around] the swamp of Moeris strongly believe that they are (*lit.* them to be) sacred. Both groups keep (*or* rear) one crocodile and train [it], and put rings made of glass in its ears and anklets round its front feet, and provide special food and offerings. So while the crocodiles are alive, they are treated very well, and after their death the Egyptians embalm them and bury them in sacred tombs. But those around the city [of] Elephantine actually eat them; for they do not consider [them] to be sacred. (Adapted from Herodotus ii.69.)

6.2

From this point on the definite and indefinite articles which must be supplied for translation are no longer bracketed.

(1) (*i*) The guards guarded the Persians (φυλάττω). (*ii*) Did you hide the golden horse? (κρύπτω). (*iii*) The Athenians and the Spartans joined in an expedition (cυcτρατεύω). (*iv*) He wrote many things on the rock (ἐγγράφω). (*v*) The gods will do many great things (πρᾱ́ττω). (*vi*) Socrates taught us (διδάcκω). (*vii*) They harmed the house of Pericles (βλάπτω). (*viii*) We fought a sea-battle in the harbour (ναυμαχέω). (2) Bronze is the mirror of form (i.e. of the body), wine of the mind. (3) Hand washes hand, fingers [wash] fingers. (4) Speech is silver, silence is golden. (5) O God, how mortals have no escape from evils [which are] innate or (*or* and) sent by the gods! (*lit.* how there is not to mortals [an] escape . . .). (6) (*i*) You are writing on (*lit.* into) water. (*ii*) You are building on (*lit.* into) sand. (*iii*) [You are bringing] an owl to Athens (*cf.* coals to Newcastle).(*iv*) You are measuring the waves. (*v*) You are looking for bird's milk. (*vi*) You are teaching iron to float (*lit.* sail). (*vii*) You are lending light to the sun. (*viii*) You are pouring wine for frogs. (*ix*) You are beating the air. (*x*) You are making an elephant out of a fly (*i.e.* a mountain out of a molehill). (7) (*i*) The mind is a great check on (*lit.* bit of) the soul. (*ii*) The Greeks [are] always children, an old Greek does not exist. (*iii*) For a mother (*or* for mothers) children are the anchors of [her] life. (*iv*) Lions at home, but foxes (*i.e.* cowards) in battle. (*v*) The mind sees and the mind hears. (*vi*) The arms (*lit.* hands) of tyrants [are] long. (*vii*) Ares (War) [is] a friend of falsehood (*lit.* friendly to false things). (*viii*) Athens [is] the Greece of Greece. (*ix*) You are comparing a bee with a cicada. (*x*) A daughter [is] a difficult possession. (8) The wind [kindles] fire, intimacy kindles love. (9) According to Socrates no-one errs willingly. (10) The wise man should not think after (*i.e.* repent) but before (*lit.* it is necessary for the wise man not to . . .). (11) The Athenian ambassadors withdrew to the army, but the generals built a wall around the Melians. Later, a small garrison of the allies remained there and continued to besiege (*lit.* was besieging) the place, while the rest of the soldiers withdrew both by land and by sea. Afterwards the Melians pulled down the Athenians' blockading wall, since not many of the guards were present. But later the Athenians sent out another army from Athens, and they now vigorously prosecuted the siege. There was treachery (*or* treachery broke out) among the Melians, and they capitulated to the Athenians. And they (*i.e.* the Athenians) killed the men among (*lit.* of) the Melians, and enslaved the women and children. And later they sent out many settlers and colonised the place. (Adapted from Thucydides v.114–116.)

7.2

(1) The proverb bids us not to move the immovable (*lit*. unmovable [things]) (2) [It is] altogether not easy to find what is right (*or* justice). (3) Ischomachus said, "Socrates, in winter a house should be well exposed to the sun, but in summer well-shaded." (4) We do not have either weapons or horses (*or* we have neither weapons nor horses). (5) No falsehood spreads for long (a length of time). (6) So for one day the Athenians encamped there. But on the following day Alcibiades called an assembly and ordered them to fight both at sea, on land and against the fortifications. "For," he said, "we have no money, whereas the enemy have plenty." (7) All human beings die (*lit*. no-one of human beings does not die). (8) (*i*) One swallow does not make a spring. (*ii*) Old men [are] children for a second time. (*iii*) You see three things in two. (*iv*) One man [is] no man. (*v*) One day does not make [a man] wise. (*vi*) The tongue leads many [people] to destruction. (*vii*) In war it is not possible to make a mistake twice. (*viii*) It is possible to recognise a lion from his claw-marks (*i.e.* to judge a person from a characteristic mark). (9) Cyrus marched forth three stages (*or* days' march) through Lydia, [a distance of] twenty-two parasangs, to the river Maeander. Its breadth was two plethra. (10) The world [is] a stage, life an appearance: you come, you see, you depart. (11) Someone said to Socrates, "Megacles speaks ill of you." And he replied, "Yes, for he does not know how (*lit*. has not learnt) to speak well." (12) Callicratidas held the right wing of the Peloponnesians. His steersman, Hermon, said, "It is a good [idea] to retreat (*lit*. sail away); for the Athenian triremes are very strong." But Callicratidas said, "It is shameful to flee." The triremes fought [for] a long time, at first in close order, and then scattered. When Callicratidas fell overboard into the sea and was drowned (*lit*. died) and Protomachus the Athenian and his men (*lit*. those with him) defeated the left wing with [their] right wing, thereupon the Peloponnesians fled (*lit*. there was a flight of . . .) to Chios and Phocaea, while the Athenians sailed back to Arginousae. And so of the Athenians the Spartans sank 25 triremes, whereas of the Peloponnesians the Athenians [sank] nine Laconian [triremes], and of their allies as well about 60. (Adapted from Xenophon *Hellenica* i. 6.32.) (13) For, when Simon came to my house at night, he forced (*lit*. knocked out) the doors and entered the women's apartments, where my sister and nieces were. At first the men in the house ordered him to go away, but he refused. Then they forcibly pushed him out. But he discovered where we were dining and did a thing most extraordinary and incredible. He called me out from inside, and as soon as I had come out, he immediately attempted to strike me; and when I pushed him away, he began to pelt me with stones (*or* throw stones at me). Although he missed me, he hit Aristocritus with a stone and gashed his forehead. (Adapted from Lysias *Against Simon* 6–8.)

8.2

(1) God and Nature do nothing without reason. (2) [It is] not easy to change a wicked nature. (3) Wicked slander wipes out whole cities. (4) Jesus Christ, son of God, Saviour (*the symbol is the fish,* ἰχθύς *being an acronym of the phrase*). (5) Gold does not tarnish (*lit*. is not stained). (6) Do you think that others will save Greece, but you will run away? (7) As a result of looking at [someone] people fall in love. (8) The possession of virtue alone is secure. (9) Alas, alas, how true the old saying is: we old men are nothing but (no other thing except) noise and [outward] appearance; we creep along [as] copies of dreams; there is no sense in [us] but we think we are sane. (Euripides, fragment 25.) (10) An elephant does not bite a mouse. (11) For most people the search for truth [is pursued] without taking pains, and they turn rather to

what is ready to hand. (12) The Lacedaemonians sent a herald and carried across the corpses (*or* had the corpses carried across). (13) It was wonder which made men begin to pursue philosophy both now and originally (*lit.* because of the fact of wondering men both now and at first began . . .). (14) The mountain was in labour, and then gave birth to a mouse. (15) Hunger is (*lit.* becomes) the teacher of many [things.] (16) The Scythians do not wash with (*or* in) water. (17) (*i*) In the beginning God made the heaven and the earth. And the earth was invisible and unformed, and darkness [was] upon the abyss, and the spirit of God moved upon the water. And God said "Let there be (*lit.* be born) light." And there was light (*lit.* light came into being). And God saw that the light was beautiful. And God made a division between the light and the darkness. And God called the light day and the darkness he called night. (*Genesis* 1.1–5.) (*ii*) I turned about and I saw beneath the sun that the race [is] not to the nimble, nor war to the strong, nor bread to the wise, nor wealth to the intelligent. (*Ecclesiastes* 9.11.) (18) Zenothemis contrived a wicked crime in collaboration with Hegestratus. They went around borrowing (*lit.* were borrowing) money in Syracuse. When they got the money, they used to send it home to Marseilles, and they loaded (*lit.* brought into) nothing on board (*lit.* into) the ship. Since the contract stipulated repayment of (*lit.* was to repay) the money after the arrival in port of the ship, they plotted to sink the ship; for they wished to defraud their creditors. Accordingly, when they were two or three days out from land (*lit.* had sailed away a voyage of . . . days), Hegestratus began to cut through the bottom of the ship during the night, while Zenothemis passed the time on deck (*lit.* above) with the other passengers. But when a noise was heard (*lit.* happened), those on the ship perceived that some mischief was taking place down below, and went to the rescue. As Hegestratus was being caught and assumed that he would be badly treated, he took to his heels (*lit.* fled) and jumped into the sea. In this way then, as he deserved, a bad man, he came to a bad end (*lit.* he died badly). ([?Demosthenes] *Against Zenothemis* 4–6, slightly adapted.)

9.2

(1) Death [is] beautiful [for those] to whom life brings humiliation. (2) The wise man carries round his substance within (*lit.* in) himself. (3) Mighty in war [was] Timocritus, whose tomb this [is]; Ares spares not the brave, but the cowardly. (*A.P.* vii. 160.) (4) Cleon said that not he himself but that man was a general. (5) The same [people] [say] the same [remarks] about the same [subject] to the same [people]. (6) You are telling me my [own] dream (*i.e.*, nothing I don't already know). (7) Then that man said, "Well, if there is need of anything else (*lit.* another thing) in addition to what (*lit.* these things which) Xenophon says, it is possible to do it immediately." After this Xenophon spoke as follows: "[It is] clear that we must march where we will have supplies; and I hear that there are fine villages which are twenty stades away." (Xenophon *Anabasis* iii.2.33–34.) (8) A friend is another self (*or* alter ego). (9) Pythagoras first named philosophy and himself a philosopher. (10) [We] must compare them with each other; for thus we will consider if they will differ from each other. (11) The Greeks mistrust each other (*lit.* are mistrustful towards themselves). (12) After dinner Cyrus asked, "Tigranes, where then is that man who used to hunt with us? You seemed to me to admire him very much". "My father here put him to death," he said. "For he said that he was corrupting me. And yet, Cyrus, he was a fine man, for even when he was about to die, he summoned me and said, 'Tigranes, you must not be angry because your father is putting me to death; for he does this not because of malice, but because of ignorance. And what (*lit.* which things) men do wrong through ignorance, I believe [they do] this against their will'." (Xenophon *Cyropaedia*, iii.1.38, adapted). (13) Demosthenes, who saw that the Lacedaemonians

intended to attack by land and by sea (*lit.* both with ships and with infantry), began to make his own preparations (*lit.* make preparations himself also), and hauled up under the fortification the triremes which remained to him, and armed the sailors from them with shields of poor quality and mostly made of osier; for it was impossible to procure arms in [this] deserted place, and even these (*sc.* which they had) they got from a thirty-oared pirate-ship and a pinnace belonging to (*lit.* of) [some] Messenians, who were there. Of these Messenians there were about forty hoplites. Accordingly, he posted the majority of his own men at the strong points of the place facing the mainland, while (*lit.* and) he himself picked out sixty hoplites and a few archers and began to go outside the wall (*sc.* of the fortification) towards the sea, [to the point] where he particularly expected that the enemy (*lit.* those men) would attempt to land. So he posted his hoplites at this point right beside the sea (*lit.* towards the sea itself). (Thucydides iv.9, adapted.)

10.2

(1) A fat belly does not generate a subtle mind. (2) How sweet [it is] to look at the sea from the land. (3) Time will explain everything to posterity (*lit.* those [who come] later). (4) Happiness is an activity of the soul. (5) O Menander and life, which one of you then imitated which? (6) Who knows if life is death, and down below death is considered life? (7) Life [is] short, art long (*i.e.* the art of medicine is extensive and requires a long time to master), opportunity fleeting (*lit.* swift), experiment perilous, and judgement difficult. (8) Wickedness [is] quick, virtue slow. (9) Where a man fares well, there [is his] native-land. (10) Whoever of mortals wishes to arrive at (*lit.* go/come into) hateful old age, does not reckon well; for a long life begets countless woes. (11) How sweet [it is] for slaves to get decent masters and for masters [to get] a well-disposed slave in [their] house. (12) Everything [is] burdensome except to rule over the gods. For no-one is free except Zeus. (13) Ignorant [people] are carried along in life as if on the high sea and in darkness. (14) The woman said, "My husband's virtue is sufficient adornment for me." (15) Where a man has a pain, there he applies (*lit.* has) his mind too. (16) (*i*) I hate a drinking-companion who remembers (*lit.* a mindful drinking-companion). (*ii*) Hostile [is] the eye of neighbours. (*iii*) Even a sheep bites an unlucky man. (*iv*) An unskilled man is a slave of (*lit.* to) everyone. (*v*) War [is] sweet to the inexperienced. (*vi*) Time decides everything (*lit.* everything is decided by time). (*vii*) Bright in darkness, but useless in daylight. (*viii*) Hands wash each other. (*ix*) Under every stone sleeps a scorpion. (*x*) Everything [is] easy for God (*or* a god). (*xi*) Every hedgehog [is] prickly. (*xii*) The whole of time cannot whiten the man (*lit.* this [man]) whom Fate paints (*lit.* will paint) black. (17) (*i*) Diogenes was once begging [alms] from a statue. [When he was] asked why he was doing this, he said, "I am practising failure (*lit.* to fail to obtain)." (*ii*) [When he was] asked what kind of wine he liked to drink (*lit.* drank gladly), he said, "Someone else's." (*iii*) He was begging [alms] from a miser. When he hesitated (*lit.* was slow), Diogenes said, "Fellow, I'm begging [alms] from you for food, not for burial." (*iv*) [When he was] asked where he was from, he said, "[I am] a citizen of the world." (*v*) When someone said that life was bad, he said, "Not life, but a bad life."

10.3

For, gentlemen of Athens, I have this reputation for no other reason (*lit.* on account of nothing else) than a certain wisdom. What sort of wisdom [do I say] this [is]? [Just that] which is perhaps human wisdom. For in reality I am likely to be (*or* I am probably) wise in this wisdom. But these men, whom I was just now mentioning, are wise in a sort of superhuman wisdom, which I am unable to describe. For I, at any rate, do not understand it, and (*lit*. but) whoever says [that I do], is lying and speaking to arouse prejudice against me. I hope, men of Athens, that you will not interrupt me, even if I seem to you to be saying something extravagant (*lit*. big). For the story which I will tell is not mine, but I will refer [you] to someone who is worthy of credit. For I shall furnish you with the god of (*lit*. at) Delphi [as] witness of my [wisdom], [as to] whether it is actually some sort of wisdom and of what sort it is. Chaerephon was familiar to you, I think. He was a comrade of mine from youth and a partisan of the democracy. And it is well-known to you what sort [of a person] Chaerephon was, how impetuous in all respects. As a matter of fact, he actually went to Delphi once and dared to ask the oracle if anyone was wiser than I. The Pythian [priestess] answered that no-one was wiser. (Plato *Apology* 20d–21a, slightly adapted.)

11.2

From this point on the relevant part of the verb to be *which must be supplied for translation is not normally bracketed.*

(1) Tyranny is the mother of injustice. (2) The dice of Zeus always fall luckily (*lit.* well). (3) There is some degree (*lit.* measure) of pleasure even in troubles. (4) And the story is not mine, but [comes] from my mother, that heaven and earth were one shape; but when they were separated apart from each other, they brought forth everything and sent up to the light trees, winged creatures, wild beasts and [the creatures] which the sea nourishes and the race of men. (Euripides, fragment 484.) (5) Concealment (*lit.* the act of hiding) is wicked and not the mark of a well-born man. (6) Someone said to Socrates, "The Athenians condemned you to death," and he said, "And Nature [is condemning] them [to death]." (7) The wagon pulls the ox. (8) (*i*) An old woman is dancing. (*ii*) You are graciously giving a mirror to a blind man. (*iii*) You are hunting the wind with a net. (*iv*) You are throwing stones at the sun (*lit.* pelting the sun with stones). (*v*) The/a tortoise is calling the oxen slow-footed. (*vi*) You are striking a peg with a sponge. (*vii*) You knocked out a peg with a peg (*i.e.* in solving one problem you created another). (*viii*) You are blocking up (*i.e.* repairing) the chamber-pot with a sandal. (*ix*) You are driving out wine with wine. (*x*) You yourself are striking your own door with a stone. (9) For, for all mankind, not only for us, either straightaway or in [the course of] time, God trips up [one's] life, and no-one is happy throughout (*or* forever). (Euripides, fragment 273.) (10) For none of these things will distress me. But if you do not do this (*lit.* these things), you will inflict (*lit.* throw) grief upon all the Argives (*i.e.* Greeks). For if we do not get this man's bow (*lit.* this man's bow will not be taken), it is not possible for you to ravage the land of Dardanus. (Sophocles *Philoctetes* 66–69.) (11) Thus the venture (*lit.* things) of the Greeks came to naught (*lit.* was destroyed). And out of many a few made their way through Libya to Cyrene and were saved, but most were killed. Egypt again came (*lit.* became) under the control of the King [of Persia], except Amyrtaeus, the king in the marshes. They (*i.e.* the Persians) were unable to capture him both because of the extent of the marsh and at the same time [because] the marsh-people are particularly warlike. Inaros the Libyan king (*lit.* king of the Libyans), who had conducted (*lit.* done) the whole Egyptian venture (*lit.* everything with respect to Egypt), was captured by treachery and impaled. Fifty triremes from Athens and the rest of the confederacy sailed [as a] relieving [force] to Egypt and put in at the Mendesian arm [of the Nile]. But foot-soldiers attacked them from the land and a fleet of Phoenicans from the sea and

destroyed most of the ships. So ended the great expedition (*lit.* the [things] with respect to the great expedition) of the Athenians and their allies against (*lit.* into) Egypt. (Thucydides i.110, adapted.)   (12) When we had transferred to the other ship, we began to drink. It is clear that Herodes disembarked from the ship and did not re-embark (*lit.* go on board again). I did not disembark at all from the ship that night. On the following day, when the man was not to be seen, he was looked for in no way more [vigorously] by the others than by me (*i.e.* I looked for him as vigorously as anyone); and if it (his disappearance) seemed serious to any of the others, [it did so] equally to me (*i.e.* if anyone considered it a serious matter, I did). Not only (*lit.* both) was I responsible for a messenger being sent to Mytilene, but (*lit.* and), since no-one else was willing to go, either of those on (*lit.* from) the ship or of the companions of Herodes himself, I was prepared to send my own servant. But when the man did not appear either in Mytilene or anywhere else, and the wind was fair (*lit.* sailing [time] was coming into being) for us and all the other ships were putting out to sea, I too departed. (Antiphon *Murder of Herodes* 23–24, slightly adapted.)

12.2

Where participial phrases have been expanded into subordinate clauses (e.g. in 1–5; see 12.1/2a) the words added in English have not been enclosed in square brackets.

(1) The man who runs away will also fight again (*or* lives to fight another day).   (2) When a bear is present (*or* around) one need not look for tracks.   (3) If you love yourself too much you will not have a friend.   (4) Although he does not feed himself, he feeds his dogs.   (5) The person who does not marry has no troubles.   (6) In trying to flee (*lit.* fleeing) the smoke you fell into the fire.   (7) A man who is running away does not wait for the sound of the lyre.   (8) It is said that dogs burnt just once are afraid of fire (*lit.* dogs . . . are said to fear . . .).   (9) For I have come to bury Caesar, not to praise [him].   (10) No-one who is hungry sings sweet songs (*lit.* beautiful things).   (11) Am I a bumpkin (*lit.* boorish) if I call a trough a trough?   (12) The man who has been bitten by a serpent fears even a little rope.   (13) The man who is illiterate (*lit.* inexperienced in letters) sees nothing although he has sight (*lit.* does not see [although] seeing).   (14) It is difficult to speak to [one's] belly, since it does not have ears.   (15) Prometheus: "You behold [this] spectacle, [me] this friend of Zeus, with what woes I am bent by him". Ocean: "I see, Prometheus, and I wish to give you the best advice (*lit.* advise the best things to you), subtle (*or* ingenious) as you are (*lit.* though being)." (Aeschylus *Prometheus Bound* 304ff.)   (16) From there Cyrus marched out though Lycaonia five stages, [a distance of] thirty parasangs, and he allowed the Greeks to plunder this country on the grounds that it was hostile.   (17) Once when turning a book of Hesiod beneath my hands I suddenly saw Pyrrha approaching; and throwing the book to the ground with my hand I shouted this, "Why do you give me trouble, old Hesiod?" (*A.P.* ix.161)   (18) Child of Phoenician-born Europa and great Zeus, ruling over Crete of a hundred cities, I have come leaving sacred (*lit.* very holy) temples . . . And we have led a chaste life since I became a mystic of Idaean Zeus, and, having conducted feasts of raw flesh as a herdsman of night-roaming Zagreus and held up torches for the mountain-wandering mother with the Curetes, I was sanctified and called an initiate of Bacchus. (Euripides, fragment 472.)

12.3

(1) A man, finding [some] gold, left a noose; but the man who did not find the gold which he had left, fastened the noose (*i.e.* to hang himself) which he had found. (*A.P.*

ix. 44) (2) The Cyprian, seeing [the statue of] the Cyprian (*i.e.* of herself) in Cnidos, said, "Alas, alas, where did Praxiteles see me naked?" (*App. Plan.* 162) (3) All Cilicians are bad men; but among the Cilicians [there is] one good man, [viz] Cinyres, but even Cinyres is Cilician. (*A.P.* xi. 236) (4) Once Antiochus laid eyes on (*lit.* looked at) Lysimachus' cushion, and Lysimachus never again (*lit.* no longer) laid eyes on his cushion. (*A.P.* xi. 315) (5) Although he produced twenty sons, Eutychus the painter has no likeness even among (*lit.* from) his children (*i.e.* he has as little success in producing lifelike paintings as in fathering children from a faithless wife). (*A.P.* xi. 215) (6) You [with] the roses, you have a rosy charm. But what are you selling, yourself, or the roses, or both together? (*A.P.* v. 81) (7) As I was kissing Agathon, I checked my soul at [my] lips; for it had come, poor wretch, with the idea of crossing over. (*A.P.* v. 78) (8) I who laughed haughtily at Greece, I, Laïs, who kept the swarm of young lovers in [my] porch, [dedicate] [my] mirror to the Paphian; since such [as I am now] I do not wish to see myself, and such as I was formerly I am unable [to see myself]. (*A.P.* vi. 1) (9) Someone told [me], Heraclitus, of your death, and brought tears (*lit.* a tear) to me, and I remembered how often both of us laid the sun to rest in conversation. But you, I suppose, my friend from Halicarnassus, are ashes long, long ago. But your nightingales (*i.e.* poems) live on, upon which Hades, the ravisher of all things, shall not lay his hand. (Callimachus epigram 2.)

13.2

(1) [It] is a fine [thing] indeed to be master of one's belly and one's desire[s]. (2) Both common-sense and proper deliberation (*lit.* deliberating on what it is necessary [to do]) are accustomed to accompany old age. (3) This is bravery (*lit.* the brave thing), [that is to say] forethought. (4) Everywhere the land which feeds [you is your] native-land (5) Old age, you know, has a certain wisdom (*lit.* something wise) indeed with respect to deliberation (*or* planning), since indeed it has seen and experienced much (*lit.* as having seen and experienced many things). (6) O unfortunate virtue, you were [a mere] word then; yet I practised you as something real (*lit.* a fact, *i.e.* as though you really existed). But you were a slave to chance after all. (7) Oedipus, the son of Laius, is my father (*lit.* father for us), and Iocaste, the daughter of Menoeceus, bore me; and the Theban people call me Polyneices (Euripides *Phoenissae* 288–290). (8) There is no temple of Persuasion other than speech, and her altar is in the nature of man. (9) He who chases two hares catches neither. (10) Cyrus, inasmuch as he was a child and liked elegance and distinction, was pleased with his clothes. (11) Not even the gods fight against necessity. (12) Obedience to one's stomach is a necessary evil. (13) In escaping Charybdis you have fallen into (*lit.* in with) Scylla. (14) A hungry ass pays no heed to the cudgel. (15) No-one desires life as much as the man who is growing old. (16) Death alone of the gods does not desire gifts. (17) The man who does no wrong needs no law. (18) Sailors (*or* those who sail) are [only] four fingers away from death. (19) You have a need of spring since you have an old cloak (*i.e.* spring, and not winter, is the right season for the threadbare cloak you are wearing). (20) The Spartan [woman] Gorgo, asked by an Attic (*i.e.* Athenian) [woman], "Why do you Spartan [women] alone rule your men (*or* husbands)?" said, "Because we alone also give birth to [real] men." (21) In reply to a certain lad who was intending to attend his classes and enquired what he needed (*lit.* of what things there is a need to him), Antisthenes the philosopher said, "A new book and a new pencil and a new writing-tablet", stressing the nous. (*The pun on* καινοῦ *and* καὶ-νοῦ *is virtually untranslatable, although in American pronunciation it comes across in 'new' and 'nous'*.) (22) The black earth drinks, and the trees drink it (*i.e.* from it); the sea drinks the streams, the sun the

sea, and the moon the sun. Why do you fight with me, [my] friends (*or* comrades), when I myself wish to drink? (Anacreontea 19.)

13.3

(*i*) I was making my way from the Academy straight to the Lyceum along the [road] outside the wall, close under the wall (*lit.* beneath the wall) itself. When I came to (*lit.* was in the region of) the postern gate where the spring of Panops is, there I fell in with Hippothales, the [son] of Hieronymus, and Ctesippus of Paiania, and [some] other young men [who were] with them. Seeing me approach, Hippothales said, "Socrates, where are you going and where [have you come] from?" "From the Academy", said I, "on my way (*lit.* I'm making my way) straight to the Lyceum." "[Come] over **here**," said he, "straight to us. Aren't you going to come over (*lit.* do you not come near)? Yet it's worthwhile." "Where do you mean," I said, "and who are you to whom [I am to come]?" "Over here," he said, showing me right opposite (*lit.* in the [spot] right opposite) the wall a sort of enclosure and door. "We spend our time here," said he, "both we ourselves and a lot of other fine [fellows]." "And what **is** this [place] then, and how do you spend your time (*lit.* what is [your] manner of spending time)?" "A new wrestling-school," he said. "And we usually spend our time in discussions, in which we wish you to share." "That's very kind of you (*lit.* doing well indeed)," I said. "And who teaches here?" "Your own friend," said he, "and admirer, Miccus." "My goodness (*lit.* by Zeus)," I said, "he's not unimportant (*lit.* the man [is] not insignificant), he's a competent teacher." "Well then, do you want to follow [me]," he said, "and to see those who are here?" (Plato *Lysis* 203a–204a.)

(*ii*) *Eucleides.* Just [in] from the country, Terpsion, or [did you arrive] some time ago? *Terpsion.* Quite some time ago, I was looking for you in (*lit.* throughout) the agora and was surprised that I could not find [you]. *E.* [No you couldn't], for I was not in the city. *T.* Where [were you] then? *E.* As I was going down to [the] harbour I met Theaetetus being carried to Athens from the camp at (*lit.* from) Corinth. *T.* Alive or dead? *E.* Alive, but only just (*lit.* and very hardly). For he's in a bad way actually because of some wounds, but more [than that] the disease which [has broken out] in the army is afflicting him. *T.* You don't mean dysentery, do you? *E.* Yes, I do. *T.* What a man [this is who] you say is in danger. *E.* A real gentleman (*lit.* fine and good), Terpsion, and (*lit.* since), you know, just now I was listening to some [people] singing his praises (*lit.* praising him very much) in connection with the battle. *T.* And [that's] not at all strange. But how [is it that] he did not stay (*or* lodge) here in Megara? *E.* He was hurrying [to get] home. I asked him and advised him [*sc.* to stay], but he refused. In fact, as I escorted [him] I recalled with admiration how prophetically Socrates had spoken in particular about him (*lit.* I recalled and marvelled at Socrates how prophetically he had spoken both other things indeed and about this man). For I think that (*lit.* he seems to me to . . .), a little before his death, he (Socrates) met him when he was a lad, and after being with [him] and conversing [with him], greatly admired his character. (Plato *Theaetetus* 142a–c.)

14.2

The abbreviations P.S. (Primary sequence) and H.S. (Historic sequence) are used in defining the uses of the subjunctive/optative here.

(1) For there is a certain pleasure even in words, if (*lit.* whenever) they create a forgetfulness of [one's] existing troubles (*indefinite, P.S.*).   (2) How then am I, a [mere]

mortal (*lit.* being mortal), to fight against divine fortune (*or* fortune sent by the gods)? (*deliberative subjunctive*). (3) [It is] the mind [that one] must look at, the mind; what advantage [is there] in (*lit.* of) bodily beauty, if (*lit.* whenever) a person does not have a beautiful (*i.e.* noble) mind? (*indefinite, P.S.*). (4) Whoever is shipwrecked twice, blames Poseidon without reason (*i.e.* he should have taken Poseidon's hint the first time) (*indefinite, P.S.*). (5) Socrates said that most men live in order that they may eat, whereas he himself ate in order that he might live (*purpose, subjunctive retained in H.S.*). (6) Let us eat and drink; for tomorrow we die (*jussive subjunctive*). (7) God plants (*lit.* produces) a fault (*lit.* blame) in mortals whenever he wishes to ruin a family completely (*indefinite, P.S.*). (8) What a charming creature (*lit.* how charming) is man when (*lit.* whenever) he is a [real] man (*indefinite, P.S.*). (9) *A.* Who is this man? *B.* A doctor. *A.* What a bad state every doctor is in if (*lit.* if ever) no-one [else] is in a bad state! (*indefinite, P.S.*). (10) Our life is very like wine: whenever what remains (*or* the remains) is small, it becomes vinegar. (*Indefinite, P.S.*). (11) Those who are afraid that they may go into exile from their native-land and those who, being about to fight, are afraid that they may be defeated are not able to take (*lit.* get) either food or sleep because of their fear; but those who are already in exile or (*lit.* and) already defeated can eat and sleep even more (*or* better) than those blessed with good fortune (*fear for the future, P.S.*). (12) A monkey is a monkey even if it has golden sandals (*indefinite, P.S.*). (13) The Greeks were afraid that the Persians might advance against the wing and, outflanking them on both sides, might cut them to pieces (*fear for the future, H.S.*). (14) When the man whom they had seized was asked from what country he came (*lit.* was; *indirect question, H.S.*), he said that he was a Persian, and that he was proceeding from Tiribazos' army in order that he might get provisions (*purpose clause, H.S.*). (15) When Diogenes saw an archer with no natural skill, he sat down beside the target saying, "In order that I may not be hit" (*purpose clause in direct quotation, hence **not** H.S.*). (16) Through inexperience of death every man is afraid to leave this light of the sun. (17) A man was running so as not to get wet, and was drowned in a hole (*purpose clause, H.S.*). (18) When the generals assembled at daybreak, they were surprised that Cyrus neither sent someone else to tell [them] what to do (*lit.* it is necessary to do) nor appeared himself (*indirect statement, H.S.*). So they decided to pack up what they had and put on their full (ἐξ-) armour and move forwards. When they were already on the point of starting, at sunrise there came Procles, the ruler of Teuthrania, and Glus, the [son] of Tamos. They reported that Cyrus had been killed, but that Ariaeus was at the halting place with the rest of the barbarians and was saying that they would wait for them throughout this day (*indirect statement, H.S.*). (Xenophon *Anabasis* ii. 1.2–3, slightly adapted.) (19) If ever he saw the soldiers going in good order, he praised [them] (*indefinite, H.S.*). (20) If you fear the law (*lit.* fearing the law) you will not be troubled by the law.

15.2

(1) [While] avoiding [the] ashes I have fallen into [the] fire (*i.e.* out of the frying-pan into the fire). (2) No-one does wicked [deeds] without the gods' knowing (*lit.* no-one escapes the notice of the gods doing wicked things). (3) A crab has not learned (*i.e.* does not know how) to walk straight. (4) We are all wise in giving warnings (*lit.* with respect to warning), but we do not realise when we ourselves make mistakes. (5) The trap has caught the mouse. (6) For the man who takes pleasure in constantly speaking does not realise (*lit.* escaped his own notice) that he is wearisome to his companions (*lit.* those who are with [him]). (7) He has eaten scorpions. (8) Whoever devises treachery (*lit.* crafty things) against another is doing this against himself unawares (*lit.* escapes [his own] notice doing this himself against himself). (9)

The hoplites happened to be sleeping in the agora. (10) It was clear that Menon desired (*lit.* Menon was obvious desiring) to be exceedingly rich. (11) So they took Jesus; and carrying his own cross (*lit.* the cross for himself) he went forth to the so-called Place of a Skull, which in Hebrew is called Golgotha, where they crucified him, and with him two others one on each side (*lit.* from this side and from this side), and Jesus in the middle. Pilate also wrote a title (*or* inscription) and placed [it] on the cross, JESUS OF NAZARETH THE KING OF THE JEWS. Many of the Jews read this title, because the place where Jesus was crucified was near the city. Accordingly, the chief priests of the Jews said to Pilate, "Do not write 'The King of the Jews', but 'He claimed to be the King of the Jews'" (*lit.* but that, "he said, 'I am the King . . .'"). Pilate replied, "What I have written, I have written." (John 19. 16–22) (12) For all seven days during which they were marching through [the territory of] the Kurds they continued to fight. (13) When Clearetus had encouraged his soldiers, he began to lead them to the place, but day broke while he was still marching (*lit.* day happening anticipated him marching). (14) When Archimedes was washing himself, so the story goes (*lit.* as they say), he discovered from the overflow (*sc.* of the water-level in his bath) how to measure (*lit.* the measuring of) the crown, and as if possessed or inspired (*lit.* just as from some possession or inspiration), he jumped out shouting, "I've found [it]," and went about saying this over and over again (*lit.* often). But we have heard neither of any glutton shouting so passionately, "I have eaten", nor of any lover [shouting], "I have kissed", though countless sensualists existed in the past and [still] exist [now]. (Plutarch *Moralia* 1094C.) (15) *A.* He is married, I believe. *B.* What are you saying? Is he really married, [the man] whom I left alive and on his feet (*lit.* living and walking about)? (16) They stopped building the large wall because they feared (*lit.* fearing) that it would not be sufficient to hold out. (17) I see that for the majority of people former prosperity gives birth to insolence.

15.3

Might. We have come to [this] distant region of the earth, to [this] Scythian tract, to [this] wilderness where no men live. Hephaestus, you must concern yourself with the commands (*lit.* it is necessary that the commands be of concern to you) which the Father (*i.e.* Zeus) enjoined on you, to bind fast this wrong-doer on [these] rocks with lofty cliffs in unbreakable fetters of adamantine bonds. For [it was] your glory, the flame of fire on which all arts depend, [which] he stole and bestowed on mortals. [It is] for such a wrong, you know, [that] he must pay the penalty to the gods, in order that he may be taught (*or* learn) to accept the sovereignty of Zeus, and cease from his man-loving ways. *Hephaestus.* Might and Violence, for you two the command of Zeus has indeed fulfilment (*or* has been fulfilled) and nothing is still in [your] way, but I lack the heart to bind by force to [this] stormy ravine a god [who is my] kinsman. Yet for all that, I must (*lit.* there is necessity for me to) get the heart for this; for [it is] a grievous [matter] to disregard the words of the Father. O lofty-minded son of straight-counselling Themis, against your will and mine (*lit.* you being unwilling I being unwilling) will I fasten you in (*or* with) inextricable brazen bonds to this rock far from men, where you will perceive (*lit.* see) neither the voice nor the shape of anyone of mortals, but grilled by the sun's radiant flame you will alter the bloom of your skin; and you will be glad when (*lit.* to you being glad) night with her embroidered cloak will hide the light and [when] the sun will scatter the morning frost again; the burden of your present suffering (*lit.* the present trouble) will continually distress you; for the one who will relieve [it *or* you] is not yet born. (Aeschylus *Prometheus Bound* 1–27.)

16.2

(1) When they had come to their tents, the rest (*sc.* of the soldiers) were busy about the provisions, while generals and captains met together. And at this point there was much despondency. For on one side there lay (*lit.* were) very high mountains, and on the other side the river was so deep (*lit.* of such a size) that not even their spears were above [the water] when they tested the depth. (2) When Diogenes was asked why athletes were stupid, he said, "Because they have been built up with pork and beef." (3) One must marry [only] after making a [proper] choice. (4) We are involved in constant (*lit.* we continue being in) dangers throughout all our life, so that those who talk about security do not realise (*lit.* have escaped their own notice) that they are preparing for war for the whole of time. (5) You are flaying a flayed bitch (*i.e.* you are flogging a dead horse). (6) The Potideans, waiting for the Athenians, were camped on the isthmus on the side towards Olynthus, and they had established a market outside the city. And the allies had chosen Aristeus [as] general of the whole infantry and Perdiccas of the cavalry. (7) When the barbarians had left their land, the Athenians began to make preparations to rebuild their city. For of the houses most had collapsed, although a few survived, in which the chief men of the Persians had themselves lodged. (8) The goat has come to knives [already] sharpened (*i.e.* one is asking for trouble). (9) They passed the night there. But when day began to break, they proceeded to march in silence against the enemy, drawn up in battle-order; for a mist had also appeared, so that they came up close without being seen (*lit.* escaped notice approaching near). (10) Then an agreement was made (*lit.* comes into being (*vivid pres.*)) with respect to all those with Demosthenes as well, on condition that no-one would die either through violence (*lit.* violently) or imprisonment (*lit.* bonds) or lack of food. (11) Tiribazus said that he wished to make a treaty on condition that neither he himself would harm the Greeks nor would they burn the houses but (*lit.* and) would take the provisions that they needed. These [terms] were accepted by (*lit.* seemed good to) the generals and they made a treaty on these terms. (12) Nor is it still the time, Socrates, to be deliberating but to have finished deliberating. There is [only] one plan: all this must be completed (*or* over and done with) within this night. (13) So boldness and courage are not the same thing. Consequently the result is (*lit.* it results) that the courageous are bold but not that the bold are all courageous, for boldness, like strength, comes to men from art and from anger and from madness but courage from nature and proper nurture of the soul (*lit.* souls). (14) The Spartans considered that the Athenians were first in violation of (*lit.* to be in a state of having broken) the treaty. (15) The goat has not yet given birth (*i.e.* don't count your chickens before they're hatched). (16) Philip, the father of Alexander the Great, wanted (*lit.* wanting) to capture a strong fort. When his scouts reported that it was difficult in all respects and impregnable, he asked if it was so difficult that not even an ass carrying gold could approach [it].

16.3

I am alive and I behold what I ought to, the sky, the earth and these shafts of sun[light]. But what a terrible turmoil (*lit.* wave, surf) and confusion of mind I have fallen into (*lit.* in) and what warm breath I breathe, shallow, not steady from my lungs. Look, why am I sitting anchored like a ship with bonds on (*lit.* with respect to) my sturdy chest and arms to this stone-carved pillar (*lit.* chiselled work made of stone) broken in half, sitting next to corpses (*lit.* having a seat neighbouring corpses)? My winged weapons and bow lie scattered on the ground, which formerly shielded my arms and protected my flanks and were protected by me. Surely I have not descended back to [the house] of Hades again, having [just] completed (*lit.* having gone) the double course from Hades set by Eurystheus? But neither do I see the stone of Sisyphus or Pluto nor yet the sceptre of Demeter's daughter. I am indeed bewildered. Wherever am I in my helplessness? Help, who is there of my friends near or far who will cure my bewilderment? (Euripides *Heracles* 1089–1107.)

17.2

(1) (*i*) If (*or* when) you are wronged (*lit.* being wronged), settle your differences. (*ii*) Keep away from other people's property. (*iii*) Don't hurry when you undertake something (*lit.* undertake slowly). (*iv*) Don't rush into marriage (*lit.* delay getting married). (*v*) Know yourself (*i.e.* your human limitations). (*vi*) Respect your parents. (*vii*) Think [only] mortal thoughts (*lit.* mortal things). (*viii*) Don't laugh over a corpse. (*ix*) Know the right moment. (*x*) Nothing in excess. (*xi*) When you drink, don't talk too much (*lit.* prattle many things). (*xii*) Use your wealth fairly (*lit.* be wealthy justly). (*xiii*) Believe in fortune. (*xiv*) If (*or* when) you are insulted, avenge yourself. (*xv*) Don't curse your sons. (2) Train your children; for you will not train [them when they are] men. (3) An army of deer led by a lion is more frightening than an army of lions led by a deer. (4) Fear old age; for it does not come alone. (5) Choose a good reputation rather than wealth (*lit.* wish to be well spoken of rather than to be rich). (6) When you have passed a rose do not seek it any longer again. (7) We have two ears but one mouth, in order that we may hear more but speak less. (8) (*i*) Neighbours have sharper eyes (*lit.* see more sharply) than foxes. (*ii*) When you are walking on foot do not fear the waves. (*iii*) Let a lion eat me, not a fox (*i.e.* if I come to grief may it be at the hands of a worthy opponent). (*iv*) Be both a lion where it is required (*lit.* necessary) and a monkey in turn (*i.e.* be prepared to assume a role suited to a particular situation). (*v*) What[ever] bread a man has kneaded, let him eat it as well. (*vi*) When the general is present, let all the officers stop (*sc.* giving orders). (*vii*) The man who desires more is also deprived of what he has (*lit.* the things which are present). (*viii*) Don't throw food into a chamberpot. (*ix*) When you are a foreigner follow the local customs. (*x*) Don't speak ill of your friend or well of your enemy. (*xi*) If (*or* when) you are prosperous, don't despise the poor. (*xii*) Judge not, that you be not judged. (*xiii*) Second thoughts are somehow wiser. (*xiv*) Most people are rogues. (*xv*) Things last year were always better. (9) One of the Saii exults in my shield, which I left unwillingly, a blameless weapon, by a thicket. But I myself escaped the doom of death; to hell with that shield; I'll get another just as good (*lit.* once more I shall obtain [one] not worse). (Archilochus 6.) (10) The royal cubit is three fingers greater (*or* longer) than the standard cubit. (11) (*i*) When Eudamidas saw Xenocrates, who was now rather old, studying philosophy in the Academy with his students and ascertained that he was searching for virtue, he said, "So when will he [be able to] use it?" (*ii*) When a certain Argive was saying that the Spartans became worse when they were abroad (*lit.* during their absences from home), he (*i.e.* Eudamidas) said, "But **you**, when you come to Sparta, do not become worse but better." (*iii*) To a wretch who was asking [him] who the best Spartan was Agis said, "The one who is most unlike you." (*iv*) When a teacher was about to read out an encomium of Heracles, Antalcidas said, "Well, who's criticising him?" (*v*) When Thearidas was sharpening a sword he was asked if it was sharp, and he said, "Sharper than slander." (*vi*) When a garrulous barber asked Archelaus, "How would you like it, your Majesty (*lit.* how am I to cut your hair, o King)?" Archelaus said, "In silence (*lit.* keeping quiet)." (12) When Aristotle heard that he was being abused by someone, he said, "Let him also whip me when I'm not there (*lit.* being

absent).'' (13) Although they are wise in other respects, the sophists do something extraordinary *viz* (*lit.* do an extraordinary thing [viz] this) they claim to be teachers of virtue, yet they often accuse their students of wronging them (*lit.* that they wrong them), by withholding their fees, although they have been well-treated by them (*i.e.* if the sophists had really been able to teach their students virtue, the latter would not have failed to pay their fees). (14) Much enmity and mutual hatred is innate in our citizens, on account of which I am always fearful that some disaster too great to bear may fall upon the city. (15) The Lacedaemonians kept sending embassies to the Athenians to make complaints, in order that they might have (*lit.* there might be to them) as great a pretext as possible for going to war, in case they (the Athenians) did not pay any attention. (16) Cleander was tyrant of Gela for seven years, but he was killed by Sabyllus, a man from Gela. (17) Hope and you, Luck, a long farewell; I have found the harbour. There's nothing [more] between you and me. Have your fun with those [who come] after me.

17.3

Hermes. You there, the clever one, bitterly bitter to the extreme, you who offended against the gods by giving honours to mortals, you the thief of fire I mean; the Father orders you to tell [him] of the marriage of which you boast and by which he is [to be] cast out of his power. And what is more, do not [tell] it (*lit.* these things) in riddling fashion, but explain each detail as it is, and do not inflict a double journey on me, Prometheus. You see that Zeus is not softened by such behaviour. *Prometheus.* Haughty and full of arrogance is your talk, for a lackey of the gods. New you are and new your power (*lit.* you [being] new wield new power), and you think indeed that you dwell in citadels free from woe. [Yet] have I not seen two rulers cast out from them? And as the third I shall behold the present lord (*sc.* cast out) most shamefully and most speedily. You don't imagine, do you, (*lit.* surely I do not seem to you in some respect), that I am terrified and cower before these new gods? I'm far removed, indeed completely removed, from that. Hasten back along the road you came; for you will find out none of the things which you question me about. (Aeschylus *Prometheus Bound* 944–963.)

18.2

(1) A man from Cyme was selling honey. When someone tasted it and said, "It's very nice", he said, "[Yes,] for if a mouse had not fallen into it, I would not be selling it." (2) A Spartan woman, in answer to her son who was saying that the sword which he had was short, said, "Add a step" (*i.e.* take a step closer to your enemy to make up for the shortness of your sword). (3) (*i*) If the lion-skin does not suffice, put on the fox-skin (*i.e.* if behaving like a lion doesn't help, behave like a fox). (*ii*) You are giving a dog bran, and an ass bones (*i.e.* you are doing things the wrong way). (*iii*) You keep your love on the tip of your tongue. (*iv*) If we hate our friends, what shall we do to those who hate [us]? (*v*) If I had cheese, I would not want a cooked meal (*i.e.* the small luxury of cheese would be enough—spoken of those who did not indulge themselves overmuch). (*vi*) [When] a friend [is] in trouble do not betray [him] because of anger. (*vii*) Gain is sweet, even if it comes from lies. (*viii*) Give something and take something. (*ix*) Wandering makes life more reasonable (*i.e.* travel broadens the mind). (*x*) [It is] disgraceful to betray one's benefactors. (*xi*) If we have money, we will have friends. (*xii*) Let matters proceed as God wills (*lit.* as is dear to the god). (4) A man came

asking the seer Olympicus whether he should sail to Rhodes and how he would sail in safety; and the seer replied, "First, have a new ship, and put out to sea not in winter but in summer; for if you do this, you will go both there and [back] here, unless a pirate captures you at sea." (*A.P.* xi. 162.)   (5) Once an old man had cut some wood and was walking a long road carrying it. Because of fatigue he laid aside the load and called upon Death. When Death appeared and asked for what reason he was calling upon him, the old man said, "So that you may lift up this load and put it on me."   (6) Every gift which is given, even if it is small, is very great, if it is given with goodwill.   (7) If a snake does not eat a snake, it will not become a dragon (*i.e.* to rise in the world one must be ruthless).   (8) Naked I set foot upon the earth, and naked I shall go away below the earth; and why do I vainly toil when I see the end naked?   (9) (*i*) When someone was surprised at [the number of] the dedications in Samothrace, he said, "There would be far more if those who were not saved had also made dedications." (*ii*) When he came to Myndus and observed that the gates were big whereas the city was small, "Men of Myndus", he said, "Shut the gates lest your city gets out (*or* escapes)." (*iii*) He was asking a bad-tempered man [for alms]. When [the latter] said, "[Yes,] if you persuade me", [Diogenes] replied, "If I were able to persuade you, I would have persuaded you to hang yourself." (*iv*) Lighting (*lit.* having lit) a lamp in broad daylight, he used to go about saying, "I'm looking for a [genuine] human being."   (10) The Syracusan generals trusted the fellow much too incautiously and immediately agreed upon a day on which they would be present and sent him back, while (*lit.* and) they themselves gave warning to the Syracusans beforehand that they would all go out in full force. When their preparations were complete and the days were at hand on which they had agreed to come, proceeding in the direction of Catana they encamped at the river Symaethus. When the Athenians perceived that they were approaching, they took all their own army and, putting it on board the ships and boats, sailed under cover of night against Syracuse. (Thucydides vi. 65, slightly adapted.)

18.3

They arrived at the mountain on the fifth day; the name of (*lit.* to) the mountain was Theches. When the vanguard got on to [the summit of] the mountain and looked down at the sea, much shouting arose. Hearing [this], Xenophon and the rearguard thought that other enemy forces were attacking up in front. But when (*or* since) the shouting was becoming greater and closer and those who kept coming up in succession were running quickly towards those who were continually shouting and the shouting became much louder in proportion as the numbers increased (*lit.* they were becoming more), it seemed to Xenophon to be something more serious. He mounted his horse and taking the cavalry set off to the rescue. And very soon they heard the soldiers shouting, "The sea, the sea!" and passing the word along. Thereupon all the rearguard also began to run, and the draught animals and the horses were driven along. When they had all arrived at the summit, they then began to embrace each other in tears, including generals and captains. (Xenophon *Anabasis* iv. 7. 21–25, slightly adapted.)

19.2

(1) Heraclitus says somewhere that everything is in motion (*or* flux) and nothing stays still, and likening existing things (*lit.* the being [things]) to the stream of a river he says that you could not (*or* cannot) step twice into the same river.   (2) Keep sober and remember to distrust; these (*i.e.* sobriety and distrust) are the limbs of the mind.   (3) Pyrrho said that there was no difference between life and death (*lit.* being alive and

being dead differed in no way). And when someone said, "Why then do you not die?", he said, "Because it makes no difference." (4) Do you think that crimes (*or* sins) leap up with wings to the gods, and then someone writes them on the leaves of Zeus' tablet, and Zeus looks at them and gives judgements for mortals? The whole of heaven would not suffice if Zeus were writing [down] the sins of mortals nor would he (*i.e.* Zeus) examining [them] [suffice] to send a penalty to each man. No (*lit.* but), Justice is here somewhere near, if you wish to see. (Euripides, fragment 506.) (5) (*i*) If you are able to travel (*sc.* by land), do not go by sea (*lit.* sail). (*ii*) You were caught by your own feathers (*i.e.* hoist with your own petard). (*iii*) A [statue of] Hermes cannot (*lit.* could not) be made out of every (*or* any) log (*i.e.* you can't make a silk purse out of a sow's ear). (*iv*) If you drink water you will (*lit.* would) produce nothing wise. (*v*) The man who knows what is useful (*lit.* useful things), not the man who knows much (*lit.* many things), is wise. (*vi*) If God gives [it], you cannot (*lit.* could not) escape evil (*lit.* evil things). (*vii*) All men naturally (*or* by nature) strive after knowledge (Aristotle). (*viii*) Whenever you are having a fine voyage, be especially mindful of squalls (*lit.* a squall). (*ix*) Give me somewhere to stand (*lit.* where I am to stand) and I shall move the earth (Archimedes). (*x*) Much learning does not teach [one] to have wisdom; for (*sc.* otherwise) it would have taught Hesiod and Pythagoras (Heraclitus). (*xi*) That which exists by nature does not change. (*xii*) [One] must bear lightly [one's] present (*lit.* standing beside) fortunes. (*xiii*) Despondent men never yet (*lit.* not yet) set up a trophy (*cf.* faint heart never won fair lady). (*xiv*) Remember that you are a human being. (*xv*) If you set a trap, you will be caught in a trap. (*xvi*) Although he stands far off God sees from near at hand. (*xvii*) He stands on the razor['s edge] (*i.e.* he is in a difficult situation). (6) How sweet [it is] for those in distress to forget their present troubles even for a short time. (7) (*i*) To a man who said, "Except for the fact that you are King you are in no way different from us," Leonidas said, "But I wouldn't be King if I were not better than you." (*ii*) When he arrived at Thermopylae, to a man who said, "Because of the barbarians' arrows it is not even possible to see the sun," he said, "So [it will be] nice, if we fight (*lit.* will fight) beneath the shade." (*iii*) When Xerxes wrote to him, "It is possible for you by not fighting against God but by ranging yourself with me, to be sole ruler of Greece," he wrote in reply, "If you knew (*i.e.* understood) the fine things of life, you would have refrained from the desire for other people's possessions; for me death on behalf of Greece is better than being sole ruler over my own race (*lit.* those of the same stock)." (*iv*) When Xerxes wrote again, "Send (*i.e.* surrender) your arms," he wrote in reply, "Come and get them!" (*v*) Stranger, tell the Spartans that we lie here, in obedience to (*lit.* obeying) their commands (*lit.* words). (8) I shall not revolt from the people of Athens (*lit.* of the Athenians) either in any way or means or in word or deed, nor shall I obey anyone who revolts (*lit.* the revolting man), and if anyone tries to stir up revolt, I shall denounce [him] to the Athenians; and I shall pay to the Athenians whatever tribute I persuade the Athenians [is appropriate]; and I shall be as excellent and just an ally as I am able (*lit.* I shall be an ally of whatever sort I may be able best and most just), and I shall come to the help of the people of Athens and I shall ward off anyone who (*lit.* if anyone) does wrong to the people of Athens, and I will obey the people of Athens. (*Inscriptiones Graecae* i³ 40. 21–32.)

20.2

(1) Once a young man fell sick and said to his doctor that he was in such pain that he was unable either to sit or lie [down] or stand; the doctor said, "My friend, you have no alternative but (*lit.* there is no other thing left to you than) to hang." (2) Who knows

if what is called death [is] life, and life is death? Except, however, [that] those of mortals who are alive (*lit.* see [*sc.* the light of day]) fall sick, whereas those who are dead never (*lit.* not at all) fall sick nor suffer ill (*lit.* possess troubles). (Euripides, fragment 833.) (3) (*i*) He started to play the flute for a drachma, and stops (*sc.* playing it) for four. (*ii*) The camel who conceived a desire for horns lost his ears too. (*iii*) There is no man who is fortunate in all respects. (*iv*) Many generals lost Caria (*cf.* too many cooks spoil the broth). (*v*) Do not let go what is visible and choose what is invisible. (*vi*) Time alone shows a just man. (*vii*) You are in no way different from an elephant. (*viii*) God does not stand aloof from a just deceit. (*ix*) A visit from (*lit.* entrance of) many doctors destroyed me. (*x*) Your appearance is like a lion's but your life is like an ass's (*lit.* you are a lion as regards your hair, but an ass as regards your life). (4) I see the nose of hook-nosed Nico, Menippus; however, he himself seems to be still far off; but he'll come, let's wait after all. For if [he is] far [away], he is not, I suppose, five stades from (*i.e.* behind) his nose. But, as you see, it precedes [him] itself. If we stand on (*lit.* on to) a high mound, we'll see him too. (*A.P.* xi. 406.) (5) When he was dyeing his head (*i.e.* his hair) a man lost his hair itself, and although he was very hairy he has completely become an egg. (6) Thereupon, Cleanor stood up and spoke as follows: "Come, gentlemen, you see the perjury and impiety of the King, and you see the faithlessness of Tissaphernes, since, although he used to say that he was a neighbour of Greece and that he would consider it most important to save us, and although he himself swore an oath to us to confirm this (*lit.* upon these things) and himself gave pledges, he himself deceived and seized our generals, and he did not even respect Zeus God of Hospitality, but after actually sitting at the same table as Clearchus deceived him by these very means and has [now] destroyed the men." (Xenophon *Anabasis* iii. 2.4.) (7) Well, Socrates, obey the laws and regard (*lit.* obeying the laws, regard) neither children nor life nor anything else more highly than justice, in order that, when you go [down] to [the house] of Hades you may be able to plead all this in your defence to those who rule there. (8) Socrates manifestly longed not for those who were naturally sound in body with respect to beauty but for those who were naturally sound in soul with respect to virtue. (9) The daughter of a grammarian, after making love (*lit.* having mingled in sexual intercourse), produced a masculine child, a feminine [child], [and] a neuter [child]. (10) For Zeus gives thought to the greatest [affairs] of mortals, but leaves unimportant [matters] to other gods and lets them be. (11) While it was summer, the soldiers who were in Chios with Eteonicus supported themselves both from [the produce of] the season and by working for hire around the countryside. But when winter came on, and they had no sustenance and they were badly clothed and without shoes, they began to conspire amongst themselves (*lit.* with each other) to attack Chios. (12) *Polymnestor.* Alas, what will you say? Is she really somewhere nearby? Show [me], tell [me] where she is, in order that I may seize [her] with my hands and tear [her] apart and bloody [her] flesh. *Agamemnon.* What's this, what's wrong with you? *Po.* In the name of the gods I beseech you, let me lay my raging hand[s] on her. *Ag.* Stop; cast [this] savagery from [your] heart and speak, so that, when I have heard both you and her in turn, I may fairly decide for what reason (*lit.* in return for what thing) you are treated thus (*lit.* suffer these things). (Euripides *Hecuba* 1124–1131.)

21.2

(1) When a certain Spartan came to Athens and saw men sitting on stools in a [public] toilet, he said, "May it not happen to me to sit in a place from which (*lit.* there from where) it is not possible to rise up for (*i.e.* to give my seat to) an older man." (2) (*i*) You are stirring the brine before you catch the fish (*cf.* first catch your hare, then cook

it). (*ii*) A tortoise is not concerned about flies. (*iii*) May such enemies always pursue me. (*iv*) One should (*lit.* it is fitting to) scold children indoors. (*v*) One's speech reflects one's way of life (*lit.* of what sort [is one's] way of life, of such a sort [is one's] speech). (*vi*) Count no man fortunate (*lit.* consider no-one to be fortunate) until he dies. (*vii*) Dogs resemble their mistresses (*lit.* of what sort the mistress, of such a sort also the bitch). (*viii*) It is fitting for a child to be silent rather than to chatter. (*ix*) Oh, what a head, and it does not have a brain! (*x*) Slaves share their masters' sickness. (*xi*) May I not have (*lit.* may there not be to me) what I want but what it is advantageous (*sc.* for me to have). (*xii*) May you fall into (*lit.* in with) Hades' anus! (*i.e.* may you die!) (*xiii*) Would that (*or* I wish that) the offspring of wretched men were dumb. (3) Whoever of mortals fears death too much, is by nature stupid; [for] this (*lit.* these things) is the concern of Chance. But whenever the moment of death chances to come, he could not escape [it] even if he went to the halls of Zeus. (Sophocles, fragment 865.) (4) All who marry above themselves (*lit.* as many as marry marriages better in race) do not know [how] to marry. (5) A man's character is of necessity affected by the sort of people with whom he spends most of his time (*lit.* with what sort of [a person] a man associates for the greatest part of the day, of such a sort as regards to character it is necessary for him too to become). (6) Next stood up Thorax the Boeotian, who was struggling with Xenophon about the generalship, and said that, if they got out of the Black Sea, they would have (*lit.* there would be to them) the Chersonnese, a beautiful and blessed country, so that it was possible for anyone who [so] wished to dwell there, and anyone who did not to go off home. It was ridiculous, when there was much bountiful land in Greece, to be searching for [it] in the [country] of the barbarians. "And until you get (*lit.* become) there, I too promise you pay." (Xenophon *Anabasis* v. 6.25–26.) (7) Once when Diogenes saw [some] women hanging by nooses from an olive-tree, he said, "I wish that all trees had borne such a fruit." (8) Whoever does (*or* tries to do) many things if it is possible not to do [them], [is] foolish, if it is possible to live a quiet (*lit.* free from business) life pleasantly. (9) In deliberation (*lit.* deliberating) the generals decided to reply as follows (*lit.* the following things) and Cheirisophus was their spokesman (*lit.* spoke): "We are resolved, if we are allowed (*lit.* someone allows us) to go off home, to proceed through the country doing the least possible harm; but if anyone [tries to] hinder us from the journey, to fight it out with him as vigorously as possible." (10) Indeed [it is] with difficulty [that] you would bear my ordeals, to whom it is not fated to die (*or* since it is not fated for me to die); for this (*i.e.* death) would be a deliverance from [my] woes; but as it is, there is no end of toils appointed for me until Zeus is cast out from [his] sovereignty. (Aeschylus *Prometheus Bound* 752–756.) (11) When Cyrus had listened to such words from Gobryas he spoke to him as follows. (12) Well, what will you do, [my] heart? Consider well before you err and make most hateful what is [now] most dear (*lit.* the dearest things). Wherever did you rush forth, you wretch? Check [your] arrogance and strength hated of the gods. And why (*lit.* with a view to what) do I lament like this (*lit.* these things), seeing my life desolate and abandoned by those who should least (*sc.* have abandoned me)? Do we then become cowards when we suffer such evils? Do not betray yourself, [my] heart, in [the midst of] troubles. Alas, it is decided; children, go away from [my] sight (*lit.* eyes); for already a new frenzy has entered my bloody heart; O [my] hands, [my] hands, for what a [terrible] task we are preparing ourselves; alas, wretched [that I am] because of [my] daring, [I] who go to destroy in a brief moment the [product of] my great labour. (Neophron, fragment 2.) (13) When a man came to Lacedaemon and beheld the respect shown by (*lit.* of) the young towards the old, he said, "In Sparta alone it is profitable to grow old." (14) We should meet together and (*lit.* making a meeting) lament over a new-born baby (*lit.* the one [just] born) for all the troubles it is coming to, and in turn farewell with sounds of triumph the man who has died and is freed from troubles as we send him forth from his house (*lit.* farewelling [and] shouting in triumph send forth). (Euripides, fragment 449.)

21.3

(1) What life [can there be], what joy without golden Aphrodite? May I die, when these things are no longer my concern (*lit.* a care to me), [viz] secret love and gentle gifts and bed (*or* sex), the sorts of things which are the attractive flowers of youth for men and women. But when distressing old age comes on, [old age] which makes a man both ugly and base, evil cares always distress him in his heart (*or* mind), nor is he glad when he looks upon the rays of the sun, but [he is] hateful to boys and dishonoured by women. So painful did God make old age. (Mimnermus 1.)   (2) You, [who are] my star, gaze at the stars. Would I might become the sky, in order that I might see you with many eyes.   (3) Formerly you shone among the living [like] the Morning Star; but now you have died you shine [like] the Evening Star among the dead.   (4) I am sending you sweet perfume, [thus] doing a favour to the perfume, not to you; for you yourself are able to give fragrance even to perfume.   (5) Hail, Messenger of Dawn, Bringer of Light, and may you come [back] quickly [as the] Evening Star, bringing secretly back again [the girl] whom you are [now] leading away.

22.2

(1) You, Love, ruler of gods and men, either do not teach beauty to appear beautiful or assist lovers (*lit.* those who are in love) with good fortune, as they suffer the pains of which you are the author. (Euripides, fragment 136.)   (2) For it was evening, and someone had come to the prytaneis with the report (*lit.* announcing) that Elatea had been captured. After this some of them got up immediately in the middle of dinner, cleared out the people in the stalls throughout the market-place, and set fire to the wicker-work, while others sent for the generals and summoned the trumpeter. The city was filled with commotion. On the following day at dawn the prytaneis called the councillors (*lit.* the council) into the Council-chamber, while you proceeded to the Assembly, and before they dealt with the matter and framed a draft resolution the whole people was seated on the hill (*i.e.* the Pnyx; *lit.* above). After this, when the Council had arrived and the prytaneis had announced what had been reported to them and had introduced the messenger (*lit.* the one who had come) and he had spoken, the herald put the question, "Who wishes to speak?" And no-one came forward. (Demosthenes *On the Crown* 169–170.)   (3) (*i*) Ask even statues for [your] daily bread (*double acc.*) (*i.e.* you're not getting anything from me!). (*ii*) There is a certain Socrates, a wise man, who speculates on (*lit.* a deep thinker about) the heavens above (*lit.* things high in the air; *accusative of respect*) and has investigated everything beneath the earth (*direct object*). (*iii*) He has come to take from us even the property of [our] grandfather (*double acc.*). (*iv*) He came to the ancient tomb of [his] father (*acc. of motion towards*). (*v*) [My] long life teaches me many things (*double acc.*). (*vi*) Meletus brought this indictment against me (*direct object*; *cognate acc.*). (*vii*) Cyrus was very handsome in appearance and very humane in spirit (*acc. of respect*). (*viii*) [No], by Zeus (*acc. in oath*), I did not see a woodcutter (*direct obj.*) better than myself. (*ix*) They made a treaty and alliance for a hundred years (*acc. to express time how long*). (*x*) I swear by the holy sky, the dwelling of Zeus (*acc. in oath*).   (4) (*i*) How sweet [a thing] [is] solitude to the man who hates common people (*exclamatory adv.*). (*ii*) Hide nothing, for all-seeing (*lit.* seeing everything) time unfolds everything (*causal conjunction*). (*iii*) We bear

children for this reason [viz] that we may protect the altars of the gods and [our] native land (*conjunction introducing purpose clause*). (*iv*) He seized the acropolis to gain sole power (*lit.* as for tyranny; *adv. introducing prepositional phrase*). (*v*) [We/one] must try to bear the constraints (*lit.* the necessary things) of life as lightly (*lit.* easily) as possible (ὡϲ + *supl.*). (*vi*) Effort, as/so they say, is the father of fame (*conjunction introducing a parenthetical clause*, 22.1/1*b*(v)). (*vii*) Alas, alas, how fine a privilege is a just victory (*lit.* to win just things), but how absolutely evil is an unjust victory (*lit.* [to win] unjust things) (*exclamatory adv.*). (*viii*) How sweet is life, if a man does not understand it (*exclamatory adv.*). (*ix*) Give to the poor, in order that you find God a giver (*conjunction introducing purpose clause*). (*x*) Time judges friends as fire [judges] gold (*conjunction introducing a clause of manner*). (*xi*) When you are young remember that one day you will be old (ὡϲ = ὅτι, *indirect statement*). (*xii*) Do we not live as pleasantly as possible if we do not grieve? (ὡϲ + *supl.*). (*xiii*) They sailed away from the Hellespont separately according to their cities (22.1/1*a*(v)). (*xiv*) Really wise men (ὡϲ *with positive adv.*). (5) At first Oedipus was a fortunate man, [but] then he became the most wretched of mortals. (6) Well, as you know, I have wept for many sufferings, but now I shall speak of one [suffering] such as [I have] not yet [wept for] before. When [my] lord Heracles was setting out on his last journey from home, at that time he left in the house an ancient tablet inscribed with signs, which he had never brought himself to explain to me like this before, when he went forth on [his] many exploits, but he used to go as one who was about to do something [notable] and not as one about to die. (Sophocles *Trachiniae* 153–160.) (7) I made war first against the Thracians, driving them from the Hellespont as they wanted to take the country from the Greeks. (8) O old age, what hope of pleasure you have, and every single man wishes to live through (*lit.* come) to you. But when he has made trial [of you], he regrets (*sc.* that he has; *lit.* takes regret) because there is no worse evil among the mortal race. (Euripides, fragment 1080.) (9) For I, Cebes, when young, had an enormous desire (*lit.* desired enormously) for this wisdom which they call the investigation into (*lit.* of) nature.

22.3

(1) We congratulate you, grasshopper, when on the tops of the trees you sing like a king, after drinking a little dew; for yours are all those things which you see in the fields, [all those things] which the woods nourish. You [are] held in honour among mortals, sweet harbinger of summer. The Muses love you, and Phoebus himself loves [you], and gave [you] a shrill power of song. Old age does not distress you, o skilful, earth-born lover of song, and since you know not suffering (*lit.* [being] unsuffering), o [creature of] bloodless flesh, you are nearly equal to the gods. (Anacreontea 54.) (2) My (*lit.* to us) temples [are] now grey, and my head white, and no longer is graceful youth at hand, and my teeth are aged. No longer is there left much time of sweet life; for this reason (*lit.* on account of these things) I weep often in fear of Tartarus. For terrible is the inner chamber of Hades, and painful the path down to him; and further [it is] fixed for the man who has gone down not to come up [again]. (Anacreontea 395.)

23.2

(1) (*i*) O sweet charm of sleep (*gen. of explanation*), ally against sickness (*objective gen.*). (*ii*) He wanted to be [one] of those who remained (*partitive gen.*). (*iii*) O Poseidon, what skill! (*gen. of exclamation*). (*iv*) To bear poverty is not [the nature] of everyone, but of a wise man (*gen. of characteristic*). (*v*) Pay close attention (*lit.* apply the mind very much) to this man (*dat. of indirect object*), I beg you (*ethic dat.*). (*vi*) Many treatments have been found by doctors (*dat. of agent*). (*vii*) Sleep is naturally a safeguard of the body (*lit.*

of bodies; *objective gen.*). (*viii*) [It is the mark] of a wicked man to praise and blame the same person (*gen. of characteristic*). (*ix*) Such is tyranny for you, Lacedaemonians (*dat. of reference* or *ethic dat.*). (*x*) Olympian Zeus, dwelling in the sky (*dat. of place where*), knows this. (*xi*) They accuse him of theft (*verb of accusing, gen. of charge*). (*xii*) Men lie because of their own (*subjective/possessive gen.*) fear of death (*objective gen.*). (*xiii*) They were afraid that the Athenians might attack with a greater force (*military dat.*). (*xiv*) They will approach with much shouting (*dat. of manner*). (*xv*) The boy's name (*lit.* the name to the boy; *dat. of possession*) was Plato. (*xvi*) Art is weaker by far (*dat. of measure of difference*) than necessity (*gen. of comparison*). (*xvii*) I admire you for [your] intelligence, but I loathe [you] for [your] cowardice (*both gen. of cause*). (*xviii*) I tried to steal [some] of the meat (*partitive gen.*). (*xix*) In your eyes (*dat. of reference*) did this man do these things justly? *or* Did this man do these things justly for you? (*dat. of advantage*). (*xx*) They did these things for the gods (*dat. of advantage*). (*xxi*) He was loathsome and rough in his voice (*dat. of respect*). (*xxii*) The army arrived at Oenoe in Attica (*chorographic gen.*). (*xxiii*) You see the king's perjury (*subjective/possessive gen.*). (*xxiv*) I am not disheartened by what has happened (*dat. of cause*). (2) Diogenes went up to Anaximenes the orator who was fat and said, "Give [some] of your belly to us the poor too; for you will both be lightened yourself and will help us." (3) There was a saying that wiles are the concern of women, whereas men are of surer aim with the spear. For if the prize of victory were [won] by guiles, we would have sovereignty over men. (Euripides, fragment 321.) (4) And now I advise all younger [men] not to produce children tardily, making delays up to old age (*or* until they are old). For [this] (*i.e.* producing children in old age) is no pleasure, and an old man is a hateful thing to (*or* for) a woman. But [do it] as quickly as possible. For rearing [children] is beautiful and a boy sharing his youth with a youthful father is a pleasant [thing]. (Euripides, fragment 317.) (5) *Meletus.* This [is what] I say, that not at all do you believe in the gods. *Socrates.* You really amaze me in speaking like this, Meletus (*lit.* O amazing Meletus, why do you say this?). Do I not even believe then that the sun or the moon are gods, as the rest of mankind [do]? *Me.* [No], by Zeus, gentlemen of the jury, since he says that the sun is a stone and the moon earth. *So.* Do you think that you are accusing Anaxagoras, my dear Meletus? And do you so despise these men and think that they are [so] illiterate (*lit.* inexperienced in letters) that they do not know that the books of Anaxagoras of Clazomenae are full of such statements? And moreover the youth learn these [doctrines], do they, from me, which they can buy for a drachma in (*lit.* from) the orchestra and [then] laugh at Socrates if he claims they are his own, especially since they are so absurd? Well, for heaven's sake (*lit.* O by Zeus), is this what you think of me (*lit.* do I seem thus to you)? Do I not believe in any god? *Me.* No indeed, by Zeus, not in the very least. *So.* You are not to be believed, Meletus, and that too, as it seems (*lit.* you seem) to me, [even] by yourself. For this man appears to me, men of Athens, to be very violent and unrestrained, and simply to have brought this indictment through (*or* because of) violence and unrestraint and youthful folly. For he seems like a man making trial [of me] [by] composing a riddle: "Will Socrates the wise recognize that I am joking and contradicting myself, or shall I deceive him and the rest of those who are listening [to me]?" For he appears to me to contradict himself in the indictment, as if he were to say, "Socrates is a wrong-doer [by] not believing in the gods, but by believing in the gods." And yet this is the [mark *or* conduct] of a joker (*lit.* of [someone] joking). (Plato *Apology* 26c–27a.)

23.3

(1) I am the tomb of a ship-wrecked [sailor]; and the one opposite [is the tomb] of a farmer; for Hades lies beneath, common to [both] sea and land. (2) Here Saon, the

[son] of Dico, of Acanthus, slumbers in holy sleep (*lit*. sleeps a holy sleep); do not say that the good die.   (3) Philip, his father, laid (*or* buried) here his twelve-year-old son, his great hope, Nicoteles.   (4) These men, having invested (*lit*. placed round) their dear native-land with imperishable glory, put on the dark cloud of death; but they are not dead in death (*lit*. having died), since from above their valour glorifies them and raises them from the house of Hades. (Simonides 121 D.)   (5) This monument hides Aeschylus, son of Euphorion, the Athenian, who died in wheat-bearing Gela; but of his famous valour the grove of Marathon could tell, and the long-haired Mede who knew it.   (6) Tears I give to you, Heliodora, even below through the earth, a remnant of love [sent] to Hades, tears sorely wept; and on [your] much-lamented tomb I pour the stream of [my] longing, the memorial of [my] affection. Piteously, piteously I Meleager lament you, my dear (*lit*. dear you), even among the dead, an empty favour to (*or* for) Acheron. Alas, where is my flower (*lit*. shoot *or* sprout) [sorely] missed? Hades snatched [her], snatched [her], and the dust marred the flower of her youth (*lit*. the blooming flower). But I implore you, all-nurturing Earth, gently clasp her, all-lamented (*lit*. the all-lamented [girl]), to your bosom, O Mother. (Meleager *A.P.* vii. 476.)

24.2

(1) *Where a negative is involved, the relevant subsection of 24.1/2 is given after the appropriate explanatory term.* (*i*) The man who knows nothing (*generic* (*f*)) makes no mistakes (*statement* (*a*)). (*ii*) Consider no-one a friend (*prohibition/negative command* (*a*)) until you examine how he has treated his previous friends. (*iii*) They do everything so as not to be punished (*infinitive* (*e*)). (*iv*) Nothing (*statement* (*a*)) was done because of the fact that the archon was not present (*infinitive* (*e*)). (*v*) I do not know (*statement* (*a*)) whether to travel (*lit*. I am to travel) or not (*deliberative question* (*a*)). (*vi*) I am afraid that I do not have (*noun clause* (*d*)) sufficient [people] to whom I am to give the gold. (*vii*) Take courage, Cyrus, I shall not hide (*strong denial* (*h*)) from you [the person] to whom I wish to go (*lit*. arrive). (*viii*) And they said that they would give back the corpses on condition that [they] did not burn (*infinitive* (*e*)) the villages. (*ix*) The deed which is not just (*generic* (*f*)) does not escape (*statement* (*a*)) the notice of the gods. (*x*) What is to prevent them from dying? (*verb of preventing is virtually negative because the answer* nothing *is expected* (24.1/7)). (*xi*) He wanted to be a friend of (*lit*. friendly to) those who were most powerful in order that, when he did wrong, he might not be punished (*purpose clause* (*b*)). (*xii*) If you don't check (*conditional clause* (*b*)) your tongue, you will have troubles (*lit*. troubles will be to you). (*xiii*) You cannot (*lit*. could not) be prosperous if you do not toil (*participle used conditionally* (*f*)). (*xiv*) You **will** not be hostile to your friends (*strong prohibition* (*g*)). (*xv*). If you say what you want (*sc*. to say), [then] hear in turn what you don't want (*sc*. to hear) (*general adjectival clause* (*c*)). (*xvi*) [We/one] must either eat tortoise meat or not eat [at all] (*infinitive* (*e*)). (*xvii*) Can you tell me whether virtue can be taught (*lit*. is a teachable [thing]) or not? (*alternative question* (*i*)—μή *is also possible*). (*xviii*) No-one will deny that he knows what is just (*lit*. just things) (*negated verb of denying* (24.1/7)). (*xix*) He was afraid that he would not be able to go out of the country (*noun clause* (*d*)). (*xx*) Do not go away until you hear (*prohibition/negative command* (*a*)).   (2) We must worship the gods, benefit our friends, help the city, try to do good to Greece, cultivate the land, look after the cattle, [and] learn the arts of war.   (3) When anyone is brought to (*lit*. into) a hostile (*lit*. opposing) trial and is about to speak about bloodshed, fear brings the mouth of men to consternation and hinders the mind from saying what it wishes. (Euripides, fragment 67.)   (4) You must beware not to be obviously doing publicly any of things which you would privately guard against.   (5) All these laws have been in

existence (*lit.* made) for a long time now, gentlemen of the jury, and no-one ever yet denied that they would be good. (6) Take care not to reveal your low birth (*lit.* lest you may appear being born lowly). (7) So I greeted the two of them, since I had not seen them for some time (*lit.* as having seen [them] after a time); and after this I said to Cleinias, "Cleinias, these two men, you know, Euthydemus and Dionysodorus, are skilled not in trivialities (*lit.* little things) but in important matters. For they know all about (*lit.* the things about) war." They despised me for saying this (*lit.* when I said this I was despised by them); so they both laughed, looking at each other, and Euthydemus said, "We do **not**, Socrates, concern ourselves with these things any longer, but deal with them [as] subordinate issues." And I said admiringly, "Your business must be a fine one, if such important matters happen to be subordinate for you; in the name of the gods, tell me what this fine [business] is." "Virtue," he said, "Socrates, [is what] we think we are able to deliver as excellently and speedily as is humanly possible." "Zeus," said I, "what a [splendid] affair. Where (*lit.* from where) did you find this treasure. I was still thinking about you, as I said just now, as for the most part being clever at this, [*i.e.*] fighting under arms, and this [is what] I was saying about you; for when you visited [us] before, this [is what] the pair of you professed." (Plato *Euthydemus* 273c–e.) (8) After him (*lit.* this man) Xenophon said, "And I am of the following opinion (*lit.* think thus). If it is necessary [for us] to fight, we must make preparations to fight as vigorously as possible; but if we wish to cross as easily as possible, I think we should consider how we may receive as few wounds as possible and lose as few lives as possible." (9) We must consider whether it is right or not (*lit.* just . . . or not just) for me to try to leave from here without the permission of the Athenians (*lit.* the Athenians not letting [me] go). (10) *A.* Tell me, do you have a field? *B.* No, I don't. (11) And further if we submit and come into the power of the king, what do you think we shall suffer? He cut off the head and hand of even his brother by the same mother and [that too] when already dead, and impaled them. As for us, who have no protector and [who] made an expedition against him with the intention of making him a slave instead of a king and of killing him if we could, what do we think we would suffer? Surely he would go to any lengths so that, by inflicting the worst outrages on us, he might instill in all men fear of ever campaigning against him? But everything must be done so that we do not come into his power. (Xenophon *Anabasis* iii. 1.17f.)

24.3

Strepsiades. In the name of the gods, what is this (*lit.* these things)? Tell me. *Student.* This is astronomy. *Str.* And what's this? *St.* Geometry. *Str.* So what's it (*lit.* this thing) useful for? *St.* To measure out land. *Str.* [Do you mean land] for cleruchies? *St.* No, [land] as a whole. *Str.* What do you call as attractive (*lit.* you say an attractive [thing]). For the device is democratic (*or* popular) and useful. *St.* And this, notice, is a map of the whole world. Do you see? Here is Athens. *Str.* What do you mean? I don't believe [you], for I cannot (*lit.* do not) see [any] jurymen sitting [there]. *St.* [I assure you] that this area is truly Attic (*or* Attica). *Str.* Come now, who's this man in the basket? *St.* The master. *Str.* Who's the master? *St.* Socrates. *Str.* Ah, [it's] Socrates. You there, go [and] call him loudly for me. *St.* No, **you** call [him] yourself. I don't have the time. *Str.* Socrates! Dear little Socrates! *Socrates* Why do you call me, creature of a day? *Str.* In the first place, tell me, I pray, what you are doing. *So.* I tread the air and my thoughts centre round the sun (*lit.* I think about the sun). *Str.* Then you're looking down on the gods from [your] mat, and (*lit.* but) not from the earth, if [indeed that's what you're doing]. *So.* [Yes] for I would never have correctly discovered heavenly phenomena, except by suspending [my] perception and thought. (Aristophanes *Clouds* 200–209, 218–229.)

25.2

(1) Again mighty Hector of the gleaming helmet addressed her: "Indeed all this is **my** concern, [my] wife; but I am terribly afraid of the Trojans and the Trojan women with their trailing robes, if, like a coward, I shrink away far from the fighting. Nor does my spirit [so] order me, since I have learned always to be brave and to fight among the foremost [ranks of the] Trojans, winning great glory both for my father and for myself. For I know this well in my heart and in my soul: there will come (*lit.* be) a day when holy Ilium will be destroyed, and Priam and the people of Priam of the fine ash-spear. But [it is] not so much grief for the Trojans hereafter [which] troubles me, neither for Hecuba herself nor for lord Priam nor for [my] brothers, who, many and brave, may fall in the dust at the hands of the enemy (*lit.* hostile men), as [grief] for you, when one of the bronze-clad Achaeans will lead you away in tears, taking away [your] day of liberty; and living (*lit.* being) in Argos you will weave a web at the command of another [woman] (*i.e.* a mistress), and carry water from [the spring] Messeis or Hypereia, much unwilling, but strong necessity will be upon [you]. And one day a man seeing you shedding tears will say: 'This is the wife of Hector, who was the best of the horse-taming Trojans at fighting [at the time] when they (*i.e.* the Greeks) besieged Ilium.' Thus one day will someone speak; and for you it will be a fresh grief because of the lack of such a husband to ward off the day of slavery. But may earth heaped up cover me in death before I hear your scream when you are taken away by force (*lit.* both your scream and your being carried off)." (*Iliad* vi. 440–465.)   (2) All night long they sat with high thoughts (*lit.* thinking big) along the embankments of war, and their fires blazed in great numbers (*lit.* many). Just as when in the sky the stars are seen conspicuous[ly] around the bright moon, when the air becomes windless; and there appear all the lookout-places and the tops of the headlands and the glens; and from heaven the boundless air is rent beneath, and all the stars are seen, and the shepherd rejoices in his heart. So many shone the fires as the Trojans lit [them] in front of Ilium, between the ships and the streams of Xanthus. A thousand fires then were blazing in the plain, and beside each one sat fifty [men] in the gleam of the blazing fire. And the horses, feeding on white barley and wheat, stood beside the chariots and waited for fair-throned Dawn. (*Iliad* viii. 553–565.)   (3) Tell me, Muse, of the man of many wiles, who wandered far and wide (*lit.* very much), after he had sacked the holy citadel of Troy. He saw the cities of many men and came to know [their] minds, and on the sea he suffered many griefs in his heart, striving to win his own life and the home-coming of [his] companions. But not even so did he save [his] companions, strive as he might, for they perished by their own presumptuousness, fools, who devoured the cattle of Hyperion the Sun [God]; and he took from them the day of [their] homecoming. (*Odyssey* i. 1–9.)   (4) From there I was carried along for nine days by baneful winds over the sea full of fish; but on the tenth [day] we stepped on to the land of the Lotus-Eaters, who feed on [that] flowery food. There we set foot on the mainland and drew water, and [my] companions quickly took their meal beside the swift ships. But when we had partaken of food and drink, then I sent ahead [some of my] companions to go and find out what sort of men were living (*lit.* eating food) in [this] land, choosing two men and sending a third with [them] as herald. They went off and quickly fell in with the Lotus-Eaters (*lit.* the Lotus-eating men). Nor did the Lotus-Eaters plot destruction for our companions, but gave them [some] lotus to taste. Whoever of them ate the honey-sweet fruit of the lotus was no longer willing to report back [to us] or return, but wished to remain there with the Lotus-Eaters, feeding on lotus, and to forget [his] home-coming. Forcibly I brought them [back] in tears to the ships, and I dragged [them] and bound [them] under the benches in the hollowed ships. Then I ordered the rest of my trusty companions to embark with haste (*lit.* hurrying) on the swift ships, lest any of them might somehow eat of the lotus and forget their home-coming. They went quickly on board and sat down at the benches, and sitting in order they smote the grey sea with the oars. (*Odyssey* ix. 82–104.)

Key to Revision Exercises

Units 2–4 *1* (i) ἀκτῶν. (ii) δῶρα. (iii) νεανίᾳ. (iv) λόγοις. (v) ποιητά. (vi) *Κρονίδου.* (vii) τραπέζης. (viii) τέκνον. (ix) ὕδρας. (x) βασιλείαις.

2 s.	*Nom.*	δοῦλος	δεσπότης	γλῶττα	ζῷον	βοή
	Voc.	δοῦλε	δέσποτα	γλῶττα	ζῷον	βοή
	Acc.	δοῦλον	δεσπότην	γλῶτταν	ζῷον	βοήν
	Gen.	δούλου	δεσπότου	γλώττης	ζῴου	βοῆς
	Dat.	δούλῳ	δεσπότῃ	γλώττῃ	ζῴῳ	βοῇ
pl.	*N.V.*	δοῦλοι	δεσπόται	γλῶτται	ζῷα	βοαί
	Acc.	δούλους	δεσπότας	γλώττας	ζῷα	βοάς
	Gen.	δούλων	δεσποτῶν	γλωττῶν	ζῴων	βοῶν
	Dat.	δούλοις	δεσπόταις	γλώτταις	ζῴοις	βοαῖς

3 (i) πίπτω, πίπτεις, πίπτει, πίπτομεν, πίπτετε, πίπτουσι(ν). (ii) κελεύσω, κελεύσεις, κελεύσει, κελεύσομεν, κελεύσετε, κελεύσουσι(ν). (iii) ἐφρόντιζον, ἐφρόντιζες, ἐφρόντιζε(ν), ἐφροντίζομεν, ἐφροντίζετε, ἐφρόντιζον. (iv) ἔπαυσα, ἔπαυσας, ἔπαυσε(ν), ἐπαύσαμεν, ἐπαύσατε, ἔπαυσαν. *4* στρατεύειν, στρατεύσειν, στρατεῦσαι; πέμπειν, πέμψειν, πέμψαι.

Units 5–7

1 s.	*Nom.*	χρῆμα	μήτηρ	κόραξ	γέρων	ψεῦδος
	Voc.	χρῆμα	μῆτερ	κόραξ	γέρον	ψεῦδος
	Acc.	χρῆμα	μητέρα	κόρακα	γέροντα	ψεῦδος
	Gen.	χρήματος	μητρός	κόρακος	γέροντος	ψεύδους
	Dat.	χρήματι	μητρί	κόρακι	γέροντι	ψεύδει
pl.	*N.V.*	χρήματα	μητέρες	κόρακες	γέροντες	ψεύδη
	Acc.	χρήματα	μητέρας	κόρακας	γέροντας	ψεύδη
	Gen.	χρημάτων	μητέρων	κοράκων	γερόντων	ψευδῶν
	Dat.	χρήμασι(ν)	μητράσι(ν)	κόραξι(ν)	γέρουσι(ν)	ψεύδεσι(ν)

s.	*Nom.*	ὄρνις	παῖς	κρατήρ	Ἕλλην
	Voc.	ὄρνι	παῖ	κρατήρ	Ἕλλην
	Acc.	ὄρνιν	παῖδα	κρατῆρα	Ἕλληνα
	Gen.	ὄρνιθος	παιδός	κρατῆρος	Ἕλληνος
	Dat.	ὄρνιθι	παιδί	κρατῆρι	Ἕλληνι
pl.	*N.V.*	ὄρνιθες	παῖδες	κρατῆρες	Ἕλληνες
	Acc.	ὄρνιθας	παῖδας	κρατῆρας	Ἕλληνας
	Gen.	ὀρνίθων	παίδων	κρατήρων	Ἑλλήνων
	Dat.	ὄρνισι(ν)	παισί(ν)	κρατῆρσι(ν)	Ἕλλησι(ν)

2 (i) ἐφύλαξα, ἐφύλαξας, ἐφύλαξε(ν), ἐφυλάξαμεν, ἐφυλάξατε, ἐφύλαξαν; ἤγαγον, ἤγαγες, ἤγαγε(ν), ἠγάγομεν, ἠγάγετε, ἤγαγον; ἐποίησα, ἐποίησας, ἐποίησε(ν), ἐποιήσαμεν, ἐποιήσατε, ἐποίησαν; ἔγραψα, ἔγραψας, ἔγραψε(ν), ἐγράψαμεν, ἐγράψατε, ἔγραψαν; ἐνόμισα, ἐνόμισας, ἐνόμισε(ν), ἐνομίσαμεν, ἐνομίσατε, ἐνόμισαν. (ii) ἐφίλουν, ἐφίλεις, ἐφίλει, ἐφιλοῦμεν, ἐφιλεῖτε, ἐφίλουν; ἐδούλουν, ἐδούλους, ἐδούλου, ἐδουλοῦμεν, ἐδουλοῦτε, ἐδούλουν; ἐτίμων, ἐτίμας, ἐτίμα, ἐτιμῶμεν, ἐτιμᾶτε, ἐτίμων. (iii) ἐλπιῶ, ἐλπιεῖς, ἐλπιεῖ, ἐλπιοῦμεν, ἐλπιεῖτε, ἐλπιοῦσι(ν); κόψω, κόψεις, κόψει, κόψομεν, κόψετε, κόψουσι(ν); ἄξω, ἄξεις, ἄξει, ἄξομεν, ἄξετε, ἄξουσι(ν). (iv) ὁρῶ, ὁρᾷς, ὁρᾷ, ὁρῶμεν, ὁρᾶτε, ὁρῶσι(ν); ὀρθῶ, ὀρθοῖς, ὀρθοῖ, ὀρθοῦμεν, ὀρθοῦτε, ὀρθοῦσι(ν); καλῶ, καλεῖς, καλεῖ, καλοῦμεν, καλεῖτε, καλοῦσι(ν). *3* (i) συνελάβετε. (ii) περιήνεγκον. (iii) συνεκράτουν. (iv) ἐξεῖλον. (v) ἐνέγραφε(ν).

Units 8–10 *1* (i) παύομαι, παύῃ(-ει), παύεται, παυόμεθα, παύεςθε, παύονται.
(ii) ἐκομιζόμην, ἐκομίζου, ἐκομίζετο, ἐκομιζόμεθα, ἐκομίζεςθε, ἐκομίζοντο.
(iii) ἐδιδαξάμην, ἐδιδάξω, ἐδιδάξατο, ἐδιδαξάμεθα, ἐδιδάξαςθε, ἐδιδάξαντο.
(iv) λούςομαι, λούςῃ(-ει), λούςεται, λουςόμεθα, λούςεςθε, λούςονται. (v) δουλοῦμαι,
δουλοῖ, δουλοῦται, δουλούμεθα, δουλοῦςθε, δουλοῦνται. (vi) ἐπολεμούμην,
ἐπολεμοῦ, ἐπολεμεῖτο, ἐπολεμούμεθα, ἐπολεμεῖςθε, ἐπολεμοῦντο.

2 None of these phrases can have a vocative:

s.	Nom.	οὗτος ὁ χαρίεις μῦς	ὅδε ὁ ἀμαθής
		this charming mouse (near you)	this ignorant person (near me)
	Acc.	τοῦτον τὸν χαρίεντα μῦν	τόνδε τὸν ἀμαθῆ
	Gen.	τούτου τοῦ χαρίεντος μυός	τοῦδε τοῦ ἀμαθοῦς
	Dat.	τούτῳ τῷ χαρίεντι μυΐ	τῷδε τῷ ἀμαθεῖ
pl.	N.	οὗτοι οἱ χαρίεντες μῦες	οἵδε οἱ ἀμαθεῖς
	Acc.	τούτους τοὺς χαρίεντας μῦας	τούςδε τοὺς ἀμαθεῖς
	Gen.	τούτων τῶν χαριέντων μυῶν	τῶνδε τῶν ἀμαθῶν
	Dat.	τούτοις τοῖς χαρίεςι μυςί(ν)	τοῖςδε τοῖς ἀμαθέςι(ν)

s.	Nom.	ἐκεῖνος ὁ ὀξύς that quick person	ὁ ὄφις αὐτός the snake itself
	Acc.	ἐκεῖνον τὸν ὀξύν	τὸν ὄφιν αὐτόν
	Gen.	ἐκείνου τοῦ ὀξέος	τοῦ ὄφεως αὐτοῦ
	Dat.	ἐκείνῳ τῷ ὀξεῖ	τῷ ὄφει αὐτῷ
pl.	N.	ἐκεῖνοι οἱ ὀξεῖς	οἱ ὄφεις αὐτοί
	Acc.	ἐκείνους τοὺς ὀξεῖς	τοὺς ὄφεις αὐτούς
	Gen.	ἐκείνων τῶν ὀξέων	τῶν ὄφεων αὐτῶν
	Dat.	ἐκείνοις τοῖς ὀξέςι(ν)	τοῖς ὄφεςιν αὐτοῖς

3 (i) αὐτή *n. f. s. of* αὐτός; αὐτή (=ἡ αὐτή) *n. f. s. of* ὁ αὐτός; αὕτη *n. f. s. of* οὗτος;
ταὐτῇ (=τῇ αὐτῇ) *dat. f. s. of* ὁ αὐτός. (ii) ταῦτα *n./acc. n. pl. of* οὗτος; ταὐτά (=τὰ
αὐτά) *n./acc. n. pl. of* ὁ αὐτός. (iii) ταύτου (=τοῦ αὐτοῦ) *gen. m./n. s. of* ὁ αὐτός;
τούτου *gen. m./n. s. of* οὗτος; αὐτοῦ *gen. m./n. s. of* αὐτός. (iv) αὐτῷ *dat. m./n. s. of*
αὐτός; τούτῳ *dat. m./n. s. of* οὗτος; ταὐτῷ (=τῷ αὐτῷ) *dat. m./n. s. of* ὁ αὐτός. *4* (i)
This girl near me; that girl over there. (ii) *This woman near you; the woman herself.* (iii)
This man near you; this man near me. (iv) *This boy near you; the same boy* (αὐτός = ὁ
αὐτός).

Units 11–13 *1* (i) ἔγνων, ἔγνως, ἔγνω, ἔγνωμεν, ἔγνωτε, ἔγνωςαν. (ii) ἠμυνάμην,
ἠμύνω, ἠμύνατο, ἠμυνάμεθα, ἠμύναςθε, ἠμύναντο. (iii) ἀγγελῶ, ἀγγελεῖς, ἀγγελεῖ,
ἀγγελοῦμεν, ἀγγελεῖτε, ἀγγελοῦςι(ν). (iv) ἀπέδραν, ἀπέδρας, ἀπέδρα, ἀπέδραμεν,
ἀπέδρατε, ἀπέδραςαν. (v) μανθήςομαι, μανθήςῃ(-ει), μανθήςεται, μανθηςόμεθα,
μανθήςεςθε, μανθήςονται. (vi) ἐδουλώθην, ἐδουλώθης, ἐδουλώθη, ἐδουλώθημεν,
ἐδουλώθητε, ἐδουλώθηςαν. (vii) ἀπαρῶ, ἀπαρεῖς, ἀπαρεῖ, ἀπαροῦμεν, ἀπαρεῖτε,
ἀπαροῦςι(ν). (viii) ἐτάχθην, ἐτάχθης, ἐτάχθη, ἐτάχθημεν, ἐτάχθητε, ἐτάχθηςαν. *2* (i)
βουλεύςων, βουλεύςουςα. (ii) διδαξάμενος, διδαξαμένη. (iii) ἀποφαινόμενος, ἀπο-
φαινομένη. (iv) βαλῶν, βαλοῦςα. (v) φιληθείς, φιληθεῖςα. (vi) ςημήνας, ςημήναςα.
(vii) οἰκοδομούμενος, οἰκοδομουμένη. (viii) τυχών, τυχοῦςα. (ix) ἀλγυνούμενος,
ἀλγυνουμένη. (x) γνούς, γνοῦςα.

3	s.	Nom.	ἥρως	λαγώς	υἱός
		Voc.	ἥρως	λαγώς	υἱέ
		Acc.	ἥρωα, ἥρω	λαγών	υἱόν
		Gen.	ἥρωος	λαγώ	υἱοῦ, υἱέος
		Dat.	ἥρωϊ, ἥρῳ	λαγώ	υἱῷ, υἱεῖ

pl.	*N.V.*	ἥρωες	λαγώ	υἱοί, υἱεῖς
	Acc.	ἥρωας	λαγώς	υἱούς, υἱεῖς
	Gen.	ἡρώων	λαγών	υἱῶν, υἱέων
	Dat.	ἥρωσι(ν)	λαγώς	υἱοῖς, υἱέσι(ν)

Units 14–16 *1* (i) κρίναιμι, κρίνειας(-αις), κρίνειε(-αι), κρίναιμεν, κρίναιτε, κρίνειαν(-αιεν). (ii) γέγραφα, γέγραφας, γέγραφε(ν), γεγράφαμεν, γεγράφατε, γεγράφασι(ν). (iii) πορεύωμαι, πορεύῃ, πορεύηται, πορευώμεθα, πορεύησθε, πορεύωνται. (iv) ἐδεδουλώκη, ἐδεδουλώκης, ἐδεδουλώκει(ν), ἐδεδουλώκεμεν, ἐδεδουλώκετε, ἐδεδουλώκεσαν. (v) βῶ, βῇς, βῇ, βῶμεν, βῆτε, βῶσι(ν). (vi) ἠλλάγμην, ἤλλαξο, ἤλλακτο, ἠλλάγμεθα, ἤλλαχθε, ἀλλαγμένοι ἦσαν. (vii) ὀρθῶ, ὀρθοῖς, ὀρθοῖ, ὀρθῶμεν, ὀρθῶτε, ὀρθῶσι(ν). (viii) κέκλεμμαι, κέκλεψαι, κέκλεπται, κεκλέμμεθα, κέκλεφθε, κεκλεμμένοι εἰσί(ν). (ix) ὁρῴην, ὁρῴης, ὁρῴη, ὁρῷμεν, ὁρῷτε, ὁρῷεν. (x) φύγοιμι, φύγοις, φύγοι, φύγοιμεν, φύγοιτε, φύγοιεν. (xi) κέκρουμαι, κέκρουσαι, κέκρουται, κεκρούμεθα, κέκρουσθε, κέκρουνται. (xii) φιλῶμαι, φιλῇ, φιλῆται, φιλώμεθα, φιλῆσθε, φιλῶνται. *2* (i) gen. m./n. s. of the perf. act. pple. of βάλλω. (ii) perf. act. inf. of μανθάνω. (iii) gen. f. s. of the weak perf. act. pple. of πείθω. (iv) perf. inf. of φοβέομαι. (v) gen. f. s. of the perf. mid./pass. pple. of λύω. (vi) dat. m./n. pl. of the aor. pass. pple. of γράφω. (vii) perf. mid./pass. inf. of κρύπτω. (viii) acc. m. pl. of the perf. act. pple. of γιγνώσκω. (ix) perf. act. inf. of λαμβάνω. (x) nom./acc. n. s. of the perf. act. pple of πέμπω. *3* ἁρπάσῃσθε, βάλλοιτο, ἅψωνται, πράξαιτο, δηλῶται, βεβουλεύμεθα, λαβοίμεθα, ἐπεποιήμην, τιμῷτο, εὕρηται.

Units 17–19 *1* (i) 3rd s. aor. opt. act. of δίδωμι. (ii) gen. m./n. s. of the perf. pple. of ἵστημι (shorter form). (iii) pres./fut. inf. of ἔρχομαι. (iv) pres. act. inf. of δίδωμι. (v) *Either* 3rd pl. ind. act. of the transitive aor. of ἵστημι *or* 3rd pl. ind. of the intransitive aor. of ἵστημι. (vi) dat. m./n. pl. of the pres./fut. pple. of ἔρχομαι. (vii) *Either* 2nd pl. imp. *or* 2nd pl. subj. of the intransitive aor. of ἵστημι. (viii) 3rd pl. impf. act. of τίθημι. (ix) 1st s. pres. subj. of ἔρχομαι. (x) dat. m./n. s. of the aor. act. pple. of τίθημι. (xi) 3rd pl. pres./fut. opt. of ἔρχομαι. (xii) 3rd pl. plpf. of ἵστημι. (xiii) 2nd s. aor. imp. act. of τίθημι. (xiv) inf. of the intransitive aor. of ἵστημι. (xv) 1st pl. aor. opt. act. of τίθημι. (xvi) 2nd s. pres. imp. of ἔρχομαι. (xvii) dat. m./n. pl. of the aor. act. pple. of δίδωμι. (xviii) 3rd pl. fut. ind. of ἔρχομαι. *2* For these paradigms see **Appendix 5**. *3* (i) If you had done this (*past*), you would have suffered nothing (*past*). (ii) If you were doing this (*present*), you would be suffering nothing (*present*). (iii) If you do this (*future*), you will suffer nothing (*future*). (iv) If you were to do this (*future*), you would suffer nothing (*future*). (v) If you did this (*past*), you suffered nothing (*past*). (vi) If you are doing this (*present*), you are suffering nothing (*present*). (vii) If you were doing/used to do this (*past, continual or habitual*), you were suffering/used to suffer nothing (*past, continual or habitual*). (viii) If you had done this (*past*), you would be suffering nothing (*present*). (*In the above i, ii, iv, viii are category 1 conditional sentences (18.1/5) and hence have ἄν with their main verb; the others belong to category 2 and do not.*) *4* ἀρχαιότερος, ἀρχαιότατος; ἀσθενέστερος, ἀσθενέστατος; ἐχθίων, ἔχθιστος; κακίων, κάκιστος (or χείρων, χείριστος); κενώτερος, κενώτατος; ῥᾴων, ῥᾷστος; σωφρονέστερος, σωφρονέστατος; θάττων, τάχιστος. *5* All forms are from the comparative of πολύς; πλέονι dat. m./f./n. s.; πλειόνων gen. m./f./n. pl.; πλείους (shorter form of πλέονες or πλέονας) nom. or acc. m./f. pl.; πλείω (shorter form of πλέονα) *either* acc. m. s. *or* nom./acc. n. pl.; πλεόνων another form of πλειόνων.

Units 20–22 *1* (i) ἐφίεμαι, ἐφίεσαι, ἐφίεται, ἐφιέμεθα, ἐφίεσθε, ἐφίενται. (ii) ἀφῆκα, ἀφῆκας, ἀφῆκε(ν), ἀφεῖμεν, ἀφεῖτε, ἀφεῖσαν. (iii) ἀνοίγνυμι, ἀνοίγνυς, ἀνοίγνυσι(ν), ἀνοίγνυμεν, ἀνοίγνυτε, ἀνοιγνύασι(ν). (iv) μεθιέμην, μεθίεσο, μεθίετο, μεθιέμεθα, μεθίεσθε, μεθίεντο. (v) παρείην, παρείης, παρείη, παρεῖμεν, παρεῖτε, παρεῖεν. (vi) ἀπωλλύμην, ἀπώλλυςο, ἀπώλλυτο, ἀπωλλύμεθα, ἀπώλλυςθε, ἀπώλλυντο. (vii) ἄφες, ἀφέτω, ἄφετε, ἀφέντων. (viii) παριῶ, παριῇς, παριῇ, παριῶμεν, παριῆτε, παριῶςι(ν). 2 (i)–(iv) are all from ὄλλυμι: (i) ὤλεςε 3rd s. ind. act. of the weak (tr.) aor.; ὤλετο 3rd s. ind. of the strong (intr.) aor. (ii) ἀπολώλαμεν 1st pl. ind. of the strong (intr.) perf.; ἀπολωλέκαμεν 1st pl. ind. act. of the weak (tr.) perf. (iii) ἀπωλώλει 3rd s. of the strong (intr.) plpf.; ἀπωλωλέκει 3rd s. act. of the weak (tr.) plpf. (iv) ὄλοιο 2nd s. opt. of the strong (intr.) aor.; ὀλέςειας 2nd s. opt. act. of the weak (tr.) aor. (v) The three forms are from ἵημι: ἱᾶςι 3rd pl. pres. ind. act.; ἱῶςι 3rd pl. pres. subj. act.; ἱεῖςι dat. m./ n. pl. of the pres. act. pple. (vi) δεικνῦςι dat. m./n. pl. of the pres. act. pple. of δείκνυμι; δεικνύαςι 3rd pl. pres. ind. act. of δείκνυμι. (vii) ἵεμεν 1st pl. pres. ind. act. of ἵημι; ἵμεν 1st pl. fut. ind. of ἔρχομαι. (viii) ἱῶ 1st s. pres. subj. act. of ἵημι; ἵω 1st s. pres. subj. of ἔρχομαι. (ix) ὧ 1st s. aor. subj. act. of ἵημι; ὦ either 1st s. pres. subj. of εἰμί or the exclamation *O, ah*; (x) δεικνύναι pres. act. inf. of δείκνυμι; δείκνυται 3rd s. pres. ind. act. of δείκνυμι.

Principal parts of verbs

Present	Future	Aorist	Perfect	Perfect mid./pass.	Aorist passive
ἀγγέλλω *announce*	ἀγγελῶ	ἤγγειλα	ἤγγελκα	ἤγγελμαι	ἠγγέλθην
ἄγω *lead*	ἄξω	ἤγαγον	ἦχα	ἦγμαι	ἤχθην
(ἐπ-)αἰνέω *praise*	αἰνέσομαι (αἰνέσω)	ᾔνεσα	ᾔνεκα	ᾔνημαι	ᾐνέθην
αἱρέω *take*; mid. *choose*	αἱρήσω	εἷλον	ᾕρηκα	ᾕρημαι	ᾑρέθην
αἴρω *raise*	ἀρῶ	ἦρα	ἦρκα	ἦρμαι	ἤρθην
αἰσθάνομαι *perceive*	αἰσθήσομαι	ᾐσθόμην		ᾔσθημαι	
αἰσχύ̄νω *dishonour*	αἰσχυνῶ	ᾔσχῡνα			ᾐσχύνθην
ἀκούω *hear*	ἀκούσομαι	ἤκουσα	ἀκήκοα		ἠκούσθην
ἁλίσκομαι *be captured*	ἁλώσομαι	ἑά̄λων	ἑά̄λωκα		
ἁμαρτάνω *err*	ἁμαρτήσομαι	ἥμαρτον	ἡμάρτηκα	ἡμάρτημαι	ἡμαρτήθην
ἀμῡ́νω *ward off*	ἀμυνῶ	ἤμῡνα			
ἀνᾱλίσκω *spend*	ἀνᾱλώσω	ἀνήλωσα	ἀνήλωκα	ἀνήλωμαι	ἀνηλώθην
ἀνοίγνῡμι *open*	ἀνοίξω	ἀνέῳξα	ἀνέῳχα	ἀνέῳγμαι	ἀνεῴχθην
ἀποκρῑ́νομαι *answer*	ἀποκρινοῦμαι	ἀπεκρῑνάμην		ἀποκέκριμαι	
ἄρχω *begin, rule*	ἄρξω	ἦρξα		ἦργμαι	ἤρχθην
ἀφικνέομαι *arrive*	ἀφίξομαι	ἀφῑκόμην		ἀφῖγμαι	
βαίνω *go*	βήσομαι	ἔβην	βέβηκα		
βάλλω *throw*	βαλῶ	ἔβαλον	βέβληκα	βέβλημαι	ἐβλήθην
βλάπτω *hurt, injure*	βλάψω	ἔβλαψα	βέβλαφα	βέβλαμμαι	ἐβλάφθην ἐβλάβην
βοάω *shout*	βοήσομαι	ἐβόησα			
βούλομαι *wish*	βουλήσομαι			βεβούλημαι	ἐβουλήθην

Present	Future	Aorist	Perfect	Perfect mid./pass.	Aorist passive
γαμέω *marry* (of the man)	γαμῶ	ἔγημα	γεγάμηκα		
γαμέομαι *marry* (of the woman)	γαμοῦμαι	ἐγημάμην		γέγαμημαι	
γελάω *laugh*	γελάσομαι	ἐγέλασα			ἐγελάσθην
γίγνομαι *become*	γενήσομαι	ἐγενόμην	γέγονα	γεγένημαι	
γιγνώσκω *know*	γνώσομαι	ἔγνων	ἔγνωκα	ἔγνωσμαι	ἐγνώσθην
γράφω *write*	γράψω	ἔγραψα	γέγραφα	γέγραμμαι	ἐγράφην
δάκνω *bite*	δήξομαι	ἔδακον		δέδηγμαι	ἐδήχθην
δεῖ impers. *it is necessary*	δεήσει	ἐδέησε			
δείκνῡμι *show*	δείξω	ἔδειξα	δέδειχα	δέδειγμαι	ἐδείχθην
δέομαι *need, ask*	δεήσομαι			δεδέημαι	ἐδεήθην
δέχομαι *receive, await*	δέξομαι	ἐδεξάμην		δέδεγμαι	ἐδέχθην
δέω (A) *want, lack*	δεήσω	ἐδέησα			
δέω (B) *bind*	δήσω	ἔδησα	δέδεκα	δέδεμαι	ἐδέθην
διαλέγομαι *converse*	διαλέξομαι			διείλεγμαι	διελέχθην
διδάσκω *teach*	διδάξω	ἐδίδαξα	δεδίδαχα	δεδίδαγμαι	ἐδιδάχθην
δίδωμι *give*	δώσω	ἔδωκα	δέδωκα	δέδομαι	ἐδόθην
διώκω *pursue*	διώξομαι	ἐδίωξα	δεδίωχα		ἐδιώχθην
δοκέω *seem, think*	δόξω	ἔδοξα		δέδογμαι	
δύναμαι *be able, can*	δυνήσομαι			δεδύνημαι	ἐδυνήθην
ἐάω *allow, let alone*	ἐάσω	εἴᾱσα	εἴᾱκα	εἴᾱμαι	εἰάθην
ἐγείρω *arouse*	ἐγερῶ	ἤγειρα	ἐγρήγορα (intr.) *I am awake*		
ἐθέλω *wish, be willing*	ἐθελήσω	ἠθέλησα	ἠθέληκα		
εἴργω *imprison, prevent*	εἴρξω	εἶρξα		εἶργμαι	εἴρχθην
ἐλαύνω *drive*	ἐλῶ (= άω)	ἤλασα	ἐλήλακα	ἐλήλαμαι	ἠλάθην

Present	Future	Aorist	Perfect	Perfect mid./pass.	Aorist passive
ἐλέγχω *examine, confute*	ἐλέγξω	ἤλεγξα		ἐλήλεγμαι	ἠλέγχθην
ἕλκω *drag, draw*	ἕλξω	εἵλκυσα	εἵλκυκα	εἵλκυσμαι	εἱλκύσθην
ἐπίσταμαι *understand*	ἐπιστήσομαι				ἠπιστήθην
ἕπομαι *follow*	ἕψομαι	ἑσπόμην			
ἐργάζομαι *work*	ἐργάσομαι	ἠργασάμην		εἴργασμαι	ἠργάσθην
ἔρχομαι *go, come*	εἶμι	ἦλθον	ἐλήλυθα		
ἐρωτάω *ask a question*	ἐρωτήσω ἐρήσομαι	(ἠρώτησα) ἠρόμην	ἠρώτηκα	ἠρώτημαι	ἠρωτήθην
ἐσθίω *eat*	ἔδομαι	ἔφαγον	ἐδήδοκα	ἐδήδεσμαι	
εὑρίσκω *find*	εὑρήσω	ηὗρον	ηὕρηκα	ηὕρημαι	ηὑρέθην
ἔχω *have*	ἕξω σχήσω	ἔσχον	ἔσχηκα	ἔσχημαι	
ζάω *live*	ζήσω/ζήσομαι βιώσομαι	ἐβίων	βεβίωκα		
ἥδομαι *be pleased*	ἡσθήσομαι				ἥσθην
θάπτω *bury*	θάψω	ἔθαψα		τέθαμμαι	ἐτάφην
θαυμάζω *wonder*	θαυμάσομαι	ἐθαύμασα	τεθαύμακα	τεθαύμασμαι	ἐθαυμάσθην
(ἀπο-)θνῄσκω *die*	θανοῦμαι	ἔθανον	τέθνηκα		
θύω *sacrifice*	θύσω	ἔθῡσα	τέθυκα	τέθυμαι	ἐτύθην
ἵημι *let go, send forth,*	ἥσω	ἧκα	εἷκα	εἷμαι	εἵθην
ἵστημι *place, make stand*	στήσω	ἔστησα (tr.) ἔστην (intr.)	ἕστηκα (intr.)	ἕσταμαι	ἐστάθην
καίω *burn*	καύσω	ἔκαυσα	κέκαυκα	κέκαυμαι	ἐκαύθην
καλέω *call*	καλῶ	ἐκάλεσα	κέκληκα	κέκλημαι	ἐκλήθην
κελεύω *order, bid*	κελεύσω	ἐκέλευσα	κεκέλευκα	κεκέλευσμαι	ἐκελεύσθην
κλαίω *weep*	κλαύσομαι	ἔκλαυσα		κέκλαυμαι	

Present	Future	Aorist	Perfect	Perfect mid./pass.	Aorist passive
κλέπτω steal	κλέψω	ἔκλεψα	κέκλοφα	κέκλεμμαι	ἐκλάπην
κομίζω convey, bring	κομιῶ	ἐκόμισα	κεκόμικα	κεκόμισμαι	ἐκομίσθην
κρίνω judge	κρινῶ	ἔκρῑνα	κέκρικα	κέκριμαι	ἐκρίθην
κτάομαι acquire	κτήσομαι	ἐκτησάμην		κέκτημαι possess	ἐκτήθην
(ἀπο-)κτείνω kill	κτενῶ	ἔκτεινα	ἔκτονα		
λαγχάνω obtain by lot	λήξομαι	ἔλαχον	εἴληχα	εἴληγμαι	ἐλήχθην
λαμβάνω take	λήψομαι	ἔλαβον	εἴληφα	εἴλημμαι	ἐλήφθην
λανθάνω escape the notice of, lie hid (ἐπι-)	λήcω	ἔλαθον	λέληθα		
λανθάνομαι forget	λήcομαι	ἐλαθόμην		λέληcμαι	
λέγω (A) say	λέξω ἐρῶ	ἔλεξα εἶπον	εἴρηκα	λέλεγμαι εἴρημαι	ἐλέχθην ἐρρήθην
λέγω (B) pick up, gather	λέξω	ἔλεξα	εἴλοχα	εἴλεγμαι (λέλεγμαι)	ἐλέγην
λείπω leave	λείψω	ἔλιπον	λέλοιπα	λέλειμμαι	ἐλείφθην
μανθάνω learn	μαθήcομαι	ἔμαθον	μεμάθηκα		
μάχομαι fight	μαχοῦμαι	ἐμαχεcάμην		μεμάχημαι	
μέλει impers. it is a care (ἐπι-)	μελήcει	ἐμέληcε	μεμέληκε		
μελέομαι care for	μελήcομαι			μεμέλημαι	ἐμελήθην
μέλλω intend	μελλήcω	ἐμέλληcα			
μένω remain (ἀνα-)	μενῶ	ἔμεινα	μεμένηκα		
μιμνήcκω remind	μνήcω	ἔμνηcα		μέμνημαι remember	ἐμνήcθην remembered
νέω swim	νεύcομαι	ἔνευcα	νένευκα		
νομίζω think	νομιῶ	ἐνόμιcα	νενόμικα	νενόμιcμαι	ἐνομίcθην
οἶδα know	εἴcομαι				

Present	Future	Aorist	Perfect	Perfect mid./pass.	Aorist passive
οἴομαι (also οἶμαι) *think*	οἰήςομαι				ᾠήθην
(ἀπ-)ὄλλῡμι *destroy, lose*	ὀλῶ	ὤλεσα	ὀλώλεκα (tr.) ὄλωλα (intr. *I am ruined*)		
(ἀπ-)ὄλλυμαι *be lost, perish*	ὀλοῦμαι	ὠλόμην			
ὄμνῡμι *swear*	ὀμοῦμαι	ὤμοσα	ὀμώμοκα	ὀμώμο(c)μαι	ὠμό(c)θην
ὁράω *see*	ὄψομαι	εἶδον	ἑόρᾱκα ἑώρᾱκα	ἑώρᾱμαι ὦμμαι	ὤφθην
ὀργίζομαι *become angry*	ὀργιοῦμαι			ὤργιcμαι	ὠργίcθην
ὀφείλω *owe*	ὀφειλήcω	ὠφείλησα ὤφελον (21.1/1)	ὠφείληκα		
πάcχω *suffer*	πείcομαι	ἔπαθον	πέπονθα		
πείθω *persuade*	πείcω	ἔπεισα	πέπεικα (tr.) πέποιθα (intr. *trust*)	πέπεισμαι	ἐπείcθην
πέμπω *send*	πέμψω	ἔπεμψα	πέπομφα	πέπεμμαι	ἐπέμφθην
πίμπλημι *fill*	πλήcω	ἔπλησα	πέπληκα	πέπλησμαι	ἐπλήcθην
πίνω *drink*	πίομαι	ἔπιον	πέπωκα	πέπομαι	ἐπόθην
πίπτω *fall*	πεcοῦμαι	ἔπεcον	πέπτωκα		
πλέω *sail*	πλεύcομαι	ἔπλευσα	πέπλευκα	πέπλευcμαι	
πρᾱ́ττω *do*	πρᾱ́ξω	ἔπρᾱξα	πέπρᾱχα (tr.) πέπρᾱγα (intr. *have fared*)	πέπρᾱγμαι	ἐπρᾱ́χθην
πυνθάνομαι *ascertain*	πεύcομαι	ἐπυθόμην		πέπυcμαι	
πωλέω *sell*	ἀποδώcομαι	ἀπεδόμην	πέπρᾱκα	πέπρᾱμαι	ἐπρᾱ́θην
ῥήγνῡμι *break*	ῥήξω	ἔρρηξα	ἔρρωγα (intr. *am broken*)		ἐρράγην
ῥίπτω *throw*	ῥῑ́ψω	ἔρρῑψα	ἔρρῑφα	ἔρρῑμμαι	ἐρρίφθην
cκεδάννῡμι *scatter*	cκεδῶ (=άω)	ἐcκέδασα		ἐcκέδαcμαι	ἐcκεδάcθην
cπείρω *sow*	cπερῶ	ἔcπειρα	ἔcπαρκα	ἔcπαρμαι	ἐcπάρην
cτέλλω *send, equip*	cτελῶ	ἔcτειλα	ἔcταλκα	ἔcταλμαι	ἐcτάλην
cφάλλω *trip up*	cφαλῶ	ἔcφηλα		ἔcφαλμαι	ἐcφάλην
cῴζω *save*	cώcω	ἔcωcα	cέcωκα	cέcῳcμαι	ἐcώθην

Present	Future	Aorist	Perfect	Perfect mid./pass.	Aorist passive
τελέω *finish*	τελῶ	ἐτέλεσα	τετέλεκα	τετέλεσμαι	ἐτελέσθην
τέμνω *cut*	τεμῶ	ἔτεμον	τέτμηκα	τέτμημαι	ἐτμήθην
τίθημι *place, put*	θήσω	ἔθηκα	τέθηκα	τέθειμαι	ἐτέθην
τίκτω *beget*	τέξομαι	ἔτεκον	τέτοκα		
τιτρώσκω *wound*	τρώσω	ἔτρωσα		τέτρωμαι	ἐτρώθην
τρέπω *turn*	τρέψω	ἔτρεψα	τέτροφα	τέτραμμαι	ἐτράπην ἐτρέφθην
τρέφω *nourish*	θρέψω	ἔθρεψα	τέτροφα	τέθραμμαι	ἐτράφην ἐθρέφθην
τρέχω *run*	δραμοῦμαι	ἔδραμον	δεδράμηκα		
τυγχάνω *hit, happen*	τεύξομαι	ἔτυχον	τετύχηκα		
τύπτω *strike*	τυπτήσω	ἐτύπτησα			
ὑπισχνέομαι *promise*	ὑποσχήσομαι	ὑπεσχόμην	ὑπέσχημαι		
φαίνω *show*	φανῶ	ἔφηνα	πέφαγκα (tr. *I have shown*) πέφηνα (intr. *I have appeared*)	πέφασμαι	ἐφάνθην (*I was shown* ἐφάνην (intr. *I appeared*)
φέρω *bring, carry*	οἴσω	ἤνεγκον	ἐνήνοχα	ἐνήνεγμαι	ἠνέχθην
φεύγω *flee*	φεύξομαι	ἔφυγον	πέφευγα		
φημί *say*	φήσω	ἔφησα (ἔφην impf.)			
φθάνω *anticipate*	φθήσομαι	ἔφθασα ἔφθην (like ἔστην)			
(δια-)φθείρω *destroy, corrupt*	φθερῶ	ἔφθειρα	ἔφθαρκα	ἔφθαρμαι	ἐφθάρην
φοβέομαι *fear*	φοβήσομαι			πεφόβημαι	ἐφοβήθην
φύω *produce*	φύσω	ἔφῡσα (tr.) ἔφῡν (intr. *grew, was*)	πέφῡκα (intr. *am by nature, am*)		
χαίρω *rejoice*	χαιρήσω		κεχάρηκα		ἐχάρην
χράομαι *use*	χρήσομαι	ἐχρησάμην		κέχρημαι	ἐχρήσθην
χρή impers. *it is necessary*	χρῆσται	χρῆν, ἐχρῆν (impf.)			
ὠνέομαι *buy*	ὠνήσομαι	(ἐπριάμην)		ἐώνημαι	ἐωνήθην

Vocabulary

In using the vocabulary the following should be noted:

(a) In addition to the abbreviations explained on p. ix the sign † is used

    (i) **before** a simple verb whose principal parts are given on pp. 289 ff.

    (ii) **after** a compound verb whose simple form is included in the same list.

(b) The feminine and neuter forms of adjectives and the genitive of nouns are nearly always abbreviated and will **not** necessarily have the same accent as the form given in full, e.g. the genitive of ἄβυϲϲοϲ is ἀβύϲϲου but these are listed below as ἄβυϲϲοϲ, -ου; in these cases the accent of the abbreviated form must be deduced from the rules for accentuation given in **Appendix 9**.

(c) The form of the article which accompanies each noun indicates its gender.

ἄβατοϲ, -ον *impassable*

ἄβιοϲ, -ον *unlivable, unsupportable*

ἄβροτοϲ, -ον *without men, deserted of men*

ἄβυϲϲοϲ, -ου, ἡ *abyss*

ἀγαγ- aor. stem of ἄγω

ἀγαθόϲ, -ή, -όν *good, noble, brave*
    ἀγαθὰ λέγω *speak well of* (+acc., 22.1/2f(ii))
    ἀγαθὰ ποιέω *do good to* (+acc., 22.1/2f(ii))

Ἀγάθων, -ωνοϲ, ὁ *Agathon* (tragic poet)

ἀγάλλομαι *glory, exult in* (+dat.)

ἄγαμαι (aor. ἠγάϲθην) *admire*

Ἀγαμέμνων, -ονοϲ, ὁ *Agamemnon* (Greek commander at Troy)

ἄγαν (adv.) *too much, excessively*

ἀγανακτέω *be annoyed*

ἀγαπάω *love*

†ἀγγέλλω *report, announce*

ἄγγελοϲ, -ου, ὁ *messenger*

ἄγγοϲ, -ουϲ, τό *vessel, urn*

Ἄγιϲ, -ιδοϲ, ὁ *Agis* (King of Sparta)

ἄγκυρα, -ᾱϲ, ἡ *anchor*

ἀγνοέω *not to know, fail to understand*

ἄγνοια, -ᾱϲ, ἡ *ignorance*

ἁγνόϲ, -ή, -όν *chaste*

ἀγορά, -ᾱϲ, ἡ *place of assembly, market-place; agora*

ἀγοράζω *buy in the market*

ἀγορεύω *speak* (in assembly); *proclaim*

ἄγριοϲ, -ᾱ, -ον *fierce, cruel*

ἄγροικοϲ, -ον *from the country, rustic, boorish*

ἀγρόϲ, -οῦ, ὁ *field, country, farm*

ἀγρυπνέω *lie awake, pass sleepless nights*

†ἄγω *lead, bring*
    ἄγω καὶ φέρω *plunder*

ἀγών, -ῶνοϲ, ὁ *contest, trial, competition, exploit*

ἀδαμάντινοϲ, -ον *adamantine, of steel*

ἀδελφή, -ῆϲ, ἡ *sister*

ἀδελφιδῆ, -ῆϲ, ἡ *niece*

ἀδελφόϲ, -οῦ, ὁ *brother*

ἀδεῶϲ (adv.) *fearlessly*

ἄδηλοϲ, -ον *unclear*

ἀδικέω *be unjust, commit a crime; wrong, injure* (+acc.)

ἀδίκημα, -ατοϲ, τό *crime, wrong*

ἀδικίᾱ, ᾱϲ, ἡ *injustice, wrong-doing*

ἄδικοϲ, -ον *unjust, dishonest*

ἀδίκωϲ (adv.) *unjustly*

Ἄδμητοϲ, -ου, ὁ *Admetus* (king of Pherae, husband of Alcestis)

ἀδολέϲχηϲ, -ου, ὁ *idle talker, babbler;* (as. adj.) *garrulous*

ἀδύνατοϲ, -ον *impossible; incapable*

ᾄδω *sing*

ἀεί (adv.) *always, continually; in succession*

ἀείδω = ᾄδω

ἀεικήϲ, -έϲ *shameful*

ἀείμνηϲτοϲ, -ον *not to be forgotten*

#ἀεκαζόμενοϲ, -η, -ον *unwilling(ly)*

#ἀεροβατέω *tread the air*

295

ἀετός, -οῦ, ὁ *eagle*

ἀηδών, -όνος, ἡ *nightingale*

ἀήρ, -έρος, ὁ *air*

ἀθάνατος, -ον *immortal*

Ἀθηνᾶ, -ᾶς, ἡ *Athena*

Ἀθήναζε (adv.) *to Athens*

Ἀθῆναι, -ῶν, αἱ *Athens*

Ἀθηναῖος, -ᾱ, -ον *Athenian*

Ἀθήνηθεν (adv.) *from Athens*

Ἀθήνησι(ν) (adv.) *at Athens*

ἀθλητής, -οῦ, ὁ *athlete*

ἄθλιος, -ᾱ, -ον *wretched, miserable*

ἆθλον, -ου, τό *prize*

ἆθλος, -ου, ὁ *contest; ordeal*

ἀθροίζω *gather together*

ἀθρόος, -ᾱ, -ον *all together, all at once, in a body*

ἀθῡμέω *be despondent*

#αἰ = εἰ

#αἰάζω *bewail, lament*

#αἰαῖ (exclamation) *alas!*

Αἴγῑνα, -ης, ἡ *Aegina* (island in the Saronic Gulf near Athens)

Αἰγῑνήτης, -ου, ὁ *man of Aegina*

Αἰγύπτιος, -ᾱ, -ον *Egyptian*

Αἴγυπτος, -ου, ἡ *Egypt*

αἰδέομαι *respect; feel pity for; stand in awe of, fear*

Ἅιδης, -ου (also #Ἀίδης), ὁ *Hades* (god of the underworld)

εἰς Ἅιδου *to the house of Hades, to the underworld* (23.1/1a)

αἰδώς, -οῦς, ἡ *sense of shame, modesty, respect* (13.1/1b(i))

#αἰεί = ἀεί

#αἰέν = ἀεί

αἰθήρ, -έρος, ὁ *upper air, sky*

αἴθομαι *burn, blaze*

αἰκίᾱ, -ᾱς, ἡ *suffering, misery*

αἰκίζομαι *maltreat*

αἷμα, -ατος, τό *blood, bloodshed, murder*

Αἵμων, -ωμος, ὁ *Haemon* (son of Creon)

†αἰνέω *praise*

αἴνιγμα, -ατος, τό *riddle*

αἰνικτηρίως (adv.) *riddingly, in riddling fashion*

αἰνίττομαι *speak in riddles*

#αἶνος, -ου, ὁ *tale, story*

αἰνῶς (adv.) *terribly*

αἴξ, αἰγός, ὁ/ἡ *goat*

#αἰπυμήτης, -ου (adj.) *with high thoughts, lofty-minded*

αἱρέομαι *choose, elect*

†αἱρέω *take, capture; convict* (18.1/4)

†αἴρω *lift, raise up; set sail; exalt*

†αἰσθάνομαι *perceive, notice, realise* (+gen. or acc., 13.1/2a(iii))

Αἰσχίνης, -ου, ὁ *Aeschines* (Athenian orator)

αἰσχρός, -ά, -όν *ugly* (of people); *base, shameful, disgraceful;* (compar. αἰσχῑων, supl. αἴσχιστος)

Αἰσχύλος, -ου, ὁ *Aeschylus* (tragic poet)

αἰσχύνη, -ης, ἡ *shame, disgrace*

αἰσχύνομαι *be ashamed* (15.1/2c); *feel shame before*

†αἰσχῡνω *dishonour, disgrace*

αἰτέω *ask (for)* (+double acc., 22.1/2f(ii)), *ask alms of* (+acc.)

αἰτίᾱ, -ᾱς, ἡ *reason, cause; responsibility, blame; charge, accusation; fault*

αἰτιάομαι *accuse*

αἴτιος, -ᾱ, -ον *responsible (for), guilty (of)* (+gen.)

#αἶψα (adv.) *quickly, forthwith*

αἰών, -ῶνος, ὁ *life, lifetime; age*

Ἀκαδήμεια, -ᾱς, ἡ *the Academy* (park and gymnasium in Athens)

Ἀκάνθιος, -ᾱ, -ον *of Acanthus* (city in Macedonia)

ἀκατασκεύαστος, -ον *unformed*

ἀκήκοα perf. ind. of ἀκούω

ἀκίνητος, -ον *motionless, immovable*

#ἀκμαῖος, -ᾱ, -ον *in full bloom, at the prime*

ἀκμή, -ῆς, ἡ *prime, zenith*

ἀκολασίᾱ, -ᾱς, ἡ *unrestraint*

ἀκόλαστος, -ον *undisciplined, unrestrained, licentious*

ἀκολουθέω *follow, accompany* (+dat.)

ἀκόλουθος, -ου, ὁ *servant, slave*

ἀκολούθως (adv.) *in accordance with* (+dat.)

ἀκονάω *sharpen*

ἀκούσιος, -ον *against the will, involuntary*

†ἀκούω *hear, listen (to)* (+gen. of person, gen. or acc. of thing, 13.1/2a(iii)); *be spoken of* (17.1/5)

ἀκριβῶς (adv.) *accurately, exactly, carefully*

ἄκρον, -ου, τό *peak, summit*

ἀκρόπολις, -εως, ἡ *acropolis, citadel*

ἄκρος, -ᾱ, -ον *high; top of* (18.1/6)

Ἀκταίων, -ωνος, ὁ *Actaeon* (mythological character)

ἀκτή, -ῆς, ἡ *shore, coast*

ἄκων, ἄκουσα, ἆκον *unwilling(ly)*

ἀλγέω *feel pain, be in pain; grieve; suffer*

ἄλγος, -ους, τό *grief, pain, suffering*

ἀλγύνω *grieve, distress* (+acc.)

Ἀλέξανδρος, -ου, ὁ *Alexander* (the Great, of Macedon)

ἀλήθεια, -ᾱς, ἡ *truth*

ἀληθεύω *tell the truth*

ἀληθής, -ές *true*
  τὰ ἀληθῆ (τἀληθῆ) *the truth*

ἀληθινῶς (adv.) *truly, really*

ἀληθῶς (adv.) *truly, really*
  ὡς ἀληθῶς *in very truth*

Ἁλικαρνασσεύς, -έως, ὁ *man from Halicarnassus*

†ἁλίσκομαι *be caught; be convicted* (18.1/4)

ἀλκή, -ῆς, ἡ *valour, bravery*

Ἄλκηστις, -ιδος, ἡ *Alcestis* (wife of Admetus)

Ἀλκιβιάδης, -ου, ὁ *Alcibiades* (Athenian general and statesman)

ἄλκιμος, -ον *brave*

ἀλλά (conj.) *but; well, now*

ἀλλάττω *change*

ἀλλήλους, -ᾱς, -α (reciprocal pron.) *each other, one another* (9.1/4b)

ἄλλοθι (adv.) *elsewhere*

ἄλλομαι (aor. ἡλάμην) *leap*

ἄλλος, -η, -ο (9.1/3) *other, the rest of; as well, besides* (7.2.12 *l.*11);
  ἄλλος ... ἄλλον *one ... another* (cf. note on 5.2.5(viii))

ἄλλοτε (adv.) *at other times*

ἀλλότριος, -ᾱ, -ον *someone else's; alien*

ἄλλως (adv.) *otherwise; in vain*
  ἄλλως τε καί *especially*

ἅλμη, -ης, ἡ *sea-water, brine; sea*

ἄλογος, -ον *speechless; irrational*

ἅλς, ἁλός, ἡ *sea*

ἄλσος, -ους, τό *grove*

ἀλυσκάζω *shun, shrink away*

ἄλφιτα, -ων, τά *barley-groats; daily bread*

ἀλωπεκῆ, -ῆς, ἡ *fox-skin*

ἀλώπηξ, -εκος, ἡ *fox*

ἅλωσις, -εως, ἡ *capture*

ἅμα (adv.) *at the same time;* (prep.+dat.) *at the same time as, together with;* ἅμα μὲν ... ἅμα δέ *partly ... partly*
  ἅμα ἡλίῳ ἀνέχοντι *at sunrise*
  ἅμα (τῇ) ἡμέρᾳ *at dawn*

ἀμαθής, -ές *ignorant*

ἀμαθίᾱ, -ᾱς, ἡ *ignorance, stupidity*

ἄμαξα, -ης, ἡ *wagon*

ἁμαρτ- aor. stem of ἁμαρτάνω

†ἁμαρτάνω *err; do wrong; make a mistake;* (+gen., 13.1/2a(iv)) *miss, fail to achieve*

ἁμαρτίᾱ, -ᾱς, ἡ *fault, wrong, sin*

ἀμείβω *change, alter*

ἀμείνων, -ον *better* (compar. of ἀγαθός)

ἀμηχανέω *be at a loss/helpless*

ἀμίς, -ίδος, ἡ *chamber-pot*

ἄμμος, -ου, ἡ *sand*

†ἀμύνω *keep/ward off* (acc. of person kept off and dat. of person defended); in mid., *defend oneself against* (+acc.)

Ἀμυρταῖος, -ου, ὁ *Amyrtaeus*

ἀμφί (prep.+acc.) *about, around*

#ἀμφίαλος, -ον *sea-girt*

ἀμφιβάλλομαι† *throw around, put on*

ἀμφιδέᾱ, -ᾱς, ἡ *bracelet, anklet*

#ἀμφιμάχομαι† *besiege*

ἀμφότερος, -ᾱ, -ον *both*

ἀμφοτέρωθεν (adv.) *from/on both sides*

ἄμφω, -οιν, τώ (dual) *both*

ἀμώμητος, -ον *blameless*

ἄν untranslatable particle: in a main clause (+ind. or opt.) with a potential/conditional sense (19.1/2, 18.1/5); in a subordinate clause (+subj.) with an indefinite sense (14.1/4c(iii))

ἄν = ἐάν

ἀνά (prep.+acc.) *up, up along; throughout, over*

ἀναβαίνω† *go up; come up; mount*

ἀναβιβάζω *make go up*

ἀναβοάω† *call upon*

ἀναβολή, -ῆς, ἡ putting off, delaying
ἀναγιγνώσκω† read, read aloud
ἀναγκάζω force, compel
ἀναγκαῖος, -ā, -ον necessary, constraining
ἀνάγκη, -ης, ἡ necessity, compulsion, force
  ἀνάγκη ἐcτί it is necessary (+dat. and inf.)
ἀνάγω† bring up, raise; (mid.) set sail, put out to sea
ἀναδίδωμι† give forth, send up
ἀναζητέω investigate
ἀνάθεμα, -ατος, τό anything dedicated (especially to evil); an accursed thing
ἀνάθημα, -ατος, τό dedication
ἀναίδεια, -ᾱς, ἡ shamelessness
#ἀναιμόσαρκος, -ον with bloodless flesh
ἀναιρέω† pick up; give a response (of an oracle)
ἀναίσθητος, -ον without feeling, stupid
ἀναίτιος, -ον innocent
ἀναλαμβάνω† take up, take with one
†ἀναλίσκω spend
ἀνάλῡσις, -εως, ἡ loosening, releasing; resolution (of a problem)
ἀνάλωτος, -ον not able to be captured, impregnable
ἀναμένω† wait, stay, wait for (+acc.)
ἀναμετρέομαι measure carefully
ἀναμιμνήσκω† remind; (pass.) recall to mind, remember
#ἄναξ, -ακτος, ὁ lord, king
Ἀναξαγόρᾱς, -ου, ὁ Anaxagoras (philosopher of Clazomenae in Asia Minor)
Ἀναξιμένης, -ους, ὁ Anaximenes
ἀνάξιος, -ον unworthy
ἀναπτύσσω unfold, disclose
ἀνασπάω (aor. -έσπασα) haul up; tear up, pull down
ἀνάσσω rule over (+gen. 13.1/2a(i))
#ἀνασταλύζω weep, sob
ἀνασταυρόω impale
ἀνατίθημι† dedicate, make a dedication
ἀναφέρω† bring back, refer
ἀναχωρέω withdraw, retreat, retire
ἀνδρ- stem of ἀνήρ
ἀνδραποδίζω enslave
ἀνδράποδον, -ου, τό captive; slave
ἀνδρείᾱ, -ᾱς, ἡ manliness, courage

ἀνδρεῖος, -ā, -ον brave, manly
ἀνδριάς, -άντος, ὁ statue
ἄνεμος, -ου, ὁ wind
ἀνεξέταστος, -ον without enquiry or investigation
ἀνερ- = ἀνδρ-
ἀνερωτάω† ask questions
ἄνευ (prep.+gen.) without
ἀνέχω† hold up, lift up; intr. rise up
  ἅμα ἡλίῳ ἀνέχοντι at sunrise
ἀνήρ, ἀνδρός, ὁ man, husband
ἄνθινος, -η, -ον flowery
ἀνθίστημι† (mid. and intr. tenses of act.) withstand, resist, oppose (+dat.)
ἄνθος, -ους, τό flower, bloom; glory
ἀνθρώπινος, -η, -ον human
ἄνθρωπος, -ου, ὁ/ἡ human being, person; man; fellow
ἄνθρωπος crasis for ὁ ἄνθρωπος
ἀνιάω distress, vex
ἀνίδρωτος, -ον without raising a sweat
ἀνίστημι† raise up; restore; cause to migrate, expel, uproot; (mid. and intr. tenses of act.) rise up, stand up; migrate, go away (19.1/1)
ἀνιστορέω make enquiry about, ask about (+double acc.)
ἀνόητος -ον foolish
†ἀνοίγνῡμι open
ἀνοικοδομέω build up; rebuild
ἀνόμοιος, -ον (also -ā, -ον) unlike, dissimilar (+dat.)
ἀνταγορεύω (aor. ἀντεῖπον, 18.1/4 note 2) speak against, deny
ἀνταγωνίζομαι struggle against, vie with (+dat.)
ἀντακούω† hear in turn
Ἀνταλκίδᾱς, -ου, ὁ Antalcidas (Spartan general)
ἀντεῖπον aor. of ἀνταγορεύω
ἀντέχω† hold out, withstand
ἀντί (prep.+gen.) instead of, in return for
ἀντιβολέω entreat, beseech
ἀντιγράφω† write in reply
ἀντιδίδωμι† give in return
ἀντίθεσις, -εως, ἡ opposition, antithesis
ἀντιλέγω† argue against, oppose
ἀντίον (adv.) opposite
Ἀντίοχος, -ου, ὁ Antiochus

'Αντισθένης, -ους, ὁ Antisthenes
 (philosopher)
ἀνυπόδητος, -ον without shoes
ἄνω (adv.) above, up above
#ἄνωγα (perf. with pres. sense,
 19.1/3a) command, order
ἀνωφελής, -ές useless
ἀξιόπιστος, -ον worthy of credit,
 trustworthy
ἄξιος, -ᾱ, -ον worthy (of), deserving
 (+gen.), worthwhile
ἀξιόω think worthy of
ἀόρατος, -ον unseen, invisible
ἀπαγγέλλω† announce, report
ἀπαγορεύω forbid (18.1/4 note 2)
ἀπάγχομαι hang oneself
ἀπαγχονίζω hang by a noose
ἀπάγω† lead/take away
ἀπαθής, -ές not suffering
ἀπαίρω† sail away, depart
ἀπαλλαγή, -ῆς, ἡ deliverance
ἀπαλύνω make tender/delicate
ἀπάνθρωπος, -ον far from men,
 desolate
ἀπανίστημι† withdraw
ἀπαντάω go to meet, meet (+dat.,
 13.1/2b(iii))
ἅπαξ (adv.) once only, once
ἀπαραίτητος, -ον unmoved by prayer,
 inexorable
ἀπαρνέομαι deny
ἅπᾱς, ἅπᾱσα, ἅπαν all, the whole of
ἀπατάω deceive
ἀπάτη, -ης, ἡ deceit
ἀπέθανον aor. of ἀποθνῄσκω
ἀπεικάζω liken, compare
ἀπειλέω threaten (+dat., 13.1/2b(i))
ἄπειμι be absent
ἀπείργω† hinder, prevent
ἀπειρίᾱ, -ᾱς, ἡ inexperience
ἄπειρος, -ον ignorant of, inexperienced
 in (+gen.)
 ἀπείρως ἔχω be without experience
ἀπενθής, -ές free from grief/woe
ἀπερισκέπτως (adv.) incautiously
ἀπέρχομαι† go away, depart
ἀπέχω† be distant from (+gen.);
 (mid.) keep one's hands off, keep away
 from (+gen.)
ἀπιστέω distrust
ἀπιστίᾱ, -ᾱς, ἡ faithlessness
ἄπιστος, -ον incredible; untrustworthy,
 not to be believed; mistrustful

ἀπίστως ἔχω be mistrustful
ἄπλετος, -ον boundless, immense
ἁπλοῦς, -ῆ, -οῦν simple (6.1/2)
ἀπό (prep.+gen.) from, away from
ἀποβαίνω† land
ἀποβάλλω† throw away, lose
ἀποδημίᾱ, -ᾱς, ἡ being abroad or
 away from one's country
ἀποδιδρᾱ́σκω (fut. -δρᾱ́σομαι, aor.
 -έδρᾱν) run away, escape, flee
ἀποδίδωμι† give back, return, repay;
 (mid.) sell
ἀποθαν- aor. stem of ἀποθνῄσκω
ἀποθνῄσκω† die, be killed (17.1/5; for
 the perfect see 19.1/3a)
ἄποικος, -ου, ὁ settler, colonist
†ἀποκρίνομαι answer
ἀπόκρισις, -εως, ἡ answer, reply
ἀποκρύπτω hide from sight; (mid.)
 conceal for one's own purposes
ἀποκτείνω† kill
ἀποκωλύω hinder from
ἀπολέγομαι pick out
ἀπολεσ- aor. stem of ἀπόλλῡμι
ἀπόλλῡμι† kill, ruin, destroy, lose
 (20.1/1 note 2)
 ἀπωλόμην I was killed
 ἀπόλωλα I am lost/dead/ruined
'Απόλλων, -ωνος, ὁ Apollo (acc.
 either -ωνα or -ω)
ἀπολογέομαι defend oneself, speak in
 one's defence; plead in one's defence
 (+acc.)
ἀπολογίᾱ, -ᾱς, ἡ speech in one's
 defence
ἀπολύω free, release
ἀπομῑμέομαι imitate, copy
ἀποπίπτω† fall overboard
ἀποπλέω† sail away
ἀποπνίγομαι choke, suffocate, be
 drowned
ἀπορέω be at a loss, be in difficulty
ἀπορίᾱ, -ᾱς, ἡ lack of provisions,
 want; perplexity, difficulty
ἀποστατέω stand aloof from (+gen.)
ἀποστέλλω† send, send away
ἀποστερέω deprive of, rob, defraud,
 refuse payment of
ἀποστροφή, -ῆς, ἡ turning away from,
 escape
ἀπότακτος, -ον set apart for special
 use
ἀποτειχίζω wall off

ἀποτέμνω† *cut off*

ἀποτίθημι† *put away, bury;*
(mid.) *lay aside*

ἀποτρέχω† *run away, run off*

ἀποτυγχάνω† *fail to obtain*

#ἀπούρας (epic aor. pple. of
ἀπαυράω) *having taken away*

ἀποφαίνω† *reveal, show*

ἀποφέρω† *carry away*

ἀποφεύγω† *flee, run off; be acquitted*

ἀποχωρέω *go away, depart*

ἀποχώρησις, -εως, ἡ *privy, public
toilet*

ἀπραγμόνως (adv.) *without trouble*

ἀπράγμων, -ονος *free from business,
not meddling in public affairs*

ἅπτω *fasten, fix; light* (a lamp); (mid.)
touch (+gen.)

ἀπωθέω (aor. ἀπέωσα) *push away*

ἀπώλεσα aor. of ἀπόλλυμι

ἄρα* (inferential particle) *then,
consequently, after all*

ἆρα interrogative particle (10.1/2a)

ἀργαλέος, -ᾱ, -ον *painful, troublesome*

Ἀργεῖοι, -ων, οἱ *Argives;* (poet.)
Greeks

Ἀργεῖος, -ᾱ, -ον *Argive;* (poet.)
Greek

Ἀργινοῦσαι, -ῶν, αἱ *Arginousae
(islands)* (scene of Athenian naval
victory)

Ἄργος, -ους, τό *Argos*

ἀργός, -όν *idle, lazy*

ἀργύριον, -ου, τό *silver, money*

ἀργυροῦς, -ᾶ, -οῦν *made of silver,
silver*

ἀρετή, -ῆς, ἡ *courage; excellence,
virtue*

Ἄρης, -ου ὁ, *Ares* (god of war)

ἄρθρον, -ου, τό *joint, limb*

Ἀριαῖος, -ου, ὁ *Ariaeus*

ἀριθμός, -οῦ, ὁ *number, amount, total*

#ἀριπρεπής, -ές *very bright,
conspicuous*

ἀρισστάω *have breakfast*

Ἀριστεύς, -έως, ὁ *Aristeus*

ἀριστεύω *be best, be best at* (+inf.)

Ἀριστόκριτος, -ου, ὁ *Aristocritus*

ἄριστον, -ου, τό *breakfast, lunch*

ἄριστος, -η, -ον *best; bravest* (supl. of
ἀγαθός)

Ἀριστοτέλης, -ους, ὁ *Aristotle*
(philosopher)

Ἀριστοφάνης, -ους, ὁ *Aristophanes*
(comic poet)

Ἀρίφρων, -ονος, ὁ *Ariphron*

ἄρκτος, -ου, ἡ *bear*

ἁρμόζει (impers.) *it is fitting, it suits*

Ἄρνη, -ης, ἡ *Arne* (place in Thessaly)

ἄρνυμαι *win*

ἁρπάζω *seize, plunder, snatch*

ἁρπακτής, -οῦ, ὁ *robber, ravisher*

#ἁρπαλέος, -ᾱ, -ον *attractive, alluring*

ἄρρηκτος, -ον *unbroken, unbreakable*

ἄρρητος, -ον *unspoken, unmentioned*

ἀρσενικός, -ή, -όν *male, masculine*

Ἀρταφέρνης, -ους, ὁ *Artaphernes*

Ἄρτεμις, -ιδος, ἡ *Artemis* (goddess)

ἄρτημα, -ατος, τό *ear-ring*

ἄρτι (ἀρτίως) (adv.) *newly, recently,
just now*

ἄρτος, -ου, ὁ *bread*

ἀρχαῖος, -ᾱ, -ον *ancient, old;
former*

Ἀρχέλᾱος, -ου, ὁ *Archelaus* (King of
Sparta)

ἀρχή, -ῆς, ἡ *beginning; rule, power;
empire; office, magistracy, board of
magistrates, magistrate, officer*

ἀρχιερεύς, -έως, ὁ *high priest*

Ἀρχιμήδης, -ους, ὁ *Archimedes*
(Syracusan mathematician and
inventor)

†ἄρχω *rule, rule over, command*
(+gen., 13.1/2a(i))
(+pple.) *begin* (of something
continued by others); (mid.) *begin* (of
something continued by oneself)

ἄρχων, -οντος, ὁ *archon (magistrate)*

ἀσαφής, -ές *obscure, unclear*

ἄσβεστος, -ον (also -η, -ον)
*unquenchable, inextinguishable,
imperishable*

ἀσέβεια, -ᾱς, ἡ *impiety, irreverence*
(to gods)

ἀσεβέω *commit impiety*

ἀσθένεια, -ᾱς, ἡ *weakness, illness*

ἀσθενέω *be weak/ill*

ἀσθενής, -ές *weak*, ill

ἀσινέστατα (supl. adv.) *most/very
harmlessly*

ἀσκέω *practise, exercise, train*

ἄσμενος, -η, -ον *glad, pleased*

ἀσπάζομαι *greet*

Ἀσπασίᾱ, -ᾱς, ἡ *Aspasia* (mistress of
Pericles)

ἄσπετος, -ον *enormously great, boundless*

ἀσπίς, -ίδος, ἡ *shield*

ἀστεῖος, -ᾱ, -ον *charming, attractive*

ἀστήρ, -έρος, ὁ *star*

ἀστρονομίᾱ, -ᾱς, ἡ *astronomy*

ἄστυ, -εως, τό *city, town*

ἀσφάλεια, -ᾱς, ἡ *safety, security*

ἀσφαλής, -ές *safe, secure*

ἀσφαλῶς (adv.) *safely*

ἀταλαίπωρος, -ον *without taking pains, not painstaking*

ἀτάρ (conj.) *but*

ἀτασθαλίᾱ, -ᾱς, ἡ *presumptuous sin, wickedness*

#ἄτε (particle) *as if, as;* (causal) *inasmuch as, since, seeing that, because, as* (+pple. 12.1/2a(ii))

ἀτελής, -ές *incomplete*

#ἄτερ (prep.+gen.) *without*

ἄτεχνος, -ον *unskilled*

ἀτεχνῶς (adv.) *simply, just*

ἄτη, -ης, ἡ *ruin*

ἀτῑμάζω *dishonour*

ἀτίμαστος, -ον *dishonoured*

ἀτῑμίᾱ, -ᾱς, ἡ *dishonour; loss of citizen rights*

ἄτῑμος, -ον *dishonoured; deprived of citizen rights*

ἄτολμος, -ον *not daring, lacking the heart to*

ἄτοπος, -ον *out of place, extraordinary, strange, absurd*

Ἀττικός, -ή, -όν *Attic, Athenian* Ἀττική (sc. γῆ), -ῆς *Attica*

ἀτυχής, -ές *unlucky, unfortunate*

αὖ (adv.) *again, moreover*

αὐγή, -ῆς, ἡ *ray, beam*

#αὐδάω *speak, say, utter, tell*

αὐθαίρετος, -ον *self-chosen, self-inflicted*

αὖθις (adv.) *again; in turn, next, on the other hand*

αὐλέω *play the flute*

αὐλή, -ῆς, ἡ *courtyard, hall*

αὐλίζομαι *encamp*

αὔριον (adv.) *tomorrow*

#αὐτάρ (conj.) *but, then*

αὐτάρκης, -ες *sufficient*

#αὖτε (adv.) *again, in turn*

αὐτίκα (adv.) *at once, immediately*

αὐτόθι (adv.) *on the spot, here*

αὐτόματον, -ου, τό *accident*

αὐτόν, -ήν, -ό (pron.) *him, her, it* (4.1/2; 9.1/3c)

αὐτός, -ή, -ό *self* (9.1/3a) ὁ αὐτός *the same* (9.1/3b)

αὐτός crasis for ὁ αὐτός

αὐτοῦ (adv.) *here, there, on the spot*

ἀφαιρέω† *take away (from), remove;* (mid.) *deprive (of)* (+double acc., 22.1/2f(ii))

ἀφανής, -ές *unseen, vanished, not to be seen*

ἀφανίζω *make unseen, wipe out, destroy*

ἀφασίᾱ, -ᾱς, ἡ *speechlessness*

ἀφεῖναι aor. inf. of ἀφίημι

ἄφθονος, -ον *abundant, plentiful; bountiful*

ἀφίημι† *send forth; discharge; let go*

†ἀφικνέομαι *arrive, come*

ἀφῑκόμην aor. of ἀφικνέομαι

ἀφίστημι† *remove; make to revolt;* (mid. and intr. tenses of act.) *withdraw, revolt* (19.1/1)

Ἀφροδίτη, -ης, ἡ *Aphrodite* (goddess of love)

ἄφρων, -ον *senseless, foolish*

ἀφυής, -ές *without natural talent/skill*

#ἀφύσσομαι *draw (a liquid) for oneself*

ἄφωνος, -ον *dumb, speechless*

Ἀχαιοί, -ῶν, οἱ *Achaeans, Greeks*

Ἀχέρων, -οντος, ὁ *Acheron* (river in the underworld)

ἀχθηδών, -όνος, ἡ *burden*

ἄχθομαι *be annoyed/displeased at* (+dat.)

Ἀχιλλεύς, -έως, ὁ *Achilles* (hero in *Iliad*)

ἄχυρα, -ων, τά *chaff, bran*

βαδίζω (fut. βαδιοῦμαι) *walk, go*

βάθος, -ους, τό *depth*

βαθύς, -εῖα, -ύ *deep*

#βαθυχαίτεις, -εσσα, -εν *long-haired*

†βαίνω *go, come; walk*

Βάκχος, -ου, ὁ *Bacchus* (another name for Dionysus)

#βάκχος, -ου, ὁ *person initiated into the rites of Bacchus*

†βάλλω *throw, hit, pelt; inflict*

βάπτω *dip; dye*

βάρβαρος, -ον *barbarian, foreign*

βαρΰνομαι be weighed down

βαρύς, -εῖα, -ύ heavy; wearisome

βασίλεια, -ᾱς, ἡ princess, queen

βασιλείᾱ, -ᾱς, ἡ kingship

βασίλειος, -ᾱ, -ον royal

βασιλεύς, -έως, ὁ king; (Persian) King

βασιλεύω be king, rule (+gen., 13.1/2a(i))

#βαστάζω lift up, carry

βάτραχος, -ου, ὁ frog

βέβαιος, -ον (also -ᾱ, -ον) secure, steady

βέβρωκα perf. of βιβρώσκω

βέλος, -ους, τό missile

βέλτιστος, -η, -ον best (supl. of ἀγαθός)

βελτΐων, -ον better (compar. of ἀγαθός)

βῆμα, -ατος, τό step

βίᾱ, -ᾱς, ἡ force, violence
  πρὸς βίᾱν by force

βιάζομαι use force, force one's way

βιαίως (adv.) violently

βιβλίον, -ου, τό book

βίβλος, -ου, ἡ book

βιβρώσκω (perf. βέβρωκα) eat

βίος, -ου, ὁ life; means of life; livelihood

#βίοτος, -ου, ὁ life

βιόω live

βιωτός, -όν to be lived, worth living

βλάβη, -ης, ἡ damage

†βλάπτω hurt, injure; damage

βλέπω see, look (at); see the light of day, be alive

βληθείς, -εῖσα, -έν aor. pple. pass. of βάλλω

#βλώσκω (fut. μολοῦμαι, aor. ἔμολον, perf. μέμβλωκα) go

†βοάω shout

βόειος, -ᾱ, -ον of beef

βοή, -ῆς, ἡ shout, shouting

βοήθεια, -ᾱς, ἡ help, aid

βοηθέω (run to) help (+dat., 13.1/2b(i))

βόθρος, -ου, ὁ hole, pit

Βοιωτίᾱ, -ᾱς, ἡ Boeotia (state in north central Greece)

Βοιωτός, -οῦ, ὁ a Boeotian

βοσκήματα, -ων, τά cattle

βόσκω feed, nourish

βουλευτήριον, -ου, τό council-chamber

βουλεύω plan, resolve, determine, deliberate; (mid.) discuss, deliberate, consider; plot

βουλή, -ῆς, ἡ plan, counsel, advice; council

†βούλομαι wish, want

#βουνός, -οῦ, ὁ hill, mound

βοῦς, βοός, ὁ/ἡ ox, bull, cow

#βούτης, -ου, ὁ herdsman

βραδέως (adv.) slowly

βραδΰνω be slow, hesitate

#βραδύπους, -πουν (gen. -ποδος) slow-footed

βραδύς, -εῖα, -ύ (compar. βραδΐων, supl. βράδιστος) slow

βραχΐων, -ονος, ὁ arm

βραχύς, -εῖα, -ύ short, brief; small, little

βρέχω wet (tr.)

#βροτός, -οῦ, ὁ mortal man

βρόχος, -ου, ὁ noose

βωμός, -οῦ, ὁ altar

#γαῖα, -ᾱς, ἡ = γῆ

γάλα, -ακτος, τό milk

†γαμέω (+acc.) marry (with the man as sub.); (mid., +dat.) marry (with the woman as sub.)

γάμος, -ου, ὁ marriage

γάρ* (connecting particle) for, because, since

γαστήρ, -τρός, ἡ stomach, belly (6.1/1b)

γαστρίμαργος, -ον gluttonous

γε* (particle) at least; at any rate, certainly, indeed (13.1/3b)

γεγένημαι perf. of γίγνομαι

γεγενημένα, -ων, τά events, occurrences, the past

#γέγηθα (perf. with pres. sense, from γηθέω) rejoice

γέγονα perf. of γίγνομαι

#γεγώς = γεγονώς (perf. pple. of γίγνομαι)

γείτων, -ονος, ὁ neighbour; (as adj.+dat.) neighbouring

Γέλᾱ, -ᾱς, ἡ Gela (city in Sicily)

†γελάω laugh

γελοῖος, -ᾱ, -ον funny, ridiculous

Γελῶος, -ᾱ, -ον of Gela

γέλως, -ωτος, ὁ laughter

γέμω be full of (+gen.)

γεν- aor. stem of γίγνομαι

γένεσις, -εως, ἡ birth, coming into being

γενναῖος, -ᾱ, -ον noble, well-born, noble-minded

γενναίως (adv.) nobly

γεννάω beget, produce

γένος, -ους, τό race; kind

γεραιός, -ά, -όν old

γέρας, -ως, τό prize, privilege (13.1/1b(iii))

γέρρα, -ων, τά wicker-work

γέρων, -οντος, ὁ old man

γεύομαι taste

γέφῡρα, -ᾱς, ἡ bridge, embankment

γεωμετρίᾱ, -ᾱς, ἡ geometry

γεωργός, -οῦ, ὁ farmer

γῆ, -ῆς, ἡ land, earth, ground
    κατὰ γῆν by land
    ποῦ (τῆς) γῆς; where on earth?

γηγενής, -ές earth-born

γημ- aor. stem of γαμέω

#γηράλεος, -ᾱ, -ον aged, old

γῆρας, -ως, τό old age (13.1/1b(iii))

γηράσκω grow old

γίγᾱς, -αντος, ὁ giant

†γίγνομαι become, be, be born; happen, take place

†γιγνώσκω get to know, recognise, realize; think, resolve, decide

γίνομαι = γίγνομαι

Γλαῦκος, -ου, ὁ Glaucus

γλαύξ, -αυκός, ἡ owl

#γλαφυρός, -ά, -όν hollow, hollowed

Γλοῦς, -οῦ, ὁ Glus

γλυκερός, -ά, -όν sweet

γλυκύς, -εῖα, -ύ sweet

γλῶττα, -ης, ἡ tongue

γνάθος, -ου, ἡ jaw

γνούς, γνοῦσα, γνόν aor. pple. of γιγνώσκω

γνῶθι 2nd s. imp. of ἔγνων

γνώμη, -ης, ἡ judgement, opinion, mind, purpose

γνώριμος, (-η), -ον well-known, familiar

γονεύς, -έως, ὁ parent

γόνυ, -ατος, τό knee (5.1/1 note 1)

Γοργώ, -οῦς, ἡ Gorgo

#γουννόομαι implore, entreat

γράμμα, -ατος, τό written character, letter

γραμματικός, -οῦ, ὁ grammarian

γραμματιστής, -οῦ, ὁ schoolmaster

γραῦς, γρᾱός, ἡ old woman (11.1/4)

γραφεῖον, -ου, τό pencil

γραφή, -ῆς, ἡ writing, drawing; indictment, charge, case

†γράφω write; draw, paint; (mid.) indict, charge

γρῡπός, -ή, -όν hook-nosed, aquiline

Γύλιππος, -ου, ὁ Gylippus (Spartan general)

γυμνάζω exercise, train

γυμνός, -ή, -όν naked; lightly/poorly clad

γυναικωνῖτις, -ιδος, ἡ women's apartments

γυνή, -αικός, ἡ woman, wife (5.1/1 note 1)

γύψ, γῡπός, ὁ vulture

Γωβρύᾱς, -ᾱ, ὁ Gobryas (Persian general)

δαιμόνιος, -ᾱ, -ον miraculous, supernatural

δαίμων, -ονος, ὁ god, deity

δαίς, δαιτός, ἡ feast

δακ- aor. stem of δάκνω

†δάκνω bite; worry

δάκρυ see δάκρυον

δακρυόεις, -εσσα, -εν weeping, in tears

δάκρυον, -ου, τό tear (alternative nom. δάκρυ 13.1/1c)

δακρύω weep

δακτύλιος, -ου, ὁ ring

δάκτυλος, -ου, ὁ finger

δανείζω lend; (mid.) borrow

δανειστής, -οῦ, ὁ creditor

Δάρδανος, -ου, ὁ Dardanus (founder of Troy)

δᾱρεικός, -οῦ, ὁ daric (Persian gold coin)

δάς, δᾳδός, ἡ torch

δασύς, -εῖα, -ύ hairy, shaggy

δέ* (connecting particle) and, but;
    δ'οὖν* be that as it may (13.1/3c(ii))

δέδαρμαι perf. mid./pass of δέρω

δέδοικα fear, be afraid (19.1/3a)

#δέδορκα see, look upon (perf. of δέρκομαι)

†δεῖ (impers.) it is necessary (+acc. and infin.); there is a need of (+gen., 21.1/4 note 3)

#δείδω be alarmed

†δείκνῡμι *show* (20.1/1 and **Appendix 6**)

δειλίᾱ, -ᾱς, ἡ *cowardice*

δειλός, -ή, -όν *miserable, wretched, cowardly*

δειμαίνω (+acc.) *be afraid of, fear*

δεινός, -ή, -όν *terrible, serious, strange; clever at* (+inf.)

δειπνέω *dine, have dinner, dine on* (+acc.)

δεῖπνον, -ου, τό *dinner*

δέκα (indecl. adj.) *ten*

δέκατος, -η, -όν *tenth*

δέλτος, -ου, ἡ *writing-tablet*

δελφίς, -ῖνος, ὁ *dolphin*

Δελφοί, -ῶν, οἱ *Delphi*

δένδρον, -ον, τό *tree* (13.1/1c)

δεξιά, -ᾱς, ἡ *right hand*
   δεξιὰν δίδωμι *give a pledge*

δεξιός, -ά, -όν *on the right hand; clever*

Δέξιππος, -ου, ὁ *Dexippus*

†δέομαι *need, implore, ask* (+gen. 13.1/2a(ii))

δέον (acc. absol.) *it being necessary* (21.1/5)

δέος, -ους, τό *fear*

#δέρκομαι *see, behold*

δέρω (perf. mid./pass. δέδαρμαι) *flay*

δεσμός, -οῦ, ὁ (alternative pl. δεσμά, τά) *bond*

δεσμωτήριον, -ου, τό *prison*

δέσποινα, -ης, ἡ *mistress*

δεσπότης, -ου, ὁ *master*

δεῦρο (adv.) *here, over here*

δεύτερος, -ᾱ, -ον *second*

†δέχομαι *receive*

δέω (A) *need, want, lack* (+gen.)
   πολλοῦ δέω *I am far from*
   πολλοῦ δεῖ *far from it!*

†δέω (B) *bind, tie*

δή* (particle) *indeed, certainly* (13.1/3b)

δῆλος, -η, -ον *visible, clear, obvious*

δηλόω *make clear, show, reveal*

Δημέᾱς, -ου, ὁ *Demeas*

δημηγορέω *make a public speech*

Δημήτηρ, -τρος, ἡ *Demeter* (corn-goddess, mother of Persephone)

δημιουργός, -οῦ, ὁ *craftsman; maker, author*

δῆμος, -ου, ὁ *the people; democracy; deme*

Δημοσθένης, -ους, ὁ *Demosthenes* (fifth-century Athenian general; fourth-century orator)

δημόσιος, -ᾱ, -ον *public, of the state;*
   δημοσίᾱ *publicly*

δημοτικός, -ή, -όν *democratic, popular*

δήξομαι fut. of δάκνω

δήπου* (particle) *I presume, I should hope, doubtless*

δῆτα* (particle) *indeed; then* (13.1/3a)

δηχθ- aor. pass. stem of δάκνω

Δία acc. of Ζεύς (11.1/4)

διά (prep.+acc.) *because of, on account of;* (+gen.) *through, across*
   διὰ τί; *why?*

διαβαίνω† *cross, cross over*

διαβάλλω† *slander*

διαβατέον *one must cross* (24.1/5)

διαβολή, -ῆς, ἡ *slander*

διάγνωσις, -εως, ἡ *[act of] distinguishing, deciding*

διάγω† *carry over; pass, spend* (of time); *live, pass one's life*

διάδοχος, -ον *succeeding, relieving*

διάκειμαι (+adv.) *be in certain state/mood*

διακλέπτω† *steal and secrete, appropriate*

διακομίζομαι† *carry across*

διακόπτω *cut through*

διᾱκόσιοι, -αι, -α *200*

†διαλέγομαι *converse with* (+dat.)

διαλλάττομαι *reconcile one's differences*

διαμέλλω† *delay*

διανοέομαι *intend, plan; think, suppose*

διάνοια, -ᾱς, ἡ *intention, plan*

διαπειράομαι *make trial of*

διαπίμπλημι† *fill with* (+gen.)

διαπολεμέω *fight it out* (with someone, dat.)

διαπορεύομαι *march/proceed through* (+acc.)

διαρπάζω *plunder*

διασπάομαι (aor. -εσπασάμην) *tear apart*

διατελέω† *accomplish; continue*

διατίθημι† *dispose; put in a certain state of body or mind*

διατριβή, -ῆς, ἡ *way/manner of spending time*

διατρίβω *pass/waste* (time)

δίαυλος, -ου, ὁ *double course* (i.e. the race up the stadium and back)

διαφέρω† *differ from* (+gen.); *make a difference*; *be superior to* (+gen.)

διαφθείρω† *destroy*; *corrupt*

διαχωρίζω *separate, divide*

διδακτός, -ή, -όν *able to be taught*

διδάσκαλος, -ου, ὁ *teacher*

†διδάσκω *teach, train*

-διδράσκω see ἀποδιδράσκω

†δίδωμι *give, offer, grant* (18.1/2)

διελαύνω† *ride through*

διεξέρχομαι† *go through, relate*

διέχω† *be separated/distant from* (+gen.)

διηγέομαι *explain, relate, describe*

δικάζω *be a juror; judge, give judgement*

δίκαιος, -ᾱ, -ον *just, honest, upright*

δικαιοσύνη, -ης, ἡ *justice, honesty*

δικαίως (adv.) *justly*

δικαστήριον, -ου, τό *law-court*

δικαστής, -οῦ, ὁ *juror, dicast, judge*

δίκη, -ης, ἡ *lawsuit; (legal) satisfaction; justice; penalty; (personified, with cap.) Justice*

    δίκην δίδωμι *be punished, pay the penalty*

    δίκην λαμβάνω *punish, exact one's due from* (παρά+gen.)

δίκτυον, -ου, τό *net, hunting-net*

Δίκων, -ωνος, ὁ *Dico*

δίνη, -ης, ἡ *whirlpool*

Διογένης, -ους, ὁ *Diogenes* (philosopher)

διόλλῡμι† *destroy utterly*

Διονῡσόδωρος, -ου, ὁ *Dionysodorus*

Διόνῡσος, -ου, ὁ *Dionysus* (god of wine)

διότι (conj.) *because*

διπλοῦς, -ῆ, -οῦν *double*

δίς (adv.) *twice*

διττός (διссός), -ή, -όν *two-fold, two*

δίφρος, -ου, ὁ *stool*

δίχα (adv., or prep.+gen.) *apart, apart from*

διψάω *be thirsty* (5.1/2 note 4)

†διώκω *pursue, chase; prosecute*

#δμώς, -ωός, ὁ *slave taken in war* (13.1/1b(i))

δόγμα, -ατος, τό *opinion, belief; decision, judgement*

†δοκέω *seem, seem good; be thought; consider* (self) *to be; think*

    δοκεῖ (impers., +dat. and inf.) *it seems a good idea*; so δοκεῖ μοι *I decide* (21.1/4a)

#δόλιος, -ᾱ, -ον *crafty, deceitful*

#δόλος, -ου, ὁ *trick, guile*

#δόμος, -ου, ὁ *house, home*

δόξα, -ης, ἡ *reputation, fame; opinion*

δόξαν (acc. abs.) *it having been decided* (21.1/5)

δόρυ, -ατος, τό *spear*

δοτέον *one must give* (24.1/5)

δότης, -ου, ὁ *giver*

δουλείᾱ, -ᾱς, ἡ *slavery*

δουλεύω *be a slave*

#δούλιος, -ᾱ, -ον *of slavery*

δοῦλος, -ου, ὁ *slave*

δουλόω *enslave*

δούς, δοῦσα, δόν, aor. pple. of δίδωμι

δράκων, -οντος, ὁ *dragon, serpent*

δρᾶμα, -ατος, τό *play, drama*

δραμεῖν aor. inf. of τρέχω

δραστήριος, -ον *active*

δραχμή, -ῆς, ἡ *drachma* (coin)

δράω *do, act*

δρόμος, -ου, ὁ *race*; δρόμῳ *at a run, at full speed*

δρόσος, -ου, ἡ *dew*

†δύναμαι *be able* (19.1/3b); *be powerful*

    μέγα δύναμαι *be very powerful*

δύναμις, -εως, ἡ *power, ability, force, strength*

δυνατός, -ή, -όν *able, possible, powerful*; οἱ δυνατοί *the chief men*

δύο *two* (7.1/5a)

#δύρομαι (=ὀδύρομαι) *lament*

δύσγνοια, -ᾱς, ἡ *ignorance, bewilderment*

#δυσδάκρῡτος, -ον *sorely wept*

δυσεντερίᾱ, -ᾱς, ἡ *dysentery*

δύσθῡμος, -ον *disheartened, despondent*

δύσκολος, -ον *bad-tempered*

#δύςλυτος, -ον *indissoluble, inextricable*

δυσμενής, -ές *hostile*

δυσπετῶς (adv.) *with difficulty*

δυσσεβής, -ές *impious, ungodly, profane*

#δύστηνος, -ον *wretched*

δυστυχέω *be unlucky/unfortunate*

δυςτυχής, -ές *unlucky, unfortunate*
δυςτυχίᾱ, -ᾱς, ἡ *misfortune*
δύςφορος, -ον *hard to bear*
δυςχείμερος, -ον *wintry, stormy*
#δυςώνυμος, -ον *having an ill name,
    hateful*
δύω (A) *enter, get into*
δύω (B) = δύο *two*
δώδεκα (indecl. adj.) *twelve*
#δωδεκέτης, -ου *twelve years old*
#δῶμα, -ατος, τό *house; family*
δωρέομαι *present, give*
Δωριεύς, -έως, ὁ *Dorieus* (half-
    brother of Spartan king Cleomenes)
δωροδοκίᾱ, -ᾱς, ἡ *bribery*
δῶρον, -ου, τό *gift, bribe*

ἑ (indirect refl. pron.) *him, her, it*
    (9.1/4a)
ἑάλων aor. of ἁλίςκομαι
ἐάν (conj., +subj.) *if, if ever*
    (14.1/4c(iii))
ἔαρ, ἦρος, τό (the season of) *spring*
ἑαυτόν, -ήν, -ό (refl. pron.) *himself/
    herself/itself* (9.1/4a)
†ἐάω *allow, permit; let alone, let be*
ἔβην aor. of βαίνω
ἑβραϊςτί (adv.) *in Hebrew*
ἐγγελάω† *laugh at* (+dat.)
ἐγγίγνομαι† *be born in, appear among*
ἐγγράφω† *write in/on, inscribe; enrol,
    enlist*
ἐγγύη, -ης, ἡ *pledge, surety*
ἔγγυθεν (adv.) *from nearby*
ἐγγύς (adv., or prep. + gen.) *near,
    nearby*
†ἐγείρω *arouse, awaken* (perf.
    ἐγρήγορα = *I am awake*)
ἐγενόμην aor. of γίγνομαι
ἐγκέφαλος, -ου, ὁ *brain*
ἔγκλημα, -ατος, τό *accusation,
    complaint*
        ἔγκλημα ποιέομαι *make a
        complaint*
†ἐγκονέω *be quick, hasten*
ἐγκωμιάζω *praise*
ἐγκώμιον, -ου, τό *encomium, eulogy;
    victory-song*
ἔγνων aor. of γιγνώσκω
ἐγρήγορα perf. of ἐγείρω
ἐγχειρέω *attempt, try; attack* (+dat.)

ἔγχος, -ους, τό *weapon, spear*
ἐγώ (pron.) *I* (4.1/2)
ἔγωγε *I at least; I for my part*
ἐγῷμαι = ἐγὼ οἶμαι
#ἐγών = ἐγώ
ἔδαφος, -ους, τό *bottom*
ἐδόθην aor. pass. of δίδωμι
ἔδομαι fut. of ἐςθίω
#ἔδω *eat*
ἐδωδή, -ῆς, ἡ *food*
ἔδωκα aor. of δίδωμι
ἕζομαι *seat oneself, sit*
†ἐθέλω *am willing, wish*
ἔθηκα aor. of τίθημι
ἔθνος, -ους, τό *nation, tribe, race*
ἔθρεψα aor. of τρέφω
εἰ (conj.) *if*
        εἰ γάρ or εἴθε *would that, I wish
        that* (to introduce wishes, 21.1/1)
        εἰ δὲ μή *but if not, otherwise*
εἶ 2nd s. of εἰμί *be* or εἶμι *shall go*
εἴᾱςα aor. of ἐάω
#εἶδαρ, -ατος, τό *food*
εἰδείην opt. of οἶδα
εἰδέναι inf. of οἶδα
#εἴδομαι *be seen, appear*
εἶδον aor. of ὁράω
εἶδος, -ους, τό *form, shape,
    appearance; beauty*
εἰδώς, εἰδυῖα, εἰδός *knowing* (pple. of
    οἶδα)
εἶεν (particle) *well, well then*
εἴθε see εἰ
εἴκοςι(ν) (indecl. adj.) *twenty*
εἴκω *give way, yield* (+dat.,
    13.1/2b(ii))
εἰκώς, -υῖα, -ός *like, resembling*
    (+dat., 19.1/3a)
εἴληφα perf. of λαμβάνω
εἰλόμην aor. of αἱρέομαι
εἶλον aor. of αἱρέω
εἰμί *be* (3.1/6 and **Appendix 3**)
εἶμι *shall go* (inf. ἰέναι; impf. ᾖα,
    18.1/3 and **Appendix 3**)
#εἶν = ἐν
εἶναι *to be* (inf. of εἰμί)
εἰπ- aor. act./mid. stem of λέγω or of
    ἀγορεύω in compounds
εἴπερ (strengthened form of εἰ) *if
    indeed*
εἶπον aor. of λέγω and of ἀγορεύω in
    compounds (18.1/4 note 2)

†εἴργω *shut up, imprison; prevent, hinder, exclude*

εἴρηκα perf. act. of λέγω

εἴρημαι perf. mid./pass. of λέγω

εἰρήνη, -ης, ἡ *peace*
  εἰρήνην ἄγω *live in/be at peace*
  εἰρήνην ποιέομαι *make peace*

εἶρπον impf. of ἕρπω

εἰς (prep.+acc.) *to, into, on to; with regard to, in relation to*
  εἰς τοσοῦτο/τοῦτο (+gen. 23.1/1*d*) *to such a pitch/point/ degree of*

εἷς, μία, ἕν *one* (7.1/5*a*)

#εἷς 2nd s. of εἰμί or εἶμι

εἰσάγω† *introduce*

#εἰσαθρέω *look/gaze at*

εἰσακούω† *give ear, pay attention*

εἰσβαίνω† *go into, go on board*

εἰσβάλλω† *throw into, invade*

εἰσβολή, -ῆς, ἡ *invasion*

εἰσέρχομαι† *enter, go inside*

εἴσοδος, -ου, ἡ *entrance; visit, appearance*

εἴσομαι fut. of οἶδα

εἰσοράω† *behold, look at*

εἰσπλέω† *sail in*

εἰσφέρω† *bring/carry into*

εἶτα (adv.) *then, next*

εἴτε ... εἴτε *whether ... or*

εἶχον impf. of ἔχω

εἴωθα *I am accustomed*

εἰωθώς, -υῖα, -ός *customary, usual*

ἐκ (prep.+gen.; before vowel ἐξ) *out of, from*

Ἑκάβη, -ης, ἡ *Hecuba* (wife of Priam)

ἕκαστος, -η, -ον *each, every*
  ὡς ἕκαστος *each individually* (22.1/1*a*(v))

ἑκάστοτε (adv.) *on each occasion*

ἑκάτερος, -ᾱ, -ον *each* (of two)
  ὡς ἑκάτερος *each (of two) individually* (22.1/1*a*(v))

#ἕκατι (prep.+gen.) *on account of, for the sake of* (usually comes after word it governs)

#ἑκατομπτολίεθρος, -ον *with a hundred cities*

ἑκατόν (indecl. adj.) *100*

ἐκβαίνω† *step out, go forth; disembark*

ἐκβάλλω† *throw out, expel* (into exile)

#ἐκδίκως (adv.) *unjustly*

ἐκεῖ (adv.) *there*

ἐκεῖθεν (adv.) *from there*

ἐκεῖνος, -η, -ο (pron. and adj., 9.1/1) *that*

ἐκεῖσε (adv.) *(to) there*

ἐκκαίω† *kindle*

ἐκκαλέω† *call (someone) out*

ἐκκλησίᾱ, -ᾱς, ἡ *assembly*

ἐκκόπτω *knock out*

ἐκκρούω *knock out*

ἐκλέγω *pick out* (18.1/4 note 1)

ἐκμανθάνω† *learn thoroughly*

ἑκουσίως (adv.) *willingly*

ἐκπέμπω† *send out*

#ἐκπέρθω *destroy utterly*

ἐκπίπτω† *fall out; be thrown out; be banished, be sent into exile* (17.1/5)

ἐκπλέω† *sail out/off*

ἔκπληξις, -εως, ἡ *panic, consternation*

ἐκπλήττω *strike with panic, frighten; amaze*

ἐκπράττω† *bring to pass, accomplish*

ἐκτός (adv., and prep.+gen.) *outside*

ἐκτροφή, -ῆς, ἡ *bringing up, rearing*

Ἕκτωρ, -ορος, ὁ *Hector* (Trojan hero in *Iliad*)

ἐκφαίνομαι† *appear, shine out/forth*

ἐκφέρω† *carry out*

ἐκφεύγω† *escape*

ἑκών, -οῦσα, -όν *willing(ly), wittingly*

ἑλ- aor. act./mid. stem of αἱρέω

ἐλάᾱ, -ᾱς, ἡ *olive-tree*

ἔλαβον aor. of λαμβάνω

ἔλαθον aor. of λανθάνω

Ἐλάτεια, -ᾱς, ἡ *Elatea* (town in Phocis)

ἐλάττων, -ον *smaller; fewer; less*

†ἐλαύνω *drive* (tr. and intr.); *drive out; march*

ἔλαφος, -ου, ὁ/ἡ *deer*

ἐλάχιστος, -η, -ον *smallest, least; fewest*

ἔλαχον aor. of λαγχάνω

†ἐλέγχω *test, examine*

ἑλεῖν aor. inf. act. of αἱρέω

ἕλειος, -ον *living in the marshes*

Ἑλένη, -ης, ἡ *Helen*

ἐλευθερίᾱ, -ᾱς, ἡ *freedom*

ἐλεύθερος, -ᾱ, -ον *free*

ἐλευθερόω *set free*

Ἐλεφαντίνη, -ης, ἡ *Elephantine* (city in Egypt)

ἐλέφᾱς, -αντος, ὁ *elephant*

ἐλήλυθα perf. of ἔρχομαι
ἐλήφθην aor. pass. of λαμβάνω
ἐλθ- aor. stem of ἔρχομαι
ἔλιπον aor. of λείπω
ἑλίccω turn (tr.), twist
#ἑλκεcίπεπλοc, -ον with trailing robes
#ἑλκηθμόc, -οῦ, ὁ [act of] being
  carried off, seizure
†ἕλκω pull, drag
Ἑλλάc, -άδοc, ἡ Greece
ἐλλείπω† be lacking in, fall short of
  (+gen.)
Ἕλλην, -ηνοc, ὁ a Greek
Ἑλληνικόc, -ή, -όν Greek
Ἑλλήcποντοc, -ου, ὁ the Hellespont
ἕλοc, -ουc, τό marsh
ἐλπίζω hope, expect
ἐλπίc, -ίδοc, ἡ hope
ἔμαθον aor. of μανθάνω
ἐμαυτόν, -ήν (refl. pron.) myself
  (9.1/4a)
ἐμβαίνω† step on/into, embark, board
ἐμβάλλω† throw in, put in
ἔμολον aor. of βλώcκω
ἐμόc, -ή, -όν (poss. adj.) my, mine
ἔμπειροc, -ον experienced, skilled
ἐμπίμπλημι† fill
ἐμπίμπρημι burn, set on fire
ἐμπίπτω† fall into/on/upon
ἔμπνουc, -ουν alive
ἐμποδών (adv.) in the way (+dat.)
ἔμπροcθεν (adv.) in front, ahead
ἐμπρόcθιοc, -ον in front, fore
ἐμφανήc, -έc open, obvious
ἔμφυτοc, -ον inborn, innate
ἐν (prep.+dat.) in, on, among
  ἐν τούτῳ meanwhile
ἐναγκαλίζομαι take in one's arms,
  clasp
ἐναντίον (+gen.) opposite, facing; (as
  adv.) face to face
ἐναντιόομαι oppose, withstand (+dat.)
ἐναντίοc, -ᾱ, -ον opposite, facing,
  opposed to
ἔνδεια, -ᾱc, ἡ lack
ἐνδίδωμι† give in, surrender
ἔνδικοc, -ον just, legitimate
ἔνδοθεν (adv.) from inside
ἔνδον (adv.) inside
#ἔνδυτα, -ων, τά clothes
ἐνεγκ- aor. act./mid. stem of φέρω
ἐνεδρεύω lie in ambush
ἔνειμι be in (+dat.)

ἔνεcτι (impers.) it is possible
  (+dat.)
ἕνεκα (prep.+gen.) because of, for the
  sake of (usually follows its noun)
ἐνέργεια, -ᾱc, ἡ activity, operation
ἔνθα (adv.) thereupon
ἐνθάδε (adv.) here
ἔνθεν (adv.) from there; thereafter;
  ἔνθεν μὲν . . . ἔνθεν δέ on one
  side . . . on the other
#ἐνί = ἐν
ἐννέα (indecl. adj.) nine
#ἐννέπω (and ἐνέπω) tell, tell of
#ἐννῆμαρ (adv.) for nine days
ἐννοέω consider, understand; discover
ἐνοικέω dwell in, inhabit
ἐνταῦθα (adv.) here, there, at this
  point
ἐντεῦθεν (adv.) from here/there; from
  then, thereupon
ἐντολή, -ῆc, ἡ order, command
ἐντόc (prep.+gen.) within, inside
#ἔντοc, -ουc, τό weapon
ἐντυγχάνω† fall in with, meet with,
  come upon (+dat., 13.1/2b(iii))
ἐξ = ἐκ
ἕξ (indecl. adj.) six
ἐξαγορεύω (fut. ἐξερῶ, 18.1/4 note 2)
  make known, speak of; speak out,
  utter aloud
ἐξάγω† lead, bring out
ἐξαιρέω† take out, remove
ἐξαΐccω rush forth
ἐξαίφνηc (adv.) suddenly
ἐξακόcιοι, -αι, -α 600
ἐξάλλομαι (aor. ἐξηλάμην) jump out
ἐξαμαρτάνω† make a mistake; do
  wrong against (εἰc+acc.)
ἐξανίcτημι (mid. and intr. tenses of
  act.) stand up from, get up from (a
  table)
ἐξαπατάω deceive, trick
ἐξαπίνηc (adv.) suddenly
ἐξαρκέω be quite enough, suffice
#ἐξαῦτιc (adv.) once more, anew
ἐξείργω† shut out from, drive out
ἐξελαύνω† drive out, expel, exile;
  (intr.) march out
ἐξέρχομαι† go out, come out
ἐξερῶ fut. of ἐξαγορεύω
ἔξεcτι (impers.) it is allowed/possible
  (+dat. and inf., 21.1/4a)
ἐξετάζω examine

ἐξευρίσκω† *find out, discover*

ἑξήκοντα (indecl. adj.) *60*

ἑξηκοστός, -ή, -όν *sixtieth*

ἐξηλάμην aor. of ἐξάλλομαι

ἑξῆς (adv.) *in order, in a row*

ἐξικνέομαι (principal parts as for
ἀφικνέομαι) *suffice*

ἐξόν (acc. absol.) *it being
permitted/possible* (21.1/5)

ἐξοπλίζομαι *arm oneself completely*

ἔξω (+gen.) *outside*

ἔξω fut. of ἔχω

ἔοικα *resemble, seem* (+dat.,
13.1/2*b*(iv)) (19.1/3*a*)
ἔοικε (impers.) *it seems*

ἑορτή, -ῆς, ἡ *feast, festival*

ἐπαγγέλλομαι† *profess, make
profession of*

ἔπαθον aor. of πάσχω

ἐπαινέτης, -ου, ὁ *admirer*

ἐπαινέω† *praise, commend*

ἔπαινος, -ου, ὁ *praise*

ἐπανέρχομαι† *return*

ἐπανορθόω *remedy* (a situation)

ἐπάνω (prep. +gen.) *upon*

ἐπαχθής, -ές *burdensome*

ἐπεγείρω† *awaken, rouse up*

ἐπεί (conj.) *since, when*

ἐπείγομαι *hurry, hasten; be eager*

ἐπειδάν (conj. +subj.) *when (ever)*

ἐπειδή (conj.) *when, since, because*
ἐπειδὴ τάχιστα *as soon as*

ἔπειμι† *be upon*

ἔπειτα (adv.) *then, next*

ἐπεξάγω† *lead out against*

ἐπέρχομαι† *go against, attack*
(+dat.); *come on, approach*

ἐπερωτάω† *ask* (a question)

ἐπέχω† *hold back, check*

ἐπί (prep.) (+acc.) *on to, to, against;*
(+gen.) *on; in the direction of; in the
time of;* (+dat.) *at, on, upon; with a
view to; in the power of*

ἐπιβαίνω† *step on to* (+gen. or dat.)

ἐπιβάλλω† *throw upon, impose upon*

ἐπιβάτης, -ου, ὁ *passenger*

ἐπιβιβάζω *put on board*

ἐπιβουλεύω *plot against*

ἐπιβουλή, -ῆς, ἡ *plot*

ἐπιγίγνομαι† *come after*

Ἐπίδαμνος, -ου, ἡ *Epidamnus* (town
on the east coast of the Adriatic)

Ἐπίδαυρος, -ου, ἡ *Epidaurus* (town
in southern Greece)

ἐπιδείκνῡμι† *prove, show,
demonstrate; exhibit, display*

ἐπιδημέω *come to stay in a place, visit*

ἐπιδίδωμι† *give in addition*

ἐπιεικής, -ές *reasonable, moderate,
fair*

ἐπιεικῶς (adv.) *fairly, quite*

ἐπιθόμην aor. of πείθομαι

ἐπιθῡμέω *desire, yearn for* (+gen.,
13.1/2*a*(ii))

ἐπιθῡμίᾱ, -ᾱς, ἡ *desire, passion*

ἐπικαλέομαι† *call upon, summon*

ἐπίκειμαι *lie upon, be upon*

ἐπικουρέω *help, remedy* (+dat.)

ἐπίκουρος, -ου, ὁ *helper, ally;*
(pl.) *mercenaries*

ἐπιλανθάνομαι† *forget* (+acc. or gen.,
13.1/2*a*(iii))

ἐπιμέλεια, -ᾱς, ἡ *concern, care*

†ἐπιμελέομαι *care for* (+gen.,
13.1/2*a*(ii)), *take care*

ἐπιμελητέον *one must take care of*
(+gen.) (24.1/5)

ἐπιορκίᾱ, -ᾱς, ἡ *perjury*

ἐπιπίπτω† *fall upon, attack* (+dat.)

ἐπίπνοια, -ᾱς, ἡ *inspiration*

Ἐπιπολαί, -ῶν, αἱ *Epipolae* (plateau
above Syracuse)

ἐπιπονέω *labour on*

ἐπισκοπέω *inspect, examine, observe*

†ἐπίσταμαι *know how to; understand*
(19.1/3*b*)

ἐπιστέλλω† *send to*

ἐπιστήμη, -ης, ἡ *understanding,
knowledge*

ἐπιστολή, -ῆς, ἡ *order, command;*
(pl.) *letter, epistle*

ἐπιστρέφω† *turn about*

ἐπιτήδεια, -ων, τά *necessities of life,
provisions*

ἐπιτήδειος, -ᾱ, -ον *suitable, useful for;
friendly*

ἐπιτίθημι† *put/place upon* (+dat.);
(mid.) *attack* (+dat.)

ἐπιτῑμάω *censure* (+dat.)

ἐπιτρέπω† *entrust; allow* (+dat.)

ἐπιτρέχω† *overrun*

ἐπιφέρομαι *move* (intr.)

ἐπίφθονος, -ον *burdensome*

ἐπιφράττω *block up*

ἐπιχαίρω† *rejoice at* (+dat.)

ἐπιχειρέω *attempt, take in hand* (+dat., 13.1/2*b*(iii))

ἐπιχώριος, -ον (also -ᾱ, -ον) *of the country, local*

#ἔπλετο 3rd s. aor. of πέλομαι

†ἕπομαι *follow* (+dat., 13.1/2*b*(iii))

#ἔπορον (aor., no pres. exists) *gave, furnished*

ἔπος, -ους, τό *word*
    ὡς ἔπος εἰπεῖν *so to speak* (22.1/1*a*(vi))

ἐπριάμην aor. of ὠνέομαι

ἑπτά (indecl. adj.) *seven*

ἐραστής, -οῦ, ὁ *lover*

ἐράω *love, desire passionately* (+gen., 13.1/2*a*(ii))

†ἐργάζομαι *work, perform, do*

ἔργον, -ου, τό *task, labour, job, deed, action; fact, achievement; field*
    ἔργῳ *in fact, indeed*
    ἔργα παρέχω *give trouble*

#ἐρέπτομαι *feed on* (+acc.)

#ἐρετμόν, -οῦ, τό *oar*

ἐρέω fut. of λέγω

ἐρημίᾱ, -ᾱς, ἡ *solitude, desert, wilderness*

ἐρῆμος, -ον *empty, deserted, desolate, devoid*

#ἐρίηρος, -όν (m. pl. nom. ἐρίηρες, acc. ἐρίηρας) *trusty, faithful*

ἔρις, -ιδος, ἡ *strife* (acc. ἔριν)

ἑρμαῖον, -ου, τό *godsend, windfall, treasure*

ἑρμηνεύς, -έως, ὁ *interpreter*

Ἑρμῆς, -οῦ, ὁ *Hermes*

Ἕρμων, -ωνος, ὁ *Hermon*

ἕρπω *creep, crawl; move about, spread; go*

ἔρρω *go to one's harm, go to hell*

#ἐρύω *drag*

†ἔρχομαι *go, come* (18.1/3 and **Appendix 3**)

ἔρως, -ωτος, ὁ *love, desire;* (personified, with cap.) *Love*

†ἐρωτάω *ask* (aor. ἠρόμην)

ἐρωτικός, -ή, -όν *amorous, in love*

ἐς = εἰς

†ἐσθίω *eat*

#ἐσθλός, -ή, -όν *brave*

ἑσμός, -οῦ, ὁ *swarm*

ἔσομαι fut. of εἰμί *(be)* (3rd s. ἔσται)

ἐσοράω see εἰσοράω

ἔσπαρμαι perf. mid./pass. of σπείρω

ἑσπέρᾱ, -ᾱς, ἡ *evening*

ἕσπερος, -ον *of/at evening;* (as masc. noun with cap.) *the Evening star*

ἑσπόμην aor. of ἕπομαι

ἔσται 3rd s. fut. of εἰμί *(be)*

ἑστηκώς, -υῖα, -ός *standing* (perf. pple. of ἵσταμαι) (or ἑστώς, -ῶσα, -ός) (19.1/1)

ἔστι *it is possible* (21.1/4 note 1); *there is*

ἔσχατος, -η, -ον *furthest, last; worst* (18.1/6)

ἔσχον aor. of ἔχω

ἑταίρᾱ, -ᾱς, ἡ *female companion; prostitute, courtesan*

ἑταῖρος (epic also ἕταρος), -ου, ὁ *companion, comrade*

Ἐτεόνικος, -ου, ὁ *Eteonicus* (Spartan commander)

ἕτερος, -ᾱ, -ον (pron. and adj.) *one or the other of two*

ἑτέρως (adv.) *in the other way*
    ὡς ἑτέρως *quite otherwise*

ἔτι (adv.) *still, yet; further*
    ἔτι καὶ νῦν *even now*

ἑτοιμάζω *get ready, prepare*

ἕτοιμος (also ἑτοῖμος), -η, -ον *ready, ready to hand, prepared; fixed, certain*

ἔτος, -ους, τό *year*

ἐτραπόμην aor. of τρέπομαι

ἔτυχον aor. of τυγχάνω

εὖ (adv.) *well*
    εὖ λέγω *speak well of* (+acc., 22.1/2*f*(ii));
    εὖ ποιέω *treat well, do good to* (+acc., 22.1/2*f*(ii))
    εὖ πρᾱ́ττω *fare well, be prosperous*

εὐγενής, -ές *noble, well-born; generous*

εὔγνωστος, -ον *well-known*

εὐδαιμονέω *prosper, thrive; be happy*

εὐδαιμονίᾱ, -ᾱς, ἡ *prosperity, happiness*

εὐδαίμων, -ον *blessed with good fortune; happy; rich*

Εὐδᾱμίδᾱς, -ου, ὁ *Eudamidas*

εὐδόκιμος, -ον *famous, glorious*

εὕδω *sleep*

εὔελπις, -ι *hopeful* (stem εὐελπιδ-)

εὐεργεσίᾱ, -ᾱς, ἡ *kindness, service*

εὐεργετέω *do good to, benefit*
εὐεργέτης, -ου, ὁ *benefactor*
εὐεργετητέον *one must benefit* (24.1/5)
εὐήλιος, -ον *sunny, with a sunny aspect*
#εὔθρονος (epic ἐΰ-), -ον *fair-throned*
εὐθύ (+gen.) *straight towards*
Εὐθύδημος, -ου, ὁ *Euthydemus*
εὐθύς (adv.) *at once, straightaway*
εὔκλεια, -ᾱς, ἡ *fame, glory*
εὐλαβέομαι *be cautious, beware, take care*
εὔλογος, -ον *reasonable, sensible*
εὐμενής, -ές *well-disposed, kindly, favourable*
#εὐμμελίης (epic ἐΰ-), *armed with good ash spear*
εὐμορφίᾱ, -ᾱς, ἡ *beauty of form or body*
εὐνή, -ῆς, ἡ *bed; marriage; sex*
εὔνοια, -ᾱς, ἡ, *goodwill*
εὔνους, -ουν *well-disposed*
#εὐπλοέω *have a fine voyage*
εὐπορίᾱ, -ᾱς, ἡ *abundance, means*
εὐπρᾱξίᾱ, -ᾱς, ἡ *prosperity*
εὑρ- aor. act./mid stem of εὑρίσκω
εὕρηκα perf. of εὑρίσκω
Εὐρῑπίδης, -ου, ὁ *Euripides* (tragic poet)
†εὑρίσκω *find; get; invent*
εὖρος, -ους, τό *breadth*
εὐρύς, -εῖα, -ύ *broad, wide*
Εὐρυσθεύς, -έως, ὁ *Eurystheus* (King of Mycenae)
Εὐρώπη, -ης, ἡ *Europa* (character in mythology)
εὔσκιος, -ον *well-shaded*
εὔστοχος, -ον *aiming well*
εὐτάκτως (adv.) *in good order*
εὐτροφίᾱ, -ᾱς, ἡ *proper nurture*
εὐτυχέω *be fortunate/lucky*
εὐτυχής, -ές *fortunate, lucky*
εὐτυχίᾱ, -ᾱς, ἡ *good fortune*
Εὔτυχος, -ου, ὁ *Eutychus*
εὐτυχῶς (adv.) *with good fortune*
εὐφημέω *shout in triumph*
Εὐφορίων, -ωνος, ὁ *Euphorion* (father of Aeschylus)
εὔχαρις, -ι *charming* (stem εὐχαριτ-)
εὐχή, -ῆς, ἡ *prayer*
εὔχομαι *pray*
εὐώνυμος, -ον *of good name or omen;*

euphemistically for *left, on the left hand* (the side of a bad omen)
#εὐωριάζω *disregard, neglect*
εὐωχέομαι *have a feast/party*
ἐφ' = ἐπί
    ἐφ' ᾧτε *on condition that* (+inf. or fut. ind., 16.1/1 note 4)
ἐφάνην aor. of φαίνομαι
ἐφήμερος, -ον *living but a day; mortal*
ἔφην impf. of φημί (7.1/2)
ἐφῑημι† *send; set on, send against; allow;* (mid.) *aim at, long for, desire* (+gen.)
ἐφίστημι† *set over, appoint*
ἐφοράω† *oversee, observe, watch*
ἔφυγον aor. of φεύγω
ἔφῡν *be naturally, was naturally* (see φύω)
#ἐχθαίρω *hate*
ἐχθές (adv.) *yesterday*
ἔχθιστος supl. of ἐχθρός
ἔχθος, -ους, τό *hatred*
ἔχθρᾱ, -ᾱς, ἡ *enmity, hostility*
ἐχθρός, -ά, -όν *hostile* (supl. ἔχθιστος)
ἐχθρός, -οῦ, ὁ *(personal) enemy*
ἐχῖνος, -ου, ὁ *hedgehog*
ἐχρῆν impf. of χρή
ἐχυρός, -ά, -όν *strong, secure*
†ἔχω *have, hold, check;* (intr.) *land, put in;* (+adv.) *be in a certain condition;* (+inf.) *be able*
ἑῷος, -ᾱ, -ον *of the morning*
ἑώρᾱκα perf. of ὁράω
ἑώρων impf. of ὁράω
ἕως (conj.) (+ἄν+subj.) *until;* (+opt.) *until;* (+ind.) *while, until* (21.1/2)
ἕως, ἕω (acc. ἕω), ἡ *dawn* (13.1/1a)

Ζαγρεύς, -έως, ὁ *Zagreus* (another name of Dionysus)
#ζάθεος, -ᾱ, -ον *very holy, sacred*
ζάλη, -ης, ἡ *squall, storm*
†ζάω *be alive, live, pass one's life*
ζεύγνῡμι *yoke, bind, join*
Ζεύς, Διός, ὁ *Zeus* (poetical also Ζῆνα, Ζηνός, Ζηνί)
ζέω *boil*
ζηλόω *admire, envy, emulate*
ζημίᾱ, -ᾱς, ἡ *fine, penalty, loss*
ζημιόω *fine, punish*
Ζηνόθεμις, -ιδος, ὁ *Zenothemis*

ζητέω   *look for, seek* (+acc.)

ζήτησις, -εως, ἡ   *search, inquiry, investigation*

ζυγόν, -οῦ, τό   *yoke; bench* (of ship)

ζώγραφος, -ου, ὁ   *painter*

ζωγρέω   *take prisoners* (alive)

ζωνή, -ῆς, ἡ   *belt, girdle*

ζῶον, -ου, τό   *animal, creature*

ζωός, -ή, -όν   *alive, living*

ζώω = ζάω   *live, pass one's life*

ἤ   *or; than*

ἦ   (particle)   *indeed, really*

ἦ   1st s. impf. of εἰμί (*be*)

ἦ δ' ὅς   *said he* (see note on 13.3(*i*) *l*.7)

ᾗ   (adv.)   *where*

ᾖα   impf. of ἔρχομαι/εἶμι

ἡβάω   *be a young man*

ἥβη, -ης, ἡ   *youth*

ἤγαγον   aor. of ἄγω

ἡγεμών, -όνος, ὁ   *leader, guide*

ἡγέομαι   *lead* (+dat.); *think, consider*

Ἡγέστρατος, -ου, ὁ   *Hegestratus*

#ἠδέ   (conj.)   *and*

ᾔδει   3rd s. past of οἶδα (19.1/3 and **Appendix 3**)

ᾔδεσαν   3rd pl. past of οἶδα (19.1/3 and **Appendix 3**)

ἡδέως   (adv.)   *with pleasure, gladly, sweetly, pleasantly*

ἤδη   (adv.)   *(by) now, already, from now on*

ἤδη   1st s. past of οἶδα (19.1/3 and **Appendix 3**)

†ἥδομαι   *enjoy, be pleased with* (+dat.)

ἡδονή, -ῆς, ἡ   *pleasure*

ἡδύς, -εῖα, -ύ   *sweet, pleasant, enjoyable* (supl. ἥδιστος) (10.1/3*a*)

#ἠέ (= ἤ)   *or*

#ἠέλιος = ἥλιος

ἦθος, -ους, τό   *custom, usage, character;* (in pl.)   *manners, customs*

ἥκιστα   (adv.)   *least of all, no, not at all*

ἠκονημένος, -η, -ον   perf. mid./pass. pple. of ἀκονάω

ἥκω   *have come* (fut. ἥξω   *will come*)

ἦλθον   aor. of ἔρχομαι/εἶμι

ἡλικίᾱ, -ᾱς, ἡ   *time of life, age*

Ἡλιοδώρᾱ, -ᾱς, ἡ   *Heliodora*

ἥλιος, -ου, ὁ   *sun;* (personified, with cap.)   *Sun-god*

ἧμαι   *be seated, sit*

#ἦμαρ, -ατος, τό   *day*

ἡμεῖς   (pron.)   *we* (4.1/2)

ἡμέρᾱ, -ᾱς, ἡ   *day*

ἅμα (τῇ) ἡμέρᾳ   *at dawn*

καθ' ἡμέρᾱν   *daily, by day*

ἡμέτερος, -ᾱ, -ον   (poss. adj.)   *our*

#ἡμίθραυστος, -ον   *half-broken, broken in half*

ἥμισυς, -εια, -υ   *half*

#ἦμος   (conj.)   *when*

ἤν = ἐάν

ἦν   3rd s. impf. of εἰμί   *be*

ἦν δ' ἐγώ   *said I* (see note on 13.3(*i*) *l*.6)

ἤνεγκον   aor. of φέρω

ἦπαρ, -ατος, τό   *liver*

ἤπειρος, -ου, ἡ   *mainland; continent*

ἠπιστάμην   impf. of ἐπίσταμαι

Ἥρᾱ, -ᾱς, ἡ   *Hera* (consort of Zeus)

Ἡράκλεια, -ᾱς, ἡ   *Heraclea* (town on Black Sea)

Ἡράκλειτος, -ου, ὁ   *Heraclitus*

Ἡρακλῆς, -κλέους, ὁ   *Heracles*

ἠρέμα   (adv.)   *gently, softly*

Ἡρόδοτος, -ου, ὁ   *Herodotus* (historian)

ἠρόμην   aor. of ἐρωτάω

Ἡρώδης, -ου, ὁ   *Herodes*

ἥρως, -ωος, ὁ   *hero* (13.1/1*b*(i))

ἦσαν   3rd pl. impf. of εἰμί   *be*

ἦσθα   2nd s. impf. of εἰμί   *be*

ἥσθην   aor. of ἥδομαι

ᾐσθόμην   aor. of αἰσθάνομαι

Ἡσίοδος, -ου, ὁ   *Hesiod* (early Greek poet)

ἡσυχάζω   *be quiet, keep quiet*

ἡσυχῇ   *quietly, gently*

ἡσυχίᾱ, -ᾱς, ἡ   *peace, quiet*

ἥσυχος, -η, -ον   *quiet, peaceful*

ἡττάομαι   *be defeated*

ἥττων, ἧττον   (compar. adj.)   *lesser, weaker, inferior* (17.1/2 note 3)

ηὗρον   aor. of εὑρίσκω

Ἥφαιστος, -ου, ὁ   *Hephaestus* (god of fire)

ἠχώ, -οῦς, ἡ   *echo* (13.1/1*b*(ii))

#ἠώς, ἠοῦς, ἡ   *dawn;* (personified, with cap.)   *Dawn*

θᾱκέω   *sit*

θᾶκος, -ου, ὁ   *seat*

θάλαττα, -ης, ἡ   (Ionic θάλασσα)   *sea*

Θαλῆς, -οῦ, ὁ Thales (philosopher from Miletus)

#θάλος, -ουc, τό shoot, sprout

θαμά (adv.) often

θάμνος, -ου, ὁ bush, thicket

θαν- aor. stem of θνήσκω

θάνατος, -ου, ὁ death

†θάπτω bury, honour with funeral rites

θαρράλεος, -ᾱ, -ον bold

θαρρέω be of good courage, take courage, be confident

θάρσος, -ουc, τό boldness

θάτερος, -ᾱ, -ον = ὁ ἕτερος

θάττων, θᾶττον quicker (compar. of ταχύς, 17.1/2b)

θαῦμα, -ατος, τό wonder, marvel; astonishment

†θαυμάζω wonder, marvel at (+gen.); be surprised; admire (+acc.)

θαυμάσιος, -ᾱ -ον wonderful, strange; extraordinary

θαυμασίως (adv.) marvellously, wonderfully

   θαυμασίως ὡς exceedingly, prodigiously (22.1/1a(iii))

θαυμαστῶς (adv.) marvellously, wonderfully

   θαυμαστῶς ὡς marvellously (22.1/1a(iii))

θε- aor. act./mid. stem of τίθημι

θέᾱ, -ᾱς, ἡ sight

θεά, -ᾶς, ἡ goddess

Θεαίτητος, -ου, ὁ Theaetetus

θέᾱμα, -ατος, τό sight, spectacle

θεάομαι watch, gaze at, look at, observe

Θεαρίδᾱς, -ου, ὁ Thearidas

θεᾱτής, -οῦ, ὁ spectator

θεήλατος, -ον sent by a god

θεῖος, -ᾱ, -ον divine, of the gods

θέλγητρον, -ου, τό charm, spell

θέλω wish, be willing (Ionic for ἐθέλω)

θέμενος, -η, -ον aor. pple. of τίθεμαι

θέμις, -ιδος, ἡ that which is meet and right; justice; right

   θέμις ἐστί it is right

Θέμις, -ιδος, ὁ Themis (mother of Prometheus)

Θεμιστοκλῆς, -κλέους, ὁ Themistocles (Athenian statesman)

Θεόκριτος, -ου, ὁ Theocritus (pastoral poet)

θεομαχέω fight against (a) god

θεός, -οῦ, ὁ/ἡ god(dess)

   πρὸς θεῶν in the name of the gods

#θεοστυγής, -ές hated by the gods

θεραπείᾱ, -ᾱς, ἡ service, treatment

θεραπευτέον one must look after/ worship (24.1/5)

θεραπεύω look after, tend; look after the interests of, protect

#θεράπων, -οντος, ὁ servant

Θερμοπύλαι, -ῶν, αἱ Thermopylae

θερμός, -ή, -όν hot

θέρος, -ουc, τό summer

θές place! put! (2nd s. aor. imp. act. of τίθημι)

θέσθαι aor. inf. of τίθεμαι

Θετταλός, -οῦ, ὁ a Thessalian

θέω run

Θῆβαι, -ῶν, αἱ Thebes

Θηβαῖοι, -ων, οἱ Thebans

Θηβαῖος, -ᾱ, -ον of Thebes, Theban

θήκη, -ης, ἡ tomb

θηλυκός, -ή, -όν female, feminine

θῆλυς, -εια, -υ female

θήρ, θηρός, ὁ wild beast

θηράω hunt

θηρεύω hunt

θηρίον, -ου, τό wild beast

Θήχης, -ου, ὁ (Mt.) Theches

†θνήσκω die

θνητός, -ή, -όν mortal

θοἰμάτιον crasis for τὸ ἱμάτιον

#θοός, -ή, -όν quick, swift

θορυβέω make a disturbance/din

θόρυβος, -ου, ὁ noise, din, clamour, commotion

Θουκῡδίδης, -ου, ὁ Thucydides (historian)

Θρᾴκη, -ης, ἡ Thrace

Θρᾷξ, Θρᾳκός, ὁ Thracian

θράσος, -ουc, τό boldness

θρασύς, -εῖα, -ύ bold, brave

θρεψ- aor. act./mid. stem of τρέφω

θρηνέω bewail, lament over

θρίξ, τριχός, ἡ hair (5.1/1 note 1)

θῡμός, -οῦ, ὁ spirit, heart; anger

θύρᾱ, -ᾱς, ἡ door

θυσίᾱ, -ᾱς, ἡ sacrifice

†θύω (A) sacrifice

θύω (B) rage

θώρᾱξ, -ᾱκος, ὁ trunk, chest

Θώραξ, -ᾱκος, ὁ   Thorax *(a
 Boeotian)*

ἰάομαι   *heal, cure*
ἰᾱτρός, -οῦ, ὁ   *doctor, healer*
ἰδ- aor. act./mid. stem of ὁράω
Ἰδαῖος, -ᾱ, -ον   *of Mt. Ida (in Crete),
 Idaean*
ἰδέᾱ, -ᾱς, ἡ   *form, shape, type*
ἰδίᾳ (adv.)   *privately*
ἴδιος, -ᾱ, -ον   *private, personal, one's
 own*
ἰδιώτης, -ου, ὁ   *private individual;
 layman*
ἰδού (adv.)   *look! here! hey!*
ἰέναι inf. of ἔρχομαι/εἶμι (18.1/3 and
 Appendix 3)
ἱερά, -ῶν, τά   *rites, sacrifices*
ἱερεῖα, -ων, τά   *offerings*
ἱερεύς, -έως, ὁ   *priest*
ἱερόν, -οῦ, τό   *temple, sanctuary*
ἱερός, -ᾱ́, -όν   *sacred, holy*
Ἱερώνυμος, -ου, ὁ   Hieronymus
†ἵημι   *let go, launch, send forth* (20.1/2);
 (mid., poet.) *be eager, strive*
Ἰησοῦς, -οῦ, ὁ   Jesus
Ἰθάκη, -ης, ἡ   Ithaca (island home of
 Odysseus)
ἴθι 2nd s. imp. of ἔρχομαι/εἶμι (18.1/3
 and **Appendix 3**)
ἱκανός, -ή, -όν   *sufficient; competent,
 capable* (+inf.)
ἱκετεύω   *beg, supplicate*
ἱκέτης, -ου, ὁ   *suppliant*
ἵλεως, -ων   *propitious* (13.1/1*a*)
Ἰλιάς, -άδος, ἡ   Iliad (epic poem by
 Homer)
#Ἰλιόθι epic equivalent of gen. of
 Ἴλιος/Ἴλιον
Ἴλιον, -ου, τό   Ilium, Troy
Ἴλιος, -ου, ἡ   Ilios or Ilium, Troy
ἱμάτιον, -ον, τό   *cloak;* (pl.) *clothes*
#ἱμείρω   *long for, desire* (+gen.)
ἵνα   (conj.) (+subj. or opt.)   *in order
 that, to* (14.1/4*c*(i)); (+ind.)   *where*
Ἴναρως, -ω, ὁ   Inaros (King of Libya)
Ἰοκάστη, -ης, ἡ   Iocasta (mother and
 wife of Oedipus)
Ἰόνιος, -ᾱ, -ον   Ionic, Ionian
Ἰουδαῖος, -ου, ὁ   Jew
ἱππεύς, -έως, ὁ   *horseman, cavalry;
 rider*

ἱππεύω   *ride*
#ἱππόδαμος, -ον   *horse-taming*
Ἱπποθάλης, -ους, ὁ   Hippothales
Ἱπποκράτης, -ους, ὁ   Hippocrates
Ἱππόλυτος, -ου, ὁ   Hippolytus
Ἱππόνῑκος, -ου, ὁ   Hipponicus
ἱπποπόταμος, -ου, ὁ   *hippopotamus*
ἵππος, -ου, ὁ   *horse;* ἡ *cavalry;*
 ἀπὸ (ἀφ᾽) ἵππου   *from horseback*
ἴσᾱσι 3rd pl. of οἶδα (**Appendix 3**)
ἴσθι 2nd s. imp. of εἰμί and οἶδα
 (**Appendix 3**)
ἰσθμός, -οῦ, ὁ   *isthmus*
ἴσμεν 1st pl. of οἶδα (**Appendix 3**)
ἴσος, -η, -ον   *equal to* (+dat.)
†ἵστημι   *make to stand;* (mid. and intr.
 tenses of act.)   *stand* (19.1/1)
ἱστορίᾱ, -ᾱς, ἡ   *enquiry, investigation*
ἱστός, -οῦ, ὁ   *loom; web*
Ἴστρος, -ου, ὁ   Danube
#ἴσχε (2nd s. imp. of ἴσχω, a form of
 ἔχω) *stop!*
Ἰσχόμαχος, -ου, ὁ   Ischomachus
ἰσχῡρός, -ᾱ́, -όν   *powerful, strong*
ἰσχῡρῶς (adv.)   *very much, exceedingly*
ἴσως (adv.)   *perhaps*
Ἰταλίᾱ, -ᾱς, ἡ   Italy
#ἰχθυόεις, -εσσα, -εν   *full of fish*
ἰχθῡς, -ύος, ὁ   *fish*
ἴχνος, -ους, τό   *track, footstep*
ἴω subj. of ἔρχομαι/εἶμι (**Appendix 3**)
Ἰώλκιος, -ᾱ, -ον   *of Iolcus* (city in
 Thessaly)
ἰών, ἰοῦσα, ἰόν pple. of ἔρχομαι/εἶμι
 (**Appendix 3**)

κἀγώ crasis for καὶ ἐγώ
Καδμεῖος, -ᾱ, -ον   Cadmean (i.e.
 Theban)
καθαιμάττω   *make bloody, stain with
 blood*
καθαιρέω†   *take down, destroy*
καθαίρω†   *cleanse, purify*
καθαρός, -ᾱ́, -όν   *free from
 guilt/defilement, pure*
καθεύδω   *sleep*
κάθημαι   *be seated* (19.1/3*b*)
καθίζω   *sit down* (tr. and intr.); (mid.)
 sit down (intr.)
καθίστημι†   *set down; put in a certain
 state; appoint; establish;* (mid. and
 intr. tenses of act.) *settle down; come*

into a certain state; be appointed; be
established

κάθοδος, -ου, ἡ   way down

καθοράω†   see, catch sight of, look
down on

καθύπερθεν (adv.)   from above

καί (conj.)   and; (adv.) also; even;
actually, in fact

καὶ . . . καί   both . . . and
τε* . . . καί   both . . . and
καὶ γάρ   in fact; yes, certainly
καὶ δή   and really, moreover; as a
matter of fact; look!; let us suppose
(13.1/3c)
καὶ δὴ καί   and especially, and in
particular
καὶ μήν   what's more; look!

καινός, -ή, -όν   fresh, new, novel

καίπερ   although (+pple. 12.1/2a(iii))

καιρός, -οῦ, ὁ   right time; opportunity;
time; crisis

Καῖσαρ, -αρος, ὁ   Caesar

καίτοι (particle)   and yet, however
(13.1/3c(iv))

†καίω   burn, kindle, set fire to

κακηγορίᾱ, -ᾱς, ἡ   slander

κακίᾱ, -ᾱς, ἡ   wickedness

κακίζω   abuse

κακίων, -ον   worse (compar. of κακός)

κακοδαίμων, -ον   unlucky, unfortunate

κακόνοια, -ᾱς, ἡ   malice

κακός, -ή, -όν   bad, evil, wicked;
cowardly; mean, lowly; (neuter used
as noun) trouble
κακὰ (κακῶς) λέγω   speak ill of
(+acc., 22.1/2f(ii))
κακὰ (κακῶς) ποιέω   treat badly;
do harm to (+acc., 22.1/2f(ii))

κακόω   ruin; wrong, maltreat

κακῶς (adv.)   badly, wickedly
κακῶς ἔχω   be in a bad
state/condition

καλεσ-   aor. act./mid. stem of καλέω

†καλέω   call, summon

Καλλικρατίδᾱς, -ου, ὁ   Callicratidas

Καλλίμαχος, -ου, ὁ   Callimachus
(Alexandrian poet)

κάλλιστος, -η, -ον   most beautiful
(supl. of καλός)

καλλίων, -ον   more beautiful (compar.
of καλός)

κάλλος, -ους, τό   beauty

καλός, -ή, -όν   beautiful, good, fine;
honourable

Καλυψώ, -οῦς, ἡ   Calypso (nymph
who detained Odysseus on the island
Ogygia) (13.1/1b(ii))

κάμηλος, -ου, ὁ/ἡ   camel

κάμνω (αορ. ἔκαμον)   toil, labour

κάμπτω   bend

κἄν   crasis for καὶ ἄν and καὶ ἐάν

κἄν   crasis for καὶ ἐν

καπνός, -οῦ, ὁ   smoke

καρδίᾱ, -ᾱς, ἡ   heart

Καρδοῦχοι, -ων, οἱ   Kurds

#κάρη, -ητος, τό   head

Κᾱρίᾱ, -ᾱς, ἡ   Caria (region in
S.W. Asia Minor)

καρκίνος, -ου, ὁ   crab

καρπός, -οῦ, ὁ   fruit, harvest

καρτερός, -ά, -όν   strong, mighty

#κασίγνητος, -ου, ὁ   brother

κατά (prep.) (+acc.)   in, on, at; in the
region of; by, according to; down,
throughout, during; in relation to, with
respect to
κατὰ γῆν καὶ κατὰ θάλατταν
by land and by sea
(+gen.)   below, down from; against

καταβαίνω†   go down, come down

καταβιβάζω   make go down, bring
down

καταγελάω   laugh at, mock (+gen.)

καταγιγνώσκω†   condemn (acc. of the
charge, gen. of the person, 23.1/1k(i))

καταγορεύω (fut. κατερῶ, 18.1/4 note
2)   denounce

κατάγω†   take/lead down; bring back/
restore (from exile)

καταδουλόω   enslave

καταδύω   make to sink, lay to rest

#καταθνήσκω†   die

κατακαλύπτω   cover over

κατάκειμαι   lie down

κατακόπτω   cut to pieces

κατακρίνω†   give sentence against (acc.
of penalty, gen. of person, 23.1/1k(i))

καταλαμβάνω†   overtake, come across;
seize, catch, capture

καταλέγω   pick, choose; recount
(18.1/4 note 1)

καταλείπω†   leave behind, bequeath

κατάλυσις, -εως, ἡ   overthrow,
destruction

καταλύω　*bring to an end, destroy;*
　finish; (intr.) *stay, lodge*
καταμείγνῡμι†　*mix in, combine*
Κατάνη, -ης, ἡ　*Catana (city in Sicily)*
καταντικρύ (prep.+gen.)　*right*
　opposite
καταπαύω　*put an end to* (+acc.)
καταπῑ́πτω†　*fall down*
καταπλέω†　*sail down/back*
κατάπλους, -ου, ὁ　*arrival in port*
καταράομαι　*call down curses on*
　(+dat.)
κατασκευάζω　*prepare, arrange*
κατάσκοπος, -ου, ὁ　*scout, spy;*
　inspector
καταστρέφομαι　*subdue, subject to*
　oneself
καταστροφή, -ῆς, ἡ　*overthrowing;*
　conclusion
#καταφθίμενος, -η, -ον　*dead*
καταφρονέω　*despise, look down on*
　(+gen.)
καταχέω　*pour down, shed*
καταψηφίζομαι　*vote against* (acc. of
　penalty, gen. of person, 23.1/1*k*(i))
κατέλιπον　aor. of καταλείπω
κατεπείγω　*press hard*
κατέρχομαι†　*go down/back; return*
　from exile
κατεσθίω†　*eat up, devour*
κατέχω†　*hold back, check*
κατηγορέω　*accuse* (acc. of charge,
　gen. of person, 23.1/1*k*(i))
κατίσχω　*hold back, check*
κατόπιν (adv., and
　prep.+gen.)　*behind, after*
κάτοπτρον, -ου, τό　*mirror*
κατοχή, -ῆς, ἡ　*possession* (by a spirit)
κάτω (adv.)　*below, down*
καυσ- fut. and aor. act./mid. stem of
　καίω
#κε(ν)=ἄν
Κέβης, -ητος, ὁ　*Cebes*
κεῖμαι　*lie; be placed* (19.1/3*b*)
κεῖνος, -η, -ο=ἐκεῖνος
κείρω　*cut (the hair), shear*
κεῖσε=ἐκεῖσε
κέκρικα　perf. of κρῑ́νω
κέκτημαι　*own, possess* (perf. of
　κτάομαι 19.1/3*a*)
#κέλευθος, -ου, ἡ　*road, path*
κελευστέον　*one must order* (24.1/5)

†κελεύω　*order, urge, tell . . . to, bid*
κέλης, -ητος, ὁ　*fast-sailing ship,*
　pinnace
#κέλομαι　*urge, order, command*
#κενεός, -ά, -όν=κενός
κενός, -ή, -όν　*empty*
κέντρον, -ου, τό　*goad*
κεράννῡμι　*mix*
κέρας, -ατος, τό　*horn; branch* (of a
　river); with gen. κέρως, *wing of an*
　army (13.1/1*b*(iii))
κέρδος, -ους, τό　*gain; profit*
#κεύθω　*hide, conceal*
κεφαλή, -ῆς, ἡ　*head*
κηδεμών, -όνος, ὁ　*protector*
κῆρυξ, -υκος, ὁ　*herald*
Κίλιξ, -ικος, ὁ　*a Cilician*
κινδῡνεύω　*be in danger, run a risk; be*
　likely to (+inf.)
κίνδῡνος, -ου, ὁ　*danger*
κῑνέω　*move*
κίνημα, -ατος, τό　*movement*
Κινύρης, -ου, ὁ　*Cinyres*
Κίρκη, -ης, ἡ　*Circe* (enchantress in
　Odyssey on island Aeaea)
κῑ́ων, -ονος, ἡ　*pillar*
Κλαζομένιος, -ᾱ, -ον　*of/from*
　Clazomenae
†κλαίω　*weep; weep for, lament;* (mid.)
　bewail to oneself
κλαυσ- aor. act./mid. stem of κλαίω
Κλέανδρος, -ου, ὁ　*Cleander*
Κλεάνωρ, -ορος, ὁ　*Cleanor*
Κλεάρετος, -ου, ὁ　*Clearetus*
Κλέαρχος, -ου, ὁ　*Clearchus*
Κλεινίᾱς, -ου, ὁ　*Cleinias*
κλείω　*close, shut*
κλέος, -ους, τό　*glory*
κλέπτης -ου, ὁ　*thief*
†κλέπτω　*steal*
Κλέων, -ωνος, ὁ　*Cleon* (Athenian
　politician)
κληθείς, -εῖσα, -έν　aor. pass. pple. of
　καλέω
#κληΐς, -ῖδος, ἡ　*rowing-bench*
κληρουχικός, -ή, -όν　*belonging to a*
　cleruchy
κλῖμαξ, -ακος, ἡ　*ladder, stairway*
κλοπή, -ῆς, ἡ　*theft*
κλύδων, -ονος, ὁ　*wave, surf; turmoil*
Κνίδος, -ου, ἡ　*Cnidos* (city in Asia
　Minor)

κοιμάομαι sleep, slumber

κοινῇ (adv.) in common

κοινός, -ή, -όν common, shared, public

κοινωνίᾱ, -ᾱς, ἡ association,
intercourse

κοινωνός, -οῦ, ὁ partner

#κοιρανέω be lord/master of, rule over
(+gen.)

κολάζω punish

κολακείᾱ, -ᾱς, ἡ flattery

κόλπος, -ου, ὁ bosom; gulf

†κομίζω carry, convey, bring;
(mid.) acquire, recover

κομπέω boast of

#κονίᾱ, -ᾱς, ἡ dust

#κόνις, -εως, ἡ dust

Κόνων, -ωνος, ὁ Conon (Athenian
admiral)

κόπος, -ου, ὁ exertion, fatigue

κόπτω cut; knock on

κόραξ, -ακος, ὁ crow

κόρη, -ης, ἡ maiden, girl

Κορίνθιοι, -ων, οἱ Corinthians

Κορίνθιος, -ᾱ, -ον from Corinth

Κόρινθος, -ου, ἡ Corinth

#κορυθαίολος, -ον with gleaming
helmet

κοσμοπολίτης, -ου, ὁ citizen of the
world

κόσμος, -ου, ὁ decoration, ornament;
order; universe; world

κοὐ(κ) crasis for καὶ οὐ(κ)

κουρεύς, -έως, ὁ barber

Κουρῆτες, -ων, οἱ Curetes (minor
divinities associated with orgiastic
rites)

κουφίζω lighten, make light

κοῦφος, -η, -ον light, nimble

κούφως (adv.) lightly

κρᾱνίον, -ου, τό skull

#κρατερός, -ᾱ, -όν hard, strong

κρατέω hold sway/power over, rule,
control; defeat (+gen., 13.1/2a(i))

κρᾱτήρ, -ῆρος, ὁ mixing-bowl

κράτιστος, -η, -ον best, strongest
(supl. of ἀγαθός, κρείττων)

κράτος, -ους, τό strength, power;
supremacy; (personified) Might
κατὰ κράτος vigorously

κρατΰνω strengthen

κραυγή, -ῆς, ἡ shouting, din

κρέας, -ως, τό meat (13.1/1b(iii))

κρείττων, -ον stronger, greater; better
(compar. of ἀγαθός)

κρεμάθρᾱ, -ᾱς, ἡ hanging basket

κρεμάννῡμι hang (tr.); (mid.
κρέμαμαι) hang (intr.)

κρήνη, -ης, ἡ spring

Κρήτη, -ης, ἡ Crete

#κρῖ (nom. and acc. s. only), τό barley

†κρῑ́νω judge, decide; select, choose

κρίσις, -εως, ἡ judgment; decision;
dispute; trial

κριτής, -οῦ, ὁ judge

Κροῖσος, -ου, ὁ Croesus (King of
Lydia)

κροκόδῑλος, -ου, ὁ crocodile

Κρονίδης, -ου, ὁ son of Cronos (i.e.
Zeus)

κρόταφοι, -ων, οἱ temples (of
forehead)

#κρουνός, -οῦ, ὁ spring, stream

κρούω strike, knock

#κρυπτάδιος, -ᾱ, -ον secret, clandestine

κρύπτω keep secret, hide; bury; cover

†κτάομαι acquire, get; (perf.) own,
possess (19.1/3a)

†κτείνω kill

κτῆμα, -ατος, τό (a) possession

Κτήσιππος, -ου, ὁ Ctesippus

κτῆσις, -εως, ἡ possession

κτίζω found, build

κτύπος, -ου, ὁ din, noise

κυάνεος, -ᾱ, -ον dark, black

Κυαξάρης, -ου, ὁ Cyaxares (uncle of
Cyrus)

κυβερνήτης, -ου, ὁ helmsman, captain

κύβος, -ου, ὁ die; (mostly in pl.) dice

#κῡδαίνω glorify

κυκάω stir

κῦμα, -ατος, τό wave

Κυμαῖος, -ᾱ, -ον of or from Cyme

Κύπρις, -ιδος, ἡ the Cyprian
(goddess), Cypris (a name of
Aphrodite, from the island of
Cyprus)

Κῡρήνη, -ης, ἡ Cyrene (city in
N. Africa)

κύριος, -ᾱ, -ον having power/authority

Κῦρος, -ου, ὁ Cyrus (1. founder of
the Persian empire; 2. younger son of
Darius II)

κύων, κυνός, ὁ/ἡ dog

κῶλον, -ου, τό limb

κωλύω *prevent, stop* (+acc. and inf., 24.1/7)

κώμη, -ης, ἡ *village*

λαβ- aor. act./mid. stem of λαμβάνω

†λαγχάνω *obtain by lot; win as a portion, get* (+gen.)

λαγώς, -ώ, ὁ *hare* (13.1/1a)

λαθ- aor. act./mid. stem of λανθάνω

λάθρᾳ (adv.) *secretly*

#λάθριος, -ον *secret, secretly*

#λάϊνος, -η, -ον *of stone*

Λάϊος, -ου, ὁ *Laius* (father of Oedipus)

Λαΐς, -ΐδος, ἡ *Lais*

Λάκαινα, -ης, ἡ *Laconian (Spartan) woman*

Λακεδαιμόνιος, -ου, ὁ *Lacedaemonian, Spartan*

Λακεδαίμων, -ονος, ἡ *Lacedaemon, Sparta*

λακτίζω *kick*

Λάκων, -ωνος, ὁ *Laconian, Spartan*

Λακωνικός, -ή, -όν *Laconian, Spartan*

λαλέω *talk, prattle, chatter*

†λαμβάνω *take, get, capture*
    δίκην λαμβάνω *punish, exact one's due from* (παρά + gen.)

λαμπρός, -ά, -όν *bright, brilliant, famous*

λάμπω *shine*

†λανθάνω *escape notice of* (15.1/2f); (mid.) *forget*

#λᾱός, -οῦ, ὁ *people*

Λασθένης, -ους, ὁ *Lasthenes*

λαχ- aor. act./mid. stem of λαγχάνω

†λέγω *speak, say, tell, mean*
    οὐδὲν λέγω *speak/talk nonsense*

λείβω *pour; let flow, shed*

†λείπω *leave, abandon*

λείψανον, -ου, τό *remnant*

λέληθα perf. of λανθάνω

λεοντῆ, -ῆς, ἡ *lion-skin*

λεπτός, -ή, -όν *subtle, fine; delicate, thin*

λέσχη, -ης, ἡ *conversation*

λευκαίνω (aor. ἐλεύκανα) *make white, whiten*

λευκός, -ή, -όν *white*

#λεύσσω *look upon, behold*

λέων, -οντος, ὁ *lion*

Λεωνίδᾱς, -ου, ὁ *Leonidas* (Spartan king)

#λεώς, -ώ, ὁ *people* (13.1/1a)

λεωργός, -όν *villainous;* (as noun) *wrong-doer*

λήθη, -ης, ἡ *forgetfulness*

λήθω = λανθάνω

ληκύθιον, -ου, τό *little oil-flask*

#λῆμα, -ατος, τό *arrogance, audacity*

ληστρικός, -ή, -όν *belonging to pirates*

ληφθ- aor. pass. stem of λαμβάνω

λήψομαι fut. of λαμβάνω

λῑᾱν (adv.) *very, exceedingly; too much*

Λιβύη, -ης, ἡ *Libya*

Λίβυς, -υος, ὁ *a Libyan*

λιγυρός, -ά, -όν *clear, shrill*

λίθινος, -η, -ον *made of stone* (see also χυτός)

λίθος, -ου, ὁ *stone*

λιμήν, -ένος, ὁ *harbour*

λίμνη, -ης, ἡ *lake* (esp. marshy)

λῑμός, -οῦ, ὁ *hunger, famine*

#λίσσομαι *beg, beseech*

λογίζομαι *calculate, reckon, consider*

λόγος, -ου, ὁ *speech, tale, word, account; argument; reason, explanation*

λόγχη, -ης, ἡ *spear, javelin*

λοιδορέω *abuse, revile;* (mid., +dat.) *abuse, scold*

λοιπός, -ή, -όν *left, remaining*

λούω *wash* (the body); (mid.) *wash oneself*

λόφος, -ου, ὁ *hill*

λοχᾱγός, -οῦ, ὁ *company commander, captain*

Λῡδίᾱ, -ᾱς, ἡ *Lydia* (territory in west of Asia Minor)

Λῡδός, -οῦ, ὁ *a Lydian*

Λυκαονίᾱ, -ᾱς, ἡ *Lycaonia* (country in Asia Minor)

Λύκειον, -ου, τό *the Lyceum* (park and gymnasium in Athens)

Λύκιος, -ου, ὁ *Lycius*

λύκος, -ου, ὁ *wolf*

Λυκοῦργος, -ου, ὁ *Lycurgus* (traditional Spartan legislator)

λύομαι *ransom*

λῡπέω *cause distress to, annoy, grieve;* (mid.) *be distressed, grieve*

λύπη, -ης, ἡ *pain, grief*

λύρᾱ, -ᾱς, ἡ *lyre*

Λῡσίμαχος, -ου, ὁ Lysimachus
λῡcιτελεῖ (impers.) it is profitable
  (+dat. and inf., 21.1/4a)
#λύccα, -ης, ἡ frenzy, raging madness
λυτήριον, -ου, τό remedy, deliverance
λύχνος, -ου, ὁ lamp
λύω loosen, release; break up
λῷcτος, -η, -ον (supl. adj.) best
λωτός, -οῦ, ὁ lotus
Λωτοφάγοι, -ων, οἱ Lotus-Eaters
λωφάω lighten, relieve

μά (particle of asseveration, affirmative
  or negative) yes by . . . , no by . . . !
  (+acc., 22.1/2h))
μᾶζα, -ης, ἡ barley bread
μαθ- aor. act./mid. stem of μανθάνω
μάθημα, -ατος, τό lesson
μαθήcομαι fut. of μανθάνω
μαθητέον one must learn (24.1/5)
μαθητής, -οῦ, ὁ student
Μαίανδρος, -ου, ὁ Maeander (river in
  Phrygia)
μαίνομαι rage, be furious, be mad
μακαρίζω congratulate
μακάριος, -ᾱ, -ον blessed, happy
Μακεδονίᾱ, -ᾱς, ἡ Macedonia
μακρόβιος, -ον long-lived
μακρός, -ά, -όν long, large, big
  μακράν (adv. acc.) far off
  μακρῷ by far
μάλα (adv.) very; quite
μαλθακίζομαι be softened
μαλθακός, -ή, -όν faint-hearted,
  cowardly
μάλιcτα (supl. of μάλα) especially,
  particularly; yes
μᾶλλον (compar. of μάλα) more;
  rather
†μανθάνω learn, understand;
  (+inf.) learn how to
μανίᾱ, -ᾱς, ἡ madness
μαντεύομαι consult an oracle
μαντικῶς (adv.) prophetically
μάντις, -εως, ὁ seer, prophet
Μαραθών, -ῶνος, ὁ Marathon (in
  Attica)
  Μαραθῶνι at Marathon
  Μαραθώνιος, -ᾱ, -ον of Marathon
#μαργῶν, -ῶcα, -ῶν (pple. of
  μαργάω) raging
#μάρπτω take hold of, seize

μαρτυρέω give evidence, bear witness
μαρτυρίᾱ, -ᾱς, ἡ evidence, testimony
μάρτυς, -υρος, ὁ/ἡ witness
Μαccαλίᾱ, -ᾱς, ἡ Marseilles
μαcτεύω seek, search after
μαcτῑγόω whip, flog
μαcτίζω whip, flog
μάτην (adv.) in vain; without reason
μᾱ́τηρ=μήτηρ
μάττω knead
μάχαιρα, -ᾱς, ἡ knife
μάχη, -ης, ἡ battle, fight
μάχιμος, -η, -ον warlike
†μάχομαι fight (+dat., 13.1/2b(iii))
Μεγακλῆς, -κλέους, ὁ Megacles
Μεγαροῖ (adv.) in/at Megara
μέγας, μεγάλη, μέγα (stem μεγαλ-;
  3.1/3) great, big; tall; important;
  loud
μέγεθος, -ους, τό size
μέγιcτος, -η, -ον greatest (supl. of
  μέγας)
μεθῑ́ημι† let go, release; give up; allow
μεθίcτημι (mid. and intr. tenses of
  act.) change, alter (intr.)
μεθύω be drunk
μείγνῡμι (also μῑγ-, aor. pass.
  ἐμίγην) mix, join; (pass.) be joined,
  mix with, have sexual intercourse with
  (+dat.)
Μειδίᾱς, -ου, ὁ Meidias
μείζων, -ον greater (compar. of
  μέγας)
#μείλιχος, -ον gentle, kind
μειράκιον, -ου, τό lad, boy
μέλας, -αινα, -αν black (10.1/3 note
  2)
Μελέαγρος, -ου, ὁ Meleager (poet
  and philosopher)
†μέλει (impers.) there is a care/concern
  (+dat. of pers. and gen. of thing,
  21.1/4b)
μελετάω practise
Μέλητος, -ου, ὁ Meletus (accuser of
  Socrates)
μέλι, -ιτος, τό honey
#μελιηδής, -ές honey-sweet
μέλιττα, -ης, ἡ bee
†μέλλω be destined to; be about to, be
  going to; intend; hesitate
μέλον (acc. absol.) it being a care
  (21.1/5)

#μέλω (for principal parts see under
    μέλει) be of concern
μέμνημαι (perf.) remember (+gen.,
    13.1/2a(iii)) (19.1/3a)
μέμφομαι blame, criticize, find fault
    with (+dat. or acc.)
μὲν*... δέ* on the one hand...
    and/but on the other (4.1/3)
μὲν οὖν no, on the contrary
    (13.1/3c(iii))
Μένανδρος, -ου, ὁ Menander (writer
    of New Comedy)
Μενδήσιος, -ᾱ, -ον of Mendes (a town
    in the Nile Delta), Mendesian
Μενέλᾱος, -ου, ὁ Menelaus (brother
    of Agamemnon, husband of Helen)
Μενέλεως, -ω, ὁ Menelaus (13.1/1a)
Μένιππος, -ου, ὁ Menippus
Μενοικεύς, -έως, ὁ Menoeceus
μέντοι* (particle) really, you know;
    however, yet (13.1/3c(v))
†μένω remain, stay, wait (for); be at
    rest, be still
Μένων, -ωνος, ὁ Meno
μέριμνα, -ης, ἡ care
μέρος, -ους, τό share, part
    ἐν μέρει in turn
#μεσηγύ (adv., and prep.
    +gen.) between
μέσος, -η, -ον middle (of), in the
    middle (18.1/6)
Μεσσηΐς, -ΐδος, ἡ Messeis (a spring)
Μεσσήνιος, -ᾱ, -ον Messenian
μέτα=μέτεστι (21.1/4 note 2)
μετά (prep.) (+acc.) after; (+gen.)
    with; (+dat., poetic) among
μεταβάλλω† change, alter (tr. and
    intr.)
μεταβολή, -ῆς, ἡ change
μεταγιγνώσκω† change one's mind;
    repent (of)
μεταδίδωμι† give a share of (+dat. of
    pers. and gen. of thing)
μεταμέλει† (impers.) there is
    repentance (+dat. of pers. and gen.
    of thing, 21.1/4b)
μεταμέλεια, -ᾱς, ἡ regret
μετανοέω think afterwards, change
    one's mind, repent
μεταξύ (adv.) in the middle; (+pple.)
    in the middle of doing something
    (12.1/2a(i))

μεταπέμπομαι† summon, send for
μετάρσιος, -ον superficial, shallow
μετεκβαίνω† go from one place into
    another, transfer
μέτεστι (impers.) there is a share
    (+dat. of pers. and gen. of thing,
    21.1/4b)
μετέχω† share in (+gen., 13.1/2a(v))
μετέωρος, -ον high in the air; τὰ
    μετέωρα things in the heaven above,
    astronomical phenomena
μετρέω measure
μέτρησις, -εως, ἡ measurement
μέτριος, -ᾱ, -ον moderate, reasonable,
    fair, average; standard
μετρίως (adv.) in moderation
μέτρον, -ου, τό measure, due measure,
    moderation
μέτωπον, -ου, τό forehead
μέχρι (prep.+gen.) until, up to, as far
    as; μέχρι οὗ until; (conj.) until
    (21.1/2)
μή no(t); (+imp. or aor. subj.) don't
    (17.1/1); (+subj.) lest (14.1/4c(ii));
    inviting a negative answer (10.1/2a);
    (on other uses see 24.1/2)
μηδαμῶς (adv.) not at all, in no way
μηδέ (conj. and adv.) nor, not even
Μήδεια, -ᾱς, ἡ Medea (wife of Jason)
μηδείς, μηδεμία, μηδέν no, no one
Μηδικός, -ή, -όν of the Medes
    τὰ Μηδικά (sc. πράγματα) the
    Persian Wars
#μήδομαι plot, plan, devise
Μῆδος, -ου, ὁ Mede; Persian
μηκέτι (adv.) no longer
μῆκος, -ους, τό length
Μήλιοι, -ων, οἱ Melians
μῆλον, -ον, τό apple
μήν* (particle) then, indeed; further
    (13.1/3a)
    τί μήν; of course
μήν, -ός, ὁ month
μηνῡτής, -οῦ, ὁ informer
μηνύω give information
μήποτε (adv.) never
μήπω (adv.) not yet
μήτε... μήτε neither... nor
μήτηρ, -τρός, ἡ mother (6.1/1b)
μητρυιά, -ᾶς, ἡ step-mother
μηχανάομαι devise, contrive; procure
    for oneself

μηχανεύομαι = μηχανάομαι

μηχανή, -ῆς, ἡ device, plan; means;
  engine of war

μιαίνω stain, pollute

μίασμα, -ατος, τό stain, pollution

Μίκκος, -ου, ὁ Miccus

μῑκρός, -ά, -όν small, short, little,
  petty

Μῑλήσιος, -ā, -ον of Miletus, Milesian

Μιλτιάδης, -ου, ὁ Miltiades
  (Athenian general)

μίμημα, -ατος, τό imitation

μιμνήσκομαι remind oneself

μίμνω = μένω

#μιν (acc. s. pron. of 3rd pers.) him,
  her, it

μῑσέω hate

μισθόομαι hire

μισθός, -οῦ, ὁ hire, pay, reward

μισθωτός, -οῦ, ὁ hireling, hired
  servant

μῖσος, -ους, τό hatred

μνᾶ, μνᾶς, ἡ mina (100 drachmas)

μνᾶμα = μνῆμα

μνῆμα, -ατος, τό monument, tomb;
  memorial

μνήμη, -ης, ἡ remembrance, memory

μνήμων, -ονος mindful, unforgetting

μοῖρα, -ᾱς, ἡ fate, lot, destiny; death

Μοῖρις, -εως, ἡ Moeris (lake in
  Egypt)

μόλις (adv.) hardly, scarcely, with
  difficulty

#μολών, -οῦσα, -όν having come/gone
  (aor. pple. of βλώσκω)

μοναρχέω be sole ruler over (+gen.)

μοναρχίᾱ, -ᾱς, ἡ monarchy

μόναρχος, -ου, ὁ monarch

μόνον (adv.) only, merely
  οὐ μόνον . . . ἀλλὰ καί not
    only . . . but also

μόνος, -η, -ον alone, only

#μόρος, -ου, ὁ fate, destiny, doom;
  death

μορφή, -ῆς, ἡ shape, form

Μοῦσα, -ης, ἡ Muse

μουσική, -ῆς, ἡ music (including
  poetry)

μοχθέω labour, toil

μόχθος, -ου, ὁ toil, hardship

μῦθος, -ου, ὁ story, fable

μυῖα, -ᾱς, ἡ fly

Μυκῆναι, -ῶν, αἱ Mycenae (city in
  S. Greece)

Μύνδιος, -ā, -ον Myndian

Μύνδος, -ου, ὁ Myndus (city in Caria)

μυρίζω make fragrant

μύριοι, -αι, -α 10,000

μῡρίος, -ā, -ον numberless, countless

μύρμηξ, -ηκος, ὁ ant

μύρον, -ου, τό perfume

μῦς, μυός, ὁ mouse

μύστης, -ου, ὁ initiate

Μυτιλήνη, -ης, ἡ Mytilene (chief city
  of Lesbos)

μυχός, -οῦ, ὁ inner chamber

μῶν (interrogative adv.) surely not?
  (10.1/2a)

μῶρος, -ā, -ον stupid, foolish

Ναζωραῖος, -ā, -ον of Nazareth

ναί (particle) yes (22.1/2h, 24.1/1)

ναίω dwell, abide

νᾶμα, -ατος, τό stream

νᾱός, -οῦ, ὁ temple

νάπη, -ης, ἡ glen

ναυᾱγέω suffer shipwreck

ναυηγός, -όν ship-wrecked

ναυμαχέω fight a naval battle

ναυμαχίᾱ, -ᾱς, ἡ naval battle

ναῦς, νεώς, ἡ ship (11.1/4)

Ναυσικάᾱ, -ᾱς, ἡ Nausicaa (daughter
  of Alcinous, King of Phaeacians)

ναύτης, -ου, ὁ sailor

ναυτικόν, -οῦ, τό fleet

ναυτικός, -ή, -όν naval

νεᾱνίᾱς, -ου, ὁ young man

νεᾱνίσκος, -ου, ὁ youth, young man

νείφει (impers.) it is snowing (21.1/4c)

νεκρός, -οῦ, ὁ corpse

νέκταρ, -αρος, τό nectar

νέμεσις, -εως, ἡ retribution

νέμω distribute, apportion, allot, assign

#νέομαι go back, return

νέος, -ā, -ον young; new; strange,
  unexpected
  ἐκ νέου from childhood

νεότης, -ητος, ἡ youthfulness,
  youthful folly

#νέρθε (adv.) beneath, below

νέφος, -ους, τό cloud

†νέω swim

νεώς, -ώ, ὁ temple (13.1/1a)

νή (particle of asseveration) *yes by . . . !* (+acc.; 22.1/2*h*)
νήνεμος, -ον *windless, calm*
νήπιος, -ᾱ, -ον *childish, foolish*
νησιώτης, -ου, ὁ *islander*
νῆσος, -ου, ἡ *island*
νήφω *be sober* (literally or metaphorically)
νῑκάω *win, defeat*
νῑ́κη, -ης, ἡ *victory, conquest*
νῑκητήριον, -ου, τό *prize of victory*
Νῑκίᾱς, -ου, ὁ *Nicias*
Νῑκοτέλης, -ους, ὁ *Nicoteles*
Νῑ́κων, -ωνος, ὁ *Nico*
#νιν* (acc.) *him, her, it, them*
νίπτω *wash*
νοέω *perceive*
νόημα, -ατος, τό *thought, perception*
†νομίζω *acknowledge, think, believe (in); treat as customary; (of a legislator) enact*
νόμος, -ου, ὁ *law, convention, observance*
νόος = νοῦς
νοσέω *be sick/ill*
νόσημα, -ατος, τό *a disease, illness, plague*
νόσος, -ου, ἡ *disease, illness*
νοστέω *return*
#νόστιμος, -ον *belonging to one's return/homecoming*
#νόστος, -ου, ὁ *homecoming*
#νόσφι(ν) (adv., and prep.+gen.) *afar off, away from*
νουθετέω *warn, rebuke*
νοῦς (νόος), νοῦ, ὁ *mind, sense, intelligence* (6.1/2)
ἐν νῷ ἔχω *have in mind, intend*
#νυκτιπόλος, -ον *night-roaming*
νῦν (adv.) *now, at present*
νυν* *well then; now then*
νυνδή (adv.; strengthened form of νῦν) *just now*
νύξ, νυκτός, ἡ *night, darkness*
ὑπὸ νύκτα *under cover of night*

Ξανθίππη, -ης, ἡ *Xanthippe*
Ξάνθος, -ου, ὁ *Xanthus* (another name for river Scamander at Troy)
ξεῖνος = ξένος
ξένιος, -ᾱ, -ον *belonging to friendship and hospitality* (used as a title of Zeus, as god of hospitality)

Ξενοκράτης, -ους, ὁ *Xenocrates*
ξένος, -ου, ὁ *foreigner, alien, stranger; guest; host*
Ξενοφῶν, -ῶντος, ὁ *Xenophon* (Athenian historian and general)
Ξέρξης, -ου, ὁ *Xerxes* (Persian king)
ξίφος, -ους, τό *sword*
ξυγ- = συγ-
ξύλον, -ου, τό *(piece of) wood, log*
ξυμ- = συμ-
ξύν = σύν
ξυν- = συν-
ξῡνός, -ή, -όν *common*
ξυρέω *shave*
ξυρόν, -οῦ, τό *razor*

ὁ, ἡ, τό *the* (2.1/2, 3.1/1)
ὁ μὲν . . . ὁ δέ *the one . . . the other, one man . . . another* (5.1/3)
οἱ μὲν . . . οἱ δέ *some . . . others* (5.1/3)
ὁ δέ *and/but he* (5.1/3)
ὅδε, ἥδε, τόδε *this* (pron. and adj., 9.1/1)
ὁδεύω *travel* (by land)
ὁδός, -οῦ, ἡ *road, way, journey*
ὀδούς, -όντος, ὁ *tooth*
ὀδυνηρός, -ᾱ́, -όν *painful*
ὀδύρομαι *lament*
Ὀδυσσεύς, -έως, ὁ *Odysseus* (hero of the *Odyssey*)
ὅθεν (rel. adv.) *from where*
οἷ (rel. adv.) *(to) where*
οἱ see ἑ (9.1/4*a*)
†οἶδα *know* (19.1/3 and **Appendix 3**)
χάριν οἶδα *be grateful to* (+dat.)
Οἰδίπους, -ποδος, ὁ *Oedipus* (son of Laius, king of Thebes)
οἴκαδε (adv.) *homewards*
οἰκεῖος, -ᾱ, -ον *related, domestic; private; one's own*
οἰκεῖος, -ου, ὁ *relative*
οἰκέτης, -ου, ὁ *house-slave*
οἰκέω *dwell (in), live, inhabit*
οἴκημα, -ατος, τό *room*
οἴκησις, -εως, ἡ *dwelling*
οἰκίᾱ, -ᾱς, ἡ *house*
οἰκίζω *colonize*
οἰκοδομέω *build a house*
οἰκοδόμημα, -ατος, τό *building, structure*
οἰκοδομίᾱ, -ᾱς, ἡ *building, structure*
οἴκοθεν (adv.) *from home*

οἴκοι (adv.)   *at home*

οἶκος, -ου, ὁ   *house, home*

οἰκτίρω   *pity*

οἰκτρός, -ά, -όν   *piteous*

†οἶμαι (=οἴομαι)   *think*

#οἴμη, -ης, ἡ   *way/power of song*

οἴμοι (interjection)   *alas! oh dear!*

#οἶμος, -ου, ὁ   *tract, strip of land*

Οἰνόη, -ης, ἡ   *Oenoë (town in Attica)*

οἶνος, -ου, ὁ   *wine*

οἰνοχοέω   *pour wine*

οἴομαι see οἶμαι

οἷον   *as, just as*

#οἶος, -ā, -ον (note smooth
breathing)   *alone*

οἷος, -ā, -ον   *what a . . . !*
(exclamation);   *of what sort, of the
kind which (21.1/3)*
    οἷός τ' εἰμί   *be able to* (+inf., 21.1/3
    note 2)

οἷοσπερ strengthened form of οἷος

οἰς- fut. stem of φέρω

ὀΐστευμα, -ατος, τό   *arrow*

οἰσύϊνος, -η, -ον   *made of
osier/wickerwork*

οἴχομαι   *be off, depart, be gone*

ὀκτώ (indecl. adj.)   *eight*

ὀλ- aor. stem of ὄλλυμαι

ὄλβιος, -ā, -ον   *happy, blessed*

ὄλεθρος, -ου, ὁ   *destruction*

ὀλες- aor. stem of ὄλλῡμι

ὀλιγαρχίā, -ᾱς, ἡ   *oligarchy*

ὀλίγος, -η, -ον   *small, few, little*

†ὄλλῡμι   *destroy, kill; lose (20.1/1 note
2)*

#ὀλοός, -ή, -όν   *destructive, baneful*

Ὄλορος, -ου, ὁ   *Olorus (father of
Thucydides)*

ὅλος, -η, -ον   *whole, complete*

Ὀλυμπικός, -οῦ, ὁ   *Olympicus (name
of a seer)*

Ὀλύμπιος, -ā, -ον   *Olympian*
Ὀλύμπια νῑκάω   *win an Olympic
victory (22.1/2g)*

ὄλυραι, -ῶν, αἱ   *a one-seeded wheat
(used as fodder for horses)*

#ὁμαρτέω   *accompany* (+dat.)

Ὅμηρος, -ου, ὁ   *Homer (author of
Iliad* and *Odyssey)*

ὁμῑλέω   *be in company with, associate
with* (+dat.)

ὁμῑλίā, -ᾱς, ἡ   *company,
companionship*

ὁμίχλη, -ης, ἡ   *mist, fog*

#ὄμμα, -ατος, τό   *eye*

†ὄμνῡμι   *swear, swear by* (+acc.,
22.1/2h)

ὁμοιόομαι   *be like, resemble* (+dat.,
13.1/2b(iv))

ὅμοιος, -ā, -ον   *like, similar to* (+dat.)

ὁμοίως (adv.)   *in the same way,
likewise*

ὁμολογέω   *agree*

ὁμολογίā, -ᾱς, ἡ   *agreement*

ὁμολογουμένως (adv.)   *in
agreement/conformity with* (+dat.)

ὁμομήτριος, -ā, -ον   *born of the same
mother*

ὁμόνοια, -ᾱς, ἡ   *agreement, harmony*

ὁμοτράπεζος, -ον   *eating at the same
table with* (+dat.)

ὁμοῦ (adv.)   *together (with)* (+dat.)

ὁμόφῡλος, -ον   *of the same race or
stock*

ὅμως (adv.)   *nevertheless, however*

#ὁμῶς (adv., accompanying two words
joined by καί)   *both*

ὄν see ὤν

ὄναρ (nom. and acc. only), τό   *dream;*
(as adv.) *in a dream*

ὀνειδίζω   *reproach, chide, insult*
(+dat.)

ὄνειδος, -ους, τό   *insult, rebuke*

ὄνειρος, -ου, ὁ (also ὄνειρον, -ου,
τό)   *dream*

ὄνομα, -ατος, τό   *name, reputation*
ὀνόματι   *in name*

ὀνομάζω   *call, name*

ὄνος, -ου, ὁ/ἡ   *ass*

ὄνυξ, -υχος, ὁ   *claw, nail*

ὄξος, -ους, τό   *vinegar*

ὀξύς, -εῖα, -ύ   *sharp, keen; quick,
swift*

#ὀπάζω   *give, bestow; make to follow*

ὅπῃ (adv.)   *in what way, how, as*

ὄπισθε (adv.)   *behind*

ὀπισθοφύλαξ, -ακος, ὁ   *member of
rear-guard*

#ὀπίσω (adv.)   *hereafter*

ὅπλα, -ων, τά   *weapons, arms*
ἐν ὅπλοις   *under arms*

ὁπλίζω   *equip, arm*

ὁπλίτης, -ου, ὁ   *hoplite*

ὁπόθεν (rel. adv.)   *from where*

ὅποι (rel. adv.)   *to where*

ὁποῖος, -ā, -ον   *of what kind (10.1/2b)*

ὁπόcοc, -η, -ον *how big, how much;*
    (pl.) *how many* (10.1/2*b*)

ὁπόταν (conj. + subj.) *whenever*
    (14.1/4*c*(iii))

ὁπότε (conj.) *when;* (+ opt.) *whenever*
    (14.1/4*c*(iii))

ὅπου (adv.) *where?* (in answer to
    ποῦ;); *where*

ὅπωc (adv.) *how?* (in answer to πῶc;);
    how; (poet.) *like, as;* (conj. + subj. or
    opt.) *in order that, to* (14.1/4*c*(i))

ὁπωcτιοῦν (adv.) *in any way whatever*

†ὁράω *see, look at*

ὀργή, -ῆc, ἡ *temperament; anger*
    ἐν ὀργῇ ἔχω *be angry with*
    (+ acc.)

†ὀργίζομαι (aor. ὠργίcθην) *become
    angry with* (+ dat., 13.1/2*b*(i))

ὀρέγομαι *strive after* (+ gen.)

ὄρειοc, -ᾱ, -ον *of the mountains,
    mountain-wandering*

Ὀρέcτηc, -ου, ὁ *Orestes* (son of
    Agamemnon)

#ὀρθόβουλοc, -ον *straight-counselling,
    wise*

ὀρθόc, -ή, -όν *straight; correct; right*

ὀρθόω *set upright; guide aright*

ὀρθῶc (adv.) *correctly*

ὅρκοc, -ου, ὁ *oath*

ὁρμάομαι *set off, start out; make an
    expedition*

ὁρμή, -ῆc, ἡ *setting oneself in motion*
    ἐν ὁρμῇ εἰμί *be on the point of starting*

ὁρμίζω *moor, anchor*

ὄρνῑc, -ῑθοc (acc. ὄρνῑν, 5.1/1 note 2),
    ὁ/ἡ *bird*

ὄροc, -ουc, τό *mountain*

ὅροc, -ου, ὁ *boundary*

ὀρρωδέω *fear, dread*

ὀρχήcτρᾱ, -ᾱc, ἡ *orchestra* (the
    dancing-space in the theatre and also
    a section of the agora where books
    were sold)

ὅc, ἥ, ὅ (rel., pron., 9.1/2) *who, which*

#ὅc, ἥ, ὅν (refl. poss. adj.) *his, her, its*

ὅcιοc, -ᾱ, -ον *holy, sacred; pious,
    devout*

ὁcιόω *sanctify*

ὅcοc, -η, -ον *how much/many/great!*
    (exclamation); *as much/many as*
    (21.1/3)

ὅcοcπερ, ὅcηπερ, ὅcονπερ *as great as,
    as many as*

ὅcπερ, ἥπερ, ὅπερ (rel. pron.) *the very
    one who/which*

#ὁccάκιc (interrogative adv.) *how often*

ὅcτιc, ἥτιc, ὅτι (indef. rel. pron. and
    indir. interrog., 10.1/2*b*) *who(ever),
    which(ever), what(ever)*

ὀcτοῦν, -οῦ, τό *bone*

ὅcῳ (+ compar.) *the more* (lit. *by how
    much*)

ὅταν (conj. + subj.) *whenever*
    (14.1/4*c*(iii))

ὅτε (conj.) *when*

ὅτι (A) (conj.) *that; because*
    (+ supl.) *as . . . as possible* (17.1/4*d*)

ὅτι (B) neuter nom./acc. s. of ὅcτιc

ὅτου = οὗτινοc

ὅτῳ = ᾧτινι

οὐ (οὐκ, οὐχ) *no(t)*
    οὐ μόνον . . . ἀλλὰ καί *not
    only . . . but also*

οὑ see ἑ (9.1/4*a*)

οὗ (rel. adv.) *where*

οὐδαμοῦ (adv.) *nowhere*

οὐδαμῶc (adv.) *in no way; not at all*

οὐδέ (conj.) *and not, nor;* (adv.) *not
    even*

οὐδείc, οὐδεμίᾱ, οὐδέν *no, no one,
    nothing*

οὐδέν (adverbial acc.) *in no respect,
    not at all*

οὐδέποτε (adv.) *never*

οὐδέπω (adv.) *not yet*

οὐδέτεροc, -ᾱ, -ον *neither of two;
    neuter* (of gender)

οὐκ = οὐ

οὐκέτι (adv.) *no longer*

οὔκουν (particle) *therefore . . . not*
    (13.1/3*c*(i))

οὐκοῦν (particle) *therefore,
    accordingly* (13.1/3*c*(i))

οὖν* (particle) *therefore, so, then;* οὖν
    δή *well, as you know*

οὖν crasis for ὁ ἐν

οὕνεκα = ἕνεκα

οὔποτε (adv.) *never*

οὔπω (adv.) *not yet*

#οὐρανόθεν (adv.) *from heaven*

οὐρανόc, -οῦ, ὁ *sky, heaven;*
    (personified, with cap.) *Uranus*

οὖc, ὠτόc, τό *ear*

οὐcίᾱ, -ᾱc, ἡ *property, wealth,
    substance, means*

οὔτε . . . οὔτε *neither . . . nor*

οὔτις, οὔτινος   *no one*
οὔτοι (adv.)   *indeed not*
οὗτος, αὕτη, τοῦτο (pron. and adj.,
   9.1/1)   *this, that;* οὗτος *can express*
   you there!
      οὑτοσί (strengthened form)   *this*
      man here
οὕτω(ς) (adv.)   *thus, so, in this way; to*
   such an extent, so much
οὑτωσί strengthened form of οὕτως
οὐχ = οὐ
οὐχί emphatic form of οὐ
†ὀφείλω   *owe; be bound, ought* (see
   21.1/1 note)
ὄφελος, -ους, τό   *help, use, advantage*
ὀφθαλμός, -οῦ, ὁ   *eye*
ὄφις, -εως, ὁ   *serpent*
ὄχλος, -ου, ὁ   *crowd, mob*
#ὀχμάζω   *bind fast*
#ὄχος, -ους, τό   *chariot*
ὀχυρός, -ά, -όν   *strong, secure*
ὀψέ (adv.)   *late*
ὄψις, -εως, ἡ   *vision, sight*
ὄψομαι fut. of ὁράω
ὄψον, -ου, τό   *cooked food, a made*
   dish; delicacies

πάγη, -ης, ἡ   *trap, snare*
#παγίς, -ίδος, ἡ   *trap, snare*
πάγος, -ου, ὁ   *crag, rock; frost*
παθ- aor. stem of πάσχω
πάθημα, -ατος, τό   *suffering,*
   misfortune
πάθος, -ους, τό   *suffering, experience*
Παιανιεύς, -έως, ὁ   *of the deme*
   Paeania
παιδαγωγός, -οῦ, ὁ   *tutor*
παιδείᾱ, -ᾱς, ἡ   *education, teaching,*
   lesson; culture; childhood
παιδεύω   *train, teach, educate*
παιδίον, -ου, τό   *child; slave*
παίζω   *play, make sport of* (+acc.),
   joke at (πρός+acc.)
παῖς, παιδός, ὁ/ἡ   *child, boy, girl; slave*
πάλαι (adv.)   *long ago*
παλαιός, -ά, -όν   *ancient, (of) old*
παλαίστρᾱ, -ᾱς, ἡ   *wrestling-school,*
   palaestra
παλαίτατος, -η, -ον supl. of παλαιός
πάλιν (adv.)   *back again, again*
παμπήδην (adv.)   *entirely, completely*
παμπλούσιος, -ον   *very rich*
πανδημεί (adv.)   *in a body, in full force*

παννύχιος, -ον   *all night long*
#πανόδυρτος, -ον   *all-lamented*
Πάνοψ, -οπος, ὁ   *Panops*
παντάπᾱσι(ν) (adv.)   *in every respect*
πανταχόθεν (adv.)   *from all directions*
πανταχοῦ (adv.)   *everywhere;*
   absolutely, altogether
πανταχῶς (adv.)   *in all ways,*
   altogether
παντελῶς (adv.)   *completely, outright*
#πάντεχνος, -ον   *assisting all the arts*
πάντοθεν (adv.)   *from every side*
#παντρόφος, -ον   *all-nurturing*
πάντως (adv.)   *in all ways, especially*
πάνυ (adv.)   *very (much)*
   πάνυ γε, πάνυ μὲν οὖν   *certainly,*
   of course (13.1/3c(iii))
πάππος, -ου, ὁ   *grandfather*
#πάρ = παρά
πάρα = πάρεστι (21.1/4 note 2)
παρά (prep.) (+acc.)   *along, beside;*
   against, contrary to; compared with;
   (+gen.) *from;* (+dat.) *with, beside, in*
   the presence of
παραβαίνω†   *transgress*
παραβάλλω†   *compare* (+παρά and
   acc.); (intr.) *come near, approach*
παραβοηθέω   *come to help* (+dat.);
   assist
παραγγέλλω†   *give an order*
παραγίγνομαι†   *be present; come to,*
   arrive at
παράγω†   *bring forward, introduce*
παραδίδωμι†   *hand over, deliver*
παραδως- fut. act./mid. stem of
   παραδίδωμι
παραινέω†   *advise* (+dat., 13.1/2b(i))
παρακαλέω†   *summon; invite;*
   encourage
παράκειμαι   *lie/be placed beside*
   (+dat.)
παρακελεύομαι†   *exhort, encourage*
   (+dat.)
παραλαμβάνω†   *take/receive from*
παραμελέω (<παρά+ἀμελέω)
   disregard, pay no heed to
παραμένω†   *remain; remain loyal*
παράπαν (adv.)   *altogether, absolutely*
   (also τὸ παράπαν)
παραπλέω†   *sail by, sail close to*
παραπλήσιος, (-ᾱ), -ον   *very similar to*
   (+dat. or καί)
παρασάγγης, -ου, ὁ   *parasang* (a

Persian measure of distance of about 30 stades)

παρασκευάζω *prepare, equip*; (mid.) *make one's preparations*

παρασκευή, -ῆς, ἡ *preparation, equipping*; *force*

παρασπίζω *bear a shield beside, shield* (+dat.)

παραυτίκα (adv.) *immediately, straight away*

παρεγγυάω *pass (the word) along*

πάρειμι *be at hand*; *be present*; *be near* (+dat.)

πάρεστι (impers.) *it is possible for* (+dat. and inf., 21.1/4a)

παρελαύνω† *drive past*

παρεμφαίνω† *emphasise*

πάρεργον, -ου, τό *subordinate issue*

παρέρχομαι† *pass, go by*; *come forward*

παρέχον (acc. abs.) *it being possible/allowed* (21.1/5)

παρέχω† *give to, provide*; *offer, furnish, cause*
πράγματα παρέχω *cause trouble*
παρέχει (impers.) *it is possible/allowed* (+dat. and inf.)

παρθένος, -ου, ἡ *girl, maiden*

παρίημι† *pass over*; *let pass*; *leave, allow, admit*

παρίστημι† (mid. and intr. tenses of act.) *stand beside, be near/at hand*

παριών, -οῦσα, -όν pple. of παρέρχομαι

πάροδος, -ου, ἡ *passage, entrance*

πάροιθε (adv.) *formerly*

παροιμία, -ᾱς, ἡ *proverb*

παρόν (acc. absol) *it being possible* (21.1/5)

πάρος (adv.) *previously*; *before* (=πρίν)

παρών, -οῦσα, -όν pple. of πάρειμι *be present*

πᾶς, πᾶσα, πᾶν (10.1/3b) *all, every*;
ὁ πᾶς *the whole*

†πάσχω *undergo*; *experience*; *suffer*
εὖ/κακῶς πάσχω *be well/badly treated* (17.1/5)

#πατέομαι (aor. ἐπασάμην) *eat of, partake of* (+gen.)

πατήρ, -τρός, ὁ *father* (6.1/1b)

πατρίδιον, -ου, τό *daddy*

πατρίς, -ίδος, ἡ *fatherland, native land*

Πάτροκλος, -ου, ὁ *Patroclus* (friend of Achilles)

πάτταλος, -ου, ὁ *peg*

παύω (tr.) *stop*; *depose*; (mid., intr.) *stop, cease from* (+gen. or pple.)

Πάφιος, -ᾱ, -ον *from Paphos, Paphian*; (as fem. noun) *the Paphian* (sc. goddess, a name of Aphrodite derived from Paphos in Cyprus)

πάχνη, -ης, ἡ *hoar-frost*

παχύς, -εῖα, -ύ *thick, stout, fat*

πέδη, -ης, ἡ *fetter*

πεδίον, -ου, τό *plain*

πέδον, -ου, τό *ground, land, region*

πεζομαχέω *fight on foot/land*

πεζός, -ή, -όν *on foot*; πεζοί *foot soldiers, infantry*
πεζῇ *on foot*

†πείθω *persuade*; (mid.) *believe, trust, obey* (+dat., 13.1/2b(ii))

πειθώ, -οῦς, ἡ *persuasion*; *obedience* (13.1/1b(ii))

πεινάω *be hungry* (5.1/2 note 4)

πεῖρα, -ᾱς, ἡ *attempt, experiment, trial*

Πειραιεύς (acc. -αιᾶ, gen. -αιῶς, dat. -αιεῖ), ὁ *Piraeus* (port of Athens)

πειράομαι *try*; *test* (+gen.)

πειρατέον *one must try* (24.1/5)

πειρᾱτής, -οῦ, ὁ *pirate*

πείσομαι fut. of πάσχω or πείθομαι

πέλαγος, -ους, τό *sea, high sea*

πέλας (adv.+gen.) *near*; *nearby*

Πελασγοί, -ῶν, οἱ *Pelasgians*

#πέλομαι (ἔπλετο 3rd s. strong aor.) *be*

Πελοποννήσιοι, -ων, οἱ *Peloponnesians*

Πελοπόννησος, -ου, ἡ *Peloponnese*

πέμπτος, -η, -ον *fifth*

†πέμπω *send*

πένης, -ητος *poor* (*man*)

πένθος, -ους, τό *grief, sorrow, mourning*

πενίᾱ, -ᾱς, ἡ *poverty*

πέντε (indecl. adj.) *five*

πεντήκοντα (indecl. adj.) *fifty*

πέποιθα (strong perf. of πείθω, 19.1/3a) *trust, rely on* (+dat.)

πέπονθα perf. of πάσχω

πεπρωμένος, -η, -ον *destined, fated*

πέπτωκα perf. of πίπτω

πέπυσμαι perf. of πυνθάνομαι

πέπωκα perf. of πίνω

περ* = καίπερ; -περ at the end of a word (e.g. ὅσπερ) is emphatic

πέρας, -ατος, τό *end*

†πέργαμα, -ων, τά *citadel, acropolis*

Περδίκκᾱς, -ου, ὁ *Perdiccas*

#πέρθω *ravage, destroy, sack*

περί (prep.) (+acc.) *about, around*; (+gen.) *about, concerning*; (+dat.) *in, on, about*

περὶ (+acc.) εἰμί *be busy with*

περὶ πολλοῦ ποιέομαι *value highly* (+acc.) (20.1/3)

περιάγω† *lead round*

περιβάλλω† *throw round; embrace*

περίβολος, -ου, ὁ *enclosure*

περιγίγνομαι† *remain over; excel*

περίειμι *survive, remain*

περιέπω† *treat*

περιεργάζομαι† *waste one's labour*

περιέρχομαι† *go round, walk round*

Περικλῆς, -κλέους, ὁ *Pericles* (Athenian statesman)

περιμένω† *wait, wait for* (+acc.)

περίοδος, -ου, ἡ *chart, map*

περιοράω† *overlook, allow*

περιπαθῶς (adv.) *passionately*

περιπατέω *walk around*

περιπίπτω† *fall in with, encounter* (+dat.)

περίπλους, -ου, ὁ *circumnavigation*

περιπτύσσω *outflank*

περιτειχίζω *build a wall round*

περιτείχισμα, -ατος, τό *wall of circumvallation, blockading wall*

περιτίθημι† *put around, bestow on*

περιφέρω† *carry round*

περιφρονέω *think about/around; despise*

Πέρσης, -ου, ὁ *Persian*

πέρυσι (adv.) *last year*

πεσ- aor. stem of πίπτω

#πετεινός, -ή, -όν *winged*

πέτομαι *fly*

πέτρᾱ, -ᾱς, ἡ *rock, cliff*

πέτρος, -ου, ὁ *stone, boulder*

#πεύθομαι = πυνθάνομαι

πεύσομαι fut. of πυνθάνομαι

πέφῡκα *be by nature, be naturally* (see φύω)

πῇ (interrog. particle) *where? how?*

πηδάω *leap, jump*

πηλός, -οῦ, ὁ *mud*

#πῆμα, -ατος, τό *woe, misery, calamity*

#πημονή, -ῆς, ἡ *woe, misery*

Πηνελόπεια, -ᾱς, ἡ *Penelope* (wife of Odysseus)

πῆχυς, -εως, ὁ *forearm; cubit*

πιέζομαι *be oppressed/distressed*

πιθ- aor. act./mid. stem of πείθομαι

πιθανός, -ή, -όν *persuasive*

πίθηκος, -ου, ὁ *monkey*

πικρός, -ά, -όν *bitter, harsh, severe*

πικρῶς (adv.) *bitterly*

Πιλᾶτος, -ου, ὁ *(Pontius) Pilate*

†πίμπλημι *fill with* (+gen. or dat.) (19.1/1 note 2)

πίμπρημι *burn* (tr.) (19.1/1 note 2)

πινακίδιον, -ου, τό *writing-tablet*

Πίνδαρος, -ου, ὁ *Pindar* (lyric poet)

†πίνω *drink*

†πίπτω *fall*

πιστεύω *trust* (+dat., 13.1/2b(ii))

πίστις, -εως, ἡ *pledge, assurance; good faith; trust*

πιστός, -ή, -όν *reliable, trustworthy, faithful*

†πλάζομαι (aor. ἐπλάγχθην) *wander*

πλανάομαι *wander*

πλάνη, -ης, ἡ *wandering*

Πλάτων, -ωνος, ὁ *Plato* (philosopher)

πλέθρον, -ου, τό *plethron* (about 100 feet)

πλεῖστος, -η, -ον *most* (supl. of πολύς)

πλείων, πλέον *more* (compar. of πολύς, 17.1/2b)

πλέκω *plait; devise, contrive*

πλέον (adv.) *more*

πλεύμων, -ονος, ὁ *lung*

πλευρά, -ᾶς, ἡ *rib, flank*

πλεύσομαι fut. of πλέω

†πλέω *sail*

πλέως, -ᾱ, -ων *full of* (+gen.) (13.1/1a)

πληγή, -ῆς, ἡ *blow, stroke, lash*

πλῆθος, -ους, τό *number, crowd; the people*

πλήν (adv.) *but, except*; (also prep.+gen.) *except, except for*

πλήρης, -ες *full*

πλησιάζω approach (+dat., 13.1/2*b*(iii))

πλησίος, -ᾱ, -ον near, close to (+gen.)

πλησμονή, -ῆς, ἡ repletion

πλήττω strike, hit

πλοῖον, -ου, τό vessel, ship, boat

πλοῦς (πλόος), -οῦ, ὁ sailing, voyage; time for sailing (6.1/2)

πλούςιος, -ᾱ, -ον rich, wealthy

πλουτέω be rich

πλοῦτος, -ου, ὁ wealth

Πλούτων, -ωνος, ὁ Pluto (god of the underworld)

πλύ́νω wash (clothes)

πνεῦμα, -ατος, τό breath

πνέω (aor. ἔπνευςα) breathe

πνί́γω choke, strangle; (root aor.) ἐπνίγην choked (intr.)

πνοή, -ῆς, ἡ breath

ποδαπός, -ή, -όν from what country?

ποθεινός, -ή, -όν longed for, desired

πόθεν (interrog. adv.) from where?

πόθος, -ου, ὁ longing, desire

ποῖ (interrogative adv.) to where?
  ποῖ τῆς γῆς; to where in the world?

ποιέω make, do; (mid.) make, think, consider
  ἀγαθὰ (εὖ) ποιέω treat well, do good to (+acc., 22.1/2*f*(ii))
  κακὰ (κακῶς) ποιέω treat badly, harm (+acc., 22.1/2*f*(ii))

ποιητέον one must make/do (24.1/5)

ποιητής, -οῦ, ὁ poet

#ποικιλείμων, -ον with embroidered coat

ποικίλος, -η, -ον many-coloured; subtle, ingenious

ποιμήν, -ένος, ὁ shepherd

ποῖος, -ᾱ, -ον; of what sort?

πολεμέω make war

πολεμικός, -ή, -όν military, martial

πολέμιοι, -ων, οἱ the enemy

πολέμιος, -ᾱ, -ον hostile, enemy

πόλεμος, -ου, ὁ war

πολιορκέω besiege

#πολιός, -ά́, -όν grey

πόλις, -εως, ἡ city, city-state

πολῑτείᾱ, -ᾱς, ἡ citizenship; constitution

πολῑτεύομαι be a citizen

πολῑτης, -ου, ὁ citizen

πολῑτικός, -ή, -όν political

πολλάκις (adv.) often

πολλός Ionic for πολύς

#πολύκλαυτος, -ον much lamented

πολύλογος, -ον talkative

πολυμαθίᾱ, -ᾱς, ἡ much learning

Πολυνείκης, -ους, ὁ Polynices (son of Oedipus)

πολύς, πολλή, πολύ (stem πολλ-; 3.1/3) much (pl. many); long
  πολλοῦ δεῖ far from it!
  πολλοῦ δέω I am far from
  πολλῷ by far; πολύ (adv. acc.) very much
  οἱ πολλοί the majority; the mob
  ὡς ἐπὶ τὸ πολύ for the most part (22.1/1*a*(vii))

#πολύτροπος, -ον of many wiles (or much travelled)

πολύφιλος, -ον having many friends

πονέω toil, labour

πονηρίᾱ, -ᾱς, ἡ wickedness

πονηρός, -ά́, -όν wicked, bad; of poor quality; wretched

πόνος, -ου, ὁ toil, labour; distress, trouble, stress, suffering

πόντος, -ου, ὁ sea; (with cap.) the Black Sea

πορείᾱ, -ᾱς, ἡ course, passage

πορεύομαι march, journey, travel

πορθέω destroy, plunder, sack

πορίζομαι procure

πόρρω (adv.) far away

πορών pple. of ἔπορον

Ποσειδῶν, -ῶνος, ὁ Poseidon (god of the sea) (acc. Ποςειδῶ)

πόσος, -η, -ον; how big?, how much?; pl. how many?

ποταμός, -οῦ, ὁ river

ποτέ* once, ever

πότε (interrogative adv.) when?

Ποτείδαια, -ᾱς, ἡ Potidea (city in northern Greece)

Ποτειδαῖται, -ῶν, οἱ Potideans

πότερα=πότερον (introducing alternative questions, 10.1/2*a*)

πότερον ... ἤ́ ... whether ... or ... ?

πότερος, -ᾱ, -ον; which (of two)?

#ποτής, -ῆτος, ἡ drink

#πότμος, -ου, ὁ fate

που* somewhere, anywhere; I suppose

ποῦ (interrogative adv.) where?

πούς, ποδός, ὁ foot
πρᾶγμα, -ατος, τό thing; business,
negotiation; affair; (in pl.) trouble
πράγματα παρέχω cause trouble
Πραξιτέλης, -ους, ὁ Praxiteles
(sculptor)
πράσσω = πράττω
†πράττω do, carry out; get on, fare
εὖ (or καλῶς) πράττω fare well, be
prosperous
κακῶς πράττω fare badly, be in
distress
πρέπει (impers.) it befits, it is proper
for (+dat., 21.1/4a)
πρέπον (acc. absol.) it being fitting
(21.1/5)
πρέσβεις, -εων, οἱ ambassadors
(8.1/4 note)
πρεσβεύομαι send an embassy
πρεσβευτής, -οῦ, ὁ ambassador
πρεσβύτερος, -ᾱ, -ον older, rather old
Πρίαμος, -ου, ὁ Priam (King of
Troy)
πρίασθαι aor. inf. of ὠνέομαι
πρίν (adv.) before, formerly; (conj.)
before, until (21.1/2)
πρό (prep.+gen.) before, in front of
πρὸ τοῦ previously
προαγορεύω (aor. προεῖπον, 18.1/4
note 2) proclaim
προάγω† lead on/forward
προαιρέομαι† choose in preference
προαισθάνομαι† perceive beforehand
προβάλλω† put forward; expose
πρόβατον, -ου, τό sheep
προβουλεύω make a preliminary
resolution (of the Council, for
reference to the Assembly)
πρόγονος, -ου, ὁ forebear, ancestor
προδίδωμι† betray
προδοσίᾱ, -ᾱς, ἡ treachery
προεῖπον aor. of προαγορεύω
προέρχομαι† go forward, advance
προθῡμέομαι be ready, eager
προθῡμίᾱ, -ᾱς, ἡ desire, eagerness,
goodwill
πρόθῡμος, -ον ready, eager, willing
πρόθυρον, -ου, τό porch, front door
προΐημι† send forth
προκείμενος, -η, -ον proposed,
appointed
Προκλῆς, -κλέους, ὁ Procles
προμάχομαι† fight in defence of

Προμηθεύς, -έως, ὁ Prometheus
(giver of fire to mortals)
προμηθίᾱ, -ᾱς, ἡ forethought
προνοέω think beforehand
πρόνοια, -ᾱς, ἡ foresight, providence
προπέμπω† escort
προπορεύομαι go in front, precede
πρός (prep.) (+acc.) to, towards;
(+gen.) in name of, by; under the
protection of, at the command of;
suiting, befitting, the mark of; (poet.)
by (=ὑπό); (+dat.) near, in addition
to
προσαγγέλλω† report to
προσαγορεύω (aor. προσεῖπον, 18.1/4
note 2) address
προσάγω† bring towards/forward;
(intr.) advance
προσαπόλλῡμι† lose in addition
προσάπτω fasten on, put on
προσαυδάω speak to, address
προσβάλλω† attack, assault (+dat.)
προσβλέπω look at
προσδέομαι† be in want/need of
besides
προσδέχομαι† await, wait for, expect
προσδίδωμι† give in addition
προσεθίζομαι accustom oneself
πρόσειμι be present/at hand
προσεῖπον aor. of προσαγορεύω
προσέρχομαι† go/come towards,
advance, approach
προσέχω† bring near, apply to
προσέχω τὸν νοῦν pay attention to
(+dat.)
προσήκει (impers.) it concerns, it is
fitting (+dat. and inf., 21.1/4a)
προσῆκον (acc. absol.) it being fitting
(21.1/5)
πρόσθε(ν) (adv.) previously; before;
(+gen.) in front of
προσκαλέω† summon
προσοράω† look at
προσπασσαλεύω nail fast to, fasten
προσπίπτω† fall upon; meet; attack
(+dat.)
προσποιέομαι claim, pretend
προστάττω assign to
προστίθημι† put to, add
προστρέχω† run towards
προσφερής, -ές similar, like (+dat.)
προσφιλής, -ές dear, beloved
πρόσω (adv.) far off

πρότερον (adv.)   *formerly, previously*
πρότερος, -α, -ον   *first* (of two); *previous*
προτίθημι†   *set before*
προτρέπω†   *urge on, impel*
πρόφασις, -εως, ἡ   *pretext, excuse*
προφέρω†   *bring forward*
προφήτης, -ου, ὁ   *harbinger*
πρόχειρος, -ον   *ready to hand*
πρυτάνεις, -εων, οἱ   *prytaneis* (the 50 members of the tribe presiding in the Council or Assembly)
πρωκτός, -οῦ, ὁ   *anus*
#πρών, -ῶνος (epic nom. pl. πρώονες), ὁ   *headland*
Πρωτόμαχος, -ου, ὁ   *Protomachus*
πρῶτον (adv., also τὸ πρῶτον)   *first, at first*
πρῶτος, -η, -ον   *first*
πτερόν, -οῦ, τό   *wing*
πτερωτός, -ή, -όν   *winged*
#πτολίερθρον, -ου, τό   *citadel*
πτυχή, -ῆς, ἡ   *leaf* (of book)
πτύω   *spit*
πτωχός, -οῦ, ὁ   *beggar*
πυθ- aor. stem of πυνθάνομαι
Πυθαγόρας, -ου, ὁ   *Pythagoras* (philosopher)
Πῡθίᾱ, -ᾶς, ἡ   *the Pythia* (the priestess of Pythian Apollo at Delphi)
πυκνός, -ή, -όν   *thick, dense*
πύλη, -ης, ἡ   *gate*
πυλίς, -ίδος, ἡ   *postern gate*
†πυνθάνομαι   *inquire, ascertain, learn* (+acc. and gen. 13.1/2a(iii))
πῦρ, πυρός, τό   *fire*; (pl. πυρά, 13.1/1c)   *watch-fires, beacons, fire-signals*
πυρά, -ᾶς, ἡ   *funeral pyre*
πύργος, -ου, ὁ   *tower*
#πῡροφόρος, -ον   *wheat-bearing*
Πύρρη, -ης, ἡ   *Pyrrha* (woman's name)
Πύρρων, -ωνος, ὁ   *Pyrrho* (philosopher of Elis)
πω*   *yet*
†πωλέω   *sell*
πώποτε*   *ever yet*
πως*   *somehow*
πῶς (interrogative adv.)   *how?*
πῶς γὰρ οὔ;   *of course*

ῥᾴδιος, -ᾱ, -ον   *easy*

ῥᾳδίως (adv.)   *easily, lightly*
ῥᾷστος, -η, -ον   *easiest, very easy* (supl. of ῥᾴδιος)
ῥᾴων, -ον   *easier* (compar. of ῥᾴδιος)
ῥέω   *flow; fall/drop off*
†ῥήγνῡμι   *break, shatter, burst*
ῥῆμα, -ατος, τό   *word*
ῥήτωρ, -ορος, ὁ   *orator, politician*
ῥῖγος, -ους, τό   *frost, cold*
†ῥίπτω   *throw*
ῥίς, ῥινός, ἡ   *nose*
#ῥοδόεις, -εσσα, -εν   *rosy*
ῥόδον, -ου, τό   *rose*
Ῥόδος, -ου, ἡ   *Rhodes*
ῥοή, -ῆς, ἡ   *stream*
ῥόπαλον, -ου, τό   *club, cudgel*
ῥοῦς (ῥόος), -οῦ, ὁ   *stream* (6.1/2)
ῥυθμός, -οῦ, ὁ   *rhythm*
#ῥύομαι (aor. ἐρρυσάμην)   *save, rescue*
Ῥωμαῖος, -ου, ὁ   *Roman*
Ῥώμη, -ης, ἡ   *Rome*
ῥώμη, -ης, ἡ   *strength, force*

Σάβυλλος, -ου, ὁ   *Sabyllus*
Σάϊοι, -ων, οἱ   *Saii* (Thracian tribe)
σαλπικτής (and σαλπιγκτής), -οῦ, ὁ   *trumpeter*
Σαμοθρᾴκη, -ης, ἡ   *Samothrace* (island in Aegean)
Σάμος, -ου, ἡ   *Samos* (island in Aegean)
σάνδαλον, -ου, τό   *sandal*
Σαπφώ, -οῦς, ἡ   *Sappho* (poetess of Lesbos) (13.1/1b(ii))
σατράπης, -ου, ὁ   *satrap* (Persian governor)
σαφηνίζω   *make clear, explain*
σαφής, -ές   *clear, plain, true*
τὸ σαφές   *the truth*
σαφῶς (adv.)   *clearly*
Σάων, -ωνος, ὁ   *Saon*
σεαυτόν, -ήν (also σαυτ-; reflex. pron.)   *yourself* (9.1/4a)
σέβομαι   *revere, worship*
σεισμός, -οῦ, ὁ   *earthquake*
σέλας, -ως, τό   *flame, gleam*
σελήνη, -ης, ἡ   *moon*
σεμνός, -ή, -όν   *revered, holy; august, majestic*
#σεμνόστομος, -ον   *haughty*
σῆμα, -ατος, τό   *mound, tomb*
σημαίνω   *signal, indicate, show*

σημεῖον, -ου, τό signal, sign
σθένος, -ους, τό strength, might
σῑγάω be quiet, keep silent
σῑγή, -ῆς, ἡ silence
σίδηρος, -ου, ὁ iron
Σικελίᾱ, -ᾱς, ἡ Sicily
Σίκελοι, -ων, οἱ Sicels (indigenous Sicilians)
Σίμων, -ωνος, ὁ Simon
#Σισύφειος, -ᾱ, -ον of Sisyphus
σῑτίᾱ, -ων, τά provisions, food
σῖτος, -ου, ὁ food (pl. τὰ σῖτα (13.1/1c))
σιωπάω be silent
σιωπή, -ῆς, ἡ silence
σκαιός, -ά, -όν clumsy, stupid
σκάφη, -ης, ἡ trough, tub, bowl
†σκεδάννῡμι (fut. σκεδῶ[-άω]) scatter
σκεπτέον one must consider (24.1/5)
σκέπτομαι examine, look carefully at, consider
σκεύη, -ῶν, τά gear, furniture
σκηνή, -ῆς, ἡ tent; stage (in theatre); stall, booth
σκηνόω lodge, take up one's abode
σκῆπτρον, -ου, τό sceptre, staff
σκιά, -ᾶς, ἡ shadow, shade
σκοπέω consider, examine, take heed
σκοπιά, -ᾶς, ἡ lookout-place
σκοπός, -οῦ, ὁ mark (at which one aims), target
σκορπίος, -ου, ὁ scorpion
σκότος, -ου, ὁ (also -ους, τό) darkness
Σκύθης, -ου, ὁ Scythian (also as adj. in poetry)
Σκύλλα, -ης, ἡ Scylla (a sea-monster)
Σκῦρος, -ου, ἡ Scyrus (island in Aegean)
σμῑκρός, -ά, -όν small, short, little
σοβαρός, -ά, -όν pompous, haughty
Σόλων, -ωνος, ὁ Solon (Athenian statesman and poet)
σός, σή, σόν (poss. adj.) your (s.)
σοφίᾱ, -ᾱς, ἡ wisdom
σόφισμα, -ατος, τό clever device
σοφιστής, -οῦ, ὁ sophist, thinker, teacher, sage
σοφός, -ή, -όν wise, clever, brilliant, accomplished
Σπάρτη, -ης, ἡ the city of Sparta
Σπαρτιάτης, -ου, ὁ Spartiate (a full citizen of Sparta)

Σπάρτωλος, -ου, ἡ Spartolus (city)
†σπείρω sow (with seed), engender; scatter
σπείσασθαι aor. inf. of σπένδομαι
σπένδω pour (a drink offering); (mid.) pour libations; make a treaty
σπέρμα, -ατος, τό seed; offspring
#σπέρχομαι hurry, hasten
σπόγγος, -ου, ὁ sponge
σποδιά, -ᾶς, ἡ heap of ashes, ashes
σποδός, -οῦ, ἡ ashes, embers
σπονδή, -ῆς, ἡ libation; (pl.) treaty, truce
σπορά, -ᾶς, ἡ sowing; begetting
σποράς, -άδος (adj.) scattered
σπουδάζω be busy about, concern oneself about (+acc.)
σπουδή, -ῆς, ἡ zeal, haste, seriousness
στάδιον, -ου, τό (plur. -α and -οι) stade (c.200 m)
#σταθευτός, -ή, -όν scorched, grilled
σταθμός, -οῦ, ὁ station, halting-place; stage, day's march
στάς, στᾶσα, στάν (intr. aor. pple. of ἵστημι)
στάσις, -εως, ἡ faction, sedition, discord
σταυρός, -οῦ, ὁ stake; cross (for crucifixion)
σταυρόω crucify
στέγω contain, hold
†στέλλω send; equip
στενάζω groan
στένω groan
στέργω love; be content with, accept
στέφανος, -ου, ὁ crown, wreath, garland
στίγμα, -ατος, τό tattoo-mark
στολή, -ῆς, ἡ clothing, clothes
στόμα, -ατος, τό mouth
#στοργή, -ῆς, ἡ love
στρατείᾱ, -ᾱς, ἡ expedition, campaign
στράτευμα, -ατος, τό army; expedition, campaign
στρατεύομαι advance with an army or fleet; wage war
στρατεύω serve in war; send a force, make an expedition
στρατηγέω be general
στρατηγίᾱ, -ᾱς, ἡ generalship
στρατηγός, -οῦ, ὁ general, commander
στρατιά, -ᾶς, ἡ army
στρατιώτης, -ου, ὁ soldier

στρατοπεδεύω *make camp, encamp* (also mid.)

στρατόπεδον, -ου, τό *camp, army*

στρατός, -οῦ, ὁ *army*

στρεπτός, -οῦ, ὁ *collar*

Στρεψιάδης, -ου, ὁ *Strepsiades*

στυγέω *loathe, hate*

στυγνός, -ή, -όν *hateful, loathsome*

σύ (pron.) *you* (s.) (4.1/2)

συγγενής, -ές *related to, relative*

συγγενής, -οῦς, ὁ *relation, kinsman*

συγγίγνομαι† *be with, have intercourse with, have dealings with* (+dat.)

συγγιγνώσκω† *pardon, forgive* (+dat.)

συγγνώμη, -ης, ἡ *pardon, forgiveness* συγγνώμην ἔχω *forgive, pardon*

συγγραφαί, -ῶν, αἱ *contract, bond*

συγκομίζω† *bring/gather together*

συγκρίνω† *compare* (something with something, acc. and dat.)

συγχωρέω *agree to/with; concede, admit; yield to* (+dat.)

συλλαμβάνω† *collect; understand; seize, arrest*

συλλέγω† *collect, gather*

σύλλογος, -ου, ὁ *meeting*

Συμαῖθος, -ου, ὁ *Symaethus* (river in Sicily)

συμβαίνω† *happen, occur, result; correspond with, fit*

σύμβασις, -εως, ἡ *agreement, arrangement*

συμβουλεύω *advise, give advice* (+dat. and inf.); (mid.) *consult, discuss with* (+dat.)

συμμαχία, -ᾱς, ἡ *alliance*

συμμαχίς, -ίδος, ἡ *alliance, confederacy*

σύμμαχος, -ου, ὁ *ally*

συμμείγνῡμι *mix together*; (intr.) *meet with* (+dat.)

συμπάρειμι *be present together*

σύμπᾱς, σύμπᾱσα, σύμπαν (=πᾶς) *all, all together, the whole*

συμπληρόω *fill up*

συμπορεύομαι *march in company with*

συμπόσιον, -ου, τό *drinking-party, symposium*

συμπότης, -ου, ὁ *drinking-companion*

συμφέρει (impers.) *it is useful/expedient* (+dat. and inf., 21.1/4a)

συμφορά, -ᾶς, ἡ *event; disaster, mishap*

σύν (prep.+dat.) *together with; with the help of*

συναγορεύω (aor. συνεῖπον, 18.1/4 note 2) *advocate* (a course of action) *with* (someone)

συναιρέω† *to bring together* ὡς συνελόντι εἰπεῖν *to speak concisely, in a word*

συναμφότερος, -ᾱ, -ον *both together*

συνδόξαν (acc. absol.) *it having seemed good also* (21.1/5)

σύνειμι *be with, be joined with* (+dat.)

συνεκπονέω *assist* (+dat.)

συνελών see συναιρέω

συνέρχομαι† *come together, assemble*

συνετός, -ή, -όν *intelligent*

συνήθεια, -ᾱς, ἡ *acquaintance, intimacy*

σύνθημα, -ατος, τό *sign*

συνθηράω *hunt with* (+dat.)

συνίημι† *understand*

συνίστημι† (mid. and intr. tenses of act.) *conspire* (+dat.)

#συννεάζω *be young with* (+dat.)

συντάττω *arrange, draw up in battle-order*

συντίθημι† *put together*; (mid.) *arrange, agree upon*

σύντομος, -ον *concise, brief*

συντρίβω *smash, gash*

συντυγχάνω† *meet with* (+dat.)

Συρᾱκόσιος, -ᾱ, -ον *Syracusan*

Συρᾱκοῦσαι, -ῶν, αἱ *Syracuse*

συσκευάζομαι *pack up; contrive, concoct*

σύστασις, -εως, ἡ *composition, constitution*

συστρατεύω *join an expedition, fight alongside*

σφαγή, -ῆς, ἡ *slaughter, slaughtering*

σφάζω *slaughter, sacrifice*

σφαῖρα, -ᾱς, ἡ *ball*

σφαλερός, -ά, -όν *perilous, precarious*

†σφάλλω *trip up, make to fall*; (pass.) *be tripped up, stumble, fall; be baffled/disappointed*

σφᾶς (σφῶν, σφίσι) see ἕ (9.1/4a)

#σφε (dat. σφι(ν)) (pron. acc. s. or pl.) *him, her, them*

σφέτερος, -ᾱ, -ον (poss. adj.,

strengthened by αὐτῶν, 25.2.3
l.7) *their own*
cφόδρα (adv.) *very much, exceedingly*
cφοδρός, -ά, -όν *impetuous*
cφώ, cφῷν (pron.) *you two* (dual of
cύ, 24.1/4)
cχ- aor. act./mid. stem of ἔχω
cχεδόν (adv.) *nearly, near, almost*
#cχεθεῖν poet. aor. inf. act. of ἔχω
Cχερίᾱ, -ᾱc, ἡ *Scheria* (land of the
Phaeacians)
cχῆμα, -ατοc, τό *form, shape,
appearance; character*
cχήcω fut. of ἔχω
cχοινίον, -ου, τό *little rope*
cχολή, -ῆc, ἡ *leisure, rest*
cχολῇ *in a leisurely way, tardily*
†cῴζω *save, keep safe*
Cωκράτηc, -ουc, ὁ *Socrates*
(philosopher)
Cωκρατίδιον, -ου, τό
(diminutive) *dear little Socrates*
cῶμα, -ατοc, τό *body, person*
Cωcιγένηc, -ουc, ὁ *Sosigenes*
cωτήρ, -ῆροc, ὁ *saviour*
cωτηρίᾱ, -ᾱc, ἡ *safety*
cωφρονέω *be discreet/prudent*
cωφροcύνη, -ηc, ἡ *good sense,
moderation*
cώφρων, -ον *sensible, temperate,
reasonable, moderate, discreet*

ταλαιπωρίᾱ, -ᾱc, ἡ *hardship, distress*
τάλαντον, -ου, τό *talent* (6,000
drachmas)
#τάλᾱc, -αινα, -αν *miserable, wretched,
unhappy* (10.1/3 note 2)
τἆλλα (or τἄλλα) crasis for τὰ ἄλλα
ταμιεῖον, -ου, τό *storeroom*
Ταμώc, -ῶ, ὁ *Tamos* (13.1/1a)
ταξίαρχοc, -ου, ὁ *taxiarch, brigadier*
τάξιc, -εωc, ἡ *arrangement, rank,
battle-array*
#τάραγμα, -ατοc, τό *confusion*
Τάρᾱc, -αντοc, ὁ *Tarentum* (town in
southern Italy)
ταράττω *trouble, disturb*
ταραχή, -ῆc, ἡ *confusion, disorder*
ταριχεύω *embalm, mummify*
ταρρόc, -οῦ, ὁ *mat*
#Τάρταροc, -ου, ὁ *Tartarus; the
underworld*

τάττω *station, draw up; appoint, place
in order; order, instruct*
ταύτῃ *here; by this route; in this way*
ταφή, -ῆc, ἡ *burial*
τάφοc, -ου, ὁ *grave, tomb*
τάχα (adv.) *quickly*
ταχέωc (adv.) *quickly, soon*
τάχιcτοc, -η, -ον *quickest* (supl. of
ταχύc)
τὴν ταχίcτην *the quickest way*
ἐπειδὴ τάχιcτα *as soon as*
τάχοc, -ουc, τό *speed*
ταχύc, -εῖα, -ύ *quick, fast*
τε* *and*
τε* ... καί/τε* *both ... and*
τέθνηκα *I am dead* (perf. of θνῄcκω
19.1/3a)
τείνω *stretch; lead* (a life)
#τείρω *oppress, distress*
τειχομαχέω *fight against
walls/fortifications*
τεῖχοc, -ουc, τό *wall* (of a city)
τεκ- aor. stem of τίκτω
τεκμαίρομαι *conclude, infer*
τεκμήριον, -ου, τό *evidence, proof*
τέκνον, -ου, τό *child*
τεκνόομαι *beget, produce*
τελευταῖοc, -ᾱ, -ον *last*
τελευτάω *end, finish; die*
τελευτή, -ῆc, ἡ *end, death*
†τελέω *accomplish, fulfil, complete;
conduct*
τέλοc, -ουc, τό *end, consummation,
fulfilment*
τέλοc (adv. acc., 20.1/5) *in the end,
finally*
διὰ τέλουc *through to the end,
throughout*
†τέμνω *cut; ravage*
#τέοc = cόc
#τέρμα, -ατοc, τό *end*
τερπνόc, -ή, -όν *delightful, pleasant*
τέρπομαι *enjoy oneself*
Τερψίων, -ωνοc, ὁ *Terpsion*
τέταρτοc, -η, -ον *fourth*
τέτοκα perf. of τίκτω
#τετράπαλαι (adv.) *long, long ago*
τετταράκοντα (indecl. numeral) *forty*
τέτταρεc, -α *four* (7.1/5)
τέττιξ, -ῑγοc, ὁ *cicada, grasshopper*
Τευθρανίᾱ, -ᾱc, ἡ *Teuthrania*
τέχνη, -ηc, ἡ *skill, art, expertise; way,
manner, means; trick, wile*

τῇδε (adv.) *here*

τηλικοῦτος, -αύτη, -οῦτον *so great, so important*

#τηλουρός, -όν *distant*

τήμερον (adv.) *today*

τηρέω *watch, guard; watch for, observe*

τί; *what? why?* (10.1/1 note 1); *in what respect?*

Τιγράνης, -ου, ὁ *Tigranes*

†τίθημι *put, place; make, render* (act. and mid.) (18.1/2)

  νόμους τίθημι *lay down laws*

  νόμους τίθεμαι *make/adopt laws*

†τίκτω *bear, beget, give birth to*

τῑμάω *honour; value, reckon;* (+dat.) *fine*

τῑμή, -ῆς, ἡ *honour, privilege, respect*

  ἐν τῑμῇ ἔχω *respect, honour*

τῑμιος, -ᾱ, -ον *held in honour*

Τῑμόκριτος, -ου, ὁ *Timocritus*

τῑμωρέω *avenge* (+dat.); (act. and mid.) *take vengeance on, punish* (+acc.)

τῑμωρίᾱ, -ᾱς, ἡ *revenge, vengeance*

Τιρίβαζος, -ου, ὁ *Tiribazus*

τις, τι* (indef. pron.) *a certain, someone, something* (10.1/1)

  τι (adv. acc., 20.1/5) *to some extent*

τίς; τί; (interrogative pron.) *who? which? what?* (10.1/1)

Τισσαφέρνης, -ου, ὁ *Tissaphernes* (Persian satrap)

τίτλος, -ου, ὁ *title, inscription*

†τιτρώσκω *wound*

#τλάω (aor. ἔτλην) *venture, bring oneself to do something*

τλήμων, -ον *wretched, unfortunate; patient, resolute*

τοι* (particle) *in truth, be assured*

τοίνυν* (particle) *now then, well now* (13.1/3a)

#τοῖος, -ᾱ, -ον = τοιοῦτος

τοιόσδε, -άδε, -όνδε *of this sort, of such a sort, such* (21.1/3)

τοιοῦτος, -αύτη, -οῦτο(ν) *of this sort, of such a sort* (21.1/3)

τόκος, -ου, ὁ *offspring*

τόλμα, -ης, ἡ *daring*

τολμάω *dare, be daring; undertake*

τόξον, -ου, τό *bow* (also in pl. τόξα, *bow [and arrows]*); (poetry)

ray/shaft (of sunshine)

τοξότης, -ου, ὁ *archer*

τόπος, -ου, ὁ *place, region; topic*

#τόςος, -η, -ον = τοσοῦτος

τοσόςδε, -ήδε, -όνδε *so much, so large, so great* (pl. *so many*) (21.1/3)

τοσοῦτος, -αύτη, -οῦτο(ν) *so much, so large, so great* (pl. *so many*) (21.1/3)

τότε (adv.) *then, at that time*

του = τινος *of someone/something*

τοῦ; can = τίνος; *of whom/what?*

τοὔνομα crasis for τὸ ὄνομα

τούτῳ dat. of οὗτος

  ἐν τούτῳ *meanwhile*

τράπεζα, -ης, ἡ *table; bank*

τραῦμα, -ατος, τό *wound*

τράχηλος, -ου, ὁ *neck, throat*

τραχύς, -εῖα, -ύ *rough, prickly*

τραχύτης, -ητος, ἡ *roughness*

τρεῖς, τρία *three* (7.1/5)

†τρέπω *cause to turn, put to flight*

†τρέφω *rear, raise, feed, nourish*

†τρέχω *run*

τριάκοντα (indecl. numeral) *thirty*

τριᾱκόντερος, -ου, ἡ (sc. ναῦς) *thirty-oared ship*

τριᾱκόσιοι, -αι, -α *300*

τρίβω *rub*

τριηραρχέω *serve as trierarch*

τριήραρχος, -ου, ὁ *trierarch*

τριήρης, -ους, ἡ *trireme*

τρίς (adv.) *three times*

τρισχίλιοι, -αι, -α *3,000*

#τρίτατος = τρίτος

τρίτος, -η, -ον *third*

τρίχες, αἱ nom. pl. of θρίξ

Τροίᾱ, -ᾱς, ἡ *Troy*

τροπαῖον, -ου, τό *trophy*

τρόπος, -ου, ὁ *way, manner, way of life;* (in pl.) *ways, habits, character*

  τίνα τρόπον; (adv. acc., 20.1/5) *in what way?, how?*

  τοῦτον τὸν τρόπον (adv. acc.) *in this way*

  τούτῳ τῷ τρόπῳ *in this way*

τροφή, -ῆς, ἡ *food, nourishment*

τρύω *wear out, distress*

Τρῳάς, -άδος, ἡ *Trojan woman*

Τρῶες, -ων, οἱ *Trojans* (13.1/1b(i))

Τρωικός, -ή, -όν *Trojan*

  τὰ Τρωικά (sc. πράγματα) *the Trojan War*

†τυγχάνω (+gen. 13.1/2a(iv) *hit (the mark), succeed; chance/happen upon, obtain;* (+pple.) *happen to –, be actually* – 15.1/2e)

#τύκιϲμα, -ατοϲ, τό *working or chiselling in stone*

τύλη, -ηϲ, ἡ *cushion*

τύμβοϲ, -ου, ὁ *tomb*

τυπείϲ aor. pass. pple. of τύπτω

†τύπτω *strike, hit, beat*

τυραννεύω *be tyrant*

τυραννίϲ, -ίδοϲ, ἡ *sovereignty; tyranny*

τύραννοϲ, -ου, ὁ *absolute ruler, sovereign; tyrant*

τῡρόϲ, -οῦ, ὁ *cheese*

τυφλόϲ, -ή, -όν *blind*

τυχ- aor. stem of τυγχάνω

τύχη, -ηϲ, ἡ *chance, luck, good or bad fortune;* (personified, with cap.) *Chance, Fortune*

τω = τινι *to/for someone/something*

τῷ; can = τίνι; *to/for whom/what?*

τῷ ὄντι *in fact, really*

ὑβρίζω *treat violently/disgracefully; humiliate*

ὕβριϲ, -εωϲ, ἡ *aggression, violence, insolence, insult, humiliation*

ὑβριϲτήϲ, -οῦ, ὁ *violent/insolent person*

ὑγίεια, -αϲ, ἡ *health*

ὕδρᾱ, -αϲ, ἡ *hydra (water serpent)*

ὕδωρ, -ατοϲ, τό *water*

ὕει (impers.) *it is raining (21.1/4c)*

ὕειοϲ, -ᾱ, -ον *of pigs, pork*

υἱόϲ, -οῦ, ὁ *son (13.1/1c)*

ὕλη, -ηϲ, ἡ *wood, forest*

ὑλοτόμοϲ, -ου, ὁ *woodcutter*

ὑμεῖϲ (pron.) *you (pl., 4.1/2)*

ὑμέτεροϲ, -ᾱ, -ον (poss. adj.) *your (pl.)*

ὑπάρχω† *be; begin (+gen.)*

ὕπειμι *be beneath (+dat.)*

ὑπέρ (prep.) (+acc.) *beyond;* (+gen.) *for, on behalf of*

ὑπερβαίνω† *step over, cross (mountains)*

ὑπερβάλλω† *pass over, cross*

Ὑπέρεια, -αϲ, ἡ *Hypereia (a spring)*

ὑπερέχω† *be above, stick out above*

Ὑπερίων, -ωνοϲ, ὁ *Hyperion (the Sun-god)*

ὑπερμαχέω *fight for*

ὑπέρπικροϲ, -ον *exceedingly bitter*

ὑπερφρονέω *be overproud, look down on*

ὑπέρχυϲιϲ, -εωϲ, ἡ *overflow*

ὑπηρετέω *perform a service*

ὑπηρέτηϲ, -ου, ὁ *servant*

†ὑπιϲχνέομαι *promise*

ὕπνοϲ, -ου, ὁ *sleep*

ὑπό (prep.) (+acc.) *under, along under, up under;* (+gen.) *from under; by, at the hand(s) of;* (+dat.) *under, beneath;* (Homeric) *at the hand(s) of*

ὑπόδημα, -ατοϲ, τό *sandal*

ὑποζύγιον, -ου, τό *beast of burden, draught animal*

ὑπόθεϲιϲ, -εωϲ, ἡ *proposal, supposition*

ὑποκαταβαίνω† *descend gradually*

ὑπολαμβάνω† *take up, answer, reply; assume*

ὑπολείπω† *leave behind*

ὑπόλοιποϲ, -ον *remaining*

ὑποπέμπω† *send secretly*

ὑποπτεύω *suspect, be suspicious*

ὑποπτήττω *cower before (+acc.)*

#ὑπορρήγνῡμι† *burst beneath*

ὑποτελέω† *pay (tribute)*

ὑποτίθημι† *place under*

ὑποφαίνω† *dawn, begin to break*

ὕϲ, ὑόϲ, ὁ/ἡ *pig*

Ὑϲτάϲπηϲ, -ου, ὁ *Hystaspes*

ὑϲτεραῖοϲ, -ᾱ, -ον *following, next* τῇ ὑϲτεραίᾳ *on the following day*

ὕϲτερον (adv.) *later, afterwards*

ὕϲτεροϲ, -ᾱ, -ον *later, last (of two)*

ὑφ᾽ = ὑπό

ὑφαίνω *weave*

ὑφαιρέομαι† (aor. act./mid. stem ὑφελ-) *steal, take by stealth*

ὑφίημι† *send;* (mid. and intr. tenses of act.) *submit, yield*

#ὑψηλόκρημνοϲ, -ον *with lofty cliffs*

ὑψηλόϲ, -ή, -όν *high*

ὕψοϲ, -ουϲ, τό *height*

φαγ- aor. stem of ἐϲθίω

#φαεινόϲ, -ή, -όν *shining, radiant, bright*

φαεϲφόροϲ, -ον *light-bringing;* (personified, with cap.) *the Light-Bringer,* i.e. *the Morning Star*

†φαίνω *reveal, declare*; (pass.) *appear, be seen, seem*; (+pple.) *obviously be*; (+inf.) *seem to be* (15.1/2*d*)

Φάληρον, -ου, τό *Phalerum* (a port of Athens)

Φαληροῖ *at Phalerum*

φάναι inf. of φημί

φανερός, -ά, -όν *clear, obvious, visible*

φάος, -ους, τό *light, daylight*

φάραγξ, -αγγος, ἡ *chasm, ravine*

φάρμακον, -ου, τό *poison; drug; remedy; potion*

φάσκω *allege, state, declare, claim*

φαῦλος, -ον (also -η, -ον) *mean, poor, low; trivial, ordinary, indifferent, cheap*

Φειδιππίδης, -ου, ὁ *Pheidippides*

Φειδιππίδιον, -ου, τό (diminutive) *dear little Pheidippides*

φείδομαι *spare* (+gen.)

φέρε (2nd s. imp. of φέρω) *come!*

†φέρω *carry, bring; bear, endure; produce; lead* (of a road)

ἄγω καὶ φέρω *plunder*

χαλεπῶς φέρω *be annoyed at* (+acc.)

φεῦ (interjection) *alas!; ah, oh!* (+gen. 23.1/1*l*)

†φεύγω *flee, flee from, escape* (+acc.); *be a defendant, be on trial, be proscribed; be banished, be in exile* (17.1/5)

†φημί *say* (7.1/2)

†φθάνω *anticipate* (15.1/2*f*)

φθέγγομαι *speak, say, utter*

†φθείρω *destroy, ruin*

#φθίμενος, -η, -ον *dead*

φθονέω *feel ill-will/envy/jealousy against, grudge* (+dat., 13.1/2*b*(i))

φθόνος, -ου, ὁ *envy, jealousy*

φιλάνθρωπος, -ον *loving mankind, man-loving, humane*

φιλάργυρος, -ον *avaricious, miserly*

φιλέω *love, like, be a friend of; kiss; be accustomed to* (+inf.)

φιλητέον *one must love* (24.1/5)

φιλία, -ᾱς, ἡ *friendship*

Φιλιππισμός, -οῦ, ὁ *siding with Philip*

Φίλιππος, -ου, ὁ *Philip* (father of Alexander the Great)

φιλόκαλος, -ον *loving beauty, fond of elegance*

Φιλοκράτης, -ους, ὁ *Philocrates*

φίλος, -η, -ον *dear, friendly; pleasing to* (+dat.)

φίλος, -ου, ὁ *friend*

φιλοσοφέω *pursue/study philosophy*

φιλοσοφία, -ᾱς, ἡ *philosophy*

φιλόσοφος, -ου, ὁ *philosopher*

φιλότης, -ητος, ἡ *love, friendship; sexual intercourse*

φιλότιμος, -ον *loving distinction, ambitious*

φιλοφροσύνη, -ης, ἡ *love, affection*

φίλτατος, -η, -ον *most dear* (supl. of φίλος)

#φίλυμνος, -ον *loving song*

φλόξ, -ογός, ἡ *flame*

φλυᾱρέω *talk nonsense*

φλυᾱρία, -ᾱς, ἡ *nonsense*

†φοβέομαι *fear, be afraid of*; φοβέομαι μή *fear lest/that* (14.1/4*c*(ii))

φοβερός, -ά, -όν *terrible, frightening*

φόβος, -ου, ὁ *fear, panic*

#φοῖβος, -η, -ον *pure, bright, radiant*

Φοῖβος, -ου, ὁ *Phoebus* (Apollo)

#Φοινικογενής, -ές *Phoenician-born*

Φοῖνιξ, -ικος, ὁ *Phoenician*

#φοίνιος, -ᾱ, -ον *bloody*

φοιτάω *go regularly to, frequent, resort to* (a person as a teacher)

φονεύς, -έως, ὁ *murderer*

φονεύω *murder, slay*

φόνος, -ου, ὁ *murder, slaughter, homicide*

φορέω *carry, bring*

φόρος, -ου, ὁ *tribute*

φορτίον, -ου, τό *load, burden*

φράζω *explain, tell, declare*

#φρήν, φρενός, ἡ *heart, mind* (pl. is used in the same sense)

φρονέω *think, consider; be wise, sensible*

μέγα φρονέω *be proud, have high thoughts*

φρόνημα, -ατος, τό *arrogance, pride*

φρόνιμος, -ον *sensible, wise*

φροντίζω *think, ponder, consider, worry; pay heed to* (+gen.)

φροντίς, -ίδος, ἡ *thought, care, concern*

Φροντιστήριον, -ου, τό *Think Tank, thinking shop*

φροντιστής, -οῦ, ὁ *deep thinker*

φρούριον, -ου, τό   *fort*
φρύγανα, -ων, τά   *dry wood, firewood*
φυγάς, -άδος, ὁ   *exile; runaway;*
   fugitive
φυγή, -ῆς, ἡ   *flight*
φυλακή, -ῆς, ἡ   *guard, guarding,*
   garrison
   ἐν φυλακῇ εἰμι   *be on guard*
φύλαξ, -ακος, ὁ   *guard*
φυλάττω (perf. πεφύλαχα)   *guard,*
   watch; (mid.) *take care, be on one's*
   guard against (+acc.)
φύρω   *spoil, defile, mar*
φύσις, -εως, ἡ   *nature, character,*
   temperament
†φύω   *cause to grow, produce*
   ἔφῡν   *was born; am naturally*
   πέφῡκα   *am naturally, am inclined by*
   nature
Φώκαια, -ᾱς, ἡ   *Phocaea* (city in Asia
   Minor)
φωνέω   *speak*
φωνή, -ῆς, ἡ   *voice, language, speech*
φῶς, φωτός, τό   *light*

Χαιρεφῶν, -ῶντος, ὁ   *Chaerephon*
   (disciple of Socrates)
†χαίρω   *rejoice*
χαῖρε   *greetings! hello! farewell!* (17.1/1
   note 7)
χαλεπαίνω   *be angry/annoyed at*
   (+dat.)
χαλεπός, -ή, -όν   *difficult, hard*
   χαλεπῶς ἔχω   *be in a bad way*
   χαλεπῶς φέρω   *be angry/displeased*
   at (+acc.)
χαλινός, -οῦ, ὁ   *bit* (for a horse's
   bridle)
#χάλκευμα, -ατος, τό   *anything bronze;*
   (pl.) *brazen bonds*
χαλκός, -οῦ, ὁ   *bronze*
χαλκοῦς, -ῆ, -οῦν   *of bronze*
#χαλκοχίτων, -ωνος   *bronze-clad*
Χᾱονες, -ων, οἱ   *the Chaonians* (tribe
   in Epirus)
χάος, -ους, τό   *chaos*
χαρακτήρ, -ῆρος, ὁ   *engraved mark;*
   characteristic, character
χαρίεις, -εσσα, -εν   *graceful, elegant,*
   charming, nice
χαριεντίζομαι   *jest, joke*
χαρίζομαι   *oblige, do a favour to*
   (+dat.); *give graciously*

χάρις, -ιτος (acc. χάριν), ἡ   *grace,*
   charm; favour; recompense, thanks
   χάριν οἶδα/ἔχω   *be grateful to*
   (+dat.)
Χάρυβδις, -εως, ἡ   *Charybdis* (a
   whirlpool)
χεῖλος, -ους, τό   *lip*
χειμών, -ῶνος, ὁ   *storm; winter*
χείρ, χειρός, ἡ   *hand*
Χειρίσοφος, -ου, ὁ   *Cheirisophus*
   (Lacedaemonian general of Cyrus)
χείριστος, -η, -ον   *worst* (supl. of
   κακός)
χειροτέχνης, -ου, ὁ   *craftsman*
χείρων, -ον   *worse* (compar. of κακός)
χελῑδών, -όνος, ἡ   *swallow*
χελώνη, -ης, ἡ   *tortoise*
Χερρόνησος, -ου, ἡ   *the Chersonese*
   (the Gallipoli peninsula)
χἠ   crasis for καὶ ἡ
χῆτος, -ους, τό   *want, lack, need*
χθές   *yesterday*
#χθών, χθονός, ἡ   *earth, land*
χίλιοι, -αι, -α   *thousand*
Χίος, -ου, ἡ   *Chios* (island and city in
   the Aegean)
χιτών, -ῶνος, ὁ   *tunic, shirt*
χιών, -όνος, ἡ   *snow*
χολή, -ῆς, ἡ   *bile, gall; anger*
χορεύω   *dance*
†χράομαι   *deal with, associate with,*
   treat, use (+dat., 13.1/2b(iii))
χρείᾱ, -ᾱς, ἡ   *use, serviceability*
†χρή   *it is necessary* (+acc. and inf.)
χρῄζω   *desire, want, need* (+gen.)
χρῆμα, -ατος, τό   *thing;* (pl.) *money,*
   goods
χρηματίζω   *deal with business* (in the
   Council or Assembly)
χρῆςθαι   inf. of χράομαι
χρήςιμος, -η, -ον   *profitable, useful*
χρησμός, -οῦ, ὁ   *oracle*
χρηστήριον, -ου, τό   *oracle*
χρηστός, -ή, -όν   *good, fine,*
   serviceable
χρῆται   3rd s. pres. of χράομαι
χρῑστός, -ή, -όν   *anointed*
χροιᾱ, -ᾱς, ἡ   *skin*
χρόνος, -ου, ὁ   *time*
   διὰ χρόνου   *after a time*
χρῡσίον, -ου, τό   *a piece of gold, gold*
χρῡσός, -οῦ, ὁ   *gold*
χρῡσοῦς, -ῆ, -οῦν   *golden*

#χρώς, -ωτός (also χρόα, χροός, χροΐ),
ὁ   skin, flesh

χυτός, -ή, -όν   poured; melted (with
λίθινος,   made of glass); piled, heaped
up

χύτρᾱ, -ᾱς, ἡ   pot

χὦ crasis for καὶ ὁ

χώρᾱ, -ᾱς, ἡ   land, country

χωρέω   go, come; be in motion

χωρίζω   separate

χωρίον, -ου, τό   place, space; region;
farm

χωρίς   without, apart, separately
(from) (+gen.)

ψάλια, ων, τά   curb-chain of bridle,
bridle

ψάμμος, -ου, ἡ   sand

ψέγω   blame, censure

ψευδής, -ές   false, lying

ψεύδομαι   lie, tell lies; cheat, deceive

ψεῦδος, -ους, τό   falsehood, lie

ψευδῶς (adv.)   falsely

ψηφίζομαι   vote

ψήφισμα, -ατος, τό   decree

ψῆφος, -ου, ἡ   voting-pebble, vote

ψῑλοί, -ῶν, οἱ   light-armed troops

ψόγος, -ου, ὁ   blame

ψόφος, -ου, ὁ   noise

ψύλλα, -ης, ἡ   flea

ψῡχή, -ῆς, ἡ   soul, life, spirit

ψῦχος, -ους, τό   cold, period of cold
weather

ψῡχρός, -ά, -όν   cold

ὤ   what! (+gen.)

ὦ   O (addressing someone); ah!
(exclamation of surprise)

Ὠγυγίᾱ, -ᾱς, ἡ   Ogygia (island of
Calypso)

ὧδε (adv.)   thus, as follows; (poet.) to
here, hither

ὠδίνω   be in labour (of childbirth)

ὠή (exclamation)   help!

Ὠκεανός, -οῦ, ὁ   Ocean (son of
Heaven and Earth)

#ὠκύς, -εῖα, -ύ   swift, quick

ὠλόμην aor. of ὄλλυμαι

ὤμην impf. of οἶμαι

ὤμοι (exclamation)   ah me, woe is me,
alas

#ὠμοφάγος, -ον   eating raw flesh, where
raw flesh is eaten

ὤν, οὖσα, ὄν pres. pple. of εἰμί
τὸ ὄν   reality, τῷ ὄντι   in fact,
really

†ὠνέομαι (aor. ἐπριάμην)   buy

ᾠόν, -οῦ, τό   egg

ὥρᾱ, -ᾱς, ἡ   season (of the
year); time; beauty

ὡρμισμένος, -η, -ον   perf. mid./pass.
pple. of ὁρμίζω

ὡς (adv.)   as; like (for a summary of
the uses of ὡς see 22.1/1)
(exclamatory) howl! (+adj. or adv.)
(+numerals) about, nearly
(+pples.) on the grounds that, under
the impression that; with the
intention of (fut. pple.) (12.1/2a(ii)
and (v) (restrictive) for, considering
that; (+supl.) as . . . as possible
(conj.) that (= ὅτι); in order that
(= ἵνα, ὅπως); when, as (ὡς
τάχιστα as soon as, lit. when
quickest, but if this expression is
used adverbially it means as
quickly as possible, 17.1/4d); since
(prep.) to, towards, to the house of

ὥς (adv.)   thus, so

ὡσαύτως (also ὡς αὔτως) (adv.)   in
the same way, just so

ὥσπερ (adv.)   like, as, as if

ὥστε (conj.)   so that, that, with the
result that, consequently (+inf. or
ind., 16.1/1)

ὠτ- stem of οὖς   ear

ᾦτε see ἐφ'

ὠφελέω   help, assist, be of use to,
benefit

ὠφελητέον   one must help (24.1/5)

Index

Abbreviations p. ix
Accents **1**.1/2; **Appendix 9**
Accusative **2**.1/3*c*; **22**.1/2
  absolute **21**.1/5
  adverbial **20**.1/5
  cognate **22**.1/2*g*
  double **22**.1/2*f*
  and infinitive **8**.1/3*a*; cf. **16**.1/1
  motion towards **2**.1/3*f*; **22**.1/2*i*
  in oaths **22**.1/2*h*
  with prepositions **2**.1/3*f*; **3**.1/5*a*
  of respect or specification **20**.1/5
  space **7**.1/7*d*
  time **7**.1/7*a*
Adjectival clauses **9**.1/2
  indefinite **14**.1/4*c*(iii)
Adjectives
  agreement **3**.1/3
  instead of adverbs **4**.2.9 note
  with article, as noun equivalent **5**.1/3
  without article, as noun equivalent **5**.1/3 note 1
  comparison of **17**.1/2
  declension: 1st and 2nd **3**.1/3; contracted **6**.1/2; irregular **3**.1/3; two termination **3**.1/3; 3rd **10**.1/4; 1st and 3rd **10**.1/3
  demonstrative **9**.1/1; **21**.1/3
  exclamatory **21**.1/3
  indefinite **10**.1/1
  interrogative **10**.1/1; **21**.1/3; indirect interrogative **10**.1/2*b*
  numerals **7**.1/5*a* and *b*; **Appendix 8**
  position **3**.1/3*a* and *b*; attributive and predicative **3**.1/3*b*; **18**.1/6
  possessive **9**.1/5
  relative **21**.1/3
  verbal **24**.1/5
Adverbial clauses of
  cause **22**.1/1*b*(iii); cf. **14**.1/4*d* note 1 condition **18**.1/5; manner **22**.1/1*b*(v); purpose **14**.1/4*c*(i); **22**.1/1*b*(ii); result **16**.1/1; time **14**.1/4*c*(iii); **21**.1/2; **22**.1/1*b*(iv)
Adverbs
  adverbial καί **4**.1/3
  comparison of **17**.1/2
  emphasized with ὡς **22**.1/1*a*(iii)
  formation of **3**.1/4
  indefinite **10**.1/2*b* note 3
  interrogative (direct and indirect) **10**.1/2
  numerals **7**.1/5*c*
  position of **2**.1/6*a*(i); **3**.1/4
Agent **11**.1/2
Agreement
  between adjective and noun **3**.1/3
  between article and noun **2**.1/2 note 1

between double subject and verb **11**.2.4 note
between neuter plural subject and verb **3**.1/1 note 2
between participle and noun **12**.1/1
between subject and verb **2**.1/4
Alphabet **1**.1/1
Antecedent (in adjectival clauses) **9**.1/2
  omission of **9**.1/2 note 1
  attraction of relative pronoun to case of **9**.1.2 note 2
Article **2**.1/2; **3**.1/1
  with abstract nouns **2**.1/2 note 1
  generic **2**.1/2 note 1
  neuter plural of +genitive **5**.1/3
  to create noun equivalent **5**.1/3
  with proper nouns **2**.1/2 note 1; +genitive of proper nouns **5**.1/3 note 2
  omitted with predicative noun or adjective **5**.1/3
  omitted in proverbs and poetry **4**.2.3 note
  with participles **12**.1/2*a*(vi)
  equivalent to 3rd person pronoun **5**.1/3
Aspect **4**.1/1
  in imperative **17**.1/1
  in infinitive **7**.1/4
  in participle **12**.1/1; **15**.1/2*f*
  in subjunctive/optative **14**.1/1; **21**.1/1*a*
Attributive position **3**.1/3*b*; **18**.1/6
Augment **4**.1/1 note 1
  double **7**.1/1 note 4
  irregular **7**.1/1 note 4; **15**.1/1
  optional **12**.3.1 note
  syllabic **4**.1/1 note 2(i)
  temporal **4**.1/1 note 2(ii)
  in perfect tense **15**.1/1
  in pluperfect tense **16**.1/2 and 3
  in verbs compounded with prepositions **6**.1/3*e*
  in compound verbs with no prepositional element **6**.1/3 note 3
Cases
  basic uses of **2**.1/3
Commands
  direct **17**.1/1
  indirect **7**.1/4
Comparative
  meaning of **17**.1/3
  construction with **17**.1/4*a–c*
Comparison
  of adjectives **17**.1/2
  of adverbs **17**.1/2
  constructions with **17**.1/4
  meaning of **17**.1/3
Conative imperfect **4**.1/1 footnote 1

Conditional sentences **18**.1/5
Conjugation, see Verbs
Contracted futures **5**.1/2 note 3
Contracted verbs, see Tenses (-ω verbs contracted)
Crasis **11**.1/5
Dative **2**.1/3*e*; **23**.1/2
  of accompaniment **9**.1/3*a*(ii), **23**.1/2*k*
  of advantage/disadvantage **23**.1/2*d*
  with adjectives **23**.1/2*b* (cf. **9**.1/3*b*)
  with adverbs **23**.1/2*b*
  of agent **23**.1/2*g*, **24**.1/5*b*
  of attendant circumstances **23**.1/2*j*
  of cause **23**.1/2*i*
  ethic **23**.1/2*f*
  with impersonal verbs **21**.1/4
  of instrument **11**.1/2
  of manner **23**.1/2*j*
  of measure of difference **17**.1/4*b*
  with nouns **23**.1/2*b*
  of place where (without preposition) **10**.2.11 note; **23**.1/2*n*
  of possessor **23**.1/2*c*
  with prepositions **2**.1/3*h*
  of reference or relation **23**.1/2*e*
  of respect **23**.1/2*m*
  of time when **7**.1/7*b*
  with verbs **13**.1/2*b*; **23**.1/2*a*
Declension, see Adjectives, Nouns, Pronouns
Deponent verbs **8**.1/2
  deponent futures **8**.1/1 note 1
  passive deponents **11**.1/1 note
Dialects **1**.3; **25**.1/1–2
Diminutives **24**.1/3
Direct object, see Accusative **2**.1/3*c*
Dual **24**.1/4
Elision **2**.1/6*b*
  in verbs compounded with prepositions **6**.1/3
Enclitics **3**.1/6; **4**.1/2; **4**.1/3; **Appendix 9**, *d*
Exclamations **22**.1/1*a*(ii), **23**.1/1*l*
Fear: constructions after verbs of fearing **14**.1/4*c*(ii)
Gender **2**.1/1
Genitive **2**.1/3*d*; **23**.1/1
  absolute **12**.1/2*b*
  of cause **23**.1/1*k*(ii)
  of characteristic **23**.1/1*b*
  chorographic (geographic definition) **23**.1/1*d*
  of comparison **17**.1/4
  of exclamation **23**.1/1*l*
  of explanation **23**.1/1*e*
  objective **23**.1/1*c*
  partitive **23**.1/1*d*
  possessive **2**.1/3*d*; **23**.1/1*a*
  with prepositions **2**.1/3*g*; **3**.1/5*b*; **11**.1/2
  of price or value **20**.1/3
  of separation **20**.1/4
  subjective **23**.1/1*c*
  time within which **7**.1/7*c*

  with verbs **13**.1/2*a*; **23**.1/1*k*
Gnomic aorist **5**.2.10 note
Historic
  endings: of active **4**.1/1 note 1; of middle/passive **8**.1/1*f*
  optative classed as **14**.1/3
  sequence **14**.1/4*c*(iii)
  tenses **4**.1/1 note 1
Imperative **17**.1/1
Impersonal verbs **5**.1/2 note 5; **21**.1/4
Inceptive imperfect **4**.1/1 footnote 1
Indefinite clauses **14**.1/4*c*(iii); **21**.1/2
Indirect command **7**.1/4
Indirect object, see Dative **2**.1/3*e*
Indirect question **10**.1/2*b*
Indirect speech **7**.1/3
  virtual indirect speech **14**.1/4*d* note 1
Indirect statement **8**.1/3
  with finite verb **8**.1/3*b*
  with infinitive **8**.1/3*a*
  use of optative mood in historic sequence **14**.1/4*d*
  with participle **15**.1/2*a*
  with verbs of hoping, promising, swearing **8**.1/3*a* note 5
Infinitive
  -ω verbs (uncontracted):
    present active **2**.1/5
    future active **2**.1/5
    aorist active: weak **4**.1/1; strong **7**.1/1; root **11**.1/1
    perfect active **16**.1/4
    present middle/passive **8**.1/1
    future middle **8**.1/1
    aorist middle **8**.1/1
    perfect middle/passive **16**.1/4
    future passive **11**.1/1
    aorist passive **11**.1/1
  -ω verbs (contracted) **5**.1/2 note 1
  -μι verbs **18**.1/2; **19**.1/1; **20**.1/1; **20**.1/2
  articular **5**.1/3
  as imperative **17**.1/1 note 5
  in indirect command **7**.1/4
  in indirect statement **8**.1/3*a*
  negative with **7**.1/4; **8**.1/3
  in parenthetical phrases **22**.1/1*a*(vi)
  in result clauses **16**.1/1 (cf. **17**.1/4*c*)
  subject in accusative **8**.1/3*a*; **16**.1/1; **21**.1/2
  with verbs of knowing/learning how to **15**.1/2*a*
Ingressive aorist **20**.2.1 note
Instrument, dative of **11**.1/2
Intervocalic sigma **5**.1/2 note 2; **6**.1/1*c*; **8**.1/1*e*; **20**.1/2
Middle voice **8**.1/1
Motion
  from **2**.1/3*g*
  towards **2**.1/3*f*
Movable nu
  in nouns **3**.1/1 note 3; **5**.1/1
  in verbs **2**.1/5 note 4; **5**.1/2 note 6

Negatives **24**.1/2
  accumulation of **7**.1/6
  in conditional clauses **18**.1/5
  with deliberative subjunctive **14**.1/4*a*(ii)
  in direct questions **10**.1/2*a*
  in indefinite clauses **14**.1/4*c*(iii)
  in indirect command **7**.1/4
  in indirect statement **8**.1/3
  with jussive subjunctive **14**.1/4*a*(i)
  in noun clauses after verbs of fearing
    14.1/4*c*(ii)
  with participles **12**.1/2
  position of **2**.1/6*a*(i)
  in purpose clauses **14**.1/4*c*(i)
  in result clauses **16**.1/1
  in wishes **21**.1/1
Nominative **2**.1/3*a*
  after copulative **3**.1/6
  with infinitive **8**.1/3*a* (cf. **21**.1/2*a*)
Noun clauses
  after verbs of fearing **14**.1/4*c*(ii)
  in indirect question **10**.1/2*b*
  in indirect statement **8**.1/3*b*
Nouns **2**.1/1
  1st declension: **2**.1/2; **3**.1/2
  2nd: **3**.1/1; contracted **6**.1/2; 'Attic'
    13.1/1*a*
  3rd: **5**.1/1; **6**.1/1; consonantal stems
    5.1/1; **6**.1/1; stems in εϲ **6**.1/1*c*; stems
    in ι and υ **8**.1/4; stems in ευ, αυ and
    ου **11**.1/4; in -ωϲ, -ω and -αϲ **13**.1/1*b*
  declined in two ways **13**.1/1*c*
  plural place names **4**.2.9 note
Numerals **7**.1/5; **Appendix 8**
  adverbs **7**.1/5*c*
  cardinals **7**.1/5*a*
  ordinals **7**.1/5*b*; **9**.1/3*a*(i)
Oaths **22**.1/2*h*
Oblique cases **2**.1/3
Optative **14**.1/1; **14**.1/3; **16**.1/4 note 1
  in adverbial clauses of reason **14**.1/4*d*
    note 1
  in conditional clauses **18**.1/5
  use of future **14**.1/4*d*
  in indefinite clauses **14**.1/4*c*(iii)
  in indirect speech **14**.1/4*d*
  in potential clauses **19**.1/2
  in purpose clauses **14**.1/4*c*(i)
  after verbs of fearing **14**.1/4*c*(ii)
  in wishes **21**./1*a*
Participles **12**.1/1; **16**.1/4
  causal **12**.1/2*a*(ii); **22**.1/1*a*(i)
  concessive **12**.1/2*a*(iii)
  conditional **12**.1/2*a*(iv)
  in genitive absolute **12**.1/2*b*
  as noun equivalent **12**.1/2*a*(vi)
  of purpose **12**.1/2*a*(v); **22**.1/1*a*(i)
  temporal **12**.1/2*a*(i)
  with verbs **15**.1/2; of beginning, stop-
    ping, continuing **15**.1/2*b*; of emotion
    15.1/2*c*; of knowing, perceiving
    15.1/2*a*

Particles **4**.1/3; **13**.1/3
  interrogative **10**.1/2*a*
Patronymics **3**.1/2 note 4
Perfect tense
  meaning of **15**.1/1
  with present meaning **19**.1/3*a*
  transitive and intransitive **15**.1/1 note 2
Pluperfect tense, meaning and use of
  16.1/2
Possession **9**.1/5
Postpositives **4**.1/3
Potential clauses **19**.1/2
Predicative position **3**.1/3*b*; **18**.1/6
Prepositions
  with accusative **2**.1/3*f*; **3**.1/5*a*
  with dative **2**.1/3*h*
  with genitive **2**.1/3*g*; **3**.1/5*b*
  placed after noun they govern **11**.2.4
    note
  pregnant use of **9**.2.13 note on *l*.11,
    22.2.2 note on *l*.3
  with pronouns **4**.1/2
Primary
  endings: of active **4**.1/1 note 1; of
    middle/passive **8**.1/1*f*
  sequence **14**.1/4*c*(iii)
  subjunctive classed as **14**.1/2
  tenses **4**.1/1 note 1
Prohibitions (negative commands) **17**.1/1
Pronouns
  demonstrative **9**.1/1; **16**.1/1 note 1
  emphatic **9**.1/3*a*
  indefinite **10**.1/1
  indefinite relative **10**.1/2*b* note 2
  interrogative **10**.1/1 and 2; **21**.1/3; in-
    direct interrogative **10**.1/2*b*
  personal: 1st and 2nd person **4**.1/2; 3rd
    4.1/2; **9**.1/3*c*
  possessive **9**.1/5
  reciprocal **9**.1/4*b*
  reflexive (direct and indirect) **9**.1/4*a*
  relative **9**.1/2; **21**.1/3
Pronunciation **1**.1/1
Purpose expressed by
  adverbial clauses **14**.1/4*c*(i); **22**.1/1*b*(ii)
  future participle **12**.1/2*a*(v)
Questions
  alternative **10**.1/2*a*, **24**.1/2*i*
  deliberative **14**.1/4*a*(ii)
  direct **10**.1/2*a*
  indirect **10**.1/2*b*
Reason
  adverbial clauses of **14**.1/4*d* note 1
Reduplication **15**.1/1 (and note 3)
Result
  clauses and phrases of **16**.1/1; **17**.1/4*c*
Root aorist
  imperative **17**.1/1 note 2
  indicative and infinitive **11**.1/1
  optative **14**.1/3 note 2
  participles **12**.1/1 note 4
  subjunctive **14**.1/2 note 2

Spatial extent
  accusative of **7**.1/7*d*
Strong aorist
  imperative **17**.1/1 note 1
  indicative and infinitive **7**.1/1
  optative **14**.1/3 note 1
  participles **12**.1/1 note 3
  subjunctive **14**.1/2 notes 1 and 2
Strong perfect **15**.1/1
  with intransitive sense **15**.1/1 note 1;
    20.1/1 note 2
Subjunctive **14**.1/1–2; **16**.1/4 note 1;
    18.1/2 note 1
  deliberative **14**.1/4*a*(ii)
  jussive **14**.1/4*a*(i)
  in indefinite clauses **14**.1/4*c*(iii)
  in negative commands **17**.1/1
  in purpose clauses **14**.1/4*c*(i)
  after verbs of fearing **14**.1/4*c*(ii)
Superlative
  construction with **17**.1/4*d*
  meaning of **17**.1/3
Temporal clauses **14**.1/4*c*(iii); **21**.1/2
Tenses
  -ω verbs (uncontracted):
    indicative active: present **2**.1/5;
      future **2**.1/5; contracted future
      5.1/2 note 3; **11**.1/3; imperfect
      4.1/1; **7**.1/1 note 4; weak aorist
      4.1/1; strong aorist **7**.1/1; root
      aorist **11**.1/1; perfect **15**.1/1;
      pluperfect **16**.1/2; future perfect
      16.1/4 note 2
    indicative middle: future **8**.1/1;
      aorist **8**.1/1
    indicative middle/passive: present
      8.1/1; imperfect **8**.1/1; perfect
      16.1/3; pluperfect **16**.1/3
    indicative passive: aorist **11**.1/1;
      11.1/3; future **11**.1/1
  -ω verbs (contracted):
    present and imperfect **5**.1/2; **14**.1/3;
      17.1/1 note 3
    other tenses **5**.1/2 note 2
    irregular futures **5**.1/2 note 2
    irregulars in -αω **5**.1/2 note 4
    disyllables in -εω **5**.1/2 note 5
    rules for contraction **5**.1/2*a–c*
  -μι verbs:
    definition **18**.1/1
    δίδωμι **18**.1/2
    ἵημι **20**.1/2
    ἵcτημι **19**.1/1
    τίθημι **18**.1/2
    verbs in -νῡμι and -ννῡμι **20**.1/1
    deponents in -αμαι **19**.1/3*b*
Thematic vowel **2**.1/5 note 3; **8**.1/1*d*
Time
  adverbial clauses of **14**.1/4*c*(iii); **21**.1/2

how long **7**.1/7*a*
  when **7**.1/7*b*
  within which **7**.1/7*c*
Tmesis **12**.3.9 note
Transitive and intransitive senses
  in aorist **11**.1/1; **19**.1/1
  in perfect **15**.1/1 notes 1 and 2
  in same tense **11**.1/1
  of ἵcτημι **19**.1/1
Verbs **2**.1/4
  aspect **4**.1/1; **7**.1/4; **12**.1/1; **14**.1/1;
    15.1/2*f*; **17**.1/1
  augment, see Augment
  compound with prepositional prefixes
    6.1/3
  conjugation **2**.1/4
  deponent **8**.1/2; **11**.1/1
  of hindering, preventing, forbidding,
    denying **24**.1/7
  moods **14**.1/1
  oddities **19**.1/3
  of precaution and striving **24**.1/6
  principal parts **7**.1/1 note 3; from dif-
    ferent roots **18**.1/4
  stems in palatals, labials, dentals **6**.1/4;
    11.1/1*b*; **16**.1/3; in λ, μ, ν, ρ **11**.1/3;
    16.1/3
  syntax: with dative **13**.1/2*b*; with geni-
    tive **13**.1/2*a*; with participles **15**.1/2
  tenses: primary and historic **4**.1/1 note
    1
    relationship: of imperfect and
      aorist **4**.1/1; of present and
      aorist: infinitive **4**.1/1; **8**.1/3*a*
      note 1; imperative **17**.1/1;
      subjunctive **14**.1/1, **17**.1/1;
      optative **14**.1/1; **14**.1/4*d*;
      participle **15**.1/2*f*
    transitive/intransitive **13**.1/2; **19**.1/1;
      20.1/1 note 2
  voice: active **2**.1/4; middle and passive
    8.1/1
    active verbs with a middle future
      8.1/1 note 1
    active verbs with passive sense
      17.1/5
Yes and *no* **24**.1/1
Vivid present **7**.2.13 note on *l*.7
Vocative **2**.1/3*b*
Weak aorist **4**.1/1
Wishes **21**.1/1
Word order
  with adjectives **3**.1/3*a*, *b*
  with adverbs **2**.1/6*a*(i); **3**.1/4; **4**.1/3
  first person before second **4**.1/3
  with genitive of unemphatic personal
    pronouns **4**.1/2 note
  (See also Attributive/Predicative posi-
    tion; Postpositives)